LASTING VISIONS

One of nine children, the author grew up on Cherry Hill Farm, in the heart of Kentucky. Nestled in the historic bluegrass region, the farm was located three miles west of Springfield. Here there was lots of southern hospitality and the community rich in history and tradition. Farming was the only source of income for many large families and the only sustainment for his family. They lived on a bare bones income. He had just finished high school. There would be no money for college. It was time for him to face the world and to make a new life for himself. He had a destiny to fulfill. His older brothers had served in the United States Marine Corps and he was determined to uphold the family tradition.

On the farm the daily routine and sometimes monotonous lifestyle was driven by the chores. Under his father's strict and watchful schedule the farm chores were determined by the changing seasons. He was to escape the harsh routine of the farm life and seek other challenges away from the farm. After helping his father with the crops during the summer of 1969 he enlisted in the Marine Corps and underwent boot camp at Parris Island, South Carolina. The Marine drill instructors were ruthless and relentless.

After graduating boot camp he trained as a machine gunner and eventually ended up in Vietnam. Never had he realized what he was about to face at the young age of 19 in a war torn country; the dense jungles, rice paddies, and mountains of South Vietnam. Cherry Hill Farm gave way to such names as LZ Baldy, Fire Support Base Ryder, Firebase Ross, Que Son Mountains, Happy Valley, Elephant Valley, Antenna Valley, and Sniper Valley.

His true story is about the camaraderie and esprit de corps of a Marine rifle squad in Vietnam. This story is about the unsung heroes of the Vietnam War. It is a story about life and survival in a nation at war. The thoughts of the author are captured in letters to his mother who prayed night and day for his safe return. His lasting visions are being told in a story that will capture your attention and fill the void that is not found in history books. This story takes you to ground zero in the Vietnam War and gives you an insight into the lifestyles of the Orient as seen through the eyes of a young Marine combat infantryman.

Lasting Visions

With the 7th Marines in Vietnam 1970

Frederick Fenwick

Bennington, Vermont
2010

— Lasting Visions —

First published in 2010 by the Merriam Press

First Edition (2010)

ISBN 978-0-557-50831-0 (paperback) #MM113-P
ISBN 978-0-557-50841-9 (hardcover) #MM113-H

Printed in the United States of America.

This work was designed, produced, and published in
the United States of America by the

Merriam Press
133 Elm Street Suite 3R
Bennington VT 05201-2250
USA

E-mail: ray@merriam-press.com
Web site: merriam-press.com

Both the author and the Publisher welcome and encourage
comments and corrections to the material appearing in this work.
Please send them to the Publisher at the above address.

The Merriam Press is always interested in publishing new manuscripts on
military history, as well as reprinting previous works, such as reports, documents,
manuals, articles and other material on military history topics.

Contents

Dedication

TO my mother, Floy Fenwick, who unselfishly prayed day and night for my safe return from Vietnam. Through her faith, courage, and personal letters, she was my inspiration and gave me hope. Her endless caring and love will never be forgotten. To my father, Elmer Fenwick, who provided for the family on a modest farmer's income and who first instilled the discipline, work ethic, and family values that served me well throughout my career. To my brother, Donald Fenwick, who served two complete tours in Vietnam. To my wife, Celina, who inspired me to write about my experiences.

To all the servicemen of the Armed Forces who participated in the battles of Vietnam in support of our country to resist communist aggression. An honorable mention goes to the Marine Corps infantrymen, "the grunt," who fought and died in that unpopular war half a world away from home. Moreover, to the families who endured the hardships, the loss of life of their loved ones, and the agony of war.

This dedication is also in memory of the servicemen and women who have gone to their rest, the present who believe in the freedom for all, and the future who will continue to strive for peace.

Last but not least, I dedicate this book to my best friend and "foxhole buddy" who I served with in Vietnam. The memories that we both shared will always remain a part of our lives and "Lasting Visions."

Disclaimer

THIS book is based on my true life story. To protect the rights and identity of those whose lives I have come in contact with I have changed some of the characters real names with fictitious ones. It was the hardest thing I had to do in writing this book. Locating the characters and obtaining written permission to use their real names was not practical or feasible as I have simply lost contact with them. The actual events, dates, and places remain unaltered and are true to life.

Foreword

THIS is my true story based on actual events. The timeline of some events may be slightly off as I simply cannot recall exact details of events that happened many years ago. I have relied heavily on my personal experiences, memory of events, photos, unit command chronologies, and saved personal letters to accurately depict this time in our nation's history, the Vietnam War. The personal letters that I wrote home while in Vietnam were saved by my loving mother. I have included excerpts of those letters in this book. They proved to be very useful in organizing my story in chronological order.

I graduated from high school in the spring of 1969. Three older brothers had joined the United States Marine Corps and I was destined to do the same. Instead of waiting to be drafted, I volunteered for military service in order to choose a distinct service branch that suited my personal preference. Nine months later I found myself as a Marine in the Republic of Vietnam. I was 19 years of age when the Vietnam War became a reality for me. Life as I knew it would take a dramatic turn and my thoughts of Vietnam and the Marines who I served with would remain a part of my life, never to be forgotten.

My career in the Marine Corps continued after Vietnam. About ten years later I contemplated the possibility of putting my thoughts about my personal experiences down on paper. I began to peck away on an old IBM Selectric typewriter. After completing the first twelve pages, of the very first chapter, I temporarily gave up on the idea. Then one day my wife bought me a starter computer with a 5.25 floppy disk drive. I was once again off and running putting my thoughts into type on an old MultiMate word processor. Through the years I reformatted my manuscript several times to the most current version of word processing software in order to keep it up to date.

I began researching facts and updating my story only to be sidetracked with my working career. I put it on the back burner and did not concentrate on it much for years. Then one day when I was on a visit to my mother's house, she showed me the saved letters that I had written home, while I was in Vietnam. She gave them all back to me and that was my inspiration to take my manuscript even more seriously. I felt that I needed to share my story. That became my goal, to see it in print before I pass from this earth. Writing my story has been good therapy for me, but the thoughts remain.

The stories are real and I have attempted to portray the adult language as it was spoken during this time period in history. The dialogues of expressions and quotations throughout the story have been regenerated as accurately as humanly possible. I hope that by reading my story that you gain a deep appreciation for what the servicemen and women do for our country. They come from all walks of life and from all corners of this great nation. The tradition lives on with our new generations who are the defenders of our freedom. Let us never forget their unselfish sacrifices.

Location Quick Reference Guide

Hill 51 .... FSB Ross, 3rd Bn, 7th Mar CP (from 5 July 1970).
Firebase Ross was located about 10 miles southwest
of LZ Baldy. It was just west of the Que Son District
Town and commanded the Que Son Valley. Grid
AT025343.

Hill 55 .... 7th Marine Regiment CP. Located about 10 miles
southwest of Da Nang. Grid AT970620.

Hill 63 .... LZ Baldy, 3rd Bn, 7th Mar CP (until 5 July 1970).
Located at the intersection of Route 535 and Route 1
about 20 miles south of Da Nang. Grid BT132453.

Hill 90 .... Not a designated hill on a tactical map. Referred to
as Hill 90 based on topographic elevation. Located
approximately 1.5 miles southeast of FSB Ryder at
the foot of the Que Son Mountains. Indicated as
mortar incident on the map. Vicinity of grid
AT965335.

Hill 185 .... Observation Post, Nui Loc Son. Located about 3
miles south of FSB Ross. Mike Company worked
this area just prior to going on R&R at China Beach.
Grid BT022288.

Hill 270 .... Observation Post established by the 7th Marines as
Outpost Lion. My squad found 10 NVA/VC caves
on the northwest side of hill. I was a tunnel rat at
Grid 995318.

Hill 327 .... Freedom Hill, 1st Mar Div HQ, Da Nang. One of the
largest entertainment facilities that served thousands
of off-duty Marines, Soldiers, Sailors, and Airmen
each day. It catered largely to rear-area personnel rather than frontline combat infantrymen. Grid
AT971738.

Hill 484 .... FSB Bushwack, Artillery Position. Located about 8
miles west of LZ Baldy. Grid BT016464.

Hill 579 .... FSB Ryder, Artillery Position. Fire Support Base
Ryder was located on a hilltop in the Que Son
Mountains about 5 miles west of FSB Ross. We had

a birds eye view overlooking the Que Son Valley and Antenna Valley. Grid AT948346.

Hill 800 .... LZ Crow, Que Son Mountains. Landing Zone Crow was about 5 miles northwest of Firebase Ross. Grid AT975416.

Hill 845 .... LZ Buzzard, Que Son Mountains. Landing Zone Buzzard was located about 6 miles northwest of FSB Ross. It was one of the highest elevations in the central Que Son Mountains. Grid AT982434.

Antenna Valley ...... Antenna Valley started about 2 miles northwest of FSB Ryder (See Route 535). There were different stories on how the valley got its name. For the Marines of Mike Company, we had to extend our radio whip antennas to communicate across the high mountain ranges. The extended antennas became a prime target for enemy snipers. Vicinity of Grid AT926369.

Elephant Valley...... Located about 15 miles northwest of Da Nang. Vicinity of Grid AT818859.

Happy Valley .... Located about 6 miles northwest of Hill 55 and about 12 miles southwest of Da Nang. Vicinity of Grid Square AT8865. A grid square is 1,000 meters square on a standard military tactical map.

Route 535 .... A highway that ran westward from the intersection of LZ Baldy and Route 1 to the Que Son District Headquarters. There the road branched with Route 535 continuing southward. The northern fork became Route 536 which was a little larger than a footpath that climbed over a pass through the Que Son Mountains into Antenna Valley and then opened out northwestward into the valley of the Thu Bon River.

Sniper Valley .... Located about 4 miles southwest of FSB Ross. Sniper Valley was located between Hill 441 and Hill 270. These prominent terrain features provided excellent hiding positions for enemy snipers. Vicinity of Grid Square BT9830.

Rockcrusher .... A quarry located about 3 miles southwest of LZ Baldy and about 6 miles southeast of FSB Bushwack. From on top of FSB Bushwack, a high Que Son Mountain peak, we had a good view of the Rockcrusher and valleys below. Vicinity of Grid BT105428.

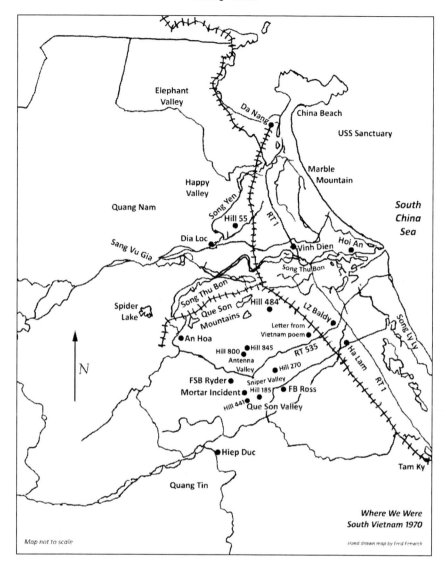

Notes
1. 3rd Battalion, 7th Marines Command Post was located at LZ Baldy
    until they relocated to FSB Ross on 5 July 1970.
2. Distances are approximate.

Chapter 1

Life on Cherry Hill Farm

APRIL 1969, 4:00 a.m. I awake to hear the banging on my bedroom door.

Wham! Wham! Wham!

"Freddy, are you awake?"

"Huh?"

"I said, are you awake?"

"Yeah, I'm awake."

"Well hurry up, eat breakfast, and get down to the barn so you can help me milk the cows."

"Uh-huh."

"Let's go. Get out of that bed!"

"Daddy, what time is it?"

"Four o'clock. C'mon now, we're wasting daylight."

"Okay, I'm coming."

This was a typical early morning wake up ritual when I was growing up on the farm and my father woke me up to help with the farm chores. My father had a certain knack of impolitely coaxing me to my feet every morning by banging loudly on my bedroom door. He would awaken me well before daylight so we could milk thirty Holstein dairy cows.

I was now eighteen years old and just finishing up my senior year at Washington County High School in Springfield, Kentucky. I was raised on small farm of 122 acres in central Kentucky known as Cherry Hill Farm. I never knew why it was called Cherry Hill Farm, but we did have several cherry trees in the back yard. There were also an abundance of apple trees and peach trees around the barnyard and house.

The farm was located three miles west of Springfield on Highway 150. The old farm house would be home for the Elmer and Floy Fenwick family for over 40 years. Although I loved growing up on the farm, I dreamed of the day that I could leave the farm work behind and explore other worlds. It was now my time to move on. After all, my older brothers and sisters had since moved away from home, except for my younger brother. It was now just my father, mother, Larry, and I to carry out the daily farm chores. All my other brothers and sisters had already put their fair share into the hard farm work and had moved away from home to start families of their own.

In 1914, my parents were born. My father was born on a farm near

Springfield and my mother was born in Harrodsburg, Kentucky. They met and married when they were in their late teens and spent an entire life providing for a family of nine. I used to count the family first names down on my fingers from the oldest to the youngest. There was Bobby, Nancy, Joann, Donald, Jimmy Howard, Carolyn, Janice, Freddy, and Larry. A still-born baby between Larry and I had been named Gary. Although my older brothers and sisters had spent some of their early childhood on other family owned farms near Springfield, Kentucky they all considered this old farm-house their home.

The farmhouse was quite a large structure. It had twelve rooms of which five were bedrooms. There were a total of five large rooms downstairs and four large rooms upstairs. These large rooms were approximately 20 feet wide by 25 feet long and about 12 feet high. There were hardwood floors throughout the house. Only two rooms on the first floor were heated in the winter months, the kitchen, and the living room. The rooms were heated by using the fireplaces in both rooms during the fall of the year and then chang-ing over to wood burning stoves at the onset of winter. We used firewood and coal to heat the rooms. My parents had their bed, dresser, couch, chairs, and TV in the living room that was adjacent to the kitchen.

My bedroom was a very small room on a north side corner of the house. It was just enough room for a twin bed and a dresser; however, a built-in closet proved to be satisfactory for storing blankets and clothes. The room had a nice fireplace but it was never used. This was mainly due to safety concerns and the fact that two wood stoves were more than enough to keep fueled during the winter months. I would sleep under about eight blankets during the winter in order to keep warm.

Just on the outside of my bedroom was the only small bathroom that the entire family used. There was one more bathroom upstairs, but my father had turned off the water since it was never used much. Our downstairs bath-room had a bath tub and a commode, but nothing else. The water used in the bathroom was pumped up from the lake that was just over the hill from the stock barn. The water smelled during the summer as algae would grow across the lake and the farm animals would wade into the lake to drink and wallow. The ceramic tile sewage pipes ran underground and through the back yard down to an old septic tank. During the extreme cold in the winter, both the water pipes coming from the lake and the sewage pipe could freeze. A few times the sewage pipe got clogged and it was a real mess digging out the tiles in an attempt to unclog it.

We also had an old outdoor outhouse as a backup in case we had a prob-lem with the bathroom plumbing. It could be used year round. If we were fortunate enough to have enough money, my mother would put toilet paper in the outhouse. When times were hard, she would go to town and pick up some JC Penny and Sears and Roebuck catalogs. We used the pages in the catalogs as toilet paper. If for some reason she could not get her hands on

Cherry Hill Farm House built in the 1860s. This was the author's childhood home for 18 years. The family income consisted mainly of selling the tobacco crop and milking 30 Holstein cows.

any catalogs, we could always resort to corn cobs. These were the cobs that remained after the hogs ate the ears of corn. We had a tin corn crib in the barn lot. It was a matter of picking the cobs off the ground and stuffing them into a burlap bag to take to the outhouse.

The indoor bathroom was very convenient for me but it was very cold in the winter. I would get dressed under my blankets as much as possible. Then I would dart into the bathroom to conduct my business before walking briskly through the adjoining dining room and into the heat of the kitchen. The old wood stove in the kitchen was a common gathering place for family members to warm their hands and backsides. It felt good after sleeping in a very cold room during the winter and after completing the chores at the barn.

My mother stored groceries and kitchen utensils in a small pantry that was next to the kitchen. It had several shelves and she normally kept it full with supplies. It was very convenient for her when she was preparing meals. Joining this pantry was another large room that we called the Back Room. It was used exclusively for hanging meat such as smoked ham and sausage. We would dress out about six hogs each fall of the year to keep the hanging meat plentiful. I used to love the aroma as I entered the room where the meat was hanging and curing.

Another first floor room that was used quite a bit was just off the dining room. We gave it the name of the Front Room mainly because it faced the front of the house. This room was always cool, both winter, and summer. It was where my mother had her piano that she played quite frequently. All the kids would bang on it as well, but when our mother sat down to play, we all took notice of her most precious talent and skills of playing this old Louismann New York Piano. We also kept our family photos here so guests could flip through the pages and reminisce about the good old days. There was a couch and soft back chairs in the room as well. The room had a nice looking vintage fireplace, but we never had a fire in it since the chimney went up past the upstairs room and the fireplace in that upstairs room. It was thought that it was too dangerous to have a fire in the Front Room with children sleeping upstairs.

In addition to the large rooms throughout the house we had a full basement with a dirt floor. Here my mother kept canned fruits and vegetables that had been processed from the garden. Once canned the old fashioned way, the food was stored in glass mason jars of various sizes. There was a large wooden bin in the basement for storing country grown potatoes. My father had also installed an electric pump in the basement that pumped drinking water from the well to the kitchen.

A deep cistern was close to the house near the back yard. It had an old fashioned hand pump that we could use to pump drinking water on the outside of the house. My father always made sure that there was a tin drinking cup hanging from the pump in order to pump a cool drink of water. The only source of replenishing the well water was rainfall. A house gutter was directed down into a concrete container on the ground that contained charcoal. The rain water ran through the charcoal for purification and into the well. Local farmers and relatives had tasted the water that came from the well. I heard them say over and over again, "This is the best tasting water in the country."

We had a very large front and back yard of about two acres. There were several large locust trees and sugar maple throughout the yard. Our favorite shade tree was a large sugar maple just a few feet from the front porch. We spent many hours under this old shade tree kicking back and relaxing after a hard days work. Just to the left of the front porch was a huge American Elm. It was a very old tree and had survived many wind storms through the years.

The Kentucky fescue was beautiful in the summer time and the kids loved to romp and play in the grass. In my early days the kids would take turns pushing an old manual reel lawn mower. We also had a gasoline-powered mower. At times it would take us two or three days to mow the yard in this manner depending on how busy we were with other farm chores. After my father bought a bush hog mower to attach behind the farm tractor, he would mow the majority of the yard, while we pushed the other mowers around the house and buildings. The bush hog had three large blades under the carriage and could cut the yard in about an hour. When I got old enough to drive the tractor I loved to mow the yard while bouncing around on our red Massey Ferguson 150.

The old house had somewhat of a unique history behind it. This five-bay, two-story house was built in the 1860s. It was believed that slaves and horses had been kept in the basement during the Civil War. Slabs of stones were stacked to form partitions and there was evidence of a small enclosed area where unruly slaves were kept until their masters decided to release them. There were no windows and only very narrow strings of light that came through the cracks of the stone walls. The doorway was about two and one half feet wide and approximately six feet high. It had been sealed with stone.

The hand-me-down stories indicated that this old house was built of poplar timber that once grew on the back acres of the farm. When we lived on the farm, there were no visible signs that a forest of popular trees had ever existed. No forests of poplar trees or stumps, just pasture land, and fields of crops. The story was also told that moonshine, commonly known as white lightning, had been stored in the attic of the house. There was a visible sign of cylinder patchwork on the drywall ceiling where a keg of moonshine had fallen through.

We had moved to this farm when I was about one and a half years old. I had been bitten in the face by a black and tan coonhound on the previous farm and had the scars to prove it. It all came about after the dinner meal. My sister, Janice, and I were sitting on the porch of this old farmhouse when my mother came out to throw away the table scraps. She always saved some food scraps for the coonhound. She threw the scraps to the dog and told us to leave him alone while he ate. We noticed that the coonhound had pretty good table scraps; chicken bones, mashed potatoes, gravy, and unfinished biscuits.

"I'm hungry," my sister said to me. "Jump down dere and git me one of dose biscits."

"You just ate," I replied. "Dat old dawg mite bite me if I take a biscit away."

"No he won't," she insisted. "You're just chicken to get me a biscit."

"No, I don't wanna," I said.

"Chicken! Chicken! Freddy is a little scaredy-cat!"

"I am not," I retorted. "I'm not scared."

"Yes you are," my sister continued on. "You are a little chicken."

"I'll show you," I replied as I leaped off the porch and reached for a biscuit from under the dog's mouth. Before I knew what was happening, the coonhound had his top teeth deep inside my forehead and his bottom teeth on the left side of my cheek. He was growling and shaking me from side to side as if I were a groundhog he had caught. My sister started screaming and my mother came outside to investigate as to what was going on.

My mother managed to beat the dog off and picked me up in her arms. I was a bloody mess. She called for my father and they were soon in the car rushing me to the doctor. My mother's dress was saturated with blood by the time we arrived at the doctor's office. The doctor stopped seeing his other patients and took me back to the examination room. He cleaned my wounds and put stitches in my forehead and cheek. It was a scar that would be with me for life.

A few days passed and my father decided to kill the coonhound for fear that he might bite one of the kids again. On the day he was about to shoot the dog a man drove up in the driveway to see my father. It was the Sheriff of a nearby town called Lebanon. He heard through the grapevine what had happened to me and asked my father not to kill the dog. He wanted to purchase him for three hundred dollars, because in his words, "That dawg is the best coon huntin dawg in the country." My father sold the man the coonhound and was relieved that he did not have to kill him.

I had worked hard during my years of growing up on Cherry Hill Farm. Some of the farm chores included such things as milking the cows, feeding the cows hay and silage, hauling cow manure, feeding the hogs, slaughtering hogs for meat, feeding and caring for sheep, raising chickens and gathering the eggs, cutting and storing hay, plowing and mowing the fields, putting up fences, raising and cutting tobacco, and tending to the garden. It was always work to be done on the farm.

I also had some pretty close calls while growing up. I once was running down the feed way in the barn to head off some cantankerous pigs when I jammed a rusty pitchfork in my right foot. It had gone through my shoe and penetrated about half an inch into my foot. My mother took me to the doctor and I received a tetanus shot that hurt more than the pitchfork in the foot. After I got home my father cut a hunk of fatback off a ham that was hanging in the back room and told me to tape it to the puncture wound. The old wives tale was that the fatback would draw out the poison. I was in a lot of pain.

A couple of days later my oldest brother, Bobby, and his sons stopped by to go fishing in the back lakes. I still had the fat back taped to my foot but I was walking on it. My brother asked me if I wanted to go fishing with them. I grabbed my favorite cane pole and we went just below the barn lot to dig for earth worms. When we got a small coffee can full of worms we headed to the back lake. The walk back to the lake was painful, but I could tolerate it. We fished and caught a stringer of blue gill and crappie. My brother also caught a couple of large mouth bass that were keepers with his favorite fish lure called a jitterbug.

We started back to the house and I became very sick to my stomach and light headed. We made it up the hill from the lake and just passed an old Tennant House. I veered off the usual trail and sat down in the shade under a large locust tree. There was a clump of locust trees just above the old lake and Tennant House that my father used for firewood. I was really sick and I held my foot as it was aching something fierce. Bobby came over to where I was sitting.

"Freddy, what's the matter?" he asked.

"Awh this foot is really hurting me," I replied.

"Take that old fat back off of it and let me see it," he said.

I unwrapped the dressing and removed the piece of fat back.

"My Goodness, Freddy!" he exclaimed. "That is an awful looking wound. It looks like it might be infected."

"I don't know if it is or not," I responded, "but it really hurts."

"Well, can you make it to the house?" he asked.

"No, I don't think so," I replied. "I will just sit here and rest for awhile. I am too sick to walk to the house. You all go on and I will walk back a little later."

"No, I'm not leaving you here by yourself," he said. He called for his sons to carry his fishing rod and fish string. "Now get on my back Freddy. I am going to carry you back to the house."

"No that's okay," I insisted. "I'm okay. I'll be all right."

Bobby had already served an enlistment in the Marine Corps. I guess his military training and background kicked in at this moment.

"Now Freddy, you listen to me," he commanded. "You get on my back and I mean right now. You are in no shape to walk back to the house on your own."

I did as my oldest brother instructed. I felt guilty having him carry me on his back all the way back up to the house. It was almost a quarter of a mile, but he knew he had to take charge of the situation. We made it back to the house and my mother had me lay on the couch in the living room. She got some ice from the freezer and wrapped a few pieces in a dishrag. Then she placed the cooling rag on my forehead. She then removed the wrapping and fat back from my foot.

"I swanie to you," she said with excitement. "Freddy, I don't know how you made it back to the lake on that foot. It is all swollen up. You have to stay off that foot for awhile until it heals up."

I was beginning to feel better with the cold rag on my forehead. Bobby told my mother that we ought to take me to see the doctor because the wound might be infected. My father overheard him and commented that I had already been to the doctor. It wasn't any use paying for another doctor's bill.

"I told Freddy to keep the fat back on his foot and that it will draw out the poison," my father said. "He needs to get that back on his foot."

My mother interrupted with a little anger in her voice. "Freddy don't need that old fat back on his foot. I am going to keep it off. I will put some hydrogen peroxide on it to help keep it from getting infected."

"Awh, do whatever you want to do," my father remarked. We can't afford another doctor's bill. He will be all right."

My brother and mother looked at each other and shook their heads in dismay. He decided he had better get home and said his goodbyes. He told me to keep an eye on my foot until it got better. If it hadn't been for Bobby that day I would have stayed under that old locust tree and probably passed out. I never forgot that kind act of unselfishness and brotherhood that my oldest brother had displayed that day.

Another time I almost drowned while seining in a lake on our farm. I must have been about ten years old when a group of relatives and friends decided to seine for fish in their farm lakes. Everything we caught worth keeping would be divided up equally for our families. Our old lake was the last stop. We already had a gunny sack half full of fish. In the bag was large catfish, crappie, bass, blue gill, and a few carp. They were all keepers, some weighed about 6-7 pounds.

It was my turn to carry the sack of fish. I would follow along in the water behind the men pulling the seine. When they drug the seine into the bank, three or four bystanders would wade out into the water and start splashing around like madmen in order to scare the fish toward the net. When they raised the seine, I would be there so they could put the large fish in the gunny sack.

We were at the deepest part of the dam. The men manning the wooden poles on each side of the seine raised it up. Fish trapped inside the net began jumping up and over the net. They quickly called for me to come with the sack. There was a low hanging willow tree just off the dam that blocked my way through the shallow water. I decided to go around the back of the seine which proved to be an error in judgment. I was now in the deepest part of the lake. Suddenly I could not feel the muddy bottom of the lake beneath my feet. I sank into the murky water as I held my breath. The heavy sack of fish was dragging me down to the bottom. I struggled to swim with the sack of fish to the surface. Just as I reached daylight I sank slowly back into the cold depths of the lake.

I could feel the large fish swimming inside the bag. They were actually pulling me into deeper water. The whole time I was holding my breath and the thought crossed my mind that I should let go of the sack and swim for it. I was a very good swimmer and I knew I could have saved myself by letting go of the fish. Then I knew that if I surfaced without the prized catch of fish, it would be hell to pay with condemnation. I held on tight to the sack.

I counted the times that I almost made it to the surface only to sink back down. I was going down for the third time when a large hand grabbed the top of my hair and lifted me to the surface. Then I felt these hairy and massive arms wrap around me and lift me from the water. It was my father that had saved me. I had taken some lake water into my lungs and coughed and gagged for a few seconds. Finally I began to breathe normally but my lungs were on fire from the lack of oxygen. I heard my father comment that my face was blue when he pulled me out. Then I heard a voice come from one of the other men they sometimes called Bear.

"I'll bet that boy has done gone and let those fish go. Where is the sack of fish? Does anyone see it? It's a shame to loose all those fish."

My father replied, "Freddy still has the sack in his hands. He never let go!"

"He best not let go," came a response from a man who used to bail hay for us. "That's a lot of work for nothing if we loose the fish. Now let's get going and finish seining this lake."

My father held me and started walking me to bank. I was still dragging the sack of fish behind me.

"Let's get the hell out of here," my father replied. "I've had enough for one day."

Everyone could tell that my father was mad at this point and didn't want anything else to do with seining. We all rolled up the seine, went to the house, and divided up the fish. It was a close call.

I was once milking a cow and was kicked square in the chest by her right hind leg. The cow kicked me so hard that I bounced off the milking parlor wall that was about ten feet away. We had nicknamed this cow "Old Kicker." We called her this because the huge Holstein cow had a reputation of kicking while we were milking her unless we put on a cow kicker. The cow kicker had two iron cups that fitted over the back legs just above the knee and pulled tight with a chain. This prevented a mean cow from kicking while either milking by hand or by milking machine. In my case, in my haste to get the cows milked in time to catch the school bus, I had forgotten about putting on the cow kickers.

After the cow had kicked me against the wall the bucket of milk went everywhere. My father left the milking machine he was tending to in order to see what had happened. I told him "Old Kicker" had kicked me in the chest. After he saw that I was bruised, but okay, he went in between the two cows and started to beat the cow with his bare fists. My father was a very strong man with a very mean temper. In my amazement, he brought the cow down to her knees as slobbers ran from her mouth. He got me up out of the way and then released the cow from the cattle stanchion without completely milking her. From that day forward, I never forgot to put the cow kickers on her again.

My school years started with first grade at Saint Rose Elementary School, a Catholic School that was about two miles from the farm. It was run by Dominican Nuns. The grade structure was from first through eighth grade. We had old wooden 1960s style student desks that were supported by metal frames. Sometimes as many as three desks were attached to two wooden slats that ran across the floor. A student's desk consisted of a wooden top with a round recess on the top right hand corner for a pen and ink bottle. It also had a cut out groove to hold pencils. The top of the desk was on hinges that allowed it to be lifted up in order to store and retrieve a limited amount of books and school supplies. Under the seat was compartment open on one side where a student could stow extra books and carrying satchel.

When I had just started the sixth grade, I had a Dominican Nun for a teacher. She was tall, thin, and mean. For some unknown reason she was very harsh with me. It seemed that she did not treat the other kids the way she treated me. I was a tough kid at the time but I became terrified just to go to school and be around her all day.

My mother had bought me all new pencils, pens, paper, and other school supplies for the school year. Right from the start this teacher singled me out and picked on me. She would come by and look at my work on my desk and throw it onto the floor. At other times she would walk up to me and start yelling that I wasn't doing things right. She would break my pencils in half and throw them on the floor and then make me pick them up in front of the class. She would also come by and kick my books out onto the floor. She did this day after day.

After about the third week I just couldn't take her meanness anymore. She came by my desk one morning and broke my pencils. I did not say a word. She then ripped up all my work I had on the desk right in front of my face. She threw the pieces on the floor and then kicked all my books on the floor. All the while the class full of kids were watching what she was doing to me and keeping very quiet. She then told me that I would have to stay after school for one hour. That meant that I would miss my school bus and would have to walk home.

"Sister," I said, "I can't miss the bus. My father will be waiting for me at home to help him milk the cows. If I don't get off the bus it will be too bad."

"Oh now, isn't that a crying shame," she replied. You will remain after school today and any other day I tell you to. I will teach you a lesson young boy to do what is expected of you in school."

"Can I at least go home tonight and tell my father that I am supposed to stay after school. Then maybe I can do it tomorrow afternoon."

"You don't seem to listen very good young man!" she snapped. "You are going to have to learn who is boss while you are in my class. I have a whole lot of erasers for you to take outside and beat after school. Then after that, you will write on the blackboard 300 times, "I will do what my teacher tells me. Do we understand each other?"

Yes, Sister," I replied.

"Hold out your hand!" she demanded. I did as she said. Then she took a wooden ruler and smacked it hard across my hand. "Did that hurt?" she asked.

"No," I said, "just a little."

She reared back with the ruler and hit me hard two more times. Now did that hurt?" she asked angrily.

"Yes," I answered.

Unexpectedly she smacked me across the back of my head. It stunned me somewhat. I felt a lot of anger, but I was too embarrassed being in front of the class to take any kind of action. I wanted to stand up and punch her right in the mouth, but I feared that my father might whip me if I did. He had some leather straps at home that were meant for shaving with a straight razor but he had used them on us kids when we got out of hand. I didn't want any part of that.

During morning recess I told a friend of mine that I was running away from school. He told me that the teacher would be really mad if I did. It was a choice I had to make, stay and miss my bus to satisfy her or get a whipping from my father. I decided to walk home. I was really scared on my way home. When I approached the front yard around noon time, some men started coming out on the front porch to relax and let their stomachs settle before they went back to work in the fields. They had just finished a big lunch that my mother had fixed.

I climbed up a small maple tree out of sight to wait for them to leave. My father was telling stories and all the men were talking and laughing. I thought they would never get up from underneath the huge sugar tree by the front porch and go back to work. If my father had seen me up the tree it would have been bad news. Finally, their break was over and they headed back to the field. I climbed down the tree and entered the front door to the house and into the kitchen. My mother was in total surprise to see me back from school so early. She wanted to know what happened and I told her everything. The more I told her about the Dominican Nun, the angrier she got. She assured me that I would not have to fear any punishment from my father and that she would talk to him about it.

My mother pulled out her old ringer washing machine and added some clothes to it for washing. She put in some lard soap and started the washer. Then she went and fetched an old wash tub and sat it on a wooden chair in front of the washer. We had seen her wash clothes in this fashion many times before. Once the washing was done the clothes had to be put through the washer ringer to get out all the excess water. They were then hung on the clothesline for drying in the sun. My mother consoled me so much that day that I decided to help her with the washing of clothes and hanging them on the clothesline.

That night she told my father what had happened at school. My father was very angry, but thankfully, not with me. They had talked about it and had decided to take me out of Saint Rose. The next morning my mother made arrangements to transfer me to another elementary school in nearby Fredericktown, Kentucky. It was about eight miles west of our house on Highway 150. She then drove me to Saint Rose Elementary School so we could get my books and supplies out from the desk. My mother went straight to the classroom door. I could see that class was in session and could hear the Dominican Nun teaching the class. My mother knocked on the door and after a few seconds the Nun opened the door. She was stunned to see my mother and me by her side.

"Well, you must be Mrs. Fenwick," she said nicely to my mother. "We missed Freddy at roll call this morning. Is everything all right?"

"I need to discuss something with you outside the classroom," my mother responded.

"Well, sure," the teacher said. She closed the door behind her. The class remained very quiet. "How can I help you Mrs. Fenwick?" she asked.

"My son Freddy has told me all about what you have been doing to him," was my mother's reply. "We live on a farm and have a large family. All my children work very hard and they have very little money to spend. I bought Freddy all new school supplies for this school year and now I hear you have been breaking his pencils and tearing up his papers. Is that right?"

The face of Nun turned a beet red. "Well, Mrs. Fenwick," she commented. "We try to instill a little discipline in the kids here at Saint Rose. I didn't mean to hurt Freddy in any way. We do things like that for the children's own good."

"Let me tell you something, Sister," my mother interrupted. "My children get all the discipline they need at home and I don't need a Dominican Nun breaking my son's pencils, tearing up his papers, throwing his books on the floor, hitting him across the hands with a ruler, and hitting him in the head. I cannot believe that a Catholic Dominican Nun would ever do such a thing. You are a disgrace to your habit. We are here to get Freddy's belongings from his desk and I am taking him out of Saint Rose and transferring him to Fredericktown."

"Please Mrs. Fenwick," the teacher pleaded. "I will be nice to your son. Just give me another chance. Just don't pull him out of Saint Rose."

Just then the Principal, another Dominican Nun, showed up. She wanted to know what was going on. My mother explained the situation to her again and told her that this sixth grade teacher needed to be removed from her job before she hurt any other kids. The Principal also tried to talk my mother into letting me stay and told my mother that she would monitor my progress.

"Monitor his progress?" my mother snapped angrily. "Lord have mercy, what kind of a school are you running here, Sister?"

That was enough to put my mother over the edge. She refused the principal's offer. She told me to go inside the classroom and get all of my belongings. I walked through the door. All the student's eyes were wide open. They were amazed that I was getting my books and leaving. Without looking at anyone in particular, I collected my belongings and departed through the classroom door without looking back. My mother took me by the hand and we walked out of the school and drove home.

The following day I started sixth grade at Fredericktown and was well received by the Franciscan Nuns. I completed the sixth grade that year at Fredericktown and then returned to Saint Rose in order to finish up my last two years of elementary school there. I did not have any contact with the Dominican Nun who had previously mistreated me. At times during my life I wished that I could be present at that Dominican Sister's death bed so I could personally tell her to go to hell.

I attended Fredericktown High School for my freshman year from 1965-1966. During that school year I played on the varsity basketball team as a starting guard. I came to the team after gaining experience on the floor in the seventh and eighth grade and had honed my shooting skills up in the barn loft by shooting thousands of set shots and layups. I was the only freshman on the varsity team and I felt privileged that I was good enough to play with the juniors and seniors. It was a proud day for me when the coach issued our basketball uniforms and I drew the number 21. Our high school basketball team was called the Fredericktown Blue Jays. I had heard one of the cheer-leaders chants over and over at the games. When the crowd got behind them it was really motivating for me. It went something like this:

Oh when the Fredericktown Blue Jays fall in line,
We're gonna win this game another time.
For the dear old school we love so well,
For the blue and gold we'll yell and yell and yell.
We're gonna fight fight fight for every score,
We're gonna rip and run down the floor.
We're gonna roll old [name of school] on the floor, out the door,
Rah, Rah, Rah!

We had a very good team and could give the more polished teams a run for their money. One disadvantage that we had was the fact that we did not have an indoor court. We had to practice on an outdoor court made of asphalt. It made practicing in the winter very difficult when our hands were numb from the outside temperatures. Practice was held during the last period of the school day so we would be finished in time to catch the school bus home. The coach was really good about that. He knew that there were a lot of farm boys in the school and that they had work to do at home.

The following year the county had consolidated the high schools into one large school. It was named Washington County High which was located right inside the Springfield city limits. I attended the first basketball meeting they had at the beginning of my sophomore year. It was a brand new and very nice indoor gym with lockers, showers, restroom facilities, and they had fancy basketball uniforms and varsity jackets. I was thrilled that I was going to get to play inside for a change and hone my skills even more.

It was announced by the coach that basketball practice would go after school. This meant that I would miss the bus and would either have to walk home or hitch a ride with someone else. I thought about it and got up enough courage to ask my father if I could play basketball at the new school. I also told him that the practice would have to be after school. He did not like that idea but he agreed just to see how it went. I attended the first few practices and managed to catch a ride home. About the third practice I could not find anyone to take me home so I walked the three miles home from school. My father was not very pleased when I showed up at the barn and he had almost finished milking the cows by himself.

"This damn playing basketball has got to stop," he told me in an angry voice. "You need to be here to help me milk these cows. I can't put up with you coming in late all the time. You tell that Springfield basketball coach you are not playing anymore."

"Okay Daddy," I responded. I did not argue because I feared that I might make him even angrier. He was the type of person that you did not want to make mad. So I went about my farm chores thinking about what had just happened. My heart sank when he had told me I could no longer play on the basketball team, I was devastated. All my hard work and practice had been for naught. My basketball career ended that day. I really loved the sport and I was very good at sinking those thirty foot set shots from half court.

I remember when the day came that I could get my drivers license. I spent many hours bouncing around on my father's tractor and even driving it up and down the highway. I figured it couldn't be much different than driving a car. I used to practice in the car by driving it back and forth on our gravel driveway and sometimes taking it through the barn lots and through the fields. After I got my learner's permit, my mother would have me drive her to town when I wasn't working in the fields. We had a black 1957 Chevrolet with a red interior. It was in mint condition and I just loved driving it.

My mother went with me to the court house so I could take the road rest. A State Trooper got in the car with me and we rode around town while he was grading me on my performance. I was a bit scared just by his mere presence in the car. Every time I made a movement, he would write something down on his clipboard. When we returned to the courthouse, he told me that I had passed with flying colors. I was elated that I could finally drive the car on my own. When I drove the old 1957 Chevrolet through town, I felt like all eyes were upon me. I was beginning to become independent and I knew that my childhood days were rapidly passing me by.

While I was in high school, a farmer's organization began to get a lot attention by the surrounding counties. It impacted just about all the farmers. It was named the "National Farmers Organization." The idea was that if you joined the NFO you stood together unified against food processors to help get higher prices for their goods. There was a lot of debate and a lot of threats that a farmer must abide by the rules of the NFO. It seemed that overnight the movement spread to all our neighbors. They wanted my father to join the NFO and without selling milk so that they could negotiate higher prices. My father elected not to join the NFO because he had a family to feed and felt it was a shame to milk thirty cows just to pour out the milk and not sell it.

One spring morning I was at the barn helping my father milk the cows. A neighbor about two miles up the road had been trying to convince my father to join the NFO, or else. He arrived at the barn right at the crack of dawn and approached my father who was tending to the milking machine. He approached my father and started to tell him that he had best join the NFO like all the other farmers.

"I can't afford to milk my cows and not sell the milk," my father told him while still squatting behind the milking machine. "I have a family to feed and I need the money to support them."

"The man said in reply, "If you don't join the NFO, I will personally come down here and pour your milk right down the piss trough."

My father looked up at the man who had a red tint to his hair. "Let me tell you something," my father said, "if you pour my milk down the piss trough, it will be red milk from the blood of your head. If you touch my milk I will split your head wide open."

With that the man left the barn and did not return. In the meantime we were hearing stories that trucks transporting milk to the market were being stopped in the middle of the road and forced to dump all their milk out on the ground. Farmers were uniting at certain points of the highways and setting up camps and bonfires to catch trucks trying to sneak to the market after dark. It was crazy times. I feared that my father would let his temper get the best of him and do something he would regret. I wished that I had never heard of the NFO.

When I was a junior in high school I bought a Honda 50 motorcycle. I was lucky to get it up to fifty-five miles per hour going down hill. Larry and I had some good rides on it during the summer. I had bought a motorcycle helmet for myself, but could not afford a second one. I made a fake plastic helmet for my brother so he could ride on the back. That turned out to be a bad mistake. One day we were zooming up and down the highway in front of our house. My parents and Janice were in the front yard watching us. Each time we passed in front of the house I would beep my motorcycle horn. We were having a blast.

About 600 feet beyond the entrance of our driveway was a motherhouse for Dominican Nuns called Saint Catharine, after St. Catharine of Siena. I decided to turn left into the entrance of St. Catharine. I put out my left hand to signal my turn. I checked my left side mirror. It was all clear except that there about six cars behind me waiting for me to make my turn. I started into the turn and once again checked my left side mirror. I saw a car speeding towards me from behind the line of cars. I knew we were going to hit so I veered to the right in order to get out of his way. The car sideswiped the rear of my motorcycle and sent us tumbling on the highway.

I felt my helmet scooting down the pavement until I finally came to a stop. I looked up and everything was a daze. I tried to locate Larry, but he was several feet away from me on the side of the road. He looked like he was in bad shape. I cursed the driver of the car under my breath. It wasn't long until my parents and my sister were on the scene. My mother made efforts to get us to a doctor. One woman came up and handed her the license plate number of the driver of the car. She had jotted it down on a piece of paper. The driver was nowhere in sight as it was a "hit and run."

Larry and I received medical attention and it was several weeks before we got back to normal. I felt really bad and thought it was my fault for getting my younger brother hurt. The State Police had caught the one driving the hit and run vehicle. It was a teenage boy. We made arrangements to go to court. My father took the two of us to the Springfield Court House one day to file suit against the boy. The boy and his father were there. They were farmers just like us.

As the discussions began, my father and the boy's father asked to talk outside. They went outside of the court house for awhile and then returned. They had agreed that both of us would receive two hundred fifty dollars each for our injuries. The case was dropped. My father told us later that the boy's father was really poor, had a family to support, and couldn't afford to go to court. Since we were not disabled, my father decided that if the man compensated us financially, all would be said and done. I never rode the motorcycle on the road again after that incident.

I also had some good times growing up on the farm. We did some fun things like going "rock fishing" in the rivers during the spring and summer. This technique of catching catfish from under a rock with your bare hands is commonly known as noodling. Not only did we have fun catching the cat fish in the rivers but also the sport of hiding from the game warden if he happened our way. The game wardens could write us up with a small fine if we were caught rock fishing.

I also enjoyed swimming in the lakes and rivers, playing baseball in the front yard, playing basketball up in the hay loft, going camping in the woods, coon hunting, sleigh riding, hunting for deer, squirrel, rabbit, and groundhogs. I was a good shot with the rifle and shotgun and enjoyed outings on my own away from everyone else. I remember going ground hog hunting with my older brothers while riding in a car through the country roads. It was just something to do.

I remember the time Donald and Jimmy Howard gave me some Oertels 92 Beer while groundhog hunting. When we got home for lunch my mother wasn't too happy that I was a little tipsy. Everything was going okay while I was eating lunch until my mother insisted that I have some of her freshly baked jam cake. I ate a big slice of cake, which was a mistake, after having a few beers. I went out to the back yard and vomited. My mother gave my older brothers a lecture, but they were too busy laughing to care.

There was an outdoor drive-in theater just outside the city limits. When the kids could scrounge up some extra cash we would on rare occasions load into someone's vehicle and go to the drive-in to watch a movie. Sometimes four or five of us would hide in the trunk of the car so we did not have to pay the admission fee. Sometimes we would get caught if the attendants became suspicious. They would then have the driver open up the trunk. When this happened we would all bail out laughing and carrying-on. Some attendants would let us go without paying, but others would not let us enter the theater until we did.

It was just a lot of fun as it was a definite break from the farm chores. Once inside the drive-in, the car would pull up beside a pole with two speakers attached and place the nearest one on the driver's side window. We would adjust the volume and then head for the snack bar. The concession stand had the best hamburgers, cheeseburgers, and fries. A coca-cola to wash it all down and we were in hog heaven.

My father did not like to venture too far away from the farm. We managed to convince him one time to go see The Ten Commandments starring Charlton Heston as Moses. He really liked that movie. Almost a year passed and we once again bugged him until he went to the drive-in with us to see the movie that was playing. The movie was titled, "Ma and Pa Kettle." He got so bored that he never went to the drive-in theater again. He said he wasn't going to waste his hard earned money to see such nonsense.

We had an old black and white TV in the living room. A twin flat wire ran from the back of the TV to an antenna attached to the chimney that ran up from the fireplace. In our spare time we would watch the local programs and get such TV shows as The Lone Ranger, Howdy Doody Show, Mighty Mouse, I Love Lucy, The Three Stooges Show, Popeye, Have Gun Will Travel, and The Adventures of Rin Tin Tin. One show that my mother and father really liked was The Red Skelton Show, a comedian who appeared on both radio and TV. Every night my father made sure the TV was turned off at exactly 9:00 p.m. It did not matter if you were in the middle of a show or doing homework. At 9 o'clock the TV went off and everyone was sent off to bed.

I had spent many cold winter nights sitting in my unheated bedroom trying to finish my homework after "lights out" on Cherry Hill Farm. I would start the farm chores as soon as I got home from school and sometimes they would last up until 7:00 or 8:00 at night. Then we would sit down and have supper. After supper I would start my homework only to be run off to bed at 9:00. I would sit in my room trying to do homework with my fingers numb from the cold and seeing a cloud of haze with every breath.

The teachers really knew how to pile on the homework. I wished that I could take them all home with me after school, have them do all the farm chores that I did, and then try to complete several school assignments at once before bed time. Of course, I would have to wake them up at 4:00 in the morning to go to the barn and milk thirty cows before school. It was no wonder that I hated school.

My father was a story teller. We loved to sit around and listen to all his stories about farming and what it was like when he was a kid. He would tell us about courting our mother in a horse and buggy. He told us of when he first got married and shocked corn for twenty-five cents a shock. He would tell us about spending twenty-five cents for my mother and him to go see a movie. The cost included the fee for seeing the movie, popcorn, and drinks. His father asked him one morning at the breakfast table how much he had spent the evening before after courting my mother. My father told him twenty-five cents. My grandfather had said to him, "Ain't that a damn sight! Spend all your money in one day. You will never grow up to be anything." My father was used to a hard life and his stories drove home to us the virtue of working hard to make a decent living.

Every morning and night I would help my father milk the cows which was at the time one of our main sources of income. I remember milking the cows twice a day starting at around 4:00 in the morning and again at 4:00 in the afternoon. The farm chores were an everyday routine, seven days a week and three hundred sixty five days a year. We had to rush to milk the thirty cows during the school months so that I could catch the school bus at 7:00 in the morning. We normally got up at the same time to milk the cows on the weekends and through the summer.

We had one old Choreboy milking machine that we used to help milk the cows. While it was plugging away on one cow, we would be milking another cow by hand and squeezing the milk into open stainless steel buckets. We could milk a cow by hand about as fast as the milking machine. It had four teat cups connected to a plastic see-through hose. You could see the milk being sucked into the stainless steel bucket. A black rubber hose was attached to the milking machine and to a suction pipe that ran the length of the milking parlor. A handle in between every other stanchion was used to turn the air pressure on or off to the milker.

The suction pipe ran across the wall, into the milking room, and was attached to a compressor pump. The bucket of the milking machine held the milk of about three cows before it had to be emptied. We would take off the cover of the milker and hang the suction cups onto the side by an attached hook. The milk was then strained into stainless steel milk cans through a large white filter. We had a small trolley that held exactly two milk cans. When they were full, they were rolled into the milking room and lifted into a chilled cooler. The water inside was maintained at a very cold temperature to keep the milk from spoiling. It could hold about 16 full milk cans. A truck showed up about every other day to gather the milk cans and to drop off empties. My father had it down to a fine science. Everything had to be coordinated just at the right time. He had been milking cows for a very long time.

Sometimes we would open the milk cans and skim the cream off the top and put it in a mason jar. Then we would fill the jar about half full of milk and start to shake it up. After about five minutes of shaking the cream with

An aerial view overlooking part of Cherry Hill Farm near Springfield, Kentucky. Photo was taken in 1975 and includes the house, stock barn, tobacco barn, and lakes. We grew a large garden just to the right side of the house.

the milk you would think that nothing was happening. Then you would notice a lump in the jar sloshing back and forth. That's when we would shake the mason jar even faster. The result was fresh home made butter for the table. We did a lot of chores the old fashioned way and sometimes the most difficult way.

Of course, there were other chores that had to be done on the farm as well. Some of my favorite chores on the farm were slaughtering and dressing out hogs in the fall of the year, filling the silo with freshly chopped corn stalks, harvesting the hay, tending to the garden, mowing, plowing, and disking the fields. Our Massey Ferguson 150 tractor really got the job done. I loved that old tractor. I could ride on it all day and not get tired.

Every summer we planted and grew a large sized garden. We had it fenced off so varmints could not get in and tear up our vegetables. Additionally, my father would plant tomatoes, watermelons, cushaw, and pumpkins in the open fields. Our garden consisted of such vegetables as potatoes, green beans, lettuce, beets, cabbage, carrots, kale, okra, onions, peas, radishes, spinach, turnips, green peppers, and cucumbers. We always had a corn crop to fill the silo with silage and to feed the hogs. During the summer the ripened ears of corn would be gathered from the fields to serve during lunch and dinner. My mother also canned a lot of fruits and vegetables and stored them in the basement. If it had not been for the garden, I do not know if we could have survived.

We had about eight rows of potatoes down through the garden. When they were ready for harvesting we rounded up the two old gray mules so we could hook then to a single point plow. As the mules pulled the plow down the long rows of potatoes my father would guide the plow right down the center of the row. Potatoes would roll out of the ground on both sides of the plow. As soon as the mules were out of our way, we carried our buckets and large wash tub and started gathering the freshly dug potatoes.

After we filled the tub and all our buckets with potatoes we would carry them to the basement and then pour them into a wooden bin. The buckets and tub were very heavy. We did not have work gloves to cushion the metal handles of the buckets or wash tub so we would stop and switch hands as we transported the potatoes to the basement. It made for a long day digging and gathering the potatoes. The only break would come during lunch time and then we were back at it again.

One summer day my father had planned to dig potatoes in the garden. It would be my father, mother, Carolyn, Janice, and Larry to help out. My father told me to round up the two gray mules from the field in order to hook them to the plow. I found them grazing in an open field and started to herd them toward the barn. Every time I got them close to the gate leading into the barnyard, they would bolt and run back to the pastures. My father was getting a little fed up with me and the mules. He decided that he should not send a boy to do a man's job so he tried to herd them up himself. As soon as the mules got close to the barnyard gate, they bolted away from him. He was very mad. I heard him say over and over.

"Hot damn, the damn luck!"

I thought we were going to try to round the mules up again when he told me, "Freddy, let's get to the garden."

On the way to the garden I asked him, "Daddy, how are we going to dig the potatoes without the mules?"

He replied, "Don't need no damn mules to dig potatoes. We'll dig them by hand."

We got to the garden and he walked directly over to the single point plow that was sitting next to the fence. He dragged it to the beginning of a potato row.

"Grab hold of that single-tree," he commanded.

"What?" I asked. "I can't pull that plow."

"Sure you can," was his reply. "Now grab hold of it and let's get going down this row of potatoes."

I stood with my back toward the single-tree and squatted down to pick it up. I grabbed the left side with my left hand behind my back and reached and grabbed the right side with my right hand.

"NOW PULL!" he yelled in a deafening voice.

I heaved forward dragging the plow behind me. My father struggled to keep the plow down the center of the row. Once in awhile he would stop me and pull back on the plow because he had not hit the exact spot just underneath the plant. I pulled the plow down the entire length of the potato row which was about one hundred feet. When we got to the end of the row and turned the plow around, I thought we were going to stop and start putting the unearthed potatoes into buckets and fruit baskets. Instead, he told me to head back down the second row. I got about half way down the row and stopped. I was exhausted. The morning sun, the humidity, and my pulling the plow were getting to me. I wiped my sweaty face with my white T-Shirt. I had dirt all over it.

"What are you stopping for?" my father asked.

"My back hurts!" I exclaimed.

"You are not old enough to have a back," he responded. "Wait until you are my age, and have worked as hard as I have, then you can say you have a back. Now grab that single-tree and let's get these potatoes dug!"

I grabbed the single-tree and continued down the row. I was pulling a plow that normally two stout mules would be pulling. After the second row I just could not pull any longer. I was completely out of breath and my lungs burned from the lack of oxygen. My father threw the handles of the plow onto the ground and went to fetch a bucket to start gathering the potatoes.

"Ain't this a damn sight?" he said. "We never will get these potatoes dug."

At that moment I started looking toward the house to see if my other siblings were on their way to the garden. They had not yet made their way from the house. I wished that they would hurry up and finish breakfast or whatever they were doing and get to the garden to lend us a hand. If not, my father was about to kill me pulling a single-point plow. He was angry and I knew that I did not stand a chance alone. If my brother and sisters were in the garden he would be more lenient with me, because the more kids there were, the less I got yelled at.

Some of the farm chores were not exactly my favorite type of work. I did not care for jobs such as weeding the tobacco beds, hauling cow manure, cleaning the chicken house, ringing the hogs, and "swapping out."

Weeding the tobacco beds involved getting on our hands and knees over a covered bed of sown tobacco seeds, and with a pocket knife plucking out the weeds one by one to enable the tobacco to grow better. This was very tedious and monotonous work and usually took days to accomplish.

Hauling cow manure was a backbreaking job surrounded by the always present stench. Cows were housed in the barn during the winter months until spring. By the beginning of spring, there would be an accumulation of about a foot of cow manure throughout the barn. My father, younger brother, and I would use a scoop and pitchfork to load the manure into a spreader to be scattered onto the field as fertilizer.

Cleaning the chicken house was a nasty job as well. We used to raise baby chickens under heated lamps. As the chicks grew in size they created a covering of poop on the wooden floor. On occasion we would use shovels to clean out the chicken house. When we did we would get chicken lice on our body and especially in our hair. The cure all was old fashioned lye soap in the bath tub.

Ringing the hogs consisted of clamping copper coated steel hogs rings in the hog's snout. We had special hog ring pliers suited to fit the hog rings. We put hog rings in their nose to help prevent them from grubbing through the dirt and under wire fences. They could really tear up a field of nice grass if we didn't. My father found other uses for the hog rings as well such as repairing my shoes when they were worn out and the shoe sole began to separate. He would clamp hog rings along the soles of my shoes to keep them together. Since my father had to spend the money he earned from the farm sparingly, we were allowed one pair of shoes each year. I must have looked comical getting on the school bus and going to school with copper coated steel hog rings in my shoes.

To swap out meant that my father would help the neighbors, friends, and relatives to harvest their crops and in return they would help us with our crops. The old farmers around Washington County coined the phrase "Swapping out." One of the benefits to helping thy neighbor was that each farmer would use their own tractors, wagons, and farm machinery to help with each other's crops. The entire evolution took place during the summer and would last for at least four months. The downside of swapping out was that if your crops were ripe enough to be harvested first, you were in luck. If not, yours could be the last crop to be put in the barn. It comprised many hours away from our own farm chores and was hard and strenuous work.

During the summer months when we were swapping out, my father could have as many as thirty farmers helping to get our crops harvested. They would begin at the crack of dawn and sometimes work until 9:00 p.m. Needless to say, they worked up a robust appetite. My mother would slave in the kitchen and prepare a full noon meal and sometimes sandwiches when we worked late at night. She would fix such items as cornbread, biscuits, country ham, sausage, green beans, country gravy, mashed and fried potatoes, pinto beans, fresh garden tomatoes, fried chicken, chicken and dumplings, and the list could go on and on. In addition, there was always dessert. Some of my favorites were cherry, apple, blackberry, coconut, pumpkin, and pecan pies. She also made banana pudding, strawberry shortcake, banana croquettes, and one of my father's favorites, rhubarb pie. She always was complimented on her very own recipe for jam cake.

Besides being a superb cook, my mother had talents that amazed everyone. She never had a music lesson in her life and could not read sheet music, but she could play tunes on the family piano that would make a person proud to be alive. She had an unusual knack of hearing a song for the first time and then sitting down behind the piano and adding her own personal touch. Her music was an inspiration for the entire family and we always loved to hear her play.

My mother and father were always there for the family. They provided for us, comforted us, and taught us core values. It is hard to imagine how my mother and father, while living on a small farm in Kentucky, provided for a family of nine during some very hard times. Together they had five sons and four daughters. Brothers and sisters alike helped on the farm. As the children were growing up, a special bond was formed unequaled by many families.

Besides selling the milk from the thirty Holstein cows, our other main source of income was selling our tobacco crop in the fall of the year. The tobacco season ran from around April through mid September. This was from the very beginning of sowing the seeds in the ground to selling the crop at the market. Growing tobacco was a full time job during the summer months. There was lots of work to go around for everyone. The evolution of growing tobacco started in the early spring by preparing the fields with a tractor by disking and plowing a plot of land for the amount of acres we were allowed to grow. A tobacco bed was then plowed approximately 12 feet wide and 300 feet long.

Sometimes we would burn wooden slabs, unusable strips sawed from logs. They would be placed over the entire length of tobacco beds and set afire. It was believed by the farmers that this burning on top of the ground would help to prevent weeds from growing when the tobacco seeds were sown. At other times we would steam the tobacco beds using a locomotive steam engine. The steam engine was fueled with coal that was shoveled into the belly of the locomotive. The generated steam was dispersed through a hose and into a metal hot box. It covered a section of soil approximately 12 feet by 12 feet. The area was gassed for weeds for about 20 minutes and then the locomotive and hot box were relocated to the next spot. This procedure would continue until the entire length of the tobacco beds had been gassed. This was another old-fashioned method of preventing the rapid growth of weeds. I failed to see that either technique of burning wooden slabs or gassing the tobacco beds did much good to prevent weeds.

Disking of the soil was the next step followed by sewing the seeds, raking the ground, and then the beds packed down by walking all over it. Wooden stakes were placed approximately 12 feet apart and a wire tacked from one end to the other throughout the length of the tobacco beds. Canvas would then be placed over the beds and secured on each side with wire pins. This would keep the canvas off the ground and helped to prevent the growth of fresh weeds. Once the tender tobacco plants began to grow the canvas also helped to protect them from frost.

Depending upon the weather conditions we would at times need to water the tobacco beds. With a tractor and wagon that had a large water tank attached, I would drive along the sides of the beds while my father watered the beds using a large hose attached to the tank. A rear valve at the base of the tank controlled the water flow. My father would cup his hands at the end of the hose to regulate the amount of pressure.

As the tobacco plants grew in the beds, it was a ritual for my father, to check the growth once a week. Even with the gassing of the beds, the plowing, and the burning of slabs over the beds, there would still be the annoying weeds that managed to survive. This was the time when we got on our hands and knees and carefully plucked out the weeds with a small pocketknife throughout the entire footage of beds. God forbid, if I mistakenly pulled out a small tobacco plant while weeding. My father would not hesitate to give me a mouthful. "Hot damn, Freddy," he would say. "Don't you know the difference between a tobaccer plant and a weed?" I would glance down the 300 feet of tobacco beds with pocketknife in hand and know that there would be no breaks until dinner time. I would make it a point to be more careful.

Once the tobacco plants grew approximately eight inches tall they were ready for transplanting. They had to be pulled out of the tobacco beds one at a time in order to separate the roots that were tangled together. The plants were then placed onto burlap sacks and the ends tied together with common nails. A nail that was woven in and out like a needle surprisingly was strong enough to secure the bundle of plants for the journey from the beds to the field. Once enough sacks were filled to get started on the actual transplanting they were placed on a wagon for transport to the tobacco field.

Our old Massey Ferguson 150 tractor had a two-seater tobacco setter attached to the back. Just in front of each seat was a metal box that was large enough to hold two burlap sacks of plants. The wagon loaded with the freshly pulled plants was positioned at one end of the tobacco patch. The ones on the back of the setter could get a resupply of plants from the wagon once the tractor made the return trip down the long rows. A few sacks were also placed on the tractor itself in case someone ran out of plants in the middle of the patch.

Each man on the setter placed a plant in every other rubber cup with the roots facing outward. As the wheel rotated on the ground, the rubber cups closed around the stem of the plant, and the roots continued down into the ground. As the tobacco plant was released, a gush of water would squirt around the roots, and the two wheels of the setter packed the dirt around the plant. The tractor driver moved very slowly down the field so the two men on the back of the tobacco setter could perfectly time the rotation of the rubber cups.

Someone was always designated to walk behind the tractor and tobacco setter with a hand full of plants. If a cup was missed by one of the two men on the back of the setter, the person walking would replant the missed spot by hand. He did this by bending over or kneeling down in the soft soil. Then he would make about a seven inch hole in the dirt where the water had squirted underground. The roots of the tobacco plants were placed into the hole and then loose dirt was pulled around the stem of the plant. This was done with all missed plants throughout the entire tobacco field. I was assigned this job at an early age until I was old enough and fast enough to ride on the tobacco setter.

Sometimes the one following the tobacco setter just used his fingers to dig into the soil and plant the missing spot. The best method was with a wooden tobacco peg. Tobacco pegs were made from knots of pine or any other suitable wood. Farmers formed them to fit their palm. A tobacco peg was about ten inches long and one and a half inches round. I had watched my father whittle them out with a pocket knife.

A few weeks later we would plow in between the rows to kill any weeds. The plants were spaced approximately 18 inches apart down the rows. The weeds in between the plants were cut using a garden hoe. When the tobacco plants reached about knee high, we could no longer plow by tractor. This was because the wheels of the tractor would strip the leaves off the tobacco stalks. My father would then plow the soil in between the rows with the help of two old gray mules.

It was a challenge in itself to keep the mules going straight down the rows. An unruly mule could damage some of the delicate plants by stepping on them. At the end of each row one particular mule always became cantankerous and would try to bolt in a direction that would lead the mule team back to the barn. I watched my father many times pull and jerk on the leather straps that went from his hands on the plow to the bit in the mule's mouth. He would eventually get both of the mules turned around and headed down the right rows. Once the mules were guided into certain rows, they walked directly down the center.

A wooden hitch connected the plow to the harnesses that draped the mule's backside. We called the wooden hitch a single tree. It was also known as a whippletree. The single tree was directly beneath the butts of the two mules. When nature called and the mules had to relieve themselves, the waste normally ended up on the single tree. Sometimes as my father proceeded down the rows behind the plow, he would sing his version of lyrics to the song "The Old Gray Mule." Instead of singing that the old gray mule ain't what she used to be, he would sing that the old gray mule doobled on the single tree. We liked to hear him sing it, because when he did, we knew he was in a good mood.

There was a constant battle to kill the insects that would literally eat the plants to nothing. There were tomato hornworms, aphids, grasshoppers, beetles, and the like that we sprayed for with insecticides. At times we would pluck off the worms by hand, hurl them to the ground, and step on them. When we did the greenish liquid would ooze their withering bodies. Using hand sprayers we also sprayed the crop or sometimes used a vehicle called a high boy which had very thin wheels designed for spraying. One other method was by airplane in which my father used only as a last resort. Spraying by airplane was very expensive for farmers on limited incomes.

After tender loving care during the growing process, the tobacco would get about shoulder height. It would then bloom and suckers would appear at the base of each leaf. These suckers and blooms would have to be plucked by hand which would allow the leaves to widen and spread. The plants would then start to ripen and turn a yellowish gold color. When the bottom leaves turned golden brown, we knew it was time for harvesting.

Cutting tobacco was the next chore. It involved dropping tobacco sticks about a foot apart and end to end down the center of two rows of plants. The tobacco sticks were approximately five feet long and about an inch thick. After we dropped the sticks throughout the entire length of two rows, we would return to the beginning in order to start cutting the tobacco by hand. A spear was placed over the top of the stick and a plant whacked off about three inches from the ground. The tobacco stalk was placed on the tip of the spear. With a forceful motion downward the tobacco stalk was speared and guided down the length of the stick. Each stick would hold six to eight tobacco plants depending on the size of the plants. The larger the tobacco leaves, the more the crop weighed at the market.

It was a struggle at times spearing the tobacco because the stick might fall over, the spear could be knocked off the stick by the leaves on the plant, or the stalk would split all the way out the end. This would cause the individual cutting the tobacco to re-spear it. An experienced tobacco cutter could cut and spear in a continuous fluid motion. A certain rhythm would have to be established and maintained throughout the cutting of the two rows. The cutter maintained a certain charisma that was an art in itself. It used to be sort of a competition to see how many sticks of tobacco an individual could cut in a day's time. If a farm hand could cut 400 to 500 sticks of tobacco in one day, he was considered a top-notch tobacco cutter and well sought after by other farmers. I always considered myself quite good at the task and found myself helping other county farmers, sometimes against my will.

The cut tobacco was left on the sticks for an entire afternoon and allowed to sun cure. The sun caused the plants to wilt, which made for easier handling and the leaves less likely to break off. At around dusk the cut tobacco was stacked into various piles in the field and left to remain overnight. Early the next morning all the farmers gathered together with their farm tractors and wagons to start the harvesting. Wagons would be loaded to the maximum capacity and then transported to the barn.

At the barn, men would scurry up into the rails and take their places for the tobacco to be off loaded from the wagons. Usually the fastest and more energetic individuals would race to the top of the barn by climbing frantically up the rails. If an individual got to the top first he would not have to pass up any tobacco beyond his own railings. Those less fortunate had to lift the tobacco sticks over their heads and pass them on to the next individual for hanging and spreading of the tobacco stalks.

The rails built throughout the barn were approximately fifteen feet above the ground and four feet between each one. In the very center it could be as many as twenty rails high. A man would straddle two rails, pass some of the tobacco sticks up to the next individual above him, and as the handling of the tobacco descended down to him he would spread the stalks on his rails. One was at shoulder height and the other was the rail he was standing on. The spreading of the tobacco on the sticks prevented rotting. It also allowed the tobacco to cure faster.

Once all the swapping out farmers got their crop in the barn, the remainder of the curing process, stripping, and taking the tobacco to market became an immediate family responsibility. Over the next couple of months, the tobacco would cure while hanging in the barn. It changed colors from green to yellow and then to golden brown. Once it turned golden brown we would climb up into the barn and toss the sticks down one by one onto the ground below. The stalks were then pulled off the sticks, placed into a large stack, and covered with a tarpaulin. This would keep the leaves moist for stripping without crumbling to pieces.

Stripping took place in an enclosed area of the barn referred to us as the stripping room. The tobacco stalks were moved into the stripping room by armloads at a time and stacked in the far-left corner of the long workbench. This was my father's usual position in the stripping room. He would separate the various grades of leaves by pulling the leaves off one at a time and placing the leaves in separate piles on the bench. There would be one pile for "trash" leaves which was the bottom of the stalk, one pile for "lugs" which was in the center of the stalk, and one pile for "tips" which was at the top of the stalk.

The family members would stand in front of a pile of leaves and make a handful with the stems. Another leaf was used to wrap around the base of the stems and then tied by wrapping the leaf through the center of the hand. The hands of tobacco were then placed on a regular tobacco stick that protruded from an opening at the top of the workbench. After about fourteen hands of tobacco were placed on the stick, it was placed in a hand press. After the tobacco leaves were pressed they were placed in a big stack and again covered by a tarpaulin. We then waited until the last of November or the first week of December to take the tobacco crop to market to sell.

At the warehouse, auctioneers would auction the crop in the same fashion as they would auction a house or farm tools. On the average tobacco would bring approximately eighty cents a pound. Considering the amount of money put into just raising one tobacco crop and the backbreaking work involved, the profits seemed very limited. As it turned out it was barely enough profit to help sustain a growing family on the farm. The miscellaneous payments during the year for fertilize, pesticides, fuel and tractor expenses, and hired hands, seemed to me at the time that I was working my hands to the bone for nothing. However, my father would receive a substantial paycheck from his tobacco crop.

This would be my last year working on the farm. I had received a letter from the Selective Service System just prior to my eighteenth birthday to report to the Springfield Draft Board to register for the draft. I drove into town to locate the draft board office as directed by the letter. I went up a set of wooden steps and entered the door. Sitting behind a table was the man that had told my father that he would pour out his milk if he didn't join the NFO. He was accompanied by a couple of women.

"Have a seat," the man said to me.

I had worked side by side with this man for many years helping him with his crops when we all swapped out together. I had spent a lot of time on his farm and he knew me well. Since the little incident at the barn about pouring out my father's milk, I hadn't seen much of him anymore.

"So you are Frederick Fenwick," he said while looking over some paperwork. "Is that correct?"

"Yes," I responded. "That's my name."

"Do you know why you are here?" he asked.

"Yes," I replied, "I am here to register for the draft."

"You are already registered with the draft," was his reply. "I am here to tell you that as soon as you finish high school, you will be drafted into the Army. After boot camp you will be going to Vietnam. Do you understand?"

"No," I responded. "I'm not going into the Army. All of my older brothers went into the Marines and I plan to do the same."

He became irritated and his face became red. "I don't care what you plan to do," he retaliated. "You will be drafted and you will be drafted into the Army. Uncle Sam will decide which branch of service you go into. Is that understood?"

"Not really," I answered. "Looks like I would have a choice of Army, Navy, Air Force, or Marines. I want to keep the family tradition and join the Marines after high school."

"You don't get your way around here," he commanded. "I will personally make sure that you get drafted into the Army and be sent straight to Vietnam."

At this point the women sensed his anger and hostility toward me. One of the women leaned over and whispered into the man's ear. She told him that was all they needed from me and that I should be allowed to leave. I knew he was just trying to get even with my father by giving me a hard time. The lady said I could leave so I stood up and walked out. I was angry as I went back down the wooden steps and onto the sidewalk of Main Street Springfield. I got in our car and drove off. All the way home I thought to myself, it would be a cold day in hell before I am forced to join the Army. We were a Marine family and I intended to keep it that way.

In late summer of 1969 we were swapping out and we ended up cutting tobacco in our own tobacco field for a change. I knew that this would be my last crop to cut before I left home. I would not take on any other jobs of helping other farmers harvest their tobacco crops. I was getting tired of helping others without compensation. It was here, on my father's farm, that I officially revealed my intention of joining the United States Marine Corps. My story about Vietnam begins on Cherry Hill Farm and in the tobacco patch.

Chapter 2

Destined for Glory

MY first cousin and I were cutting tobacco beside each other in the summer of 1969. We were fresh out of high school. We had our freedom. No more worries, or so we thought.

My cousin looked at me and asked, "Freddy, what are you going to do now that you are out of high school?"

"Well, I'm gonna join the Marines," I responded.

"Join the Marines?" he asked.

"Well," I said, "as you know my older brothers have been in the Marine Corps and I want to follow in their footsteps. You know, carry on the family tradition."

"You know you may end up going to Vietnam," he replied. "You don't want to go over there, do you?"

"Aaahh," I said. "Don't really matter."

"You just want to go in the Marines because you think they are rough and tough. Right?" he asked.

Not missing a stroke or breaking my rhythm I murmured, "Naw, not really. Then I spoke up with confidence, "I would like to learn a little judo, fire some Marine Corps weapons, and in general learn how to take care of myself. There is nothing left for me anyway once I help Dad put in his crops this year. Now that I am out of high school, I suppose it is time for me to get out on my own. I can't expect Mom and Dad to support me forever. Why don't you join the Marine Corps with me?"

"Uuugh, not me, I ain't gonna join the Marines," my cousin replied.

"I don't know, you might like it," I responded. I was talking to the Marine Corps Recruiter and he told me that we could go in on the Buddy Program. He called it a Buddy Plan."

"What's a Buddy Plan?" my cousin asked.

"Well," I continued, "the recruiter told me that if two people signed the enlistment contract at the same time and enlisted on the Buddy Plan that they would be guaranteed to go through boot camp and get assigned a duty station together."

Doubtfully my cousin exclaimed, "Ahh, that sounds pretty good."

"Yeah, why don't you try it with me?" I asked.

"I don't know," he said. I may end up looking for a public job. I hate to leave my family and friends, especially all my girlfriends."

The author cutting tobacco on Cherry Hill Farm. Photo was taken several years after the timeline of the story. This scene depicts country life in the tobacco patch where he made his decision to enlist in the United States Marine Corps and ultimately serve his country in Vietnam.

"Hell, your girlfriends will still be here when you get out," I said."

"Naah, I don't think so. I got other plans," he replied.

"Okay then, but I'm going," I spoke with authority.

"When are you going to see the recruiter again?" he asked.

"Next week," I proudly announced.

At this particular instant I could not convince my cousin to join the Marines with me. We continued to cut tobacco and I challenged him to a race to the end of our rows in which he eagerly accepted. I managed to beat him to the end by about twelve full sticks and then glanced down between the rows while he continued to sweat and struggle with the oversized plants.

"Slow poke!" I yelled.

Not wanting to admit defeat, he replied, "Hot out here, ain't it?"

I helped him finish cutting his rows, meeting him half way.

With the last stalk of tobacco on the stick, he asked, "Are you really serious about going into the Marines?"

"I sure am!" I exclaimed. "I should be signed up and ready to go by September."

"Well hell," he replied. "I might as well go in with you."

"Good," I said. "Tell you what. I will go to Danville next week and I will let you know what comes out of my discussion with the recruiter."

"All right," he said.

The following week I drove to Danville, Kentucky and talked with the Marine Corps Recruiter. I told him I was interested in joining the Marines along with my first cousin. He told me to go back home and think about it and when it came time for that giant step in our lives to come back and take the entrance exam.

During the next few weeks, I began receiving brochures, posters, and the like all about the Marines. The more I glanced at some of the photos of Marines in training and the various uniforms, the more motivated I got in regards to joining. We confirmed our plans to sign up for the Marines together and enter on the Buddy Plan Program. The way it was presented to us by the recruiter was there was no way we could be separated from each other once we finished boot camp, if we only knew. We signed the papers for the Marine Corps Delayed Entry Program which meant we would have a few months to think about it and could even back out if we wanted to. Our projected month for actually enlisting in the Marine Corps was set for September 1969.

The months passed quickly and before we realized it September had rolled around. It was time to sign the enlistment contract to serve in the United States Marine Corps, just as my three brothers before me had done. No more hanging on to my mother's apron. I was about to enter another world. We both drove to see the recruiter after calling him on the phone first to verify that we would be in his office at a certain time. When we arrived the recruiter was not in his office. We asked an Army Recruiter in the same building where he could be located. We were told that the Marine Corps Recruiter was home and that he had taken the rest of the day off. I was allowed to use the office telephone to call him at his house.

When he answered the telephone, he said to me, "Come on over and have a drink."

I could tell that by the way he was acting and slurring his speech on the telephone that he had been drinking alcohol. He gave me directions to his house and after driving around for awhile we finally found it. He told us to make ourselves at home and to have a beer. The more we sat and talked the more he tried to convince us not to join the Marine Corps. He began praising the Army, Air Force, and Navy, saying that the Marine Corps was all messed up. He told us that we should let someone else fight this stupid war.

The more my cousin and I listened to this blasphemy the more disgusted we became. I knew that maybe the beer and alcohol was doing the talking for him, or maybe, it was just reverse psychology. At any rate, we decided that if he was not interested in helping us enlist, that we would go see a different recruiter. More and more the recruiter was becoming irritating to us as he continued to degrade the Marine Corps. I began to feel my ears getting red and face flushed which was the sign of anger within the Fenwick family.

He was walking on my fighting side because my older brothers had all been in the Corps. One brother was still on active duty.

"Look!" I finally said. "If you are not going to enlist us, we will go to Louisville and see a recruiter there."

The recruiter replied, "I'm not trying to talk you out of it, I just think it's a bad move right now because of the Vietnam War."

"Well look," I said. "That's why we are here, to join the Marines, not to hear some cock and bull story."

"Okay, Okay," the recruiter retracted his comments. "Come back on Monday and you can take the exam and sign the contract, but I still think it's bad timing for you to go in now."

My cousin and I looked at each other in dismay. We decided to drive back home and to think about it over the weekend.

"So what if we go to Vietnam?" my cousin had said during the drive back. "After all, that's what the Marine Corps is all about, isn't it?"

"Yeah," I agreed. "My brother has served two tours in Vietnam and he made it back. We can't hide from the Draft anyway, and if it comes down to that, I'd rather be in the Marines of my own choice, not being forced as to what branch of service I must enter. I suppose if we do go to Vietnam we will just be fulfilling our patriotic duty."

We began to become excited about going through training and the possibility of war. The next Monday we arrived at the recruiter's office, took the entrance exam, and signed the enlistment contract. The next thing we knew we were on a Greyhound bus headed for the MEPS (Military Entrance Processing Station) in Louisville, Kentucky. We were to stay the night in a crappy barracks style building that was near to the MEPS. I can recall the body odor that filled the communal squad bay that night. It seemed as though these men had never seen a shower.

We were awakened at around 4:00 the following morning and told to eat breakfast and report to MEPS for processing. Our paperwork was checked for accuracy and we underwent a series of physicals. I recall that all of the individuals getting ready for induction into the various services were talking about how rough it was in one service as compared to other branches of service. Of course, the Marine Corps had a reputation of being the meanest outfit anywhere. My cousin and I were amused at listening to some of the rumors and sea stories we heard from others conversations.

During the initial physical all the inductees were lined up in two rows facing each other down a long hallway. My cousin and I managed to get next to each other. Someone came out and told us to strip down to our skivvy drawers. We removed our shoes, trousers, and shirts. Then we were instructed to turn around with our backs toward them and to drop our skivvy drawers around our ankles.

A doctor came out and announced that he would be coming down the line starting with the port side and sticking a finger up each rectum. He started on the opposite side from us. He instructed that side to bend over and spread the cheeks of their asses real wide. He worked his way down the row of naked men carrying out his doctoral duties. I glanced back over my left shoulder to see what he was doing. I never saw the doctor change his rubber glove. There were two other men accompanying the good doctor. One of them announced in a loud voice that everyone could hear.

"Damn! He's got dingle-berries. Look at the fuckin dingle-berries!"

Then we heard laughter on the other side. My cousin and I glanced over our left shoulders to see what was going on. We both saw that some boy who was there to join the military service had little balls of feces hanging off his ass. It was disgusting! Then we happened to make eye contact with each other and burst out laughing.

We could not resist a wise crack between us. "He must be going into the Army," my cousin said with a chuckle.

"Yep," I replied, "I hope they teach him how to wipe his ass."

The doctor found a few more with dingle-berries. We just couldn't imagine how people could be so filthy. After the processing was completed we were finally ready to prepare for our trip to the recruit training depot at Parris Island, South Carolina. There was one more thing to do, recite the Oath of Enlistment. All the ones that were going to Parris Island were gathered into a small room. It was standing room only. One of the permanent personnel at the MEPS told us to raise right hands and repeat after him:

I, (Full Name), do solemnly swear that I will support and defend the Constitution of the United States against all enemies, foreign and domestic; that I will bear true faith and allegiance to the same; and that I will obey the orders of the President of the United States and the orders of the officers appointed over me, according to the regulations and the Uniform Code of Military Justice. So help me God! At the time, I did not realize how true this was to become.

We were bused to the airport and soon were on a plane heading for Charlestown, South Carolina. From Charlestown we were going to be bused to Parris Island. The plane ride was a quick one. We found ourselves wondering through the Charlestown airport with our baggage not knowing which way to go. It wasn't long until a Marine sergeant in uniform approached us and asked if we were going to Parris Island. After we confirmed that we were, he told us to get on the bus that was parked outside. Soon everyone was aboard the bus. The Marine sergeant started the bus and told us our next stop would be the world famous Marine Corps Recruit Depot, Parris Island, South Cakalaki. We were going to meet our friendly drill instructors there who would take real good care of us.

By now it was evening and dark outside. As the bus rolled along, some dimly lit interior lights was enough to read a book, if we wanted to. But who could read a book at this hour, I thought. He had heard horror stories about Marine Corps Drill Instructors. We knew we were in for the surprise of our lives. The atmosphere on the bus was filled with mixed emotions, uneasy expectations, and a fear of the unknown.

Some of the boys were making wise cracks about the drill instructors and telling others that they would teach the drill instructors not to mess with them. They had grown up tough and mean and no Marine DI was going to give them a hard time. We arrived at the Main Gate of Parris Island. The bus driver proceeded through the dimly lit gate and for the first time in my life I saw palm trees swaying in the breeze. It was a bit foggy outside but I caught a glimpse of a street sign with the inscription of Malecon Drive. I could also see that on both sides of the road was swamp land.

My cousin and I talked about not being able to see outside that Main Gate for quite some time. We expected to see a different world awaiting us. As the bus slowed down and pulled up next to old white wooden barracks everyone suddenly became quiet. We came to a stop and you could have heard a pin drop on that bus. We could feel the anticipation in the air of what was to happen next. It was dark but we tried to see out of the foggy windows at what awaited us. The date was 23 September 1969, a date that I would always remember.

A sign hung just above the entrance door. It had a red background with yellow lettering that read, "Through This Portal Pass Prospects For The Worlds Finest Fighting Force, United States Marine Corps." A Marine Corps sergeant, different from the one that had driven us from Charlestown, stepped outside the front doors of the barracks and into the glistening light given off by the streetlights and moonlit sky. He was dressed in tropical trousers and a khaki shirt. Rows of ribbons decorated his chest and were very colorful. He had spit-shined shoes, a shiny brass waist plate with Marine Corps emblem, and he was wearing the infamous "Smoky Bear" hat. The Marine Corps called it a Campaign Cover. He had wide shoulders, narrow hips, appeared very robust, and had a cold furious gleam in his sunken eyes. We could just barely make out the empty squad bay behind his rigid posterior. Just for a moment, he resembled a statue, but he began to move closer to the door of the bus. He meticulously proceeded up the steps of the bus, paused nonchalantly, put his two hands on the bars at the front of the bus, and with a rough bellowing voice, began to speak.

"What are you looking at crazies? I didn't give you permission to eyeball me! Keep your head and eyes straight to the front! Sit up straight! Roll them shoulders back, get those heels together! I said keep your fuckin eyes off me pukes! You maggots do not rate to look at me! When you get off this bus, there will be some yellow footprints that you will place both feet on and you will freeze at the position of attention! You will not move a muscle! Do you understand maggots?"

In shocked unison and with low voices we all responded, "Yes, Sir."

"I can't hear you ladies!" he yelled. "What's the matter, not used to sounding off like you got a pair of gonads? You had better sound off from the diaphragm of your lungs! Do you understand?"

"YESSIR!" we screamed.

"Ladies you have approximately 10 seconds to get off this bus with all of your belongings and get on the yellow footprints marked on the pavement and 9 seconds are already gone. God help the poor bastard who is the last one off this bus. Now move it ladies!"

As we hurriedly grabbed our clothing bags and started scuffling to the front of the bus we could hear other drill instructors on the outside yelling. "Move it sweethearts! Faster! Faster! Faster! Asses and elbows ladies! Asses and elbows! You best be moving it you bunch of slimy ass civilian pukes! Hurry up!"

Some recruits tripped trying to be the first off the bus, others ran over the ones that did. I reached the bottom of the steps only to encounter a drill instructor with his face inches from mine. "You'd better be moving it dirt-bag. I don't speak for my health. Hurry up and get on those yellow footprints at the position of attention. Hurry up!" I had lost all conception of where my cousin might be during all this confusion.

Moments later we were all standing on the yellow footprints with our bodies frozen and rigid in what we thought was the position of attention. I did not dare to move a muscle for the drill instructors were ranting and raving all around me. Their thundering voices sounded like the crack of a whip. They were sharp and piercing. They were all yelling and screaming, walking through the ranks, correcting positions of attention, and chewing ass like there was no tomorrow. I had heard profanity before, but nothing like this. Everyone was scared shitless. Those that moved ever so slightly or eyeballed the area were ganged up on by the drill instructors and ripped up and down from head to toe.

The drill instructor that had originally first boarded the bus caught one new recruit looking around in a daze. "What are you looking at crazy? Keep your fuckin eyeballs straight to the front! Who do you think you are? Huh? Do you think you are in charge of this unruly mob? Huh? Well, do you? Answer me you piece-ah-shit!"

"Nossir!" came the reply.

"Who is in charge here recruit?"

The recruit yelled out, "You are, Sir!"

"You! You! Do you know what a ewe is boy? A ewe is a female sheep, and the last time I looked, I didn't have wool on my ass! Are you calling me a fuckin female sheep, boy? Are you?"

"Nossir!"

He turned away and spoke to the entire platoon. "You slimy ass civilians will never refer to your drill instructors as YOU! You will call your drill instructors exactly that, drill instructors! You will not speak, eat, shit, pick your ass, scratch your balls, or wipe your ass until you are told to do so. Do you understand ladies?"

"Yessir!"

"I can't hear you sweethearts. Louder!"

"YESSIR!" we screamed.

"Listen up you bunch of maggots. I will now explain the position of attention. You will assume the position of attention any time you are standing around doing nothing like slimy ass civilian pukes. The position of attention is when your toes are on line, your heels are together, your feet are spread at a 45 degree angle, and your body weight is evenly distributed on both legs. Your knees are straight but slightly bent. Both hands form a fist and the thumbs are placed along the seams of your trousers. Your gut is tucked in, your chest is out, your shoulders are rolled back. Your chin is tucked in slightly, and your head and eyes are straight to the front. You will freeze at the position of attention without movement. Do you understand me."

"Yessir!"

"Now when I give you the word, I don't want to see nothing but asses and elbows heading for that hatch. A hatch for you civilian pukes is a door. Do you understand?"

"Yessir!"

"Once you clear the hatch, you will double time, that means run, sweethearts, up the ladderwell, that means stairs. At the top of the ladderwell you will proceed into the open squad bay and assume the position of attention in front of one of the double racks. Only two recruits in front of each double rack. Now, move it, girls! Hurry up! Hurry up! Faster! Faster! You're moving too slow ladies! I said, HURRY UP!"

There was a mad dash for the hatch, recruits being tripped, trampled, drill instructors screaming from the diaphragm of their lungs, "asses and elbows." We double timed up the steps and pushed our way through the open hatch at top of the stairs. Recruits jockeyed for position in front of the racks. Two recruits assumed the position of attention in front of each double rack. Some of the racks had three recruits standing in front of them. The drill instructors were running up and down both sides of the squad bay ranting and raving and squaring us away.

One recruit was caught moving too slow for a drill instructor. He was immediately reprimanded. "Why are you moving so slow recruit?" the drill instructor demanded.

"I don't know, Sir," was the recruit's reply.

"I, huh? Left eye, Right eye, Private Eye! You a goddamn Detective boy?"

"Nossir!"

"From now on you will refer to yourself as a private. Do you understand, Private Eye?"

"Yessir!"

"Get back on line you worm." The drill instructor then demanded all eyeballs be placed on him. "If you want to speak to the drill instructors you will say, Sir Private Smuckatelly, or whatever your fuckin last name is, and request permission to speak to the drill instructor. Do you ladies understand me?"

A response was bellowed from all the recruits in unison with a force that rattled the walls, "YESSIR!"

Then we played bedtime games. Hit the rack, get out of the rack, hit the rack, get out of the rack. The drill instructor that had greeted us at the bus then got our attention.

"Girls, you will lay in those racks at the position of attention. You will sleep at the position of attention. I will be back in a few minutes and I had best not hear one sewer mouth talking or one peter breath whispering. Do you understand what I'm saying to you, sweethearts?"

"Yessir!"

Then there was silence as we lay in the bunks with all our slimy civilian clothing still clinging to our slimy civilian bodies and heard his footsteps creaking down the steps. One of the drill instructors turned out the lights in the squad bay. There were sounds of other drill instructors as they conversed among one another. I heard one of them say, "Got anymore coffee downstairs?" I had a sudden disbelief that the drill instructors just might be human after all.

It was after midnight, in the early hours of the morning. I realized that it was well past this country boy's bedtime. A few minutes passed and even after all the commotion that had erupted during the past hour, I drifted off into a light sleep. At some point I heard yelling downstairs. Another bus load of recruits must have arrived. Then the bright lights in our squad bay were turned on again by one of the drill instructors.

"GET OUT OF THOSE GODDAMN RACKS. HURRY UP! MOVE IT!" For a split second, I thought my father was hollering at me to get up and milk the cows. Then it dawned on me that the merciless drill instructors were back, raising all hell again. Everyone scrambled to their feet lining up on a yellow line that had been painted down both sides of the squad bay. Some were still swaying because of their sleepiness.

"Assume the position of attention, worms! Hurry up douche bags! The time on deck is 0300, that's 3 o'clock in the morning for all you maggots. You will, at my command, double time down the steps and make a head call. That means you will get the chance to have a pee-pee call. Do not let your peckers dangle too long ladies. You are on my time now, Uncle Sam's time. Everyone will piss at the same time, like I said before, you will not do anything while aboard Recruit Training Depot, Parris Island, until you are told to do so. You have two minutes to get downstairs, piss, and return to your racks. Now move!"

Since there were over eighty recruits, I figured each one had less than two seconds to accomplish emptying their bladders. We bolted from our positions with the drill instructor inspiring us on. We trampled down the steps and into the rest room. From now on it would not be called a rest room. It would be called a "Head." We were about to become familiar with Naval terminology.

Recruits lined up behind eight urinals. There were three to four individuals at one time standing in the stalls for the commodes. The lines to the urinals backed up all the way outside the door. It was total chaos. When I got to within the third person back from a urinal, I heard a demeaning voice.

"Clear the head! Clear the head! Goddamit, I said clear the head! When I say clear the head, I don't care if you are in the middle of a shit, you will cut it off and get the hell out of my head, ladies. Now move it! On the double!"

With my fly still open I ran out, up the steps, and froze at the position of attention in front of my rack. I wondered when the next head call might be, for I definitely had to go. I would not dare ask one of the drill instructors for permission. I would just have to hold it until the next head call.

We were back into the racks again. I lay on the mattress and could not force myself to go to sleep. I glanced at my watch. It was 4:45 in the morning. I could hear a platoon on the outside of the barracks and I managed to get a dim view of them running and forming a platoon of four ranks. Then they all sounded off in unison, dragging out the words in a rhythmic manner.

"Sir, Platoon 2040, the count on deck is, eighty-seven, highly motivated, truly dedicated, ass kicking, name taking, United States Marine Corps Recruits, Sir!"

A drill instructor in the darkness barked an order, "Riiight, Face! Forward, Harch!" Then with a musical rhythm and chant the drill instructor began calling cadence while the recruits stepped off in perfect harmony.

"HWAN, HUP, THREEP, FO, YO LEF."

I knew this was the heavy cadence of the drill instructors heard by the recruits from dawn until setting sun. All recruit bodies and minds moving in unison across the parade deck.

Then there was a distinct different sound coming from yet another platoon. "Platoon 2049, Ah-Ten-Hut!"

These recruits were obviously new to the game, as they sounded off in girlish like manner. The drill instructors appeared and one of them stepped in front of the platoon at the position of attention. I could hear the other drill instructors chewing ass somewhere within the formation. Then there was silence and the drill instructor in front of the formation began to speak with a frog voice.

"Get your eyeballs up here on me, you broke dicks. When I give you the command Right Face, everyone will face to the right at a 45-degree angle. I will give you the command For-ward, March. When you hear the command of execution March, every swinging dick will step off with the left foot and continue to march."

He gave the command, Riiight, Face! Unlike the first formation, when I had heard a distinctive pop, this platoon had a thumpty-thump-thump sound. Then the command "For-ward March," was given and the figures in the formation stepped off, some with the left foot, others with the right, and with no uniformity whatsoever. I realized that the first platoon had been on the Island a few weeks longer than this platoon had, and that my platoon would have the thumpty-thump sound. As they passed by the barracks the recruits were sounding off, "Step Two, Three, Four, Left, Right, Left!"

What a sorry bunch of slimy civilian puke, I thought to myself while inwardly grinning. My thoughts were interrupted by a sudden thunder bolt voice coming from the center of the squad bay.

"Reveille girls, Reveille! Drop your cocks and grab your socks! Get out of those goddamn racks! On the double!"

While weaving back and forth on the yellow line still in a daze, the drill instructor granted us another chance at making a head call. This time I bolted my way through all the slow pokes and muscled my way to the urinals. I barely managed to ease my overfilled bladder. When I was about half way through urinating, the drill instructors gave the command to "Clear the Head." What a relief! I wondered if I could be able to squeeze out a stool in only a second when the pain hit me. Oh well, I thought, just take a day at a time. Little did I realize that I would be constipated for the entire first week of boot camp because of the initial shock of this regimented schedule and the total fear of the drill instructors.

We then formed on the bottom floor along long rows of tables and were instructed to take our duffle bags and dump all the contents out onto the tables in front of us. The drill instructors went up and down the rows of recruits checking for contraband and instructing them on the do's and don'ts while aboard Parris Island. My cousin and I were standing in a rigid position waiting for our turn to be reamed out by the drill instructors.

A staff sergeant drill instructor came up to me from behind. I had caught a glimpse of him earlier and noticed that he wore several ribbons over his left breast pocket. On the table I had a green Marine Corps Guidebook that my brother Jimmy Howard had given to me in order to help me study and learn as much as possible about the Marines. He had served in the Marine Corps and had shared some of his stories about the treatment he had experienced while undergoing boot camp at Parris Island. I was expecting harsh ridicule for having the guidebook on the table and thought that maybe I should have left it at home.

"What is this recruit?" the drill instructor yelled. "Who gave you permission to have a Marine Corps Guidebook, huh?"

"Sir, my brother gave it to me, Sir," I responded.

"Your brother, huh?" the drill instructor asked. "Is your brother in the Marine Corps?"

At the time my brother, Donald, was in the Marine Corps on active duty.

In order to keep things less complicated, I merely responded, "Yessir!"

"Well, just because you have a brother in the Marine Corps, don't think that's gonna get you over in recruit training. Get rid of it!"

"Yessir," I yelled.

"What is your fuckin brother's rank, Numbnuts?" the drill instructor yelled out in my ear."

"A staff sergeant, Sir," I responded.

"Oh, a staff sergeant, just like me, huh?" he asked.

"Yessir," I yelled.

"I'll bet he has never seen combat, has he, Shit-for-brains?" the drill instructor questioned. "I'll bet he's one of them stateside Marines who has never been overseas. Is that right Scumbag?"

"No Sir," I bellowed. "My brother has served two tours in Vietnam."

The voice of the drill instructor suddenly dropped to a conversational tone. "Very well, you can keep your Marine Guidebook," he responded. "You are gonna need all the help you can get to make it off this Island in one piece. Understand me, Maggot?"

"Yessir!" I nervously answered.

My cousin was on my right side and he too got a dose of the drill instructor's chewing out session. Some personal items such as shaving gear and toiletries we were allowed to keep but other items were confiscated. This was the first time that anyone had ever taken away my personal belongings. I did not know exactly how to react. One thing was for sure, I was not going to buck the system. Who was I to question Marine authority?

About the time the sun began to rise we were marched to the mess hall for the morning meal. We were herded into the mess hall with one recruit immediately behind the other in single file.

"Tighten it up! Tighten it up!" a drill instructor commanded. "Asshole to belly button. You scumbags better make that private in front of you smile. Now tighten it up!"

When we got to the chow line we were told to grab a metal tray and eating utensils and start through the chow line. One of the drill instructors commenced ranting and raving.

"This morning we are having duck for breakfast. Duck in and duck the fuck out. You had best be sidestepping through my chow line with your head and eyes straight to the front, Worms! Hurry up! Faster! I had best be hearing the pop of your heels slamming into each other as you sidestep through my chow line! This ain't no picnic, you Shitbirds!"

As we sidestepped through the chow line we were served food by the more seasoned Phase Two recruits. They had already fired their weapons on the rifle range for qualification and were now in their week of Mess and Maintenance. "Stick it out if you want it privates, stick it out if you want it," they could be heard saying. If you didn't stick your tray out far enough and closer to the food containers they would not put food on your tray. I stuck my metal tray out and a recruit slammed some scrambled eggs onto my tray. I heard and felt the clang of his metal spoon hit my metal tray. Then another messman placed a piece of toast on my tray followed by another slamming down some creamed beef on top of the toast. I would learn later that the Marines called this S.O.S. or "Shit on a Shingle."

After we received our food and eating utensils we were directed to stand on each side of a table facing one another. There were about six recruits side by side on each side of the tables. No one was allowed to sit down until the drill instructors told us to.

Then one drill instructor came to our table and commanded, "Ready, Seats!"

We all sat down with our trays plopping on the table. We were not fast enough for the drill instructor so we were told to stand back up with trays in hand.

"Ready, Seats!" he yelled out.

This time we were faster but he made us sit at the position of attention until given the order to eat.

Then he commanded, "Ready, Eat! You maggots have exactly five minutes to finish your chow and duck the fuck out of my mess hall and four minutes are already gone. Hurry Up!"

We were then allowed to fill our small cups at the milk machines. I started to dig in but I couldn't get past the taste. The food was so different from Mom's home cooking that I could not eat it. I sat at the table just pecking at my food.

Then I heard another drill instructor command, "You're done, get the hell out of my mess hall."

We stood up and took our trays to the pot shack for cleaning. Recruits were dumping large portions of food because we were not given enough time to eat it. A drill instructor hollered out as we were rushed out of the mess hall.

"You maggots may not like this good old Marine Corps chow, but by God there will be the day when you will eat everything on your tray and want more!"

An uncle of mine had once told me that the military added salt-peter to chow in order to keep recruits from getting horny, so I figured that was why it tasted so bad. Thoughts went through my mind of Mom's cooking and what they might have to eat this morning for breakfast. She would have been astounded at the difference of taste if she could have tasted the good old Marine Corps chow we were being served. I supposed that from all the stress we were enduring at boot camp that even Mom's cooking would not taste the same under similar conditions.

After chow we went back to the barracks to field day the heads and the squad bays. Then the drill instructors played some more games just to harass us. The morning progressed on and before we knew it we were herded into formation. I had my head and eyes straight to the front as we marched in formation to the cadence of our drill instructors. None of the recruits seemed to be in step. We were definitely "boots." Our forward movement abruptly came to a halt. We had stopped in front of a small Post Exchange and barbershop. The drill instructor had us form a single line one behind the other. My cousin and I remained rigid in line at the position of attention. I could feel the recruit in the back of me breathing down my neck and I was sure that my cousin felt me breathing down his neck.

A drill instructor yelled, "Tighter! Tighter, you Scumbags! Asshole to belly button! Close it up!"

A glance at the recruits coming out of the barbershop revealed that they had no hair on their heads. We shuffled inside the barbershop and lined up against the far right wall. It seemed the barbershop was very small for over eighty recruits but the fact remained that each recruit only spent seconds in the barber chair. There were four barbers cutting hair. A couple of quick strokes across the top of the scalp, a couple of passes around both sides of the head, and all of a recruit's hair had fallen to the floor. All the recruits were treated the same. The barbers, without missing a stroke, shaved off mustaches, goatees, and beards. The barbers seemed to take joy in the fact that they could cut a recruit's hair in a matter of seconds. I did not see an unhappy face among the civilian barbers. They seemed to enjoy their job. I thought for a moment that we might as well be sheep. It was now time for my cousin and me to get into the barber chairs.

"Hurry up Maggots and get in those chairs!" a drill instructor yelled at us."

I scrambled into an empty chair and the barber proceeded to run his hair clippers from the front of my scalp directly down the center and rolling back the cut hair. It was just like shearing sheep. I had several moles on my head when my barber started. He sheared me so fast that the moles were caught in the clippers and were cut off at the base of the scalp. My family barber back home would have taken better care to prevent nicking the moles. The barber who cut my hair for the first time at Parris Island ridded me of the annoying things all in a few strokes. What a way to have head moles removed, I thought.

My cousin was out of his chair first. As he passed in front of me, I caught a glimpse of his white scalp. He looked so different without any hair. I mentally pictured him as a hairless Martian. I inwardly smiled not daring to show facial expression and risk being caught by a drill instructor. On my way out the door I could feel blood trickling down the back of my neck. I thought the moles might bleed profusely since we were not allowed to move our hands from our sides. As we stood in platoon formation, at the position of attention, I could feel the blood oozing down my head and neck and trickling down the center of my back. It was very humid that morning and we were all sweating from the heat. My blood was now mixed with perspiration

Private Fenwick, Marine Corps Boot Camp Photo, September 1969.

so I did not really know how badly I was bleeding.

We returned to the squad bay and stood on line at the position of attention. It seemed like hours standing rigid and not moving a muscle. Then there was an interruption in the silence. A recruit had arrived late off another bus and was assigned to our platoon. The drill instructors ganged up on him ranting and raving like there was no tomorrow. They wanted to make sure he was fully indoctrinated into our little band of slimy civilian puke.

The recruit's hair was long, dangly, and down to his shoulders. He also had a full beard. Out of the corner of our eyes we could see the drill instructors making mince meat out of this guy. He was instructed to get a razor out of his ditty bag and then fetch a metal bucket. He was ordered to go into the head and to dry shave his beard off without using any shaving cream or water. All hell broke loose inside the head. The drill instructors were screaming and yelling while continuously taunting the recruit.

"Get that bucket over your head, Scumbag!" we heard one drill instructor yell. "Now shave that fuckin hippie beard off your face! Hurry up! Faster! Faster! You're moving too slow recruit! Faster!"

He was commanded to do side-straddle hops, commonly known as jumping jacks, while dry shaving under the bucket. He finally emerged from the head running to get on line with the rest of us while the drill instructors were up in his face. We could see that he had cut his face all over and looked like a stuck hog ready to be gutted. I could tell that he had a problem with acne, but there was not a bump left on his face. The drill instructors ridiculed him some more and then gave him band aids to put all over his face. He was an unsightly figure with a bloody face and hair still down to his shoulders. At this point, the drill instructors cut his hair with a pair of scissors.

We arrived at this recruit receiving barracks on a Tuesday and were to remain there for six days while waiting for a sufficient quantity of men to form a full platoon. Our permanent drill instructors were scheduled to pick us up the following Monday for eight grueling weeks of training. In the meantime the recruit receiving drill instructors kept us busy by assigning us mundane jobs such as making signs and posters, painting the interior walls and exterior of the building, conducting field days of the heads, and continuously sweeping and swabbing the hardwood floors. I managed to write a short letter home to my parents on the third day. Although one six cent stamp was enough for a letter, I placed two stamps on the envelope to make sure my letter got through to them.

During this time at recruit receiving we were marched to a building they called the Classification Section and were told that we would be taking the Area Aptitude Tests. We were going to spend a complete work day here. We were dismissed from our platoon formation and double timed up the outside stairway to the second floor. As I entered the doorway I saw that there were many tables joined together with chairs. The chairs were placed about twelve chairs across the front and twelve chairs deep, enough to accommodate over one hundred recruits. We were hurried to our seats by our drill instructors.

A sergeant from the Classification Section walked into the room and began to give us instructions for taking the tests. He explained that we would be interviewed about our background and practical experience before entering the Marine Corps. We would be tested on our general ability to learn and given special aptitude tests to measure our civilian experience and skills in the use of office machines, radio, electronic equipment, etc. Results of these tests and interviews would become a part of each recruit's official record and stay with us throughout our Marine Corps career. These tests would be used for classification and assignment purposes in determining the duty assignments for individual recruits after boot camp. They would also help determine our military occupation and measured mental-abilities.

A test and answer sheet was handed out to the recruits along with number 2 pencils. Once we got started with the tests the drill instructors convinced the sergeant administering the exams that they would keep an eye on us so we wouldn't cheat. They encouraged him to go back to his desk and get some work done instead of standing idly around watching us. The sergeant agreed and departed the room. As soon as they shut the door behind him the drill instructors started harassing the recruits.

We had been told by the sergeant that we would have peace and quiet in order to put forth our best effort on the exams. The drill instructors had different plans. One drill instructor would go from one recruit to the other and whisper threatening remarks in their ears. Another started walking on top of the tables. As he passed recruits working on their tests he would kick their paperwork around with his foot and sometimes their material would fall off the table. Then he would rant and rave about nothing in particular. I found it very difficult to concentrate on the examination with all the ruckus going on around us. Later when the Marine administering the tests returned and the drill instructors became quiet again. It was if there had been silence the whole time.

Finally in a few days we went to a supply building to receive our initial uniform issue. I could see green uniforms and accessories placed in bins as we entered the building. We were instructed to strip down and take showers before putting on the military uniforms. There would be no slimy civilian smell to stink up the newly issued Marine uniforms that already reeked of mothballs.

When we began to strip down in this small room the smell of raunchy body odor filled the air. It dawned on me that we had not been allowed to take showers since we arrived at Parris Island. The body odor was overwhelming. It made me sick to my stomach. Here we were in cramped quarters with over eighty recruits that were naked as jaybirds.

We were rushed in and out of the showers and then ordered to file by the bins to receive our utility coats, utility trousers, web belts, utility caps, white boxer skivvy shorts, white crew neck T-shirts, green field socks and two pair of black leather field boots. We also received a pair of black converse sneakers. Several supply Marines were on hand to measure our feet and give us the sizes we needed.

We loaded our arms with the uniforms and made our way to our assigned bins. I dumped the uniforms and quickly started putting on a pair. It felt good to be clean and in fresh clothes even though they smelled of moth balls. Hurriedly we tried on each pair of boots. One pair was too small for my feet, but after seeing another recruit get royally chewed out for asking a drill instructor to switch boots for the same reason, I decided against having them chastise me in the same way. Why make waves, I thought? Maybe I could break-in the smaller sized boots as I wore them.

After we got in our first sateen utility uniform we moved to an area and were told to stand in single file, asshole to belly button. We did as instructed and were told by one of the drill instructors that we would be receiving our "Bucket Issue." We moved single file past some large wooden bins with shelves stacked four high. It looked as though there were wooden pallets on the floor that had a shelf spaced directly above them and then another pallet with a shelf above it. Galvanized buckets were positioned on the four shelves filled with 782 gear, the Marine vernacular assortment of straps, buckles and poles. We were told to pick up one bucket and to fall outside in formation so each item could be inspected.

The new recruits shuffled about trying to get into some kind of formation. The drill instructors ranted and raved and finally got us into four ranks on a grassy area just outside the supply building. One drill instructor had us dump all the contents of the buckets out onto the ground. He held up each item and made us do likewise. Once he was convinced that every recruit had the item we were instructed to put it back inside the bucket.

I looked at each item as we raised them up high over our head and then dropped them into the bucket. I counted out one canteen, a canteen cup, canteen cover, cartridge belt, meat pan (with knife, fork, and spoon), knapsack, haversack, shelter half, three tent poles, six tent pins/pegs, guideline rope, and other sundry items. When we had finished we were told to get back inside and place the bucket on the floor next to us. I did not know how I managed to get all of the gear stuffed back inside that small galvanized bucket, but I did.

Once inside the supply building our "Initial Issue" was given to us. We dumped the items in the bin in front of us to inspect them. One of the drill instructors called off the items in rapid succession for us to raise them above our heads for accountability. As he named them off quickly I rummaged through the contents in my bin to try and find everything.

The drill instructor yelled out in a menacing frog voice, "Grab one pair of black socks in your mouth and one pair of green socks in each hand. Get 'em up!"

The drill instructor called off items such as running shirt, running shorts, white socks, shower shoes, shaving kit, pipe cleaners, towel, letter writing pad with envelopes, a green Guidebook For Marines, wash cloth, laundry bag with two large diaper pins, soap, soap dish, Crest toothpaste, two toothbrushes, scrub brush, boot laces, sewing kit, Gillette retractable razor with blades, shaving cream, foot powder, band aids, flashlight with batteries, one inch paint brush, Carter's Liver Pills, chap stick, Kiwi boot polish, two combination locks, Q-Tips, and a comb. I inwardly smiled when I saw the small black comb. I figured I would not need it for awhile. It got a little overwhelming for me so I just stopped trying to keep track of all the items the drill instructor was calling off and hoped I had everything. We had also drawn pillows, pillowcases, sheets, and wool blankets.

The bin in front of us also contained a red Marine guidebook which was unlike the green one that my brother had given to me. It was known as the "Red Monster." We were told that any time we were standing around for a split second without doing anything constructive, that we would have the Red Monster six inches from our face and our eyes glued to the pages. We were to read and study everything that the guidebook contained and was told that all of its contents would be testable while undergoing recruit training. It contained the eleven General Orders, Close Order Drill, The Code of Conduct, Field Sanitation, First Aid, and various other essential military subjects.

We were forced marched back to the recruit receiving barracks with all our newly issued gear. After we packed our gear into our seabags and haversacks, in a standard orderly fashion, we stood on line with the Red Monster six inches from our faces. We were all at the position of attention with the exception of the guidebook directly in front of our eyes. How were we to study, I thought, with the drill instructors always coming in and raising hell with us?

The first Monday came upon us quickly. We were told that our permanent drill instructors would be picking us up that afternoon and that we were now formed as a recruit platoon and commence training. We were given cardboard boxes and told to pack our civilian clothes and shoes in order to mail them home. To the drill instructors, we were as low as whale shit, and whale shit was on the bottom of the ocean. They did not want any slimy civilian clothing contaminating Parris Island.

The recruits were herded to the mess hall for noon chow. I still could not quite stomach the different taste of a Marine Corps gourmet meal. When we returned to the barracks we were forced to stand at attention in front of our uniform bins with the Marine Guidebook up in our faces. At around one o'clock, I could hear a group of drill instructors talking outside the squad bay. One told another, "They are all yours, staff sergeant."

A senior drill instructor casually walked to the center of the squad bay and took his position up on a wooden platform that was about three feet off the floor. He was dressed in tan tropical trousers, khaki shirt, campaign cover (commonly referred to as a Smokey Bear), black belt, and wore chevrons that were three stripes up, one rocker at the bottom, and crossed rifles in the center. The senior drill instructor who had taken his position on the center platform wore a glistening black belt. It represented full authority over us.

I noticed two other sergeant drill instructors quietly taking their positions in the squad bay with one on each side. We would soon learn the Marine Corps rank structure forward and backward. The other sergeant drill instructors wore green web belts with a shiny brass waistplate. It had a Marine Corps emblem in the center with eagle, globe, and anchor. The senior drill instructor began to speak to all the recruits in a stern and meticulous manner.

"All right recruits, get your eyeballs up here on me! DO IT NOW!" There was an instant turn of the heads on both sides of the squad bay. The inflection of his voice sounded like the snapping of a whip. "I will be your senior drill instructor for the next eight weeks. Some of you will be with me at the conclusion of eight weeks, some of you will not. For the time that you are on this Island, I will be your mother, your father, your brother, your sister, and your girlfriend back on the block, but you had best not try to fuck me! Do you understand?"

"Yessir!" we replied.

"I can't hear you ladies. LOUDER!"

"YESSIR!" we bellowed.

"When I give you Numbnuts the word, you will put your cover on your head. That means hat for all you civilian pukes. Then we will prepare to move outside on the yellow footprints." There was a pause and then he commanded in a loud and stern voice, "Put your covers on your head, DO IT NOW!"

Being raw recruits, some did not fully understand the Marine Corps lingo. Some recruits grabbed their wool blankets and placed them on top of their heads, for the last thing they had heard the senior drill instructor say was to put their covers on their heads. I realized then that "cover" in the Marine Corps meant "hat." The other drill instructors had a field day with those recruits who had placed their wool blankets on their heads. The drill instructors ranted and raved about their stupidity. They did look comical, but it was not a time to laugh.

The senior drill instructor continued. "On my command, you will face to the left or the right depending upon which side of the squad bay you are on and face the rear hatch." He pointed to the door that he meant. "You will put your packs on your back, sling your seabags over your right shoulder, and move quickly outside that hatch. Once you are outside, you will find yourself a spot on the yellow footprints, drop your seabags by your right foot, and assume the position of attention. I had better not see one asshole pucker. Do you hear me ladies?"

"YESSIR!" we yelled in unison.

"MOVE IT!" he barked with authority. "MOVE IT!"

As usual there was a massive cluster of bodies trying to get through the doorway at the same time. All the drill instructors were yelling for us to move faster. My cousin and I quickly pushed our way through the tangled bodies, down the four steps, and managed to find some yellow footprints so we could stand close to one another. Then the senior drill instructor approached the formation and demanded for us to look left and look right and to take notice what recruit we were standing next to. This was how we were to fall in from now on. My cousin and I figured that we had lucked out by being next to each other in formation. After all, we had come into the Marine Corps under the "Buddy Plan."

We were given orders to pick up our seabags which contained our military uniform issue, then drop them, and then pick them up again. We were moving too slow for our drill instructors so they commenced to get it through our heads right from the start that when they barked orders, we obeyed. It was just like our senior drill instructor had explained to us; "instant, spontaneous, response to orders, without question and without hesitation." With our seabags on our shoulders and our packs on our backs, we began moving like a herd of cattle, toward a designated temporary barracks in 2nd Recruit Training Battalion area. In fact, one of the drill instructors made us moo like cows.

It was a hot and humid September day. As we crossed a large parade deck covered with asphalt, recruits began to get out of breath and began dropping their seabags from their shoulders. Some of the drill instructors from the recruit receiving barracks were following along the sides of us as we carried our gear. They were ranting and raving at us as we proceeded across the large parade deck that was across the street from recruit receiving. They were assisting our permanent drill instructors to instill the fear of God into us even more. The senior drill instructor was leading the platoon while walking extremely fast and not saying much except yelling, "CLOSE IT UP!" Anyone who dropped his seabag was scolded and reprimanded in a very humiliating and degrading manner by the other drill instructors.

We were herded into an old white wooden barracks in which the squad bay floors creaked at the slightest movement. We were now positioned in front of our racks that were stacked two bunks high. The drill instructors aligned us in alphabetical order starting from the front right side nearest the DI Hut and ending up at the same spot on the opposite side. We were told that the left side of the squad bay was called Port and the right side of the squad bay was called Starboard. Anytime we were "On Line" with Port and Starboard side recruits facing each other we would assume the position of attention.

Luckily, my cousin and I got racks on the Port Side that was adjacent to one another. He was assigned the top bunk with another recruit occupying the rack below him. I was assigned a bottom bunk with another recruit occupying the bunk above me. I managed to glance at the length of the squad bay and the number of double racks. There were about twenty-two double racks on each side. This must be home, I thought. Home for over eighty recruits, room and board furnished at government expense, free chow at the mess hall, and physical training to get into shape. A deal that many civilians would pay a fortune for. What more could we ask for?

The drill instructors from the recruit receiving barracks were dismissed by our senior drill instructor. It was now just the senior drill instructor and his two assistant drill instructors in the squad bay. It was finally beginning to fall into place and make sense. I realized that the drill instructors that greeted us when we first got off the bus six days earlier, and who took us through initial processing, were different than the drill instructors we had now.

These permanent drill instructors were to be with us throughout training for the next eight weeks. They were the ones that would teach us close order drill, physical training, manual of arms, pack and equipment, guard duty, history, customs and courtesies, rifle assembly and disassembly, marksmanship, hand to hand combat, bayonet training, and all the discipline and motivation we could stand. During this era in history, the Marine Corps placed emphasis on preparing us for combat in Vietnam, no matter if it killed us.

We stood on line still gasping heavily to catch our breath. Beads of sweat rolled off our foreheads and streamed down the sides of our faces. Our sateen utility jackets were now saturated with sweat from the force march across the parade deck to our barracks. Our drill instructors referred to the barracks as a "barn." The senior drill instructor walked into the center of the squad bay. There was the usual ritual of correcting positions of attention and degrading our very soul.

"Ladies, I've been on this Island for over two years training recruits and never in my entire tour have I seen such a bunch of lazy, good for nothing, hoggy assed, civilian slime. And the Marine Corps expects me to train you to be combat effective Marines! You've gotta be shitting me! I don't see that I have a hell of a lot to work with! But you Numbnuts will learn! You will all learn to be killers and protect this great nation of ours! Do you understand?"

"Yessir!"

He went on to explain the procedures for making a head call and that we would do everything as a platoon, in unison and as one unit. He told us that upon his command of Center, March, that we would take one step with the left foot and bring our right heel smartly along side of the left heel. Then we were to face 45 degrees to the right or left facing the direction of the head, bringing the other heel along side the pivot foot and freeze at the position of attention. On his command of Forward, March, we would step off with the left foot and continue to march in unison into the head. When "Clear the Head" was given, we were to stop what we were doing, double-time back to our racks, and stand on line facing toward the center of the squad bay.

Surprisingly enough, when he gave us the command of Forward, March, we stepped off to what seemed in step with his cadence. Once inside the head everyone bolted to a urinal to try to do his thing before we were ordered out. No sooner had I finished, the word was given to get out and back on line. We all ran as fast as we could with the drill instructors up in every recruit's face that passed them by. It reminded me of a very mean dog we used to have back on the farm.

Suddenly everyone was stopped in their tracks by the senior drill instructor. I could hear the heavy breathing of the recruits as they stood frozen in place.

"Listen up, Numbnuts! When I say clear the head, everyone will sound off from the diaphragm of your lungs, Aye, Aye, Sir! That means that you understand the order and will obey to the best of your ability! Do you understand girls?"

"Yessir!"

"Now let me hear you say it!"

"Aye, Aye, Sir!"

"I can't hear you ladies. LOUDER!"

"AYE, AYE, SIR!" we yelled.

"Hurry up and get back on line. Move it!"

Everyone then scrambled back to their positions in front of their racks facing the center. To our dismay someone had taken a crap in the toilet and had not flushed the commode. We were all threatened that if it ever happened again, the turd would be passed around on both sides of the squad bay and that we would scrub the toilets until the drill instructors got tired, and we were assured that they would not tire easily by supervising the cleanup.

My cousin and I thought this was a bit funny. Not because of what had happened in the head, but rather the continuous chewing out we were receiving on the subject of a floating turd. We smiled at each another and it did not go unnoticed. One of the smaller drill instructors was suddenly in our face, spitting, slobbering, and waving his hands back and forth. His teeth were clenched and I recall that he had to tiptoe in order to meet us eye to eye. About every third word was the "F" word. I began to smile at his style of speech which was a terrible mistake. He got up very close to my face and starting yelling at me.

"Do you fuckin think something's fuckin funny you fuckin puke? Well do you, you fuckin maggot? Answer me you fuckin pimply faced fuck!"

"NOSSIR!" I screamed.

After reprimanding me for what seemed like a few minutes, he finally stepped over to my cousin and started screaming and yelling at him. The same type of language continued. At least now I knew not to drop my eyes down to make eye contact with a short DI. In fact, no eye contact was allowed. All head and eyes were to be straight to the front at all times. Even if your eyes did happen to be on the same eye level as the drill instructors, you were to stare a hole right through him without following his head or eye movements. I knew the drill instructors were serious and would not tolerate the simplest form of disrespect.

We were instructed in routine barracks procedures and were given a class on how to properly make a rack. The drill instructors told us they wanted the blankets and sheets so tight they could bounce an elephant off of them. One of the drill instructors also set up barracks security throughout the night called fire watch. Two recruits were assigned times in which to stand security by walking back and forth down the center of the squad bay. They were assigned two-hour shifts. Since the drill instructor had started the roster by alphabetical order, I did not draw fire watch the first night in the platoon. We were assigned laundry numbers which also went in alphabetical order. Most of the time we were called by our laundry numbers instead of by our last names. My cousin became Laundry #14 and I became Laundry #15.

It felt good to take showers that night and finally getting to hit the rack. The fresh sheets felt good to the skin although they had a distinctive scent and seemed to be half starched. As I lay back in my bed still at the position of attention, I wondered what my mother and father might be doing back home. If they only knew what I had gotten myself into. For me, however, it was too late. No turning back now. I was a prisoner of my own desires.

Reveille the next morning went much too soon as far as I was concerned. I was used to getting up early on the farm, but it seemed very difficult to hop out of the rack and start another day as I had the previous days. I knew if I did not however, that I would have one of the drill instructors breathing down my neck. With one heave I hit the wooden floor as soon as the lights came on. We were run into the head and commenced our daily morning routine. "The Three S's," the drill instructors called it, "Shit, Shave, and Shower." However, the luxury of a shower would have to wait until late evening when we were about to hit the rack for the day. First we had to work up a sweat during the course of the day in order to rate a shower at night. Cleanup was conducted in the squad bay and then the order was given to fall out in platoon formation.

While standing in formation, the senior drill instructor approached us in the darkness of the morning and began to speak.

"Listen up, Numbnuts. While you are a recruit on Parris Island, you will be in Platoon 3049. My job is to train you to become combat effective Marines. Upon graduation from boot camp, 95 percent of will be shipped to Vietnam. If you listen to your drill instructors, you may have a chance in hell to survive in a combat environment. That is my mission. To help you survive combat without coming back home with your dick blown off. You won't be any good to Suzy Rottencrouch if your balls are blown off because you didn't pay attention in boot camp. So you had best retain in your brain-housing group everything that your drill instructors teach you. Do you understand?"

"YESSIR!" we yelled."

"You will act and train as a team. Teamwork, goddamit, Teamwork! If you train as a team, you will act as a team in combat. The more you sweat in peacetime, the less you bleed in war. Now we are going to march to chow and by God every swinging dick had best hold his head up high and be proud of this unique fighting force we call the United States Marine Corps."

I felt a sudden boldness as we stepped off on our way to the mess hall. I seemed to be energized by the senior drill instructors concern for our welfare. The pride part would probably come later. Right now, I was still a bit scared of the unknown that lay ahead in recruit training. I heard the many sets of heels hitting the pavement in ragged unison. The senior drill instructor called cadence for the platoon. "HWAN, HUP, THREEP, FO, YO, LEF. AH LEFTY RIGHTA LEF." Although we were new on Parris Island, the rhythm of the cadence seemed somewhat in step. It motivated me.

We stayed in this old white wooden barracks at 2nd Battalion for about two days. One morning at reveille we were run into the head and told to make head calls and to shave. Inside the small head about eighty recruits were bumping into each other trying to use the commodes, urinals, and sinks. My cousin and I figured we had better shave first and allow the long lines to use the commodes and urinals a chance to die down. We stepped up to the sinks and jockeyed for a position at the sinks side by side. We used the sink stopper and ran some hot water into the sink. My cousin had a heavy beard. He began lathering up with a can of boot camp issue shaving cream. I saw him put a new blade in his double edge safety razor and he started to shave.

I never had a heavy beard during high school. I only managed to get a little peach fuzz on my face so I rarely shaved since I did not have much to shave. I lathered up with shaving cream but did not put a blade in my razor. I quickly went through the motions as if shaving and I was finished in a jiffy. I started to wash my face. My cousin looked at me in amazement because I had finished so quickly. Just then one of the drill instructors came up to me from behind and caught me totally off guard.

"How did you finish shaving so fast recruit?" he barked.

"Sir, the private only has peach fuzz!" I yelled out.

"The drill instructor responded, "Let me see your razor."

I handed my double edge razor to the drill instructor and then watched as he opened it up to check if a blade was inserted. "What are you looking at crazy!" he yelled. "Get your eyeballs off of me and straight to the front. Lock your body at the position of attention, Scumbag!" I did as he ordered while staring at myself in the mirror hanging above the sink. "You little Dirt Bag!" he continued. "You don't have a blade in this razor. Did you think you could pull the wool over your drill instructor's eyes you Little Puke? Well, did you Maggot?"

"NOSSIR!" I yelled.

"Then put a fuckin blade in this razor you Little Ass before I dry shave you myself. Do you understand me?"

"Yes Sir!"

"Louder Worm, you better sound off like you got a pair of gonads."

"YESSIR!"

"Then MOVE IT!" he snapped at me.

I nervously searched inside my shaving kit for a double edged blade. I inserted one into my razor and closed the opening. I started to shave.

"From now on, Scrotum, you will always shave with a blade in that razor, is that understood?"

"YESSIR!" I bellowed out.

"Carry on!" the drill instructor said as he turned and walked away from me.

I was thankful the drill instructor decided to reprimand some other recruit. I shaved with the brand new blade in the razor and cut my face in several places. After I washed the shaving cream off my face I dried it with the white towel that I had around my neck. There were blood stains all over it. I figured that if I was to shave with a blade in the razor that I should not push as hard against my face and to go around any acne. Otherwise I would look like a stuck hog every morning when we had to shave.

One morning we were marched down to the Naval Medical Clinic, the drill instructors called sick bay, to receive physicals and inoculations. It was a grueling experience for us. During the time we were not physically being seen by medical personnel, we were rigid at attention "asshole to belly button," with our Red Monster in front of our faces. It came time to get our inoculations. The recruits were formed in two rows facing inboard. We were instructed to strip off our utility jackets and T-shirts. Using a black magic marker, the Navy corpsmen marked our bare chests with our laundry numbers.

The corpsmen started coming down both lines giving shots with a jet injector, commonly known as an air gun. The jet injector is a medical injecting syringe that uses a high-pressure narrow jet of injection liquid instead of a hypodermic needle to penetrate the skin. It is powered by compressed air or gas, either by a pressure hose from a cylinder or from a built-in gas cartridge. I had never seen an air gun before and I always hated getting shots back home. We were warned not to move a muscle while we were receiving the shots with the air gun or the force coming from the gun would cut us. We were told to remain very still and not to flinch.

The corpsmen walked down both lines very quickly. Two of them came on both sides of me and gave me a shot with the air guns in both arms. They then continued on down the line. I felt the sting of the shots but I did not think it hurt too much as I tried to relax as they had told us. Then two more corpsmen came up to me and gave me a shot with a needle in both arms. The needle shots began to sting but I still did not move. I felt that should be the last of the shots as we had already received four shots.

Then two more corpsman came down the line and put the air guns up to my shoulders in the same place as I had received the other shots. I jerked away slightly and they cautioned me that I must remain very still. They placed the air guns on both shoulders and then as in unison, hesitated for a few seconds. The corpsman on my right side shot first and I flinched just as the one my left gave me a shot. They laughed and moved on to the next recruit. I managed to sneak a peak at my shoulders and noticed that blood was oozing out from the last shots and trickling down my arm. I still did not move.

I was beginning to feel a bit dizzy and light headed. Then I heard a corpsman holler out, "Drop your trousers and your skivvy drawers down to your ankles and standby for a knockout. You will each be receiving a Gamma globulin injection in the ass." He walked down in front of me and I noticed a very large and long needle. He walked back up to the beginning of the line and started down behind our row. As the Navy corpsman and a drill instructor walked behind us I could hear the corpsman ask the drill instructor, "Point to the recruits that you want me to really jab hard." The drill instructor was more than glad to point out the recruits that he thought were misfits.

All of a sudden, I felt the long needle sink into my right cheek of my butt. I started to feel very sick and nauseated. I could feel that my knees were buckling and that I was about to pass out. I bent over slightly at the waist to catch my breath. By now the concrete floor looked white to me. Just then a drill instructor was in my face scolding me to get back to the position of attention. I tried but I could not force myself to stand up straight. Then another drill instructor was yelling in my face and ears. My knees buckled and they both stood me upright yelling at me to stay at the position of attention. Then the senior drill instructor came over to where I was. Now there were three drill instructors around me.

"Oh what's the matter you little pansy," one of them said. "Does your pussy hurt? You little Maggot, you had best get with the program, do you understand me Worm?"

"Yes Sir," I said in a low voice.

"Louder! Louder!" the drill instructor commanded. "I can't hear you, Scumbag!"

Just then I started falling towards the floor and the next thing I knew the senior drill instructor had me sit down with my legs crossed in front of me with my head down.

"Just let him sit there for a few minutes until he comes around," the senior drill instructor told the other two. "He should be okay in a few minutes. When he does, get him back on his feet." After a minute or so I felt somewhat better and the white floor that I had seen before came back to the original color. I started to get to my feet. The senior drill instructor came over to me and said, "Well Shit-for-brains, you gonna pass out on me again?"

"No Sir!" I yelled out.

"You better not," he said. "The next time you'll be going to the Dentist with all your teeth knocked out because I won't be here to catch you. Do you understand me, Crazy?"

"Yes Sir!" I responded.

We were marched back to the barracks and as soon as we got in front of our racks we had to do pushups and side straddle hops. The exercises were to massage and loosen up our shoulders after the shots. "We will do pushups until you puke," one of the drill instructors said. The next day I could hardly get out of the rack because my arms were so sore. They were bruised and swollen. We had to drop down and do more pushups before we were allowed to make a head call.

Later that morning we packed our seabags and haversacks in order to relocate to our permanent barracks. We moved in platoon formation across the northwest corner of the 2nd Battalion parade deck and crossed the main road. As we were heading into the barracks area I noticed the old oak trees and Spanish moss dangling from them. I had never seen anything like it before. Then the brick barracks came into sight. We crossed a road called Wake Boulevard and I saw a row of six barracks side by side. Each barracks had three decks with a squad bay on each level. We were run into one of the squad bays and directed to take our positions in front of the racks. Our senior drill instructor told us that we were now in Hotel Company, 3rd Recruit Training Battalion. We were in the elite platoon known as Platoon 3049.

The squad bay was set up in the same fashion as the one we had just vacated, two rows of racks that were stacked two bunks high. We were placed in the bunks by alphabetical order once again. My cousin was in the double rack right next to mine. When we got on line in front of our racks, my cousin stood to my right, because his first name began with a "D" and mine was "F." We would also fall out in platoon formation side by side. When the drill instructors faced us to the right and gave us Forward, March, my cousin was directly in front of me. I stepped on his boot heels a lot.

Now the training would begin on a Wednesday and I looked forward to the challenges ahead. We had to memorize our service numbers, rifle serial numbers, and lock combinations, or else. I realized what I was getting into. I knew that we would be trained to fight in a combat zone. I took the training to heart, for I felt that one-day I might end up in Vietnam where everything I had learned in boot camp may in fact pay dividends. Although the drill instructors were sadistic and ruthless at times, I respected them for what they were doing for God, Corps, and Country.

We learned of the pride and traditions that motivate a fighting force and that these traditions are as much a part of a Marine's equipment as his pack or rifle. These traditions, loyalty to country and to the Corps, self-sacrifice, devotion to duty, discipline and versatility, all of which are summed up in the phrase "Esprit de Corps," or "Working Together" made us all feel like brothers in arms. We were told that the pageantry and worldwide service of the Marine Corps is symbolized in its insignia and that we were the keepers of tradition. We were beginning the process of becoming United States Marines.

We were taught to forget everything we learned in school about telling time. We were to use military time. The terms a.m., p.m., and o'clock were to be eradicated from our memories. Instead, we had to quickly memorize the 24 hour clock and use it as long as we were in the Marine Corps. I learned for example that if reveille went at 5:00 in the morning, that the Marine Corps time was 0500, and if we hit the rack in the evening at 10:00, that the Marine Corps time it was 2200.

We learned that the Marine Corps emblem consists of an eagle clenching the Marine Corps motto in its beak, the globe (Western Hemisphere), and the anchor. The emblem was adopted from the British (Royal) Marines and was modified by Brigadier General Jacob Zeilin in 1868 to depict the Marines as both American and maritime. The globe and anchor signify the worldwide service and sea traditions. The spread eagle represents the nation itself. The motto, "Semper Fidelis" is Latin for "Always Faithful" and was adopted about 1883. The Marine Corps emblem has been the pride of every Marine since the founding of the Marine Corps on 10 November 1775.

While undergoing boot camp, my cousin and I stayed close together. It made the stressful environment easier to cope with knowing that we were there for one another. We managed to sneak a conversation from time to time without being caught by the drill instructors. It seemed as though every minute of every day we were involved in some type of training. Besides the discipline, motivation, classroom instruction, numerous personal hygiene inspections, and equipment inspections, the drill instructors conducted close order drill over and over. The least bit of idle time was quickly consumed by conducting drill movements and executing the manual of arms with the rifle. Our drill instructors made us smack and pop our rifles so hard in performing precision drill movements that I thought we would break them half into. We disassembled, assembled, cleaned, and polished our M14 rifles.

We were taught how to assemble the different field packs of the M1941 pack system. It consisted of three main parts, the haversack, knapsack, and belt suspenders. The pack system could be converted into five different configurations which included the Light Marching Pack, Marching Pack, Field Marching Pack, Transport Pack, and the Field Transport Pack. The Field Marching Pack seemed to be the preferred pack for the drill instructors when going on long conditioning hikes. It consisted of the haversack, belt suspenders attached to the cartridge belt, and a blanket roll attached. The blanket roll was made by rolling our green military blanket, along with three tent poles, six tent pegs, and guideline rope inside the shelter half and then fastening it to the haversack. We went on many conditioning hikes with helmets, packs, and full combat gear.

We were required to wear "Chrome Domes" during the first and second phase of training when we were outside. The Chrome Dome was the liner for the old steel pot helmet. We spray painted them silver. They were always getting in the way during the manual of arms with the M14 service rifle. The drill instructors just loved to hit us up side our heads and send the Chrome Domes bouncing off the floor or parade deck. About the only time we wore the green sateen utility covers was when we were going to the mess hall to eat chow. The drill instructors called them soft covers. The utility covers were folded up in thirds and placed in the right rear trousers pocket while side stepping through the chow line.

When I wrote home to my parents, my letters were all generalized with not much detail as to what we were going through during boot camp. Sometimes we would be given only five minutes to write a letter. If you did not have your letter finished, sealed in an envelope, and a stamp affixed in that amount of time, you were just out of luck for that evening. One time it took me four nights just to write a three page letter.

In one letter I reveled that we had to enlist in the Marine Corps for three years vice the two years that the recruiter had promised. My cousin and I didn't know what to do at the time so we signed the papers anyway. I wrote that we were only authorized to keep five dollars in our footlockers at any given time, about the rough physical training, that we were allowed to go to church on Sundays, and that the chow was good. I told them about firing the M14 Service Rifle for qualification on the rifle range, standing fire watch in the middle of the night inside the barracks, about being a "Milk Man" at the mess hall during our week of Mess Duty, and that I had to get up at 0315 to get to the mess hall in order to stand chow guard. A chow guard's responsibility was to clean off the tables and sweep and swab the floors as the hordes of platoons came dashing in and out of the mess hall.

I informed my parents about preparing for exams, personnel inspections, about running the confidence course and obstacle course, going to Elliot's Beach for Essential Subjects Testing, about putting up a hog board with girl friends pictures on it, and how we went from over eighty recruits to sixty-two in a little over a month. I cautioned my parents not to send gum or candy to me in the mail. Several recruits had to perform many exhausting exercises such as side straddle hops and bends and thrusts because they received "pogey bait" (candy or sweets) in the mail.

I told them about standing on line reciting the Chain of Command and the Eleven General Orders, all in a cadence of learning. If our drill instructors said the words General Orders, we would yell out in unison, "General Orders, Aye Aye Sir. Sir, the private's first General Order is, to take charge of this post and all government property in view. Sir, the private's second general order is, to walk my post in a military manner, keeping always on the alert, and observing everything that takes place within sight or hearing." Then we would continue with the next general order and so on.

My short letters revealed some of our training evolutions. I mentioned running three miles with packs and full combat gear and then having to do the rope climb with all that heavy gear on. I talked about the Physical Readiness Test and Final Drill Competition. I told them I had qualified as a 1st class swimmer after having to stay in the pool for thirty minutes and making a life preserver out of our trousers for the test. The recruits also had to swim 80 yards with a M14 service rifle around our necks. I told them about attending Field Meets, studying for the 2nd and 3rd Phase tests, and our final Command Inspection conducted by the colonel in charge of the battalion.

The letters that I sent home did not include things that I thought would upset my mother. I did not write about one of our drill instructors forcing us to do pushups and "Up and On Shoulders" with the M14 rifle immediately following inoculations and into the following morning. Our shoulders were so sore we could hardly move. I didn't tell them about doing so many pushups in the squad bay that the entire floor was wet from our sweat. We would slip and slide in our own sweat to the point that we couldn't perform the pushups any longer. A drill instructor would make us swab the deck with mops and then dry it with our white towels. Once the floor was dry, we would commence doing pushups again.

The drill instructors loved to punish us with an exercise called "Up and On Shoulders." It was a physical drill movement with arms that was taken from the Landing Party Manual, United States Navy, 1960. It was conducted with our M14 rifles. The original purpose of the exercise was to build the muscles of the arms and of the side and front walls of the chest. The starting position was at the ready which meant the rifle was held chest high with both hands, the right hand grasping the stock of the weapon, and the left hand grasping the hand guard. It was a four count movement. For the count of one, the rifle was pushed horizontally overhead. For the count of two, the rifle was lowered to the back of the shoulders, head up, and elbows well back. For the count of three, the rifle was raised up again horizontally overhead. For the count of four, the rifle was brought back to the ready position. Since the M14 weighed eleven and a half pounds, it did not take long to become extremely fatigued. The drill instructors also enjoyed having us place our M14s on the back of our fingertips, palms facing downward, and then extending our arms straight out. God help the poor recruit who managed to drop his weapon.

I also did not tell anyone about certain recruits being forced to eat a cigarette, drink a canteen of warm water, and then perform side straddle hops while under a bucket. This unusual punishment was usually reserved for those smokers caught in the act. The intent was to make the recruit sick to his stomach and throw up. They were ridiculed as being weak when they finally puked in the bucket. I did not convey to my mother about the time I got hit in the stomach twice by the senior drill instructor when I requested to wear tennis shoes out for physical training. I risked it because I had blisters on my feet the size of quarters.

I did not mention the fact that sometimes they would give us five minutes to shit, shave, and shower, nor did I mention the term blanket party that was designed to square away a non-performing recruit. I also never said that our senior drill instructor got relieved of duties because one of the recruits had made allegations to higher authority that the senior drill instructor had been beating him. His punishment was relief from being a senior drill instructor and made an assistant DI for our platoon.

I did not tell them about me being sent to the Motivational Platoon for a day only because the new senior drill instructor had a quota to fill. This new black senior drill instructor came walking down the squad bay one morning pointing to various recruits and telling them they were going to the Motivation Ditch to get some discipline. He had a quota of twelve recruits and had to get just one more designated to go. He paced back and forth up the two rows of recruits on line. He couldn't decide who else to send. He got close to me and then looked me dead in the eye.

"And you too, you pimply faced mother fucker," he said. "Now all of you Dirtbags get your packs and rifles and get your asses outside. There will be a bus waiting for you to take you to the Motivation Platoon. Now, HURRY UP!"

The Motivational Platoon would stick in my mind for a long time afterwards. The recruits designated to fall out that day had grabbed our rifles, cartridge belts, and packs and ran down the steps of the barracks. We loaded aboard the bus and we rode past the rifle range. Then we veered off the main road and the bus came to a stop. We were greeted by three drill instructors ranting and raving at us. We first formed up and our equipment was checked. We were given one C-Ration meal to put in our packs. We started on a 12 mile hike. It was fast and brutal. It would be hell to pay for any recruit who fell behind. We were supposed to take a break at the half way point but we never stopped. All the while the drill instructors were running up and down the formation yelling at us.

We returned from the hike totally exhausted. The sand fleas were out and biting us all over. We were not allowed to swat these little critters that were put on this earth by God himself. So we let them bite and draw blood. Then we were divided into two groups and forced to fight one-on-one with pugil sticks. We were so tired we could hardly hold the pugil up to chest level. After the pugil stick bout we were forced to crawl through a ditch filled with mud with our packs, cartridge belts, and rifles. We were covered from head to toe with the gunk in the ditch.

After crawling through the ditch for about an hour the drill instructors told us to eat our one C-Ration meal. We did this without having a chance to wash our hands. For me that was a treat because we got to sit down and stuff our faces. I wondered what might be next. It wasn't long until the buses arrived and took us back to our platoon. We were paraded up and down the squad bay in our muddy uniforms and equipment as a warning to other recruits. Then we were sent to the wash rack to hose off with water hoses. We were a mess and I had never smelt so bad. After we cleaned our gear we were allowed to take showers. The warm shower water was heaven to me. I hoped that I never again got sent to the Motivation Platoon.

Every night we had to go through a ritual of getting into bed. We would all be standing on line with our M14 by our right side and facing the center of the squad bay. The drill instructor would start it off.

"Prepare to Mount," he would sing out.

We would respond, "Prepare to Mount, Aye Aye Sir! If we were not loud enough we would have to scream it out again.

The drill instructor would then command, "Mount."

We would scramble into bed with our rifles in a matter of seconds.

The drill instructor would then command, "Freeze at the Position of Attention." The rustling noises would cease almost immediately. It would be extremely quiet.

The next command from the drill instructor was, "Adjust."

All the recruits would slap their hands over their chest in a crisscross manner and then yell out "Marine Corps!"

He would then have us pray or recite the creed of the Marine and his Rifle. Sometimes we would sing the Marines' Hymn. Upon conclusion, he would tell us, "Good Night Ladies."

We would all respond, "Good Night Sir." It was only then that we could crawl under the sheets and blankets and sleep with our trusty M14 service rifle.

The creed of a United States Marine and his Rifle was pounded into our brain housing groups at the beginning of boot camp. It went like this.

MY RIFLE

"This is my rifle. There are many like it but this one is mine. My rifle is my best friend. It is my life. I must master it as I would master my life.

"My rifle, without me is useless. Without my rifle, I am useless. I must fire my rifle true. I must shoot straighter than my enemy who is trying to kill me. I must shoot him before he shoots me. I will...

"My rifle and myself know that what counts in this war is not the rounds we fire, the noise of our burst, nor the smoke we make. We know that it is the hits that count. We will hit...

"My rifle is human, even as I, because it is my life. Thus, I will learn it as a brother. I will learn its weakness, its strength, its parts, its accessories, its sights, and its barrel. I will keep my rifle clean and ready, even as I am clean and ready. We will become part of each other. We will...

"Before God I swear this creed. My rifle and myself are the defenders of my country. We are the masters of our enemy. We are the saviors of my life.

"So be it, until victory is America's and there is no enemy, but Peace!"

A few days prior to graduation I was called down to the Classification Section for an interview with a male civilian. He started asking all sorts of questions about my background and told me that I was being considered for security guard at the White House after a one year tour of duty. He told me that only thirty Marines out of three thousand were hand picked for this type of duty. He said that they would really investigate my background. He also told me that I could participate in ceremonies and perform the rifle manual for audiences. I was fingerprinted and then dismissed back to my platoon. I was elated that this ole country boy from Kentucky was being considered for such an assignment.

The proud day finally arrived when we could graduate from Marine Corps boot camp. Ironically, the recruit who had been forced to dry shave under a bucket while doing side straddle hops when we first arrived at recruit receiving, was made Honor Man of the platoon. He was issued the Dress Blue Uniform and promoted to private first class.

It was all behind us now. The date was Wednesday, 26 November 1969. We had made it! It would be the last time Platoon 3049, in the year 1969, would march across the parade deck. Through loyalty, pride, confidence, and dedication to our country and Corps, we had earned our place in the long history and heritage of the Marine Corps. What I had endured and accomplished at Parris Island would leave an indelible mark and bestow the title that I would bear forever, "Marine." I had learned from our drill instructors in boot camp, "Once a Marine, Always a Marine." This chapter in my life was now history. With the training behind me, I felt I had the basic knowledge to survive combat and in the Marine Corps. It was time to move on. The grass had to be greener on the other side. It would be all down hill from now on, at least, I thought.

The following morning on Thursday, 27 November 1969 we departed through the Main Gate of Parris Island headed for Camp Lejeune, North Carolina for infantry training. I recall glancing back over one shoulder with a sigh of relief. I wondered about the next platoon that our drill instructors would be picking up at recruit receiving and the adventures that awaited the civilian scumbag recruits.

After about a six hour bus ride from Parris Island we arrived at Camp Lejeune, North Carolina. It was around noon when we pulled through the front gate of Camp Geiger. This was an adjoining base to Camp Lejeune where all the new Marines fresh out of boot camp went through infantry training. It was called Infantry Training Regiment and we were going to be assigned to Tango Company. Here we would specialize in our occupational specialties that had been assigned to us at boot camp. My cousin and I became Military Occupational Specialty (MOS) 0331, Machine Gunner.

Within the company that was formed, there was a machine gun section, mortar section, law section, flame-thrower platoon, and the basic riflemen platoon. We started our training on 2 December 1969 after a full company had been formed. Tango Company turned out to be a huge infantry company. While going through training, I remember the long chow formations. There were over three hundred Marines in our company alone. The formations would be so large that the Troop Handler's would give the command Right, Face, Forward, March and we would only march a few feet until we were given the order to Halt. Then a column of files from either the left or right side of the formation would march forward to enter the mess hall to eat chow.

One thing that was "taboo" here was for a Marine to walk through another unit's formation. The Marines in that unit would gang up on an unfortunate soul who wondered through their ranks and beat the living crap out of him. We saw some bloody faces because of it. For the Marine Corps Troop Handlers, it was just another lesson that a boot Marine had to learn the hard way.

Our training included about fifteen days of Individual Combat Training (ICT) where we all trained together regardless of what our MOS was. At ICT we were given classes on the various weapons and map reading. We also conducted hands-on training while firing the weapons. We fired the machine guns, mortars, claymore mines, flame throwers, 3.5 rocket launchers, fired the M16 on automatic fire, conducted night defensive fires, ran the infiltration course, and went through the gas chamber. In the gas chamber we had to remove our gas masks and sound off our name, rank, serial number, and date of birth before being lead outside to recover from the tear gas.

One of the highlights was the throwing of grenades. Once an individual was in the grenade pit he was supervised by an instructor. There were a series of commands given to make sure it was done properly and safely. The instructor would command, "Both hands into fists on your chest and facing me. Take grenade, Squeeze, Pull pin, Prepare to throw, Throw grenade." Then both would drop down into the throwing pit. You didn't want to stand upright and watch a grenade detonate unless you wanted a face full of shrapnel.

ICT was followed by Basic Specialist Training (BST) where we trained with our specialty weapons. In our case it was the M60 Machine Gun. The training lasted for about thirty six days. Since the training was over the Christmas period we were allowed to take a few days of annual leave and go home for Christmas. My cousin and I took the opportunity to fly home. It was enjoyable meeting the family again, but we dreaded coming back to Camp Geiger to finish up our training. On 10 January, two days after my birthday, it was 9 degrees Fahrenheit. We qualified with the M60 machine gun on Tuesday 13 January 1970. It was a very cold day but I managed to fire expert with the M60.

I have vivid memories of the training that was conducted at Camp Geiger. I remember firing the M60 machine guns on the ranges, which lasted for several weeks and the forced marches out to the training areas. Our troop handler, a short stocky black staff sergeant, was sadistic and at times seemed even worse than our drill instructors. He made our life miserable both in garrison and out in the training areas. He would at times carry around a huge club that looked like a baseball bat and would not hesitate to hit someone over the head with it for a minor infraction. He was just meaner than hell.

On one occasion I reported to pay call to receive cash payment along with the other members of our platoon and forgot my Armed Forces Identification Card on the table next to the troop handler. It was procedure that each Marine would report to the pay officer, watch him count out the money due the Marine, and respond, "Sir, the private's pay is correct." The Marine would then retrieve his ID card from the troop handler, execute an about face, and march out of the office. I had practiced this routine a few times before going over to the office and thought that I had mastered the procedure. During my pay call, in my haste to return to the barracks, I mistakenly executed an about face and marched out leaving my ID card behind.

It took me awhile to get up enough nerve to return to the building where pay call had been conducted. I knew I had to face the troop handler in order to claim my ID card. My cousin and I were sitting on our footlockers cleaning our M16 rifles and M60 machine gun, and I mentioned to him about my ignorance.

"Are you going to go back and ask for it?" he asked.

"I'm afraid to," I replied.

"Well, you have to get it sometime. They may end up coming and looking for you."

"Yeah, I know. I suppose I was trying to postpone the inevitable."

I decided that I would finish cleaning my weapon and then go over to the office to retrieve my ID card. I had to get up enough courage to face the music, so to speak. I entrusted my rifle to my cousin for safekeeping and I proceeded to the office. I walked into the doorway and stood in front of the desk where I had received my pay. Pay call had concluded, thus the pay officer was no longer there. Sitting behind the desk was our troop handler, the staff sergeant.

"Sir, Private Fenwick requests permission to speak to the staff sergeant, Sir!"

"What do you want?"

"Sir, the private left his ID card on the table when he received his pay from pay call, Sir! The private would like to have it back, Sir!"

"Ooooh! You just go around leaving your government ID card laying all over the area, huh, Private Fenwick? Well, I'm gonna teach you a lesson. You're little mistake is gonna cost you. What do you think I should do, just give it back to you?"

"Nossir!" I replied.

"Get away from the front of my desk and stand over there in my corner."

I moved quickly to an open area next to some olive drab wall lockers and faced the wall. The troop handler made me face about so that I was facing the doorway entrance.

"Now, private, BEGIN! Bends and thrusts until I get tired of watching your dumb ass and I don't get tired of watching. Hurry up! MOVE!"

I began my most dreaded exercise. Bends and Thrusts was an exhaustive physical exercise we had learned in boot camp. A four-count movement started at the position of attention. For the count of one, the individual conducting the exercise would bend down and touch the floor with the palms flat on the floor. For the count of two, both feet were kicked back fully extended to the rear. For the count of three, both feet were brought back up to about twelve inches from the hands. For the count of four, the individual would stand up and assume the starting position. This four-count exercise was conducted all in one fluid motion without a break in momentum. The exercise was repeated many times until told to stop by someone in a position of authority. While I was doing the exercise the troop handler yelled at me for moving too slow.

"You'd better hurry it up crazy or I'll come over there and knock your teeth out! Faster! Faster, Private Fenwick! You do bends and thrusts like an elephant shits, slow and sloppy! Hurry up!"

The troop handler then told me he was leaving the building for five minutes. "I'll be back, you Worm, and you had best not quit on me! Do you understand me?"

"YESSIR!" I yelled.

The troop handler left the office and was gone for about a half hour. I did not dare to stop doing the exercises without his permission. He finally walked into the office and saw me still doing the bends and thrusts.

"You still here, Private Fenwick?" he asked. "I thought you would be in an Unauthorized Absence status by now. That's a shame you didn't go over the hill. Now you'll have to suffer even more. Do you want to go U.A. on me now, Private Fenwick?"

"Nossir!"

"Do you want to quit doing bends and thrusts now private?"

I could barely respond as I was completely out of breath and physically exhausted. "Nossir!" I replied. I knew that if I responded yes, the troop handler would punish me even more.

"Good, keep doing them. I'm not tired yet anyway."

It was difficult to maintain my balance while doing the bends and thrusts because by now I was slipping and sliding in my own sweat. I continued for about another ten minutes before he finally told me to stop. He threw my ID card on the floor next to my feet in a puddle of sweat.

"Pick up your ID Card and get the hell out of my house!" he yelled.

I picked up my ID card and bolted for the door.

I heard him say on my way out, "Let this be a lesson to you Shithead, not to leave government property laying around."

I returned to the squad bay, sat down on my footlocker, and immediately commenced cleaning my rifle. Perspiration was dripping from my forehead and onto my rifle parts. I wiped the sweat away with my right forefinger and onto the floor.

My cousin looked over at me and asked, "What happened to you?"

"It's a long story," I replied. "Don't want to talk about it." I was afraid I might be caught talking and forced to do bends and thrusts again. I had had enough exercise for one day.

I tried to keep a low profile throughout the rest of the training. I did not want to call attention to myself. All I wanted to do was to finish infantry training in one piece. I was not that fortunate however, because the same staff sergeant reprimanded me again later during a training evolution at the firing range. Although two small pieces of chewing gum was included in the C-Ration meal the troop handler would not allow us to chew it. On this one occasion, he decided to give us permission to chew gum during the meal, but we had to dispose of it prior to going back up on the firing line.

As I finished my meal I started chewing the gum to help clean my teeth. I heard the machine gun instructor up on the firing line call for me to get behind a machine gun to start my training. I grabbed my cartridge belt and other equipment and started up to the firing line. As I passed the troop handler he reached out and grabbed me by my throat. In my haste to get into position behind a machine gun I had forgotten about having the chewing gum in my mouth. I was ordered to dig a hole, 6 feet deep, 6 feet wide, and 6 feet long. As it was cold that day, I wore my long johns and a field jacket. Having come from the farm, I was used to hauling cow manure and throwing silage out of the silo. I dug the hole with my entrenching tool as quickly as possible with no problem.

The North Carolina sandy soil was a lot easier to dig in than the soil back on the farm, I thought. When I was finished, the troop handler instructed me to fill it back in, which I did with little effort. Now I can get back to the firing line, I thought. The troop handler had other plans, however. I was told to dig another hole. I began to dig in the same hole that I had first dug. I was immediately corrected and reprimanded for my stupidity. I was to dig the same size hole in another location that was not as sandy as the first. I was getting very hot while digging the hole and began to shed my top layers of clothing, but was told by the troop handler to keep them on. This little excursion lasted all afternoon and I missed firing the machine gun that day. All the while I was asking myself, which is more important, firing the machine gun or digging holes in the sand? It was discipline, I reckoned. "Instant, Spontaneous, Response to Orders."

The troop handler would usually hold mail calls in the squad bay. He would yell out, "Mail Call! School Circle!" School circle was boot camp slang, which meant that all the Marines would gather around in a tight group and wait for our mail to be passed out by the troop handler. "Asshole to belly button," he would say, in order for us to tighten it up even more. Our particular troop handler would call the names and say, "Air Mail." He would then fling the letters over our heads in every direction. As the letters fell in our midst, everyone would fight their way to find out whether the letter belonged to them. On some occasions when a Marine's name was called and he did not sound off loud enough, he would be ordered to come to the front. When he eventually reached the front after bumping and elbowing others, the troop handler would then double his fist and punch the Marine in the mouth.

After infantry training at Camp Geiger we were authorized home leave prior to reporting to our next command. After a few weeks at home telling stories about our training and about the Marine Corps, my cousin and I were to report to Staging Battalion in Camp Pendleton, California. We arrived at Camp Pendleton on Saturday 7 February 1970 and we got in touch with my sister, Janice, the next day. We spent the weekend with her at her apartment in San Clemente. We told her stories about the airlines losing our seabags on the way out. They were located in Chicago and sent out to us. We had to go to the San Clemente bus station to pick them up on that Monday. I told my sister that on our way from Chicago to San Diego we saw Pikes Peak in the Rocky Mountains and flew over the left side of the Grand Canyon. This old farm boy was excited about that.

Staging Battalion was formed to train Marines in jungle warfare. We were assigned to the 4th Replacement Company, Unit 4457. We learned techniques of patrolling, recon, listening posts, observation posts, mines, booby traps, and in general, techniques on how to survive in Vietnam. This course of training lasted approximately four weeks. Marines even today still refer to one specific hill at Camp Pendleton as Mount Mother Fucker in which Marines hiked to and from the training areas. It was a very steep hill to climb.

While coming back from a training range over this hill one day, a sergeant behind me told me to close up the gap. I responded "Yessir!" He then told me not to call him Sir, because he worked for a living. It made me realize that I was no longer a recruit. I believed I had reached a point that my drill instructors had always told us about, that of being a trained killer and a basic Marine. The training was good and the chow was bad. It seemed as though they were preparing us for Vietnam, because the only menu we seemed to have was rice, salads, noodles, and occasionally chicken. Of course, any breakfast tasted the same day after day.

I felt that three good things happened while my cousin and I were at Camp Pendleton. First, we were promoted to private first class. Second, we received weekend liberty so we got the chance to go into the town of San Clemente and visit my sister. Third, we received the essential training to familiarize us with the various Viet Cong and North Vietnamese Army jungle tactics.

My sister's apartment was about fourteen miles from the base. The good times she managed to show us on the weekends helped relieve some of the pressures we had endured during training and the thought of going to Vietnam. We visited Disneyland and a variety of other sights. Of course, there was always time for beer drinking, and reminiscing about the good old times back home in Kentucky.

Before my cousin and I realized it, we were on a plane heading for Okinawa. This was our first time out of the good old USA. We arrived at Kadena Air Force Base on Okinawa and were bused to a Marine base called Camp Hague for administrative processing. We were now totally separate from the basic training, the drill instructors, Infantry Training Regiment, the troop handlers, and the relentless harassment. We stayed at Camp Hague approximately five days while we were being processing for further transfer. After a day of work details and accountability at formations, we would go to the enlisted club at night for a few beers. After a couple of nights downing the brew at the club, I decided to stay in the barracks and work on my uniforms.

It just so happened that my older brother, Donald, was stationed in Okinawa at the time. He had served two tours in Vietnam and was now stationed on Okinawa. I called him on the telephone a few days earlier. On this particular night he arrived to take me out on the town. I met him at the door and he followed me back to my rack. I started digging through my seabag to see what type of uniform I could wear for the evening. I had no civilian clothes with me although we were now authorized to wear civilian attire on liberty. I guess I felt that I had no need for them since I was carrying around a seabag full of Marine Corps uniforms.

I searched and tried to match up my uniform items. I felt a bit like a greenhorn when I asked my brother whether I should put emblems on my shirt collar. This was not in accordance with the uniform regulations and he was quick to correct me. I knew better, but I guess I was a bit nervous about going out on liberty and felt somewhat intimidated since my brother was a staff sergeant. I had seen old pictures of an earlier generation of Marines, who wore emblems on their shirt collars, and for some reason it just stuck in my head. I wanted to make sure I was within uniform regulations. With his assistance, I managed to hurriedly get dressed and we ended up in Kin Ville, Okinawa. The entire night was spent barhopping from one bar to another. I had never seen so many bars in one place.

The next morning after muster we were formed into ranks one behind the other and proceeded into a building. Here we would receive our Permanent Change of Station Orders. When my cousin and I got inside the doors, we could see Marine clerks endorsing the paperwork for each Marine. There were about eight lines of Marines waiting to have their orders processed and the same amount of clerks. In front of the line that we were in, we could hear the clerk announce aloud as he stamped each Marine's Orders.

"Okinawa, Okinawa, Vietnam! Vietnam, Vietnam, Okinawa! Okinawa, Vietnam, Okinawa!"

To me there seemed to be no consistency whatsoever, but my cousin began talking to me about devising a plan.

"You want to stay in Okinawa with your brother, don't you?" he asked.

"Yeah, I'd like to stay here," I responded.

"Well I want to go to Vietnam," he said."

"Well I do too," was my reply. "I would rather stay on Okinawa for just awhile and spend some time with my brother. I can always go to Vietnam later on."

My cousin suggested that we could switch places in line so that his orders would be stamped Vietnam and mine would be stamped Okinawa. He was confident that we could make the switch just in the nick of time. I was very skeptical and argued with him that I did not think it would work. He kept telling me that he had the system all figured out and that we both could get the orders we wanted by switching places in line at precisely the exact moment. I finally agreed to give it a try.

As we approached the counter he nodded for us to switch places in line. We did and he was the first one to reach the counter. The clerk took his orders and with a heavy blow on the counter top, stamped his orders.

"Okinawa," the clerk announced.

My cousin seemed somewhat shocked. "But I want to go to Vietnam," he retorted.

The clerk then reached out for my paperwork. I handed it to him.

"You're going to stamp him Okinawa, ain't you?" my cousin asked.

The clerk looked at my cousin and then looked back at me. With a forceful downward stroke, the stamp came down on my orders and in a sarcastic voice said, "Wrong, VIETNAM!"

"Wait a minute," I said. "Can't you change these around? My cousin wants to go to Vietnam and I want to stay in Okinawa. Can't you just re-stamp our orders?"

"Look!" the clerk said angrily. "The orders stay as is. Now move away from the counter."

My cousin decided to add his two cents to the conversation. "Listen," he interjected. "Freddy has a brother stationed here on Okinawa and wants to spend some time with him. I want to go to Vietnam. Can't you just change the orders for us?"

The clerk began to look at both sets of orders again. "Which one of you is Fenwick D.M. and which one of you is Fenwick F.W.?" the clerk asked.

We both spoke at the same time in unison. "I'm D.M. and I'm F.W."

The clerk started reviewing the names at the top of the orders. He seemed very confused and irritated that things had to be so complicated in stamping two sets of orders.

"Who the hell is D.M.?" the clerk asked abruptly.

"I am," my cousin replied.

"Well, you are staying on Okinawa," the clerk said. "F.W. is going to Vietnam."

"But you don't understand," my cousin added.

"The clerk threw the orders down on the counter. "Pick up your orders and get out of the line. You don't argue with me. I'm a corporal, you're a private first class. What I say goes. Now step aside! Then he called for the next Marine in line. "Next!"

The corporal was right. We were PFCs, and he was a corporal, a non-commissioned officer. What could we say? We figured we had best follow his orders or risk getting into trouble. We both walked slowly out of the building and paused on the outside steps. We looked at the stamps on our orders.

My cousin seemed to be dismayed that his plan had failed and I was a bit disappointed. "Man," I thought we had the system all figured out in there," he said. "I still don't know what went wrong."

"Did you say we? You mean you, don't you?" I replied. "I will never trust you again to figure things out.

"Sorry it didn't work out so you could stay here on Okinawa with your brother," he said. "I really wanted to go to Vietnam."

"Oh well," I replied. "So much for the Buddy Plan. Tomorrow I head out for Vietnam and you get to stay on this tropical island they call Okinawa. Let's go to the enlisted club and have one last celebration together."

My cousin looked at me as though I should not have said one last celebration, but we started to walk away together, with the intentions of getting commode hugging drunk that night. We accomplished the mission because the next day our heads ached bitterly.

My cousin watched from a short distance as I picked up my seabag and got in the back of a flat bed truck. It was a large truck that the Marines called a 6-by or 6x6 mainly because it had six large wheels and all six were powered. The real name for this truck was M35A2 2½ -ton cargo truck that was commonly referred to as the "deuce and a half." It had a row of wooden seats on each side of the vehicle and could seat approximately twelve Marines in the back. There were about nine of us that were going to the Kadena Air Force Terminal in order to catch a flight to Vietnam.

I was the last one on the truck and sat next to the tailgate. I had a good view of my cousin because the truck bed was about five feet off the ground. As the driver jerked forward, I heard my cousin yell, "Give em hell, Freddy!" We exchanged smiles and waved to each other. I felt a lump in my throat. This was the first time we had been separated since joining the Marine Corps. We had endured a lot together but the time had come for us to seek our own destiny. As the truck sped toward the main gate of Camp Hague, my cousin disappeared from sight.

After processing and a long wait at the Kadena Air Terminal, we eventually got on the plane and were airborne. I managed to get only a few intermittent winks of sleep through the early morning hours of flying. While half-awake and half-asleep, I heard the flight attendant say, "We have now started our descent into Da Nang, South Vietnam. We will be landing in approximately 20 minutes. Please fasten your seat belts and return your seats and trays to their upright position. We appreciate you flying with Flying Tiger Airlines and hope you have a pleasant stay in Da Nang."

Some of the Marines who were awake sounded off, "OOORAAH!" I wondered what my future might hold. Was I destined for glory or would this place called Vietnam snuff out my life at a very young age? Only time would tell. I began to pray silently.

Chapter 3

Medevac Mike

0700, Friday, 6 March 1970. The plane began to descend from high altitude as the flight approached Da Nang from Okinawa. I peered out a window and was able to see some mountains, rivers, and rice paddies. We landed on the tarmac at Da Nang. The plane full of servicemen was fairly quiet and calm. As the plane taxied to the gate I looked out to get a glimpse of my new surroundings but could see only the terminal. The plane came to a rolling stop and the passengers began to claim their personal belongings from the overheads. As we moved forward and out of the front hatch of the aircraft, I immediately felt the change in the temperature as compared to Okinawa. The air was hot and humid with no breeze at all. I felt my forehead become clammy as I descended the steps.

The Marines offloading the aircraft were directed into a small holding area. It was a shed supported by wood 4X4s, with tin roof, no sides, and wooden benches on a dirt floor. Off in a distance I could see Marines laying a helo pad for helicopters, which was adjacent to the runway. After about an hour a truck pulled up. We boarded the vehicle with our seabags. We arrived at a wooden barracks and were told that it would be temporary until our units were assigned. We were to spend the next couple of days having formations, cleaning the barracks, burning feces from the outhouses, racking gravel, emptying trash cans, filling sandbags, and other miscellaneous garrison duties.

I was introduced to the art of burning feces which was known to the Marines as burning shitters. Wooden outhouses were pre-positioned throughout the base camp at Da Nang. Back home on the farm we had an outhouse, but it was only a one-holer. These would seat three to four men. There was a door with latch at the rear of the structure and half-cut fifty-five gallon drums were placed inside on top of a plywood floor. When the drums were full, a detail was formed to dispose of the waste. Basically, the drums were pulled out from the back, moved away from the outhouse, the drums filled with diesel fuel, and the contents set on fire. Normally we would use a stick with a rag on the end, soak it with fuel, and light the drums in this manner. After all the feces burned, the drums were then placed back into the outhouse to await its next customers. When the platoon sergeant called for a "shit detail" at morning formation, we all knew what he meant.

During this layover in Da Nang I managed to get a piece of paper and an

— 91 —

envelope so I could write home while I had the chance. I would not need a stamp as the mail was free if sent from a war zone. We could simply write the word "free" in the upper right hand corner of the envelope in place of a stamp. I thought that was a good deal. It would be my first short letter home from South Vietnam.

March 7, 1970

Dear Mom, Dad and Larry,

I got in Da Nang yesterday morning about seven o'clock. I'm going to the 7th Marines, which is about twenty miles from here I guess, but I don't know my address. I will write again when I find out where I am.

I saw Donald in Okinawa. I will write you about it when I get my address. We had a pretty good time. I may get myself a camera later on if I can. Don't worry about me being over here in Vietnam because I'm not. And if I don't worry, neither should you all. You all have too much to worry about now. Just remember I'll think of you all wherever I go or whatever I do.

Yours truly,
PFC FENWICK

The next morning we ate morning chow and were divided into various work details that consisted of outside police. After we were finished it was our own time to pack our gear in preparation to join our assigned units. That afternoon the platoon sergeant had us all fall out of the barracks and into formation. With a clipboard in his hands he began to address the Marines in ranks.

"The following Marines will fall into a separate formation to my left when I call off your name," he said. "You Marines will be going to Marble Mountain. The second group will step to the rear of the formation, you will be going to the DMZ. The third group will fall in to my right and will be transported to LZ Baldy." Some Marines were left in the original formation because they had not yet been assigned units. He then spoke to each group separately.

When he got to my group he said, "Okay listen up! You Marines are to be taken to the helo pad for further transportation up to LZ Baldy. That is the base camp for the 3rd Battalion, 7th Marines. Have all your gear ready to go within the hour. Are there any questions?" No one responded. Then he told us, "All right then, get in there and do a quick cleanup of the barracks and prepare to move out. Let's get it done people!"

We spent less time on the cleaning of the squad bay than we normally would and stuffed our seabags with gear that we had taken out for personal use. In about thirty minutes we grabbed our seabags, slung them over our shoulders, and proceeded from the barracks to the trucks. The awaiting deuce and a half drivers revved their engines as we heaved our belongings up and onto the bed of the truck. We scampered aboard and took our seats facing across from one another. Some were quiet with their heads down, others were merely staring off into space in a daze. Still others were chatting about anything and everything. Guess it was easier putting on a brave front than being brave. These Marines were from all walks of life heading toward a combat zone of unknown fate. Some were from farms like me, some from the big cities.

We all came from different backgrounds, different beliefs, and had different goals in life. It was while I was in boot camp that I realized that we all joined the Corps for different reasons. Like it or not we were to become a part of the Vietnam War. We now realized that the entry level combat training was over and that we were in Vietnam to serve our country. From here on out it would be on the job training in real world combat operations. Trickles of sweat began to slowly roll down my chest from the heat of the morning sun. I recalled what my first senior drill instructor had once said, "The more you sweat in peacetime, the less you bleed in war."

We arrived at the helo pad and staged our gear in one pile while waiting the arrival of a CH-46 Sea Knight helicopter. Before long some helicopters were circling above our heads and then began to descend. We picked up our seabags as the gusts from the propellers stirred up a huge cloud of dust. Through the commotion one gunnery sergeant who was coordinating the airlift yelled, "Okay, this is your bird people, Saddle up!"

The Marines that were going to LZ Baldy boarded the chopper and it lifted into the air. I had been lucky to get a window seat and peered out at the surroundings. I could now see the entire base camp at Da Nang. I watched the buildings and the movement of the Marines below as we cruised out further away and over the surrounding hillsides and rice paddies. Soon the buildings were out of sight and the pilot leveled the aircraft on a straight course.

As we flew along I peered out the window to see what sort of terrain we were flying over. I could see the Vietnamese farmers working in the rice paddies, villages with thatched roofs, dirt roads with Vietnamese traveling on them, mountains, and dense jungles. The thing that intrigued me the most were the clumps of banana trees near the edge of the rice paddies. I thought they were pretty to watch swaying in the breeze. I noticed a convoy of military vehicles on a dirt road that seemed to be heading in the same direction as the chopper.

It seemed as if half an hour had passed when the pilot began to circle another base camp. This one was a lot smaller than the base camp I had seen from the air when I left Da Nang. I could see Marines moving about below. Some had shirts on while others did not. Some were not wearing any headgear while others were wearing either the standard utility cap or helmets. Some were carrying weapons while others were not. I was somewhat surprised to see very little uniformity throughout the base camp. Sandbag bunkers were visible around the perimeter of the base camp. The chopper began to descend.

A corporal awaited us as we disembarked the chopper. He wanted to know what company we were going to. I told him I was going to Mike Company. He looked at my orders and said, "That's correct, Mike Company, 3rd Battalion, 7th Marines. It is just up at the top of this hill. Follow me and I will take you all to your respective companies."

We followed the corporal down a dusty road and it began to incline up a small hill. At the top of the hill was the base camp. There were M274A2 (Mules) and M151A1 (Jeeps) running all over the place and kicking up a lot of dust. The Mule was also known as the Mechanical Mule. It was a 1/2 ton, 4X4 lightweight carrier with a flat bed that could be used for many infantry tasks including the transport of personnel, patients on stretchers, or cargo. They could even be used as a platform for a recoilless rifle. I was intrigued at the ingenuity of this particular vehicle and wished that I had something like it back on the farm.

This base camp of LZ Baldy looked busy, very busy. As we walked through the base camp I noticed through the door openings that the structures had plywood sides, tin roofs with sandbags evenly spaced, and the floors that were supported by wooden poles about three feet high. Suddenly we stopped and the corporal said, "This is Mike Company."

There was a red sign next to the entrance with yellow and white lettering that read, A COMPANY CALLED MIKE. The story that was told to the new joins was that at an earlier time during the Vietnam War, Mike Company had engaged with the enemy and completely ran out of ammunition. The Marines of Mike Company had to resort to hand to hand combat. We were told that a training film was made based on the valor of those brave men. Consequently the title of the film became known as "A COMPANY CALLED MIKE."

The corporal told us to wait outside while he talked to the company first sergeant. I overheard the first sergeant tell him that there was no room in the company area and that the newly arrived Marines would have to be billeted at the Noncommissioned Officers (NCO) Club. I heard the first sergeant tell the corporal, "Get them settled in and have them report back here first thing in the morning to start checking in."

We then proceeded to the hooch that had been designated as the NCO Club. In Vietnam, Marines referred to all living quarters as hooches. It could be a structure with a tin roof over your head as the ones in the base camp, a fighting hole, a bunker, or one made by the individual Marine with a poncho or poncho liner. Whatever the configuration, it was still hooch to all the Marines.

We stepped inside the hooch and I could see that cots had already been spaced about a foot apart down both sides of the building. It was dark inside although the sun was shining. The cots were canvas with aluminum frames and about two feet wide. I placed my seabag on a cot that I thought to be vacant. To my surprise a Marine in a different cot and who had obviously been in Vietnam for awhile said, "Move your shit, that's my rack!"

I sensed his irritation so I reluctantly moved my gear to the next available cot. He lay back down, obviously on another Marine's cot, placed his utility cover over his eyes and folded his arms over his chest. I heard him mumble, "Fuckin newbies, fresh out of the world and think they own the goddamn place."

I decided to ignore his rudeness and began to gaze at my new living quarters. Some of the other Marines that I had flew in with me moved to the rear of the hooch and I heard one say, "Hey look you guys, we've got a bar right here by our racks." I walked back to join them and as I went through the door, I could see that a plywood bar had been set up in the back room with wooden benches and tables. The "slop chute" had a musky aroma of spilled beer and cigarette smoke that lingered in the air.

"Yeah," I said, "this is going to be all right. Here we are waiting to go out to the field in a few days and we have a club right here in the barracks. Not far to stumble back to our cots, huh?" The others agreed.

The Marine who had earlier told me to move my seabag from his cot spoke up. "Field?" he questioned. "You must think you're still in Infantry Training back in the world. In the Nam, we call it the Bush."

Without responding to the Marine I began to unpack my seabag feeling a little irritated by his attitude. Although we had the club and all the beer you could drink at our fingertips, I did not realize at the time the trouble it would pose for the new joins. The first night we began sitting around talking about our uncertainties, not knowing what we would be getting into and discussing what sort of combat action we would encounter. The club opened for business in the back room so we decided that we should partake in a few beers.

The old salts in the bar were crazy as hell. They were drinking Black Label Beer like there was no tomorrow and stacking the cans on the tables high as they would go. Eventually all the stacked cans would come tumbling off the tables and onto the floor. There were roars of laughter and excitement over the routine, which seemed to be a ritual. There was more drinking and more stacking of cans throughout the night. They did not seem to give us new joins much eye contact. It was as if they were intentionally ignoring us.

After having a few beers myself and laughing along with the others, I decided to call it a night. The beer had gone to my head and all I wanted to do was to lie down in my cot and go to sleep. I stumbled in the darkness and managed to find the cot in which I had claimed. I had no pillow or blanket so I took off my utility jacket and folded it up for an impromptu pillow. I would not need a blanket because it was so hot and humid in the hooch. Even at night it was hot. I tried to mentally shut out the sounds of talking and the noise that was coming from the bar. I just needed a good night's sleep. Suddenly the bar door came crashing open and about seven rowdies made their presence known in our squad bay. They began kicking our cots, turning over our gear that lay on the floor, and yelling profanities.

"You bunch of fuckin newbies, you are in the Nam now and you're all gonna get killed." They laughed and joked among themselves as they continued their boisterous behavior of terrorizing all the new Marines. For awhile they would disappear back into the bar for more drinks but it would not be long before they were back in the squad bay again. "Newbies, newbies, you're all a bunch of fuckin newbies and you're gonna get zapped by the gooners. Charlie is out there waiting for you, you're all gonna die."

Although I was mad from within I did not say a word. I knew if I said anything to the old timers that there would surely be a fight right there in the squad bay. I just was not in the mood. Besides, the other new Marines seemed to ignore them also. I guess we were somewhat intimidated by their behavior and the fact that they had been in country longer than most. It turned out to be a very long night without much sleep.

The next morning a Marine from the company office came into the squad bay and woke us up. We were instructed to get dressed and go to the mess hall for chow. After we finished getting dressed and making head calls in a nearby outhouse, we fell into formation and the Marine had us route step to the mess hall. It was within close proximity of our squad bay and the company office.

As I entered the hatch to the mess hall, I could smell the aroma of eggs and potatoes. I stepped into the line and saw a Marine cooking eggs in a puddle of grease. Small metal containers were spaced on the counter containing bread, bacon, and creamed beef (Shit on the Shingle). I told the Marine cooking the eggs that I would have a hard egg. After only a few seconds he placed the greasy egg on my paper plate. Then I moved down the line and put some bread and bacon on my plate. There was a Marine serving the creamed beef. I said to the Marine cook, "I'll have some of that S.O.S." He scooped up some creamed beef with a long handled spoon and covered my egg, bacon, and bread with the creamed beef. I found a vacant spot at a chest high bench and with a plastic knife and fork began to devour my first gourmet meal of the day. I did not mind eating while standing up. I heard a Marine say, "It may not look too appetizing, but it beats the hell out of C-Rations."

After breakfast we were instructed to take our seabags to battalion supply. We were to tag them with our names and unit and turn them in for safekeeping. A corporal at the battalion supply told us that our seabags would be stored there until we left the country, no matter how long it might be. I figured that my uniforms would all be molded and mildewed by the time I got ready to claim them at the end of my tour. When every seabag had been turned in, we went through a door to the outside and were issued our 782 gear. The Marine Corps terminology was duoce gear. This consisted of canteens, pack, cartridge belt, poncho, helmet, flak jacket, poncho-liner, and a host of other combat equipment.

At a distance and up on a hillside within plain view we could see some fixed wing aircraft flying low and dropping bombs. Tracer rounds were visible bouncing off the ground and into the air. We heard the firing of various weapons from all directions.

"I wonder who is up there," I commented.

The Marine corporal issuing my 782 gear said, "That's Mike Company. They don't call them Medevac Mike for nothing."

"What do you mean by Medevac Mike?" I asked.

"You'll soon find out," he replied. "I see from your custody receipt card that you are going to Mike Company. They sort of adopted that nick-name because they are always getting hit by Charlie."

"How often do they have to medevac Marines?" I asked the corporal.

He laughed aloud. "You'll find out. They are always in the shit!"

Before I had signed for all my gear, I looked up on the hill and two choppers were circling where all the firing was taking place.

"See, I told you," the corporal said to me. They must have some KIA or WIA in the company now. Stick around and you'll see the body bags being brought in."

With that I kept quiet. I picked up my duoce gear and headed back to the hooch. I knew that my time was coming and that I would soon be in a similar situation. I began to see some choppers landing on the same landing zone that I had arrived on. I could see the causalities being off loaded from the choppers. They were rushed to the Battalion Aid Station where the corpsmen and doctors would try to piece them back together. Before the choppers lifted off, I could see some black body bags being off loaded. I knew the body bags contained dead Marines. I turned away and proceeded inside my hooch.

The day ended far too soon for me. I did not particularly care for going through another night of being harassed by the Vietnam vets in the NCO Club. It seemed strange to me that they would act that way towards the new Marines, after all, we had been taught during training about Marine Corps camaraderie and taking care of our own. I just hoped that the Marines in Mike Company would treat us better than the ones back at the base camp. I decided to write a letter home again before all the daylight in the squad bay disappeared.

8 Mar 1970

Dear Mom, Dad and Larry,

I got my address today so thought I'd drop you a few lines while I have time. The only thing that will change later on is that I will put a platoon number on it. Right now we're staying in the club so you can imagine what goes on. They gave us drinks on the house last night and one this afternoon. It's been several people come in today and drink up. They even cleaned out the bar. What time we weren't outside I just lay in my rack. It's one of the fold-up types. We're supposed to go to our company tomorrow and I'll sure be glad when we do. It will be "Mike Company."

Well I can hardly think around here for the radios, but will try to tell you what happened in Okinawa. First of all, when we got there they separated my cousin and me. He will stay in Okinawa unless he gets foolish and tries to come here. I phoned Donald later on that night and a sergeant told me he was on liberty, but that he would tell him I called. The next night I called again and he told me that Donald was on his way to find me. So I stood by the entrance and in about ten minutes he drove in. I don't think he actually recognized me. I guess it was because all the guys on the base were wearing jungle utilities. Anyway he got me a special liberty pass and I went to his house. It's just a three-room house, but is real cozy. It's the typical Japanese house.

We arrived in Da Nang at seven o'clock Friday morning and the next day I got on a chopper and flew about twenty miles. I don't know for sure, but I believe its southwest of Da Nang. I'm in the 7th Marines and on a place called Mount Baldy. I doubt if it's on the large Vietnam map you have, but at least you know I'm not too far from Da Nang. I think things are kindly quiet now, at least it has been since I got here.

It's about 75 to 80 degrees here now and kind of dusty. I don't guess it's rained for several days. Other than that, it's not too bad yet, but I'll be glad when I get to my company.

Well I'll close now and hit the rack. I didn't get much sleep last night. So write real soon and take care I will always think of everyone.

Bye for now,
Freddy

During the initial few days at LZ Baldy our time was occupied on work details and getting checked in to our company. The clerks at the company office screened our Service Record Books to ensure they were correct and that our record of emergency data was updated. This was important in case we were either wounded, captured, killed in action, or in case our parents or next of kin had to be notified. At night, we were assigned Hole Watch, which was security around the perimeter of the base camp, and weapons passed from one relief to the other. We had not yet drawn our own individual weapons. Hole watch was conducted in bunkers or just dug out holes fortified with sandbags. This type of security was vital in case of sudden attacks by the Viet Cong or the North Vietnamese Army

My first night on hole watch started when a sergeant took about twelve of the new Marines to our fighting holes. We were assigned one sector while other groups would cover the remaining sectors on all sides of the base camp. We were placed four men to a fighting hole. He gave us some claymore mines, instructed us in their use, some grenades, trip flares, and ammunition for the weapons. We had also carried out a M60 machine gun and had it mounted on a tripod. I asked the sergeant if we should fire the M16 rifles before we stood watch to make sure the sights were properly adjusted. He said, "Nah, you don't need no battle sight zero on these weapons, all you have to do is point and aim. With all the ordnance I have given you, plus the machine gun, you should be able to suppress any gooks that try to come through the wire."

We commenced to set out the claymore mines in front of our defensive positions, inserted an ammunition belt in the machine gun, placed trip flares in likely avenues of approach, and then found a spot on the hard ground to settle in for the night. The M18A1 Claymore Mines were olive green in color, was command detonated, and was loaded with about 700 steel balls backed by a composition explosive. A blasting cap ignited the 3.5 pound mine which sent the steel balls in a fan-shaped arc out to 100 meters. Two bipod prongs could be extended from the base which was used to implant the device into the ground. The outboard side was placed toward the enemy and an electrical wire was connected from the body of the claymore to the hand-held firing device which ran back to the fighting hole. It was our first line of defense in case of a night time enemy attack.

The corporal explained to us that we had to be careful with the claymores because Charlie would sneak up to them at night and face them back toward our position. Then they would back up and either fire on our position or make a commotion in order for the Marines to fire the claymore. If the Marines had their heads sticking over top of the sandbags they could catch a face full of the steel balls. He warned to check them carefully in the morning since Charlie would also booby trap the claymores during the night. He then headed off with the other Marines to post them around the perimeter.

The early hours of the night seemed to pass rapidly because we were all talking and preparing a watch roster for the night. At around 2200 the others decided to crash, a terminology used by Marines meaning sleep. I had the first watch and it was not long until I could hear a Marine snoring away. I thought to myself, how was I to defend this position, with the Marines loudly sawing logs in their sleep? As things began to quiet down, I started to listen for every sound around me and watched the distant treeline with great alertness. I kept my eyes peeled for even the slightest movement not knowing what to look for during my first night on hole watch.

As I gazed at the treeline that was approximately two hundred meters to my front, I began to fantasize about the enemy's possible presence in the trees. I moved my eyes in a rhythmic motion back and forth across the treeline, across the open rice paddy, and along the adjacent holes. I strained my eyes to determine if I could see the Marines in the fighting positions on both sides of me. It was very quiet except for the mosquitoes swarming around my ears. While fanning my ears to keep these pests away, I broke my concentration momentarily. I looked around me to see the other Marines fast asleep on the ground.

I began to daydream about my mother and father and peered at the moonlight sky. There was not a cloud in the sky. I attempted to locate the North Star and the Big Dipper. For a moment, I thought I might one day have to rely on my navigational abilities in case I ever got lost. To my surprise, I counted three falling stars before I realized that my alertness was not on the treeline. A sudden fear came over me as I focused my attention once again on the trees. I felt for my rifle ever so slowly to avoid any unnecessary sound and meticulously placed it in my lap. I looked to locate the selector switch on the weapon for reassurance and confirmed that the M60 machine gun was still mounted and ready to go.

My four hours of watch seemed to drag by but I had to make radio checks every fifteen minutes which was a relief to know there were other Marines on my side of the wire. I woke the next Marine for his watch and I settled down on my poncho to get a few hours of sleep. The dew was now thick and my poncho was wet from where I had unrolled it for my bed. I curled up inside of it, attempted to relocate some of the bigger stones that invaded my bed on the ground, and covered my head to keep the mosquitoes away from my face. I must have managed to doze off for a few minutes when I heard the Marine on watch say, "Hey you guys, there's somebody out there. Wake up!" We scampered to our feet and tumbled into our fighting hole.

"Listen," he said. "Hear that?" As we listened intently, we heard a low menacing voice come from the treeline.

"Hey, Manine… .Manine, tonight you die."

We began talking about firing into the area that the voice was coming from, but remembered that we should call in to let the Corporal of the Guard know what was going on. We used the radio to contact him and we were told to just hold our fire and not to fire unless fired upon or saw distinct movement. The Corporal of the Guard communicated to us that it was one of Charlie's tricks to probe the lines and see where our positions were or to draw fire so he could pinpoint our automatic weapons. We waited cautiously and the voice appeared again only this time in a different location in the treeline.

"Hey Manine…Manine! Tonight you die. Tonight you die, Manine," the eerie voice said.

Then we could hear him laugh as if to taunt us. We finally decided to continue our watch as scheduled since we were not to fire on this intruder and give our position away. The voice continued for a few hours and then disappeared. The night passed without incident and we were relieved at around 0800. I felt tired and sleepy, however I knew we had another full day ahead of us.

After morning chow we were told to form a working party and fill sandbags to beef up the fortification of the perimeter fighting holes. We boarded a truck and were driven to the same fighting hole where I was the night before. We started our tedious task of filling the sandbags with dirt, rocks, and sand. It was now mid morning and the sun was beating down. The air was hot and muggy. We took off our utility jackets and worked with just our green T-shirts on. The task of the day was soon accomplished and we headed for the NCO club for a few drinks to quench our thirst.

The next day all the new Marines signed for our own individual M16A1 service rifle at the armory. I looked it over carefully to determine if it was functioning properly. As I inspected my weapon from the butt stock to the end of the barrel, I began to think of the creed we had learned in boot camp. "This is my rifle, there are many like it, but this one is mine."

It was not long until a 6x6 truck pulled up next to the armory and a short and slightly overweight staff sergeant stepped out from the passenger side. He told us that all the "newbies" were to receive an Orientation and Indoctrination Course and part of the training was to get our battle sights on our M16s. Battle sight zero is a term used by the Marine Corps in which adjustments are made on the front and rear sights of the rifle in order to hit a target at three hundred meters. All the Marines simply called it BZO.

He told us to load on the truck and that we were going to be transported out to the firing range. We traveled on some very dusty roads and then came to an abrupt stop in the middle of nowhere. The staff sergeant got out of the passenger side of the vehicle and told us to form a working party in order to break open the metal ammunition cans from the small wooden crates. We each received thirty rounds of ammunition, enough for ten rounds in three magazine clips. We were then told to form a single line facing down range away from the truck. We were on top of a hill that gradually sloped down and into a ravine. We all formed a single line facing away from the truck.

"Lock and Load!" the staff sergeant commanded.

All the Marines began seating a magazine of ammo into their M16s.

"Take your weapons off safe and commence firing!

We all sort of paused and looked at each other a bit confused.

"Where are the targets?" I boldly asked.

"Ain't got no targets," the staff sergeant replied. "Just pick you out a bush or a rock to fire at. This will be the last chance you Marines get to obtain your battle sight zero on your weapons before you go into combat. So make sure you put the right dope on your rifle. Now, commence firing!"

The Marines down the line commenced firing their weapons at rocks or into bushes. I could see some rounds ricochet off the rocks about twenty-five feet away.

"I'll give you a few minutes to get your sights adjusted!" the staff sergeant yelled out over the loud firing of the M16 service rifles.

I figured I had better start firing if I was going to get my sights adjusted in time. I would have preferred silhouette targets and wondered why the staff sergeant had not brought any from the base camp. Maybe it was because in Vietnam there was not a need for paper targets when you had "Charlie" to shoot at. For me, this was an important event to get the right adjustments on my sights before joining Mike Company in combat. Evidently, the staff sergeant did not think it was critical enough to be overly concerned.

I picked out a bush up close and started to fire into it. I could not tell exactly where I was hitting. I loaded the second magazine. This time I aimed for a rock in the distance. I still was unsure where I was hitting to make any accurate adjustments. I loaded the third magazine and picked out a small rock that was closer to me. I made two adjustments before I heard the staff sergeant's voice.

"Cease fire! Cease Fire!" he commanded. "If you ain't got your battle sight zero by now, you are just shit outta luck. Make sure you remember your BZO and keep it on your weapons. Now file by me with your weapons on safe and the bolt to the rear so I can check your chamber. Once I have determined your weapon is safe, get back on the truck."

I had been used to cleaning up expended brass on the training ranges, but not here in the Nam. We picked up the wooden boxes and metal ammo cans and we were soon headed back toward the base camp. As I rode in the back of the truck, I remained quiet while the other Marines were busy talking. I was very concerned about facing the enemy and not knowing if I had the correct sight adjustments on my weapon. I felt cheated so I silently cursed the staff sergeant for being so careless with our lives.

Instead of going straight back to the base camp, the driver pulled up beside a rice paddy. The staff sergeant got out of the vehicle and said, "Okay, out of the truck Marines. It's time for a bath, Vietnam style."

There was clear running water and a pool of water just below a paddy dike. We all stripped down to our skivvies and waded into the water. We managed to wash the sweat off our bodies and rinsed our sweat-stained T-shirts. There was no telling what creatures lurked in the water, but we did not care. At least it was cooling, wet, and clear. I managed to put my anger aside. It was not long until we were splashing and carrying on in the water as if we were boys back home playing in a river. After our swim we headed back to LZ Baldy in order to clean our weapons, go to chow, have a few classes, and settle in for the night back at the hooch. I decided to write a letter after everything was done before it got dark.

11 March 1970

Dear Mom, Dad and Larry,

I just got back from chow and from taking a swim and feel pretty good, so thought I'd drop you a few lines. This may seem a little soon but this is my last sheet so I'll use it up. I'll have to go to the PX tomorrow and get some more paper and envelopes. I wish I could write to some of my kinfolk and neighbors but right now, we're busy with classes during the day. That's right, we have a week of classes before we go out to the bush. When we get in we have to write a letter within two hours or it will get dark and where we're staying now does not have any lights. We're supposed to move into our company sometime this week. I was sure glad to get out of the NCO Club though because it was always a mess to clean up.

I mentioned earlier that I went for a swim. Well if you want a shower around here, you have to pour some water into a small tank and take it to a four feet square enclosure. So instead of going to the trouble, most of us go to a hole of water that flows from a rice paddy. It's clear water running in at all times and is about chest high. I washed my under clothes in it also. The temperature seems to rise a little every day but I don't imagine it's got over 85 degrees yet. It gets pretty cool at night here. I even lay my field jacket out to cover me at night.

Well I got hold of a map today and found out where I am. I am south of Da Nang on Mount Baldy. The name you all might find on the map is Nui Huong Que. That is the section I'm in, although when we go into the bush, we will cover a larger radius.

I'm running out of things to tell you all so will let you get back to what you were doing. Whatever you do, take it easy.

Sincerely,
Freddy

During the next few days our time was occupied by cleaning our weapons, having accountability formations, undergoing personnel and equipment inspections, and in general preparing to go to the bush. By now I was familiar with the terrain on LZ Baldy. I could find my way to the mess hall, supply, armory, PX, and check cashing facility with no problem. I also knew the boundaries of the perimeter from the concertina wires and the positions of most the fighting holes.

As I spent my first few days at LZ Baldy, I began to feel more comfortable with my new surroundings. The Marines that arrived with me, although we would end up in various companies, worked and played together. There were times at the club that some of the old salts would share some of the horror stories of combat and they began to accept us more freely. I still felt the need however, to get settled in to my new company.

I observed an infantry company, from within the 3rd Battalion, return from the bush and noticed how tired and dirty the Marines looked. Some seemed to be in a daze while others were joyful to be back in the rear. I tried to avoid going to the club when they first came in, for I felt that I might receive the "newbie tease" again. In the meantime, we continued to have hole watch every night.

The personnel in the rear only stood hole watch if all the companies were in the bush or there were no newbies to do it for them. It seemed to be a skate job to be in the rear and never have to go into the rice paddies, jungles, or mountains, like the grunts. The term grunt was a slang nickname given to the infantry units that represented Marines on the front lines. I tried to write letters home to reassure my mother and father that I was okay.

13 Mar 1970

Dear Mom, Dad and all,

I don't have anything to do so will drop you a few words. I've been pretty busy today filling sandbags to place around bunkers. It was pretty hard work because we had to stack them a few yards away and it was pretty hot. I even got sunburned today. Last night we had perimeter watch so I had to sleep out. It was all right except for the mosquitoes. They brought around coffee at about 10:00 p.m. and sandwiches at about 1:00 a.m. I had an AN/PRC 77 Radio Set that I could talk to different Marines in their holes. The PRC-77 is portable radio with a VHF and FM combat-net radio receiver that is used to provide short-range, two-way voice communication. It also provides secure voice transmissions. It was sort of fun. This is my night off so I will try to write a few letters.

Nothing is new around here, it's just the same thing going on. I will be going out to my company in a few days which will give me more exciting things to do. To make sure your mail gets to me a little quicker just put 3rd Platoon on the address like I have it on the envelope.

What are Dad and Larry doing these days? I imagine they can find plenty to get into especially now that spring is around the corner. I can imagine it now. Larry, the time over here is just a little bit different from back in the world. Right now its seven o'clock Friday evening here, while in Kentucky it is about eight o'clock in the morning. Therefore, I'm about eleven hours ahead of him. Ha!

Well I'll let you all go now, I've found out there are no lights in these barracks. Oh well, I'll get around to writing. Tell everyone I still think of them although I can't seem to get a letter to them.

Bye now,
Freddy

The time came for me to join my company in the bush. They were only about three miles southwest of LZ Baldy near the Suoi Cho Dun River. Upon command, we loaded onto 6x6 trucks with our packs, helmets, M16s and miscellaneous combat gear. Once all the Marines were in the back of the trucks the drivers revved their engines and jerked the trucks forward. We began our trek to locate Mike Company. As we rode along the dusty road the terrain seemed to be mostly flat. After riding for about thirty minutes the drivers pulled up into the company's defensive perimeter and came to a stop. I had finally made it to Mike Company.

All the new Marines were told to off load. After I got off the truck with my gear I looked around and could not believe my eyes. There were a few Marines walking around in their skivvies who had just returned from swimming in the river. There was a jeep and trailer with beer and sodas stacked to the top and on ice. On top of that, the Marines of Mike Company were barbecuing steaks, hot dogs, and hamburgers. Some Marines were basking in the sun. The atmosphere was similar to a beach party and one could tell that these men were having a great time. For a moment, I wondered if I was in the wrong place.

A corporal approached the truck and asked, "Who are the Marines being assigned to 3rd Platoon?"

"I am," I responded, "and there are one or two others going to 3rd platoon."

"Come with me and I'll introduce you to your squads," he said.

The corporal escorted us to the platoon area and the two other Marines were introduced to their squad leaders. A couple of Marines within the squads shook our hands and said, "Welcome to Vietnam, welcome to Mike Company." Others did not say much and just lay back on the ground with what seemed like resentment. By now I was used to being looked down upon simply because I was new to a unit. It was as if the new Marines were intruders. The corporal gestured for me to follow him again and we came upon the 3rd squad. He then told the squad leader that I had been assigned to his squad.

"Go ahead and grab you a beer, go swimming, get you a steak, and just relax today," the squad leader said. "Early tomorrow morning we are heading out on an operation." Then he turned and walked away

"I found a flat spot on the ground amidst the other squad members. After moving a few small rocks aside I pulled my poncho out of my pack and spread it out on the ground. I would bed down here for the night. Then I folded my poncho liner several times and placed it at the head of the poncho. My poncho liner would initially serve as my improvised pillow and I could later cover myself during the hours of darkness.

I made my way to the jeep trailer containing the beer and soda. I reached into the melting ice and pulled out a Black Label Beer. Then I returned to my pack and sat down on it. As I slowly sipped my beer I peered around at my new surroundings. I was amazed that the company was in such a relaxed state. I managed to get a barbeque hamburger and hot dog and made a couple of trips to the jeep trailer to quince my thirst. Most of the Marines sat around on their packs and continued to eat and drink. As I was getting ready to call it a night, some Marines built a bonfire, right in the middle of the command post. They carried on outlandish conversations as though they were on some kind of camping expedition. I just hoped that there was no enemy close by.

I dozed in and out of sleep on the hard ground. To my surprise, reveille was sounded early the next morning at about 0430. It was still dark when the squad leader came by to arouse us from our sleep. He sent a couple of Marines to fetch a few cases of C-Rations and when they returned they were passed out to us in equal shares. I figured that since it was early morning I would dine on a small can of ham and eggs and crackers. As time passed the sun began to rise in the east. The warmth of the sun felt good compared to the dampness of the night.

The squad leader started coming by and dropping off ordnance and supplies to various members of the squad. He dropped off claymore mines to selected individuals, supplied us with hand grenades, ammunition, and told us to refill our canteens. He dropped off quite a bit of ordnance for me to carry, plus a plastic water jug, M60 machine gun ammo, and mortar rounds. I could not believe the amount of equipment that lay in front of me.

Finally, I said, "Hey, what do you think I am a pack mule? I can't carry all this stuff."

"Well, you're gonna carry it, cause everyone else has had their fair share. Now it's your turn in the barrel. You will carry every piece of gear you see in front of you," the squad leader commanded.

I silently cursed at the squad leader under my breath as I knelt down and started cramming the gear into my small pack. I sensed a shadow of a man approaching me and looked up to see who it was. I thought it might be the squad leader with more equipment to carry.

"Hey, my name is PFC Hawkeye. I'm in your fireteam. Don't worry about carrying all this stuff, I'll help you. The squad leader is a real asshole sometimes. He is always giving us more gear than we can carry."

"My name is Fenwick," I said. "Where are you from Hawkeye?"

"Oregon," he replied.

"I've never been to Oregon," I said, "but I've always heard it's a pretty State."

"Yeah, it is a pretty State, and its home to me."

"Well, I'm from Kentucky," I said.

"Kentucky, huh? I've never been to Kentucky either, but I've heard a lot about the bluegrass there," Hawkeye said.

We both chuckled at our clumsiness in starting a conversation for the first time.

The next thing I heard was "Saddle up!" The voice I heard was stern and authoritative.

"Who was that?" I questioned Hawkeye.

"Oh, that's the company gunny. When he says saddle up, that means get all your gear on and get ready to move out. He has been a drill instructor, and is an all right guy, but you don't want to rub him the wrong way," Hawkeye replied."

"Where are we moving to, do you know?" I asked.

"I don't know, but wherever it is, it's bound to be hot. They normally fatten us up on beer and steaks before a big operation."

"I guess I'm in it for the glory," I said with a smile.

Hawkeye winked and said, "Join the crowd."

I stood up, slung my pack over my shoulders, adjusted the fit, and picked up my rifle. I saw Hawkeye place his bayonet on his weapon and I decided to follow suit.

The squad leader walked over and stood beside me. "Fenwick, you are walking point today," he said. "It's our squad's turn to take the lead when we move out."

"Point? Do you mean up in front of the column?" I asked innocently.

"Yeah, I mean up front, fuckin point man, goddamit!" he cursed. "You are going to move along and check for mines and booby traps. Jesus H. Christ, I have to teach these fuckin newbie's everything."

I was feeling a bit agitated and could not figure out why the squad leader was making me walk point. This was my first full day in the company.

I hesitated for a moment and then asked the squad leader, "Don't you think that I'm a little bit new in country to be walking point?"

At this point he pointed his finger at me and retaliated. "Hey, everyone else in my squad has walked point, and since you are a newbie, you're going to walk point. You don't need any experience, just get out there and walk. Just watch where you're stepping," he said with a smile.

Our platoon guide, a sergeant, overheard the commotion. He walked over to us and told the squad leader, "You can't do that, he is new in the squad. Put him as tail end Charlie and put someone with more experience up front."

The squad leader's face turned a shade of red. He turned facing the sergeant. "Fenwick is in my squad, and I say he's walking point," the squad leader retorted!

"No he's not!" the sergeant snapped back. "You put him as tail end Charlie on his first day out, and that's an Order!"

Tail end Charlie was a term used to identify the very last man in a squad or platoon formation. The squad leader began to argue with the platoon guide but the sergeant was not giving in. "Look, if you make Fenwick walk point on his very first day, I'll make sure you are the first one designated as a tunnel rat when we find a spider trap," the platoon guide said.

A tunnel rat was someone who crawled into tunnels, bunkers, caves, or holes to search for VC. There could be poisonous snakes, pungi stakes, mines, or booby traps in these hidden places.

The squad leader glared at me while answering the platoon guide. "Aaah, fuck it, fuck it, walk goddamn tail end Charlie then, Chickenshit!"

By this time we were joined by the platoon sergeant, a short stocky staff sergeant. "What the hell is all the arguing about over here?" he asked.

The platoon guide informed him what the commotion was all about. After hearing the platoon guide's explanation the staff sergeant confirmed that I would walk tail end Charlie and not be put up front leading the entire company. Needless to say, the squad leader was very angry. He cursed to himself as we moved out slowly over a trail and across a rice paddy. As we moved along in a single column spaced approximately ten meters apart, Hawkeye stopped and gave a gesture for me to move up to where he was.

"Hey Fenwick," Hawkeye said. "Notice that I have my rifle facing outboard to the left and that the Marine ahead of me has his weapon facing to his right?"

I looked ahead at the Marine up front and replied, "Yeah!"

"Well, there is a reason for that," Hawkeye said. "You see, if we think we are getting ourselves in a world of shit, we stagger the weapons. This allows us to return fire in all directions rapidly in case we are hit from the flanks or are caught in an ambush. So no matter if you are right handed or left handed, you can still put rounds down range at Charlie. You can worry about sight alignment, sight picture, and trigger control after you clean the crap out of your skivvies."

"I understand," I responded.

Hawkeye began to move past me back up to his original position in column.

"Hey Hawkeye," I said. "Thanks a lot."

"Any time," he replied.

In a half hour or so we entered a wooded area and began traveling up along the banks of a river. Our platoon was then halted and the 1st and 2nd platoons by-passed us as they took the lead. We walked slowly beside the river and all of a sudden I heard, WHAM! WHOOM! Rat-tat-tat! There was a tremendous firefight going on somewhere up in the front of the company. As I steadied my rifle I began to look all over to see where I could return fire. All I could see up front were some of the Marines in the squad taking cover. Bullets commenced cutting through the trees above my head and leaves began to trickle down to earth. I took up a position behind a huge boulder still trying to find a field of fire. I could only sense that the platoons in the front were being hit from across the river.

The platoon sergeant suddenly approached my position from the rear. He was a Samoan and his skin was really dark from being exposed to the hot Vietnam sun. There was one other Marine behind me now that had just joined the company the day before. The platoon sergeant calmly barked orders. "Get down behind these big rocks! Take cover! Keep your heads down!"

It just so happened that there were these big boulders along the river where I had stopped. The platoon sergeant told me to stay low and assured me that I could not return fire with the Marines just in front of me. Besides, the main firefight was so far up ahead in the column that we could not see what was going on. As I leaned up against this big rock wishing I could be of some assistance, the enemy rounds coming from across the river continued to zing overhead cutting leaves and branches off the trees. Then we started receiving mortar rounds. The Marines in the platoon ahead of me were returning fire with M16s, M60 machine guns, and M79 grenade launchers.

The platoon sergeant asked me, "You know what kind of rounds those are cutting off those leaves?"

"No," I responded nervously.

"That's the sound of AK47s. The gooks must have hit the leading platoon. Sounds like there is a bunch of those slant-eyed commie bastards over there. Just stay down low, it will be over soon. 1st platoon is giving them hell. "Get some, 1st!" He then looked at me and asked, "You have just joined the company, haven't you?"

"Yes Sir," I replied, "just yesterday."

"Well, welcome to Vietnam. Don't worry, just keep your head down behind this boulder. Can't ask for better cover. Ain't no bullet gonna penetrate this thang. "Where are you from back in the world?"

"Kentucky," I responded.

"What is your name?"

"PFC Fenwick, Sir."

"Well, Fenwick," he said. "From now on I'm gonna call you Kentucky. You're scared ain't cha Kentucky?"

"No Sir." was my reply.

He then looked me in the eyes and repeated, "Kentucky, yor scared ain't cha?"

Again I said, "No Sir."

"Goddamit, Kentucky! he yelled out. "You're scared, ain't cha?"

"Yes, Sir!" I bellowed out.

"I'm scared too," he calmly said. "You don't have to deny it. It's only natural. I'm scared, you're scared, and so are the other Marines out here. Every time we get into a firefight, I feel like shittin my drawers. Just take it easy, it'll all be over before long."

I nodded in agreement but could not imagine that a man that was as calm as he could have the least bit of fear. He settled me down and made me feel like I belonged to a unit that needed me as much as I needed them. I still could not see the action that was going on up ahead of me. While I crouched down below the rock, I could hear the squad radio blaring with transmissions. The operator was only a few feet away from me. He was just listening to the receiver so I assumed it was the platoon radio operator who was doing all the talking.

I heard the squad radio operator say, "The company commander is calling in an air strike. The word is to keep your heads down low."

As we waited for the jets to arrive on the scene, there was now only sporadic firing and then no firing at all.

The squad radio operator yelled out, "We've got some wounded Marines up front, there will be some choppers coming in after the air strike for a medevac! Sounds like about four of our guys got their tickets back to the rear. Just wounded though, I believe."

After about twenty minutes, I heard some Phantom Jets screaming across the sky. The platoon radio operator yelled out, "Keep your heads down, they are going to be dropping some five hundred pound bombs on the target!"

I hugged the rock as two jets made their first sweep down low over the treetops. The bombs hit on the other side of the river and they shook the ground with terrific force. I could hear the sound of metal whizzing through the air. The jets circled in the air and made two more strikes, then they disappeared out of sight and sound. A few minutes later I could hear the sound of choppers approaching. I could see two CH-46 Sea Knight helicopters and four UH-1 Huey Gunships. The gunships veered off and began spraying the area across the river with automatic fire. The CH-46s came in low and landed up ahead of me out of sight. I could hear the engines slow the acceleration of the rotors and some Marines yelling to get the wounded aboard.

Both choppers lifted into the air. As they passed over my head I could see one of the door gunners swinging his M60 machine gun and putting rounds on the enemy position. The Hueys joined them and they were on their way back to the base camp taking the wounded with them. I learned later that four Marines had been wounded, but none seriously.

The word was given to dig in and that we would remain in our positions the rest of the afternoon and through the night. We were instructed by the squad leader to dig fighting holes, post security, and set out a listening post. Watches were set up for the night. The squad leader ensured that I had the 2400 to 0200 watch because of the previous confrontation we had that day.

I began to dig my foxhole and noticed that Hawkeye was digging a spot about six feet long, two feet wide, and looked about twelve inches deep.

"Hawkeye, what are you digging that for?" I asked.

"It's my sleeping hole," he replied. "What you need to do is dig a hole the length and width of your body and deep enough so that your chest and head is below the ground surface. That way if Charlie sneaks in at night while we're sleeping and lobs some chi-coms on us, or we get hit by mortar or rocket fire, the shrapnel will go over your body instead of through it. Gives you a better change of survival."

A chi-com was the VC crude version of a hand grenade that contained nails, glass or anything else that would inflict casualties. The term chi-com was slang that stood for anything Chinese Communist. I began digging frantically in order to dig my sleeping hole for the night. When I had finished I noticed that I had blisters on both hands from digging. My palms began to sting. I placed my poncho in the hole and lay down to check and see if my body was below the ground. Just right, I thought.

By now it was getting to become dusk and the squad leader told us to set our watches for the night. Two other Marines went out for the listening post. I figured since I had the midnight watch that I would try to get some sleep. As I lay in my sleeping hole I opened a can of ham and eggs that I had in my pack and began to chow down. The word was given not to use heat tabs for heating our C-Rations or any other sources of light like flashlights or cigarette lighters that may give our positions away.

I ate the can of ham and eggs cold along with a few crackers. We had been supplied with six days of rations the day before and it seemed my pack was full with the rations alone. I looked at the mortar rounds, the trip wire devices, pop up flares, and the other assortment of ordnance that I had received and wondered how I had managed to fit it all in or on my haversack. I figured that if I ate a little chow I would not have to carry as much weight. The fact remained however, that we did not know when we would get resupplied again. Little did I realize that there was almost never enough time in the Nam to adequately heat my chow. As I ate, thoughts crossed my mind that I could have been one of the Marines medevaced earlier, if I had been walking point. I was restless through the night but finally managed to doze off.

At around 2345 a Marine woke me and told me it was my turn for watch. Still half asleep I asked what exactly I had to do for watch. He explained to me that every fifteen minutes the platoon radio operator would call for a SITREP (Situation Report). When he called me on the radio, all I had to do was to key the handset twice. That would let him know that everything was all secure at our squad's location.

"How do I know if he's calling me?" I asked.

The Marine explained to me that since our unit was Mike Company each platoon and squad had their own call sign. The company Command Post was Mike. Mike 1 was the 1st platoon, Mike 2 was the 2nd platoon, and Mike 3 was the 3rd platoon.

He told me, "Since we are in the 3rd platoon and the 3rd squad, our call sign is Mike 3 Charlie meaning the 3rd squad. Now do you understand?"

"Yeah, I think so," I replied.

As he walked away to his sleeping hole he gave me one other piece of advice. "Just remember your call sign is Mike 3 Charlie. When they call you on the PRC-77 just key your handset twice and above all stay alert." He pointed to a Marine who was laying in his sleeping hole and told me that he would be the one to relieve me from watch. Then he crawled to his own sleeping hole to try and get some sleep. I did not know his name but I thought he showed a lot of patience with me.

I moved to the fighting hole I had dug while carrying the radio and my rifle. I sat down with my feet dangling inside the hole. I positioned the radio next to me and laid my rifle on the ground ensuring the barrel or chamber would not be vulnerable to dirt. I put the handset up to my ear but could only hear a low hissing sound. I stared in the direction across the river not being able to see anything in the darkness.

Then over the handset came a low voice from the 3rd platoon radio operator.

"Mike 3 Alpha, Mike 3 Alpha, SITREP, Over." Then I heard two hissing sounds as the 1st squad security watch keyed his handset twice.

The platoon radio operator then said, "Mike 3 Bravo, Mike 3 Bravo, SITREP, Over."

Again, the handset was keyed twice by the 2nd squad security watch.

"Mike 3 Charlie, Mike 3 Charlie, SITREP, Over."

It was now my turn. I knew that Mike 3 Charlie was my 3rd squad, but I hesitated for a couple of seconds longer than I should have. I feared that I might key the handset at the wrong time. I did not want to mess up my first night on watch with the squad.

The voice was now more pronounced and commanded in a more firm manner, "Mike 3 Charlie, Mike 3 Charlie, if you can hear me, key your handset twice!"

I keyed the handset twice hearing the pisst, pisst sound on the hand receiver.

The radio operator then said, "Roger, understand all is secure at your pos. Stay awake out there!"

POS was an abbreviated version for our position or location. I then heard him call for Mike, the company radio operator. "All is secured at this time, Over." I heard the familiar pisst, pisst sound on the receiver and I knew that the company radio operator had acknowledged the platoon's report. I felt around for my grenades and then waited intently for the next SITREP.

I began to think about the squad's call sign. Not only did the squad have a call sign but each Marine in the squad had a call sign. The first acronym was the phonetic alphabet for our enlisted rate, then our enlisted rank, then the phonetic alphabet word for our last name. My call sign was Echo Two Foxtrot which meant enlisted, rank of an E-2 (private first class), and Fenwick for the last name. Little did I realize that the call sign "Mike 3 Charlie" would have such a significance and lasting impact on me for the rest of my life. For the time being, I would get to know my squad members inside and out. We were to be brothers-in-arms for the time we were together in Vietnam.

As the night passed I did a few more SITREPs in a more confident manner and began to feel more at ease. Just then I heard a noise coming from about thirty meters to my front. There was an embankment leading down to the river's edge and we were about fifty meters from the water. I froze my bodily movements and tried to pinpoint where the noise was coming from. I heard a branch snap and then another one. Someone must be out there, I thought. I knew there were no friendlies to my immediate front so I decided to call to the platoon commander to get permission to throw a grenade. I took the handset off the radio, squeezed it, and started to speak in a very low voice.

"Mike 3, Mike 3, this is Mike 3 Charlie, Over."

A voice came over the net, "Mike 3 Charlie, this is Mike 3, Over."

"Roger," I said. "Be advised I have movement to my direct front. Request Outgoing, Over."

"Wait one," came the reply.

I waited while the platoon radio operator checked with the platoon commander to see if he would grant permission. In about a minute a different voice came back on the radio.

"Mike 3 Charlie, This is the Mike 3 Actual. What exactly do you have in front of you, Over?"

I knew that the Mike 3 Actual was our platoon commander, a first lieutenant. I replied, "Be advised I have some sort of movement approximately thirty meters to my direct front. Request to throw a grenade."

"You have no friendlies or a listening post to your front, do you?" he asked.

"That's a negative, Over," I replied.

"Very well, you have permission to throw a grenade."

I then transmitted, "Mike 3, this is Mike 3 Charlie, Roger Out."

I felt for a grenade in the darkness, placed it against my chest, pulled the pin with my left hand, and drew back my right arm to throw. I threw it with as much force as I could, taking care to aim it right down the center of my clear field of fire. I was cautious not to throw it to the extreme left or right and take the chance of hitting a tree limb. I lunged down in my fighting hole as the grenade went off. KA-WOOM! All the Marines around me jumped from their sleeping holes and dove into their fighting holes.

"Who threw that fuckin grenade?" A Marine yelled in the darkness. "What's out there?"

I spoke up and said, "I threw the grenade. I heard movement and got permission from the platoon commander for Outgoing."

The squad leader came over to me in the darkness cursing and yelling. He asked, "What do you have out there, Fenwick?"

"I don't know," I said. "I heard rustling and some branches snap so I called the platoon commander to get permission to throw a grenade."

"Jesus Christ, Man," he quipped. "When you get ready to throw a grenade you had better holler, OUTGOING, and then throw the frag. Fuck, you scared the shit out of us, you fuckin newbie!"

We waited silently for a few seconds and I could hear no further sounds.

I was hoping that something would be out there because I had caused all the commotion. Finally the squad leader told the other Marines to go back to sleep and warned that I had best get my shit together. My pride was hurt somewhat. I was only trying to do my duty, but got yelled at instead. I wondered how long it would take me to be as calm as Hawkeye and a veteran at this sort of thing. I hoped that it would not take too long for me to learn this new way of living.

Morning came and the squad leader woke us. He told us to chow down if we wanted to and that we would be providing a blocking force for the company. I ate quickly and placed any gear that I had taken out the night before back inside my pack. The word came down that we were to move out, and once again, our platoon moved out in a column formation. Only this time we were not with the other two platoons. A blocking force was when one unit got on one flank while a separate unit swept through an area from another direction. As the "gooners" ran out in retreat from the lead combat element, the blocking force would have open season on the fleeing VC or NVA.

My platoon waded across the river and set up in defensive positions as we waited for 1st and 2nd platoons to sweep through the area pushing the enemy toward our flank. From looking at a map, the squad leader had revealed to us that there was a village close to where the Marines had been hit. The 1st and 2nd platoons were to move through the ville looking for signs of Charlie. The squad radio operator kept us informed of what was going on as the other platoons were moving. Suddenly we heard a firefight coming from the village and the squad leader told us to be on the lookout for running VC. Next thing I knew, I saw a group of Vietnamese carrying weapons and running from the ville in our direction. We patiently watched them until they got within range.

"OPEN FIRE!" the squad leader yelled.

Almost immediately four of the fleeing VC fell to the ground. The others turned and began running away from us. As we fired, the squad leader was shouting and directing our fields of fire. I heard him yell out, "Get some 3rd! Get some!" By now the village was in flames. The other two platoons were setting fire to all the hooches. We began to move forward in order to get a body count.

I heard the platoon operator say, "No casualties in the ville. Mike Company has waxed their asses but good."

We moved forward checking the bodies and collecting their weapons. I came upon a dead VC. He was the first human being I had seen whose life had been taken since my arrival in Vietnam. I peered down at his body next to my feet. He had on what looked like black pajamas and his AK47 rifle was laying about three feet away. He had on a cartridge belt with some magazines, one canteen, and his left leg had been shot almost in half. His upper body was rippled with bullet holes and part of his head was blown off. I stared at the dismembered figure. It suddenly dawned on me that this must be the reality of war. I began to picture me laying there instead of the dead VC. I helped the others collect weapons and stacked them in one pile. The bodies were stacked up and we went off and left them. The villagers would claim their fathers or brothers later and cart them away for burial.

As we began to reconsolidate with the other platoons, I noticed what I thought was a VC, talking to the platoon commander. To my disbelief, this Vietnamese had a M16 rifle slung across his shoulder. For the life of me, I could not figure out what was going on. Then Hawkeye explained to me that he was what they called a Kit Carson Scout. These Vietnamese scouts were assigned to various American units that assisted in locating Charlie. They were originally VC who had surrendered to the Americans. They in turn would hunt down their own people, a traitor, so to speak. They also helped to interrogate and act as translators for those VC or NVA whom we captured. Depending upon the source of information, some of the prisoners were sent back to the rear for more thorough interrogation. These Kit Carson Scouts stayed with the units, and for the most part seemed reliable even though they were viewed as traitors.

As days passed I became closer to my buddies in the squad. We were there for one reason in my mind, to look out for each other, at least that is what I thought. One night I was laying in my sleeping hole and my fireteam leader, Travieso, was on watch.

I could hear him mumbling to himself, "Damn, I can't get this pin back in. Son of a bitch. This stupid damn thing."

"What are you doing Travieso?" I asked.

"Oooh, I pulled the pin on this grenade and now I can't get it back in."

"What did you do that for?" I asked. Were you going to throw it out? Did you hear some movement?"

"No, I didn't hear nothin. I pulled the pin out just to see if I could put it back in."

He continued to wrestle with the grenade while attempting to get the pin back in the grenade. "Damn this thing, just won't go back in. I don't know why." Travieso was biting the pin with his teeth trying to straighten it.

"You mean to tell me you pulled the pin just to see if you could get it back in?" I asked.

"Yeah, I got bored with nothing to do, no excitement going on," he mumbled.

"What do you think you are doing?" I asked. "Don't you know you could blow the entire fireteam to pieces?"

"Calm down, calm down," Travieso said. "Can you see if you can get it back in for me?"

"Maybe we should just call the Actual to see if we can throw it out of the perimeter as outgoing. We will just tell him that we heard some movement."

"Nah, we can't do that," Travieso replied. I can get it back in eventually. C'mon you try it."

He handed me the grenade with his thumb pressed against the spoon. "Now hold this spoon real tight so it will not release. If you don't, it will go off."

I wrapped my right palm around the grenade ensuring that I had a tight grip on the spoon. I was actually squeezing it so hard that my hand was shaking. My palms were getting sweaty and I could feel beads of perspiration running down my forehead.

"Let me try to straighten this pin with my teeth first," Travieso said. He tried to straighten the prongs with his teeth and then handed me the pin. With the grenade in my right palm and the pin in my left hand I tried to insert the pin back into the grenade. I did not seem to get much success either because of the darkness and the fact that the prongs on the pin had been bent back slightly. I could barely just see the hole from the moonlight.

"Travieso, I can't seem to get this pin back in either," I said. "My hands are all sweaty now and I am holding it so tight that I might drop it. If I do it will kill us both. Why don't we just throw it out of the perimeter?"

"Let me have it back and I'll try it again," Travieso suggested.

He wrapped his palm over my hand and slowly slid his fingers down to the spoon and body of the grenade. "Now you can let go," he said. Then he held the grenade against his chest.

"Let me see if I can insert the pin while you hold the grenade," I told Travieso. I manipulated the pin trying to insert it back into the hole. It was not working. Travieso then took the pin from my hands and with unbelievable ease slid the pin right back into the hole. He bent the prongs back to hold the pin in place and then held the grenade in the palm of his hand for me to see that the task had been accomplished. He began to laugh and snicker at the concerned look on my face.

"What the hell!" I exclaimed. "You put the pin back in with no problem."

Travieso laughed. "I just wanted to see how scared you would get."

"You Shit-For-Brains," I retorted. "Don't you ever do that shit again!" I started punching him on his back and arms. He eased away from my reach while laughing uncontrollably.

"Cool it man, Cool it! You're gonna get the platoon commander down here in a minute and you're gonna be in a lot of trouble. Knock it off!"

"I'm gonna be in a lot of trouble?" I asked. I reached out and pulled his shirt up towards me so I was now looking straight into his eyes. "If you ever pull this shit on me again, I will beat your ass no matter if you're the fire-team leader or not."

He continued to quietly snicker and laugh. I let him go and he took his position back on watch. I lay back down in my sleeping hole shaking my head with disbelief. It was difficult enough to get a good night's sleep in

Vietnam and now I had a fireteam leader who wanted to play games. I realized that my heart was pounding loudly and with a tremendous rate of speed. I tried to calm down so I could try again to get some sleep.

Just as I was about to fall asleep, Travieso came over and shook me. "Okay Fenwick, it's your watch. Wagenbaugh is your relief. And oh, by the way, thanks for making my watch go by a lot faster. Once in awhile you need a little excitement in your life." I called Travieso a few dirty names as I assumed security watch in my fighting hole.

The next day we cleaned our weapons and wrote letters. Around 1700 the platoon commander called up the squad leaders for a brief. The squad leader returned from the squad leader's meeting and informed us that our squad was going out for an ambush that night. The squad radio was checked and the batteries replaced with new ones. Everyone also checked to make sure we had sufficient ammo. We were then briefed by the squad leader. He gave us a Five-Paragraph Order. As Marine Corps infantrymen, we used the acronym SMEAC; Situation, Mission, Execution, Administration and Logistics, and Command and Signal. We were to set in our ambush approximately four hundred meters from the perimeter along a well used trail to see if there was any VC moving around during the night. As the sun sank behind the western sky our squad walked slowly along the trail and set up our ambush in a graveyard.

The Vietnamese buried their dead by collapsing the corpse and placing it into a hole about three feet deep. They stacked a mound of dirt on top that was about three feet off the surface of the ground. These mounds made excellent defensive positions on an ambush because we could get in behind them and use them for some protection. We then set the watch. The way it turned out was that the ones who had been in country the longest would take the first watch. That way they would be able to get more sleep than the newer Marines that were given the later shifts.

As it happened everyone was talking in low voices and not anyone settling down yet for some sleep. We were talking about home and how long it would be before we went back to the rear for showers and beer. One of the Marines in the squad was a real character.

Stark suggested, "Let's start our own firefight. That way they will pull us back inside the perimeter. I don't know about you guys, but I don't want to stay out here all night on this fuckin ambush."

It appeared to me that Stark was very arrogant and cocky. He persisted with his idea of firing our weapons at absolutely nothing so we could rejoin the company back inside the perimeter. His plan was to tell the platoon commander that we saw some VC crossing the trail and start firing at will. He continued talking about how we could pull it off and get away with it. While we were firing our M16s, throwing grenades, shooting the M79 grenade launcher, firing off illumination, and the machine gun, he would tell us when to stop firing for a moment. Then he would fire his .45 caliber pistol in the air. He reckoned that his .45 pistol would sound like an enemy AK47. That way it would put more realism into the phony firefight.

Most of the Marines protested this sort of behavior, but the squad leader decided that he would cast the vote for everyone and agreed with Stark. He thought it was a good idea to get pulled off the ambush. Stark called back to the company perimeter on the radio and got the 3rd platoon Actual. Stark told the platoon commander that we had five VC in the open and without hesitation said that we were commencing fire at this time. The squad leader started to fire at virtually nothing and then some others joined in. During the firing Stark was coaching them on.

Then he yelled out "Okay, you guys, slow down your rate of fire, I'm going to fire my .45 and they will think that it is an AK47."

He fired off a few rounds into the air and then our small arms fire would pick up again. No one knew if the command post thought it was an actual firefight or not. This phony firefight went on for a couple of minutes and then Stark called back to the platoon commander and said that the VC had run off and that we could not see them any longer. He asked the platoon commander permission for our ambush to come back into the perimeter since our ambush position had been compromised.

"That's a negative," came the response. "Stay out there in case they come back. Your ambush is on a trail that leads right into the CP and we don't want Charlie in our perimeter."

The Marines who had not condoned the phony firefight from the very beginning began to grumble. We all thought it was a hairbrained idea that could get us in a lot of trouble. The squad began to bed down for the night. I heard one Marine mumble, "Now see what you've done, you gave away our position. Now Charlie knows exactly where we are."

"Aaah, shut the fuck up," said Stark.

I stood my watch and got off at around 0300. As soon as I wrapped up in my poncho liner for a little shut-eye, the Marine on watch yelled, "Gooks! Gooks! Wake up everyone!"

I started to reach for my rifle and then remembered the trick that Stark had tried to play earlier that night. I hesitated momentarily, thinking he was up to his old trick, when suddenly a round landed next to me throwing dirt on my poncho. Then there were the sounds of machine gun fire, someone was firing the M79 grenade launcher, and some of the Marines were firing frantically into the darkness. Someone fired off an illumination flare and I saw about five Vietnamese with rifles running down the trail away from us. I commenced firing my rifle but was too late. They had disappeared out of sight. The Actual called over the radio and asked if we had any casualties. Stark told him that we did not have any squad casualties and that we did not hit any of the fleeing VC. He began to plead with the Actual to allow us to return to the perimeter. He yelled into the radio handset, "This place is crawling with gooks!"

Permission to reenter the company perimeter was not granted by the platoon commander. We stayed on full alert until the sun came up. At daybreak we moved back within our front lines and went to our original positions that connected the other two squads in the platoon. About as soon as we sat down to eat some C-Rations we got the word that the company was moving to another location. I had planned on getting a little sleep, and some time to write letters during the day, but that was not to be. I felt a sudden urge to choke Stark but I got on with the business at hand.

That day the company moved about five klicks (5000 meters) and set up on a small knoll. Squads began patrolling around the company perimeter but they had returned finding nothing. Our squad was then designated to go out on patrol on our side of the perimeter and given certain checkpoints. By now the sun was straight over our heads at around noon time and it was very hot, humid, and muggy. I wore a helmet, flak jacket, cartridge belt with canteens and grenades attached, and a bandoleer of M16 ammunition strapped around my shoulders. Under my flak jacket I wore a green short-sleeve T-shirt.

As we proceeded down the hill in single file from our CP we moved along a trail. The elephant grass was tall and leaning over onto the trail. I twisted and turned trying to avoid the cutting edges of the elephant grass but it was senseless. The elephant grass was cutting my arms with every step I took. I saw blood trickling down my sweating arms. I got a sudden furry of rage and anger to where I didn't care anymore. I would just let the sharp blades of the elephant grass cut me to pieces. I began to bolt forward for a few feet keeping my arms down at my sides and letting the grass cut across my arms. It was more of an act of defiance. I said aloud, "Go ahead, cut me, who cares. I can take the pain."

It was not too long into our patrol that we came to a sudden stop. Word was passed back through the squad from one Marine to another that a booby trap had been spotted on the trail by the point man, Travieso. After a few minutes we started to move again. The Marine in front of me stopped moving forward and then gave a motion for me to come up beside him. When I reached the Marine he pointed to the booby trap that Travieso had spotted on the trail. I looked down and saw a thin green wire stretched across the trail.

One end the wire was tied to a bush and on the other end was connected to the spoon of our own M26 hand grenade. The killing radius of the grenade was 16 feet however, the casualty-producing radius was 50 feet. The grenade was placed upside down in a rusty C-Ration can that some Marine had discarded. I was told to be careful and step over it because the pin was out of the grenade. The least amount of pressure on the wire would enable the grenade to fall out of the can thus detonating the device. I slowly placed my left foot over the wire followed by my right foot. The other Marine then moved slowly away and I stayed there to show the Marine behind me the booby trap. After going through the procedure again, I moved on up slowly to catch up with the patrol.

It was not long until we were stopped again. The word was again passed back that another booby trap had been discovered. We remained in position while Travieso inspected the device and continued with his forward progress. This time when I got to the booby trap it was the same type of trip wire but was connected to a chi-com grenade, which was the VC version of a grenade.

That was the first time I had seen a VC grenade. It had a wooden handle connected to a round salmon can. The spoon was intact but I noticed that the pin was missing. Old Charlie is really trying to inflict some casualties, I thought. Hawkeye began explaining to me that sometimes they would just wait along a trail and would hand detonate a booby trap or land mine from a distance and disappeared out of sight either in tunnels or spider traps.

We began to move around it and then I heard Travieso say, "Fuck this shit, here's another fuckin booby trap. This area has the bastards all over it. We had best hold up here for awhile until I can check this trail out and see if there is an alternate route." The next thing I heard Travieso say was, "I can't believe this shit! The gooks even have them planted off the trail in the grass, in the bushes, all over this goddamn place!"

The squad leader spoke up and said, "All right, listen up, don't anybody move off this fuckin trail. There are booby traps all over the place. We'll stop here, call in to let the Actual know what we have out here, and see how many of these fuckers are in our way."

I could hear the squad leader on the radio telling the platoon commander that we were going to try to blow some in place. I wondered how we were to manage that since we did not have any combat engineers attached to us. We were all instructed to lie down and take cover and be careful about tripping any booby traps. Travieso was pulled back from his search and about four Marines started throwing rocks at one booby trap in the trail up ahead. They would throw a rock and then get down covering their heads with their helmets. Someone managed to make a direct hit on one and it detonated. WHOOM! Dirt and rocks flew in the air and I could see a blue smoke where it had exploded. Just to think that one of us could have stepped on the thing was enough to make me cringe.

Now there were about four Marines throwing rocks at the booby traps. Of course, Stark had to be a part of it. All of a sudden he came of with a mastermind of an idea. He decided that he would try to get some shrapnel from one of the booby traps so he could be medevaced out of the bush. Stark got back about twenty feet from the booby trap with some rocks in his hands. He told us all, "Watch this shit. I'm gonna get me a Purple Heart. A stateside wound. One that I will be medevaced out of the bush and never be back to this fuckin Nam ever again."

He threw a rock at the device and then faced away, bent over, and tucked his head down on his chest. The rock hit close by the device but it did not explode. He grabbed another rock and threw it. Again he faced away and bent down at the waist. Still there was no explosion.

One Marine said, "Stark you are crazier than hell!"

"I don't care what you say!" Stark snapped. "I'm gonna get me a state-side wound and get out of the bush. I can't stand it no more. I'm getting tired of looking for Luke the Gook. All I need is just a couple of little wounds in my ass and I have my ticket out of this shit."

He started to throw another rock and Hawkeye said, "Yeah, but what if it blows your balls off?"

We all started laughing.

"Oh shit, I never thought of that," Stark replied.

He backed up about another five feet away from the device. Then he threw the next rock. As soon as he released the rock he bent over at the waist and placed his helmet over his gonads. The booby trap still did not go off. We reckoned that it had been out in the weather for so long that the damned thing must have rusted.

"Dammit!" Stark snapped angrily. "Just my luck. I can't even get wounded even when I try. I gotta get out of this fuckin Nam, that's for sure!"

We were still only about two hundred meters from the perimeter and had counted seventeen booby traps. The squad leader called back and spoke with the Actual. He told him how many booby traps we had seen on that trail and were not even at Checkpoint One yet. The word from the platoon commander was to turn the patrol around and start back into the perimeter. He told us to be damned careful not to trip any on our way back. Travieso took the lead again and we walked back into the CP talking about what an idiot Stark was. I could not believe that the squad leader would allow him to do such a thing. I hoped that I would never get that insane during my time in the bush.

That night as our squad was moving to a night time ambush site we spotted six NVA/VC. Five of the enemy had packs and were about 75 meters away from us. We took them under fire with small arms and received return fire from the enemy. Then they disappeared into the darkness. The squad leader called back to the platoon commander to report the incident and it wasn't long until the company 60mm mortars were dropping rounds onto the area where we had seen the enemy. Then a 105 illumination mission was called for. We swept through the area under the light of the illumination drifting down from the sky under small parachutes. It gave off enough light to see where we were going but not enough to detect any mines or booby traps. We did not find any uniforms or weapons so we regrouped to set up in our ambush position. It was quiet for the remainder of the night.

The next day we moved to yet another location. We moved out in a column, one man behind the other, about fifteen meters apart. We walked through rice paddies and we could see the hill where we were to set up our company defensive position for the night. I glanced at the Marine in front of me and all of a sudden there was a loud explosion. KAH-WHOOOM! He had stepped on a booby trap. I saw a puff of bluish black smoke rise slowly into the air where he had been standing. His body went hurling into the air and fell back to the ground. The Marine was screaming and yelling, "God, help me. Please save me. Get me a corpsman!"

I yelled as loud as I could, "Corpsman up! Corpsman up!"

His legs were in really bad shape. I tried to calm him down and keep his mind off his wounds, but I felt that he would most likely lose a leg, maybe both. A Navy corpsman retraced his steps running back toward us and attended to him immediately. He applied a tourniquet to his legs and gave him a shot of morphine. I held on to the Marine and yelled to Stark to give us a hand.

Stark said, "Ugh ugh, not me! I ain't doing that shit no more, I can't stand it no more, I gotta get the fuck out of here."

He continued walking forward so another Marine came back to offer assistance. The squad radio operator radioed the platoon commander. The platoon knew someone had hit a booby trap and had stopped moving forward. A medevac chopper was called in. It seemed like a long time before the bird arrived, but it must have been only about twenty minutes. They medevaced the Marine out and that was the last time I ever saw him. He was well liked within our squad and was a good Marine.

We moved up to the top of a hill. We could tell that another Marine unit had been here before because there were old fighting holes on top of the hill that were partially filled in with dirt. Our perimeter was set up with our platoon on one side of the hill and connecting to the other two platoons in a 360 degree defensive position. We began to clear fields of fire. A couple of the Marines decided that instead of digging different fighting holes that they would just dig the dirt out of the existing holes. All of a sudden we heard an explosion. WHOOOM! A booby trap detonated in an adjacent foxhole where two Marines were digging about thirty meters away. Both Marines collapsed wounded from the detonation.

Our squad leader ran over and yelled to us, "Don't dig in the existing foxholes, they may be all booby trapped! Make sure you dig your own holes and watch where you're steppin!"

Although there was a large fighting hole that had been pre-dug right at my position, I started digging another one adjacent to it. The soil was dry and hard as rocks. Our entrenching tools, that we carried on our packs and used for digging, had picks on one side and a spade on the other. They all had wooden handles. With the pick I dug out a fighting hole as deep as I could. I did not know if the pre-dug fighting hole next to me was booby trapped or not but I was not about to take any chances. We heard that seven other Marines had been wounded by the initial blast and that a medevac chopper had been called. Word traveled throughout the company that another booby-trapped foxhole had been found.

Medevac chopper lands to evacuate a wounded machine gunner who stepped on a booby trap.

After about twenty minutes the choppers arrived at our position and the nine medevacs were taken back to the rear. One of Charlie's booby traps had done its job of inflicting casualties on the unsuspecting Marines. It was later determined that a homemade mine made of C-4 and shell fragments in a can rigged with a trip wire had done the damage. The trip wire used for detonation was about three inches off the ground and connected to a clump of grass a short distance away from the explosive that was buried about three inches below the surface of the ground. It has resulted in three emergency and six priority medevacs.

I noticed that Stark was not digging a fighting hole. He was just starring off into space. He was mumbling to himself, "I can't stand it no more, gotta get out of here, I'm too short for this shit. I've been in country longer than any of these boots and here I am still fuckin around with this shit. I want to get out of here and go home." A couple of the Marines tried to talk to him but saw it was no use. We figured he would snap out of it in time.

The night passed without any further incident. Bright and early the next morning we were told that we were going to move northwest about five klicks. This was equivalent to about five thousand meters. As we started moving out the word was passed to make sure everyone watched out for booby traps. In front of my fireteam was a machine gun team that was attached to the squad. Just watching them move along with the machine gun and the accessories, reminded me of ITR and the training that I had with the M60 machine guns. I was trained to be a machine gunner, but since my arrival in Vietnam, I had been assigned as a rifleman.

I wished that I could be in the machine gun team so that it would enable me to use my expertise in the specialty in which I was trained. I watched the team move along and we proceeded down an embankment. The walk was slow and everyone seemed to be on edge. I overhead the radio operator say that they were crossing a creek up front. I looked up and saw one of our machine gunners carrying a M60 on his shoulder. He took a turn, dropped down into an embankment, and disappeared from sight. The elephant grass seemed to be about five feet high in this area and was hard to walk through because of its thickness. All of a sudden, I heard an explosion.

KAH-WHOOOM!

Everyone dropped to the ground thinking that we were being hit. There was screaming and yelling coming from down in the embankment. Someone yelled, "CORPSMAN UP!"

Then word came back through the squad that the machine gunner had tripped a booby trap. Hawkeye and I walked forward cautiously looking at the ground for more booby traps. When we got to the machine gunner, he was being attended to by the corpsman and we noticed that he had one leg really mangled up and his left arm blood soaked. I saw that his weapon had nicks from the explosion. I thought to myself that he had his ticket back to the States. He was not going home the most pleasant way, but nonetheless, he was going home alive. I was beginning to understand how Mike Company earned the nickname of "Medevac Mike."

Chapter 4

China Beach R&R—
Rest and Relaxation

THE sun began to sink slowly in the western sky. I sat quietly in my sleeping hole on top of my spread out poncho. The elephant grass provided some concealment for me but I could still see part of the squad to my left and right. Hawkeye was immediately to my left. I decided to reorganize my pack, equipment, and ordnance so that I knew exactly where everything was located before it got dark. No sense of fumbling around in the dark for weapons and ordnance if Charlie happened to creep up on us. My mind wondered and I began to think of home and the farm. I thought about my mother and father and my brother Larry and what they might be doing at that very moment. My thoughts were interrupted by Hawkeye's voice.

"Hey Fenwick, have you heard the good news?" Hawkeye asked.

"What good news?" I replied.

"Mike Company is going to China Beach for R&R, three glorious days of rest and recuperation. I hear they have a beach, club, and hot chow. Sounds good don't it?" he asked.

"I don't know," I responded. "I was just getting used to the bush. I may not want to come back after all that relaxing."

"We will be humping back to LZ Baldy tomorrow morning and from there head out to China Beach," Hawkeye said enthusiastically. "I can't wait to relax for a few days, catch up on my letter writing, and swim in the ocean."

"Yeah, sounds really nice," I said. "Where exactly is this China Beach?" I inquired.

"We'll," Hawkeye replied, "I hear the Americans gave it that name. I think it is close by to Da Nang and Marble Mountain. We should have a good time on the sandy beaches."

"Yeah Hawkeye," I said. "I haven't been in country as long as you have but I could use a little R&R right about now. Maybe I can scrub a little of this dirt and crud off my body. How far do you think we have to hump back to the base camp?"

"Oh, about five klicks, I reckon," Hawkeye responded.

"Yep," I said. "We should be ready for a little R&R after a five klick hump back to the rear. Hell, I've only been here less than a month and already I've been swimming in the rice paddies, had a cookout, almost shot by

Charlie, saw Marines get blown away, and now we're going to a beach where we can swim in the ocean, down some beers at the club, and get some hot chow. What's next?"

"Just stick around," Hawkeye said. "You will see more excitement over here in a month than you have in your entire lifetime. It will make a man out of you real fast."

"I know," I replied, "that's what I'm afraid of."

The next morning the Marines of Mike Company prepared to move out. We donned our heavy packs in order to start our long walk back to the base camp. We crossed over some hills and ended up walking along a road known as Highway 535 heading northeast toward LZ Baldy. As we came within a mile or so of the base camp, some Vietnamese kids began to tag along with us from a nearby village. They were bare footed, filthy, and were barely clad. Most of them were about the ages of six to nine years old. The kids were approaching various Marines and saying, "Manine give babysan cigmo, hokay, hokay? Manine give babysan chop-chop. Manine numba wan."

A Marine in front of me gave one of the kids a small packet of four cigarettes that came with the C-Rations. Another boy approached me and asked for some chop-chop. I told him to Didi Mau. At least that was the way I had learned to say it in Vietnamese, which meant to go away.

The boy then said to me, "Manine no give babysan chop-chop, Manine numba fuckin ten."

When the Vietnamese asked the Americans for a cigmo, they meant a cigarette and when they asked for chop-chop, they meant C-Rations. Number one meant you were an okay guy, number ten meant you were much disliked. I learned later that we would be plagued by their presence whenever we were close to a village. It amazed me how little of the English Language the kids had to speak in order to convey their desires for food or cigarettes.

We stopped along the road for a ten-minute break. The sun was beaming down directly above us and scorching hot. The road was dusty and we had walked for a couple of miles without shade from any trees like we were used to in the bush. We began to feel exhaustion drawing our energy from within us. I noticed a couple of teenage Vietnamese girls with baskets in their arms approaching us. They had sodas and cups of crushed ice and were going from one Marine to the other trying to sell their refreshments. The sight of some refreshments at this moment made me feel the dryness in my mouth. I was hot, smelly, and tired from the journey.

"Cold soda, Manine," I heard a young girl ask a Marine who was about ten meters back from me. She approached him with her styrofoam cooler of goods. She carried two on a bamboo pole. I felt the desire to purchase a cold soda from her but I figured that we would be arriving at the base camp before long. I also longed for a hot meal, cool swim in a river or rice paddy, or better yet a nice bucket shower. I settled for a drink of warm water from my canteen that tasted like iodine. As I quenched my thirst with the warm liquid, I looked around with envy at the Marine who was about to relieve his thirst with an ice-cold soda.

As we sat on the side of the road we watched one of the girls pop open a bottle and pour the soda into a paper cup filled with crushed ice. Without hesitation the Marine gulped down large mouthfuls of the soda. The word was passed to saddle up and to move out. We began our walk down the dusty road again and soon the village was out of sight. Suddenly from behind me came cries of moaning. The Marine who had bought the soda was holding his stomach in pain while a few others gathered around him. One yelled out for a corpsman. The column was halted while the corpsman attended to the Marine. A medevac chopper was called for and in about fifteen minutes the Marine was evacuated back to the rear.

I did not immediately know what had happened to the Marine except to speculate heat exhaustion. Then the squad leader began questioning the squad members if we had bought any food or drinks from the Vietnamese during our breaks.

One of the squad members at the very end of our squad spoke up. "I saw him drinking a cup of soda that a Vietnamese girl was selling at our last stop."

"That stupid idiot!" the squad leader snapped. "He probably drank some crushed ice along with the soda. Listen up people! From now on nobody is to buy any kind of food or drinks from the Vietnamese. You cannot trust any of these communist bastards. That includes women and children. Noooo-one! Do you hear me?" As he walked away the squad leader continued to rant and rave about how stupid a Marine could be to trust the Vietnamese.

We arrived at LZ Baldy and heard that the Marine had been medevaced to the Regimental Aid Station. Rumors circulated through the squad that the Marine had supposedly consumed chipped glass from the ice. I thought to myself that we were in South Vietnam to help the people defend their country and they repay us with such gratitude. You could not be too cautious of things even as minor as purchasing a cup of soda from the Vietnamese. In their haste to ease their thirsts, many Marines fell victim to this trick of the Viet Cong. Some failed to realize that a smiling face from a young girl selling soda along side a road could be the devil himself. You never knew if the crushed ice or soda contained slivers of glass that could cut your insides to bits.

We spent the rest of the day cleaning weapons, taking showers, and packing the gear we needed for China Beach. We were all excited about our trip. The squad mingled around our cots inside our hooch. We got engrossed in planning our days of relaxation. I knew that some of the Marines in the company had green shorts and I wondered how they got them. I didn't have any swimming trunks and thought I would look comical laying out on the beach in my camouflage utilities trying to get a tan.

The next day on 23 March, we gathered and packed our personal belongings that we would need at China Beach. We checked out our weapons from the armory and replenished our rifle ammunition. We then humped down to the helo pad and boarded choppers for the trip to Da Nang. I managed to get a seat near the exit ramp. I was curious what the country side looked like from LZ Baldy to Da Nang. Once in awhile I could get a glimpse of the landscape below. The chopper first started off flying over the rice paddies, rivers, valleys, and villages. We were also flying across some mountain ranges. They seemed to be quite steep and some had visible trails running across the top of them. As we neared Da Nang I could see buildings with tin roofs up on the hillsides that the Americans had built. I figured they were observation posts that aided in the security of the Da Nang area of operation.

When we landed in Da Nang we loaded onto 2-1/2 ton cargo trucks and traveled from the landing zone through the streets of Da Nang. We then came to the sandy roads leading into the China Beach area. Upon arrival we noticed structures and general purpose tents that were set up. We were assigned the tents right next to the beach and we moved inside to stow our gear on and under our cots. A few Marines pointed out to the rest of us that there was a club at China Beach where we could go and down some cold beers. Once the squad had settled in the tents one Marine was assigned gear guard in order to guard our weapons so the rest of us could venture out onto the beach. We called our little excursion of rest and relaxation as "Stack Arms."

There were some Army soldiers swimming in the ocean and sea gulls were flying overhead. I hoped that the Army and the Marines would be able to get along together on the same beach without getting into fights. I decided to take a walk on the thick white sand and for a brief moment I realized that I was taking each step cautiously as though I was looking out for booby trap wire. It then dawned on me that we were now in an area where there were no firefights and no mines or booby traps, just good times ahead. I kicked off my jungle boots and felt the warm sand beneath my feet. I was convinced that there was nothing to fear.

We got organized very quickly and we spent the afternoon swimming in the ocean. A grill was set up for a barbecue. We drank soda and beer to our hearts content. We lay out in the sun and everyone began to look forward to the evening at the club. We also heard that there was to be a live band. After a good swim, clean clothes, and hot chow, I had time to write a letter home.

March 23, 1970

Dear Mom, Dad and all,

You can never guess where I am at this time. I'm at Stack Arms, a place where a company goes to relax for three glorious days. It's called China Beach and is on the outskirts of Da Nang. The beer is free, the sodas are free, the food, movies and just about everything is free. We even got a rack with a mattress, blankets, and sheets. Sounds like I'm crazy but we've been sleeping on the ground for the last month. It's a nice place here and is set up just for people who come out of the bush for some relaxation. I'm aiming to go surfing tomorrow which will be my first time. They have a real nice beach here. It looks like I joined Mike Company just in time to come to Stack Arms. I think a company might come here every three months or so. Anyway I'll have a good time here for three days.

As you know I've been in the bush for awhile. It's not so bad out there except for the insects and the humping. We practically move every day to a different position and we all look like pack mules. I don't hump the machine gun because they put me where they needed me most. So I'm just a rifleman now. If someone from the gun team leaves though, I'll probably get in the team. When we go back after Stack Arms we'll be going into the mountains. Where, I don't know. We spent about two days on Hill 185, but we were moving most of the time.

I got a letter from Larry, Nancy and Janice yesterday. When I opened Janice's, I thought I had a book. She had been writing off and on since the 7th of March. I was sure glad to get them. It takes seven days for a letter to get to me and if I'm out in the bush, we have to wait three days for resupply to come in. So when I get a letter I really enjoy it. Maybe I can catch up on some of my writing while I'm here at Stack Arms if I don't get too loaded on the beer.

The beer here is available from nine o'clock in the morning until midnight and to get one you just have to show the man an empty can. There is no limit to how many you get either. Just six at a time but no telling how many times these guys pays him a visit. I like the soda myself. Ha!

Well I'll close for now and let you all read the daily paper you get along with the other mail. I know that's a daily ritual for you. I just wanted to let you know that I'll be having a good time for awhile. So until next time, be good and stay well.

Yours truly,
Freddy

We put on our jungle utilities that we had washed by hand during the day. It did not take long for the sun to dry them out. We went to the club that night and the place was packed with Marines. It was standing room only to say the least. It appeared that everyone from the entire company was at the club to include another Marine unit as well. I feared there would be trouble between the two units. There was plenty of draft beer and canned beer for all of us. It did not matter what age you were. If you were old enough to fight a war, you were old enough to drink beer.

It was not long until an oriental band took their places on a small stage and began playing rock and roll music from the late 60s. The music sounded good to me for I had not heard live music in quite some time. The band was made up of Filipinos who traveled to South Vietnam on a tour from the Philippines. As the night progressed, the drunker, and crazier we got. I had been drinking off and on all afternoon and was beginning to feel no pain.

There was cheering and yelling coming from a far corner of the room. The Marines were holding something up and were passing it around. Each man took turns drinking beer from it. The beer was quickly refilled and the process continued from one Marine to another. Everyone was drinking from it and hollering words of excitement as they passed it on to the next Marine. As the passing of the container came closer to me, I noticed the drinking mug was a human skull.

I asked a Marine who was standing close to me, "What the hell are they doing?"

"It's a VC skull, Man! Somebody got him a VC skull and has been carrying it around in his pack. We're gonna drink beer out of the fuckin thang," he said.

"Oh, that's just great," I commented. Now we have a VC skull drinking mug. What's next?"

The VC skull made its way through the crowd of Marines and was passed my way. The thought crossed my mind that it might be a good time to move from my position to avoid the passing of the skull. Then without warning one of the Marines handed me the skull as he tried to yell out over the loud music. "Have a drink Marine!"

The club full of crazed Marines began to chant, "Drink! Drink! Drink!" Some had been drinking since 0900 in the morning and were half crazy. I took the skull and tried to hand it off to another Marine standing next to me without taking a drink from it. Loud boos came from the crowd.

I heard a Marine yell out, "Hey asshole, you had better drink beer from that VC skull."

The Marine that I tried to pass the skull on to pushed it back to me without taking it. "You had best do what they say. "Payback is a Medevac."

I knew that all eyes were upon me and I knew what payback meant so I dared not to chicken out. I grabbed the skull with both hands keeping the chin and teeth orifice upright so the beer would not spill out. I could not believe that I was holding a skull that once encased the brains of a living human being. I imagined the oriental face that had accompanied this bony surface in his past life. The skull had a tint of yellowish color and was half full of beer. I hesitated, feeling a sudden churn in my stomach and the beer began to spill out of the sockets of the teeth and onto my utility jacket.

In the meantime there was cheering and laughing from those all around urging me to take a drink. I looked around the club and I could see that hundreds of Marines were staring at me waiting to see me drink from the skull and getting impatient that I was taking too long. If I refused to take a drink from the skull, I knew that I would have been ridiculed, made fun of, or even beaten up. Most likely I would have been forced into a fight for being a coward. I could not see me being harassed by the Marines of Mike Company so I decided to go ahead with the ordeal.

"What the hell?" I finally yelled out in despair.

I closed my eyes, held the skull up to my mouth, and began to sip the beer from the openings of the teeth cavity. Some of the beer gushed out and soaked the front of my freshly washed utility jacket and trousers.

A Marine from the crowd yelled, "Hey, Man! You've got to know how to drink out of a VC skull. Tongue it man! Tongue it!"

Everyone around me roared with laughter. I placed my right forearm across my mouth and chin wiping away the spilled beer. I then passed the skull onto the next Marine. He in turn began to drink from the skull.

The yelling and cheering continued. "KILL, KILL, KILL! KILL, KILL VC. OOORAH! OOORAH!"

Never in my life had I expected to do something so grotesque. Since I was smack dab in the middle of hundreds of drunken and wild Marines, I felt threatened, had I not drank beer from the skull. I hated to imagine what might have happened to me if I had refused. The Filipino Band started playing "We Gotta Get Out Of This Place" by the rock band, the Animals. The Marines began to dance to the music among themselves while chugalugging beer like there was no tomorrow. Some were singing out loud to the lyrics with the band. The warm beer was working fast now and going to my head. I was on cloud nine but I began to feel a self-inflicted headache coming on.

I decided to get out of this place and call it quits for the day. I stumbled back to my tent and plopped down on my cot. While I lay back in the prone position on my back I wished that the pain in my head would go away. I could feel my head pounding with every heartbeat. It felt like a sledgehammer hitting the back of my head. I wanted an aspirin badly, but I would just have to suffer. After all, it was of my own doings that I was in this state. No one forced me to drink the warm Black Label Beer in the hot sun on the beach. I started drinking in the middle of the afternoon only because everyone else was and the fact that the beer was readily available and free. I thought that possibly I would learn from my mistake.

A member of my fireteam had gotten so drunk and incoherent that he kept yelling that he wanted to kill something. He stumbled into the partially lit tent and started to rummage through his pack. He pulled out his .45 caliber pistol, locked and loaded the weapon, and started waving it in the air.

"I'm going to kill somebody!" he yelled.

"Put that damn pistol back in your pack!" I commanded.

"I'm going to kill somebody. Don't get in my way or I'll do you in!" he cried out. He began waving the pistol back and forth stopping at random to aim at virtually nothing in particular. I feared he might fire the pistol by accident.

"What the fuck are you doing?" I asked angrily. "Extract that round out of the chamber, remove the magazine, and put that pistol back in your pack."

"Fuck you Fenwick! Leave me alone! I want to shoot something!"

He stumbled past my cot and went outside the tent. POW! POW! There was the sound of the pistol firing outside of the tent.

"Holy crap!" I yelled. I scrambled to get in an upright position and then sprang to my feet. I stumbled over packs and equipment while finding my way to the tent entrance. I found the Marine outside the tent pointing his gun down toward the ground. He had fired two rounds into the soft sand. Two other Marines appeared from nowhere out of the darkness. They had also heard the shots and came to investigate. We all wrestled him down to the ground and managed to grab the pistol away from him. He began kicking and screaming. Between the three of us we finally managed to calm him down. We got to our feet leaving him laying in the sand. I stuffed his pistol into my pack so he could not get to it. In a few minutes he stumbled back inside the tent.

"Where's my fuckin pistol?" he asked. I ignored him. "Fenwick, I said, where's my fuckin pistol?"

"I've got it," I replied. "I'll keep it for you overnight and give it back to you in the morning."

"I want it now!" he demanded.

"Oh, no you don't," I replied. "I'm not giving it back to you tonight. I'm not taking the chance of getting shot by a crazed Marine who's drunk on his ass. I will give it back to you in the morning and that's final."

For about the next twenty minutes he stumbled around in the darkness trying to locate his pistol. He tried looking through my gear and under my cot. Each time he seemed to be getting close to the pistol I would force him to back off. At one point he began to rummage through my pack. I grabbed it away from him and placed my pack under my head. He swore obscenities toward me but finally made it back to his cot and collapsed into a deep sleep. He snored so loudly that it sounded like an old buzz saw that we used to have on the farm.

The next morning we all felt our hangovers from the previous night. My head was hurting because of over indulging in alcohol. I managed to eat a C-Ration breakfast and then gave the Marine back his pistol who had the bad attitude the night before. I then joined a small group of Marines from the tent and headed out for the beach. The Marine who had fired off his pistol during the night elected to stay behind and clean his pistol. I thought he might do something stupid but the others convinced me to leave him alone. Our little group walked down the beach. It was a beautiful sight with the sun glistening on the ocean and the white sand on the beach. It reminded me of some photos I had seen somewhere along the way that advertised a vacation getaway to a foreign tropical island.

Just like the day before Marines had already made their way to the beach. Some were swimming while others just basked lazily in the sun. Transistor radios were blaring away and there was laughter of the Marines mixed in with the music. Some were trying to sing with the music that they heard coming from their small radios. We talked about the previous night at the enlisted club and looked forward to going back to the club again that night. I would have to drink moderately this time and pace myself. One thing was for sure, there would be no drinking of warm beer in the middle of the afternoon for me. I would bask in the sun instead and try to recuperate from my hangover. So this is what R&R is all about, I thought. Forget about all your fears and worries in the Nam. Rest and Recuperation!

It was a memorable three days of R&R. On the third day while everyone was still suffering from hangovers, we boarded the trucks again and headed to the LZ at Da Nang to be heli-lifted back to LZ Baldy. We realized that our party was over. The Marines were mostly silent on our return trip because we all knew that we were heading back to the bush. It seemed to be a very short journey back to the LZ Baldy base camp.

When we arrived at LZ Baldy we noticed that the main roads within the battalion area had been covered with what looked like burned oiled. It was to be done about three times a week to help cut down on the dusty road conditions. As the vehicles such as jeeps and mules ran up and down the roads it wasn't long until the dust reappeared. It may have cut down on the dust within the battalion area but it was nasty to get the oil on our boots.

We were told to get our war gear ready in order for us to mount out the following morning. There were rumors of us going into the Que Son Mountains and then other Marines were saying that we were going into the lowlands. No one seemed to know for sure.

"Have you been to the Que Son Mountains before?" I asked Hawkeye.

"Yeeaah, a few times," he replied. "You haven't been there yet, have you?"

"Not yet, but I imagine it is my destiny since Mike Company seems to go all over the place," I said.

"Yep, you will get there sooner or later," Hawkeye responded. "It is very beautiful up in the mountains but still a lot of NVA and VC running around."

"Guess time will tell whether we go to the lowlands or the Que Sons. Either way, I don't want you too far away from me so you can keep this old Kentucky boy out of trouble," I said.

"We'll have to look out for each other," Hawkeye replied. "You cover my six and I'll cover yours."

"Roger that!" I said.

March 26, 1970

Dear Mom, Dad and all,

This may seem a little soon but thought I'd write before I go into the bush again. We got back from Stack Arms yesterday and think we are going back to the hills again today. I really had a good time and I hated to leave but it's just one of those things. If you would, the next time you write, send me Donald's address as I guess maybe there has been a change.

We're supposed to have an inspection today at 12:30 p.m. and then leave LZ Baldy around 3:00 p.m. It is now about 11:00 a.m. and I've just finished eating chow. We had meatballs and spaghetti. I stuffed myself pretty good because that will be our last hot meal for awhile. Instead of going into the hills again I think we're going to some lowlands around a river. We were supposed to go into the mountains, but that may have changed.

I got a letter from Mom and Nancy yesterday. The one Mom sent was post marked the 17th and it took about eight days to get here. Seems like a long time but guess I'm pretty far from home. You don't have to write so often because the cost of stamps mounts up after awhile. I have a book of stamps in my seabag but won't be able to get them this trip. If I ever do I'll send them home. I want you to tell Nancy and Larry, thanks for the letters. I really appreciate it.

Well, now that spring has come I guess Dad and Larry will be pretty busy. Wish I was back there to help out. Just take it easy and don't work too hard. I'll try and do the same. Bye for now. Everyone stay well and be good.

Sincerely,
Freddy

P.S. Wish you all the happiest Easter ever.

Chapter 5

A Taste of Survival

THE mission to the Que Son Mountains would have to come at another time. We moved to an area that was about three klicks southwest of LZ Baldy. From here we would send out patrols and ambushes and relocate our company position from time to time. The Marines of Mike Company prepared the company's defensive position by establishing principle directions of fire for each squad and digging fighting holes, sleeping holes, and camouflaging the perimeter. The Marines placed folded ponchos on the ground inside the sleeping holes and arranged their gear to their own individual liking. We had heard that we would be in this area for more than three days, possibly a week or longer. Because of this, everyone was putting forth a little more effort in order to make their surroundings as comfortable as possible.

The first day was a bright and sunny day with a gentle breeze blowing. The humidity was high and I was sweating from digging my fighting hole and sleeping hole. I stood up to take a break from the digging and peered around the defensive perimeter. All the Marines were steadily at work. Very little talk could be heard but I could see a couple of small groups talking in low voices. I thought about how the Marines bonded with each other although they never knew one another before arriving in Vietnam.

Throughout the perimeter there were rows of camouflaged poncho liners blowing in the breeze that had been tied to small trees, shrubs, and bushes. Some of the poncho liners retained the just off the shelf look which meant they belonged to the ones who had recently joined Mike Company. The majority of the poncho liners however, were faded out by days of being exposed to the hot sun and tropical climate. This signified the old timers of the unit who had been in country for several months. The parapets of the fighting holes had been nicely concealed and the Marines had begun settling in. Claymore mines and trip flares had been placed immediately in front of the fighting holes in likely avenues of approach. It seemed like such a peaceful atmosphere.

I went on the first patrol led by a full-blooded Navajo American Indian whom we all called Chief. The entire squad considered him a hotshot point man. He had an uncanny knack for locating mines and booby traps and had a certain intuition when the enemy was about. Chief was sensitive to the enemy's unique odor and the smell of sardines or mackerel, which was a favorite food with rice for the VC and NVA. He could smell the enemy from a distance and provide a warning to the rest of the squad before we got too close.

We waded through rice paddies and moved cautiously into a treeline. We came upon a dead VC laying on the ground. He was dressed in what looked like a pair of black pajamas. His swollen body was black in color and covered with dried blood and flies. It appeared that the decaying body had been at this location for a few days. The stench was overpowering and almost nauseating to me. There was no weapon near the corpse. As we spread out in search for more dead bodies Chief moved on to the opposite side of the trees and out of our sight. Then we heard the rapid succession of rounds being fired by Chief's M16 rifle. Rat... a... tat... tat!

At the sound of rifle fire we instinctively dove behind available cover and hastened our weapons to the ready. We nervously refrained from any return fire because we knew it had been the sound of Chief's M16. The silence was broken within a few seconds of the firing with Chief's voice coming from behind the trees.

"You better be dead now, you bastard."

There were sighs of relief as the squad got to our feet, eager to witness Chief's kill. We all slowly gathered around Chief to peer at the dead Vietnamese. Chief had come upon a badly wounded NVA who had been half asleep and sitting upright against the base of a tree. He probably had been lapsing in and out of sleep when Chief stumbled upon him. His left foot was completely mangled with only shreds of flesh that remained attached to his leg. Flies were feeding hungrily on his wounds. His face was white as sheet and we could tell the NVA had lost a lot of blood. The slumped body must have been barely alive when Chief opened fire on him. According to Chief, the NVA woke up and suddenly realized that Chief was upon him. The startled NVA made a last minute move to get his weapon. That is when Chief opened fire and put him out of his misery.

The squad leader ordered us to spread out and set up a 360-degree perimeter, commonly known to us as a hasty defense. We scouted the area to see if there was any more VC or NVA in the vicinity. It was finally concluded that these were the only two. It seemed strange to me that we had come upon a dead VC and close by was a seriously wounded NVA. We did not take the time to investigate.

"Good job Chief," Hawkeye said as he patted Chief on the shoulder. "Gotcha self a NVA. He ain't one of the local yokels. This one here is from the north."

"Yeah, look what I got," Chief said as he held up his left hand with a shiny 9mm German Lugar pistol.

We gathered around and gazed at Chief in admiration.

"This one is mine," Chief said with a snarl.

Hawkeye responded, "No problem, Chief. That pistol is yours to keep.

Finders, Keepers! You've got yourself a souvenir from the Nam."

The pistol must have been a prized possession for the now deceased NVA. How a German Lugar found its way to South Vietnam and into the hands of the NVA, I had no idea. Nonetheless, Chief had himself a fine souvenir. A couple of the Marines searched the body to see if there was anything that might be useful to our intelligence Marines in the rear. There were various pieces of paper in his pockets. Inside a brown leather satchel next to the body was an undetermined amount of Vietnamese currency. The excitement grew among us as we hurriedly counted the money. At one point we stopped counting and estimated that the notes exceeded over one thousand U.S. dollars. The NVA must have been traveling through South Vietnam paying the VC for their services and loyalty to the NVA.

We began to jokingly debate whether to split the cash among ourselves or turn it over to higher authority. About half of the squad proposed to divide the money in equal shares amongst us. We argued back and forth for a couple of minutes debating what we were going to do with the money. To his credit and better judgment, the squad leader made the decision to turn over the cash to higher-ranking officials in order to avoid any repercussions. We had also found map sheets in his pocket.

Curiously, we gathered around trying to get a glimpse of the maps and charts. There were various hand markings and sketches drawn on each map sheet. We could see that the sketches also contained notations in a foreign language. I assumed it was Vietnamese writing. One of the maps indicated the location in which we were now standing. We returned to the perimeter feeling quite elated with our findings. Upon our arrival, the cash, identifications, and other papers were turned over to the platoon commander for disposition. Our Kit Carson Scout confirmed that the pieces of paper were identification that the NVA had been a paymaster. The maps were sent back to the rear on the next available chopper. The Battalion S-2 Intelligence staff would examine the documents for any useful information.

Chief's find was the main topic of conversation throughout Mike Company that day. Everywhere he walked in the perimeter he received a congratulatory pat on the back and thumbs up from the rest of the Marines. The company commander promised Chief to reward him with R&R (Rest and Relaxation) to another country or some other type of recognition.

The next day various patrols were sent out from the perimeter. Two squads would go out together patrolling both opposite sides of the perimeter, intersecting, and rotating around in a clockwise manner. During the night the squads would take turns setting up ambushes.

On the second night our casual routine was abruptly interrupted. WHOOMPH! WHOOMPH! Mortar rounds were being fired from an unknown location and dropping just outside the CP. Marines started scrambling out of their sleeping holes and diving for cover inside their fighting holes. I heard some Marines yelling, "INCOMING! INCOMING!"

I had grabbed my M16 and bandoleers while scurrying from my sleeping hole into my fighting hole. I readied my rifle for what seemed like an imminent enemy attack. It seemed as though that for a few seconds there was complete silence. A strange eerie feeling came over me. As I peered out from my hiding place, I saw consecutive flashes of light coming from up high on a hillside to my direct front. I realized the incoming mortar barrage was coming from that position. The silence was interrupted with enemy mortars rounds pounding the base of our position. They were landing just outside the perimeter toward my ten o'clock direction. Each explosion moved closer to the perimeter as the enemy adjusted their fire. The rounds were walking right into the CP.

I believed there had to be more than just one mortar tube out there, but I could only make out one flash. By now everyone was riveted to their fighting holes. There was nothing we could do except keep our heads down. The mortar rounds were now getting closer to my position. Shrapnel was zinging overhead and ricocheting off the ground and rocks. Each round would violently shake the ground on impact and I could feel my teeth chatter. With my head down inside my fighting hole and pressed against my helmet, I began to taste the Vietnam dirt. I must have forgotten to close my mouth. I spit out the foul taste and cradled my weapon even more tightly with both arms. Without realizing it, I began to pray.

"Our Father, who art in heaven, Hallowed be thy name; thy Kingdom come; thy will be done on earth as it is in heaven. WHOOMPH! Give us this day our daily bread; and forgive us our trespasses as we forgive those who trespass against us; and lead us not into temptation, but deliver us from evil. Amen." WHOOMPH! WHOOMPH!

I feared that this heavy curtain of mortar fire might eventually work its way directly over my fighting hole and a round drop right on top of me. My fate was in God's hands. I remembered what I had been taught when Jesus was praying to God in the garden grove in Gethsemane just before he died on the cross. "My Father, if it is possible, let this cup be taken away from me. But not my will, but your will be done."

Meanwhile the company commander had called back to the base camp for artillery support. The enemy barrage had lasted for about ten minutes but it seemed like a lifetime. The commander's request was answered with artillery rounds being dropped several meters from the flash of the mortars. It was close enough however, to silence the aggressors. We figured they had packed up and were on the run. On the second attempt, the artillery rounds fell closer to where the enemy had positioned themselves up on the hillside. Flying debris had grazed a few Marines but none were seriously wounded. The company commander directed a one hundred percent watch for the remainder of the night. This meant that everyone would stay awake and alert for any enemy aggression.

During the hours of darkness we intermittently fired off the M79 Grenade Launchers around the perimeter. The M79 was also known as a "Blooper." Every squad had a Marine who was designated as the "Blooper Man" who carried the breach-loaded M79, a .45 caliber pistol, and all the assorted rounds for the blooper. It fired a 40mm grenade that was either HE (high explosive), the flechette (Bee Hive), Buckshot, WP (white phosphorus), smoke cartridges, and illumination. The HE round produced over 300 fragments that traveled 1,524 meters per second within a lethal radius of 5 meters and could engage targets to approximately 430 yards. The Bee Hive fired 45 10-grain steel flechettes and the Buckshot contained twenty or twenty-seven pellets of #4 buckshot. The WP had a burning effect and the buckshot was used for close range.

On this particular night we fired off illumination rounds about every twenty minutes to try and detect if Charlie was moving toward our perimeter. Our 60mm mortars would also fire illumination and an occasional HE round outside the circumference of the perimeter. The illumination from the mortars gave a lot of light for a longer period of time. I wondered why our own mortar section had not returned fire on the enemy instead of calling for artillery fire. I assumed they were too busy trying to take cover during the heavy enemy barrage. The outgoing around the perimeter continued through the night in case the enemy decided to probe our defensive posture.

At about 0300 I heard a commotion and then a lot of mumbling farther around the perimeter to my left. I listened intently as the noise grew even louder. It seemed as though a Marine had heard noises in the bushes and was alerting his squad to get ready for an attack. Suddenly my side of the perimeter opened fire without warning. Our squad likewise commenced firing to our direct front and some of the squad began to spray the area with automatic fire. Hand grenades were being thrown from positions around the perimeter and illumination lit up the night sky. We had heard only a few of the enemy return fire and believed they had been taken by surprise and were now running in retreat. The order was given to cease-fire. Soon the perimeter was quiet once again except for the firing of illumination.

"Gooks are in the perimeter!" a Marine suddenly screamed out.

Then almost immediately I heard another Marine yell out, "It's not gooks, it's a fuckin pig!"

From my fighting hole I spotted the pig. It ran right in front of me from my right front to my left and it was about ten feet away. It was heading straight for the CP. I never saw a pig run so fast. The frenzy beast was running for its life. It was very scared and was attempting to get out of our perimeter and away from these Marines in a hurry. I could hear laughter from the Marines as the pig bolted through the perimeter. One Marine in the distance yelled out for someone to catch the pig so we could have it for lunch. I imagined what a feast it would make instead of the usual C-Rations. It was a good size pig and was about three feet long and two feet wide. From my experience on the farm, I estimated the pig to weigh about one hundred pounds.

Cleaning my rifle gave way to reading a letter from Mom.

At the first sign of daylight patrols were sent out around all sides of the perimeter. Reports filtered back over the squad radios that eight dead NVA regulars had been found. With telltale signs of heavy bloodstains on the ground and a few abandoned weapons, it was suspected that some of the wounded enemy had been hurriedly dragged away by their comrades. The rest of the day was to pass without further contact with the NVA. The Marines guessed they were laying in wait up in the hills for another opportune time to attack.

I was very tired from being awake all night but managed to eat a C-ration meal. I seemed hungrier than usual for some reason. It must have been the stress of the night's incoming mortar rounds. My squad also got a chance to go down to a nearby stream to wash off. The water was clear and very comfortable. It felt good to relax for a bit and to get the dirt and grime off us. When I got back to my foxhole, I shaved my face, and cleaned the grit from my M16 rifle. After last night's encounter with the enemy, I wanted to make sure my weapon was functioning properly for our next contact.

Since I did not have to go out on patrol that morning, I managed to get a catnap before the sun got too hot. I collected all my loose equipment that was strung about my sleeping hole and fighting hole and partially packed my haversack. The latest word from the CP was that the company was getting ready to move to another position. After organizing my gear I sat in the open sun and decided to answer a few letters. At mail call the night before, I had received a letter from two of my older brothers and one from my older sister. I took the time to answer the letters as quickly as I could because I also wanted to write a letter home to my parents. Along with the other letters, I had received an Easter card from my mother during mail call. As I re-read the card for about the fourth time before answering it, I softly whispered to myself, "What great timing Mom has!" For today was Easter Sunday.

Easter Sunday
2:00 p.m.

Dear Folks,

How does this find you all? In good health and spirits I hope. Since today is Easter, we're just sitting around but will be moving again about four o'clock this afternoon. We move from hill to hill about every day and set up new positions. I got your Easter card last night while I was digging me a fighting hole and really liked it. I also got a letter from Bobby, Jimmy Howard and Janice. Sure did enjoy reading them. I answered them this morning but don't know if I'll be able to do it every time.

Chief, some more guys, and I went in the stream this morning to wash off. Chief is an American Indian and our squad's clown. He's just a little guy and we have a lot of fun out of him. The water was perfect and I felt pretty good then, but now I'm sitting in the sun while some from other platoons are going down for a swim. I would put my poncho liner up for shade but we'll be moving pretty shortly. You should see the tan on my arms now. I look like I've been to Florida. Guess the weather back home is warming up now since spring has set in. I can imagine what it's like.

Well, since I can't tell you all much news, I'll describe my surroundings. Right now we're on a small hill about ten miles from LZ Baldy. All I can say is that it's plenty of hills, bushes, and rice paddies. Also there are several villages around us. We go through a ville about every day and about all you see is old mamasans and small children. Old papasans must be out tending the fields but half of them are what we have to watch out for. The kids are cute to watch and they make you laugh. They'll take a cigarette, candy, and anything else you give them. When we talk to them as we walk

along they sometimes say "no bic," which means they don't understand. It's really interesting to watch them. We dig in different positions through the hills each day and move out the next day.

Here's a coin I had found on a trail that Larry can have as a
souvenir. Also the paper bill I am enclosing is the kind the military
uses over here, if you get the chance to use it. I should be able to
save money over here because there's nothing to spend it on. I'm also sending my promotion warrant home, where by I made private
first class. You can throw it in a drawer for safe keeping because I
don't think I'll need it over here.

Well since we'll be moving out in awhile, I'll close for now until a later date. Just wanted you all to know I was thinking about you
this Easter. Hope you had a good time. Excuse my pen, the darn
thing will hardly write. No wonder, I got it over here.

Yours truly,
Freddy

I decided that I should put my poncho liner back up for shade although I
had already packed it. The afternoon rays of the sun were really beaming
down now. The poncho liner would serve to keep the hot sun off my head.
The poncho liner had two strings at the four corners and down two sides for
tying it to whatever a Marine could find. In all, there were six points that
could be used to tie it up. I tied the four corners to a couple of bushes. Since
I was now in between the two bushes and under the poncho liner, instant
semi-cool shade appeared. What a nice little place, I thought to myself.
Home Sweet Home! Maybe I should give my temporary residence a name, I
thought to myself. Apartment Number 9 would sound nice.

Whenever I was in my sleeping hole or under my poncho liner, I got
accustomed to meticulously laying out my clothing, equipment, weapon, and
ordnance in the same fashion everytime. Things were easier to find in the
dark if I knew where to feel for them. I used my pack as a pillow and sometimes fluffed up my utility jacket for added comfort. I gathered all the letters
I had written, placed them in a waterproof bag, and placed them under my
pack. They would go out with the next resupply chopper. I felt good knowing that I had the chance to write so many letters in one day. As I knelt down
over my pack oblivious to anything going on around me, the squad leader
approached me from behind and said, "I need someone else to go out on patrol."

Without turning around to face him I said, "Don't look at me, I went out
on a patrol yesterday. I had planned to stay back today to sleep and write
letters."

He responded, "There's nobody else who is available, looks like you're
it."

I turned around and sat down on the ground facing him. "Wait a minute," I said, "I went out on a patrol yesterday. Someone else from the squad should go out today. Not everybody has had their turn."

"Look Fenwick," he replied angrily, "it's your turn to go on patrol and even though you went yesterday, I say you're gonna go again. So, get your ass in gear. We're moving out in ten minutes."

"Dammit, I don't get no huss around here," I complained.

"As long as you're in my squad you ain't gonna get no huss!" the squad leader snapped. He then walked away abruptly mumbling something to himself about fuckin newbies.

I began to organize the gear I would take on patrol. I got a bandoleer of ammo from my fireteam leader, loaded extra M16 magazines, placed two grenades inside the pockets of my flak jacket and fastened two others to the outside. I ensured the two canteens on my cartridge belt were full of water. I put my soft utility cover in the left cargo pocket of my trousers and placed the helmet on my head. I always carried my soft cover with me in case I got the chance to take off my helmet. The helmet was heavy and awkward and gave me headaches from time to time. I put on a soft cover every chance I got. I grabbed my M16 and joined the rest of the squad who had assembled in a little group awaiting our combat mission instructions.

We received our Five-Paragraph Order and the squad leader checked everyone to determine if we had the proper equipment to suit the mission. Once satisfied, the squad leader assigned a point man and we headed down a sloping embankment on patrol. We were one behind the other in a column and slowly began to spread it out until we maintained an interval of about twenty paces between each Marine.

We were to hit six different checkpoints at the grid locations indicated by the platoon commander to the squad leader. The squad leader had already plotted the six digit grid coordinates on his map. When we reached each checkpoint, we were to call back and let the platoon commander know that we had arrived at each specific checkpoint. We walked for about half an hour and arrived at Checkpoint One. The squad leader radioed back to report our location. We all sat down in little group next to a small stream and started to fill our canteens.

After the squad leader had filled his canteens he sat down by a small boulder with his back propped up against the rock. He began to scan over his map. "Tell you what," the squad leader said. "Instead of us going to all these checkpoints, let's just sit right here and call in every half hour or so. I'll radio back to the lieutenant and tell him that we have reached all six checkpoints without having to sweat our asses off in this heat. He'll never know the difference. By the time we are supposed to be at Checkpoint Six, we will ask permission to return to the perimeter. That way we don't have to be out here walking around all day long."

Some of the squad members seemed a little surprised and rather confused at his antics, especially the new Marines. A Marine who had been in the squad longer than the squad leader spoke up.

"That's a crock of shit, if you ask me," he said. "If we were assigned a mission to hit six checkpoints, then we should do just that."

Stark could not resist the urge to chime in and mouthed off in retaliation. "You people are so goddamn gungy! Let's just sit right here and do what the squad leader tells us. You're not in command, he is.! You never know what's out here, mines, booby traps, fuckin NVA, or gooks. Fuck it! I agree with the squad leader, lets stay put. I'm too short for this shit."

We began to moan and groan among ourselves for a moment until the squad leader interrupted our arguing and told us all to shut up. Someone quickly changed the subject and the next thing I knew we were all talking about the good old USA. We had lost track of the time until the squad leader barked at the squad radio operator.

"Gimme dat handset!" he commanded.

He took the handset from the radio operator and attempted communication with the platoon commander's radio operator who was back in the company perimeter. The squad leader spoke into the radio handset.

"Mike 3, Mike 3, Mike 3 Charlie, Over." There was a slight pause and then a response came over the radio from the platoon radio operator.

"Mike 3 Charlie, this is Mike 3."

The squad leader began his transmission. "Be advised that Mike 3 Charlie is now at Checkpoint Two, Over."

"Roger, Mike 3 Charlie. I copy that you are at Checkpoint Two. Roger, Out."

The squad leader handed the handset back to the squad radio operator with a big grin on his face. After about a minute we heard another transmission. It was the Actual, our platoon commander.

"Mike 3 Charlie, this is Mike 3 Actual. Are you at Checkpoint Two, Over?"

The squad leader replied, "Mike 3 Actual, that's affirmative, Over."

"Mike 3 Charlie, this is Mike 3 Actual, be advised that you had best be at Checkpoint Two because there will be some HE rounds drop on Checkpoint One within a few minutes. Out."

We all looked at each other in disbelief and Hawkeye said, "Shit, they're gonna drop HE on this position. Let's get the hell out of here!"

The squad began to slowly rise to their feet except for the squad leader and Stark.

"Nah! He's just bull-shitting us," the squad leader said. "They ain't gonna drop no rounds on this position."

Hawkeye replied, "You know, the lieutenant must be on to you now. He's probably testing you to make sure we are at Checkpoint Two. Maybe he's got the suspicion that you're not following his orders like you're supposed to. Just like the make believe firefight not long ago."

Ignoring Hawkeye, the squad leader got to his feet and gazed around.

He laughed and said, "Nah, Nah, he ain't gonna do something like that. He won't drop no HE rounds on this position. Hell, there's nothing here to shoot at. Besides, we're still here," he laughed.

"Hell, the lieutenant don't know that," I said.

The squad leader gave me an evil eye and nonchalantly lit a cigarette. We began discussing and complaining about what was taking place. Our arguing was suddenly interrupted by another radio transmission.

"Mike 3 Charlie, Mike 3 Charlie, this is Mike 3 Actual. Be advised incoming HE rounds will be dropping on Checkpoint One in five mikes, Over."

One of the newer Marines seemed a bit more panicky. "We've got less than five minutes to get outta here."

Unconcerned, the squad leader replied back to the platoon commander. "Mike 3 Actual, this is Mike 3 Charlie. We are now proceeding on to Checkpoint Three, Out."

While finding a comfortable seat on a rock the squad leader mumbled, "I wonder if that man is serious about dropping HE rounds on Checkpoint One? The hot sun must have melted his brain housing group."

I figured I would put in my two cents worth and spoke out in defiance. "Let's don't take no chances, let's just get the hell out of here."

Stark could not resist the urge of lashing out at me. "Here we go again, somebody else trying to take charge. If you ever become a squad leader, Fenwick, then you can make the decisions. But for now, you're just a low-life rifleman. A peon like the rest of us and nobody cares what the hell you think."

"Rifleman or not," I retorted. "If we do get some HE rounds on this position, they will wax all our asses."

Hawkeye added, "He's right, let's go now before it is too late. We ain't got no business here, lets move on to Checkpoint Two. That way if they do drop those rounds we will be out of the way."

"Listen to these pansy-asses," Stark said. "They always want to be so goddamn Gung-ho."

The squad leader finally rose to his feet, reached for his cartridge belt and rifle, and said, "Maybe we better go, that asshole might just do it. Grab your gear and let's move out."

As the squad formed in single file and began moving, Stark began complaining. "This squad is such a bunch of fuckin pansies," Stark said. "Nobody got no balls. These goddamn newbies think they're in charge. They're gonna end up getting us all killed. I can't fuckin wait until I get the fuck outta here."

"Shut up, Stark!" the squad leader commanded. "Just shut the fuck up!"

Our squad radio operator could be heard saying, "Hey you guys, Shot Out." HE rounds are on the way."

A Marine behind me in column spoke up. "See, the platoon commander is wise to the squad leaders shit now."

I was too concerned about quickly getting out of the area to put a voice to a face. Besides, now was not the time to chastise the squad leader. We started to pick up the pace and then began to run. We were not looking out for mines or booby traps as we should have been. We were just trying to get out of the area as fast as we could.

WHOOMPH! WHOOMPH!

We glanced behind us. Checkpoint One was being bombarded with HE rounds. We could see smoke and dust in the exact spot where we had just been sitting. Rounds whistled over our heads. We ducked down slightly as we ran in an attempt to avoid flying debris and shrapnel. The artillery barrage soon lifted and we moved rapidly on to Checkpoint Two. Without stopping, we moved expeditiously proceeding on to Checkpoint Three. The squad radio operator called in to report that we were at Checkpoint Three. He could barely speak into the handset since he was almost out of breath from moving at a double time. The lieutenant came over the radio and asked the squad radio operator if he was sure that we were at Checkpoint Three.

"Roger that!" replied the squad radio operator.

The lieutenant transmitted, "Well, you had best be at Checkpoint Three because HE rounds will be dropping on Checkpoint Two in five mikes."

Needless to say, we hurried on to Checkpoint Four. The squad leader and Stark remained quiet as we moved along. We all knew that we had almost made a fatal mistake, had we not questioned the squad leader's authority. I wondered how much longer I could last in Vietnam under the command of an incompetent squad leader. I wanted a different one.

I heard more HE round blasts coming from the area where we had just traveled. Just then out of nowhere appeared a VC with a rifle slung across his shoulders to our direct front. He darted across an open area and disappeared into the ground. It happened so fast that we did not have time to open fire.

We radioed back to report the sighting. Very cautiously, we approached the area where the VC had ducked underground and we saw that it was a well-used tunnel. We threw some grenades into the hole. There were sounds of rumbling under the ground. We suspected that he was still in there and perhaps more like him. A couple more grenades were tossed into the hole as we yelled, "Lai day, Chieu hoi." (Come here and surrender). There was no response.

"Come here, Fenwick,! the squad leader commanded. "Now you have a chance to be a tunnel rat. Get down inside this hole and see what we have in there."

"I can't get through that hole," I replied. "It's too small for me."

"Then grab a fuckin E-tool and widen the hole!" he snapped in an angry voice.

"We didn't bring any E-tools," I responded.

"Then use your goddamn hands!" he yelled.

As I moved forward toward the entrance of the tunnel, Hawkeye walked up to the squad leader and said, "I'm smaller than him, I'll go. Someone give me their .45 pistol and I'll go in."

"I can't let you do that Hawkeye," I said, "the squad leader wants me to go in. Besides, you have already had your fair share of being a tunnel rat."

"It just don't mean nothing," Hawkeye replied. He took a .45 caliber pistol from one of the other Marines and proceeded into the hole before I could say anything else. I felt a sudden surge of guilt that Hawkeye had assumed my responsibility without hesitation. The squad leader said nothing. He just looked at me with hateful eyes. I stood there not believing that I had let Hawkeye take my place. It had happened so suddenly. I feared that something terrible might happen to Hawkeye in the tunnel. I knew if it did, I would never live it down. I anxiously awaited some sort of sign from the tunnel that Hawkeye was okay.

After a couple of minutes Hawkeye emerged from the hole and got to his feet. "There's more than one of the bastards," he said excitedly. "I'm sure there are two or three. I can hear them back further in the tunnel but I can't get to them. One of them sounds like he's wounded." He then asked for his M16 and started back into the hole again. This time we heard some shots fired in the hole.

"I'm bringing one out! Clear the hole!"

Hawkeye exited the hole dragging a VC by a leg. We got on our knees and helped him drag the first VC out of the hole. I noticed that the VC did not have shoes on. As he was being pulled out of the hole he was screaming, "Chieu Hoi! Chieu Hoi! The VC's skin color was as white as a sheet with a yellowish tone. It was obvious he must have spent a lot of his time underground in tunnels. Hawkeye crawled back into the hole and dragged out two more VC. They were wounded from Hawkeye's fire. A chopper was called in and they were taken back to the rear for interrogation.

As we continued on our patrol we spotted one male and one female at a distance moving to our front. The male was carrying an AK47. We opened fire and then swept through the area. The male had managed to escape but we found the female who was wounded in her back. She had an AK47 magazine, a poncho, medical gear, and some rice in her possession. The female and her equipment were medevaced back to the rear. Results like this kept the squad leader from getting into trouble with the platoon commander. Our squad believed that the platoon commander suspected that the squad leader was not fully complying with all of his orders although the lieutenant never really said anything.

By now we were proceeding on to our next checkpoint. We finally arrived at Checkpoint Six and the squad leader called back and told the Actual that we were coming back into the perimeter. We were told a few days later that we would be getting a different squad leader. We heard that the new squad leader had already been in country for about 9 months and was a seasoned combat veteran. Mike 3 Charlie was ready for a change of leadership.

Chapter 6

Letter from Vietnam
(A Poem of Love and Fear)

WE continued to work in our Area of Responsibility (AOR) in the lowlands. This suited well with the Marines of Mike Company as we did not have as many hills to hump up and down. It seemed to be a quiet place and we could even dig our fighting holes and sleeping holes in the soft soil without too much difficulty. The time when we were not moving from one location to the other or sending out patrols and ambushes we would sit around and talk about anything and everything under the sun.

There were conversations about Susie Rotten Crotch (girlfriends) back in the States, about why the hell we were fighting this war, about any up-coming operations, and when the next rehabilitation in the rear might be. Normally it was about thirty days or more out in the bush before we went back to the base camp for rest and rehabilitation. We made everything cozy because we thought we would be in this area for a couple of weeks.

Our platoon went on a daytime patrol one day and ended up detaining 3 females and 1 male. All of them did not have any identification which was in itself made us suspicious. They were wearing blue shirts and white trousers and ranged in age from 25-35 years old. We brought them back to the perimeter with us and safeguarded them until we could send them back for interrogation on the next resupply chopper.

One morning our squad was moving around lazily and digging through our packs to find some C-Rations to chow down on. We heard over the radio that a squad from the 1st platoon was going out on patrol. It wasn't long until they were taken under fire by enemy AK47s and 60mm mortars from about one hundred meters away. Another squad from the same platoon was sent to reinforce them. All the while they were still receiving mortar rounds. The two squads ended up detaining 5 Vietnamese males that were wearing black pajamas. One had pack burns on his shoulders. The youngest was about 15 years old and the oldest was about 40 years old. The 1st squad then started to receive small arms fire.

Our 3rd platoon, Mike 3, was told to proceed to their location and to assist with their efforts. We had to put our C-Ration meals aside so we could hasten to their aid. As we approached the position of the 1st platoon squads, an OV-10 was called on station to aid the 1st squad on the scene. On each contact with the enemy the squads would open up with M16s, M60 machine guns, and M79 grenade launchers. By now the 1st squad was running low on ammunition.

Our platoon relieved the 1st squad and set up a perimeter to medevac the wounded Marines. The OV-10 expended its ordnance that resulted in two secondary explosions and then supported the 1st and 3rd platoons while a medevac was called. While we waited for the medevac chopper, the Aerial Observer and gunships worked the area where the enemy fire had come. Our platoon swept the area and did not find any enemy dead. This action resulted in one priority and two routine medevacs.

That afternoon, while Mike 3 was returning to the perimeter from a sweep, a Marine in our platoon tripped a booby trap while coming through a hedgerow. It was a M26 grenade placed inside the bushes with a trip wire strung across the trail about two inches off the ground. The explosion resulted in one emergency and two priority medevacs. I began to wonder if this area in the lowlands was quiet and peaceful after all. It seemed that the enemy was lurking around every turn.

I was compelled to sit down while I had the chance and write a letter to my parents. I would do it in the form of a poem. I knew I could never be a poet, but I thought I would at least give it a try. At this moment in Vietnam, I wasn't scared of the fact of dying as much as I was of dying without one last chance of expressing my thoughts and feelings for my parents. If I was to die on this Vietnamese soil, I at least wanted one last letter to my mother and father to show my love for them. It would be a quick one, but it would come from the heart. By writing this simple poem I thought that they would understand how much I really loved them.

April Fools Day, 1970

Letter from Vietnam

To Mom and Dad who are so true,
Who understands the way you do.
Although I may be far from home,
I'll never really be alone.
For what we think and what we know,
We'll be close wherever we go.

To you Mom, who works so hard,
And never seems to get too tired.
Who slaves in the kitchen day after day,
And never does it for reward or pay.
Yes, you're always doing for others needs,
And always have been doing good deeds.
The things you've done, I'll never forget,

Early morning April 1, 1970. This was my location when I wrote the poem to my parents titled "Letter From Vietnam." I had feared that I would not make it out alive. On the back of the photo I wrote, Hill 360 looms in the background with Sniper Valley at the base.

Even though I'm part of the so-called jet-set.
I'm just plain ole me all the way,
Wish there was a way I could repay.

To you too, Dad, I want you to know,
I'll remember you and your ways wherever I go.
The farm life for me was really grand,
Hope some day to have some land.
Thanks for bringing me up on the farm,
And keeping me from all harm.
Although at times there was hard work,
I'll always love it, wherever I lurk.

Wish I were there to help you out,
But duty calls me on and about.
If ever I can do anything,
Just let me know, I'll certainly spring.

Well this ends my lines of wit,
Hope you two liked it a bit.
While I'm waiting and nothing to do,
Thought I'd send my thoughts to you.
But soon I'll be moving out on my way,
To finish another glorious day.
While I'm in the Corps, you can bet your life,
I'll remember you both, and all of your strife.
So "you all" be good and all be well,
While your son serves his time… in hell.

Love you always,
"Plain ole Fred"

I managed to get my poem in an envelope and sent out on the next re-supply chopper. That night our squad was set in a night time position and observed two NVA/VC moving across our front. It appeared as though they were carrying weapons but we could not tell for sure since it was dark. We opened fire and then called for 60mm mortar illumination. We swept through the area but the NVA/VC was long gone.

On the third day in this position the word was passed down through the chain of command that we would be moving. A working detail from the various platoons dug a big hole for the entire company to bury their trash. I was part of the working detail. Each platoon gathered up all the company's trash that included empty C-Ration boxes, cartons, and open and unopened C-Ration cans. Marines that just did not like the contents like beef and potatoes, for example, threw the unopened cans away. If they threw away unopened cans they were supposed to punch holes in them with their Ka-Bars or bayonets. This would ensure that the food would spoil before the VC could get to it. There were always some cans found that had not been punctured because the Marine discarding the can was either too lazy or just did not care. A fire was set to burn up the trash. After the blazes subsided the working detail covered the hole by throwing in dirt to fill it up. Then they returned to their assigned platoons and we prepared to move out.

All of Mike Company started moving in a column formation along a cleared trail. The company moved out in an accordion effect with the front of the column moving away slowly. My squad had been assigned as tail end Charlie for the company so we waited patiently for our turn to start moving. The squad leader told me that I was to be tail end Charlie for the squad. I would be the very last Marine in the company formation.

I began to ponder in my mind about the possibility of the VC rummaging through the garbage that we had just buried. The Vietnamese villagers had done this many times before whenever the company moved from one position to the next. No matter how hard we tried to burn our rubbish, destroy the C-ration cans, or bury the site with dirt, the villagers would hoard around after we left uncovering everything they could get their hands on. Any unused or left over food in the C-Ration cans was quickly eaten. It was only a matter of brushing off the majority of the dirt. If there were any unopened cans the kids would bash them against rocks in order to get to the contents.

Most of these full cans were taken back to the village. They would also use any unburned cardboard sleeves off the C-Ration cartons and use the cardboard to make hats and sleeping mats. It was comical to see a papa-san out in the rice patties with a hat made of C-Ration cardboard. The hats would still have the writing on them. Our worst fear was that if the VC went through our trash they could use the cans to make booby traps. Additionally the VC would pick up any ordnance that may have been left behind. You could not tell if any of the old papa-sans or women were VC unless they were seen with weapons.

I imagined that I might be able to sneak back undetected to the position where we had just left and possibly get a lucky shot at a Viet Cong. As the squad kept creeping forward I decided to turn around and check the area. I eased up ever so quietly to our original position and hid behind a large hedgerow next to the hole that we had dug. Soon I began to hear noises, so I concealed myself even more and slowly brought my weapon up to the ready. Just in case, I placed the selector switch on automatic.

Some kids came out of the treeline and started digging up the hole where we had put our garbage. They were digging out cans while jabbering away in Vietnamese. As suspected, some of the larger kids were trying to get the food out of the cans by hitting them on rocks. Juices seeped out of some of the cans as the kids dug them from the ground. They were pulling out the sleeves of the C-Ration cases that had not completely burned up looking to uncover more cans. Then a couple of women appeared from the trees. None had weapons, but I figured that any minute now a VC armed with a weapon might come out into the open and I could get me a "confirmed kill."

I waited for a few minutes and got so engrossed in trying to spot a VC that I lost all track of the time. I must have been hiding behind the hedgerow for at least twenty minutes. All of a sudden, it dawned on me that I was all alone. The company had continued to move and my squad was now completely out of sight. I looked around and didn't see anyone. I thought to myself about the possibility of becoming a prisoner of war if I was not very careful. What would happen if I was suddenly surrounded by armed VC or perhaps even the NVA? Here I was trying to be a hero and get a confirmed kill not realizing the dangerous situation I had caused for myself. What a stupid mistake, I thought. I figured that the best thing that I could do at this point would be to try and catch up with the squad and forget about killing any VC.

As I eased down the trail not a soul was in sight. I completely forgot about checking for mines and booby traps along the trail. My concentration was focused on trying to catch up to the squad and nothing else. I began to fear the thought of being captured and began to walk a little faster. My fast pace turned into a slow run. My heavy pack was bouncing awkwardly up and down on my back. I began to sweat in the heat of the morning sun.

I came upon a fork in the trail and I had no way of knowing which way the company had gone. I began to look for signs on the trails such as boot prints, broken twigs, lost gear, or anything else that would give me a clue as to their direction of march. I decided to take the trail leading off to the left. The further down the trail I went the denser the vegetation became. Then the trail seemed to vanish altogether. It was no longer a frequently traveled trail. I began to wonder if I would ever catch up to the company unless I yelled out for someone. I realized that I could not do that since any enemy lurking in the immediate vicinity would hear me.

I turned around and hurried back to the junction in the trail. This time I took the trail to the right. I began to think that this trail could end up a dead end like the other one. To my amazement and disgust the trail forked off yet again in another direction. I stopped and visually scanned the trail behind me. I could hear noises growing louder that were coming from the area where the company had vacated. I figured the villagers were still digging up the garbage and wondered if a VC may have joined them by now. I just wanted to see a Marine, any Marine.

My heart began to thump in big beats. My palms were sweating and beads of perspiration trickled down my cheeks and forehead. It was the first time since I had been in country that I had been in the bush by myself without sight or sound of my comrades. I felt so all alone and stupid. I decided to take the trail leading off to the right. As I traveled along looking for clues of the company's whereabouts, I suddenly noticed a boot print in the trail. My heart sank. A boot print, an honest to goodness Marine boot print! I did not know I could get so excited about a boot print.

I was now on cloud nine. I began to run at a double time. Then my better judgment told me that I had best start watching out for mines and booby traps. I walked along still faster than the usual pace. My eyes focused on the trail searching for trip wires, cans attached to bushes, or raised dirt in the trail that could signify a mine. I began to stop periodically and jump into the air attempting to spot a helmet, flak jacket, weapon, or anything else that could be associated with a Marine.

I proceeded further down the trail and jumped up again. I saw some movement in the bushes. "Oh Sheeiitt!" I murmured under my breath. "I'm surrounded by VC." Cautiously I inched forward but then recognized the back of a Marine's head who was a member of our squad. I then saw Hawkeye just ahead of him. I had made it. I had caught back up to Mike Company. I walked up to the Marine in front of me and asked angrily, "Don't you ever look behind you to see if there is anybody there?"

The Marine replied nonchalantly, "No need to look back, I'm not tail end Charlie."

I felt like punching him in the face but decided to move on up to greet my best friend Hawkeye.

Hawkeye turned around and saw me approaching. "Where the hell have you been?" he asked. "I was just getting ready to go back and look for you. Thought maybe you had to a take a shit or something."

"Don't ask no questions," I replied.

I put my arm around his neck. "Hot damn, am I glad to see you," I said.

"Hey, take it easy," Hawkeye replied. "I'm not your girlfriend you know."

I began telling him about my plan to sneak back and get a confirmed kill while the company was on the move. I explained that I had lost sight of the squad and that the trails all branched off in different directions. I told him I did not know which trail to take in order to catch up with the company.

"That's not a plan, that's a brain fart," Hawkeye said. "Hell, Fenwick, don't ever do that again. We'll go off and leave you behind and you'll be out here in the bush all by yourself."

"You got that right," I responded. "From now on I'm sticking right on your ass."

"As long as you don't make me smile we'll be all right," Hawkeye replied. We got a chuckle out of that and I had learned a very valuable lesson.

While in a night time defensive position just before sunset our 81mm mortars were registering their defensive fires. One erratic round landed in the perimeter. A "Check Fire" was immediately called for. Soon the medevac choppers were on their way to take out the wounded. There were 4 emergency, 2 priority and 2 routine medevacs. For some reason we just couldn't seem to get away from the nickname, "Medevac Mike." I never knew what was going to happen from one minute to the next.

As the company moved onward, during the daylight hours, we noticed that our pace became very slow and then stopped completely. The brush and vegetation was very thick now. We would move forward a few feet and then wait for several minutes before moving again. Each time was for a very short distance. The Marines in the squad began to tire of standing in place with their heavy packs on their backs. About the time they wrestled with their gear and plopped down on the ground to rest the company column would start moving again.

I could hear cussing and swearing as Marines lifted themselves back to their feet and adjusted their packs and equipment only to move a few feet before stopping again. Everyone was becoming quite frustrated with the situation. I kept turning about to ensure the rear of the column was secure. We got word that the reason for the slow movement was that the bush was so thick the squads up front were using machetes to hack a path through it. Each squad was taking turns.

Eventually our squad received word from our platoon commander that is was our turn to help out in clearing the path for the company. We gathered our individual equipment and began moving to the front of the company column past the maze of Marines waiting one behind the other. I noticed that some were standing while others were sitting on the ground and resting. Some took advantage of the downtime to eat a can of C-rations, some were just staring at nothing in particular, and some were smoking cigarettes. All of them seemed to be in a pissed off mood. As our squad got closer to the front, the Marines who had been hacking their way through the elephant grass, bamboo, and thick brush were soaked with sweat. Their faces were red and their eyes sunk back in their heads with exhaustive faceless expressions.

It was now our squad's turn to swing the machetes. I moved forward and was handed one of the knives by a Marine who had been using it. I felt the cutting edge of the knife blade with the thumb of my right hand. It was so dull I reckoned that it would not cut hot butter. It was so hot under all the elephant grass and bushes that I could hardly breathe. I took off my flak jacket and T-shirt and I began to swing the machete back and forth. Perspiration soon soaked my entire body. I compared it to being in a sauna.

We got into a little clearing and edged our way around a big boulder on the side of a hill. It had water dripping down the sides. I took the palms of my hands and gathered up some running water and splashed it on my face. It felt so cool to my skin. Some of the Marines were so hot and tired they started to throw their gas masks off into the bushes. One threw a live mortar round down an embankment. Some started throwing away extra gear they felt they didn't need.

I thought to myself, no wonder the VC ended up with our explosive devices, the Marines discarded them at will. Some Marines began to take the flak out of their flak jackets, which was the material that was more or less shrapnel resistant. They tossed them off into the bushes. I assumed the rationale behind all of this was because they were so over burdened with combat gear and it was so hot and humid in this thick vegetation. I believed the heat was getting to them. Some were almost at the point of heat exhaustion and heat stroke. With all the complaining and arguing I knew that most just did not care.

Instead of proceeding through this area any farther, the company commander decided to turn around and go back in the direction we had come from. Everyone began to cuss and swear since we had chopped down so much brush and now we were backtracking. It just didn't seem to make a lot of sense. The afternoon sun began to slowly sink in the west. We knew we had only a few hours of daylight to dig in for the night. We rounded a small hill and set up defensive positions. We got word of our next little venture for the next day. We would be humping to a place called LZ Bushwack. After I dug my fighting hole for the night I sat down on my pack and started a letter.

April 7, 1970

Dear Dad,

Well how does this find you and the farm? I hope everyone is doing fine. I got your second letter yesterday and was glad to hear from you. Sorry your pigs didn't turn out too well but guess that's life. It seems to me as though you have several cows and calves and have about all the fences put up. I know you all put a lot of work on the fences, but now maybe you'll be through for awhile. I laughed when I got Larry's letter several weeks ago saying that when you all got the fence tight, it was fifteen feet above the hollow. I bet it was really tight when you all finally got it steepled. Ha!

When you said it snowed on Easter Day, I didn't know what to think. Guess it was pretty hard on your canvas and tobacco beds. Hope the tobacco plants do all right and come on out of the ground. Wish I were there to help with the crop this year but I'll be thinking of what you're doing.

You asked how many goes with me when we go to the bush. Well all of Mike Company goes to the bush which is about sixty or so. The trouble is the company seems to get smaller all the time. Either they are sent back because of some sort of illness or due to something else. Some go to school in Da Nang for five days. Right now our original squad is only five people so we usually tie in with another squad or the gun team. They were going to make me a radio operator the other day but there was a guy who went to radio school and he got it. I didn't want it anyway because I have enough to carry now.

I don't know about the Marine Corps. Here I was trained to be a machine gunner and they try to make me a radio operator, but over here they put you wherever they need you most. I'm just a rifleman now but I carry all sorts of ammunition. They've got a new thing going now. We stay in one place for about two days, go out to the bush for sixteen days, and come back to the rear for three days. I'd rather stay out because they're always messing over us with inspections and other petty stuff in the rear. We will be going to a place called LZ Bushwack up on a mountain tomorrow to spend a week or ten days. That will be pretty decent.

Sure wish I could get a camera to take some pictures but I guess all I'd have is rice paddies, mountains, bushes, and villages. But now where we're at we see very few villes. It's a "free fire zone" and there's not supposed to be any friendly gooks here.

Wish I could send you all a cassette tape but I'll never get a tape recorder while I'm here. They hardly have anything at the PX. Well I'll close now and eat some of my C-Rats. Maybe I'll get a chance to heat it up for a change. So be good and don't work too hard. I'll be thinking of you.

As Always,
Freddy

P.S. How did you and Mom like my poem?

The resupply choppers arrived at our position at around 0800 one day at a place called the "Rockcrusher." We got resupplied with ammunition, but not chow. I supposed that this area had been called the Rockcrusher because it had been used in previous years as a rock quarry. There was also a railroad track that ran through the valley and passed by what used to be a mine. This cleared out area of crushed rock and gravel was nestled in a valley formed by huge mountains.

We were supposed to hump to the top of LZ Bushwack from the quarry. Seemed logical! Get loaded down with all sorts of ammo and then hump to the top of a mountain. But who was I to question the strategy. We made our way to the top through the heavy brush and dense vegetation on the sides of the mountain. When we got to the clearing at the top I could see that there was a small artillery battery on top. We were to run patrols and act as security for the fire support base.

We were all exhausted from our climb with packs, weapons, and ordnance. Even though we were physically strained we wasted little time in preparing our fighting positions. Someone in the squad said, "Hey you guys, we must be pretty far out. We can see the border of Laos and Cambodia from up here. I heard the platoon commanders talking about it."

Hawkeye and I got with Travieso, our fireteam leader, in order to locate our position on the map. As we studied the map, Travieso pointed to a string of mountains and said, "Over to the northwest is Laos and over to the southwest is Cambodia."

"Seems like we are a long way from home," Hawkeye said.

"Yeah, a long way from home," Travieso responded. "This is a free fire zone up here which means we can kill anything that moves. We don't have to wait for Charlie to fire at us first."

I looked out to the west over the ridge of mountains to the west. They looked so serene, peaceful, and majestic. A soft blue haze covered the valleys below us. I wondered what we might get into being as this was a free fire zone. Time would tell, I reckoned. Patrols were sent out around the perimeter. Each time we would have to bring along machetes and chop our way through the thick foliage. One day after a patrol I was sitting in my foxhole looking out across the mountains and admiring the view. The clouds could be seen below our positions. Corporal Ka-Bar, our new squad leader, came over to where Travieso, Hawkeye, and I were sitting.

"You guys are not going to believe this," he said, "but we have to dig a trail around the perimeter." The other platoons have squads out on the other side digging right now. It seems the lieutenants want them dug so they don't fall off the mountain when they are checking positions during the night."

"What a crock-a-shit," retorted Travieso. "Don't these lifers have nothin better to do. Maybe they should cut through the bush every time we go out on patrol. Put the dumb asses as fuckin point men!"

"I know it sounds stupid," Corporal Ka-Bar replied, "but we had best get started before they are breathing down our necks. Don't worry, I'll give you a hand."

"Oh, no you don't," Travieso blurted out. "We'll do it! Besides, we just got rid of a screwed up squad leader. We all like you and want you to stick around for awhile. We can't have our squad leader pass out from heat stroke. Common you guys, grab your E-tools and we'll satisfy the lifers."

We followed Travieso's lead. We began to dig a path in front of our positions in a combined effort to connect the path with the other squads on our left and right flanks. What a pain in the ass, I thought. Here we were digging a trail so the lieutenants don't fall off the mountain. What next? Guess we'll have to build them a shitter too. The digging was extremely difficult. The ground was so full of roots that we had to break, twist, hack, and pull them apart in order to dig the trail with our E-tools. It was hot and muggy and we soon became soaked with sweat. Corporal Ka-Bar came by to check on our progress.

"You guys need anything when we get resupplied again?" Corporal Ka-Bar asked. "I'm putting in my order now."

I stopped digging momentarily and rose up to respond to Corporal Ka-Bar. "Yeah, I'd like a pair of gloves," I said. "The kind I used to use back home on the farm while hauling hay. My hands have blisters all over them from digging this damn trail. I had blisters on them before I started digging and now this has opened the old ones and started new ones." I spoke merely with sarcasm because of the task we had at hand.

"Let me see those farm hands," Corporal Ka-Bar said to me. I raised both hands with the palms facing toward him. "Yeah, you do have blisters, blisters on top of blisters! I'll order you a pair of real digging gloves," he said with a grin.

"Is there such a thing in the Nam?" I asked.

"Sure," he replied. "Just leave it to me and I'll get you some."

"Damn, Corporal Ka-Bar," I said. "I thought you were kidding about getting gloves. I wouldn't expect supply to issue out gloves to the grunts."

"You gotta know the system," he responded. "I'll order you a pair of gloves that will be even better than your farm gloves.

"Wow," thanks a lot Corporal Ka-Bar," I told him. "You are all right in my book."

"I'll take good care of you," he said.

It was comforting to know that we now had a squad leader that cared about us. My former squad leader would not give me the time of day. He had always talked down to me and treated me with disrespect. I also felt that he placed the squad in jeopardy by placing us in dangerous situations that could have been avoided. I was glad that I had Corporal Ka-Bar as my new squad leader. We all liked him and respected him. I did not actually think that Corporal Ka-Bar would manage to get me any gloves out to the bush but he seemed sincere and for that, I was grateful.

April 12, 1970
8:00 a.m.

Dear Mom, Dad and Larry,

Well today is Sunday and we worked pretty hard yesterday, so we get today off. Thought I'd write and let you know where I am and what I'm doing. We're up on a mountain called LZ Bushwack and believe me it sure is a huge mountain. I think it's probably 12 miles or so from LZ Baldy. We got here two days ago and will be here for about another week. It's an artillery camp on top with about six big guns. When they go off we all know it.

Yesterday we went on a patrol around the top of it, dug a trail around part of it, and dug a little deeper on the fighting holes. You may wonder why we dug a trail around part of it. Well it seems that the captain of the artillery battery and our lieutenants wanted one around it to keep from sliding off. Of course when the lifers, as we call them, want something done we're the ones that do it. What gets me is that this camp has been up here for no telling how long and we have to be the ones to dig a path on it. We do have pretty good living quarters though.

We have little huts that are about a six feet square and are made out of ammo boxes and sandbags. There are three of us in this one and we make out all right. We're all one little family, in fact our whole squad is. It's hard to believe how well we all get along together. Of course we have to work together when we're in the bush. Well what I was going to tell you is that our hut is beside a big rock and we can see all over the place. We've got plastic around it to keep the wind out and we put our poncho over the top for shade. It's really very comfortable. I could stay in the bush the rest of the time if we could live like this. We've got it pretty easy up here but will be going over the mountains in a few days.

You can't imagine what it's like up here. It's like being on top of the world. Sure wish I could take some pictures from up here.

This morning the clouds were coming over the top of us and once in awhile balls of white clouds would come in our hut. It was really something to see. I can look out the entrance and see a lot of lights at night. In the day I can see a long way but can't distinguish anything. When all the lights come on at night, I can only imagine what is down there. Maybe if the 7th Marines pull out in a couple of months, I could go to Da Nang. I sure would like that. We got re-supplied yesterday and besides our regular C-Rations, they brought bread, juice, apples, oranges, and sardines. They sure tasted good for a change.

Well how's the weather back home now? Seems like when I hear from someone that you're having bad weather. Right now it is hot and dry here in Vietnam. What puzzles me is that it gets cool at night. It feels pretty good though after a hot day.

Mom, I just remembered that you had a birthday this month. Sorry I couldn't get you anything but you know how it is. Maybe if I ever get to where it's civilized I can send you all something. Wish I could get a tape recorder so I could send you a tape but guess it will be awhile before I can. Anyway, I hope you had a nice birthday. Hope you have a nice year.

Well I just got the word that we are moving across the mountains tomorrow. The Marine Corps never does what it says. I was hoping to stay here a week but now I'll have to get packed up for tomorrow. We'll be doing the usual in the mountains, going on patrols and ambushes, and moving from place to place.

Guess I'll let you all go now and get back to business at hand. As I look out of my entrance to this hut, I am looking into the east and I'm imagining what you all are doing at this very minute. Being as its afternoon now, everyone is probably in the bed. At night when I'm on watch, I imagine you're up and working. Just take it easy, be good, and enjoy life when you can.

Yours truly,
Freddy

P.S. I have Donald's address. It's the same as it was, except you add "Embark Team #2" to it.

The next day we were told that we were going to cross over a string of mountains on an operation that would last about ten days. Resupply choppers flew in and landed with what looked like a ton of ordnance. Here we go again, I thought. Load up the old pack mules and hump across the mountains. After the choppers lifted off, we began to divide out the supplies among the other platoons, then squads, then fireteams, and then to the individual Marine.

I received six meals of C-Rations, eight bandoleers of M16 ammunition, a can of M60 machine gun ammo, five trip flares, three claymore mines, ten grenades, six mortar rounds, two bandoleers of M79 grenade rounds, and an assortment of other ordnance. I wondered if I would have enough room in and on my pack to carry all the stuff. I took the C-Ration cans out of the cartons and slid them into a few of my green socks and attached them on the sides of my pack. After I got everything organized, I threw my pack over my shoulder to check for fit and to see how much it weighed. I estimated that I had at least eighty pounds on my pack alone.

Just then Corporal Ka-Bar approached me with one hand behind his back.

"Fenwick, I have something else for you to carry," he said.

I glanced at him with what must have been my most pitiful facial expression. "Corporal Ka-Bar," I replied, "I don't have room for another grenade, flare, mortar round, machine gun ammo, chow, or nothin else. Give it to the lieutenant. After all, I had to dig his trail for him didn't I?"

"Take it easy," Corporal Ka-Bar interjected. "Here are the gloves you wanted."

He threw me two gloves that he had hidden behind his back. I caught them in mid air and began examining them in detail. The gloves were green and tan, had a velvety texture with very tiny holes throughout, was reinforced in the palms and fingers, and had a wrist strap in order to tighten them if necessary. I figured the purpose of the small holes was to allow air ventilation so the hands could breathe and expel perspiration. I knew they would do the trick at least for awhile until they wore out.

"Damn! Thanks a lot Corporal Ka-Bar," I said. "I really appreciate it."

"Don't mention it," he replied.

He walked away nonchalantly as if it was no big deal but for me I was thrilled to have a pair of gloves I could use for digging. As Corporal Ka-Bar proceeded back to attend his own gear on the ground, I heard someone in the squad say, "Hey Corporal Ka-Bar, do you think you can get me a pair of those farm gloves?"

Corporal Ka-Bar turned around and said, "You should have said something when I asked Fenwick if he wanted some gloves the first time. Now it may be awhile before we get resupplied or any special requests go back to the rear."

The Marine responded by saying, "That's okay, I can wait. Can you get me some?"

"All right," Corporal Ka-Bar said with a sigh. "How many of you guys want gloves?" The entire squad raised their hands.

"Roger that," Corporal Ka-Bar said. "I'll put in the order."

We all heard the echo of the company gunnery sergeant as he shouted out, "Saddle Up!" The company began a slow pace as we started moving out. The weight of my flak jacket, cartridge belt, and pack seemed overpowering. I could feel the pack straps pinching into my shoulders and had to lean forward to keep the weight balanced on my back. If I stood straight upright the weight could topple me backwards.

As we moved slowly over the top of the mountain I began to daydream back to a time on the farm when my father could not round up the old gray mules to dig potatoes in the garden. That's when he told me to grab the singletree that was attached to the plow and start pulling. He decided that if we couldn't round up the old gray mules that I would do just fine. Carrying all this combat gear on my back reminded me of that day on the farm but I would have gladly pulled the plow again if given the option.

I awoke from my daydreaming and came back to the reality of war. I imagined about what we were about to encounter in the days ahead. I figured that we must be heading for either Laos or Cambodia but no one would say for sure. As we made our way across the top of the mountains I noticed that the vegetation was sparse. The vegetation was a lot denser along the sides of the mountain. It was almost as if we were walking in a clearing at the very top of the mountains. There was also a well used trail across the top. The word had been passed down through the chain of command to walk on the sides of the trail in order to avoid mines and booby traps but the Marines did not seem to pay it any attention. Most walked right down the middle of the trail. The company would stop occasionally and send out patrols down off the sides of the mountains. At night ambushes were sent out.

It soon began to rain both night and day. It seemed the summer monsoon season had come early. We did not know how long it would rain but we knew that we would be miserable while we were wet. We were either hot and wet or cold and wet, but always wet. If we were not wet from our own sweat during the heat of the day, or wet from the settled dew at night, we were wet from the rains. There was one thing about Vietnam we could count on during the summer monsoon season, there would be plenty of rains.

During this particular operation it rained constantly. Everyone was soaked from head to toe. We began to have cases of trench foot and jungle rot. Jungle rot was the Marine jargon for a fungus condition contracted in tropical climates. The continuous wetness of the skin caused sores to form and become filled with pus. The sores would break open exposing the skin to unsanitary conditions and then become infected. Scabs would form on the arms, legs, feet, chest, and other body parts exposed to extremely wet conditions. Regardless of how much topical antifungal creams a Marine used to heal the jungle rot, most were fruitless attempts, since the medication would wash off. The skin had to be dry for the medicine to become effective. It was virtually impossible to keep the skin dry under these wet conditions.

Some Marines had very bad symptoms of jungle rot. Their skin would become infected and the pus seemed to eat away at their arms and legs. Some had ugly scabs with the pus oozing out of them. I tried to dry and powder my feet and to keep my arms and legs as dry as possible every chance I got. My first symptom of jungle rot appeared on my right forearm. I thought I would carry the scars for the rest of my life, but with constant attention and care, I managed to keep jungle rot under control. Some other Marines were not as fortunate.

By the end of the second day we thought that resupply choppers would fly in the following day to replenish our food supply. Some of the Marines ate two and three cans of C-Rations that night in anticipation of the next day resupply. For some reason I decided to save some of my chow and not carelessly glutton myself just because we thought resupply was imminent. Instead, I gorged myself on a can of beans and meatballs. I dug around in the bottom of my pack to determine exactly how much chow I had left. There was one can of ham and eggs, a can of peaches, a can of pound cake, a can of crackers, and a small can of peanut butter.

Early the next morning we could hear the company gunny on the radio requesting a resupply of food, water, and juice. There was no need for any type of ordnance or ammunition since we had only fired illumination rounds during the night while in a defensive posture. A response was heard over the radio from someone back at the base camp.

"There will be no resupply today because the choppers cannot fly in this inclement weather."

I felt as though the general feeling throughout Mike Company was that this was just one more disappointment of many to come in Vietnam. Most took the bad news in stride. They felt that tomorrow would be another day and that it was no big deal.

"Oh well, what's another day when we're starving to death out here," I heard a Marine say. "No biggy! We'll get resupplied tomorrow. Right you guys? The Marine Corps will take good care of us, right?" No one answered him.

The initial two days of rations were beginning to dwindle throughout the company. Increasingly we could hear Marines grumbling that they were hungry. I decided to eat only one can of C-Rations per day until we managed to be resupplied. I began to discipline myself in this regard until the fifth day. We finally received word that the choppers would be flying out from the base camp to our position. It was good news and some of the Marines began to rejoice and get motivated. I now had a can of crackers, pound cake, and peanut butter. I ate the crackers and pound cake and was tempted to eat the peanut butter, but I decided to wait until the choppers actually landed.

After about two hours of waiting anxiously for the choppers to arrive the Marines began to complain about the choppers not yet being at our position. Some began to strain their ears in the direction of the base camp in order to catch a faint humming sound of either helicopter rotors or engines. There was no visibility as the fog and rain was now heavier than it had been a couple of hours earlier. We began to fear that the helicopters would be grounded once again. As our squad gathered around in the pouring rain near the squad radio we listened intently to get an update on the resupply status. We heard a faint and distorted voice come over the net.

"Mike, Mike, There will be no resupply at your pos today because the choppers cannot fly. The weather is just too bad. We will attempt another lift tomorrow, weather permitting."

We could hear the company gunny on the radio giving someone hell on the receiving end. Even with all the "You Will and You Better" from the company gunny, the fact remained that we were not to receive any chow that day. The squad members just looked at one another in disgust and walked away.

The days dragged by and it kept pouring rain. We were all drenched to the bone. The weather was worse now than it had been when we first requested resupply. We were going on our eighth day and still no food. For certain, there was no water shortage. All a Marine had to do was to open the cap on his canteen, roll a make shift funnel out of his poncho, and let the water drain into the canteen. The canteen would be filled to the brim in only a couple of minutes. However, we knew that we could not survive on water alone. Understanding the dilemma the company was in, the company commander authorized squads to go out on patrols for the sole purpose of finding food.

My squad's lucky day came when we went on a patrol through a mountain village and ate the rice that an old mamasan was cooking. We then went out back and found a lonely watermelon next to a hooch. We divided it up amongst ourselves, and as we were devouring it, an old papasan came running out jabbering away in Vietnamese and waving his hands in protest. We couldn't understand what he was saying, but we knew he wanted us to leave his watermelon alone. One of the Marines shoved the old man aside and pointed his M16 service rifle in his face.

"I'll kill you old man, you fuckin gook!" he yelled.

Corporal Ka-Bar intervened and told the Marine to leave the old man alone. Nevertheless, he also told the Marine to keep an eye on him. All we wanted was his watermelon. A couple of Marines began to provoke the old man with bodily gestures while eating his melon. The old papasan was swearing away in Vietnamese but we did not care. We looked for more melons but there were none to be found. We filled our canteens from a well that was nearby to the old papasan's hooch and then continued on our way. Our extreme hunger had overpowered our sense of moral principles.

Our stomachs being partially full, we would not die of starvation, just yet. I began to sense an overpowering instinct for survival. I had the feeling that I would do just about anything now just to stay alive. Our squad frequently volunteered to go out on patrols from the mountaintop down through the ridgelines and into the gentler slopes to try to locate more mountain villages.

We took from the villagers only what we needed to sustain ourselves for a day since we were still hoping for resupply. We felt like the merry old men of Robin Hood. We would take from the rich and give to the poor. The Vietnamese were not rich by any means, but with the squad being without food, we were definitely the poor ones. It seemed odd to me that the villagers become more curious of us than angry. I guessed they realized that we meant them no harm and that we were just in search of food.

Our whole platoon went out on patrols as well. We would have preferred to go it alone as a squad patrol so we could forage for food. While the platoon was moving on a patrol through the mountains someone found a trail along a stream showing extensive use. We followed the trail through the wilderness in an attempt to locate any enemy but we did not find any NVA/VC. They could have been hiding almost anywhere and we wouldn't have seen them because of the heavy vegetation.

The rain seemed to subside and by the seventh day resupply was requested again. By now, the Marines were always at each other's throats. There was anger, fear, and mixed emotions. Even as we listened intently to the radio transmission back to the rear for resupply arguing Marines could be heard throughout the company. Finally an incoming transmission came over the radio net.

"Resupply choppers are on their way. They will be at your pos in approximately one hour. How copy?"

Our company radio operator could be heard saying, "Roger, I copy loud and clear."

The entire mountain suddenly erupted with yells of excitement and enthusiasm. The Marines were in a state of jubilation. The resupply choppers were finally coming in. Hawkeye and I moved away from the radio and returned to our packs on the ground. I sat on the pack itself to keep from getting the cheeks of my ass muddy. I looked over at Hawkeye. He was a pitiful sight.

"Hawkeye, do you think the choppers will actually fly this time?" I asked.

He mumbled, "I don't know, but it looks pretty good. I know one thing, I'm starving."

Wearily I said, "Yeah, you're not the only one. I've never been this hungry in my life."

After what seemed like an eternity we heard the faint humming of the helicopter engines from afar. Moments later we heard the distinctive whop whop sounds of the rotors. Then we knew for sure that this time the choppers would make it in. Ah yes, who would have ever thought the Marines would be cheering the arrival of C-Rations.

I reached deep inside my pack and fumbled around searching for my last small can of peanut butter. After locating it I brought it up to the height of my chin in order to open it with my John Wayne can opener. I always carried a John Wayne on my dog tag chain. I punctured a hole in the small can and the trapped air and aroma rose to my nostrils. I paused to savor the smell for a moment before proceeding to open the lid. With every stroke of the can opener the aroma got even stronger. I thought that was the best smell ever. It smelled so good. My mouth became moist and saliva began to drip from my bottom lip. I reached for a plastic spoon in my flak jacket pocket, dipped the spoon in the peanut butter, and took one very small taste. I let it melt in my mouth as if it were ice cream.

"Chow! I smell chow!" one of the Marines in my squad said. "Hey, who's got the chow over here? What are you eatin over there, Fenwick?"

While still looking down at my can of peanut butter, so as not to draw attention to myself, I responded in a low voice, "Peanut Butter!"

"Well why the hell didn't you tell us you had some fuckin chow," was his reply. "We're fuckin starving here and you're hoarding all the chow."

"Well hell," I retorted. "I've been carrying this little can of peanut butter around for the last seven days. Been saving it as a last resort."

Hawkeye stood up and began to approach me. As he walked toward me he said, "Fenwick, you ass! You ass! Give me a taste of that peanut butter!"

"No problem Hawkeye," I said with a smile. "Got a spoon?"

"Spoon hell!" he cried out. "Don't need no damn spoon ta eat peanut butter. I'll use my fingers."

I began to laugh as Hawkeye poked his right forefinger into the peanut butter, scraped up a tiny bit, and inserted it into his mouth.

"Hummm, Niceee!" he said.

The next thing I knew there were about four Marines hovering around me wanting a taste my peanut butter. We all took turns dabbing our fingers inside the small can and allowing the peanut butter to melt in our mouths.

Corporal Ka-Bar was there also. He reached in between outstretched arms for his helping of peanut butter. As he dipped his finger in he said, "You've been holding out on us, Fenny. What else you got stashed away?"

"Nothing," I said. "Honest, nothing at all, except this little can of glorious, scrumptious, delicious, fantastic, mouth watering, creamy, little can of peanut butter."

We were so engrossed in the moment that we lost all perception of what was going on around us. A chopper was now hovering overhead and soon landed. Some Marines on working parties scurried to off-load the C-Rations and jungle juice.

"What do you know!" someone yelled out. "We even got SP packs. Alleluia!"

SP was the abbreviation for Special Packs. They were cardboard boxes packed with all sorts of goodies that were sent out from the rear periodically. The SP's contained cigarettes, candy, chewing gum, letter writing gear, toothpaste, and miscellaneous items that made our survival in the bush a little more comfortable. It was always a welcome sight to see the SP's off loaded from the resupply choppers.

There was plenty enough help to unload the chopper. Meanwhile, Hawkeye and I were still trying to savor the last bits of peanut butter from the tiny can.

"Hey Hawkeye, save some for me," I said. "Let me lick the can."

We both snickered. Here it was the seventh day and finally the chow had arrived. I had carried around that little can of peanut butter for the entire time. From that day forward, I always had a special taste for peanut butter. We ended up getting six C-Ration meals for each Marine. Usually I would just eat only one can from any particular menu when I sat down to eat a meal. This time I decided to eat the contents of an entire carton for my first decent meal in seven days. Although I was extremely hungry the individual carton of rations quickly filled me up. My stomach seemed to have gotten smaller. Corporal Ka-Bar came by and asked if anyone wanted an extra meal because they had brought out extras.

"Hell yeah, I'll take one!" I exclaimed.

Hawkeye immediately spoke up with enthusiasm, "Me too!"

We both commenced to find additional space in our packs for another precious little box of goodies. This time we did not mind the extra weight. Soon Mike Company was on the move again. We moved out in single file down the sides of the mountains and ended up in what we called the lowlands. It was more humid at the base of the mountains and the visibility was somewhat better. I could now see that there was a small Vietnamese village in the clearing and that we were about to head across some open rice paddies. As we trudged along a trail near the village, I heard a young Vietnamese boy speaking directly to me.

"Hey you, Manine, Manine! Manine numba one, where you been? Huh? Where you been? Manine numba one! Souvenir babysan chop-chop. Huh? Thuoc la, Thuoc la!"

"Speak English," I responded without taking my eyes off the trail in front of me. "I don't understand Vietnamese."

"Souvenir babysan cigmo, hokay, hokay?" the boy asked.

I looked up and peered at a small boy about seven years old that wore khaki colored shorts with no shirt and barefooted. He continued to jabber away in order to get my attention.

"Didi Mau!" I commanded. I just wanted the boy to go away and leave me alone.

"You go buc buc VC? Huh, Manine? Boo coo buc buc VC? Huh? Sovineer babysan cigmo! Hokay? Hokay, Manine? Sovineer babysan cigmo. Manine numba one!"

Buc buc was Vietnamese which meant to fight. Knowing that he also wanted food and cigarettes I told him, "No chop-chop today."

He asked again and I told him the same. There was no way I was going to give this kid any of my C-rations after going for seven days without food myself. I tried to explain using broken English and body language that I needed the food for myself.

"Manine numba fuckin ten!" the boy said angrily. "No give babysan cigmo. No give babysan chop-chop. Manine numba fuckin ten!"

"Don't go away mad, just go away," I said. "Didi, you little shit! Didi Mau!"

As he walked away with an arrogant attitude, I heard him say in English, "Hope you get Bino!" In other words, he was saying to me that he hoped I stepped on a booby trap.

I could feel my inherited temper begin to rise and take control of my emotions. Now he had made me very angry.

"Get the fuck outta here!" I commanded. "Didi Mau, you little bastard!" I yelled.

I switched my rifle from my right hand to the left and with one fell swoop I reached down, picked up a rock in my right hand, and hurled it at the boy. Since I had a rifle in one hand and a heavy pack on my back, I missed him by a few feet. The boy ducked only slightly and with a resentful look on his face he began to wonder off toward the village. He was still belligerent and defiant as he jabbered away in Vietnamese. I had wished I could leave my position in column to go after him and kick his ass. Instead, I tried to take my mind off the situation in order to refrain from getting too mad and doing something crazy.

As I walked along slowly I began daydreaming about my mother and father raising a family of nine on a farmer's income. I recalled an occasion while growing up on the farm when my mother did not know what our next meal might be. The finances had depleted to a stage where we living on pure hope and what foodstuffs remained in the pantry and basement. Since my mother canned fruits and vegetables from the garden each summer, we still had canned goods and a bin full of potatoes. We would not starve, but the niceties of a meal such as bread and condiments would have to wait until our finances improved. One thing was for sure, we had plenty of milk from milking the cows. The fact remained, however, that there was no money to buy flour to make biscuits.

At the time I was still in grade school. I remembered getting off the school bus at the end of our driveway on a cool and brisk autumn afternoon. It was not a cloud in the sky and the sun was shining bright in the western sky. I heard the rustle of dry tree leaves beneath my feet as I walked through our large front yard to the house. The fallen maple and locust tree leaves that blanketed the yard during this time were particularly a pretty sight with all the fall colors. What a gorgeous day it was.

I walked through the front yard that was more or less three hundred feet from the main road. I stopped at the well and started pumping up a fresh taste of cool well water. I daydreamed as I moved the pump handle up and down. I could almost taste the water before it made its way up through the long pipe in the well. It had the best taste in the county as far as our family was concerned. Pure rainwater drained from the roof gutters of the house and filtered through some charcoal before draining into the deep well. I cupped both hands under the running water and took a few gulps. We always had a tin drinking cup that was attached with a small chain and fastened to the pump. For us kids, drinking out of our hands just came natural.

I proceeded up the steps of the back porch and entered the back door and into the kitchen. I figured I would follow the same routine and get a bite to eat before I went to the barn to help my father milk the cows. I noticed my mother sitting at the head of the table with her back toward me and her head down. She was sitting in the chair normally reserved for my father which seemed a little odd to me. Nevertheless, I paid her no mind, went straight to the refrigerator, and opened the door. I scanned the sparse contents looking for some Miracle Whip salad dressing to have it on crackers.

"Momma, we got any tatty detty?" I asked. I was tongue-tied at the time and therefore pronounced salad dressing as "tatty detty." It wasn't until after several years of mispronouncing my speech that my parents took me to the family doctor. The doctor finally snipped the base of my tongue and I was then able to speak normally. I had liked the taste of salad dressing on bread and it was my favorite sandwich. My mother had not answered right away so I turned around to face her and get her attention. I saw that she was wiping some tears from her face with a tissue while sobbing softly.

"What's wrong Momma?" I asked.

"I don't know what to fix for supper," she said. "I've run out of just about everything and we do not have the money right now to buy any more groceries."

I walked over to where she was sitting at the table and stood close to her. "Well, we've got some potatoes don't we?" I asked my mother.

She replied, "Yes, but we can't just eat potatoes. How would I fix them? I thought you all might be tired of potatoes by now."

"Why don't you fix potato soup? I like that," I said.

"Do you really, Freddy?" my mother asked.

"Yeah," I responded. "You fix it real nice."

"Very well then, potato soup it is! That's what I'll fix. We are all out of Miracle Whip but there is blackberry jam in the basement if you want to have that on crackers," she added.

"Naw, that's okay," I said. "I'll just eat some potato soup when I get back from the barn."

My mother had stopped sobbing and I remembered her going down the steps from the dining room and into the basement to gather some potatoes. After milking the cows the family sat down to supper. I remembered how good her potato soup had tasted. She had it seasoned just right. I wished that I had some of her soup at that very moment while I was still daydreaming. It seemed as though I had already seen my fair share of tribulations throughout my short life. I imagined how hard life must have been for my mother and father while raising a large family on a farm. My thoughts returned to reality and I mumbled to myself that I would not share my life sustaining C-Rations with the Vietnamese kids. I felt as though I was fighting their war and that I was not there to give them handouts. There would be no sympathy for them, so I thought.

After moving for most of the morning the company finally stopped around midday and set up a defensive position in a graveyard. Our squad was then sent out on patrol in order to find out if the Viet Cong were storing rice in the area. We came upon a village and began checking each hooch. We questioned the mamasans and papasans in our best broken Vietnamese language. We checked for spider traps, tunnels, and weapons. We asked where their rice was stored but did not get any cooperation or useful information.

One Marine found a tunnel and started to go down into it. He cautiously checked the entrance for booby traps and snakes. The VC would tie poisonous snakes to the entrance of tunnels, so that when an unsuspecting Marine entered a tunnel carelessly, he had a good chance of being bitten. Those types of casualties had happened before. After reassuring himself that there were no such obstacles he proceeded down into the tunnel. He was gone a few minutes and then suddenly he sprang up out from inside one of the hooches.

"Hey you guys!" he exclaimed. "Here is the end of the tunnel. Comes out right under this hooch! They have all sorts of rice stored down below."

We began the tedious task of carrying all the bundles of rice out of the tunnel and finally stacked them in a pile on the outside of the tunnel. We set fire to the rice, stood back, and watched it go up in flames. Although it was true that Vietnamese living in the villages used the rice for their own daily consumption, such an over abundance hidden underground was a sure indication that the Viet Cong and North Vietnamese Army regulars were nearby. Consequently, we burned what we considered excess so the enemy would not have access to it. Maybe by burning their food supply the VC and NVA might move away from this village and prevent the innocent villagers from being in harms way. It was just another way of getting back at Charlie. It seemed crude for the villagers but who was I to question policy. My boyish soft heart was becoming numb and hard. I had no real feelings for what we were doing, just another day in the Nam, and a day closer to going home.

It was the peak season for harvesting the rice. We walked into a nearby rice paddy where they had rice stalks tied in bundles and set fire to that as well. Old mamasans and papasans were protesting loudly but we ignored their demands to leave the rice alone. We continued on our way leaving the village behind us. Looking back, I saw the bellowing blazes and black smoke rising into the air. We were just beginning to come out of the rice paddy and onto solid ground by a treeline when the Marine in front of me caught my eye.

Suddenly, the same Marine who had gone berserk at China Beach by firing his .45 caliber pistol in the sand, stopped dead in his tracks.

"I just heard a click," he said softly. "I think I'm standing on a fuckin mine!"

I was only a few meters behind him. "Whatever you do, don't lift your foot!" I commanded. "If that is a pressure device we'll all be blown to smithereens!"

"Thanks a lot, Fenwick, for the encouragement. Don't give a shit about me. I'm the one standing here on a mine. Easy for you to say!"

"Hey, take it easy," I responded. "I'll see if we can get you out of this mess in one piece. Keep the pressure on that one foot. Think survival!"

I yelled up to the next Marine in column that something was wrong and that I suspected we had a Marine standing on a mine. He passed the word up the chain of Marines and Corporal Ka-Bar was alerted. He stopped the squad's forward movement to take charge of the situation.

Corporal Ka-Bar emerged from the vegetation back tracking along the squad. There was no sense of urgency. He moved slowly and nonchalantly toward the Marine who was up to his ankles in rice paddy water. He stopped next to the Marine and stood there gazing down at his feet for what seemed like a long time.

"Ain't you gonna do something?" the Marine asked.

Corporal Ka-Bar said nothing. Instead, he continued to stare at the Marine's feet as if he was mentally assessing the situation to determine the best course of action to take. No one in the squad offered a solution probably because they felt at any minute we would be calling in a medevac chopper. They were content with keeping quiet while Corporal Ka-Bar figured out a way to get this Marine out of his predicament.

"Fuckin shit," the Marine began cursing. "I've been over here only two months and now I'm gonna end up in a body bag with probably both legs blown off. Somebody get me off this thang!"

"Take it easy," Corporal Ka-Bar finally responded. "Me and Fenwick will help you outta this mess."

Corporal Ka-Bar directed me to move forward and stand on the other side of the Marine. I mentally thought what a lucky guy I was that day to be handpicked by the squad leader. What an honor! I wondered why he had not chosen someone else for this risky business at hand. Nevertheless, I trusted and respected Corporal Ka-Bar. I moved through the rice paddy mud and came along the opposite side of the stunned Marine facing Corporal Ka-Bar. He directed me to kneel down into the murky water and feel around the Marine's feet to determine if there were any signs that this might be a pressure device or if any wires were attached. We knelt down into the mud and began to slowly feel around his feet. The rice paddy mud had a foul stench that almost made me gag. We determined that the device he was standing on was limited to his right foot.

"Keep all your body weight on your right foot and don't you dare lift it Marine!" Corporal Ka-Bar demanded.

I could tell that the Marine was following orders by gently leaning his body onto the right foot. The water was about six inches deep now. It seemed that the device was sinking in the soft mud. I felt the rice paddy water ooze around my legs and backside. It had a cooling effect, but I could think of better ways to cool off than kneeling in rice paddy mud.

"What the hell is this thing anyway?" I asked Corporal Ka-Bar. "It's got teeth around the outer edge and seems to go all the way around. I don't feel any wires though, do you Corporal Ka-Bar?"

"No wires on this side either," he responded. Then with a little more excitement in his voice than usual he peered around the Marine's legs and looked me straight in the eye. "Fenwick, this is a fuckin bear trap!" he exclaimed.

My facial expression was one of disbelief. "Come on now, Corporal Ka-Bar," I replied nervously. "A bear trap in Vietnam? There ain't no bears over here are there?"

Corporal Ka-Bar answered while remaining in his usual calm demeanor. "No, but there are tigers and that is what the Vietnamese set these traps for. The tiger population has thinned out since the war so now the bastards set the traps for the unsuspecting Marine in order to inflict more casualties. You see, they think we're some kind of animal. As long as they believe we're animals we might as well live up to our reputation." Corporal Ka-Bar then smiled as if nothing unusual was happening.

The Marine sanding on the bear trap was getting frustrated and annoyed by all the seemingly casual small talk. He could hold back no longer.

"Here I am standing in the middle of a fuckin bear trap and you two wise guys are acting like everything is just fine and dandy," he blurted out. Get me outta here, will ya!"

"Shut up!" Corporal Ka-Bar snapped. "If this damn thing closes on your leg it will cut all the way to the bone. Now keep quiet and keep the pressure on that right foot!"

"Fenwick," Corporal Ka-Bar ordered, "you grab that side and hold down with all your might. Whatever you do, do not let go until I tell you to."

He looked over his shoulder and yelled for another Marine to bring us two full M60 machine gun ammo cans. The full ammo cans were collected and delivered to us quickly. Corporal Ka-Bar took one and passed it to me and he kept the other one. He told the Marine who had delivered the cans to move back out of the way.

"Okay, Fenwick, now you place your ammo can on top of the outer jaw of the bear trap, put all your weight on it, and I will have him lift his foot. Then he can step off of it."

"I don't know if this is a good idea or not Corporal Ka-Bar," I said. "What if the damn thing is booby trapped after all."

"It's the only thing we can do under the circumstances," Corporal Ka-Bar replied. "Any last minute prayers say them now."

Without haste we placed both ammo cans on the outer jaws of the bear trap and adjusted our body weight so that as much weight as possible was bearing down of the top of the cans. The tops of the ammo cans were barely sticking out the top of the rice paddy water that had become very muddy at this point.

"Listen up!" Corporal Ka-Bar said to the Marine standing on the trap. "On my command, you are to lift your foot off the trap and quickly dive forward face down in the rice paddy for cover. Fenwick, when he is clear of the trap, we will both dive backward in opposite directions. Hit the deck for cover. If it is booby trapped underneath we might have a chance by diving away from it."

"What cover?" I asked quickly. "Ain't nothin here but rice paddy!"

"Just get as low to the ground as possible," Corporal Ka-Bar replied.

"Might as well say my prayers now, cause this don't look too good," I said out loud.

At that very instant I remembered something that one of my teachers in grade school, a Dominican Nun, had told the class one day. She stated that at the time of death, a person should think of Jesus and meditate on a crucifix. Then you should repeat three times, "Who is suffering? What is he suffering? Why?" By saying this at the hour of your death, she stated that the gates of heaven would open for you even though you may be with sin. I began to repeat it silently to myself.

Corporal Ka-Bar looked up at the Marine standing on the trap. He spoke in a commanding voice. "When I count to three, I want you to dive for cover. Fenwick, I will say GO, when we are to release our pressure on the ammo cans and get away from this thing as rapidly as possible. Do we all understand?"

"I'm ready," I said hesitantly.

The Marine standing on the trap began moaning again. "Yeah, I understand. I'm going home in a body bag. Who gives a shit?"

"All right," Corporal Ka-Bar interrupted, "here we go, on the count of three, One... Two... "

"Wait a minute! Wait a minute! the Marine on the trap blurted out. "Am I supposed to lift my foot and dive for cover on the count of Three or when you say Go?"

"On the count of three," Corporal Ka-Bar said angrily.

"Okay! Okay!" the Marine replied. "Just let me catch my breath first!" He took a deep breath, then let it out slowly. "I'm ready!"

Corporal Ka-Bar started his count again. One... Two... THREE!"

The Marine quickly lifted his foot and clumsily dived to his direct front and landed face down in the rice paddy. I wanted to dive at that very instant myself but my better judgment and discipline forced me to hold back until I had heard my squad leader's command.

Corporal Ka-Bar then looked me square in the eyes. "Okay, Fenny, this is it. Ready, Set, GO! His command of execution sounded like the cracking of a whip.

We both dived backward away from the device. I feared that any second the device would explode. I closed my eyes as I hit the rice paddy water and the soft layer of mud. I managed to keep my head up out of the mud but my helmet flew back on my head and was covering the back of my neck. The chinstrap on the helmet was pressed firmly against my throat but I would have to wait to see if there was going to be an explosion before releasing the pressure. I thought that the positioning of my helmet covering the back of my neck was as good as any for protection. It could have come off completely had I not had the chinstrap fastened. I remained motionless a couple of seconds, then realized the vulnerability of my exposed private parts. I had landed in the rice paddy with both legs spread wide open. My butt was wide open to the device. I quickly closed my legs tightly together for added protection of my family jewels. I had not heard an immediate explosion so I raised my head slightly and wiped away the dirty water from my eyes.

Just then I heard Corporal Ka-Bar's calm voice. "Hell, Fenwick, you gonna stay submerged in that rice paddy mud all day. Get the hell up! We're okay!

Nothing had happened. "Thank God it didn't go off," I said with a sigh of relief.

Corporal Ka-Bar and I moved back to the trap to recover the ammo cans and to fully inspect the device. I noticed that my ammo can had fallen off the outer jaw of the trap. "At least it ain't gonna snap shut," I said with confidence.

We began to feel around the base of the trap again. Corporal Ka-Bar found a small anchor chain that was connected on to the body of the trap. He traced the chain through the rice paddy mud gently pulling it up. The chain had another short rusty wire that was attached to the chain and staked in the ground. The chain and wire were easily pulled to the surface. We began to see the details of the trap for the first time as Corporal Ka-Bar lifted it out of the water. I cupped my hands and threw some water on it to wash off the mud and get a better look. The trap was huge. Corporal Ka-Bar tried to drag it to the nearby rice paddy dike but was struggling.

"Give me a hand with this Fenwick," he said. "This thang is heavy!"

Having had experience with beaver and muskrat traps back on the farm, I knew that the safest place to grab the trap was by the handle. If the trap closed shut, at least my hands would be out of the way of the teeth. We drug it up onto the rice paddy dike and inspected it further.

"Look what a trap!" I exclaimed. It seemed to be rusted shut. The Marine that had been standing on it came over and peered down at this large trap.

"That was a close call," he said without looking at either of us. "You guys just saved my life."

"It's all in a days work," Corporal Ka-Bar responded.

"No," the Marine insisted, "You guys really saved my life!"

Corporal Ka-Bar and I laughed and then he suggested that we carry the trap out of the rice paddy and onto solid ground for all the squad to see. The Marine who had been standing on the bear trap held on to one side and I grabbed the other side. Together we sloshed through the rice paddy mud to the clearing on dry land. There our squad gathered around to take a look at the bear trap. We placed it on the ground and backed away.

The rescued Marine got a stick that was about four feet long and began jabbing the release device in the center of the trap. The trap would not close shut. Out of curiosity, I picked up a small rock and hit dead center of the trap's release device. Still nothing! I got a larger rock and got the same results. Then the Marine put down his stick and began to madly look for rocks. He started throwing them in the center of the trap with much force. Still the trap did not close. It was totally rusted shut.

Corporal Ka-Bar began to laugh at the Marine's antics. "Ha ha ha! A fuckin elephant couldn't spring this trap!"

The entire squad began to laugh. Only minutes earlier my heart was beating rapidly in fear of getting injured or killed by an explosion, but now I was relaxed and joined in the laughter. The Marine decided he was going to keep the bear trap for a souvenir. He strapped it across his back as our squad proceeded back to the company CP.

After awhile the Marine carrying the trap said, "Goddamn, this trap is heavy! I can't tote this on my pack with all the other gear!"

"No sheit!" I said. "Why don't you throw it away? I'll be damn if I would carry it, too much extra weight. Why do you want a bear trap anyway?"

"Well, I would just like to take it home and show my friends that I had stepped on a bear trap in the Nam. Tell war stories! Tell them that Fenwick and Corporal Ka-Bar saved my life!"

"Yeah, saved your life all right," I replied. "That damn thing wouldn't close shut if you put a pound of TNT under it."

He snickered and said, "Yeah, guess you're right." He stopped, took the trap off his pack, and tossed it into the weeds. This souvenir was not to be.

That evening as our platoon was moving to a night time ambush site a Marine spotted movement parallel to us that was about 50 meters away. We opened fire with small arms and then swept the area but the enemy had eluded us. We had not received any return fire so we proceeded on to our ambush site. We spent the night on the hard ground fighting off the mosquitoes.

The next morning our 3rd platoon rejoined the company and we started moving again. It wasn't long until we heard the piercing sound of an explosion up in front in the column. I ducked down slightly and tried to see where the blast had come from. A small puff of bluish smoke raised into the air. Someone yelled out, "It's Stark, he's been hit." There was no need to call for a corpsman because one had not accompanied us on our patrol."

Corporal Ka-Bar walked forward and discovered that Stark had tripped a booby-trapped chi-com along the trail. He had been walking point. We all moved a little closer being careful not to trip any more. Stark was laying on the ground moaning and groaning. Both his legs were slightly bleeding from shrapnel but he had not been seriously wounded. He was very lucky. The homemade booby trap did not have sufficient force in the explosion to cause major damage. Given the fact that Stark was the same Marine, who had once backed his butt up to a booby trap and threw rocks at it just to get wounded and get out of Vietnam, it seemed that destiny had sealed his fate. He finally got his wish.

"So-long fellers," Stark said excitedly. Then he began rambling on talking to no one in particular. "I finally got my stateside wound! I'm going home boys! Been nice knowin ya! He paused and grimaced as if in pain. Oh shit, the pain, the pain! It feels good though. Pain is good! I'm going home!"

We paid little attention to his theatrical behavior and remarks. We began to improvise a makeshift litter out of bamboo poles and a poncho. Having completed the task, Stark was placed on the litter. Two Marines on each end of the litter raised Stark off the ground and we began to carry him back to the company perimeter. All the while he was carrying on about how he was finally leaving the bush and getting the hell out of Vietnam. He had little regard for the Marines carrying his litter.

He was medevaced out on the next available chopper that day. It took a couple of hours for the medevac chopper to arrive. All the while, Stark had been bragging and boasting that he was going home. His telltale smiles and jokingly gestures assured us that he was pretending his wounds hurt more than they did. He boldly cussed the choppers for not arriving sooner.

At one point, Travieso made the comment, "A routine medevac, for a routine guy."

The day came when Mike Company went back to LZ Baldy for rehabilitation. When we got to the base camp we heard that Stark had been treated at the Battalion Aid Station and released. He would not be returning to the bush or to Mike Company. Instead, he had been assigned to Headquarters and Service Company as the battalion commander's driver. He would serve out the rest of his time in Vietnam driving a jeep for the colonel and hanging out with the rest of the pogues. A pogue was Marine slang for office personnel back at the base camp who did not go to the bush. Now we had a real decent squad, now that two of the careless Marines were gone.

The following morning Corporal Ka-Bar came into our hooch. "All right, listen up, Mike 3 Charlie!" he commanded. "We will have a company formation at 1600. Everyone must be clean-shaven and be in buff shined boots. Bring along your weapons and I will inspect after the formation."

We began to complain and voiced our dislike of having to shine our boots after being in the bush for almost a month.

"That's a crock of shit," one Marine blurted out. "They get us back to the rear and then we have to be spit-shine Marines. Hell, we're in the Nam."

Corporal Ka-Bar assured us that it was for a good cause and that it wouldn't hurt us to get cleaned up. We commenced cleaning our weapons and applying Kiwi boot polish to our faded out jungle boots. As I was about to dab some polish on the toe of one of my boots, I noticed that the surface of the leather had been completely scuffed down to the hide. I did not have any leather dye so the polish on its own would have to suffice. For a moment I wondered if my boots would hold a good shine being as they were all worn down. To my surprise however, the polish was absorbed well into the leather and the toes turned out black and partially shiny once again. I was a bit disappointed, as I liked the scuffed and salty look of the worn and faded jungle boots. We shaved as well.

It came time for us to straggle down to where the company was forming up. We took our places in ranks in the 3rd platoon. If we had known what type of formation we were going to have we would have shined our boots without question. Corporal Ka-Bar informed us that it would be a memorial formation to honor our fallen comrades. Out in front of our company formation were three M16 rifles with bayonets that were planted into the ground. Helmets were placed and resting on top of each rifle butt plate. We formed up as a company facing the company gunnery sergeant. All the platoons were on line and consisted of four ranks each.

The company gunnery sergeant yelled out, "Company, Ah-Ten-Hut!" He said it with such authority that we all knew that he had been a drill instructor. He then commanded, "Report!" The platoon sergeants standing in front of the platoons echoed down the line starting from the 1st platoon, "Sir, All Present or Accounted For." If a platoon had any KIA, the platoon sergeant would announce the name of the KIA Marine. I could not imagine the grief and sorrow that the mothers and fathers would have over the loss of their sons in Vietnam. It was a sad moment for me.

The company gunnery sergeant then faced about and turned the formation over to the first sergeant. He in turn faced about waiting for the company commander to approach the formation while the company gunnery sergeant took his position behind the formation. The company commander approached the company first sergeant to receive the report. He was a tall and lean first lieutenant with a huge handlebar mustache. It suited his scruffy face to a tee. I had watched him twirling his handlebar mustache out in the bush while talking on the PRC-77 radio. He always wore some military issue wide rimmed eye glasses and his handlebar moustache distinguished him apart from the other officers. The Marines of Mike Company depended on him to lead us into combat. To us he was known as the company commander of "Medevac Mike."

He received the report from the first sergeant and gave the command, "Post!" At that time the platoon sergeants marched to the rear of their platoons and the other first lieutenant platoon commanders marched in front of their platoons. The company commander then gave the command, "Parade, Rest!" We all stood at a modified parade rest which basically put us at ease. The company commander said a few words and then introduced the Battalion Chaplain. The Chaplain came forward, asked us to bow our heads, and he began with prayer. We had a moment of silence for the dead Marines whose lives had been snuffed out so abruptly. They were young men, still teenagers. I wondered how many more invocations for the dead would follow in the days ahead.

April 24, 1970

Dear Mom, Dad and Larry,

How are things back on Cherry Hill Farm? I hope everyone is doing fine. You all are probably enjoying the weather since it's about May. Guess everyone is running around like chickens with their heads off. I realize there is a lot to be done in the summer months, but it's no better place to be than Kentucky in the summer. Mom said the grass was getting green and was ready to cut. I can imagine what the yard would look like after being mowed for the first time. Wish I were there to mow it with the tractor. Won't be long until Larry will be mowing the yard with the tractor and bush-hog, I don't guess. His first time the yard will probably look like a plowed field. Ha! Is he still running the gas out of the car? Guess Dad will have to put new tires on the car after Larry peels out in the gravel driveway all the time.

I guess Dad is pretty well caught up on his fencing. It seems like every time I hear from someone, he's fencing all the time. He'd go crazy over here putting up fences because there's no fence as far as you can go. There's a strand of concertina wire around landing zones, but that's about it. When I say landing zone that means the rear for us which is LZ Baldy. Of course, there are several LZs around here by different names but they are kindly far apart.

I just about know what's going on back there now since I spent most of my life on Cherry Hill. Whatever you all do this summer I hope you have a good season and enjoy life. Don't work too hard but I guess that goes along with depending on livestock and crops to make a living.

As far as over here, I'm doing fine. It stays pretty hot now especially when we go climbing around the mountains. We'll be in the lowlands for awhile and then will go back into the mountains. There are a lot of hills. Of course, I don't write much about the war over here. I don't think Marines care to talk about it, only to each other. I'll let you all in on some stories when I get home. Okay?

There's no need to worry about me over here because I don't and neither should you all. I have all the confidence in the world in the "Man" upstairs. I figure that's a pretty good start. It really isn't too bad. In fact, I kindly like in the bush. It's just some of the silly things that we sometime do like moving so often and other petty things. I guess though its part of the program. It seems like every time we get resupplied, we move to another position with all the extra gear. It don't mean nothing to me though because I'm pretty well used to it.

When we get to a position we dig in and dig sleeping holes. They're just the size of our bodies and nothing fancy, but we can make them pretty comfortable during the day by putting our poncho down and putting our poncho liners up for shade. While we're not doing anything we just lay back and take it easy. Since we have watch at night, it gives us a chance to catch up on our sleep unless we go on patrols or ambushes. When we go outside the perimeter it's just our squad. We have seven in our squad at the moment. Sometimes we take two men from the machine gun team along with us. Wish I could get in the gun team, but they have enough right now. Maybe if someone goes home I can take his place.

So things are going pretty well for me so far. Just hope it continues. I think of you all real often but at times, I can't write as much as I'd like. Sometimes I start a letter and they tell us to do something so I usually end up not finishing it.

I thought I could wait and write when my paycheck comes in, but it doesn't look like that will be for another week or so. I left my last pay check on the books but will send it all home when I get it. My paycheck is about $92.00 now. Mom said something about a war bond. Well I don't know anything about it unless it was something I took out in boot camp or should I say forced to take out. I doubt if it's any good or important, so I don't care what you do with it. You can throw it away for all I care unless you think it might come in handy. [Note: Little did I know at the time that the war bond my mother mentioned was actually Savings Bonds.]

Well we're taking it easy right now but will moving to another position before long. Mom, you don't have to send me a cake because I doubt if I'd eat much anyway. The squad would probably end up getting most of it. Whenever anyone gets a package from home, it just comes natural to pass it around and share it. Anyway, it would probably be half melted by the time it got to me or mashed up into a pizza.

Well I'll let you go now so you all be good and take care. I'll write later on.

Bye for now,
Fred

P.S. I got the Springfield Sun and saw my poem titled "Letter from Vietnam" in the newspaper. I didn't think you would put it in the paper but I don't mind. The guys in the squad didn't see the poem but they got a kick out of the paper, especially the picture of the old school house. They all know I live on a farm and that the town has a population of about 3,100. They all come from big cities except for a few that live in the south.

Chapter 7

Foxholes, Fields of Fire, and Firefights

URING our rehabilitation at LZ Baldy for the month of April the Marines of Mike Company spent the time taking showers, visiting the small exchange for health and comfort items, patronizing the club, writing letters, and in general just relaxing. Once in awhile we would have to go out to the perimeter of LZ Baldy and stand hole. I was in our hooch on our last day of rehab prior to the company heading back to the bush. I had readied my pack and equipment for the next day and decided I would just take it easy while I had the chance and relax on my cot. I sat on the side of the cot and decided to chow down on a can of C-Ration peaches. I opened the can of peaches with my John Wayne can opener, fetched a plastic spoon from my pack, and mixed in a little coffee creamer. The creamer gave the peaches a soothing taste. I began to chow down slowly savoring every mouthful.

I heard someone entering our hooch and looked up to see who it was. The first thing I noticed was the deep dark tan of the arms and face. It was Lance Corporal Travieso. He was of Hispanic decent and all the days in the hot sun of Vietnam had made his skin color very dark. He came walking toward me across the squeaky plywood floor of the hooch. He stopped about three feet away and peered down at me.

"Fenwick, you skate, you fuckin skate!" he said briskly.

"What-are-yer-tawkin-bout?" I murmured with a mouthful of peaches.

Travieso proclaimed as if jealous, "You're going to Da Nang for two and a half damn days, that's what! Gonna leave us behind while we head back out to the bush. You won't have to put up with all the bullshit for awhile."

"Say what?" I asked. I looked up at Travieso towering over me. "I still don't know what are you talking about?"

"They're sending you down to the Land and Mine Warfare School at Da Nang, you skate," Travieso said. "I've been trying to go to that school for I don't know how long."

"How did this all come about?" I inquired.

"Corporal Ka-Bar recommended you to go," Travieso responded. "He said that you need more expertise with mines and bobby traps so that when you come back you can be our point man."

"Hey, that's great!" I said, while still shoveling peaches into my mouth. "When do I leave?"

"Tomorrow morning," Travieso replied. "There will be a chopper coming in at 0700. Have all you gear packed and ready to go. You will be taken down to Da Nang where you can skate, drink beer, and have a good old time."

"I really don't want to go after all," I said jokingly. "Why don't you go in my place?"

"Nah, hell no! You go," Travieso said with a grin. "I sorta like it here in the bush anyway. Besides, this is my kind of life." He walked away murmuring something to himself about the bush being where he belongs.

Hawkeye had overheard our conversation. He came over and sat down across from me.

"Da Nang, huh?" he asked.

"Yeah, Da Nang," I responded with a sheepish look.

"You'll like it there," he said, "it beats the bush!"

"Yeah, I'm looking forward to it," I responded.

Hawkeye began to brief me about what the school would be like and that I would be able to get to the Club at Freedom Hill in Da Nang. Freedom Hill was an area on the military base at Da Nang with a club, Post Exchange, snack bar, and the amenities provided military personnel who were lucky enough to be stationed at a large base camp. I relished the idea, especially about being able to get out of the bush for two and half days. Hawkeye and I enjoyed our conversation about something other than being in the bush.

The next morning as Mike Company prepared to go back to the bush; I went down to the landing zone and boarded a CH-46 chopper. Soon I was flying toward Da Nang. When I arrived at the landing zone in Da Nang a 6x6 truck was there waiting to transport the Marines to the Land and Mine Warfare School. I rode in the back of the truck with other Marines who had been assigned to the school. It seemed to be out on the beach. My classes started almost immediately after we checked in. It was a two and a half day course and the instructors did not want to waste any time.

We were instructed in the techniques of probing for mines and booby traps, how to disarm booby traps, and the procedures to follow when blowing a mine or booby trap in place. We used detonation cord, C-4, and dynamite. We were shown how blasting caps were used in conjunction with C-4 and other explosives.

Probing consisted of the students getting on our hands and knees and inserting the tip of a bayonet at a forty-five degree angle into the sand. This was done every six inches apart. If the blade hit something metal we would then feel around the sides with our hands to try and locate the dummy mine. Then we would take action to disarm it by disconnecting the wires attached to the device. The whole idea of probing a bayonet into the soft sand reminded me of plucking the weeds out of the tobacco beds back on the farm.

It was a very professionally run military school. The Marine instructors of the 1st Engineer Battalion were top-notch and they made the course of instruction demanding but enjoyable. They knew that the students, especially the infantry Marines, would go back to the bush and put the training to good practical use. I learned more about the mines and booby traps commonly found in Vietnam than I had previously realized.

Not only were we taught how to disarm devices but the students were also introduced to the various other implements of war that Charlie used to inflict casualties upon their enemies. The instruction covered pungi sticks, swinging spike balls, manually operated electronic mines, and a host of other clever devices that the Vietcong had designed over the many years at war. We were taught how the VC and NVA used such devices as the grenade booby trap, the cartridge trap, mud-encased grenade, and improvised satchel charges. We even learned about bear traps which seemed a bit coincidental since I had already had a personal experience in the bush with one.

We learned to be aware of lost or discarded combat equipment and ammo. A pair of binoculars or lost rounds laying on a trail would most likely be booby trapped. We were taught not to pick up souvenirs no matter how tempting. Any equipment laying about, we were instructed to automatically think booby trap. Charlie would take a M16 round, place it into the ground on a hard surface, and position a nail under the detonator or use a spring operated device to ignite the trap. When an unsuspecting Marine stepped on the trap the round would go off into his foot.

They would place obvious wires of booby traps on trails for the Marines to see and then place another booby trap behind a rock, tree, or gully. When a Marine took cover behind these natural barriers while attempting to blow the devices in place, the second booby trap could be detonated. An objective of the VC was to inflict as many casualties as possible on American servicemen causing a state of confusion, disorganization, and fear within the unit. The enemy ensured that they provided the American servicemen a constant barrage of menacing harassment devices.

The two and a half days at the Land and Mine Warfare School gave me a chance to unwind from the daily pressures and uncertainty of being in the bush. I managed to get to the enlisted club only once but I really enjoyed the break. The chow in the mess hall also tasted good compared to the hum drum routine of eating C-Rations. I was beginning to feel like the old salt and an experienced combat veteran. I felt more confident than I had when I first arrived in country. I was comfortable with my level of combat expertise that was to sustain me through my ordeals in this God forsaken country.

April 28, 1970

Dear Mom, Dad and Larry,

Well, guess what? The first sergeant sent two men to a Land and Mine Warfare School in Da Nang for two and a half days. They send either one or two Marines about every month. Anyway, I was one of them. We learned about VC booby traps and how to work with demolitions, setting off explosives, and so forth. We'll have a test tomorrow and then I'll go back to the bush and join the rest of the company.

A buddy of mine needed some money so he sold me his Insta-matic 124 camera for $5.00. Guess that was a pretty good deal, huh? Anyway I have a camera now, but no film. He said he'd give me his film when it comes in. I might get to send some pictures home after all.

Guess when I get back to the company I'll have plenty of mail since I've missed two mail calls. I never will catch up on my writing. It's getting to where I don't write letters much anymore because I can't find very much time but I'll always manage to get a few lines home.

Well I'll let you all go now, so don't work too hard. I'll be thinking of everyone and hoping for your best.

Yours truly,
Freddy

Upon completion of the school I received a completion certificate. It read, "1st Marine Division FMF, This is to certify that PFC Fenwick, F.W. has completed a three day course of instruction in Basic Combat Demolitions, Land Mine Warfare and V.C. Booby Traps on 29 April 1970." It was signed by the U.S. Marine Corps Commanding Officer of the 1st Engineer Battalion. I folded it twice and tucked it away in my letter writing gear for safe keeping.

I boarded a chopper close to Freedom Hill and flew back to the base camp at LZ Baldy. When I checked my mail at the company office, I had a small box from my mother. I went just outside the company office doorway and sat down on the sandbags that encircled the structure. I opened the box and found a jam cake wrapped in waxed paper. I cut a piece of cake with my bayonet. It sure tasted good and the cake was still moist. Such a delight, I thought.

Immediately I broke out my letter writing gear in order to write a quick note thanking her for her thoughtfulness. While writing the note, a few Marines began coming in and out of the doorway. They noticed that I had an open box with something to eat. Some of them I had seen before and others I had not. They all asked what I was eating and if they could have some. I gave each of them a piece of the cake until it was all gone. I had initially intended on sharing it with my squad in the bush, but I figured I might as well let the Marines in the rear taste some real homemade cake. Besides, I would have had to hand carry it on the next chopper out with all my other combat gear and I just didn't have that many hands. I vowed not to tell my squad for they would have surely chastised me for not sharing the jam cake with them.

April 30, 1970

Dear Mom, Dad and Larry,

Guess this letter is a little sooner than expected, but thought I'd let you know how good that jam cake was. Of course I didn't eat it all. Some of the Marines at the company office helped me eat it. They told me to tell my Mom that it was delicious. It was real moist and fresh. Guess putting it in the tin can helped to keep it that way. It was real good. Thanks a lot Mom, it was really thoughtful of you. It got here April 29th so guess it took about eight days to get here which isn't too bad.

Dad, I also got the letter you put in with the package. Sounds like your cattle are multiplying a lot. That's good, maybe you'll have a lot to sell this fall. Hope all the crops do fine this summer. Just think of me when you wish you had some help. Larry's probably working his butt off but he'll enjoy it when he gets out of school.

Well, I'll close for now, I'm going to catch a chopper out to the company. Guess you know I've been to Land and Mine Warfare School so I'm going to join the rest of the company now. So everyone be good and I'll be thinking of you all.

Yours truly,
Freddy

I caught a CH-46 chopper along with other Mike Company Marines at LZ Baldy. We were escorted by two Huey Gunships. We flew over, what we called the lowlands, for half the time we never knew exactly where we were or where we were going. The chopper began to circle prior to landing. I looked out a side window and saw Marines on the ground walking about and poncho liners tied to bushes. It seemed a small perimeter for Mike Company. The chopper touched down at about midday and I grabbed all my gear and shuffled to the rear door. The ramp of the chopper dropped and I walked into the loud noises of the engines and heavy blasts of wind from the rotors. The other Marines remained on board the chopper. I thought that was a little strange.

I was momentarily disorientated until I looked around and saw Lance Corporal Travieso waving his hands to signal me in his direction. I knew that the rest of my squad would be close by. As I walked toward Travieso the propellers from the chopper seemed to push me along. It then lifted into the air and I stood there motionless just trying to keep my balance from the wind gusts while dust and debris kicked up around me. Soon the chopper leveled off in the air and continued to fly in a direction away from LZ Baldy.

As quiet and calm returned I began to hear the familiar sounds of Marines around the perimeter. Some were talking among themselves, some were digging with their entrenching tools, some were fixing their hooches, while others were listening to small transistor radios.

"Hey Skate," Travieso said without a handshake. "Come here and let me show you where our squad is. How have you been doing down there in Da Nang? Been going with all those oriental ladies?"

"No, I've been working," I replied.

"I'll bet you've been working," Travieso said doubtfully. "How did it go?"

"It was real good," I said. "I learned a helluva lot. Wished they had taught me something like that before I first came over to the Nam."

"Well, now you gotta put your training to good practical use. Maybe you could keep me from being blown up," Travieso said.

"You look after me and I'll look after you," I replied in response. "Maybe we can make it through Nam in one piece."

"You gotta deal," Travieso responded.

I took off my pack and laid it on the ground. Then I dropped my helmet on top of my pack and reached in my utility trousers cargo pocket to get my green sateen soft cover. I shook it out and put the cap on my head. It felt much better getting that steel pot helmet off my head.

"Hey Travieso, where is everybody?" I asked. "All I see is Mike 3. Where's the rest of Mike Company?"

Travieso reached into his camouflaged utility trousers pocket and pulled out his folded map. As he held the map in his left hand he scanned the military map with his right forefinger. "We split up," he responded. "Guess they thought the platoons could cover more area if we broke away independently from the main group while we are in the lowlands. The other two platoons are about a klick from here. Right now it is just our 3rd platoon in this pos between the Song Yen Ne River and the Song Yen River. There's a railroad about a klick to our east. We have this area all to ourselves."

I was impressed with his map reading skills. "Great," I replied. Maybe we can stay in this one pos for a few days instead of humping to another position every day.

"Yep, maybe," Travieso said. "When you left for Land and Mine Warfare School they made us OpCon to 2nd Battalion, 1st Marines. It is a good possibility that we will remain under their operational control for about two weeks."

"That would be great," I responded. "It looks so peaceful and serene here in the lowlands. By the way Travieso, how do you know all this stuff about where we are located and what we are doing? I always seem to be left in the dark most of the time."

Travieso responded, "Ya just gotta be nosy and ask a lot of questions of the right people. Otherwise, they won't tell you jack about what is going on."

"You are all right in my book," I told Travieso jokingly, "No matter what Hawkeye says about you." We both laughed and then Travieso went and plopped down on the ground next to his pack.

I looked around our platoon perimeter and caught a glimpse of our platoon commander's head and his radio operator close by. The Marines of Mike 3 seemed to be in a relaxed state of mind. They went about their tasks nonchalantly in an almost melancholy manner. My three days in Da Nang was short lived. I was now back to where I belonged while I was serving in Vietnam, back to Mike Company, Mike 3, and Mike 3 Charlie. I found a spot near Hawkeye to dig my sleeping hole. He told me that he already dug the fighting hole and that we could share it during the night.

I had the last watch the following morning before the sun rose slowly in the eastern sky. It was a beautiful sight watching it rise above the banana trees that were scattered around the border of the rice paddies. Marines were already stirring about and putting up poncho liners in preparation for the hot sun that was to follow. The Marines lackadaisical mannerisms seemed to rub off on everyone. It was as if everyone was in slow motion. No one was in a hurry. They all just enjoyed the peaceful serenity. If you had to be in the bush, you might as well make the most of it.

My squad could be heard offering to trade various C-Ration meals for the ones they could tolerate. The Marines had nicknames for some of the C-Ration meals to fit their Gyrene Gyngle terminology. They began to break open cans of Ham and Lima Beans (Ham and Mother Fuckers), Beef Slices & Potatoes with Gravy (Beef and Rocks), Spaghetti and Meat Balls (Spaghetti and Gonads), Fried Ham Slices (Rump Roast), Beans w/Frankfurter Chunks in Tomato Sauce (Beans and Dicks), Chopped Ham & Eggs, Pork Steak, Beef with Spiced Sauce, Boned Chicken, Meat Balls with Beans in Tomato Sauce, Turkey Loaf, BeefSteak, and Boned Chicken and Noodles.

I reached for one of my canteens and downed a cool swig of water. It tasted best early in the morning due to the drop in temperature during the night and after the damp dew settled on the canteens. Since I mixed a halogen tablet in each canteen for purification, the water was more palatable when cool than when warm or hot. I decided that I would eat a good breakfast, something that would fill me up. I broke out my John Wayne can opener and opened up a can of Spaghetti and Meatballs. Along with it I would have crackers and some grape jelly.

I used the small can that the crackers came out of and made a heating stove out of it. I did this by cutting holes in the side of the can with the can opener and a slit at the bottom on each side of the can. I bent the sides inward from the slits at the bottom of the can to allow oxygen to get to the heat tab. I would also have a can of fruit cocktail and used the empty can to brew me some coffee.

What a life, I thought to myself. Spaghetti and Meat Balls for breakfast!

It just doesn't get any better than this. Normally I would only eat one can of chow before beginning the daily routine; however, seeing as we were going to be in this position for awhile I decided to eat more than usual. After all, I figured that I had to replenish my energy level from not eating hardly anything for a period of ten days when we were in the mountains.

As I was chowing down, six Vietnamese kids approached just outside the perimeter. They appeared to be between the ages of five and seven years old. There were four boys and two little girls. They were squatting down and watching me eat. Soon they began to ask for some chop-chop. I knew that they wanted me to give them some chow. I hollered at them to Didi, but they ignored me. I felt uneasy eating in front of them knowing that their diet mainly consisted of rice and fish, but I was determined not to give in. After a little while I uttered to myself, "Oh, what the hell! Let's see if they will go for a pack of cigarettes."

The cigarettes were included in all the C-Ration meals. This particular meal contained four Pall Mall non-filtered cigarettes. I threw the pack out to them hoping that they would just take the cigarettes and leave me alone. They scrambled and tried to catch the small pack of cigarettes even before it hit the ground. I figured that they might take the cigarettes back to their village and give them to their mamasans or papasans, but that was not the case. The oldest boy opened the pack and took out a book of matches that he had obviously gotten from discarded C-Ration packets. He lit a cigarette and gave the rest to the other children. Eventually they were all toking away and fighting among themselves for a chance to puff a cigarette. Then they began to ask for chop-chop once again.

"Manine give babysan cigmo, Manine numba one," the oldest boy said. "What-se-name you, Manine? What-se-name you? My name, Tom! What-se-name you?"

I hesitated a bit and then responded, "My name, Fred." That was a mistake because he then began to carry on jabbering away and speaking fairly good English.

"My name, Tom," he said, "Tom Ming. Where you been "Fled?" Huh? Where you been?"

I knew that he was trying to pronounce my first name Fred as best he could by saying Fled so I ignored it. Then I responded, "I go Buc Buc VC." This meant that I had been fighting the Viet Cong.

"Manine go Buc Buc VC? Boo coo Buc Buc VC, huh?" he asked.

"Yeah," I replied. "Boo coo Buc Buc!"

"Souvenir babysan one chop-chop. Hokay? Hokay? Souvenir babysan one chop-chop, hokay, Fled?" he asked in rapid succession.

"No souvenir chop-chop," I responded.

This conversation went back and forth until he finally said, "If you give Tom Ming chop-chop, I show you bino. Hokay? Hokay?"

Hawkeye was sitting on the ground about fifteen feet from me. "Hey

Hawkeye," I said, "this little guy wants to show me a bino for some chop-chop. Sounds like a pretty good deal!" Hawkeye looked up from eating his C-Ration meal and just smiled.

"Where bino?" I asked the boy.

Tom said, "Give me one chop-chop and I show Fled bino. Hokay?"

I thought about it for a few seconds and thought that the kid was trying to bullshit me. "Didi," I said. "Go away!"

"Tom be friend with Fled. Hokay? No Didi Mau! Babysan show Fled bino. Hokay?"

Hawkeye came over and sat down beside me. "What's going on between you and the boy?" he asked.

I replied, "He said he would show me a booby trap for some chop-chop. What do you think?"

"I don't know," replied Hawkeye. "Sometimes if you get on the right side of these Vietnamese kids, they treat you right."

Travieso was sitting on the ground in a cross-legged position next to his pack. He was eating chow from a C-Ration can when I asked him if he would mind if I walked just outside the perimeter to see if the boy could show me a booby trap.

"No!" he snapped. "Don't you go out there by yourself. You can't trust these people. You never know what will happen. If you want to do something like that, go along with the fireteam."

"Well, how about if I get a few volunteers and inform the platoon commander what I want to do?" I asked Travieso.

Without looking up from eating his chow that he had prepared with a heat tab, Travieso replied, "Yeah, that's okay." He did not seem too overly concerned about a Vietnamese kid wanting to show me a booby trap, only that he had time to eat his hot chow and he was going to take advantage of the opportunity.

"Hawkeye, would you go with me on patrol if you knew that we could find a booby trap and disarm it?" I asked.

"Yeah, I'll go, Hawkeye replied. "If it's gonna save a Marine's life, I'm all for it."

Travieso told our squad leader what I wanted to do and he in turn informed the platoon commander. In a matter of minutes the lieutenant approached me from behind and walked directly to me.

"What's going on here, Fenwick?" the lieutenant asked. "Don't be giving these kids any C-Rations. They will pester you for eternity and we don't need them hanging around the perimeter."

"Sir," I responded, "this boy said that if I give him some chop-chop that he will show me a booby trap. I told him that he will have to show me the booby trap first and then I will give him a can of C-Rations."

"That's crazy," the lieutenant said. "You can't trust these people."

"Sounds like I heard that line before," Travieso interjected.

"Well," I said, "wouldn't it be worth it if he did show us a booby trap? It would prevent a casualty or even the death of one of our Marines."

"You've got a point there," the lieutenant agreed. "All right, I'll form a squad size patrol and we will see if this kid is on the up and up."

"Outstanding!" I said. "Can I walk point?"

Travieso heard me and sounded off, "Listen to this you guys. Fenwick goes to two and a half days of school on mines and booby traps and now he volunteers for point man. Gungy, huh?"

"Yeah," Hawkeye replied, "he's a real go getter! Gung Ho!"

"Hey lieutenant," Travieso said. "Does this mean that I don't have to walk point anymore? Fenwick is a highly trained and highly motivated booby trap sniffer-outer!"

"Not hardly," the lieutenant replied. "You've saved our ass many times before. I want you walking point until I rotate out of this place."

We all laughed out loud while Travieso was mumbling some kind of obscenities under his breath. "Finally Travieso said, "Okay, who wants to join Fenwick and the others on a squad patrol?"

Another Marine in our squad answered up and said, "I'll go, I need a break from all this sitting around and waiting for Charlie to find us." Then another Marine piped up as well, "I'll go too, you can count me in."

We formed our little make-shift squad and brought along two machine gunners just in case Charlie was close by. The machine gunners were commandeered by Travieso from another squad. He simply walked up to them while they were eating C-Rations and told them they were needed for our patrol. Without question, the two machine gunners joined us for the hunt.

I took point. It was the first time I had led a patrol. I tried to remember everything they had taught me at the Land and Mine Warfare School. I moved across the rice paddy dikes very cautiously along with Tom. I told him to walk about twenty paces in front of me on the trail. I was no dummy! If this kid was for real we would soon find out. All of a sudden Tom stopped and became excited. He was pointing his finger and saying, "Bino! Bino!"

I gave a hand and arm signal for the squad to stop. It felt good being in charge for a change and taking on more responsibilities as a leader. I walked up to where Tom was standing. I looked to where he was pointing off the side of the trail. There was a C-Ration can the same size that my spaghetti had came from. It had a trip wire running across the trail. Inside the can there was a grenade with the pin pulled. It was the same kind of M26 grenade that I was carrying. Charlie had managed to get his hands on an American grenade. An unsuspecting Marine could trip the wire and the grenade would fall to the ground and detonate.

"Tom, you are number one," I said.

"Souvenir me one chop-chop," Tom replied.

"I souvenir boo coo chop-chop if you show me another bino," I said.

"Hokay!" he replied excitedly.

The lieutenant came forward and looked at the booby trap.

"Nice going, Fenwick," he said. "I'll get some people to blow this thing in place."

"Don't thank me Sir, Tom Ming is the one that led me to it," I said. "He is willing to show us some more."

"Great!" the lieutenant responded.

The booby trap was blown in place as we hid behind the dikes for cover. Then we proceeded along the trail and Tom pointed out another booby trap. This one was blown in the same manner and we were off to find some more. After blowing four booby traps in place, Tom Ming pointed out a fifth booby trap.

"Here's another one!" I hollered back to the platoon commander.

Finally, the lieutenant said, "Shit this area is covered with booby traps. We will be out here for the rest of the war looking for these fuckin things. We'll blow this last one and then head back to the CP!"

When we approached our defensive perimeter I instructed Tom to wait outside our front lines. I found my pack and pulled out a can of beef slices & potatoes with gravy. I figured I could manage to give up one of my less desirable C-Ration meals. I tossed it to Tom in a softball pitch fashion.

Tom caught the can before it hit the ground. He was very excited and said, "Manine give babysan chop-chop, Manine numba one!"

I replied, "Tom, you're pretty numba one yourself!"

As the lieutenant passed by my fighting hole on his way back into the perimeter he said, "Fenwick, why don't you give him a full meal, he deserves it. But that's all. No more chop-chop. Tell him to Didi Mau immediately."

"Roger that, Sir!" I responded. I gave Tom a full C-Ration meal still in the box and told him to Didi.

"Hokay, bye Fled!" Tom yelled out as he walked away.

In Vietnamese, he aggressively scolded some of the other children lingering nearby for them to move away. They followed him out of sight and into a nearby village begging all the way for a portion of the C-Ration meal.

I thought to myself that Tom Ming's father could possibly be a VC. How else would Tom know where to locate the booby traps? We found a total of five booby traps that day with the help of Tom Ming. I felt satisfied with the job I had done on my first experience of walking point man. For the rest of the squad patrols I would be without the help of Tom Ming, but I was confident I could handle the increased responsibility.

The next morning my squad went out on a patrol. As we crossed the rice paddies I looked and saw Tom Ming riding on top of a water buffalo in the muddy paddies. An old papasan was trudging along behind the plow. Tom began to yell and wave.

"Hey Fled! Fled! Manine numba one! Manine numba one! This my papasan." He pointed to the man behind the plow, but the old man never looked up.

"Where you go Fled? Where you go? Buc Buc VC? Huh? Buc Buc VC?" Tom yelled out.

"I go Buc Buc boo coo VC!" I yelled back to him. "Your papasan VC?" I asked.

"No! No!" he responded quickly. "Papasan no VC! Papasan numba one!"

The squad moved out of sight of the rice paddies and into a village. We checked every hooch. There were only old papasans, mamasans, and small children. I supposed that the younger men were either in the fields or were VC hiding from us. When I returned to my fighting hole I found that the kids had returned wanting more food. It took me awhile to shoo them back away from our perimeter to a comfortable distance. When things got quiet, I managed to find time to write home before the sun went down. All the while I was writing my letter, my every movement was being watched by the kids, but they kept fairly quiet while talking among themselves. I ignored them.

May 3, 1970

Dear Mom, Dad and all,

Well how's things back at home right now. I hope everyone is doing fine. For myself, things are going pretty well. We are working in the lowlands. It sure is decent because we don't have to move so much. I think we'll be here until about the 10th and then head back around LZ Baldy. We spend most of our time going on patrols and ambushes. The ambushes are at night but we set up watches so we get a little sleep. We have one for two straight nights and then stay back in the perimeter for one night. The reason we're keeping so busy is because the company isn't with us. It's three platoons but ours is about a mile from the rest.

The kids around here run us crazy. I'll be glad when we get away from them. You can hardly run them away. They're always wanting something. Sometimes they show us dud rounds and booby traps which is good, but you can't take a good healthy dump unless they're watching you. Of course all the mamasans are in the fields too. It don't mean nothing to us though, it's just the principle of the thing, if you know what I mean.

Well we got paid today so thought I'd better send the check home before something happens to it. I got $92.00 for this pay day. I kept out some but I really don't need it out here in the bush. Say Mom, if you could, can you send me a couple of Kodak Instamatic 124 film and I'll take a few pictures. Just take enough money out of the check to cover it. Also I'd like to have some way of sending them home in the roll because I can't develop them over here. You don't have to be in any hurry, just when you're in town and have the time.

Well I'll close now because I can't think of much to say right
now. It's getting dark and I haven't ate chow yet. I have to keep my
mind on what's going on over here. Besides the kids are outside my
position jabbering away. I ran them away earlier, but now they're
back begging for food. Some speak pretty good English. I had a
pretty good little buddy, but the lieutenant is always making us run
them away which is good in a way. Well this is hoping everyone
back home is doing fine. Take care and I'll be thinking of you all.

Guess who,
Freddy

P.S. Let me know if you get the check. I haven't had any mail for a
bit, but it's just that they don't bring mail out very often. I did get
the cake though. It was really good.

Our platoon was assigned an AOR to provide security for the 1st Engineers. We were to provide two-man teams along a dirt road that they were
reconstructing near the Song Yen Ne River. As the Combat Engineers
worked with their bulldozers and mine sweepers, two Marines were placed
at intervals about a mile apart along the road. The two-man teams were to
stay out on the road for two days at a time. We would also guard the engineer's equipment so that Charlie could not booby trap them. After two days
as security we would be relieved by two different Marines and then go back
to our platoon's position down by the river.

Hawkeye and I were dropped off by a 6x6 not too far from a pagoda.
This is where the Vietnamese came to pray. We decided that the pagoda was
so close to the road that we might as well set up our position inside the temple. We laid our packs inside the pagoda and then stood at the doorway to
look out. There was a clear view up and down the road as the ground was
level. We put our war gear on and grabbed our M16s to walk around the
surrounding area in order to check for anything suspicious.

Hawkeye and I walked several meters around the pagoda and came to a
haystack. We thought it was a little suspicious as there was concertina wire
strung next to it and there were signs of the hay being disturbed and scattered on the ground. Then on the back side of the haystack, we noticed a
small hole about two feet off the ground, leading into the haystack. We began to take our rifles with fixed bayonets and jab them into the haystack.
While we were jabbing our bayonets into the haystack we yelled, "Lai day,
Lai day" for any VC to come out. To our surprise the hay started moving
and out came a small Vietnamese male.

The Vietnamese was about forty years old, unarmed, and had no identification. I patted him down while Hawkeye held his rifle on him. After he
was checked for any weapons or devices, we checked the haystack even fur-

Fenwick taking a break in the shade of a Pagoda. Hawkeye and I were providing security for Combat Engineers along a roadway. We had unexpected guests. Found suspected VC in a haystack nearby.

ther to determine if there were any hidden booby traps or weapons, but did not find any. We suspected him to be VC and called back to our platoon commander. A couple of Marines came by in a 6x6 and took the suspected VC back toward our platoon position for questioning by the Kit Carson Scouts. Hawkeye and I were glad we had found him in the haystack when we did as he could have sneaked up on us during the night.

We went back inside the pagoda and plopped down on the floor next to our packs. It was not long until a group of Vietnamese kids came to the pagoda begging us for cigmos and chop-chop. We ignored them at first but as time went on we became friendly with them. We still however, resisted giving them any cigarettes or food. Since I was not a habitual smoker, I always gave Hawkeye all of the cigarettes that I got from my C-Ration accessory packs.

As the construction of the road progressed we kept on alert during the day. At night we took turns standing watch while the other slept inside the temple. One morning about six of the villagers arrived for their morning worship. Two were elderly men and the others were middle aged women. They had with them little brass urns which they placed up on the altar next to the statues of Buddha. Then they lit some sticks of incense which almost immediately filled the small temple with a distinctive odor. I turned to Hawkeye and told him that I wouldn't mind having one of the statues as a souvenir.

"You better not remove any of these statues in here," Hawkeye warned. "These people may find some of their Vietnamese friends to hurt you if they found out that you stole something."

"I'm just kidding," I replied. "Hell, what's new? They hurt Marines on a daily basis. The ones who come in here are most likely VC anyway."

"Yeah, maybe so," Hawkeye said, but we'd best not take anything out of here. Besides, there are only two of us."

"Yeah, okay Hawkeye," I replied. "You're right about that."

The Vietnamese knelt down, clasped their hands above their heads, swayed their bodies to a rhythm, and began to chant. It sounded a bit spooky as we did not speak the Vietnamese language. Their mental state seemed as though they were in a trance where their soul was taken over by the spirits. After awhile their chanting did not bother us as much as our mere presence seemed to bother them. After all, we were Americans, foreigners to them. We sat on the floor with our M16s at hand and silently watched them with great interest. We wondered what they might be chanting about in Vietnamese. Save the crops, protect the family, get these two Americans out of our temple. Hawkeye and I didn't have a clue.

About thirty minutes later they got to their feet, turned around, and started to leave. For the first time since their arrival into the temple the women looked at us and smiled on their way out the door. The old men who had at first given us the evil eye, managed to force a hand shake on their way out the open entrance. It was as if they were grateful that we had not interrupted them while they were praying in the temple.

On the third day and early in the morning we saw a 6x6 approaching. Two Marines sat in the front seat. We thought we were getting relieved but did not see any other Marines sitting in the back of the deuce and a half. The driver pulled up to us and told us to put all our gear in the back as he was taking us to another strategic location along the road. After we loaded in the back of the truck, the driver jerked the vehicle forward and proceeded down the road. He was to pickup up and transport other security Marines along the way.

We stopped and picked up two Marines standing by the roadside. They hoisted their 782 gear up on the back of the truck and commenced to climb up. I reached out to give them a hand as the bed of the truck was quite high. The two Marines sat down on the troop seats and began to tell Hawkeye and me what a crappy night they had while sitting out in the open night air. They had red welts all over their arms from mosquito and red ant bites. Hawkeye and I just looked at each other without comment and smiled, for the pagoda had provided us with shelter from the damp night air the night before. The burning of incense in the pagoda also seemed to help keep the annoying mosquitoes at bay, at least for the night. In Vietnam, there was never shelter from hungry mosquitoes.

After about twenty minutes of riding the truck finally stopped. The driver yelled out from the cab of the vehicle that this was where Hawkeye and I were to dismount. This would be our new position along the road to provide security for the Combat Engineers. We scrambled from the back of the truck with all our gear. Instead of climbing down using the foot rung like Hawkeye had, I decided to jump to the ground from the bed of the truck. I hit the ground with a thud and I felt a sharp pain in both feet. I remembered my father used to tell me not to jump off high things because I could cause a stone bruise. I would make it a point to climb down off a 6x6 in the future instead of jumping. That would be a good way to break a leg with a full pack on your back.

The truck jerked and bounced away and headed down the road with the other two Marines being thrown around in the back. I wondered if the Marine Corps taught the M35A2 2-1/2 ton cargo truck drivers in Motor Transport School to pop their clutches with every gear they shifted. I had never seen one driver that could shift the gears smoothly. Soon the truck was out of sight but it left a cloud of black smoke from the exhaust lingering in the air. Hawkeye and I looked at one another and gave each other that "Well, we better start digging" look. We were now out in an open area. It wasn't as good as the position we had just left at the pagoda but we would have to make due.

Without further delay we dug our fighting hole. Then we reported to the platoon commander over the radio indicating the grid of our new location. Hawkeye plotted the grid and gave me the coordinates. Hawkeye was good at that. He could definitely read a map. If you wanted to know your location in the bush, be it day or night, a Marine only had to ask Hawkeye, Travieso, or Corporal Ka-Bar. They were all good at land navigation with map and compass. It was good to have a friend like Hawkeye with me who was so confident and trustworthy. While he read me the grid coordinates, I called them in over the radio to report our location to the platoon commander.

The platoon commander informed us that there would be a spotter round fired in the vicinity of our position in order to verify the map coordinates. In case we took on enemy fire during the night, we could call for artillery and fire support that would already have the grid. This way the artillery battery would not have to waste valuable time in the dark locating and plotting our position on the map.

We waited for the spotter round but it did not come right away. We were sitting at the edge of our fighting hole talking about things back home, how much time we had left in country, and at the same time swatting the pesky insects around us. Just after sunset we rubbed insect repellent all over our arms, neck, and face to avoid being eaten alive by the vicious mosquitoes. We received a call on the radio and were informed that the artillery battery would be firing one spotter round, an air burst, in our general vicinity. I acknowledged over the radio that we received the transmission and within a few seconds we heard the radio operator back at the artillery battery say, "Shot-Out!"

"Roger, I confirm Shot-Out," I replied over the radio.

About three hundred meters from our position there was an air burst of white smoke. I immediately reported on the radio, "Right on target, maintain those coordinates, Out!"

About two hours later while we sat around talking, we heard the hissing sound of a round traveling through the air from a distance and immediately followed by the sound of a 105mm Howitzer back at the artillery battery. For a moment we thought that they were firing at a target way beyond our position. Then there was a loud explosion only about thirty feet above our heads, "BOOOM!"

We immediately dived into the fighting hole expecting the worst. The first thought that crossed our minds was that they were going to drop high explosive rounds on our position. Hawkeye and I were packed in like sardines in this small make-shift fighting hole and I realized we should have made it a little wider. I noticed that Hawkeye had grabbed his helmet out of instinct but mine lay on top of the ground next to where I had been sitting. Wouldn't do me much good up there, I thought to myself. I reached for it and put it on my head.

"That scared the crap outta me!" I blurted out to Hawkeye.

"You're not the only one," Hawkeye replied while barely catching his breath. "Damned asses! They shot that spotter round right above our heads. I thought they would at least be three hundred meters away from us."

We braced ourselves for more anticipated spotter rounds but all was quiet. We settled back down and got on with the business at hand. It was dark now and I couldn't see anything beyond our fighting hole. Here we both were out in the middle of nowhere all by ourselves. The other pairs of Marines providing road security on our left and right flanks were out of sight even during the daylight hours. Our only communication was the PRC-77 radio. I hoped that our batteries lasted until we could get relieved by other Marines. During the remainder of the night I kept a keen ear and stayed alert hoping that we would be prepared and not get caught off guard again by another exploding spotter round.

Hawkeye and I were relieved of this position and rejoined our 3rd pla-

Hawkeye reading a letter from home. If it was one thing we looked forward to it was mail call.

toon by a larger river called the Song Yen River. It was about 6 klicks (6000 meters) north of Hill 55. While we were bivouacked next to the river it was an opportune time for us to fill our bellies with C-Rations, write letters, and swim in the river. Hawkeye and I put up our makeshift poncho hooch right beside the river bank. We did not realize at the time while we were erecting our field living quarters that we were putting it in a Vietnamese garden. From time to time an old mamasan came by to tend to her garden but she never said anything to us about it. She probably figured it was not worth her trouble to try to communicate with us. So we stayed where we were but tried not to trample her garden too much.

Occasionally our platoon was visited by some local prostitutes. One day as we were swimming in the river two prostitutes suddenly appeared. They were asking a fee of $5.00 U.S. dollars for their services. They were quickly taken up on the offer by a few Marines trying to get their money's worth behind the bushes. They must have serviced ten to twelve Marines that afternoon. I stayed away from them because I had heard the stories about the venereal diseases these Vietnamese prostitutes transmitted to their partners. I made up my mind earlier on that I would not fall for this type of temptation and to live the life of celibacy while I was in Vietnam. There were, however, other Marines who didn't care about the risks.

I reckoned they enjoyed the sexual encounter for the few minutes of pleasure until they ended up diagnosed with the clap. That was the term Marines used loosely to describe any type of venereal disease. After being away from home for so long and out in the bush, a prostitute was probably the next best thing compared to old "Suzie Rotten Crotch" back stateside. Our drill instructors called recruit's girlfriends that name. The appearance of the prostitutes made the Marines start talking and day-dreaming about their fiancés and girlfriends back home. Just to see a fairly good looking Vietnamese woman was enough to start idle minds wandering and fantasying.

There were several Marines who received Dear John letters from their girlfriends who could not wait any longer. This ruined the moral of a few good Marines. Most of their girlfriends back in the States did not believe there was justification in fighting the Vietnam War and it made things more difficult to keep a lasting relationship. Not only that but some girls just could not keep a long term relationship with Marines who were thousands of miles from home.

One day an incident occurred that seemed funny to the Marines, but not to the victim. We were watching a group of Kit Carson Scouts, Vietnamese soldiers who aided the American Servicemen. They had been assigned to our platoon. During their free time they would walk along the river bank searching for fish and then lob hand grenades into the water. After each explosion dead fish could be seen floating to the surface. They would then wade into the water and gather up the catch of the day to go along with their South Vietnam version of the C-Ration meal. The fish were more suitable to their palates.

There was an old papasan drifting down the river in his paddle boat. It was about three feet wide and eight feet long. As he got closer one of the Marines said, "Look at old papasan out in the river. I would like to throw a grenade out there and sink his ass!"

We laughed out loud and another Marine said, "Yeah, No balls! You ain't got no balls!"

"I'll show you what balls I have. Watch this," the Marine said in reply. He grabbed up four of his grenades and headed down to the river bank to join the Kit Carson Scouts.

"Papasan!" he yelled out to the old man. "Lai day, Lai day, mother fucker!"

The old man shook his head and waved his hands across his face saying,

"No com bic, no com bic!"

"Oh yes, you understand Lai day!" the Marine yelled back to him. "You come here old man or I'll BINO your dumb ass!"

He could not wait to toss the grenades while the rest of the Marines laughed and continued to edge him on. The old man was rattling away in Vietnamese and waving his hands at the same time. The Marine threw a grenade in the direction of the old man's boat. It exploded in the water right next to the boat making a big splash in the river. This time the old man was not waving his hands. He held up both fists and continued to rant and rave at the Marine. We roared with laughter at his mannerisms and antics.

The Kit Carson Scouts thought it was funny too so one of them decided to toss a grenade in the direction of the old man. It exploded in the water about twenty feet from the boat. The old man began to talk rapidly in Vietnamese and shake his fist at the Kit Carson Scout who had thrown the grenade. They laughed about what the old man was saying.

The Marine who had thrown the first grenade and who did not want to be out done by the Kit Carson Scout hurled another grenade at the old man. This time the grenade landed in the boat and the old man jumped into the water to save his own life. The boat floated down the river as the old man surfaced from the water. The grenade exploded inside the boat. We could see a cloud of smoke coming from the inside of the boat as it drifted downstream. The ole man began swimming after it. He continued to yell loudly cursing at the Marine who had thrown the grenade. As soon as he neared the partially capsized boat it sank into the depths below.

We all roared with laughter as the episode unfolded. It had started with an innocent old Vietnamese man, who was minding his own business and floating down the river in his boat, only to be attacked by some crazy Marine with frag grenades. The old man headed for the river bank struggling now just to keep his head above the water. He looked like a wet rat swimming to shore. The lieutenant became aware of what was going on down at the river and came down from his make-shift shelter to tell us to stop harassing the old man. Everyone took the lieutenant's warning with a grain of salt and continued to roll with laughter. Then one by one we all went down by the river bank and dived into the water for a swim, clothes and all.

After enjoying this comical situation with a Marine sinking an old man's boat and our dip in the river, Hawkeye and I decided to sit down in the warm sun and write some letters home.

May 16, 1970

Dear Mom, Dad and Larry,

Well how are things back home? Guess you all are pretty busy now with things to do on the farm. As for me, I'm fit to fight and am doing just fine. We've been pretty busy these last few weeks providing security for the Engineers. I'm guessing I'm about six miles from Da Nang but don't know for sure. We will be going back to LZ Baldy about the 20th. Anyway we've been acting as security for the 1st Engineers while they clean out a creek. We go on road security for a day, then watch the equipment for a day, and then stay at our platoon's position the next day. So we don't have it too bad right now. Once in awhile we get to go swimming in the river which is right beside us but that is just one day out of three. The other two days we're out on the road.

Two men are dropped off at different spots along the roads. Our main purpose is to see that Charlie don't put any mines on the road. They're pretty good at that. A small dozer and another big machine, which I don't know what it is called, hit a mine the other day. It did not do too much damage. Actually they hit two different mines. So we have to watch the roads and the men operating the equipment. Really, we've had it pretty easy.

I hate to go back to the hills around LZ Baldy. We are in the flatlands but there are mountains all round us. It really is pretty over here in a way. There is some good scenery in Nam, but of course, you have the bad scenes too. I learn something new every day. It seems that I'm now used to this country and feel pretty much at home. It's like I'm on a big camping trip. Ha! Most of my good friends left from the squad but I still have some pretty good buddies. We've got a few more new people last week.

I got a letter from Donald the other day and he seems to be doing fine. He was talking about one thing and then the other. He is on a cruise away from Okinawa at the moment. He said he was going to take a seven day leave after his cruise and go camping up north in Okinawa.

I sure would like to travel but I'm pretty well satisfied over here in Vietnam. At least there's no such thing as spit-shined boots, polished brass, and keeping squared away. Of course we have to be squared away over here too in a way because the least little thing you might get busted or given office hours. In other words, nonjudicial punishment. In case you don't know what office hours mean, it's just a bad mark in your service record book. I don't worry about nothing though because you almost have to not care at all to get something like that.

What was funny today was that a guy sank a papasan's boat in the river. He was charged twenty dollars for the boat and received office hours that cost him sixty-six dollars. He shouldn't have been messing with the civilians anyway. We all had a good laugh out of it.

I saw something the other day which was interesting. Hawkeye and I were dropped off by the road next to a small temple. We went inside and just laid around in the shade. We could see the road because both walls were halfway out. Anyway, about noon along came three Buddhist priests to worship. Us being so thoughtful, we moved our gear onto a little porch under the shade. They were beating on pots and pans, wooden sticks, and singing all at the same time. It was quite interesting to watch. After it was all over they shook our hands and were real friendly. Of course we couldn't understand a thing they were saying to us although we'd catch a few words here and there. Most of the time these people just smile at you but we can tell they don't mean it. The women over here really work hard. They can carry things that I can't carry and they are so small in size.

Well, enough about this place over here. I don't know if I'll interest you all in telling you these things or not. I could talk and talk about this place but there's no way I could ever write letters about it unless I write a book. And I'll never take time for that.

Oh! Happy Mother's Day, Mom. I don't know when it is but at least it's in the month of May. Mom you said you lit candles for me at Church. I really appreciate it but you don't have to worry a bit about me. I have a feeling I'll come through okay. I don't worry so neither should you all. After all, the Marine Corps will take care of what I need, and God will see me through. So don't worry about me even though I may not write for awhile. I'll be thinking of everyone anyway.

Well, I'll let you all go now so be good and take care. Don't work too hard on the farm. Guess by the time you get this letter the tobacco will be ready to plant. Hope you have good luck with it. Bye for now, I'll write later. Tell all I said hello.

Yours truly,
Freddy

P.S. Mom, forget about the 124 Instamatic film for my camera if you have not already sent it. I'll manage to get some. Thank you anyway.

During this time by the river our platoon bivouac encampment did not change much. We were glad that we did not have to hump with our packs as much although we did go out on patrols and ambushes. There were a few incidents within Mike Company that Hawkeye and I took note of. In the early part of May a squad while in an ambush site observed three enemy and engaged them. Another squad while in a night time ambush after midnight observed the launch of four enemy mortar rockets. They swept the area and found the launch site. Another squad engaged the enemy killing two enemy and confiscating an AK47 and a 9mm pistol.

Hawkeye getting his canteen cup ready to chow down on some C-Rations. We fixed our hooch with C-Ration cardboard in anticipation of rain.

One afternoon while a squad was on patrol by the river they observed one enemy body wearing a green shirt and shorts floating in the river. The body was missing the head. We knew that even though our platoon position by the river seemed serene that there were enemy about. We ended up killing about nine enemy in this area and confiscating various enemy rifles and pistols. With regard to the other platoons in Mike Company, we also had some unfortunate Marines who stepped on mines or booby traps and had to be medevaced out.

Hawkeye and I thought one thing a little strange during a time of war. Our platoon was informed that there would be a truce from noon to noon from 18-19 May. There was to be a temporary cessation of offensive operations in celebration of Ho Chi Minh's birthday. We were not too keen on the idea of a cease fire for two days. "Tell that to Charlie," we joked among ourselves.

After about two weeks by the river away from the rest of the company we joined the other two platoons. Mike Company relocated a few miles northwest of Da Nang and fell under the operational control of 3rd Battalion, 1st Marines. There we worked in an area called Elephant Valley. On 23 May we were heli-lifted back to LZ Baldy for three days of rehabilitation. It was the same routine for us back in the rear. We stood hole watch for the office pogues, had cook-outs, conducted rifle and equipment inspections, and during the nights we drank beer and soda to our hearts content. Some Marines even got a chance to see some x-rated movies that a Marine staff sergeant in the rear had managed to commandeer. They watched it merely for amusement. Most importantly, it afforded us the opportunity to shower at the outdoor shower cubicles and wash a month worth of dirt and grime from our filthy bodies. We hand washed our uniforms and hung them on poles, sandbags, and the outside of the hooches to allow them to dry in the hot sun. A half cleaned uniform was better than the soiled and sweat stained utilities against our bodies.

May 23, 1970
8:00 p.m.

Hello Mom, Dad and Larry,

Well how are things back home? I hope just fine. I just got back to Baldy and took a shower, got clean clothes, had a hot meal, and got five letters, so I am feeling like a new man. We'll be going back out the day after tomorrow into the mountains again. I sure hate to hump my heavy pack again but we've got a few more people so maybe it won't be such a load with all the ammunition.

If you all wonder why I haven't written very much this month, it's because I really didn't have time and I was also running short of paper. I finally got this dinky stuff which isn't very strong but will serve the purpose.

We've been pretty busy this month and we've done a good job for God, Corps, and Country. The lieutenant was complementing us on what we've done. We've had some combat action which has led to some vital information. I won't tell you all about it now but I will when I get back home. Don't worry about me over here because there's nothing to worry about. I'm doing fine.

I got the film Mom sent me and I've been taking flicks one after the other. I'll send them home if I get a chance to go the post office while I'm at the base camp. If you have any questions about any of them just ask and I'll explain. One I took of the ocean when I landed near Da Nang before we were assigned to LZ Baldy.

Thanks Dad for the letter. I always like to hear what's going on back on the farm. Hope you have a good season and all the crops do fine. Just don't work too hard. Maybe Jimmy Howard will help out some. I also got a letter from him telling me about his experience when he went frog gigging. Wish I was back there to get in on the action.

Mom, you mentioned something about me going on R&R. Well, if I did get the chance to go on R&R, I'd have to save up on my money and not send it home. I really haven't thought about it much. I'd just as soon stay in Vietnam unless I can go sometime in September or October. That is, if I thought it would do me any good.

I got the locust bloom Larry sent me. When I opened up the letter I smelled something funny but didn't know what it was. I took out the plastic and smelled the aroma. It was mashed up and smelled like rotten potatoes. Ha! Anyway it was thoughtful to send them. I just hope they don't smell like that at home or else everyone would be going around wearing gas masks.

Well, I'll close for now and let you go. I'll write when I get a chance. So bye now and take care.

Have Gun Will Travel,
Freddy

We ended up having one full day of rehab at LZ Baldy. Word was passed that we were going into the Que Son Mountains on a special operation. There had been an earlier plan to spearhead an operation in the mountains but the plans had been changed at the last minute for reasons never disclosed to the squad. This time it was for real. Our mission was to locate and destroy enemy base camps and installations, capture enemy equipment and supplies, and destroy or capture enemy units and personnel that our S-2 Intelligence had reported existed in the Que Son Mountains.

Corporal Ka-Bar informed us that Lance Corporal Travieso was going to stick close to him during this operation. Travieso was to work with and observe Corporal Ka-Bar. When the time came for Corporal Ka-Bar to rotate back to the States, Travieso would take his place as squad leader. We were also told that Hawkeye would be the 1st fireteam leader. That meant that Hawkeye would be my fireteam leader during this operation and have four men under his charge. It motivated me to have Hawkeye as my fireteam leader.

In our company area we readied our 782 gear to go back out to the bush and stood a personnel and equipment inspection. At formation we were issued our ammunition, ordnance, and rations. We humped down to the landing zone loaded with our combat gear and ammunition to board the Ch-46 helicopters. Our squad was hearing a rumor that we were going to land at the base of the mountain and hump our way up one side to the very top.

We loaded aboard the choppers and were soon flying in a westerly direction toward the Que Son Mountains. Down in the valley at the base of the mountain range and on the west side was a lake known to us as Spider Lake. As we flew over Spider Lake the choppers veered upwards and we were fortunate enough to off-load at LZ Buzzard on Hill 845. It was located higher up in the Que Son Mountains. This saved us a hump up the side of the steep terrain. The choppers lifted into the air and slowly disappeared out of our sight. The roar of the engines grew faint in the distance.

I mentioned to Hawkeye, "This is all right. At least we don't have to hump up the side of the mountain."

"Yeah," he replied, "that's a relief."

"Any idea what's next?" I asked Hawkeye.

Hawkeye responded by saying, "The word is that we're supposed to hump over this mountain and look for a hidden cave. Charlie is out there somewhere just waiting for us."

Our squad leader, Corporal Ka-Bar, gathered us together for a brief. He began telling us what was going on. "What we're going to do as a company is to move forward slowly along these mountains right along the top. When we stop on the trail we'll send out patrols down along the sides of the mountain. After we search an area we will form back up with the main body of the company and continue to move across the top. This should be about a ten day operation."

We started humping over the hills. When we got to the top of one ridgeline I could look down the sides of the Que Son Mountains. It seemed strange that on this one particular area there were no leaves on the trees. I figured it was either from constant bombardment or a result of Agent Orange. It was quite eerie to look at. There was a heavily used trail which ran directly across the top of the Que Son mountain ranges. At night we set up OP's (observation posts), LPs (listening posts), and ambushes. Those who were not chosen to go out on specific patrols provided security along side of the trail and slept when the opportunity presented itself. Some actually lay right in the middle of the trail.

At night we discovered bits of the bark off the trees that was laying on the ground. They gave off a glow in the darkness because they were somehow covered with phosphorus. It was almost like an illuminating flash light. The larger pieces would shine bright in the darkness. Sometimes I used them to locate articles within my pack. I could move them about like a flash light; however, I did not make it a habit to move excessively in order to avoid detection by the enemy. If I needed to use the phosphorus coated bark as light to dig in my pack, I would cover myself over with my poncho so that no movement of light could be detected in the darkness. It was a fascination for me. I had not seen anything like it, not even on the farm.

Early one morning as our platoon moved across the Que Son Mountains on patrol we were accompanied by an interrogator translator. Someone found a piece of paper laying on the ground. The Kit Carson Scout interpreted the piece of paper as saying "Ridge trail between our location and Hill 945 is booby trapped." It was suspected that this piece of paper with the warning was placed there about a day before we found it. Needless to say we began to be more cautious in looking for booby traps as we walked along. We knew that the elusive enemy was lurking about somewhere close, but we would have to work at it to find his hideouts and safe havens.

Our squad was also accompanied by a Marine Scout Dog Handler. He was a black Marine corporal by the name of Corporal Martin. He was accompanied by his trusty scout dog, a beautiful German Shepherd by the name of Rebel. He had an uncanny ability of sniffing out VC and NVA. The dog would forewarn his handler and the Marines around him when the enemy was very close, but hidden so well that we could not see them. Corporal Martin and Rebel were to stay with our squad during this particular operation.

We also had a corpsman and machine gun team with our squad. At about mid morning Corporal Martin and the dog were put up front of the column with our point man while our platoon was moving toward our objective. As our platoon moved over the mountain ridges our squad came to an area with dense foliage. We began to come to the top of a crest and came upon a small clearing. As soon as the point man and Corporal Martin walked into the clearing, Rebel stopped and sniffed the air as if something was wrong. We moved down the trail about one hundred meters to see what he was alerting on and started receiving 50-60 rounds of small arms fire from our direct front. The enemy had been waiting to ambush us on a secondary trail.

The squad dove for cover while attempting to return fire but there was not much we could see because the enemy fire had come from down the ridgeline where the ground sloped downward about 75 meters away. The 1st fireteam in the front of the column spread out to return fire. I could hear Rebel up ahead growling fiercely. The machine gunner attached to the squad laid his M60 up on top of a large boulder and fired at the two enemy running away but did not get them. They managed to escape down a bluff and out of sight.

The squad leader gave us the order to cease fire. The 1st fireteam moved forward cautiously searching the area for any more enemy. They found an AK47 that had Rebel's teeth marks and two pair of Ho Chi Min sandals. The German Shepherd had been shot, nevertheless, he found the enemy that had shot him and attacked with a vengeance. The rest of the squad moved forward to assist in the search. I arrived where Corporal Martin was. He was down on the ground holding his M16 rifle with his right hand and hugging the mortally wounded Rebel with his left hand. A battle dressing had been placed over his wounds by a corpsman.

Rebel's tongue was out panting hard as Corporal Martin hugged him tight. Although fatally wounded, the dog seemed consoled with the fact that his master was still by his side. Marines from the squad gathered around to peer down at Rebel. They said very little but I knew they felt sorry for Corporal Martin and the dog. The dog had unknowingly sacrificed his life for the Marines on patrol that day as he would later die from his wounds. Rebel's tour in Vietnam had come to a tragic end. This would be his last operation. It had ended while serving the Marines of Mike Company.

Later that same day at around noon, Hawkeye and I were talking about our mission in the Que Sons. We estimated we were about a klick and a half northeast of Hill 800. The map showed a river below us called the Khe Suoi Noi. There had been other Marine units here in these mountains before Mike Company, but to our knowledge, they had not been able to make the big find that our intelligence personnel had reported. They managed to suppress enemy movement and to locate cave complexes but we were not aware of any major finds of an enemy cache of money, provisions, or weapons. Mike Company had also been in the Que Son Mountains several times before, looking for a major hospital complex, but we had heard that they had been unsuccessful as well.

We heard that the S-2 Intelligence had received their information from a VC defector, one who had surrendered and then provided information about the enemy and acted as a guide to enemy locations. They were called "Hoi Chanh." We also heard that enemy movement had been spotted throughout the area by aerial photographs and Recon teams spotting excessive enemy movement. A Recon team had supposedly reported observing wounded NVA being transported into this area.

The word was passed throughout the ranks that Mike Company was taking a short rest break. We stopped in place along the main trail. Most Marines just plopped down in the middle of the trail. It was a good opportunity to find something to eat before continuing our quest over the top of the mountains. Hawkeye was only a few yards ahead of me and had sat just off the trail next to his pack. I noticed that he was digging for some chow. I took off my pack and dropped it along side the trail in what looked like a comfortable place to rest. Then I sat on the ground and rummaged through my pack for a can of fruit. A quick snack would have to do for now. As I opened a can of fruit cocktail with my John Wayne can opener I tried to get Hawkeye's attention.

"Hell, Hawkeye," I said while still opening my can of C-Rations. "If there is a hospital cave around here there must be signs of smaller trails leading off of this main trail. If we could locate any secondary trails off of this one, it might bring us to the hospital cave after all."

"That's probably right, but no unit that I'm aware of has found it yet," replied Hawkeye. "The bush is just too dense, I reckon."

I reached into my utility cargo pocket and pulled out a plastic spoon and began eating my fruit cocktail. It was very pleasing to the palate as I was hungry from all the humping. Normally I would bury the empty cans after I had finished eating a meal to prevent the enemy from using the cans for booby traps. At this particular moment I became lackadaisical and I just tossed the empty can off behind me and into the bushes. It got hung on a tree branch up the slope of a gradual incline. Realizing what I had done, I decided to throw it further back into the bushes so it wouldn't be so obvious.

I walked over to the branch, grabbed the can, and threw it deeper into the bushes and trees. I watched the spot where the can landed and it still seemed too noticeable. I decided to retrieve the can and bury it; after all, I did not want to be the one responsible for Charlie making a booby trap out of it. Ducking under the tree branches and dodging bushes I made my way to the can several feet from the main trail. I reached down and picked up the can and then started to look around at my surroundings. My eyes were drawn to a slight clearing that looked like another trail running parallel to the main trail. Realizing that I did not have my M16 with me I made my way back through the dense foliage toward the main trail.

Walking back toward Hawkeye I pointed in the direction I had just came from and said, "Hawkeye, it looks like another trail over there."

"Nah, you're just day dreaming," Hawkeye replied.

"No, look for yourself. It does look like a trail running off this main trail," I told Hawkeye.

Hawkeye reached for his M16, stood up, and walked with me back to my pack. I grabbed my M16 and then he followed me into the bushes. We reached the top of the slope where the open area was visible.

"See, over there," I said to Hawkeye as I pointed with the tip of my rifle. "That's has to be another trail."

"Nah," Hawkeye responded, "it's not very well used and there are leaves covering it. Besides, it wouldn't be that obvious anyway."

"Let's take a closer look anyway," I persisted.

"Okay, if you insist," Hawkeye replied.

We walked over cautiously ducking through the bushes and small trees. As we got closer, Hawkeye said, "Naw this can't be a trail. If it was it looks like it hasn't been used for quite awhile."

"Let's go just a little bit further," I replied.

We walked a few more feet and then we saw a foot path that looked well used. As we moved closer the path got even wider.

"Hawkeye, this is a damn main trail here," I said. "See how it is worn down and opens wider as it gets deeper down the side of this ridge."

"Yeah, you're right," Hawkeye admitted. "It sure looks like a well used trail."

"So now what, Hawkeye?" I asked. "What are we going to do? We can't just go down there by ourselves. We may run into a whole NVA Army."

"Let's go back and tell our platoon commander," Hawkeye suggested.

"Yeah okay," I agreed.

We backtracked the same way we had come through the bushes and spindly trees and arrived to where our 782 gear was laying on the trail. Hawkeye used the chain of command and told our squad leader about it. Corporal Ka-Bar selected a couple of other experienced Marines to go and look at it. I showed them where I had found the opening of the main trail. They returned back to the squad leader and one of them said, "Yeah, it's a main trail over there, no doubt about it."

The squad leader then went to the lieutenant and explained to him that I had stumbled upon a main trail just off the trail that Mike Company was on. The platoon commander came over and started looking around and asking questions. He called the company commander on the radio and told him about the trail and requested permission to take a couple of squads down the trail to check it out. The company commander granted permission to do so and the platoon commander designated the 1st and 2nd squads to head up the patrol.

As our squad was sitting along the trail the 1st squad came past us with full combat gear. The point man looked at me and said, "Hey man, where is this fuckin trail they said someone found?"

"Its right over there behind the bushes," I said, while pointing toward the trail which I had stumbled upon.

He proceeded through the bushes and trees and came to a halt. "Shit Man," he said. "There's no goddamned trail."

"Just walk a little further," I insisted.

He walked through the bushes ducking under branches as his squad followed closely behind. They soon disappeared into the vegetation. After about twenty minutes we heard over the radio that the 1st squad had found a cave-like complex that appeared to be a hospital cave. The 2nd squad proceeded down the trail to join them. Our squad was to remain in place and to join them later for security.

I looked at Hawkeye and asked, "Ain't this a bitch? I found the trail leading to the hospital cave and the other squads get to go down and check it out. What kind of crap is this?"

Hawkeye replied, "I don't know, guess that's the way it goes sometimes."

"Yeah, that's the way it goes all right. Its bullshit, that's what it is!" I said angrily.

"Awh yeah, you just want all the glory," Hawkeye said.

"Naw, that's not it," I responded. "We found the trail, at least our squad should be the one to check it out."

Hawkeye shook his head from side to side. "Yeah, I agree with you, but the platoon commander has other ideas. That's his call, I guess."

"His call? Oh yeah, right!" I retorted. "I guess I'm just the low man on the totem pole, a low-life peon!" I continued to mumble under my breath but Hawkeye pretended not to hear. He knew I was a bit upset about how things had unfolded, but we had to live with the decision. After all, what was done was now history and I couldn't change that.

It wasn't long until the other squads had investigated the large cave complex in a rock formation. The cave was approximately 50 feet wide and 75 feet long with a stream running through the center. A search of the cave produced 3 sleeping mats, a cooking pot, and 4 chi-coms. They were all destroyed. Our squad was told to join up with the other two squads. As we caught up to them we were all taken under enemy fire wounding one Marine. We maneuvered around the hospital. We found two AK47s, 1 SKS, 1 M16, 2 chi-coms, 1 LAAW, and miscellaneous 782 gear.

Our squad set up security for the other two squads around the giant boulders that had several entrances down into the caves. As I sat down on the top of a huge boulder, facing outboard and looking for any enemy movement, I overheard some of the Marines from the 1st and 2nd squads talking among themselves. They were having conversations about the NVA hiding out down inside the caves. I thought to myself how I had initially found the trail from atop the mountain that lead to the hospital caves and now the other squads were basking in the glory and taking all the credit. I was still a bit bitter about it but I had to put my feelings aside. I noticed that a Marine in the distance was preparing to go down inside one of the caves. He grabbed his .45 caliber pistol and proceeded to crawl head first down into the cave opening in order to confront any NVA.

I could hear his muffled sound of yelling out to the NVA, "Lai day, lai day, mother fuckers!" he yelled. There was no response from inside the cave. After a short period of time, the Marine crawled back out of the opening and proclaimed, "I'm gonna shoot this mother fucker in his leg, then I'll drag his ass outta there. I can see him. I can feel him. But I can't pull him out, no matter how hard I pull. He seems to be holding on to something in there and I'm limited on the amount of space I have to maneuver in the hole."

The Marines began mumbling among themselves and the next thing I knew the same Marine reentered the cave. After a few seconds everyone around the caves heard, "POW! POW!" The Marine was then seen emerging from the hole dragging a NVA by his feet. He had shot him in the leg. The Marine then turned around and immediately went back into the hole. Another NVA was shot in the thigh. Soon the Marine emerged again dragging out the second NVA. Two other NVA were coached from the cave without any resistance. The male prisoners ranged in ages from about 13 years old to 25 years old.

It was determined that our platoon would stand down and provide a defensive perimeter as security for the other two platoons while they conducted a thorough search of the hospital cave complex. Our platoon was to also send out patrols around the hospital. The other platoons began their search of the caves on a mop-up operation. They began to investigate the hospital caves for more enemy and supplies. The hospital was approximately 150 feet long with about 3 levels that was made from the rock.

The search produced about 100 pounds of documents and about 500 pounds of surgical gear. There was about 400 pounds of rice, 20 pounds of salt, 20 pounds of different foods, 150 pounds of potatoes, 55 gallon barrel of corn, 2 M16 bipods, 1 baseball fragmentation grenade, 1 chi-com, and two 82mm mortar rounds. There was also 2 chi-com grenades tied to a sand-bag. The platoons continued through the afternoon carrying out NVA equipment and tagging them to be transported to the rear. This area was known as DUY XUINN VC Hospital.

The four NVA were turned over to our squad to guard and segregate pending the arrival of the chopper to take them back to the rear for interrogation. We were augmented with a couple of other Marines from one of the other squads. We were told to tag the POW's with capture tags. Each tag would contain the following information: 1) Who - The Capturing Unit, 2) Where – Coordinates of capture, 3) When – Date time group of capture, 4) Why – Circumstances of capture. The prisoners were to be classified as detainees and we were to keep a record of all equipment captured in order that the Hoi Chanh be accredited proper recognition for his services and information.

I began to fill out a capture tag hanging off one of the detainees. Beside the "who" line for capturing unit, I printed PFC Fenwick with my black ball point pen. I looked at it for a few seconds and wondered if I should leave it that way. Then the thought crossed my mind that I might get into trouble for not filling out the tag properly. I scribbled through my name with my pen and printed Mike Company. Then I filled out the rest of the tag.

The prisoners were lined up on the trail waiting for the chopper to arrive. We did not know how the chopper would land for there were huge trees all around the hillsides. There was one small clearing in which the choppers might possibly land. A couple of Marines went toward the clearing with smoke grenades to signal the landing zone. The only way possible for the choppers to land was to put the rear wheels on the ground first and hover the front end in mid air off the side of the hill. Radio contact was made with the inbound choppers and one of the pilots agreed to try the stunt.

While we were standing around guarding the four NVA, a Marine asked one prisoner if he wanted a cigarette while dangling a pack of C-ration cigarettes in front of his face. The NVA nodded his head indicating that he wanted a smoke. The Marine handed him a cigarette and lit it for him. As soon as the NVA took a drag from the cigarette, the Marine mashed it with his hands crumpling the burning cigarette right into the NVA's face. He then asked the NVA if he wanted another cigarette. This time the NVA shook his head no.

Some other Marines sat around mocking the NVA and another Marine grabbed the wounded leg of one of the NVAs and twisted it. "Hurt?" he asked. Every time he twisted the NVA's leg he would wince in pain and let out a whimper that sounded like, "Eeee... hhh!" The Marines standing around thought it was funny hearing a grown man sound like a woman. A couple of the Marines took turns slightly twisting the wounded leg and laughing each time the NVA let out a squeal.

The unfortunate NVA survivors were ridiculed by offering them cigarettes and then refusing to let them have one. They would also offer them a drink of water from their canteens but then poured a little over their heads. At other times they were offered C-Rations only for the Marines to open the cans and eat the food in front of them. It appeared that at this juncture in the Marines combat tour that there was no room in their hearts and minds to bestow pity on the enemy.

Time passed and before we knew it a CH-46 began to descend onto the cleared LZ as a Marine popped a yellow smoke grenade. This was done to mark the location for the chopper to set down on the ground. The chopper hovered above the designated spot blowing yellow smoke in every direction. The pilot had come right over the tree tops. He dropped the ramp on the high ground with the front wheels still hovering in mid air. The propellers were twirling at a very high rate of speed to keep the chopper stabilized. We moved the four detainees toward the chopper. Two Marines on each side of the wounded NVA helped them up the ramp and into the belly of the chopper. Two Marine escorts had been designated to accompany the NVA back to the base camp for interrogation.

Lucky bastards, I thought. Hot chow, cold showers, warm beer, and a sleeping cot awaited the escort Marines back at the base camp. At least they would get one night back at the base camp before they had to rejoin the company on the next resupply chopper. The crew chief lifted the ramp of the CH-46 and the pilot lifted the chopper into the air. I had to lean forward and brace myself by grabbing a small tree and holding on for dear life. It felt as though the wind gusts from the propellers would blow me right off this mountain top. Soon it was out of sight heading back to LZ Baldy. We never knew what happened to the NVA who were sent back to the rear for interrogation. Sometimes we had seen VC returned to the same location where they had been detained once the interrogations were completed.

We remained around the caves for security and set up ambushes that night. The next day while searching through the area Mike Company discovered a POW camp. It was located in a rock complex with about 8 levels and large enough to hold approximately 100 people. We found several documents, 135 piasters, 1 flare gun, 1 US compass, 3 M16 magazines, and 2 NVA packs containing miscellaneous gear.

Later that same day our 3rd platoon was the lead platoon for Mike Company. We found another hospital complex embedded in a rock formation. The hospital had 3 levels and an indoor waterfall. The first level was about 20X10 feet, the second level was about 30X15 feet, and the third level was about 10X10 feet. Another cave situated parallel to the hospital first level was used as an office. Mike 3 continued the search and found 10 cans and 2 bags of medical supplies, large amounts of documents, 5 shirts, 2 shorts, 3 trousers, 350 pounds of rice, 20 pounds of salt, 20 pounds of Vietnamese food, 150 pounds of potatoes, 55 gallon drum of corn, 30 pound barrel of corn, 2 M16 bipods, 2 chi-com booby traps, 1 baseball frag grenade, 1 chi-com, and 2 81mm mortars. All equipment was destroyed except the medical supplies and documents.

During the next few days Mike Company continued our mission in the Que Son Mountains. We found a bunker and another cave complex that consisted of about 25 bunkers and caves ranging in size up to 5'X8'X5'. A booby trap was found consisting of a large can filled with explosives and placed in a water hole next to the trail with a trip wire stretched across the trail. Also one grave was found with 1 NVA body. The complex also contained 6 NVA helmets, 1 US helmet, 1 AK47 magazine, 1 NVA bayonet, 6 wooden practice chi-coms, 1 bottle B1 vitamins, and miscellaneous clothing, documents, and cooking gear.

Our 3rd Platoon moved up Hill 845 to a clearing about three hundred meters away from the caves. Just beyond the clearing the Battalion Command Post had been set up for control and support. They had joined us from the rear and were called "Command Group A." With them they brought a 81 mortar Platoon for on call fire missions. Our Platoon formed a 360 degree perimeter around the top of the hill.

The next morning it was announced on the radio that every gas mask was needed at the Headquarters and Service Company Command Post so they could gas the caves. A chopper arrived with a chemical agent needed to do the job. We passed the word from squad to squad to collect all the gas masks available and to take them to the Command Post. After about an hour, a transmission came over the radio from the H&S company commander again, "Get all those gas masks up here ASAP!" The company commander of Mike Company ordered all his platoon commanders to get a count of every gas mask. All the platoons began to check within their squads. We discovered that we could only muster one gas mask within our entire platoon and that belonged to one of the newbies fresh out from the base camp.

Our squad chuckled out loud at the fact that, we as Marine warriors out in the bush, could not muster more than one gas mask. Everyone in the platoon had either thrown theirs away or never signed for one the base camp. Although Mike Company was almost ninety strong, as a whole we only managed to obtain about five gas masks. Needless to say the Command Post was not too happy about the results. This was because nobody was carrying gas masks and moreover none of the Marines really cared. For the Marine infantry grunt trudging through the mountains, jungles, and rice paddies of Vietnam, it was just an extra piece of gear to lug around. We had never had to use them before anyway.

The H&S company commander swore that every "swinging dick" in the line companies would have a gas mask in their possession for the next combat operation. We found humor in his hostility and attempt to square away the grunt Marines. "Who does he think he is?" I heard some of the Marines saying. "Just another "office pogue" officer who don't know his ass from a hole in the ground. He camps out back at LZ Baldy and very seldom comes to the bush."

Now that Mike Company had found the hospital caves the higher echelon would have to get a piece of the action. At least that is the way some of the Marines felt. They failed to realize that their mission was an important one as well. Some said that the high ranking officers would most likely receive medals for the success of this operation in the Que Son Mountains. Mike Company was constantly in the bush and now it seemed that just because something did not go right, and that it might make someone look bad, there would be hell to pay.

The chemical was finally sprayed throughout the caves by our 3rd Platoon. We were told that it would take effect right away and that it would be at least eight years before any human could survive in the caves. It was just my luck to find the trail leading to the hospital and then the other squads getting the opportunity to make the big discovery. It had taken other units many months of fruitless searching for the hospital in the Que Son Mountains. Although it was my initial discovery of finding the trail leading to the hospital caves, there would be no citations, no awards, or no medals. I was just an infantry Marine doing his job. I knew that I would never be destined for glory, but that I would always have lasting visions.

Mike Company stayed near the caves for another few days keeping watch and periodically checking the surrounding area. It was hoped that by sending out patrols and ambushes we could catch some NVA off guard traveling through the area. For some unknown reason the NVA seemed to know in advance of our operation in the mountains and departed before we arrived. The only ones left behind were the four we had captured that could not travel on foot. To our dismay, we did not encounter any other contacts with the enemy.

The remaining days that we spent on top of the Que Son Mountains gave us a chance to relax by not moving from one position to another. Hawkeye and I shared a fighting hole on the edge of a clearing. The clearing was dusty with no bushes or trees. Each time a resupply chopper landed, the gusts of wind from the rotors would blow all our gear about, and we would have to cover our faces with our hands to avoid getting dust and debris in our eyes. We finally got used to it and began to cuddle all our personal gear as the choppers landed.

The worst part was when we were in the middle of eating a meal and getting it covered with dust and dirt. Since Hawkeye and I shared the same fighting hole, our friendship began to bond even more than before. We would exchange our letters from home and share our inner most thoughts. We had some time to write letters and sent them out with the resupply choppers. We were always eager to receive letters from home. I tried to make a habit whenever possible to answer letters as I received them from mail call, especially the ones from Mom, Dad and Larry, my younger brother.

May 31, 1970
12:00 noon and 20 seconds
Que Son Mountains
(hot & cloudy)

Mom, Dad and Larry,

Well how are things back home? I hope just fine. Guess you all are busy now. I stay pretty busy myself. People probably think I've forgotten about them but I haven't had time to write. I could find the time but they hardly ever take mail out. If they do I never know which chopper.

We're on an operation in the Que Son Mountains and it sure is a wilderness. We've had good luck because we captured four gooks, found two hospitals and a POW camp. They really have been making good use of these hills. The hospitals we found had all sorts of medical supplies, rifles, gook grenades and about anything you can name. There were caves and bunkers all over the hillsides. After we got all the stuff out, we set off charges in them and later a squad gassed them. The medical supplies that we got were estimated to be worth seventy-five to one hundred thousand dollars.

Right now the 3rd Platoon is up on a hill with the H&S Company CP overlooking the place where we found the stuff. They've got a firebase up here with 81mm mortars. The reason 3rd Platoon is up here and the rest of the company is not is because we did most of the work. At least we won't be humping these mountains for a few days. We're supposed to go back to Baldy for rehab in about six days. I hope we do. Rehab is when we go back to the rear for three days to rest and clean up. We spent one day at Rehab before we came on this operation.

I get mad every time a chopper comes in up here. We're right by the landing zone and everything gets blown away every time. I have a hooch made with a poncho liner but it tears down every time a chopper comes in. About ten or twelve choppers arrive and take off each day. They blow dirt and dust everywhere and sometimes we have to go down the hillside looking for our gear.

Wish I would have saved a roll of film to take up here. I asked Janice to send me some more film so she could have some pictures. So you don't have to send any more. Hope you got the film I sent home and hope they turned out good. The blonde headed guy's name is Hawkeye and is a real good friend of mine from Oregon. He's my fireteam leader but is just a PFC like me. He was busted down a rank once. I may be picking up Lance corporal next month. I sure hope so. Send me a picture so I can see how they turned out. My hair was a little long and we were dusty and dirty but what can you expect being over here. It's not too bad though, I don't mind a bit. Don't worry about me because I'm doing just fine.

Tell Dad to let Jimmy Howard read the article I sent him. It tells exactly what we do from day to day. We've just got it easy for a few days up here. Guess we were lucky to be the ones to find the hospitals. One of the gooks we found was thirteen years old but was big enough to carry an AK47 rifle. That's all that matters to the gooks. After this operation we'll go back to our old area, back to the rice paddies, but most of them are dry now since the sun dries up the rain fast.

Well I'd better go now. I hear another chopper coming in. Maybe I can get this off on it. Tell everyone I've been getting their letters but haven't written much. I'll see what I can do when I get back to the Rear. So bye for now, I'll write later.

Your most affirm,
Hillbilly Fred
"from old Kentuck"

After a few days of patrolling around the caves and setting out ambushes it was decided that we would continue our drive across the top of the mountains. H&S Company was heli-lifted back to the rear and Mike Company began its movement to the next ridgeline. We would stop periodically and set out patrols. While the patrols were out along the sides of the hills the remainder of the company would stay on the main trail.

One day as my squad was moving through the dense foliage, we began to receive incoming fire from AK47s. The foliage was so thick we could not see the enemy. The squad began firing frantically into the trees and bushes in order to ward off the enemy attack. For a short few moments the cutting sound of the rounds through the jungle sent a cringe through my spine. As I returned fire I wondered if one of the stray bullets might strike me.

The squad leader yelled for us to fire in the automatic mode. This we all did and I remember emptying a full magazine in a matter of seconds. By now leaves and branches from trees were floating slowly to the ground. The command to cease fire was given and we began to move forward to locate any enemy dead. Luckily we did not receive any casualties. As we approached the area where we had received the enemy fire, there laid two dead NVA soldiers. Immediately we scanned the area for others.

There were no others to be found. We confiscated their rifles and packs and left the bodies to decay in the Vietnam wilderness. We radioed back to the CP and requested artillery fire in the direction which the enemy had retreated. We were told to return to the CP as the incoming rounds would be

A ridgeline in the Que Son Mountains. On the other side I found a trail that led Mike Company, 3rd Battalion, 7th Marines to a NVA hospital.

too close to remain in the area. We arrived back on the main trail and I located my pack. We sat down and began to chow down on some C-Rations and Corporal Ka-Bar got a count on how many M16 rounds each Marine had. We then distributed them equally among the squad and got supplementary ammo from the two other squads in the other platoons.

As I reloaded my magazines we heard the squad radio operator say, "Shot out, artillery is on its way." We heard the rounds bursting below us in the area where the NVA had been spotted. A readjustment of fire was made by the artillery battery and they adjusted their fire another one hundred meters. Five rounds dropped in the new location. We could tell that a forward observer near the CP was adjusting the fire. He adjusted one more time another fifty meters. Then it came over the radio "Fire for effect." Hawkeye and I laid back on our packs and listened to the horrific barrage and knowing that our aggressors would succumb to the blasts. It was a familiar and welcomed sound to the Marines of Mike Company. Another squad would patrol the area after the fire mission in search of NVA bodies.

We received word that a chopper was coming in. It landed and took off almost immediately. Then it was passed along the Marines on the trail that a pay officer had arrived from the Base Camp to give us our pay checks. I thought to myself what a way to receive pay. I was laying back on my pack with the sun shinning in my face. The warmth from the sun began to put me to sleep. Suddenly not knowing what was going on around me, a Marine first lieutenant approached me and asked,

"Hey Marine, want your pay check or not?"

I responded, "Yes, Sir!"

He reached into the brown satchel he was carrying and pulled out a stack of checks that were wrapped with a rubber band.

"Name?" he asked.

"Fenwick," I replied.

He began to thumb through the checks. "Ah, here we go," he said. "Fenwick, 92 dollars!"

I asked him if I had to receive the check in the bush or if he could take it back and have it added to my pay records.

He said, "It's up to you." You can have it now or I can have it run on the books for the next pay day. Actually it's a real pain in the ass since the check has already been cut."

"Okay, Sir," I said. "I'll take the check now and mail it out. Will you be able to take it back to the mail room if I write a quick letter?"

"Tell you what, Marine," he said. "Go ahead and sign for it. I have to deliver the rest of the checks and when I'm done I will come back up the trail and pick up your letter. Make it fast though, because I don't have much time."

"Aye Aye Sir," I said. "Can do easy."

The lieutenant went from one Marine to the other giving them their pay checks. Some stuffed them in their packs while others rapidly placed then in an envelope to be mailed home. Some of the other Marines did not receive a pay check. They had asked the rear office personnel to carry their pay over on the books from one pay day to the next.

June 3, 1970

Hello All,

Well how does this find everyone? I hope you are doing fine. Guess by the time you get this letter Dad will have finished setting the tobacco. Hope it turns out good. I've been getting the letters from home but can't find time to write very often. I owe "boo coo" letters to people now. Maybe I can catch up on some of my writing when I get back to the Rear. We're supposed to go in for Rehab around the 10th but you never can tell.

Guess I've told you all I'm on an operation in the Que Son Mountains. I don't know the name of the operation, but I don't guess they've named it yet. Anyway Mike Company has really been cleaning up. We found two Viet Cong hospitals, an R&R center and a POW camp, and all kinds of weapons. We got paid in the field again, so I'm sitting right on the side of a mountain and you can't see fifteen feet in front of you, except when we look down the trail. But it's really shady and we've stopped for about two hours. To-morrow we'll hump down into the valley.

Mom, I don't know if I have to put "Pay to the order of Mrs. Elmer Fenwick" on the back of the check or not, but I thought may-be I'd have to in order for you to put it in the bank. Anyway, thanks a million for doing it for me. I really appreciate it.

Well, sorry this is so short but I have to hand my check in so it will go out today. So bye for now, always thinking of everyone.

As ever,
Frederick

I had just sealed the envelope when the lieutenant appeared again com-ing back up the trail. He was collecting letters as he moved along slowly. I noticed the .45 caliber pistol he carried on his waist. I thought to myself, not much protection if his chopper was ever shot down. He collected my letter and I reclined back on my pack. I was thankful I was able to get a letter out that contained my pay check instead of carrying it around and risking losing it or getting it mutilated. I heard a chopper land at the LZ that one of the pla-toons had cleared and it was off again in a matter of minutes.

The following morning we began our slow movement over the mountain ranges with the intent of descending into the valley below. We had one more hill to negotiate before we began our decent. As we were struggling to climb a steep embankment with rough bushes and huge rocks, a sniper round hit in the dirt, not more than fifteen feet in front of me.

"Take cover!," Corporal Ka-Bar yelled.

We all stopped and lay down in place looking across the hillsides to see if we could spot the enemy sniper. It was quiet for about five minutes so the company began to move again.

"Pweeuu!" Another shot rang out that zinged over our heads. Then there came a "Craack," that distinctive sound of a SKS single shot rifle. It was the type that Charlie carried when he was not carrying an AK47 Assault Rifle. Mostly the VC had these types of weapons in addition to AK47s while the NVA were known to carry mostly the AK47s as individual weapons.

"That son-of-a-bitch!" Travieso yelled out. "We've got some commie VC down in the treelines taking pot shots at us. Anyone see where it came from?"

"I can't see nothin," Hawkeye replied. "He's got to be over on the next ridge. If we can spot the muzzle flash we could have a good chance of knocking him out with one of the machine guns."

Just then another round hit the dirt about thirty feet below us. "Fuckin asshole!" Travieso screamed. "You couldn't hit nothin if it was five feet in front of you, you commie bastard!"

I looked over at Travieso and saw the frustration and anger in his facial expression. "Yeah," I agreed, "he couldn't hit the broad side of a barn."

Hawkeye chimed in and replied, "That's the way to tell him Kentucky."

We both laughed at the fact that I was the farm boy with the Kentucky accent and telling Travieso that our enemy couldn't hit the side of a barn.

Corporal Ka-Bar interrupted and said, "He may not be able to hit the broad side of a barn, but all it takes is for one stray round to find its target, and we've got a casualty on our hands." Just then the word was passed down to all the radio operators that it was time to move. The radio operator relayed the message on to Corporal Ka-Bar. "Okay, let's move out!" he commanded. "Stay alert!"

I slowly stood up while crouching in a slump somewhat attempting to duck my head a little. I then realized that it was no use. If the sniper was going to hit me he would have done it with the first shot. I rose upright and continued moving forward with my squad.

Travieso yelled in the direction that the shots had come from. "Go ahead you mother fucker! Try it again! No balls, you fuckin gook!"

"Ka-powww!" Almost immediately another rifle shot rang out. It went cutting through the air just above our heads. It reminded me of pulling targets in the butts on the rifle range when first you would hear the zing of the projectile cutting through the target followed by the pop of the rifle up on the firing line.

"You stinking, slant-eyed, rice-propelled, mother fuckin gook!" Travieso screamed. "You piece-a-shit! Take this, asshole!"

Travieso began to fire his M16 into the direction where he thought the sniper was located. Then one of the machine gunners opened up and began firing frantically while scouring the entire area.

"Cease Fire! Cease Fire!" came the command from the platoon commander. "Knock it off! You can't hit what you can't see!"

The firing stopped as abruptly as it had started. The platoon commander informed us that the company commander ordered us to move out and forget about the sniper. He would call for artillery to silence the sniper once the company got to the top of a specific ridgeline where we were heading.

"What a bunch of bullshit!" Travieso said angrily. "I say we send out a patrol and wax that fucker's ass!"

"Nah," Corporal Ka-Bar replied, "We would never find him in these mountains. He's probably got tunnels and caves in these hills that would come out in China."

"Good," Hawkeye said snickering, "Let's go to China for a little R&R!"

"OOORAH," said Wagenbaugh, "I could use a little pussy right about now."

"Couldn't we all?" stated Corporal Ka-Bar.

We continued up the hillsides and the sniper would fire about every five minutes. We ignored him. I thought to myself, here we are being shot at by some VC and no one is paying any attention to him. Guess the VC never received marksmanship training as we had during boot camp.

"Couldn't hit nothin," I mumbled to myself. Just then one of the Marines in another Platoon up front caught a stray round. The VC sniper had hit his target.

"Corpsman! Corpsman up!" came a scream from one of the Marines.

We all passed the word down the line for a corpsman. Almost immediately one of the Navy corpsman came running as fast as he could past the Marines in column. As he passed close to me I said, "Go gettum Doc!"

"Fuckin gooks," he replied while almost out of breath, "I didn't join the Navy to do shit like this, you grunts are bad news!"

Hawkeye was in front of me and he looked back over his shoulder and said, "Doc, you ain't no Sailor, you're a goddamn Marine."

"Fuck you Hawkeye," the Doc quipped as he continued on up the hill at a gallop.

"Good old Doc," Corporal Ka-Bar said. "He's one hellava guy! Don't know what we would do without our Navy corpsman."

"Yep," I replied, "they are some brave men risking their lives for us. I respect the hell out of them."

"Yeah and they only carry their medical supplies and a .45 pistol," added Hawkeye. "I'd do anything for our Doc's."

Word was passed down the chain of command that the sniper had only nicked a Marine in his side. He was bandaged by the Doc and was helped to the top of the hill crest by two other Marines while the Doc assured him that he would be all right. The company commander radioed back to our Fire Support Base at LZ Ryder. He requested that HE rounds be dropped on the hillsides where we had been receiving the sniper fire.

In about twenty minutes the artillery rounds from the fire support base began exploding on target. An adjustment was called in by the company commander and we could hear his voice on the radio, "Fire for Effect!" We watched from our fighting positions as the area became saturated with artillery fire.

"Get some!" Travieso yelled. "Give that fuckin gook some lead for dinner."

As each round landed on target the Marines on the hillsides could be heard saying, "OOORAH! Get Some, Arty!"

We had hoped that the VC had been blown to pieces but there was no way of ever knowing. We didn't receive any more sniper rounds after the barrage. After the bombardment we heard choppers in the air. There was a CH-46 accompanied by four Huey Gunships. Two gunships veered off and started spraying the same area with M60 machine gun fire and rockets. The other two gunships stayed with the CH-46 and circled our position while the CH-46 landed. The chopper dropped off some M79 high explosive rounds along with other munitions and then lifted off with the wounded Marine on board. The gunships joined the CH-46 in mid air, two on each flank. It resembled a mother duck and her ducklings flying in formation.

Later in the morning our squad went on patrol around one side of the mountain. We discovered 4 chi-com grenades rigged with a trip wire and a M79 HE round set with a pressure detonating device. The chi-coms were located off the sides of the trail while the M79 was in the center. We blew them in place and soon went back to join up with the company. I knew that if I wanted to see another rehab back at LZ Baldy that I had better remain very vigilant while I was still up in the Que Son Mountains.

Word was passed down the chain of command that we would remain in a defensive posture throughout the night so the Marines of Mike Company began to dig fighting holes. We had to use the picks on our E-tools in order to dig our fighting positions in the hard rocky landscape. After continuous digging for about an hour I was satisfied that my hole was deep enough although it was only about two and a half feet deep. I decided not to dig a sleeping hole being as the ground was so hard. I felt that if we received incoming during the course of the night that my fighting hole would suffice. I would sleep there.

Throughout the night a fifty per cent watch was established which meant half the company was awake while the other half slept. Every fifteen minutes, Marines from the outer limits of the perimeter would use the M79 grenade launcher to fire HE rounds down the hillsides and into the gorges below. Marines on watch would also holler, "Outgoing" when they threw hand grenades out of the perimeter and into the darkness. At other intervals the various platoons would shoot up illumination rounds from the M79s. It helped that on this particular night the moon cast light all around the hillsides.

At around 2300 Wagenbaugh was heard speaking loudly to the squad, "Gooks, Gooks, I hear movement!"

Corporal Ka-Bar rose from his sleep and asked, "How many do you think are out there?"

"I don't know," replied Wagenbaugh, "sounds like only a couple."

Without hesitation Corporal Ka-Bar said, "Throw a frag grenade."

"Outgoing!" yelled Wagenbaugh as he threw the grenade from his fighting position and down the hillside. It exploded with a muffled sound.

"Hear anything now?" Corporal Ka-Bar asked.

"Nah", replied Wagenbaugh, "whoever it was must be booking out of Dodge City by now."

"Then I'm going back to sleep," said Corporal Ka-Bar.

I wasn't on watch during this commotion and was trying to catch a few zz's. Since I didn't dig a sleeping hole, I was laid back on the ground next to my fighting hole with poncho under me and poncho liner covering me. I rolled over to one side and attempted to find a comfortable position on the hard ground. I could hear the rest of the squad settling back down also. We figured Wagenbaugh was just hearing things because he always was a little on the jittery side. I began to think of pleasant things like being back on Cherry Hill Farm in order to relax enough to get some sleep. Then my dream world came crashing down as I awoke to reality and heard a M79 HE round explode just beyond the perimeter immediately followed by the explosion of a hand grenade.

"What the hell, Wagenbaugh?" Corporal Ka-Bar yelled. "How come you didn't warn us with "Outgoing" before you start a war?"

"Some commie bastard just threw a rock at me. I could tell it was a rock bouncing across the ground by the illumination."

Corporal Ka-Bar was his calm self as he muttered, "Oh, then it must be rock apes. They won't hurt you."

"Rock apes?" Wagenbaugh asked. "You mean fuckin monkeys?"

"Yep," replied Corporal Ka-Bar. "They have been known to lob grenades back into the perimeter after you pull the pin and throw it out. So don't give them anymore ammo so I can get back to sleep."

"Fuckin monkeys throwing grenades, that's a bunch of shit," replied Wagenbaugh. "Ain't no such thing as rock apes."

"Just ask any of the old salts around here, they will tell you the same," Corporal Ka-Bar replied while yawning."

"Have you ever seen a rock ape?" I asked Corporal Ka-Bar.

"No Fenwick, I haven't, but the rock apes are for real," he replied.

"I can't believe this," I said. "I have heard stories about rock apes from other Marines, but I always thought it was a myth. We need those monkeys on our side. With a little training they could give Charlie a hard road to travel."

Hawkeye intervened, "Yeah, we should sign them up with the New York Mets."

We settled back down, some on watch, and some trying to get back to sleep. I covered my head with my poncho liner to help ward off the never ending nuisance of the mosquitoes. I could hear the high pitched sound of the mosquitoes flying about my head and could feel them biting through the poncho liner. As I was about to doze off to sleep by mere exhaustion, I heard a voice saying, "Fenwick, it's your turn for watch." It was Wagenbaugh. I heard him say that the blooper and rounds were next to me and that I had better not go back to sleep. I heard him scurrying away so he could get some shut eye.

I rose slowly from under my poncho liner and sat up. Mosquitoes were flying all about my head getting into my ears and eyes. I reached for my pack and pulled out a bottle of insect repellant. I rubbed some on my face, neck, and arms. Then I slid down into my fighting hole for security watch. I looked at my wrist watch. It was a little after midnight. I would stand hole watch for the next two hours. The morning passed without incident and I didn't hear anymore rustling in the bushes. I was keeping a keen ear out for the so-called rock apes.

I knew that the NVA, VC, and sometimes Vietnamese kids would probe the front lines at night. I even saw the occasional pig run across our fields of fire, but I found it hard to believe that there were apes in the mountains that would lob rocks or grenades at you. So whether the story of rock apes was fact or fictional, I never saw one. Another Marine relieved me at the end of my watch and I finally could get a little shut eye before we started a new day in the Que Son Mountains.

At around 0600 I began to hear the squad steering about. I could hear the familiar sounds of C-Ration cans being opened with the aid of the trusty P-38 can opener, nicknamed the "John Wayne." Supposedly the nickname came about when the actor was shown in a training film opening a can of K-Rations. Regardless of how it came about, the name stuck. Every single Marine in Mike Company carried a John Wayne, you could count on that.

As I lay in an uncomfortable fetal position, I heard Corporal Ka-Bar say, "Okay, rise and shine. We've got another glorious day ahead of us in the Nam. Travieso, make sure the squad is up."

Travieso started to call each Marine in our squad by name. "Hey Hawkeye, reveille. Wagenbaugh, reveille. Fenwick, reveille." I didn't move and did not answer even though I had heard Travieso. "Fenwick, are you awake?" Travieso asked. I still did not answer as I was very tired from standing watch and getting very little sleep during the night. "You gonna sleep all day?"

"Naw, I'm awake," I finally responded. "I am afraid to move my poncho liner because I feel the moisture from the dew. It feels like it rained on me last night. My poncho liner is almost soaking wet. Nothin like being wrapped in a wet blanket."

Hawkeye said, "Don't worry, the sun will dry you out most rickety tick."

I took both hands and flipped the poncho liner back and away from my face. I could feel the cool moisture running down my arms. The poncho I had slept on was wet. I had slept with my utility jacket on with the sleeves rolled up. I felt a sudden chill on my bare arms and unrolled both sleeves. In the meantime, Travieso continued on with his roll call throughout the entire squad.

"Is everybody up?" Corporal Ka-Bar mumbled.

"Yeah," Travieso replied, "everybody but you, let's shake a leg."

I looked and saw that Corporal Ka-Bar was still laying under his poncho and not moving.

"Leadership by example," I said. "Rise and shine, Corporal Ka-Bar."

"I feel like laying here all day," he said.

Hawkeye replied, "If you don't get up we'll feed you to the rock apes."

"Bring them little buggers on," Corporal Ka-Bar replied. As he slowly sat up he said, "I can eat one raw right now because I'm so hungry."

We all snickered at the idea. Corporal Ka-Bar then reached into his pack and pulled out a can of ham slices and some crackers. He dug a little deeper into his pack and brought out a small transistor radio. He placed it carefully on a rock next to his fighting hole. With one hand he began to tune the radio in order to pick up a broadcasting radio station.

By now I had decided to brush my teeth even before I ate chow in order to get the morning taste out of my mouth. I had run out of toothpaste so I began to brush my teeth with the salt that I had saved from a C-Ration pack. I wondered if my teeth would ever be as healthy as when I left boot camp or if they might just rot out completely. There was no time in the Nam for dental appointments. As I was swishing my mouth with water I heard a familiar voice coming from Corporal Ka-Bar's transistor radio.

"Goooooooood Morning, Vietnam." The greeting from the radio announcer was followed by music that started off sounding like, "Doo… doot… doot… doot… doo… doot." It was a catchy little tune.

I watched as Corporal Ka-Bar began swaying his upper body back and forth to the music.

"Practicing for the two step?" I asked.

"No," he replied. "Just the watusi. Gotta keep in practice for my girlfriend back home."

Hawkeye joined in, "You remember the old chant from boot camp don't you?" He began chanting in a musical tone. "Ain't no use in going home… Jody's got your girl and gone… Ain't no use in looking back… Jody's driving your Cadillac."

When Hawkeye finished his lyrics, I finished it off by calling cadence as the drill instructors had done in recruit training. "Lo Right Leeefftt… Lo Righta Leeefftt… Left Right Leeefftt… Ah Lefty Righta… Lo."

Corporal Ka-Bar shook his head and smiled. "What a bunch of clowns I have in my squad. You guys are crazy."

"Ain't nothin but a thang," Hawkeye said laughing.

I felt a sudden sense of pride in my squad. For myself, I was happy to be a part of this elite group of brave men. Just then we heard the platoon commander call out, "Squad leaders up!"

"Oh Shhhit," said Corporal Ka-Bar, "here we go again."

He placed his can of ham slices next to his transistor, stood up, and started walking to the CP for the squad leaders meeting. Without looking back Corporal Ka-Bar said, "Don't nobody fuck with my chow!"

"Not a problem," replied Travieso. "I'll keep a real good eye on it."

"That's what I'm afraid of," Corporal Ka-Bar replied.

Some music was playing over the transistor. "That song reminds me of home," Hawkeye said. "I can't wait to get back to the world, back to the rolling hills of Oregon." Hawkeye tried to sing along and shake his head with the rhythm of the music. The song was by the Herman's Hermits released in 1965 titled "Mrs. Brown, You've Got A Lovely Daughter." I didn't think Hawkeye was doing the song justice as I listened to his version of the song.

"I wish they would play my favorite song on the radio," I said.

"What's that?" Hawkeye asked.

"The Old Gray Mare," I replied.

"Let's hear it," Hawkeye said.

Since my father had two gray mules on the farm that he used often to cultivate the corn, tobacco, and to till the garden, the tune suited him just right. I sang the lyrics like I had heard my father sing it many times before.

"Well the old gray mare, she ain't what she used to be, ain't what she used to be, ain't what she used to be, the old gray mare, she ain't what she used to be, many long years ago. Well the old gray mare, she doobled on the singletree, doobled on the singletree, doobled on the singletree, the old gray mare, she doobled on the singletree, many long years ago."

When I had finished Hawkeye laughed. "You're behind the times," he said. "Don't think I've heard that one before." Then he continued singing along with the radio.

I heard Travieso say, "Sing it again, Sam!"

We laughed at the comical way Hawkeye was singing along. Then coming from the transistor radio we heard the beginning of the song, "Sunshine of Your Love" by the British blues-rock band, Cream. I made the comment that I loved to hear Eric Clapton play the guitar. No one answered me. They were too engrossed in the music. For a few minutes we were still and quiet just trying to listen to the lyrics of the song. I heard one Marine say it reminded him of his girlfriend back in the States.

At times we felt abandoned and lonely, relying only on correspondence from home and broadcasts through the small transistor radios. It reminded us of the good old USA. It was amazing how a small transistor radio could remind you that a civilized world was still out there. For a few moments it was a way we could forget about the loneliness and isolation of being in Vietnam. Even in the most remote places we could hear the broadcasts coming from the tiny transistor radios. What a world was out there, I thought to myself.

There was music and broadcasts in different languages. As a Marine thumbed through the channels he could receive stations such as programs from the United States, Washington-The Voice of America, Australia, Philippines, London, and Paris. There were local stations as well. There were also the sounds from the enemy camps of Radio Peking broadcasting the ranting shouts of the Red Communist demonstrating against us or the reading of casualty list over Radio Hanoi read by Hanoi Hati.

We could hear Hanoi Hati broadcasting with such phrases such as "Down with the Americans! Vietnam will win this war! Long live the military friendship between the Chinese and the Vietnamese people! Long live Chairman Mao Tze Tung and President Ho Chi Minh!" This was usually followed by her audacity of transmitting over the radio network, "Radio Peking wishes you all a pleasant day!" Our favorite was the reassuring sounds of home away from home, good old Armed Forces Radio. They saluted the various units in the field, news, and sports. Some news was transmitted live, ten thousand miles away from home.

Corporal Ka-Bar returned from his squad leader's meeting with the platoon commander. He turned off his transistor and said, "Saddle up, we're moving off this hill. Gonna hump down to the valley and set up a defensive posture for a few days."

"Oh great!" Travieso said, "Nothing like a good hump in the morning with a heavy pack on your back."

"No choppers this time?" I asked.

"Nope, no choppers for you Fenwick," Corporal Ka-Bar replied. "Since you are a farm boy this should be easy stuff for you."

"It's never easy," I responded. "Even on the farm I worked my hands to the bone."

We started packing our haversacks to get ready for the hump down the side of the mountain. We could tell it was going to be a hot day. As soon as I was packed up I stood up and picked up the heavy pack to see how heavy it was.

"Good grief, my pack is heavy," I said.

"Hey Fenny!" Corporal Ka-Bar shouted out. "Come over here. I have something else for you to carry."

"Oh, no you don't," I responded. "I already have enough of gear to carry. I don't think I could fit one more thing in or on this dinky ass pack."

"You'll like this," Corporal Ka-Bar said in return. "Come on over and I'll give it to you."

"Give me what?" I asked.

"Some black and white film for your instamatic camera," Corporal Ka-Bar said.

"What?" I asked. "Film? You actually have film for my camera?"

"Yeah," he said. "My camera takes the same kind of film as yours. I bought this black and white film when I was back at LZ Baldy and haven't used it. I'm getting too short to take anymore photos anyway. By the time I get them developed, I'll be on the Freedom Bird out of Nam."

"You are not serious," I said. "You are actually going to give me your film?"

"Yep, you can have it," he said. "It is my little present to you."

I walked over to where Corporal Ka-Bar was sitting on the ground next to his pack. He handed me the film.

"You may want to take a few flicks on our way down Hill 800," Corporal Ka-Bar said. "That is if you can see five feet in front of you. The area we will be humping down is very dense."

"Thank you much Corporal Ka-Bar," I said. "I really appreciate this."

"Don't mention it," he said. "I hope you get some good flicks.

"I'll try," I replied.

I turned and walked back to my pack. I knelt down, located my 124 Instamatic camera, popped open the cover, and inserted the black and white film. I placed my camera inside my left pocket of my flak jacket so I could get to it easily when a photo opportunity presented itself. I thought about Corporal Ka-Bar giving me his film. What a genuine and personable individual he was. I then realized that he was getting short in Nam and that I needed to observe his combat prowess. I could learn from him by study, practice, and observation until he rotated back home. I felt a lump in my throat that Corporal Ka-Bar thought that much of me to give me his film. I was proud and privileged to have him as my squad leader.

We began our movement through the dense foliage and started our descent down Hill 800 which had a LZ on top of it called Landing Zone Crow. I thought it an odd name for a landing zone, but figured the name suited it well, because as far as I was concerned the birds could have it. It was very hot and muggy as we humped down through the thick trees and bamboo. I could barely see in front of me.

I stopped to take a picture of four squad members. As I looked through the lens of the camera I could not make out even one human figure and they were only a few feet away from me. I snapped the picture in hopes of proving just how thick the vegetation really was. We slowly trudged along while taking a few breaks on the way down. The humidity below the canopy of the trees made it difficult to stay cool and it made for a very exhausting journey.

We finally made it to the bottom of the hill and set up our defensive position for the night. I took off my helmet, heavy pack, flak jacket, and green T-Shirt and dropped them on the ground at my feet. I was sweating from head to toe. Hopefully I could cool off a lot faster without a shirt on. I reached inside my pack and pulled out my camera and then I asked Hawkeye to take a picture of me and Corporal Ka-Bar. We both posed for the photo and then set about digging our sleeping holes and fighting holes.

That night the enemy was probing our perimeter and throwing chi-coms at us. With all our return fire and illumination being fired throughout the night we didn't get much sleep. The next day we went out on patrol around the surrounding area. Not far from where our position was located we found seven booby traps. Corporal Ka-Bar told us that we had to be very careful in this area and to keep alert for them. Fortunately, we managed not to trip any while we were in this position.

Mike 3 Charlie started stirring around one morning as the sun began to rise. It looked like it was going to be a decent day. My poncho was wet from the night dew so I spread it out over some bushes in order for it to dry. I also shook out my poncho liner and spread it out as well. The good thing about the poncho liners was that they would dry very quickly. I then started looking for something in my assortment of C-Ration cans to eat for breakfast. I settled on some ham slices, cheese, and crackers. I also thought I might heat up some C-Ration coffee to help warm me up.

Travieso was moving around waking everyone up so they could get started with the business at hand. He came to where Corporal Ka-Bar was laying on the ground underneath his poncho. I noticed that the poncho was quivering and shaking.

"Get up Corporal Ka-Bar," Travieso said. "It's another glorious day in the Nam." Corporal Ka-Bar did not answer. Travieso grabbed the foot of the poncho and shook it a little. "Come on, get up Corporal Ka-Bar, you have to set the example for your fellow Marines," Travieso said. Still there was no answer from Corporal Ka-Bar and it was obvious that he was shaking underneath his poncho. Travieso pulled back the poncho and said, "Corporal Ka-Bar, are you okay?" Travieso saw that Corporal Ka-Bar's body was in a convulsion like state. "He's shaking like a leaf. Fenwick, go get the corpsman."

I immediately stopped stirring my coffee and went to fetch our platoon corpsman. The Doc came over with his medical bag and checked Corporal Ka-Bar's condition. "He is convulsing," the Doc said. "I'll inform the platoon commander that he needs to be medevaced out of here. It looks like he has battle fatigue."

I wondered if there was such a thing and if I would be prone to battle fatigue sometime during my tour in Vietnam. I hoped not because Corporal Ka-Bar did not look good. He was jerking and twitching violently by now and was not responding to Travieso or the corpsman. I felt totally helpless as there was nothing I could do and I hated seeing my squad leader in this state. A medevac chopper was called and Corporal Ka-Bar was taken back to the rear for some medical attention and rest. I feared that we may not see him again.

In a couple of days we were choppered back to LZ Baldy to commence a period of rehabilitation for about three days. Corporal Ka-Bar rejoined the squad after a few days of rest. I was glad that he was back with us for I trusted and respected Corporal Ka-Bar. He was a good combat leader. As we were preparing to go back out to the bush we got the word that some enemy had shot down a helicopter at FSB Ross. Mike Company was sent out that night to provide security for the firebase. They had expected a big enemy push to overrun the base camp.

"Here we go again," Travieso said. "Better check your ammo."

We packed up and soon the choppers arrived. We flew to Firebase Ross and setup defensive positions in the bunkers. The office pogues manning the fighting positions went back to their normal routine of pushing papers while the grunts of Mike Company took over security. Arrangements were made for us to get some hot chow from the mess hall but showers and clean clothes would have to wait. Somehow mail was delivered to all of us manning the perimeter at Firebase Ross. We guarded the base camp for a day. During this time we sent out patrols around the perimeter and watched air strikes pound the surrounding areas. If the enemy was planning to overrun the base camp, I'm sure that the air strikes had thwarted their plans.

June 10, 1970

Hello Mom, Dad and Larry,

I got Mom's letter tonight so thought I'd write to you before I go back to the bush. We leave tomorrow but I don't know where we're going. Somewhere in the lowlands I suppose. We were supposed to leave today but we had to go to Landing Zone Ross last night for security. Someone said a gook shot down a chopper, but I don't know if they did or not.

Well Dad, hope you are through setting tobacco by this time. I guess it's the same old story every year isn't it? Maybe you'll have a good crop this year. I sure hope so. I hope everything turns out real fine for you.

Mom, thanks for the pictures. I guess they turned out pretty good. You can have the rest. I wouldn't have room for them anyway. I put the others in my wallet in some plastic so they'll keep dry. You don't have to worry about me and the gook kids over here. I watch them pretty close even though they're no harm to us. That was just in the civilized area and mostly all they want is a smoke or chop-chop (chow). I never give them much because I can't afford to. They just give the smokes to their mamasans anyway. Wait, I'll take that back. You'd be surprised how young these kids start smoking. Usually they smoke what they can get their hands on.

Seems like you're curious about my ingrown toe nails. Well, they haven't given me much trouble over here and if they do I'll have something done about it. As long as they don't bother me though, I'll just let them go. Maybe I'll get them straighten out when I get back to the States.

Mom, I know you mean well, but don't send me another cake or any candy as far as that goes. Believe it or not, I don't like much sweets anymore. I'd much rather have some good old biscuits. Have you got any more sausage in the jar? A couple would sure go good with a biscuit. But you don't have to send sausage just because I said that. I'm doing pretty good over here when it comes to chow. It's just that eating the same thing all the time gets kinda old. We usually have good meals back in the rear but we're never back there that often.

Well, I'll sign off for now and will write later. I got a letter from Janice. Bye for now, everyone take care.

As ever,
Freddy

Mike Company deployed back to the bush the next day. We ended up in Antenna Valley. While we were getting helicopter drops at our location a chopper took enemy small arms fire from a distance. It returned to LZ Baldy without landing. The next night while we were in a night time position we received 60-80 small arms fire from the opposite side when the chopper had taken small arms fire. Mike Company returned fire with small arms and 60mm mortars. Artillery was also called for. The next day we did not find any dead enemy. That afternoon our platoon spotted 2 NVA/VC wearing green utilities with packs and weapons about 400 meters away from us. We commenced firing with small arms fire and then swept the area. Again we didn't find any dead enemy. It seemed to be a cat and mouse game between the Marines and the enemy.

Two days later and to our total surprise, we were heli-lifted to the low-lands close to a river called the Suoi Cho River. Our position was near Hill 65 and about three klicks from Route 535. Route 535 was a road that lead from LZ Baldy to FSB Ross heading southwest. We were going to send out patrols during the day and ambushes at night. On the first morning at our new position the 2nd platoon was on the move to a blocking force position. They spotted about 5 NVA/VC wearing black pajamas. They were carrying packs and weapons. Although the 2nd platoon fired at the enemy, when they swept the area they did not find anything.

Mike 3 Charlie went out on a patrol that afternoon. Travieso volunteered to walk as point man. The rest of the squad was glad that Travieso would be the one to lead our patrol for he was always very alert. Corporal Ka-Bar briefed the squad and we readied our combat gear to engage any enemy that may be lurking about. We started heading southwest, crossed over a rice paddy, and came upon a treeline. As we started to enter the treeline, Travieso halted the squad and whispered for Corporal Ka-Bar to come forward to the front of the squad patrol. Corporal Ka-Bar was about center of the squad so he could more effectively direct our firepower. He gestured for the rest of us to stay put while he moved forward to join Travieso. The rest of the squad remained very quiet as we studied and watched the reactions of our combat leaders.

Corporal Ka-Bar and Travieso were extremely cautious as if sensing immediate danger. I had previously observed the same gestures and facial expressions of Travieso. They were signs that there was risky business ahead and a time to take matters seriously. Travieso had made the comment on

Mike 3 Charlie questioning suspected VC. After checking a nearby village we found 2 VC in a tunnel. Typical rice paddy scene in the Quang Nam Province.

various occasions, that he could actually smell the enemy at a distance, as Chief had also attested. Since Chief had rotated back to the States, Travieso was now our primary point man, who had a real cunning ability to detect enemy presence. He claimed that the enemy had a certain fishy smell that he could detect by sniffing the air. Also when Travieso knew the enemy was close by or he sensed booby traps he would become silent. He would stand in one place for a couple of minutes not saying a word and not moving. Our squad knew that when this happened, we had best get our weapons at the ready. Travieso had an extraordinary instinct that we all trusted.

A few minutes later Corporal Ka-Bar and Travieso walked back toward the squad. Corporal Ka-Bar gave the hand and arm signal for the squad to gather around him and assemble. He explained that they had spotted four NVA just off the trail sound asleep on the ground. They were wearing green utilities and cartridge belts. Very quietly he told us to ensure that our magazines were fully seated and that our selector switch on our M16s were on automatic fire. He told us we were to sweep slowly through the foliage in a squad line formation. That meant we would be spread out shoulder to shoulder while advancing forward in one straight line. Travieso was to be the first one to initiate a volley of automatic fire as he had seen exactly where the enemy was sleeping. Immediately after his burst of automatic fire we were to open up as well while we swept through the area on line.

"We're gonna hold reveille on them mother fuckers," Travieso said.

We snickered at the idea and could not wait to get on with the task at hand. A couple of Marines in the squad doubted Corporal Ka-Bar's tactics of moving forward in a frontal assault while in a line formation. We had been taught the technique in infantry training but few doubted its effectiveness because the assault had everyone standing and moving forward side by side. It was much like the British troops had done in the continental days. The few that doubted Corporal Ka-Bar's tactics figured we would be sitting ducks for the enemy if they awoke quickly. I trusted Corporal Ka-Bar's instincts for he had proven himself in combat time and time again. Needless to say, Corporal Ka-Bar as the squad leader and in a leadership position got his way.

We checked our weapons and started to inch forward for the engagement. I positioned myself on the extreme right flank of our line formation. We watched where we were stepping so as not to make any noise that would spook the enemy. The squad was spaced about 5 meters apart and we could see one another out of the corner of each eye. Travieso was positioned in the center directing us forward and keeping us on line.

We got within eye sight of the sleeping NVA. Travieso placed his finger on his lips indicating for us to be very quiet. As we moved closer, I saw all four of the NVA sleeping on the ground, as Corporal Ka-Bar and Travieso had explained. Their rifles were laying next to their sides and they were resting their heads on their cartridge belts/pouches. One of them had his rifle laying against a tree. The fireteam leaders gave Corporal Ka-Bar the thumbs up that we were ready to rock and roll. Travieso signaled us to stop in place.

"Reveille... Mother Fuckers... Reveille!" Travieso screamed as he opened fire! Rrrr... aatttaaa... aaatttt!

The rest of the squad opened fire at the same time. Bbrroowww! The NVA never had a chance. Whatever they were dreaming about had come to an abrupt end. Two of them had reached for their weapons but the constant hail of bullets from our rifles was too much. They had been caught in our field of fire. Heavily embedding strings of bullets ripped into their bodies and they instantly succumbed to their wounds. We approached them cautiously and began to rummage through the pouches that were affixed to their cartridge belts. We checked for items that could be of use to our rear intelligence personnel. One of the Marines on the far left flank was lucky enough to be near the only NVA pack. Without haste he grabbed it up and said,

"Looks like I got me a gook pack as a souvenir."

I picked up a Russian made SKS 7.62x39mm semi-automatic carbine that was laying next to the dead NVA that I had shot. I knew my rounds had killed him because he had been directly in front of me on the right flank and I had watched my rounds walk through his upper torso. He had opened his eyes just as Travieso sounded reveille and had seen me approaching. As he reached for his SKS, I pulled the trigger of my M16. He was too late.

The SKS had a folding bayonet that hinged down from the end of the barrel. It was a gas-operated weapon with a tilting bolt action locking system and had an effective range of 400 meters. It was used extensively by the NVA/VC and it was a good trophy for any Marine lucky enough to kill a NVA armed with the weapon. I took my M16 and stuck the bayonet end into the ground so I could have two free hands to examine the SKS. I examined the nice wooden stock. Then I noticed that the dead NVA had a black string around his neck with a tiger tooth attached. I decided to keep the tiger tooth as the dead NVA would have no use for it. I stood up and held the SKS in front of my chest with both hands.

"Boy, I really got me a souvenir now," I said excitedly.

Wagenbaugh looked over at me from my left flank and said, "That's not yours, it's mine, and I'm taking it back with me."

"Bullshit!" I snapped back. "This NVA was on my side when we opened fire. I watched as my rounds hit him. So since I'm the one who killed him, I'm taking the SKS!"

"Don't make a shit," Wagenbaugh said quickly. "You haven't been in country long enough to take a souvenir like that, it's my turn to get a souvenir weapon."

"Oh, no you don't," I replied angrily. "It don't work that way. Whoever gets the kill, gets the weapon. It don't matter how long you've been in country."

Corporal Ka-Bar interjected, "You weren't even close to this one Wagenbaugh. Fenwick shot him, so he can keep the SKS."

"All Riiight, thank you much Corporal Ka-Bar," I said as I slung the weapon over my right shoulder.

"No problem," Corporal Ka-Bar said. "Just make sure you hang on to it or Wagenbaugh will cheat you out of it."

Wagenbaugh was a bit bitter about what had happened. He was mumbling obscenities to himself as we continued to rummage thorough the NVA equipment. After a thorough search Corporal Ka-Bar told us to take a break and rest for awhile. I put my back up against a tree and began to inspect the SKS. It was in good shape. The stock was a little nicked but other than some caked on rust everything worked. The SKS ammunition magazine was fully loaded. I placed the magazine in one of my flak jacket pockets. Then I started playing with the affixed bayonet as I opened and closed it. The squad radio operator called back to the platoon radio operator and reported that we

Mike 3 Charlie patrolling a river in the Quang Nam Province.

had four confirmed kills.

"Mike 3, Mike 3, this is Mike 3 Charlie, Over."

"Mike 3 Charlie this is Mike 3," the platoon radio operator replied. "Send your traffic."

"Roger, Mike 3, be advised that we have four Victor Charlie confirmed kills, Over," our squad radio operator said.

"Mike 3 Charlie, this is Mike 3. I copy you have four dead Victor Charlie. Get Some, Mike 3 Charlie! Get Some!" After a brief hesitation the platoon radio operator could be heard saying, "Be advised the Actual wants you to continue your mission and to keep your eyeballs peeled."

"Mike 3, this is Mike 3 Charlie, Roger Out," our radio operator replied.

One of the Marines in the squad spoke up. "Keep our eyeballs peeled? What the hell is that supposed to mean? We found these sleeping NVA didn't we?"

Private First Class Fenwick (foreground) taking a break from the heat during a river patrol.

"Awh, the lieutenant just wants to be involved," Corporal Ka-Bar answered. "We go out on patrols and risk our asses while he sits back in the CP barking orders. It must be frustrating for an officer not to be able to get into the weeds like us enlisted grunts and see some action."

We prepared to continue on our patrol. Marines in the squad were designated to carry back the 3 AK47s and miscellaneous gear that we had captured from the dead NVA. I was carrying two rifles as well, my M16 and my SKS. I just hoped that I would be able to take it back to the States. It would be a nice war trophy. As we proceeded further into the treeline we heard noises and observed three more enemy running away. We managed to capture one but the other two got away. The captured enemy was in civilian clothing. We hit all our checkpoints and headed back to the company perimeter.

Corporal Ka-Bar had the Marines with the AK47s turn them over to our platoon commander so they could be transported back to the rear. I walked up to our platoon commander and asked if it was okay for me to keep the SKS.

"Sir, I got this SKS off one of the NVA that I killed today," I informed the lieutenant. I was told by my squad leader that I might be able to keep it as a souvenir. Is that okay?"

"Sure, it's okay," he responded. "You have earned it. When we get back to the rear you can store it in the armory until you leave the country. You can take a SKS back to the States with you as long as the bolt is out of it."

"Okay, Sir, thanks," I replied. "This is all right!"

I felt so elated about the whole idea of bringing home a souvenir from Vietnam as other Marines before me had done. I thought to myself, quite an accomplishment for a private first class, E-2, with just over three months in country. The other AK47 rifles that were confiscated off the NVA had to be turned in to the authorities for disposition, but I was being authorized to hang on to my SKS carbine.

We spent the next few days running patrols and ambushes. Each time I went out on a patrol I hand picked a Marine to keep an eye on my SKS and guard it with his life. When I returned from a patrol the first thing I would do when I got back inside the perimeter was to locate my SKS and take it to my sleeping hole. I enjoyed the thought of walking around with two rifles in the bush. Some of the other Marines seemed to envy my newly acquired status.

One day our company first sergeant came out on a chopper from LZ Baldy to deliver our mail. He was making his rounds chit chatting with the Marines and telling them that they were making Mike Company proud.

As he approached me he said, "Hey Marine, what are you doing with that gook weapon? How did you get that?"

"I got this SKS off one of the NVA I killed the other day," I answered. "I was given permission to keep it by the platoon commander. I will take it back to the rear, put it in the armory, and take it home with me when I leave Vietnam."

The first sergeant replied, "Well, you can't carry two rifles with you in the bush. Go ahead and tag it with your name and platoon. Give it to me and I'll take it back and turn it into the armory for you. When you get back to LZ Baldy come see me and I'll get the proper paperwork done for you to legally transport it back to the States. Then when you do get ready to leave the country you can pick it up from the armory."

"Thank you much, first sergeant," I said, "I really appreciate this."

"Don't mention it," the first sergeant replied.

I tagged my SKS rifle and handed it over to the Mike Company First Sergeant as instructed. He continued to walk the lines and chat with different Marines. It wasn't long until we heard a chopper coming back in with resupplies and to take the first sergeant back to LZ Baldy. I watched him walk up

Airing my feet, rearranging my haversack, and preparing to "Saddle Up." Not far from this location I captured a SKS 7.62x39mm semi-automatic carbine during a frontal assault on four NVA. The rifle mysteriously disappeared from the company armory.

the ramp of the CH-46 with my SKS in hand. I was satisfied with the arrangement and thought that I was going to be leaving Vietnam with a good souvenir.

As the rotors of the chopper lifted it into the air a sudden shock came over me. In my haste to give the first sergeant my SKS, I had forgotten to give him the magazine clip that was with the weapon. I decided I would just carry it in my pack until I could store it. Then I realized that I had forgotten to look for a serial number on the weapon and to jot it down on a piece of paper. All I had tagged on the weapon was my rank, name, company, and platoon. I reckoned everything was all right, however, and that there was nothing to worry about. The first sergeant was the senior enlisted Marine in

Mike Company who advised the company commander. I felt he could be trusted with my SKS.

A few days later I had just finished eating some C-Rations and I was going to write a couple of letters. I wasn't going to say anything about me getting a SKS for I thought it was too good to be true and I had a long way to go in Vietnam. For some reason I decided to just bury the SKS magazine with the live rounds. I figured I would not need it and I really did not want to carry it around with me in my pack.

After I had buried the SKS magazine, I was approached by the 3rd squad leader of the 2nd platoon. He told me that he needed me to go out on patrol with his squad because he was short on people. We would be passing by a village and the platoon commander wanted to make sure he had enough men if the "shit hit the fan." Corporal Ka-Bar had said it was okay for me to augment their squad. I was told that we would be moving out at around 0830. I readied my combat equipment and made sure I had enough M16 rounds.

We started out on patrol and I fell in behind one of our machine gunners that we had in the 3rd platoon. He would be augmenting the patrol as well. It wasn't long until the patrol detained a boy about 14 years old. An interpreter questioned him and determined that he was working with the VC. A chopper was called for and the detainee was sent to the rear for interrogation.

We continued on the patrol and came out of a treeline and into an open rice paddy. The machine gunner in front of me took a shot directly in the center of his chest. Ahead of us we saw one male NVA/VC and a female wearing black pajamas running back into the treeline. I could see that the female was carrying a rifle and was the one who had shot the machine gunner in the chest. We started receiving AK47 fire from the village and we returned fire with our M16s and M79 HE rounds. We figured that we had missed the female.

First aid was administered to the wounded Marine by the Marines closest to him. The fleeing VC woman had shot him at such a distance that the AK47 round had penetrated one of his M16 magazines that he had secured in a bandoleer across his shoulder, went through his flak jacket, and then through his dog tags. Behind his dog tags he wore a religious medallion. The bullet had struck his religious crucifix that he wore around his neck and the medallion was embedded in the center of his chest about a quarter inch deep. The crucifix was removed by pulling on the chain attached to the ring at the top of the crucifix. The wound resembled a tattoo in the center of his chest. A battle dressing was placed over the wound. I examined the crucifix closely and saw that it was still in one piece with a slight dent in the middle. The bullet had struck the very center of the medallion.

The wounded Marine glanced at me and the other Marines hovering over him while feeling the ground around him with his hands. "Where's my gun?" he asked.

"I got your M60, I responded. "Just take it easy. You are going to be okay."

"I want my gun!" he demanded.

"Don't worry about it," I said, "we'll take care of it."

He looked at his chest and saw that he had been bandaged up. "Has anybody seen my crucifix?" he asked.

We reassured him by showing him that the crucifix was still hanging on the chain around his neck. Those of us who were close enough to witness the incident were stunned by what had just happened. It was either fate, luck, or an act of God. If you were any kind of Christian you would know that a "Miracle" had just happened. The religious crucifix had saved his life.

A chopper was called in to medevac him out. In the meantime the squad assembled to pursue the fleeing VC. Two Marines remained behind until the chopper arrived and the wounded Marine was medevaced. They received sniper fire while trying to load the wounded Marine onto the chopper. It lifted off the ground and the two Marines joined us in the chase. I figured that the chopper arrived on the scene within about fifteen minutes which was a fairly rapid medevac. I hoped that if I ever got wounded, that I could be evacuated just as fast.

The medevac chopper flew over the rice paddies and banana trees and out of sight. Our squad was now entering a treeline that was close by to the village. We tried to retrace the route in which the NVA/VC had fled. As we entered the small village we saw about five bamboo hooches. Suddenly there were two women running out of the back of a hooch and into the thick brush. One had a weapon and the other did not.

We fired at them with our M16s and the one without a weapon stopped running and put her hands up in the air. The other woman with weapon in hand fell to the ground. She was seriously wounded and we knew she wouldn't live long. We moved to where they were, confiscated the AK47, and started back into the village. Two Marines had to carry the wounded woman as the other one walked along side of her. By now there were kids running frantically all over the place. We paid very little attention to the kids since we had captured the female Vietcong who had shot the Marine in the chest.

Several more women and children were rounded up and were forced to sit on the ground. The two females that had been fleeing from the village were separated from the group for questioning. There were no males in this village to be found. They possibly escaped through tunnels or spider traps which we could not readily locate. We checked all the hooches turning over everything that was the least bit suspicious. We could not find any other weapons or Vietcong, so we were directed to torch some of the hooches in the village. The roofs were covered with dried grass. Almost immediately, the flames engulfed the flimsy structures. We moved back away from the heat, guarding our prisoners, and watched the hooches burn to the ground. It was not our concern that the villagers did not have a roof over their heads. After all, one of them had shot a Marine.

We had been given instructions over the radio that we were to bring the two prisoners back to the CP for interrogation. We had enough Marines to switch off in carrying the wounded female VC back with us. A few Marines constructed a makeshift stretcher using two bamboo poles and a poncho. The other VC woman could walk along with us. A Marine put a battle dressing over her stomach wound and then the wounded VC was placed on the litter. Four Marines grabbed the ends of the bamboo poles and lifted her with the litter. We began our journey back to the CP. One Marine who was walking along the side of the stretcher decided to tease the wounded woman. He started to fondle her breasts. The woman protested smacking his hands away and speaking in her native tongue. Some of the Marines initially laughed about it.

The more the wounded woman resisted, the more aggressive the Marine became. He decided to grab her between her legs. The VC woman began screaming and the other woman who was walking next to the litter came running to her aid. She reached for the Marine's hand to pull it away. He shoved her away and yelled, "You bitch! Don't you ever touch me!" Just then the wounded VC rolled off the litter. The Marines carrying the litter laughed. We stopped to lift her back on the litter and continued walking.

Drop that bitch, that fuckin slut," the Marine said to the ones carrying the litter. The Marines in the front dropped the bamboo poles and the wounded VC slipped off the stretcher and onto the ground. She was picked up and put back on the stretcher. The woman's stomach was bleeding through the battle dressing from her gunshot wounds but no one seemed overly concerned. No one else wanted to waste their battle dressings on a VC who almost killed a good Marine.

It became my turn to help carry the litter. I grabbed the pole at the right rear of the stretcher. After a few paces one of the Marines on the right front of the stretcher dropped the bamboo pole without warning. The woman VC rolled off the stretcher while another Marine and I were still holding on to the rear poles.

"Damn it, when I drop my pole, you all drop it at the same time!" he snapped.

"Why don't we just get her back to the rear like we are supposed to instead of playing games?" I asked.

I was feeling the intense heat and weary from our walk. We were feeling irritable from not only the heat but from the happenings that had taken place since we started this patrol. Now we had the extra burden of carrying this VC back to our perimeter. I dropped my pole and began to roll the VC back onto the stretcher. Another Marine assisted me.

The Marine in the front who had dropped the stretcher remarked, "Don't you want to play the game? Getting soft, or what?"

"Hell no," I replied. "This end back here is heavy, just dead weight. All we are doing is wasting time."

"She's looks dead already," he replied. "What the fuck, Over! What difference does it make? She tried to kill us didn't she?"

I responded, "Yeah, but she is still alive. Maybe they can get some information out of her when we get her back to the CP."

I heard the voice from the Marine who had started touching the woman in the first place. "Ooohh, you're getting soft! Why, you have a thing about killing women?"

"No! It's not that," I replied. "She is heavy and it's hot out here. I just want to get her back to the CP."

The squad leader who was up at the front of the column came back to take charge of the situation. He walked over to the stretcher and squatted down to check if the wounded VC was okay. He looked up and proclaimed, "I think she's dead."

One Marine said, "Oh how unfortunate for her. This bitch tried to kill us."

The squad leader then radioed back to his platoon commander reporting that the wounded VC woman was dead.

"How in the hell did that happen?" the platoon commander questioned over the radio.

"She was badly wounded already. We were carrying her back and she just died," the squad leader replied.

The platoon commander paused for a short while and then commanded, "Bring her back anyway."

Some Marines began moaning and complaining about the latest order we had received from the platoon commander. One of the Marines said, "Well, shit! Now we are stuck with a dead bitch and still have to carry her back to the CP. This fuckin sucks!"

As I was carrying my end of the litter, the woman walking along with us was screaming and crying, while letting out squeals and shrieks. I didn't know how much more I could take as it was really getting on my nerves. We finally reached the CP around noon. We were approached by a Kit Carson Scout accompanied by the platoon commander. The VC who was alive was interrogated. They were conversing back and forth in Vietnamese. We stood around to watch the interrogation. At one point the Kit Carson Scout slapped her and then sat her down on the ground to interrogate her further.

The lieutenant in the meantime wanted to speak with the ones that went out on the patrol. He approached the squad leader and asked, "How in the hell did this female VC end up dead when she only had a stomach wound?" It was explained that she had slipped off the litter and must have gone into shock. The lieutenant looked at the rest of us and asked, "Did you Marines have anything to do with this prisoner's death?"

"No Sir!" was the repetitive response.

He started asking us if the squad leader encouraged any wrong doings. Each Marine responded that she just died on the way back from wounds she had received when we had first opened fire. Everyone was looking at me out of the corner of their eyes when the lieutenant asked me, "What do you know about this?"

"It happened just like everyone said," I replied.

"Yeah right, are you sure?" he asked again.

"Affirmative, Sir," was my reply. "She died of her stomach wounds."

The lieutenant felt we were holding something back but he didn't question us any further. We figured someone higher in the chain of command had told him to investigate how a female VC could die on a stretcher on the way back to the CP. The other woman VC was eventually put on a chopper and taken away for further interrogation. After pondering over in my mind the moral values of the day's happenings, I convinced myself that the VC woman paid the consequences of trying to take an American life. The wounded Marine could have very well been a dead Marine. Our hearts were growing cold and hard. The reality of war was taking its toll in the minds of these nineteen year old warriors. I never knew if they buried the female corpse or just left it in the vicinity as a reminder not to become a VC.

Soon we returned to LZ Baldy for a few days of rehabilitation. It gave me a chance to sit down in our hooch and write a letter home. I would not mention that I had my very own SKS carbine because I was hoping to bring it home and surprise my mother and father. At the company office I filled out a DD Form 603-1 (War Trophy Registration/Authorization) and a DD Form 603 (Registration of War Trophy Firearm). I was fairly confident that I would be going home with my souvenir SKS 7.62x39mm semi-automatic carbine.

June 24, 1970

Hello Mom, Dad and Larry,

How is everyone getting along these days? I hope you all are in good spirits and enjoying the summer. Of course I know there is a lot to be done. I sure wish I could sit out under the old sugar tree by the front porch at night. But at least here I stay out under the stars. I always wanted to stay out all night and to go camping. Ha! Well it looks like my dreams came true. Now I get too much of a good thing.

I told Hawkeye the other day, the blonde headed guy in the picture, that if he came to visit me when I got out of the Marine Corps, that I'd buy him a case of beer and we'd go camping. He said the beer part was all right, but I thought he was going to belt me one when I said we'd go camping. Ha! He's a pretty good dude and is from Oregon. We stay pretty close out in the bush but now he has a fireteam of his own. He is a PFC and has one Lance corporal in the team. He's been over here for about six months.

Well I almost got to send a cassette tape home but we couldn't find any batteries. Hawkeye has the same kind of tape recorder as yours, the one Janice gave to you. We're going back out to the bush tomorrow so I don't guess I'll get to tape a message for you. Don't send me any batteries because it's no telling if I would ever get the chance again.

Guess you've already sent the sausage. Well Mom, if it's on its way, okay, but from now on don't send me nothing unless I ask for it. It's too much of a bother for you and besides it costs money. So if I ever need anything I'll sure call on you. Thanks a million for what you have done so far.

Well Dad, Happy Fathers Day! I didn't know anything about it until Janice told me that she might call you on that day. Glad you have the hay in the barn. Tell Larry he can't catch fish with the hook in his knee. He's got to throw it in the lake. Of course when it was in his knee, he already had a worm on it. Ha! No, Larry, just kidding. Here's a picture you can have of me even though it didn't turn out too good.

Mom asked about the monsoons. Well I don't know but it sure has been raining a lot these days. Monsoons aren't supposed to start until around September but maybe we'll have an early start. Oh well, at least we can take a shower in the bush. Ha!

Dad, did Jimmy Howard ever let you read the piece I had sent him? If he hasn't, ask him to let you read it. It's just about every-thing that goes on while we're in the field. It's about the Marine Corps grunts.

Well I've about run out of things to say so I'll close for now. So you all be good and I'll be thinking of you.

Yours most affirm,
Fred

Our three days of rehab at LZ Baldy went by way too fast. Before we knew it we were gearing up to head back out to the Que Son Mountains. While back at LZ Baldy we received a few more new joins from the States. They had been standing hole watch, and like myself when I first arrived in country, they were eager to join the company.

On 26 June Mike Company began to deploy to the Que Sons. Corporal Ka-Bar would not be going with us on this operation for he was due to rotate back to the States on 29 June. Lance Corporal Travieso stepped up from fire-team leader to our squad leader. I was comfortable with the arrangement because Travieso was a very good tactician and took pride in looking after the squad.

Company Office for Mike Company, 3rd Battalion, 7th Marines at LZ Baldy. Hawkeye takes time out for a photo.

Each squad received our usual C-Ration resupplies and all the ordnance we could carry such as hand grenades, trip flares, claymore mines, mortar rounds, machine gun ammo, and other miscellaneous items. We moved to the helo pad and lined up in helo sticks with the designated amount of Marines to load aboard each individual chopper. We sat down in place and leaned up against our heavy packs to await the arrival of the choppers.

"Guess we're gonna fly to the top of the Que Son Mountains like we did the last time," I told Hawkeye.

Hawkeye looked at me and replied, "Well, the rumor is that we're going to be heli-lifted out to Spider Lake at the base of the Que Son Mountains and then we're gonna hump up to the top."

"You mean they're gonna drop us off at the bottom of a mountain and we're gonna hump up to the top?"

"That's what I hear," Hawkeye replied.

"Ain't this a bitch!" I exclaimed. "The Marine Corps has all these helicopters flying all over the damn place and we have to be dropped off at the base of a mountain and hump up to the top. I ain't believing this shit."

"Welcome to the Marine Corps Infantry," Hawkeye replied.

"Yep," I agreed, "Good old Marine Corps grunts. Humping high and humping low, humping everywhere we go."

While we were sitting and waiting near the helo pad a CH-46 chopper landed and we noticed a recon team of eight men off loading the chopper. They were dressed in gillie suits, their faces were painted with camouflage sticks, and they carried sniper rifles in addition to M16s. A Marine within our ranks yelled out, "Holy shiiitt! Look at that!"

Two recon Marines were dragging a huge tiger by the hind legs across the helo pad. They had killed the beast while they were out on an operation. As they passed by Mike Company, Marines began to tease the recon Marines saying, "Get some! Recon! We'll kill the gooks, you kill the tigers."

"Fuck you!" a recon Marine replied. "You don't know what it's like to survive in the bush on your own."

Someone from Mike Company yelled, "Give us a break, Reeecoonnn! Your shit stinks just like ours."

We all jeered and laughed. Feeling intimidated by the mere mass of Marines waiting for the choppers, the recon Marines ignored our jeering and taunts. As they passed our squad Hawkeye said, "Mighty big cat you've got there. Where did you get him?"

"Happy Valley!" a recon Marine exclaimed.

Another Mike Company Marine asked, "How much do you think it weighs?"

"Feels like about three hundred pounds."

"What are you going to do with it?"

"Damned if I know," the recon Marine answered.

We watched as they continued to drag the beast slowly along. The coat of the big cat was slick looking with intricate patterns of camouflage. It had been quite a beautiful animal. It was a shame the recon Marines had killed it.

Shaking his head from side to side Hawkeye said, "Hope we don't run into nothin like that in the Que Sons."

The CH-53s landed on the helo pad and we boarded for our next mission. We were flown to the base of the Que Son Mountains at a place called Spider Lake. The choppers circled and landed near the edge of a treeline. The water in the marshy wetlands was only a few inches deep where our chopper set down. We stepped off the ramp of the chopper into the crystal clear water. Reeds were growing up waist high and we had to wade through the vegetation before we got to dry land.

Hawkeye looked at me and said, "Welcome to Spider Lake."

I looked out across the reeds and water and responded, "This looks more like a swamp than a lake."

"It takes on the appearance of a spider from the top of the Que Sons," Hawkeye replied, "thus the name Spider Lake."

Before Mike Company reached dry land we took a couple of pot shots

Atop the Que Son Mountains with Spider Lake in the valley.

from some lonely NVA/VA. We ignored his sniper fire and got organized to begin our ascent up one side of the mountain. The heat and humidity quickly became hot, real hot. About halfway up the mountain I looked over my shoulder and sure enough the lake resembled a spider with all the inlets flowing into the main body of water. It reminded me of a black widow spider. The water in the lake was crystal clear and I could see the reflection of the sun bouncing off the surface.

We carried our heavy packs up through the dense foliage and finally reached the top of the Que Son Mountains. For the next few days we were to move across the top and send out patrols around the mountainsides. As we moved along I heard an engine roaring high in the sky. I looked up and could barely make out the outline of a one-prop plane. I glanced down to where I was stepping and for some reason glanced back up at the plane. I saw something drop from the plane and I wondered if maybe it had lost something by mistake.

"There goes those commie bastards again," Travieso said.

"What's going on?" I asked.

"You'll see," he said. "Won't be long and you would think that it is snowing. They fly over from the north and drop little messages of propaganda distributing them in the mountains and villages so that the South Vietnamese can be persuaded to surrender to the communist rule. I wish we could blow the fuckin things out of the air but no one ever screws with them for some reason."

I sort of laughed at his attitude. It was not long until little bits of paper began drifting slowly over the tree tops and falling to the ground. A few fell to the ground directly in my path. I reached down and picked one up. It had Vietnamese writing on one side and a cartoon on the other. The only thing that I could make out was something about the Americans. I asked Travieso if he knew what it meant.

"No," he said, "but the Kit Carson Scout can interpret it. "Basically most of them say Yankee go home and leave the Vietnamese to their way of life. I hope their fuckin plane crashes."

I was going to save one but remembered how the NVA treated the Vietnamese people and decided to toss it aside. What a strange land this is, I thought. Our squad was walking point for the company and we had a machine gun team with us. We moved across some hills and started down a finger on the ridgeline. I looked all around and it seemed as though we were on top of the world. To my left were rice paddies spread out below in the valley and on my right was jungle and wilderness. I figured that we were leaving the mountains heading toward the lowlands. I became thirsty and reached for my canteen as I continued to walk. I unscrewed the top and began to drink the warm liquid.

Raaattaa... tttaaa!

I almost dropped my canteen and instantly dropped to the ground for cover. My first instinct was the thought that we had been hit by an enemy ambush. Then I realized it was one of our own machine gunners. He was firing between five to eight round bursts.

A Marine behind us yelled, "What's going on up there?"

The machine gunner continued to fire. In between bursts he yelled out, "I saw two fuckin gooks running down the trail, caught me by surprise."

Travieso came up from behind and went up to where the machine gunner was firing. "What are you firing at?" he asked.

The machine gunner replied, "I saw two gooks, didi-ing down the trail. It looked like they had AK47s."

The point man interjected, "I saw them too but you scared the hell out of me when you opened fire. I thought you were shooting in my direction."

"Be careful with that damn gun," Travieso said. "You have people in front of you."

The machine gunner replied, "Don't worry, I had a clear field of fire."

By now our squad radio was blaring again with transmissions. The platoon commander and company commander wanted to know what we were firing at. When they were informed of the circumstances, the company was halted, and our squad plus the 1st squad was sent down the finger to investigate. We dropped our packs to lighten our load as we would search for the gooks and then rejoin the company.

We got to the very end of the finger and began to spread out on both sides looking for the gooks. There was not a trace that they had been there.

"How could they have disappeared just like that?" Hawkeye asked inquisitively.

"I don't know," replied Travieso. "I don't see how they got away from us. There are steep bluffs and cliffs on both sides. Beats the hell out of me!"

Travieso radioed back and reported to the platoon commander that we could not find anything. We were told to continue looking for awhile longer. Hawkeye and I went to the very edge of a cliff almost toward the end of the finger. We walked around cautiously and noted that the ground came to a cliff that was a straight drop off. The question in our minds was how the gooks could have escaped over this embankment, unless they were so scared from the machine gun fire, that they just dove over the edge. In that case, we thought, Charlie would be no more.

Travieso told everyone to stop looking and assemble. We all gathered around him next to some huge boulders. "Are you guys sure you saw some gooks because there is nothing here? No blood stains, no lost gear! I don't even see no tracks."

The machine gunner answered, "Hell, yeah!"

"There were two of them all right," the point man interrupted. "They saw me coming and took off like a bat out of hell. That's when Machine Gun Kelly opened up. Then they just vanished."

The machine gunner began to get a little defensive that our squad leader had questioned him. He began to swear at himself for not killing the gooks when he first opened fire. "Too many big rocks in the way," he said.

"All right," Travieso interjected. "Let's take a short break before we join back up with the company."

The Marines began to plop down on the ground to take a break. I told Hawkeye that I wanted to take another look at the cliff we had stumbled upon. Hawkeye decided to join me. We walked over slowly toward the edge of the cliff again. When we got to the very end, Hawkeye said, "Jeeze, I wouldn't want to fall off this cliff, it's straight down."

I cautiously looked over the edge and the view was breathtaking. I had never seen such a drop from such a high altitude. I had previously studied a military map that Travieso used to plot grid coordinates. It appeared that at roughly the highest peak of the Que Son Mountains it would be approximately 2900 feet above sea level. I figured that if there were 5280 feet in one mile, and that distance was divided by two, the result would be 2640 feet above sea level. That would mean that the cliff was about a half mile straight down.

I looked out in the distance and I could see white puffs of clouds down below and miles and miles of rice paddies. It was a sight that I would not forget. I wanted to take a photo from this birds eye view on top of this mountain, but I realized that I had left my camera in my pack. It was back at the platoon's location. Hawkeye wondered a bit to my right through some chest high bushes to get a better view in the opposite direction. I decided to mosey to my left side and to see the view from another angle as well. I eased even closer to the edge of the cliff and lay down on my stomach. As I low-crawled on the ground it began to decline downward. I came to the very edge and looked over the cliff. It seemed to be endless.

I decided I had best not get too close to the edge or I would find myself plummeting over the side without a parachute. I started to move backwards and then felt a little of the rock gravel under the palms of my hands start to give way. I felt my heart begin to beat faster. Maybe I had ventured too far toward the edge of the cliff and couldn't get back on flat land. I slowly put pressure on both elbows and tried to dig the toes of my boots into the ground to get some traction. I moved ever so slightly. When I had moved about six inches backward, the rocky earth under my elbows slipped again and my body slipped forward a couple of inches. My heart sank. How could I have been so careless? I managed to move back a few more inches and was satisfied that I could finally stand up without going over the cliff. I grabbed a sturdy bush to help me to the standing position and walked over to rejoin Hawkeye.

"Well, we better get back to the squad," Hawkeye said. I did not answer him. "What's the matter, Fenwick," looks like you have seen a ghost!"

"No, I'm all right," I replied. "I just may have gotten a little too close to the edge of this cliff."

Didn't you enjoy the scenery?" he asked.

"Yes, but I've seen enough for one day," I replied.

"This is some mountain," Hawkeye said as he took one final look over the valley below.

"Yep," I agreed, "some more mountain!"

We returned to where the other two squads were resting and then we all proceeded back to join the company. Mike Company continued our trek over the Que Son Mountains. For the next few days the 1st and 2nd platoons began seeing all the action. The 2nd platoon found a cave complex capable of holding 40 to 50 enemy. It was believed to be a base camp and it had been recently used that day. A search of the complex produced 3 SKS, 2 chi-coms, 500 AK47 rounds, 3 RPG rounds, 1 bangalor torpedo, and 3 AK47 magazines. All were destroyed.

Then the 1st platoon spotted 7-10 NVA/VC moving north wearing green utilities and carrying packs and weapons. They called for artillery to bomb the enemy position. The next day a Marine in the 2nd platoon while on patrol tripped a grenade booby trap rigged with a trip wire across a trail. The explosion wounded four Marines including 3 priority medevacs and one non-medevac. Suddenly after hitting the booby trap they were taken under fire by 3 enemy wearing green utilities. The 2nd platoon returned fire but the enemy fled. They called in gunships and fixed wing strikes on the suspected enemy route of escape, but had negative observed results. Three Marines were wounded in this contact and were classified as routine medevacs. During the firefight, the 2nd platoon detonated another booby trap which was a pressure release type and sustained one wounded Marine who was classified as a routine medevac. All the wounded Marines were medevaced.

The Que Sons were as turning into a dangerous place. The enemy knew we were there and watched our every move. On the last day of the operation I became very hot, sweaty, and thirsty as we moved up through a mountain pass. I realized that I had almost finished eight canteens of water without a refill. Luckily, we came upon a clear stream running down the side of the mountain, with huge black boulders in the waters path. I decided that this was an opportune time to refill my canteens. There was a holdup at the front of the column so our squad stopped moving and we commenced to refill our canteens. When I had finished filling my eight canteens I retrieved my bottle of halogen tablets from my first aid kit. I started to add one tablet per canteen of water to purify my drinking water.

A Marine just ahead of me was standing in the middle of the stream. He looked back at me and said, "You're not going to put halogen tablets into this crystal clear water are you?"

I responded, "Yeah, I don't wanna take no chances. It may look clear but I don't want to catch no damn disease from stagnant water."

"Stagnant water?" he quipped. "It's crystal clear, cold, and very nice." He took off his helmet and dipped it into the mountain stream. Then he filled his helmet with water and poured it over his head. I decided that was a good idea and I did the same. The cool water over my sweaty head felt so good. Then the Marine began to fill a canteen with the stream water.

"Ain't you gonna put halogen tablets in your water?" I asked curiously.

"Hell no, not this fresh water," he replied.

"Well, hell, me neither," I said. I must have drank an entire canteen of the cool water. After I had quenched my thirst I made sure all my filled canteens were securely fastened to my cartridge belt and pack. I had not put any halogen tablets in my canteens. The Marine was right, I thought to myself. I would not need to purify the water as it was crystal clear and coming from the top of the mountain. Besides, halogen tablets would leave a bad taste in your mouth.

We received word to saddle up and the company began to move forward once again. We trudged ever so slowly up the stream bed. There was thick foliage on the right side of the stream. I watched the Marine in front of me picking his way through the tree branches that kept slapping him in his face. To avoid the hassle of wrestling with the tree branches, I veered to my half right crossing the narrow stream. I rounded a huge black boulder that must have been at least ten feet in circumference.

As soon as I got on the other side of the boulder I looked down and saw four dead VC laying partially submerged in the running water. They wore only black pajamas and their bodies were bloated and decaying in the mountain stream. The corpses stunk to high heaven and I almost gagged from the stench. One of the bodies looked disfigured and was laying across a shallow part of the stream on some surface rocks. His head was in an upward tilt position while his legs rested in the downward flow of the water. His body was so bloated that I could see that the stream water was actually running into his opened mouth and out between his legs.

"Oh…shit," I mumbled to myself. My immediate reaction was to reach for my halogen tablets and I quickly dropped two tablets into one of my canteens. Then I shook the canteen vigorously. It was a sanitary procedure to place one halogen tablet in a canteen of clear water and two tablets into cloudy or muddy water to purify it. I didn't want to take any chances with the dead bodies in the stream so I put two tablets in each canteen of clear water. The directions for purifying water with the halogen tablets was to dissolve the tablets by shaking the canteen, loosening the cap for a few minutes, and then tighten the cap back down. After thirty minutes, the iodine in the tablets would purify the water, so that it was fit for human consumption.

I peered down at the rotting corpses as I began to step over them. Then I caught sight of the Marine up front of me in column and followed a few meters behind him. I shouted up to him that I had observed four dead bodies in the stream and he passed the word up through the column of Marines. As we moved further up the mountainside word was passed over the radio to make sure we used halogen tablets to purify the stream water. The terrain was now very steep and it was a struggle to walk uphill carrying our heavy packs and equipment. I began to feel physically drained and sick to my stomach. For a few minutes I thought my mind was merely playing tricks on me after having seen the dead bodies in the stream.

I began to feel exhausted, nauseated, and my body temperature was rising. I reached for the pouch on my canteen cover and pulled out two salt tablets. I hoped that they would replenish the salt in my body and improve my metabolism after sweating so much in this hot and humid environment. I placed the salt tablets in my mouth and reached behind my right hip to get a canteen of water. I was having trouble trying to unfasten the two snaps on the canteen cover. I was too weak to bother with it so I gave up on the idea of washing the salt tablets down with water. Instead, I let the salt tablets dissolve in my mouth, sucking on them like candy. They tasted awful.

After about ten minutes I felt as though I needed to throw up. I suspected that the salt tablets had made me dizzy and sick to my stomach. I attempted to run my forefinger deep into my throat hoping to vomit but I only gagged. I could have kicked myself for not drinking water with the salt tablets. We proceeded a little further up the mountainside until we reached the crest. Word was passed down that we would take a break. I sat down on the ground feeling very weak, nauseated, and in a state of delirium. I wanted a drink of water but was too weak to reach for my canteen.

Hawkeye was the second Marine ahead of me in column. He looked back and noticed that I was about out of it. He yelled out to the corpsman in front of him, "Hey Doc, you better get back here and take a look at Fenwick, he don't look so good!"

The corpsman walked back toward me and as he passed Hawkeye he asked, "What's wrong with him?"

"I don't know," replied Hawkeye, "he looks as pale as a sheet."

The corpsman approached me and took his pack off and laid it on the ground. He squatted down next to me and asked, "What's wrong with you?"

"I don't know Doc," I said, "I took two salt tablets without water and I think it's giving me an upset stomach. My head is pounding something fierce."

"Hell, don't you know you have to take salt tablets with water?" the corpsman asked. He then placed the back of his palm against my forehead. "Damn you've got a temperature, you're burning up!"

He took out a thermometer and placed it into my mouth while he took my pulse. After a few seconds he removed the thermometer and said, "You've got a temperature of one hundred, Fenwick. We're gonna have to medevac you outta here."

"Naw, don't do that Doc, I'll be all right, just let me drink a canteen of water," I said while slurring my speech.

"Oh no," the corpsman replied. "At a hundred and five your brain will fry. We've gotta get you outta here, and now!"

"Common Doc, don't do that," I begged. "I've already humped this far. I don't want to leave my squad now. Besides they will have to carry all my extra ammo if I get medevaced out."

"Not your concern," the corpsman replied. "I make the call and I say you are going to be medevaced."

I was too weak to make any further protests. The corpsman informed the platoon commander that I had to be medevaced. The platoon commander told the corpsman to see if I could hang in there awhile longer because choppers were on their way to heli-lift the company back to LZ Baldy. India Company was to replace us in the Que Son Mountain AO. For Mike Company this operation had ended. I told the corpsman that I would be able to make it until the choppers arrived. I felt lousy and just wanted to get off this mountain.

It wasn't long until we loaded aboard CH-46s and headed back to the base camp. When we arrived at LZ Baldy I got settled in our hooch and sprawled out on my cot. I had a rough time sleeping that night as I felt really sick. The next day I mustered enough strength to write a letter home as we were preparing to go back to the bush that same day.

July 1, 1970

Hello Mom, Dad and Larry,

Well I have another month down over here. Guess that's four months now that I've been over here all together. Seems like it has been longer than that, but time seems to be passing by pretty quick for me. These last two months have really gone by fast. I just hope they all go that way.

We have been in the Que Son Mountains again climbing all over the place. It's nice and cool up on top but we move every day. It is up and down all the way. When we started out we were in the lowlands at the base but we ended up on top of the highest mountain. Sometimes I think the Marine Corps is trying to make mountain goats out of us. They've already made us pack mules. Ha!

We found some rifles, clothes, rice and different types of rounds in a cave. When we got over the first part of the mountains we had contact with some gooks but didn't manage to kill any. They told us to back away so they could call in an air strike. We just sat up on a hill and watched two big jets drop bombs down below. It sure was a sight to see. Wish I had some film so I could have taken some flicks.

Well believe it or not, when the air strike was over, a platoon went down there and there were still gooks around. This time I don't know if they got any or not. So when they returned back to our position they called in air strikes all day long. These mountains were really shaking. Also helicopters were flying down to where they thought the gooks were. It was around the same place that we found the hospital caves.

Well, all the Marines at LZ Baldy are moving to LZ Ross which is about ten miles away from here. It's a base camp just like LZ Baldy only its a little smaller. I've been there about three times when they call us for security and back ups. They're all getting packed up and say they'll all be moved by the 6th of July. So when we come in from the bush we'll go to LZ Ross instead of LZ Baldy.

How's things back in old Kentucky these days? Hope everything is going okay. I guess you all are pretty well caught up on the farm work by now. I just about know what I have to do from day to day. I sure don't have to look for things to do because we keep pretty much on the go. Guess that's why the time passes quicker.

Mom, I got a letter you wrote to me today that was dated in January! I knew I wasn't getting all my mail. In that letter you were talking about it snowing and that our next door neighbor had died. I'm getting most of my mail now I think, but we don't have mail brought to us until about every five days.

Well, I'll close for now before it gets dark. I'm going to wait until morning before I seal the envelope because we're supposed to get paid tomorrow. So until next time I'll say bye for now, and hope everyone is doing fine.

Yours most affirm,
Fred

I was all packed up and ready to go back to the bush that afternoon. An hour or so prior to departing I had a splitting headache. I asked the platoon corpsman for some aspirin and if he would take my temperature. He gave me two aspirin and then pulled out a thermometer from his medical bag. He inserted it under my tongue and after a minute or so he read off a temperature of one hundred. He advised me to sit under the shade of a hooch for awhile to see if my temperature would go down. I found a shady spot and plopped down on the ground. I could not remember a headache so bad and I felt miserable. When Mike Company was ready to board choppers the corpsman took my temperature again. This time it was one hundred one. He told me that I needed to stay back and seek medical attention at sick bay. He then cleared it with my platoon commander and squad leader.

I proceeded to sick bay with all my gear. I hated the fact that my squad was going back to the bush and I was not with them. I didn't even get the chance to give Hawkeye a proper send off on his next combat operation. Then I figured that I would be more of a hindrance to my squad in a combat situation if I was sick. When I arrived at sick bay a Navy corpsman placed an ice pack on my forehead and started an IV. The ice pack seemed to thaw quickly as I was burning up with a fever and the air was hot and muggy in the BAS tent. A Navy doctor came by to look at me and asked me a few questions. He then told the corpsmen in my immediate vicinity to watch me and keep the IV going. He said he would be back later to check on me.

The doctor turned away quickly and departed for what seemed to be more important medical duties as there were Marines in the BAS in worse shape than me. Some had been brought in who had been wounded in combat. The corpsmen continued to monitor me and take my temperature. I got tired of laying on the cot feeling helpless, so I told one of the corpsmen that I was ready to go back to the bush. Without responding, he put the thermometer in my mouth and tested my temperature once again.

"You're not going anywhere," he said. "You still have a temperature of one hundred and one degrees. I'm going to get with the doctor to see if they will medevac you outta here."

I sat up on the side of the cot as I awaited the return of the corpsman. I began to feel even worse and doubted if I would be able to hold my own in the bush with my squad. It seemed like a long time before the corpsman finally returned. Standing over me he said, "Turn your rifle into the armory and your 782 gear into supply. You're going to be medevaced to a hospital ship."

I wearily got all this accomplished. Carrying all my heavy equipment and locating the armory and supply had taken a toll on me. I was really beginning to feel delirious. I don't know how I managed to get up enough strength to turn in my equipment on my own, but I did. As I passed by the company office I dropped off the letter that I had written that day so it would go out with the next mail run. It would have to go out without my pay check since we were supposed to get paid the following day. I then headed back to BAS. When I reported back to the BAS the corpsmen seemed to ignore me as the tempo of attending patients had increased. There were more casualties arriving on medevac choppers from various Marine units. After I finally got the attention of a corpsman he went to check on my status. When he returned I was informed that I was to wait on the helo pad to be evacuated.

At 1800 I boarded a CH-46 Sea Knight along with other sick and wounded Marines. The pilot flew directly over Da Nang and out toward the coast line. As the pilot flew out over the water he veered a hard right and began to descend to the landing platform of a ship. As the chopper hovered for landing I peered out one of the windows and noticed that the ship had a huge red cross painted on the side. It was a hospital ship called the USS Sanctuary. I was not sure how I managed to find my way from the helicopter pad to the hospital ward. I must have been so delirious from my high fever that I was not aware of my surroundings. I found myself standing in front of the nurse's station. Without warning a female nurse stuck a thermometer in my mouth. After a few seconds she spoke to me in the most feminine voice. I had not heard anything like it in quite some time.

"Okay, let me see young man". She pulled the thermometer from my mouth. "Oh my Lord," she said. "You have a temperature of one hundred two. We've got to get that temperature down as fast as possible."

One of the male Navy corpsmen was standing next to the nurse's station. He told me that I needed to turn over any personal items and my jungle utilities for safe keeping while aboard the USS Sanctuary. I was allowed to keep my jungle boots. The hospital ship would provide me with health and comfort items, hospital shirt and trousers, and a white wrap around robe. I was directed behind a curtain and instructed to place my personal belongings into the bag provided by the corpsman and to get dressed in the ward clothing.

I rummaged through my utility cargo pockets. I had in my possession a few souvenirs that I had picked up in the bush. I had a VC map, six AK47 live rounds, and a tiger tooth that I had gotten off a NVA that I had killed in a frontal assault. My souvenirs caught the corpsman's eye as I placed them one by one in the bag. He began to ask me how I had obtained the items. I was too sick to go into detail so I gave him a brief synopsis of each item. He was quite interested in the VC map and tiger tooth. I bagged and tagged my personal items and handed the bag over to the corpsman.

"We're gonna store all your personal effects in this bag for safe keeping," he said. "When you leave the ship, you will be able to reclaim them."

"Okay Doc, I replied."

I wasn't too keen on the idea of parting with my personal items but I did as I was instructed. He opened the curtain and with the aid of the other medical staff they got me settled into a hospital bed. It was just inches off the tile floor. There were three other cots fastened to the braces and stacked above me. I noticed that the bed immediately above my head was empty, at least for the time being. That was a good thing because if anyone had been laying in the rack above me the mattress would sag in the middle and limit my free space.

The ward corpsmen finally got my temperature under control by using ice packs, inoculations, and an IV. A Navy doctor came by to talk to me and asked if I had been drinking unclean water out of the rice paddies. I told him that I had not recently, but if I did fill my canteens from a rice paddy, that I always used halogen tablets to purify the water. I went on to inform him that I had filled my canteens from a stream up in the Que Son Mountains and had drunk the water without using the tablets. I explained that the water was running down the side of the mountain and was very clear. He told me that I should use halogen tablets at all times because you never knew what types of bacteria were in the water.

I told the doctor, "Yes Sir, I know I should have used halogen tablets. I let another Marine talk me out of it. The water was running down the mountainside and was cool and crystal clear. I didn't know that there were four dead VC just upstream when I drank the water."

"What?" the doctor asked abruptly. "You mean you drank water out of a stream that had dead bodies in it?"

"I replied, "Yes Sir, but it was by accident. I didn't know the dead bodies were there until I passed around a big boulder and saw them laying in the stream. Then I immediately put halogen in one of my canteens, but I guess I was a little late."

"A little late is not the word for it," he remarked. "Well now it looks like it has affected you physically and the reason you are on this hospital ship."

"Yes, I know," I responded. "I guess I messed up."

I wondered why the Marine who talked me out of using the halogen tablets had not gotten sick like I had. He had drunk some of the water also. Why just me, I thought to myself. At any rate, here I was on the USS Sanctuary. I remembered how my father would express being ill, sick as a dog! But at least I had a bunk bed with clean sheets and a pillow. This was a treat in itself. I had not lain in such a nice rack since arriving in country. I felt that at least I would be in good hands and taken care of for awhile.

On the second day aboard the USS Sanctuary I met a Marine aboard the ship that I had gone to boot camp with. We talked when we could and he always wanted to know what sort of action I had seen. He was stationed near Da Nang and hadn't seen any combat action. I enjoyed his company but he always prodded me to tell him what the bush was like. I told him a few war stories based on my experiences as he enjoyed hearing about all the stuff the grunts do.

A Red Cross Nurse would usually come by my rack and try to humor me with a few jokes and games. I did not find her jokes very amusing but managed to crack a smile sometimes. I didn't want to hurt her feelings but I felt so bad that I was not in the mood for games. I would normally start a game of checkers or cards with her and then doze off in the middle of it. I was so doped up from taking all the medication.

July 9, 1970

Hello Everyone,

Just a few words to let you all know I'm okay. Don't get excited because I'm writing on this kind of paper. I'm a little sick and am on a Naval Hospital. The ship is the USS Sanctuary, and is just off the coast of Nam.

The 1st of July we were heading back for the bush and about an hour before we were to leave, I asked the Doc if he'd give me some aspirin for my headache. I also got him to take my temperature and it was 100. He told me to lie on the shade and take it easy for a few minutes. About time we were leaving he took my temperature again and it was 101, so he told me to stay back and go to sick bay. I went down there and they said they were going to medevac me. So at about 6:00 that evening I was choppered to the Naval Hospital off the coast of Da Nang.

When I got here I was feeling pretty rotten and had a temperature of 102. They started giving me all kinds of shots and pills and taking some blood. I felt like a pin cushion for the first couple of days. Believe it or not, they still don't know what I had. The doctor said I had all the symptoms of malaria but that I don't have malaria. I feel pretty good now except I'm a little weak and light headed. This rocking ship doesn't do my head and stomach any good either. Anyway, I'm a lot better now.

I'm leaving tomorrow for Cam Ranh Bay. Its further south from here. Someone said I'd go on a plane so it must be pretty far. Maybe you all can locate it on the Vietnam map you have at home. I guess it will be mainly a place to recuperate and rest. I may be on some working parties down there, but it don't mean nothin. Guess it beats roaming around out in the bush. You might say I'm taking an R&R for a couple of weeks. I sure can use the rest. Now maybe I won't have to take R&R for awhile. Besides, you only get one chance for R&R over here.

My only complaint now is that I won't be getting any mail as long as I'm away from my unit. The last time I got any mail it was the last part of June and it'll be a couple more weeks before I get any. So you don't have to write so often. I'll let you know when I get back to the unit and get squared away. It might be a possibility that some may get to me before then, but I kinda doubt if it will.

Here is a picture that a nurse from the Red Cross took of me and a buddy. She comes around every day to give us games to play and to compete in contests like drawing or making hats or some other foolish things. She had a camera and some film that the Red Cross furnished so she took pictures of everybody. The guy in the picture with me is a buddy I had throughout boot camp, ITR, and Staging Battalion. I ran into him when I got on ship and we are in the same ward. He says he's not far from Da Nang and doesn't do much. Of course I had some war stories to tell him. Don't know if he believed me or not.

I'll probably see some different sites when I go to Cam Ranh Bay tomorrow. Hope I can get some film before I leave. They even have a PX on ship. Guess what? I've been taking a shower every day. How about that? After a few more I may be able to get some dirt off. Ha ha!

Well how's life back in the world. Hope everything is going all right. Have the girls done away with dresses or are they still trying to figure out how to make them shorter? I don't care how short they get myself, do you Larry?

Well guess I've about run out of things to talk about so guess I'll close for now. Besides the Doc just stuck a thermometer in my mouth. "Cough! Cough!" Don't think nothin of me being in the hospital, at least I'm resting ain't I? Well, bye for now folks, I'll be thinking of everyone real often.

As ever,
Fred

I began to start feeling better but was still awful weak and sick to my stomach most of the time. Medical tests showed that I had amoebic dysentery and strep throat. I asked the Red Cross worker for a dictionary and she brought me a small pocket one. I looked up amoebic dysentery and found that it was the inflammation of the intestines caused by Endamoeba histolytica; usually acquired by ingesting food or water contaminated with feces; characterized by severe diarrhea. So now I knew how I had gotten amoebic

Aboard the USS Sanctuary. Medevaced from the Que Son Mountains after drinking water from a contaminated stream containing four dead VC. Fenwick is pictured on the left. Went through boot camp with the Marine on the right.

dysentery, by drinking water that was passing through the body of a dead VC. I looked up strep throat and found that some of the symptoms were sudden and severe sore throat, abdominal pain, difficulty swallowing, halitosis, rash, frequent cold chills, and a fever of 101 degrees Fahrenheit or greater.

The Navy doctor explained to me that my bowels would not pass and that the strep throat was causing the high temperature. No matter how hard I tried I could not manage to get a bowel movement and my throat was very dry and sore. The next morning I was told to get ready and that I would be leaving the ship. I figured my body's resilience allowed me to recover quickly from my illnesses. When I approached the checkout counter, a corpsman told me that I would be going to Cam Ranh Bay for rehabilitation and rest.

"Where is Cam Ranh Bay?" I asked.

One of the corpsmen responded, "It's an Army base way down south by the beach. They will take good care of you!"

"I don't want to go to no Army base," I protested. "I need to get back to my unit."

"You need more rest," the corpsman replied.

"Great," I said with sarcasm, "where do I claim my personal effects?"

"See HM1 Jones at the next counter," he said with a grin.

I walked over to the next counter. "HM1 Jones?" I asked.

"Yes, I'm Jones," he answered.

"I left some of my personal effects in a bag for safe keeping when I first arrived aboard ship. I am going to Cam Ranh Bay today and I need to get them back."

"What's your name?" the corpsman asked.

"Fenwick," I replied, "Private First Class Fenwick."

He turned about and went into a little storage room looking around at some of the personal effects that had obviously been stored for other Marines. He returned shaking his head.

"We don't have any personal effects for you Fenwick, are you sure you left them with us?"

"Of course I did," I said, "I turned in my jungle utilities, a map, tiger tooth, AK47 rounds, plus a couple of other items."

"Well," he said, "If you had AK47 rounds, they are contraband and would have been disposed of."

"Okay, I understand that," I retorted angrily, "but how about the rest of the items? Someone must have them."

Angrily he replied, "Don't be accusing us of taking anything that belongs to you, Marine."

By now I was getting a little irate and frustrated. "Hell fire!" I exclaimed. My voice was somewhat louder than the usual conversational tone. "They put them in a bag and said I could claim them when I got ready to leave the ship. What the hell is going on?"

"I'm telling you that you don't have any personal effects here," Jones replied. "If you have any bitches, take them up with the senior corpsman."

"Now I'm beginning to understand," I said as I gritted my teeth. "Some Navy Squid who has never seen combat is going to be walking around in the world one day, with my souvenirs, bragging about how he took them off a dead gook. This is a bunch of bullshit!"

In the mist of our heated argument some of the other corpsmen and nurses came over to where we were. They wanted to know what all the ruckus was about. I explained the situation and two of the Navy nurses checked the storage room again.

One of the nurses said, "Here are your personal effects. Just calm down. See, everything is all right!"

She handed me the blue, brown, red, and yellow striped bag with a draw string at the top. I immediately opened it to check the contents. Just as I feared, some of my items were there all right, but my souvenirs were gone. I became even angrier. Finally a Navy doctor came over and interrupted our argument. He directed me to take what belongings I had and to get out on the flight deck on the double. I was to wait for a chopper to fly me to Da Nang so I could catch the next plane bound for Cam Ranh Bay.

"What about my utilities?" I sounded off.

"There's no time," the doctor said. "Now get your butt moving up to flight deck."

With my little ditty bag in hand, I found my way to the helo pad and waited for a chopper to arrive. In my mind I swore and hoped that the Sailor who had taken my souvenirs would end up in the bush. I could imagine him telling war stories to his friends back in the States and showing them the tiger tooth, and VC map. What disgusted me was that someone in the armed forces would do a Marine this way. Even my jungle utilities were gone.

I knew that whoever stole from me would be sitting off the coast of Da Nang on a ship for his entire tour; sleeping in soft beds, eating hot chow, watching TV, playing card games, and taking a hot shower every day. I did not care about the AK47 rounds, I just wanted my jungle utilities, tiger tooth and VC map back. Was that too much to ask after I had risked my life each and every day in Vietnam? I thought about how much difference there was in the integrity of the corpsmen on a Navy ship versus the brave and caring corpsmen attached to Marine infantry units, especially those who went to the bush with Mike Company.

Soon I was on a CH-46 flying from the ship back to Da Nang. I caught a C-130 Hercules heading south along the coast of South Vietnam for Cam Ranh Bay. The only thing I knew was that it was an Army Base somewhere in South Vietnam. It seemed like hours of flying time in the four-engine tur-boprop military aircraft from Da Nang to Cam Ranh Bay. It must have been at least two hundred seventy miles south of Da Nang, a long way from my unit.

When I arrived I was admitted to a ward in a quanson hut that took on the appearance of a half moon. Every half hour or so an Army corpsman would come by and take my temperature and vital signs. It wasn't long until I began to feel a little better. I was told that I could check out of the ward in a log book and go to the beach, PX, and around the camp.

I began to check out and go down to the beach. I would lay out a poncho liner and sun bathe on this far eastern shore. When I finished sun bathing on the beach for a few hours each day I would go to the head in order to shower and wash the sand off of me. Inside the head there were about eight sinks, real honest to goodness toilets, stand up urinals, and a shower stall. The floor was concrete and was cool to my feet compared to the hot sand on the beach.

The Army really has it made, I thought to myself. Showers every day, a nice beach, hot chow, and an occasionally a USO (United Serviceman's Organization) show. I looked into the mirror while I was shaving and noticed that I was quickly getting a nice dark tan. I had a problem with acne in the bush, but now my face seemed to clear up and have a good tone to it. I figured that the salt water and the sun was nature's way of cleansing my skin. Little by little I began to wash dirt and stains from my body that had accumulated while in the bush without hot baths or showers. I realized, however, that my stay at Cam Ranh Bay would soon come to and end and that I would be rejoining Mike Company.

For now though, I was "Living the life of Riley." I remembered that expression from a television series in the mid 1950s. To me it meant that I was enjoying my new found state of prosperity and contentment and that I was privileged in a sense. I wished that I could have been home on Cherry Hill Farm at that time so I could strut around with my suntan. Dreams, however, are only as good as how long they last. As I walked back outside in the hot sun, reality took over, and my thoughts reminded me of my buddies back in Mike Company out in the bush. There would be no showers and sun bathing for them.

One afternoon I attended a USO Show. There was a live band playing on stage. The all male audience was medical patients from all branches of service. We sat around some wooden benches in the hot sun. The benches were built next to the beach in the soft sand. Three large parachutes were draped over the stage to act as shade and backdrop for the band. They were gently blowing in the breeze. A band from the Philippines was playing. They had a group of six in the band with a female lead singer. In addition, there were two go-go dancers swaying to the music as the band played. I could hear jeers and cat calls throughout the audience. The go-go dancers wore short mini-skirts and were not embarrassed to strut their stuff.

One of the Army guys pretended to collapse on the bench saying, "OOhhhh, I think I'm in love." Others were yelling, "I love you no shit, buy me one drinki. I love you no shit, buy me air conditioned Honda. I love you no shit, buy me electric stove." Then another jeer came roaring from the audience, "I love you no shit, I give you passport to America, land of the big PX!"

There was beer and sodas available but very few were drinking sodas. Everyone was out to have a good time. The band started playing House of the Rising Sun. The audience began to sing along with the lyrics while swaying to the music. The go-go dancers began to tease the audience by facing away, bending over, and with their hands on their knees, moved their butts back and forth in a rhythmical motion and then up and down. We could see their white panties from where we were sitting. Two men jumped up on the stage and started for the dancers with their arms stretched out. The girls ran quickly behind the drummer. Almost immediately two Army military police jumped up on the stage and scurried the two men off the edge. They fell into the soft sand. Everyone roared with laughter.

A thunder storm appeared out of nowhere and it began to pour down rain. Some of the guys who had taken their ward shirts off to bask in the sun began to put them back on. Others just continued to sing along while drinking beer like there was no tomorrow. The parachutes were now blowing wildly in the wind and the band stopped playing for a moment. We all started yelling in protest. The band moved their equipment back a few feet on the stage in order to get under the parachutes and protect their instruments. The band started up another tune while the wind was blowing gusts of rain up under the parachutes.

The song they chose was "In-A-Gadda-Da-Vida" by the rock band Iron Butterfly. Everyone was screaming, "Yeah, Yeah, Get some!" They played this song for several minutes and then immediately started another song. As I tipped up my beer I heard the lyrics of "Yesterday" by the Beatles. I began to sing along. Yesterday, I thought. Oh those yesterdays. How I wished I was back home on the farm.

The rain cloud soon disappeared and the sun popped out once again. Here came the dancers to the edge of the stage twisting and turning their buttocks. A Marine sitting next to me in his ward pajamas yelled, "Come here you L B F M's," he spelled. "Come here and sit on my face!"

"What's a L B F M?" I asked.

"Little Brown Fucking Machines," he said as he spilled his beer down the front of his chin and chest. These oriental beauties really know how to shake that thang. I'd like to pop one of these Filipina ladies just for Old Glory!"

"Yeah," I agreed, "One for Old Glory!"

The band continued to play for about three hours that afternoon and finally began to pack up their equipment. Everyone yelled in protest and we got more rowdy by the minute. We finally coaxed them into playing one last tune. The band struck up a song written by Mel Tillis which was made world famous by Kenny Rogers and the First Edition in 1969, "Ruby, Don't Take Your Love To Town." The lyrics began to flow freely throughout the audience as we all sang along with the band. The Marine next to me put his arm around my neck. We toasted our Black Label Beer cans by clanging them together and continued to sing along without missing a beat. In unison we tipped our beer cans together, raised them toward the sky, and then chugged the lukewarm beer. We raised our heads as if to sing to the heavens. I inwardly thought to myself that it was a song of the times. I went back to the ward and crawled into my rack. I slept for awhile and missed evening chow. I figured taking in the music was worth missing the Army mess hall chow. I had a good time that afternoon and also managed to get some much needed relaxation.

The next morning I was called up to the front desk. An Army sergeant corpsman was sitting behind a counter. He stood up and said, "Fenwick, I'm gonna make you a "Temp Man."

"What's a Temp Man?" I asked with uncertainty.

"A Temp Man is someone who goes around the ward and takes everyone's temperature the first thing in the morning and the last thing at night. That is, before the other corpsmen and doctor arrive in the morning and after they depart at night."

"I don't know if I'm cracked up for that job," I said. "I'm a 0331, Doc. Machine Gunner! A Grunt! Infantry! Know whut ah mean?"

"You can handle it," he said with confidence. "It's a piece-a-cake. All you have to do is take each patient's temperature and record it on this chart. If a patient's temperature is 98.6, it is normal. Anything above or below, our medical staff will follow up with the necessary care or treatment."

He then showed me how to shake the thermometer using wrist action in order to allow a starting point for the mercury inside. He explained that I should leave it in a patient's mouth for about two minutes before reading it. I took the thermometer and tried to figure out how to read it. He told me to take my temperature first to see if I knew how to do it. I read it after a few minutes.

"The corpsman said, "Great! You've got it. See how easy it is?"

"Yeah, no problem," I replied.

I started making my first rounds in the quanson hut at exactly 0600. With clipboard and a thermometer in hand I started on the left side of the squad bay working my way around in a clockwise direction. As I approached the first bed I glanced around the ward and noticed that most of the patients were still snoring away. Some were turning restlessly about and others began to get up out of bed to make head calls and brush their teeth. It appeared that the Marines on the ward were the early risers who were mostly stirring about while the Army personnel were still in the racks.

It went smooth with the first few patients. When I approached the fifth, a Marine, he was still snoring. I touched his shoulders and shook him to wake him up. He bolted up in the bed and began swinging wildly. He knocked the medical chart from my hands and it clanged to the concrete floor. I managed to block one of his blows with my forearm.

"Holy shit!" I said. "Calm down, all I want to do is take your temperature."

"Fuckin shit," he said. "Don't ever touch me again. I don't want nobody touchin me. You hear me? No one!"

"Excuse the hell out of me," I replied. "Here is the thermometer, take your own damn temperature."

"Shit man," he said as he suddenly realized what was going on. "You scared the hell out of me. I thought I was still in the bush."

"Can I take your temperature now?" I asked.

"Yeah, okay," was his reply.

I inserted the thermometer into his mouth and he lay back down. I told him that I would be back in a couple of minutes to obtain the reading. I went to the next rack and woke the next soldier. This time it went a little smoother. I then returned to the Marine after a few minutes and he had rolled over on his side with the thermometer dangling between his open lips. I decided not to attempt to reinsert it and risk another confrontation, so I began to ease the thermometer from his lips trying not to wake him. Suddenly he bolted up again swinging his fists. He barely caught me on the side of my right cheek. I jumped back and began cursing the job that I had been assigned.

"Man, if you don't knock it off," the Marine said, "I'm liable to smack you one!"

"Crap ass!" I replied angrily. "I'm not putting up with your bullshit."

"No hard feelings," he said as he inserted the thermometer back into his mouth. "I get a little jumpy at times. Been in the bush too fuckin long, I guess."

After we both settled down some, we began to talk a little about our different grunt units and after a few minutes, I was able to read his temperature.

"You've got a temperature of 99.8," I said. "Just slightly high, 98.6 is normal." I had tried to impress him with my new gained knowledge of being responsible for taking temperatures of the patients. "I will let the corpsman know you have a slight temperature and I'm sure they will take another look at you."

"Thanks man," he said.

"No problem. Just don't knock my head off in the future," I said smiling as I walked away to the next patient.

My next patient was snoring loudly. I wanted to avoid any sudden surprises so I shook the man gently; he did not respond. I shook him even harder and he just moaned. Oh well, I thought. I inserted the thermometer between his lips. He began to smack his lips as if trying to taste food or something. I managed to get it under his tongue and checked his vital signs. In a couple of minutes I began to slowly remove the thermometer. As I gently retracted it, the patient rose slowly as though attempting to keep it in his mouth. I envisioned a dead man rising from his coffin. Finally the thermometer slipped out and he slowly laid back down still sleeping. I was amused at the comical state that he was in.

Throughout my round in the ward, several of the patients acted the same way. They seemed to be in a state of shock when first awakened. The worse part was that someone would swing at me while they were still in a deep sleep. I recorded all the temperatures and returned the chart to the front desk. I told the corpsman that I did not like the job, but he said that I would only be assigned the task for one week and then he would assign someone else.

Needless to say, after a week of being a Temp Man I got a little fed up with it but it had its advantages. During the day I was allowed to check out of the ward and roam around the base. I spent most of my time on the beach. I also had some time to myself to just be alone and think of home. I managed to get a greeting card from the Army PX that had this inscription on the front, "Know what I miss most about you?" On the inside it had, "Oh well… You know…" I knew it wasn't the best greeting card to send home, but it would have to do. Quality was hard to come by in the Nam.

July 13, 1970

Well hello folks,

How are things going for you these summer days? Hope everyone is in good health and spirits. Guess its pretty warm back home now. At least you have that sugar tree in the front yard to sit under in your spare time.

I'm doing pretty good now and feel a lot better. They sent me to Cam Ranh Bay from the ship to recuperate. I bet you all can find it on the map. It's about half way down the coast of Vietnam.

The Army runs this place and boy is it nice. We have formations each morning and things to do but in the afternoon we have most of the time off. I don't even have to be at the formations or go on working parties. The sarge of the barracks made me the "Temp Man," that is, I take all the guys temperature at six o'clock in the morning and again at ten o'clock at night. Then I post the results in the log book they have. It's about forty guys in the ward now.

Well, to tell you the truth, I'm having a pretty good time. The beach is open all day, they have showers, good chow, a snack bar, a PX, and just about anything a base would have in the States. Like I said, the Army runs it.

I got some film today so I'll take a few pictures tomorrow. Still no mail yet, but they may get some to me before long. I know for sure that I'll be here until the 17th or maybe a few days more. Really I'm doing real well, at least for awhile.

As ever,
Fred

One morning at reveille I was called to the front desk. The corpsman on duty told me that I was doing fine and that I would be joining another company at Cam Ranh Bay. Now that I was over my illness they would make me work for the Army. At formation an Army gunnery sergeant told us to report to the supply building in order to be issued the olive drab Army jungle utilities. They were similar in design as the jungle utilities but were not camouflaged. I felt like I was out of uniform but the new utilities felt a lot better than the hospital garb. I inwardly cursed to myself when I thought about my Marine jungle utilities being stolen back at the hospital ship.

After our uniform issue we formed up again and the gunnery sergeant called out about six Marines and explained that we would be filling sandbags and fortifying the bunkers. Others were broken into groups to police the base for trash and litter. It seemed that the Marines were picked solely to fill sandbags while the Army personnel would walk around picking up trash. We thought that the Marines had a raw deal.

We filled sandbags in the hot sun during the morning and afternoon. We had another formation at 1600 and were told by the Army gunnery sergeant that we were to be present for formation the next morning in our fatigues, green T-shirts, and combat boots. We were to start running and exercising in order to get back in physical shape. This was the first time since my arrival in Vietnam that I was to be subjected to organized physical training. I felt that it was just another way for the Army to mess with us.

The next morning before breakfast we went on a jog around the base. The Army gunnery sergeant was calling cadence as we ran along in a straggly formation. He seemed to take joy in the fact that he was in charge of some Marines in formation. We ran along on a dusty dirt road. As our boots pounded on the dry dirt the dust was kicking up in a cloud of haze. It seemed to hover over our formation and it became very difficult to breathe. Of course the gunnery sergeant was running on the outside of the formation where there wasn't as much dust. Although we were breathing in the dust as we ran in formation we were forced to stay on the dirt road. It would have been better to have run on the beach.

I felt so out of shape even though I was breathing in the dust. My muscles were not used to this type of abuse. When we first started off I felt a deadened pain as my feet pounded inside my jungle boots. My shins began to burn as well. Although the cadence was not the same as what I was used to in the Marine Corps it sounded good to chant for a change in formation. We sounded off as the Gunny lead us in cadence. "In the Nam... he fought the dirty Cong... He fought him in the spring time ... and in the month of May... And if you ask him why the hell he fought-um... he fought um for the red, white, and blue." I would have preferred the Marine Corps cadence myself. To me there was nothing more motivating than running with Marines in formation, keeping in step, and sounding off to all the unique chants of the Marines.

After morning chow we had another formation and roll call. The Gunny picked me and three other Marines and told us that we would be going on guard duty. He told us to report to the S-2 Officer and that we would get further instructions. When the formation was dismissed, the Marines and I proceeded to the Headquarters tent and located the S-2 Officer, an Army first lieutenant. He explained to us that we were to set up on the beach about three hundred meters out of the base perimeter and would act as a listening post at night and observation post during the day. We were to question any suspicious Vietnamese outside the wire if they passed by our position and to inspect any baskets that they may be carrying for weapons or ordnance. He told us to report to a staff sergeant at the armory and draw a M60 machine gun. The S-4 office was to provide the ammunition.

We proceeded to the armory to draw the machine gun. When we arrived, a sergeant told us that we had no authority to draw a gun. We explained that the S-2 Officer had given us a brief. His reply was, "No authorization! No machine gun!" We went back to the S-2 Officer and told him what had happened at the armory. He seemed mad because of our incompetence to complete such a simple task. He gave us a staff sergeant's name and told us to go back to the armory and to talk to him personally. We arrived back at the armory and asked for the staff sergeant by name. After some deliberation with the sergeant, the staff sergeant finally appeared from within the armory cage. He told us that without the proper paperwork that we would not be allowed to sign for a gun. We explained the run around we were getting, so he gave us a form letter and told us to take it back to the S-2 Officer for signature.

By now we were getting a little perturbed. We all went back to the S-2 Officer and asked for his signature. He signed it while grumbling and complaining about Marines not being able to carry out simple instructions. Back at the armory we signed for the gun, a tripod, and spare barrel bag with all the accessories. Next we were off to see someone in S-4 for the ammunition. When we told a Spec-4 what we needed and the purpose, he told us that we did not have a written request and could not draw the ammo without it. He said that it would have to come from the Guard Officer who was located in the S-2 tent. We went to the tent looking for the Guard Officer.

"Why are you Marines back here again?" the S-2 Officer asked angrily.

"We had to come back and get a written request for ammo from the Guard Officer," one of the Marines replied.

"Jesus Christ, can't you boys do anything right?" the officer snapped.

"We are not boys," the Marine retorted. "And we're getting sick and tired of getting jerked around, lieutenant. You damn "doggies" can guard your own beach as far as I'm concerned. I didn't ask to come to this fuckin Army Base to start with!"

"You're out of line soldier! You're close to being on the border of disrespect," the officer said angrily.

The Marine did not hesitate with a response, "With all due respect Siiirrr, we are not soldiers, we're goddamn Marines and would like to be treated as such."

"One more word out of you and I will run you up on charges, on all of you," he quipped.

"Sir, we're just trying to accomplish our mission," I said. "If we can only get the ammo we'll be on our way and out of your hair."

He called for the Guard Officer. "Get these people some machine gun ammo and get them the hell out of my sight!" he yelled.

A second lieutenant who was eating a C-Ration pound cake got up and started out of the tent. "Follow me Marines," he said. We looked at each other in disbelief. We followed him to the S-4 tent. He discussed the need for ammo for us with the Spec-4 and we were given a hand written note to turn in at the Ammo dump.

"Take this down to the ammo dump," he said. "They will give you a can of ammo."

We asked soldiers along the way if they could point us in the direction of the ammo dump. I couldn't believe how many didn't know where the ammo dump was located. We finally arrived at the right bunker. There was an Army gunnery sergeant standing outside the entrance to the bunker smoking a cigarette.

"Can I be of any assistance to you Marines?" he asked.

We began explaining the circumstances and the need for ammo. He took the note from one of the Marines, read it, and began to laugh.

"You mean those idiots want you to go outside the perimeter with only one can of ammo?" he asked in disbelief.

"You got it," one of the Marines responded.

"What a bunch of ass bags," he said. "I'll give you four cans. That ought to be enough for one gun. By the way, where are your M16s?"

The Marine that had talked back to the S-2 Officer said, "Guess we're expendable items."

"That's nonsense!" the Gunny exclaimed. "Come with me to the armory and I will see to it that you take out some M16s and .45 pistols. You never know what might happen outside the lines."

We received three M16s and each drew a .45 caliber pistol. We followed the Gunny back to the ammo bunker and he gave us some claymore mines and illuminating pop up flares.

"That oughta hold you now," he said.

"Thanks Gunny," I replied. "I appreciate your help."

"Don't mention it," the Gunny said while lighting another cigarette. "When you're done just come back and see me to turn in all that stuff. What ever you do, don't leave it out there for Charlie. We've got enough problems as it is."

Just then someone approached and said, "Hey, you guys going out to set up security on the beach?"

"Yeah," we all replied in unison. It was a soldier from the S-2 tent that was going to lead us to where we were to set in. We wondered if we were going to get another run around. We followed him through the tents, around the bunkers, and through the concertina wire that was stretched around the perimeter. We had to ziz-zag our way through the wire making our own trail. We moved along the beach in the soft sand just a few hundred meters from the water. After we were about three hundred meters away from the perimeter we all stopped when the soldier did.

"Well, this is it. Set your gun up right here and face it out towards the ocean," he said calmly. We looked at each other in complete awe.

"Ah ain't believin dis shit," I quipped. "You mean to tell me we are to set up the gun on this open beach. No cover, no camouflage, no concealment, and what about fighting holes?"

"Don't worry," the soldier replied casually. "In case you do get hit you could be back inside the perimeter in a matter of minutes."

Another Marine spoke up, "Easy for you to say, you are not the one that will have to run back through that clump of concertina wire."

The soldier replied with a sneer, "Take it easy Marines, you all are too paranoid. You're only out here for security, not to take on an entire NVA

Division."

I retorted, "Evidently you haven't been in the bush lately, this fuckin lackadaisical attitude will get you killed. Tell me something, will you? What are we going to shoot at in the middle of the ocean? You all expecting a NVA invasion from the South China Sea?"

Suddenly I became aware of my boldness in hearing myself rattle on like an old salt. I had become very confident and to a degree somewhat arrogant. What did these guys know about the bush anyway, I thought to myself. Most of them will probably never see the jungles and rice paddies of Vietnam. Just kick around on the beach, eat at the mess hall, attend USO shows, drink Black Label Beer, and take showers every day while they pull duty in the Nam. And all the while writing home and telling everyone how rough they have it.

"Tell you what!" the soldier exclaimed. "I'll go back and bring out a radio so you can have communications."

"Now you're tawkin," I said.

We all looked at one another in amazement. At first they were just going to send us outside the perimeter with just a M60 machine gun and with no M16s or radio for communication. Knowing our luck we might just get that NVA invasion from the sea. The soldier walked back into the perimeter. We were determined to go ahead and set up the gun and scratch out a place in the sand for a sleeping hole. It would provide minimal protection, we thought.

Since I was trained as a machine gunner, I volunteered to set the gun up. I mounted it on the tripods, placed the T&E (Traversing and Elevating) mechanism on the gun and sighted through the rear and front sights. I set the sights at five hundred meters for grazing fire. Grazing fire meant that the rounds would not rise above the height of an average man for that distance. I checked the spare barrel bag and its components, and set the left and right lateral limits on the gun. I explained to the other Marines what I was doing as I went through the procedures.

"You really got your shit together," one of the Marines commented.

"Well," I replied, "I was trained as a machine gunner at Infantry Training Regiment, Camp Geiger, North Carolina. When I got to Nam they made me a rifleman. I've been wanting to get my hands on one of these babies ever since I got here."

"Yeah," one of the Marines said, "hope we don't have to use it."

"If we do, I'll show you how to rock and roll," I said confidently.

The soldier finally arrived with a radio and a case of C-Rations. "Here's you some chow," he said. "I'll bring you out a jug of water in the morning."

One of the Marines said, "Hey, you're all right for an Army doggie."

"Yeah," he replied, "and you Jarheads are all right too."

"Say that with respect," one of the Marines quipped jokingly. The rest of us couldn't resist from laughing.

"Hey, how long are we going to be out here on guard duty?" one of the Marines asked.

The soldier replied, "Oh, maybe a day or two."

"A day or two?" a Marine shouted. "You mean we won't get relieved for a few days. Don't you have others that can take turns with this shit detail?"

"Afraid not," came the reply, "us Army doggies have more important things to do."

"That's okay, at least we won't be getting fucked with out here," the Marine replied.

"Yeah," another Marine added, "I'd rather do this than fill sandbags."

The soldier left us and we began to orient ourselves with the surroundings and to get settled in for the night. The warm sand felt good to us. I laid my poncho liner down in the small sleeping hole that I had scrapped out with my bare hands. I lay down to test it out. The edge of the sleeping hole felt soft and comfortable. I took my hands and sculptured a pillow out of the sand as best as I could. I lay back again and said, "Ah yes. Perfect! This is the life." The other Marines followed suit and made them a pillow in the same manner.

The sun was beginning to go down and the reflection off the beach looked inviting. We took turns diving into the ocean water and going for short swims. The air was still warm enough to allow us to dry before we had to bed down for the night. Even though we swam with our skivvy drawers on it didn't take long for mine to dry out before it got totally dark.

As night fell a full moon replaced the sun. It gave off a bright and beautiful glimmer down the beach. We could see all around us. We wouldn't need any illumination flares on this clear night. The stars were shining in the sky above and the humid air was blowing gently across the beach. The sound of the incoming waves had a majestic sound, almost tranquilizing. I particularly liked the reflection of the moon on the crashing waves as they hit the shore line. We would not have to worry about the mosquitoes either tonight because of the breeze from the ocean. I felt so serene and peaceful.

As I lay back on my poncho liner gazing at the stars and conversing with the other Marines, I saw a falling star. What a beautiful sight. I began searching for the Big Dipper and North Star.

One of the other Marines shouted as he pointed towards the clear night sky, "There, did you see that? I just saw a falling star!"

"That makes two in about ten minutes," I said. "I saw one awhile ago myself."

One of the Marines asked, "Where are you from back in the world?"

"Kentucky," I responded, "why do you ask?"

"I just wondered," he said, "you gotta country accent!"

"Yeah," I responded, "and damn proud of it!"

That's all it took to spark my story telling about good ole Kentucky. I began telling them about some of the chores I used to do back on the farm. They all seemed interested in what I was telling them and encouraged me to continue. They got a good laugh when I told them about hauling cow manure and weeding tobacco beds. We took turns talking about our mothers and fathers. As I listened to the stories about their parents, I was convinced that I had the best mother and father on the face of the earth.

Suddenly I felt something crawling on top of me. I raised my head and saw a small sand crap crawling across my stomach. I immediately took my open right hand, scooped the creature up, and with a continuous motion flung it off of me. It landed on another Marine. He jumped at first and then decided to start playing with it.

Then one of the Marines said, "Just look at the fuckin sand crabs, they're all over the place."

I stirred from my prone position and noticed that the sand crabs had popped out of little small holes that they had made in the sand. There were hundreds of them scurrying across the sand. I slapped my palm down hard on the sand. The thumping sound and vibration caused the craps close to me to dive into their holes. In a few seconds they were back out again scurrying about with their pincers making a scraping sound.

We began to cover the holes while burying the crabs in them. We played games with the crabs by filling in their holes and watching them uncover themselves. We finally gave up since we were outnumbered and set up a watch throughout the night. I could feel the sand crabs crawling over my poncho liner throughout the night but decided to leave them alone. After all, they were not hurting anyone. During my watch I played with them when they came scurrying past me.

We ended up staying in this same position for three days. We were having a ball just being by ourselves. No one of authority was there to bark any orders. We basically did whatever we desired. It amazed me that we were put out on this lonesome beach without anyone from the higher echelon checking on us from time to time. It was as if they had totally forgotten about us. We ate C-Rations, played with the sand crabs, went swimming during the day, and searched a few mamasans who came walking down the beach looking for anything and everything.

None of us spoke fluent Vietnamese so it was a bit comical when we stopped and searched the mamasans. In fact we had fun doing it and the mamasans didn't seem to mind. Some were more than happy to have us peak inside their baskets to see what they had scavenged off the beach. We were looking for weapons or ammo, but never found any. There was no enemy invasion from the sea to ward off either. We were having too much fun to worry about enemy activity here on this heavenly beach. Even some of the small boats were too far off the coast for us to be concerned.

On the fourth day we were relieved by some other Marines that had been in the medical ward. I knew that it would not be long now before I would leave the beautiful beach at Cam Ranh Bay and return to my squad in the bush. We arrived back in the perimeter and turned in our weapons. The gun and ammunition was left with the Marines who relieved us. I took a shower and realized that it was Sunday.

I decided to go to church for a change and to thank the Lord for my very existence. I put on my olive drab Army utilities and went to a quanson hut where Mass was being held. I listened intently to the Priest during his sermon. He was bad mouthing the hippies back in the States something fierce. He was talking about them protesting the war and smoking dope while we were losing our lives for our country. A bunch of cowards and indecent bigots was his message to us. He got so angry at one point, I thought he might begin cursing, but he maintained his decency. I left at the conclusion of the Mass felling better that I had attended.

My thoughts went back to home and my childhood when I had attended mass at Saint Rose Church with my mother and younger brother. We would go to the 9:00 a.m. mass while my father would be the early bird and go the 6:00 a.m. mass. He did this so that he could get home early enough to start milking the cows, a chore that had to be done twice a day, seven days a week. I remembered the tasty and bountiful Sunday dinners that my mother fixed. I would have given anything for one of her chicken and dumpling meals. Instead, I went to the mess hall and feasted on fried eggs and creamed beef.

When I returned to the hooch I sat down and wrote a letter home.

July 19, 1970
11:00 a.m.

Hello Mom, Dad and all,

Well today is Sunday and we're not doing much so thought I'd drop you a few lines. I've been trying to catch up on my writing while I've been here. There sure are a lot of people to write to. Trouble is I don't hardly know what to tell them since it's the same thing day in and day out.

I went to Church today. It's been quit awhile since I've had the chance. It's just a little Chapel, but it has an air conditioner inside and is real nice. When the priest gave his sermon, I thought I was back in boot camp. He was talking about all these hippies and such and how they act toward the Church. He really knew what he was talking about.

Today we've only had one formation but tomorrow we'll have to make three or four. Oh! By the way, I'm in a different company here. They exercise us in the mornings and put us on different details or jobs until we leave. I've had guard duty for the past three days. I'll be leaving to go back to my unit maybe around the 21st. After they put you in this company, it's not much longer until you're heading back to your original unit. I'll kindly be glad when I get back. Hope I get back in time to get paid this month. Well I've "skated" for a few weeks now, that is, I've gotten by easy. But like the guys in the bush say, "You owe it to your body." I was real lucky to get such a break. I didn't think my luck would run that way. This has almost been like an R&R except during the few days that I was sick.

I guess you all are wondering what was the matter with me. Well the doctor told me I had all the symptoms of malaria but that the tests were negative. I just had a temperature, some chills, and he said strep throat and amoebic dysentery. But that was all cleared up in the few days that I was on ship. I was feeling fine when I got to Cam Ranh Bay. Guess you've gotten the picture I sent in that a Red Cross worker took of me. I can imagine what you all thought when you got the letter with Red Cross symbol stamped on the envelope.

I've taken a few pictures down here, some at the beach and some of a USO Show. There has been two here since I arrived. Some of the pictures took by accident so don't be surprised if a couple comes back with not much on them. Mom, don't worry about the money in getting the pictures developed. I'll pay you back or you can take it out of the checks I send home. I'm planning to get an album to put the photos in when I head back to the States.

Besides being hot and dry over here, I guess I have no complaints, as of now. The only thing is that they still haven't sent any mail to me but I'll be leaving soon anyhow. I keep myself occupied anyway. I don't like for the mail to pile up on me, if you know what I mean. I guess Mike Company is still getting settled from moving to LZ Ross.

Well guess that about raps up the scoop on this place. There's not much happening here, that's why I want to get back to my unit. How is everything with you all? Hope all the crops, cows, and whatever, are doing fine. Guess you're eating good ole green beans and tomatoes out of the garden. Believe it or not, the Army has tomatoes once in awhile down here. They sure do have a dog's life. Maybe that's why they call them "doggies." They go out in the field too, but on their base camps, they sure have it nice.

Do you all still have plenty of company on the weekends? I guess the grand kids are getting a little too big to be jumping up in Dad's lap now. Last month I got a letter from some of my nieces. They were all in different envelopes so I got one about each mail call. Tell them when they come over to the house that I have a buddy that likes to read their letters. He has several nieces and nephews himself and he really gets a kick out of them. It's that blonde headed guy, Hawkeye, in some of the pictures I sent home.

Well as I think about the time of the year, it seems like the time has really went by fast. Guess what Larry, your school vacation is a bit over half through. I have to keep reminding you. I don't want you to miss school. Oh well, anyway it won't be long until I'll have five months in "The Nam."

Well guess I've about said all I know to say so I'll let you all go for now. Until next time I'll say good-bye and may God bless.

Most affirm,
Fred

I continued to go on working parties, filling sandbags, and policing the area. It seemed like a never ending project to beautify the base at Cam Ranh Bay. Sometimes as a group of us Marines walked through the area picking up the trash and burning shitters we would sing a song that the Marines had managed to come up with. The tune mimicked the "Oh Christmas Tree" song that we all used to sing at Christmas time. It went like this.

"We like it here...we like it here...You fuckin A...we like it here...We shine our boots...we shine our brass...Just to kiss the lifer's ass...Although we have malaria...We still police...the fuckin area...We like it here...we like it here...you fuckin A...we like it here."

Another one of our favorites mimicked the song "Oh My Darling Clementine."

"Ship me over...Sergeant Major...I don't wanna leave the Corps...Make the next four...like the first four... and I'll live forever more."

Then we would change tunes and sing to the melody from the theme "Bridge on the River Khwai." It went something like this.

"Re-up...and buy a brand new car...Re-up...show what a fool you are...Re-up...I'd rather throw up...So take your money...And your car...And... shove it up your ass!"

Chapter 8

Back to the Bush

ON 18 July I received word that I was to pick up my orders and that I would be flying back to my unit. After all the paperwork had been processed and stamped, I said good-bye to some of my acquaintances that I had come in contact with at Cam Ranh Bay. One was another Lance corporal that I knew from Mike Company. He jokingly told me that he was a "Rogue" before he joined the Marine Corps, but to me he was a damn good guy. He accompanied me to the runway and waited with me just to keep me company.

Three different times the flight was cancelled. By the time I was sure the flight would depart as scheduled, I found myself alone on the tarmac as my fellow Marine had said goodbye so he could get back to his daily duties. After all, I was a field Marine and could manage on my own. I finally got onboard a C-130 heading for Da Nang. When I landed I caught a bus that was going to Freedom Hill. I hoped that one day I would pass back through Da Nang on my way home, but for now I would have to earn my pay for a little while longer in the rice paddies, jungles, and mountains. There would me no relief from the burdens of war for a Marine grunt.

The bus pulled into Freedom Hill. I had been there before when I had gone to the Land Mine Warfare School. I visited the PX but didn't buy anything since I didn't have room to carry much. I just walked around and felt like I was on some military base in the States. Freedom Hill reminded me of some little small town. I knew that I would be leaving soon however, back to the mines, booby traps, Charlie, and the dreaded insects. At least for awhile I felt the comforts of home.

While I was at Freedom Hill, I ran into three Marines from Mike Company that was also trying to get back to Firebase Ross. We all started talking about going down to the helo pad to catch a chopper, but one of the Marines had the bright idea that we should hitchhike back. I wasn't keen on the idea because none of us had weapons. In the end the others coerced me into going along with them. The plan was to start walking down the main road and thumb a ride to LZ Baldy and then take a chopper from LZ Baldy to Firebase Ross.

We started walking and it wasn't long until a Marine convoy approached us from behind. There were four 6x6 trucks heading our way. One of the Marines got in the middle of the road and flagged down the first driver. The driver of the leading truck came to a stop right beside me and the other two Marines. The other three trucks came to a stop as well and sat idle while revving their engines. Then the Marine who had flagged down the driver joined us on the side of the road. I looked in the cabin of the truck and noticed an A-driver sitting in the passenger seat.

"Hey Marine, going our way?" I yelled out to the driver over the loud noise of the 6x6 engines.

The driver stuck his head out the side of the window. "Dis here convoy is going to LZ Baldy if that helps!"

"That's where we're headed," I yelled back, "can you give us a lift?"

The driver replied, "Sure, go back to the fourth truck, it don't have nothin on it. You all can be comfortable back there."

We started to run along side the 6x6 trucks and I noticed cases of C-Rations and other sundry items stacked on the beds of each truck. We arrived at the last truck which was the fourth truck in the convoy. The tailgate was locked in the up position and we found it difficult to pull ourselves up and crawl into the truck bed. Once over the tailgate two Marines sat on the right side troop seats and the other Marine and I took a seat on the left side. We faced each other toward the center and placed our belongings in front of out feet.

One of the Marines on the right side of the truck yelled out to the driver, "Hey Man, thanks for the lift!"

The driver looked back over his left shoulder and out of his rolled down window and replied, "Hold on to your nuts! It's gonna be a rough ride!"

In the back of the vehicle there were two other motor transport Marines that were riding with the convoy. One short stocky Marine was manning a mounted .50 caliber machine gun that had the weapon loaded with a belt of ammo. He was also packing a .45 caliber pistol. The other Marine was his A-gunner whose responsibility was to feed him the links of ammo if needed. He was armed with a M16. We started to introduce ourselves to the other Marines but were cut short as the driver jerked the vehicle forward. We had to hold on to the back of the seats to keep from being thrown to the truck bed. I knew we were in for a very rough ride and wished that I had waited for a chopper back at Da Nang.

The convoy was now rolling down Highway 1 heading south toward LZ Baldy. The road was very dusty and we struggled to breathe in the back of the 6x6. As we rode passed the rice paddies and small villages I could see Vietnamese women on the road walking with baskets on their heads. Vietnamese men and women were on motor scooters and others were on some sort of man-made jalopy. As we moved passed them numerous kids would run along the trucks as fast as they could with outstretched hands begging for chop-chop. Luckily the convoy was moving fast enough to lose them in the dust.

As we moved along the road there would be kids that seemed to appear out of nowhere. Then a different group would be chasing the vehicles as we passed by. Once in awhile the Marine that was manning the machine gun would toss out some gum to the kids. He would laugh loudly at the scramble of kids fighting and kicking to get to the gum first. I began to scope out the scenery and to try and enjoy the ride. There were small hooches on both sides of the road, rice paddies seemed to appear as far as the human eye could see, and there were rolling hills in the background. I knew it was now a matter of time until I would be walking through this familiar territory with my squad back at Mike Company. The country side for now seemed peaceful and beautiful to the eye.

We came upon a roadside village and to my surprise the trucks pulled off the side of the road and stopped. Our driver cut off his engine and rolled out of the cab and onto the ground. He looked up at us and said, "Come on in you guys, we're gonna have us a drink!" We all looked at each other in disbelief, but we figured why the hell not. We might as well quench our thirsts while we had a chance. I could not believe that the convoy was stopping in the middle of nowhere just outside of Da Nang. I wondered about the security aspect. Would there be any VC around? Who knows? Who cares?

Most of the motor transport Marines and my little party of Mike Company Marines went into a cafe type restaurant. It had a grass roof, bamboo poles for support, and a dirt floor. There were about four wooden tables and chairs with no table cloths and a small bamboo bar centered in the back of the room. We took a seat with about five Marines around two of the tables. I made sure I got a seat by the entrance door in case I had to make a fast get away. I was not real comfortable with my surroundings and the company of the motor transport Marines. They seemed like trouble to me.

As we sat down I could smell the aroma of fish. A middle aged mamasan came over to our table and asked if we wanted some beer. We ordered a round and started to drink the lukewarm Vietnamese beer. The local beer was called Ba Moui Ba or Biere 33. As we were sipping our beers two Vietnamese girls came over to our table who were dressed in black silky pajamas. They selected two of the motor transport Marines who were nearest to them and put their arms around their necks. Then the first girl to approach the table asked her Marine if he wanted to "boom-boom."

"Manine want short time?" the frisky girl asked. "Manine numba one boom-boom. Me so Harney. Me boom-boom long time, you see. Me numba one fucky fucky."

"How much for boom-boom?" the Marine asked.

"Only ten MPC," the Vietnamese woman replied. "Me boom-boom long time. Me sucky fucky good, you see."

The Marine answered, "I give you five MPC, no more."

"Manine too cheap skate," she said. "Hokay, hokay, sucky fucky eight MPC."

"No eight MPC," the Marine responded while raising his beer to his lips. "Five MPC or nay-san didi mau."

"Manine numba fuckin ten," she said as she walked away to approach another Marine.

"Didi mau, nay-san!" the next Marine yelled. "Give the black syphilis to some gook, not me. I don't want my dick to rot off."

She returned to the Marine who had offered five MPC. In a few moments he was up, grabbed her by the hand, and she led him behind a curtain down a dimly lit passageway behind the bar. The older mamasan was speaking Vietnamese to the other girl and gave a motion for her to take a Marine behind the curtain. It was not long until one of the convoy drivers took the girl and started back behind the curtain.

"I hope your dick falls off," a Mike Company Marine yelled out.

"Not to worry," replied the truck driver. "I always have a raincoat to wear."

"Better hope it don't bust," another Marine added.

Everyone began to laugh. One of the Marines sitting at our table made a comment that wearing a rubber while getting laid was like taking a shower wearing a raincoat."

"Yep," another Marine responded, "but you had best protect your family jewels with these Vietnamese ladies of pleasure."

The rest of us were content to just kick back and have a couple of beers even if it was the local brew. I had enough MPC on my person to afford one beer. MPC was an abbreviation for "Military Payment Certificate." They were issued to military personnel to help curtail black marketing. The MPC was good in the military clubs and Post Exchange. It was sort of like Vietnamese money (Dong) that Americans could spend on the local economy instead of American currency. The Vietnamese were known to black market American currency throughout the south especially in the cities and villages.

The servicemen were paid in US dollars which they could convert to the local currency at the black market conversion rate. This appealed to the servicemen rather than the government fixed conversion rate. From this conversion rate imbalance, a black market developed where as the servicemen could profit from the more favorable exchange rate. To reduce profiteering from currency trade, the US military devised the MPC program. MPCs were paper money denominated in amounts of 5 cents, 10 cents, 25 cents, 50 cents, 1 dollar, 5 dollars, 10 dollars, and 20 dollars. Although actual US dollars were not circulating, many local establishments accepted MPC equal with US dollars, for they could use them on the black market.   We began to talk about the stories that Vietnamese prostitutes had been known to put a broken neck of a beer bottle up their private parts so an unsuspecting American going for a "short time" would be cut. I had heard the stories over and over but I just didn't see how any woman could manage to do that. What I did know was that these Vietnamese prostitutes would give the American servicemen some sort of venereal disease. I had made up my mind that the risk was far too great. I would not allow myself to be tempted, no matter how "harney" I got.

The two Marines emerged from behind the curtain with smiles on their faces and we immediately walked out and boarded the trucks. Amazing, I thought! Here we were drinking beer inside this little watering hole and the .50 caliber machine guns were left unattended except for those Marines who decided to take cat naps in the cabin of the trucks. I must make it a point to be more cautious in the future and not keep such bad company, I thought to myself. If I was to safely survive a tour of duty in Vietnam, I had best remain vigilant and not be led astray.

In the back of our truck there were a couple of opened C-Ration cases that had been rummaged through. Marine slang and lingo dubbed it as "rat-fucked." As we continued down the road the Marine manning the .50 caliber machine gun began throwing out individual C-Ration packs of cigarettes to the kids. He amused himself by watching the kids on the side of the road fight for them.

At one point on the road we began to move at a crawl because of the traffic congestion ahead of us. Once in awhile a water buffalo would be standing in the middle of the road and the lead driver would be yelling and screaming for the animal to move. He would nudge one once in awhile and at times get out of the truck, pick up a rock, and hurl it at the beast. We had heard that a water buffalo was worth more to the Vietnamese than human life. The rumor was that American servicemen had been fined for killing a water buffalo but not for the accidental death of civilians.

While stopped briefly, the machine gunner in our truck tossed out a cinnamon nut roll can from a C-Ration carton. The kids along the road fought frantically for the prized possession. One boy emerged from the heap of little bodies with the can. Then they began to beg for more. One of the Marines told the gunner that he was wasting good chow.

"Don't mean nothin," he said. "Watch this!"

He grabbed a can of apricots which was a larger and heavier can and threw it at the boy. It slipped through the boy's hands, hit him in the forehead, and bounced off. The boy grabbed his head in pain and dropped the other cinnamon nut roll can. The other kids scrambled for the two cans ignoring the injured boy. The gunner laughed uncontrollably.

"What the fuck did you do that for?" one of the Mike Company Marines yelled.

"Fuck these commie gooks," the gunner replied. "These little fuckers will grow up and become VC. We ought to mow them all down with this .50 cal!"

"You're fuckin crazy," the Marine replied.

"Who gives a shit," the gunner responded.

The vehicle lunged forward and again we were off moving rapidly down the road. The road was now clear and all the drivers were putting the pedal to the metal. I held on to the bench I was sitting on trying to hold on for dear life. I felt that the vehicle might overturn and land in a rice paddy off the side of the road in the middle of nowhere.

I yelled to the driver, "Hey, slow this thang down, you have passengers back here you know!"

His only response was, "Yee Haa!"

"Jesus H. Christ," the Marine on my left said, "The fuckin idiot's are trying to kill us!"

The gunner of the .50 caliber machine gun spoke up, "Just sit back and enjoy the ride," he yelled with inflection in his voice.

As we zoomed down the dirt road with a cloud of dust trailing behind us, the gunner spotted some Vietnamese farmers out in the rice paddies. They were wearing circular straw hats and dressed in the usual black pajamas. Some were bending over planting rice in the paddies while a couple more men were plowing behind water buffalos.

The gunner turned the .50 cal in their direction and yelled, "Watch me scare the living hell out of these gooks! Then he commenced to give himself verbal commands. "Gooks in the open, three hundred meters, right flank, fire for effect!" He commenced firing the .50 cal into a treeline and in the rice paddies kicking up mud and water into the air. He was firing three to five round bursts just to the left of the farmers. Raaattaa... tttaaa!

I yelled out over the loud popping sound of the machine gun, "What the hell do you think you're doing? They ain't VC!"

The gunner heard me, stopped firing, and turned his head my way. "What did you say, Marine?" he barked.

"I said they ain't VC!" I yelled back at him.

"What, you fuckin crazy?" he responded. "They're VC to me goddamit. Can't you see they're wearing black pajamas? We should kill them commie gook mother fuckers!"

I looked and saw that some of the farmers had dropped to the ground for cover and others running for their lives to get behind the rice paddy dikes. I mentally envisioned this truck load of Marines going up for courts-martial because of one stupid egotistical Marine behind a .50 caliber machine gun. Suddenly without warning, an enemy round hit the side of the truck. "Zzzz... iii... iiing!" We ducked down off the troop seats and onto the bed of the truck to take cover. I felt totally helpless as none of the Mike Company Marines had weapons.

"There the commie bastard is!" the gunner yelled out. "Behind that rice paddy dike. Looks like he has an AK. I'll get that mother fucker!"

I figured that since we were getting return fire that at least one of them was VC after all. The gunner was now putting hot lead into the rice paddy dike where the enemy fire had come. In only a few seconds the VC stood up with AK47 in hand and began running toward the treeline. The gunner opened fire on the enemy. The next thing I saw was the VC fell backward with his body flying one way and his weapon the other.

"Yee Haa," came the excited roar from the gunner. "I told you they were goddamn VC! Yee Haa!"

The motor transport A-gunner yelled out, "Let's stop and get that AK off that dead gook!"

"You crazy fuck!" the gunner yelled. "Those treelines are crawling with VC. I'm not getting my feet wet in a rice paddy for no commie VC. I'll just shoot'em from the truck!."

The convoy continued on down the road at even a faster speed than before. The .50 caliber machine gunner was now gloating about his intuition, combat prowess, and heroism. He looked at me with a defiant and contemptuous attitude and said, "The Marine Corps should give me a medal."

I reckoned I had learned a lesson from this experience. I had let a motor transport Marine outfox this old grunt. Oh well, I thought. Guess you learn something new everyday in this crazy mixed up war. Since hitching a ride on the convoy a couple of hours had passed but we somehow managed to arrive safely at LZ Baldy. I was so glad to get out of the back of the 6x6. I had been bouncing around for so long that I was sore and stiff. The three other Marines from Mike Company and I walked through some old familiar sites at LZ Baldy but we knew that the Mike Company office personnel had already been relocated to Firebase Ross. We would try to bed down here for the night and catch a chopper to Firebase Ross the following morning. We finally found the headquarters hooch of a unit where we could check-in to be assigned a rack for the night.

An unfamiliar Marine first sergeant told us that the only available cots were in a hooch that housed Marines pending courts-martial and nonjudicial punishment. He walked us around the side of his building and pointed to where we needed to go. We thanked the first sergeant and headed for the designated hooch. As we approached the hooch we looked at each other in a concerned manner as we could hear radios blasting away and the smell of marijuana filled the air. The Marines who were with me stopped at the bottom of the wooden steps leading up to the entrance of the hooch. They whispered back and forth and then told me that I should be the first to lead the way inside. I was so tired that I did not argue.

I climbed up the steps and opened the door. I took a quick glance inside the hooch and saw the usual two rows of cots that lined both sides with a walkway down the center. In the rear some of the cots had been covered with see through olive drab mosquito nets that were attached to sticks and poles and tied to the sides of the cots. I could smell the aroma of marijuana mixed with incense. We found four vacant cots just inside the entrance. Each of us claimed a cot and laid our gear on them. Then I sat on my cot and attempted to get settled in for the night. All of a sudden the radios that were previously blaring away started to turn off slowly one by one. Now there was silence except for the shuffle of our feet on the plywood floor. I looked around and saw that the entire hooch was occupied by about ten black Marines.

They had extremely long hair that was not in conformance with Marine Corps regulations. Most were unshaven and sporting goatees or beards with beads hanging around their necks. A couple of them toked on marijuana cigarettes. We decided to ignore them and settle in on our cots. A black Marine approached us who had faded out utility trousers, a green T-shirt with the sleeves cut off, beads around his neck that contained four tiger teeth, pins from grenades, and a large peace symbol. He had green rip cord that had been weaved into wrist bracelets and had a huge knife dangling in a sheaf off the left side of his web belt. He stopped in the center of the hooch just a few feet from where I sat on my cot.

"What you white honkeys doin in mah muthafuckin hooch?" he asked boldly.

"One of the Marines replied, "We are only here for one night and then we are going back to the bush tomorrow."

"Ah dont wan no white trash in mah hooch," the black Marine said. Dig it?"

"Look Man, we don't want no trouble. It wasn't our idea to stay here tonight," the Marine said.

"Who tode you honkeys you can stay in mah hooch, soom fookin white honkey lifer?" he asked.

"Yeah," replied the Marine, "some first sergeant said we could stay here tonight."

"Dat's tipical of dem wite honkey lifers, dey look afta der own kind. Doin't give a rats ass bout us black Marines. Dis is a soul brother hooch, dig it? No honkey's arthrized. Git yo shit and disappear."

The black Marine then reached across his waistline with his right hand and slowly pulled a bowie knife from its sheath. It had a blade about twelve inches long. He brought it up in front of his face and looked at it slowly up and down while twisting it from side to side.

"Us brotha's will cut yor dicks raight off. Understand honkey? We can cut yor heart out without yo nowin bout it. You dig?"

My temper began to take control of my emotions. I stood up to confront this individual. I was not in the mood to put up with the threats from a Marine pending a court-martial. Besides, I was there to get some sleep, not duel with a Marine who couldn't hack it in Vietnam.

"You listen to what I have to say and listen closely," I told him. "You don't scare me with your racist bullshit. We're all in this war together. It makes no difference to me if a Marine is black, blue, brown, pink, or purple. We are all still Marines."

"Yo a gutsy fuckin honkey ain't yo boy?" the black Marine replied with a sneer.

I continued on without answering him. "Some of my best friends are black. I have saved their ass and they have saved mine. It's a mutual respect for one another. I don't care what you guys did to get into trouble but you ain't gonna take it out on us."

"Man, yo don know who yor fuckin wiff, do you?" the black Marine asked. "Dis here knife will fuck up yor health record for life."

I moved out from the side of my cot, took a few steps to the center passageway, and then approached him face to face. I looked him dead in the eye. "Unless you put that knife away, I'll shove it up your ass side ways and give you a spare asshole."

The black Marine laughed out loud and slowly returned the knife into the sheath. Then he said, "Dis honkey muthafucka is fuckin crazy, don't wanna fuck wiff him."

The other black Marines in the back of the hooch began to laugh.

One said, "Yo white honkey's stay on dat side of the hooch and there won't be any blood shed tonight, Can you dig?"

"Yeah," I replied. "Wouldn't want any blood shed on your side of the hooch, now would we? After all, you must be getting pretty short in the Nam. I would hate for you to go back to your loved ones with your health records all screwed up."

I heard one of the black Marines in the far corner of the hooch mumble, "Dese muthafuckas ain't about shit. Leave dem honkeys alone fore I gotta git up and kick sum ass."

The black Marine who had put his knife away turned away from me and started walking back toward his cot. I heard him say, "Nah, dem white boys ain't worth it. They're ass is outta here come tomorrow. Charlie will wax their asses for us."

I sat back down on my cot and wondered if I had made matters worse. I would sleep lightly this night just in case a Marine non-hacker got a hair up his ass. It was one thing to be brave and yet another to be out numbered. After the other Mike Company Marines squared their cots away for the night they wanted to go to the club for a few beers in order to avoid a confrontation. I did not have any money but they told me they would buy a round of cheer. I decided that was a good idea for it was better than staying in this hooch alone. When we returned later that evening only a couple of black Marines were sitting in a back corner smoking dope and talking about their courts-martial and nonjudicial punishment. The night passed without further incident.

The next morning we woke up early, went to chow, and made arrangements to be choppered to Firebase Ross. At the landing zone we boarded a CH-46 heading for the base camp. When we lifted off, for some unknown reason, the pilot decided that he would pull a stunt in the air. He tilted the aircraft at a forty-five degree angle and then made a sharp turn upward. I could feel the pressure in the cabin and it seemed like riding a roller coaster. The two Marine crew chiefs in the back of the chopper were laughing and getting a big kick out of it. They were coaching the pilot and co-pilot to pull another stunt. The pilot made a couple more sharp turns in mid air. I assumed that the intent was to try and scare the grunts in the back of the aircraft, they succeeded.

It just so happened that Mike Company had just returned from the bush to Firebase Ross for a few days of rehabilitation. They were preparing to go back to the bush on 25 July. The company commander that I had known since my arrival in Vietnam had been transferred while I was at Cam Ranh Bay. We now had a different company commander. I immediately searched for Hawkeye. I spotted his blonde hair in a hooch where my squad was being billeted. He was sitting on a cot writing a letter home when he looked up and saw me.

"How ya doin you old codger?" asked Hawkeye.

"Awh, I'm doin fine Hawkeye," I replied. "How are you doin?"

"Just as ornery as ever," he said in a calm voice. "Welcome back to the real world! You been skating all this time, ain't you?

"Yep, been skating down at Cam Ranh Bay, I replied. "I was glad to leave though, so I could get back to the 3rd squad and be with my foxhole buddy."

"I know when you lie, Fenwick, and you are lying about that," Hawkeye said. "I bet you were having a ball."

"Yeah, the beach, the chow, the USO shows, it was all good," I responded."

Hawkeye then gestured for me to sit down on the cot next to him. Although it had another Marine's gear on it the Marine was out of the hooch for the time being. We talked about my stay onboard the USS Sanctuary and at Cam Ranh Bay. I also told him about how I almost got attacked in the hooch back at LZ Baldy. Hawkeye could not believe that the Marine senior leadership would allow Marine misfits to smoke dope in the hooches and do nothing about it. I told him that they were afraid to even go near the hooch. "Yep," I said, "LZ Baldy is going to the dogs."

After we talked for awhile Hawkeye pointed to an empty cot where I could settle in for the night. I felt really good that I was back in my squad among Marines that I knew and trusted. I decided to go get a haircut since I was looking pretty shabby by now. Hawkeye put his letter writing gear away and came with me to the barber shop. On the way he explained that he was going on R&R to Hawaii the next day. He was so excited about it. We talked about the sunny beaches of Hawaii and the half nude women frolicking in the waves. We arrived at the barber shop and there were only a few Marines ahead of us. We took a seat while waiting and continued to catch up on lost conversation.

It wasn't long until it was our turn. I let Hawkeye get a haircut first and when he had finished I jumped into the chair. The Vietnamese barber used hand clippers, the kind that cut hair by squeezing two small handles back and forth. Once in awhile he would mistakenly pull some hair out instead of cutting it while using the obsolete clippers. He seemed to give a good haircut and could speak English fairly well. I remembered that the instructors at Staging Battalion had told us, never to discuss upcoming operations in a barber shop, because the VC had good ears. So I avoided any conversation with the barber.

He was quite friendly and after he finished giving me a haircut he gave me a neck and back massage. He did this by taking both hands, joining them together as if he were going to pray, and in a constant rhythm pound the heel of his hands up and down across my neck, shoulders, and back. It felt good when he had finished. I ended up giving the old man a tip in addition to the regular price of the haircut and Hawkeye did the same. The old man bowed and thanked us for our generosity.

On our way back from getting a haircut Hawkeye and I stopped by the Mike Company armory so I could draw my M16 and magazines. We were so wrapped up in the moment that I completely forgot about checking on my SKS stored at the armory. It felt good to be carrying my M16 around with me again. Without it, I had felt somewhat naked and helpless. I would be able to draw ammunition back at the hooch and reload my magazines for combat. I also needed to visit battalion supply to resign for my 782 gear since it had been turned in prior to me being medevaced to Cam Ranh Bay.

Hawkeye and I stood hole watch that night together. One side of the perimeter got into a heavy firefight. We did not get anything on our side but there was a one hundred per cent alert throughout the night. The next day we returned back to our hooch. We were informed that sometime during the night that the barber had been killed, along with some other VC, while attempting to come through the perimeter wire. The barber whom we had gotten a haircut from the previous day turned out to be VC after all. When Hawkeye and I found out that the barber had been killed, we both snickered that he would not get any more tips from us.

Mike Company had a big beer bust while the company was back at Firebase Ross. We were allotted 32 cases of beer and soda from the recreation funds in conjunction with our rehab steak fry. That was a good time to drink, eat a juicy barbequed steak, and to build some camaraderie among the Marines of Mike Company. Everyone looked forward to the cookouts in the rear when we could just relax and not think about the Vietnam War.

Hawkeye and I woke up on 25 July and decided to eat breakfast at the mess hall before the company headed back into the bush. When we returned to the hooch, Lance Corporal Travieso was holding reveille on the squad.

"Reveille, Reveille, Reveille," he announced. "Grab your packs and rifles and get out to formation. It's time to move out."

The squad was stirring about lazily so Hawkeye and I decided to help Travieso with reveille.

"Common you guys," Hawkeye shouted. "Get out of those racks, it's time for another operation. I'll be thinking of you all cause I'm going to Hawaii for a little R&R."

Wagenbaugh sat up from his cot and replied, "Fuck you Hawkeye. Go ahead and run out on us, you buddy fucker you."

Hawkeye was smiling from ear to ear. I had not seen him so happy. I was going around shaking toes and encouraging the squad to get up and get moving.

"Look at old gungy Fenwick," Lance Corporal Travieso said. "He's already had his R&R at Cam Ranh Bay while we've been out humping in the bush.."

"That's okay though," I replied. "I'm back now and ready to keep you guys out of trouble. Now that Hawkeye is leaving to go on R&R I don't guess the squad will ever be the same."

"I may not even come back to this hell hole," Hawkeye said. "I may just go UA (unauthorized absence) in Hawaii. I could hide up in the hills and they would never find me."

"You'll be back, all right," Travieso said. "You can't keep away from us."

"Don't count on it," Hawkeye replied quickly.

As the squad began to fall out for formation, each wished Hawkeye farewell and good luck on his R&R. We were the last two remaining inside the hooch. I walked up to Hawkeye and shook his hand. I told Hawkeye that if he didn't come back to the squad that I would always remember him.

"Don't worry Fred, I was just blowing smoke," Hawkeye said. "Although I hate to come back, I've got to look out after you guys so you can get back to the States in one piece."

We smiled at each other. As I heaved my pack up to put it on my shoulders, Hawkeye assisted in getting my arms through the straps. It was very heavy. The pack seemed even heavier than before as the straps dug into my shoulders. I grabbed my M16 off my cot and headed out the door. Hawkeye followed me out and down the steps. When we got to the bottom of the steps I turned in the direction of the formation and Hawkeye turned the opposite direction in order to head down to the company office to get his leave papers.

I took a few steps and then turned 180 degrees to my left about. "See you around Hawkeye!" I yelled out. I noticed that my voice had cracked somewhat as I was saying my final goodbye.

Hawkeye looked back over his right shoulder but kept walking. "See you, Fenwick," he said. "Take real good care of yourself."

I continued on and decided to turn around one more time. When I did, Hawkeye had disappeared between the hooches. I knew that I would be awful lonely without my comrade by my side. I could always depend on Hawkeye. He was such a down to earth and humble Marine. He would do anything for you. I would miss our conversations. As I walked down to where our formation was being held I felt saddened by the fact that Hawkeye would not be with us on this operation but happy that he finally got the chance to get some well deserved rest and relaxation.

Our 3rd platoon opened ranks. This meant that the front rank took two paces forward, the second rank took one pace forward, the third rank stood fast, and the 4th rank took two steps backward. This allowed the squad leaders enough room in between ranks to walk down the line and inspect weapons, ammo, and equipment. Although we only had three squads in the platoon, when we fell into formation, we would form four ranks. This was due to being augmented by other Marines such as machine gunners.

Lance Corporal Travieso began to walk up and down our squad to make sure everything was in order. We received and evenly distributed M16 and .45 caliber pistol ammunition, extra machine gun and mortar ammo, extra M79 grenade launcher rounds, trip flares, claymore mines, and a host of other combat arsenal. Our canteens were checked to ensure that we had them completely full of water. We also received a six day supply of C-rations. Travieso told us our next operation was called "Pickens Forest." Once all of Mike Company's gear was inspected and the company commander was satisfied, we moved down to the landing zone.

While we waited for the choppers to arrive I asked Travieso, "Where are we off to this time?"

"Looks like we are going to FSB Ryder to act as security for the artillery battery, but first, we will make a detour and check out a village down in the lowlands."

"Where in the lowlands?" I asked.

"Don't know," Travieso responded, "somewhere in the Quang Nam Province.

"That could be anywhere," I replied. "Quang Nam covers all the lowlands around Sniper Valley. Oh well, guess we will find out sooner or later. I guess it will be skate city up on Fire Support Base Ryder, huh?"

"You got it," Travieso said. "At least we get one hot meal a day. Those arty Marines up there on Ryder really know how to live. They've got their own little mess hall."

"So what's our main mission up on Ryder?" I asked.

"Well," he responded, "basically we are going to put out listening posts and observation posts and run a few patrols around the sides."

"That sounds okay to me," I said. "How long are we going to stay up there?"

Travieso answered, "For about two weeks, I guess."

The 2nd platoon of Mike Company was not going with the rest of the company. Instead they had been detached and assigned to the Combined Unit Pacification Program. The mission of Mike CUPP was to assist the military training of the Popular Forces in our AO, to provide added security to the surrounding villages, and to conduct pacification operations in the area adjoining FSB Ross. Mike Company would be operating minus the 2nd platoon.

It wasn't long until some CH-46 choppers started landing on the Firebase Ross landing zone. We scrambled aboard each aircraft and lifted into the air. I was on my way back to the bush after a rest at Cam Ranh Bay. We landed in the area where we were supposed to check out a village. We reckoned that we would be flown up to FSB Ryder after patrols were sent out.

We formed up in the company defensive position and set about digging our fighting holes and sleeping holes. Once most of the digging was done I began to hear small transistor radios playing music. Some of the Marines carried them around with them so they could listen to the news and to music while out in the bush. The platoon guide had settled in not too far from my position. The song titled "Cecilia" sung by Paul Simon came over the radio. We sat quietly listening to the lyrics.

Our platoon guide made the comment, "That song reminds me of my troop handler back in Infantry Training Regiment."

I felt that it was a bit strange that the song would remind him of some senior enlisted Marine barking orders at him while he was undergoing infantry training at ITR. "Why do you say that?" I asked.

"Oh, I don't know," was his reply. "It just reminds me of him."

"Strange!" Travieso said.

"Yeah," I commented, real strange!"

We all laughed about it and carried out conversations with the platoon guide. He was a real down to earth sergeant that treated us with respect and dignity. As if in the automatic mode, we stopped our conversations and commenced placing claymore mines and trip flares out to our direct front, in order to keep any enemy from sneaking up on us at night.

The next day at about 0800 the 1st platoon while on a patrol detonated a booby trap. It was a M33 grenade hanging five feet above the trail and rigged with a vine as a trip wire. Three Marines were wounded. All were immediately medevaced. Then at about 1000 that same morning, the 2nd squad of our platoon received sniper fire from four enemy situated 300 meters to the northeast. One Marine was wounded and a medevac was called. The squad returned fired and utilized helicopter gunships against the enemy. As the medevac was being completed, one gunship was hit by enemy ground fire and went down. They then set up a perimeter around the downed aircraft until it could be lifted out.

At approximately 0730 the following day two patrols were sent out in different directions. One patrol was the 1st platoon and the other was our 3rd platoon with the exception of my 3rd squad. Mike 3 Charlie was to remain behind in the perimeter while the other squads checked the surrounding area. We heard over the squad radio that a patrol would be passing our position to check out a village. As the 3rd platoon patrol passed our fighting holes, most of the squad took notice that our platoon guide was with the patrol. It was uncommon for the platoon guide to go out on patrol. Normally the lance corporal and corporal squad leaders were responsible for patrols.

Lance Corporal Travieso yelled out to him, "Hey, Sergeant Eiland, why are you going out on a patrol today?"

"I wanna go out and get some action," the platoon guide replied.

Travieso replied, "It's about time you got some confirmed kills. All you've been doing is sitting back on your haunches giving orders. Why don't you take point man?"

"Aahh, the hell with you," the platoon guide said jokingly.

We all laughed. It was good to see that the platoon guide was taking an interest in our platoon's combat actions. Because of his rank and position he did not have to go on patrol but he did because he was a very dedicated Marine. Soon the patrol disappeared across a rice paddy and into a treeline.

A few minutes later the 1st platoon detonated a booby trap. The device was a M26 grenade buried in the center of the trail and rigged with a trip wire about three inches above the deck. One Marine was wounded. He was classified an emergency medevac and promptly taken to the nearest medical facility for treatment. After the medevac the 1st platoon continued their patrol and found the body of a 12 or 13 year old male laying face down. The boy had been killed by shrapnel approximately two days prior. A search for the child's parents revealed nothing.

Then at approximately 0800 the same morning, our 3rd platoon received about 10-15 rounds of extremely accurate sniper fire from 200 meters to their west. One Marine was struck by the snipers rounds and was killed instantly. The 3rd platoon returned fire and called in an aerial observer. The AO worked the area of the sighting with its ordnance and then called in a fixed wing strike. The air strikes arrived and delivered a thundering bombardment. From where my squad was positioned we could not see exactly what the target was.

After the air strike our squad, Mike 3 Charlie, was listening intently to the squad radio as the events unfolded. Our squad knew that the patrol our platoon guide had decided to join had made contact with the enemy. While listening to the action over our squad radio we heard the patrol radio operator.

"Break Break! Mike, Mike, this is Mike 3."

"Mike 3, this is Mike," was the reply from the company radio operator.

"Roger, be advised that we have one KIA, need a medevac chopper, Over."

"Roger, I copy that you have one KIA," the company radio operator responded. "Request you transmit the name of the KIA phonetically."

"Mike, Mike, this is Mike 3. Be advised one KIA, Echo Five, and I spell phonetically, Echo, India, Lima, Alpha, November, Delta. How copy, over?"

In an instant Travieso spoke out loud to our squad, "That's Sergeant Eiland!"

My squad became very quiet in order to hear the radio transmissions between the company radio operator who was back with us in the CP and the 3rd platoon radio operator. The facial expressions of our squad were of total shock and disbelief. As the company radio operator repeated the message back to the 3rd platoon radio operator to confirm the message, we began to whisper each letter of the phonetic alphabet, as the company radio operator spoke into the handset of his PRC-77.

"Roger, I copy one KIA, Echo 5, and I spell phonetically, Echo, India, Lima, Alpha, November, Delta. Will request medevac, Out!"

After a few minutes a sobbing 3rd platoon radio operator with an emotional voice came back on the net. "Hurry up with that goddamn medevac chopper! I don't want Sergeant Eiland bleeding on this fuckin Vietnamese soil!"

Our squad sat silently and just stared at each other in a daze. We knew that our platoon guide, who had joked with us less than an hour ago, was now dead. His life was snuffed out at a young age for he was only 20 years old. He had died from small arms fire on 27 July 1970 while serving his country in Mike Company, 3rd Battalion, 7th Marines, in the Quang Nam Province. He would be added to the Mike Company list of KIA.

Our platoon guide's home state was Alabama. He was a very well liked and respected by the entire platoon. He was professional, dedicated, and the epitome of what a Marine should be. He would be missed by all. I was particularly heartbroken by the fact that he was no longer with us to lead us, guide us, and provide for us. In a moment of silence, I raised my thoughts to heaven and said a few prayers for him. He would become a lasting vision for me as I would play out the events of that day over and over in my mind. If only he had stayed back that day from going on patrol. After all, he was a sergeant and did not have to go on patrol. He did it because of his love for his fellow Marines and the love he had for his country.

We heard the whomp whomp sound of a CH-46 helicopter flying in from a distance. One chopper landed well beyond the treeline and out of sight. In a few minutes the chopper was back in the air heading away from us. "God bless you, Sergeant Eiland," I whispered to myself as the medevac chopper disappeared out of sight. The squad became very quiet as each of us seemed to reflect on what had just happened.

I was in a daze after our platoon guide's death. There was movement and activity within the unit but I didn't seem to take much notice. I wanted to talk with my best friend, Hawkeye, but he was on his R&R. I just held it in and wondered if I would be the next Marine to be medevaced out. After awhile I decided that I had better get a grip on myself if I were to survive in this hostile environment. It was extremely difficult to go on with my regular duties as if nothing had happened.

The following day the 1st platoon was again back out on patrol. At around 1530 they observed two men sitting under some trees about 150 meters to the northwest. As the 1st platoon approached, one of the men tried to flee. The 1st platoon fired a warning shot and the man returned. One man was 22-25 years old, the other man was about 40 years old and had pack marks on his shoulders. Both men were detained and one man then pointed out a mine field. Both detainees were sent to the Interrogator Translator for further interrogation.

On 30 July in the afternoon someone in the 1st platoon detonated a booby trap while set in a daytime position. It was a M26 fragmentation grenade set for pressure detonation. It had been positioned under a shade tree by Charlie three feet off the trail and was camouflaged with tree bark and a C-Ration accessory pack wrapper. The explosion wounded two Marines causing one priority medevac. The other Marine was not evacuated. They were also on patrol when they observed three enemy sitting under a tree 100 meters away. The enemy was wearing black clothing and had weapons. The 1st platoon took them under fire with small arms, but the enemy fled to the west. The platoon searched the area of the sighting and found documents and miscellaneous gear left behind by the enemy due to their haste. The documents and gear were sent to the rear for further evaluation.

On 1 August we were choppered up to FSB Ryder. The Marines settled into their designated bunkers. From the top of FSB Ryder we could look out over Antenna Valley, Happy Valley, and the Que Son Mountains. The artillery battery had sandbagged bunkers set up with steps made of ammo crates. Inside the bunkers there were cots set up on the dirt floor. The roofs of the bunkers were made of plywood and covered with sandbags. These bunkers would be our home for the next two weeks. Three other Marines and I went into our bunker and began to set up the conveniences of home away from home. Although it was dark inside, a ray of light would peep through the entrance.

I made the comment, "Hey, this is gonna be all right. Got cots to sleep on, one hot meal a day, and we only post out security."

"Yeah, another Marine said, "but we'll be burning shitters, going on working parties, and doing all the other shit details that the arty guys don't want to do.

"Yeah, you're right," I agreed, "guess that comes with the territory."

Travieso came by later and checked to see if everything was going okay. "Watch out for the rats up here," he said, "they'll eat you alive."

"Yeah, I see signs of them already," I answered. "As long as they keep away from me we can share this hill."

Travieso responded, "Fenwick, these rats are so big they can carry you right off your cot."

"That's all right," I responded. "I was born on the farm where we had rats running around in the corn crib. I used to kill them with a shovel. They don't bother me none."

"Yeah, I hear you tawkin," Travieso replied. "But you didn't have to sleep with the critters either when you were down on the farm." The Travieso addressed the entire squad, "Just stay up on your cots so they don't take a plug out of your hide."

We laughed about the rat conversation we were having. Travieso departed for his hooch but then in a matter of minutes he was back again. "Fenwick, I need you to go on a working party."

"Don't tell me, its burning shitters, right?" I asked.

"How did you know?" Travieso questioned me while grinning.

"Well, I just managed to figure it out based on the conversations we were having a few minutes ago about working parties."

Skate City, I thought to myself. I must learn to keep my mouth shut. I joined three other Marines from the platoon to go on the working detail. We met up with an artillery corporal who took us to where they had an outdoor shitter, a two-holer. We pulled out the cut fifty-five gallon drums with all the feces, got some diesel fuel, poured it into the drums, set fire to it, and then stood back and watched them burn. After the flames went out we placed the drums back inside and moved to the next shitter. That ended up being our working party for the rest of the day. Some party, I thought. I always wondered how Marines who had preceded me in the Marine Corps had managed to change the term from working detail to working party.

That afternoon we finished our toilet burning assignment and we were released back to our unit. I went back to my bunker and entered into the darkness. It took me a few minutes to adjust to the darkness inside the bunker as I had been out in the bright sunlight all day. I grabbed a canteen of water so I could wash my hands and I managed to locate my letter writing gear inside my pack. Since the sun was still out, I decided to sit outside on the top of the bunker, air my feet, and write a letter home. There would be no mention of our platoon guide in my letter for I did not want my parents to worry about me.

August 2, 1970

Hello Mom, Dad and Larry,

Well how does this find everyone back in Kentucky? Hope things are going smooth for you. For myself I'm doing just fine. I got back to the company on 20 July and went to the bush the next day. I was kinda glad in a way to get back.

When I was medevaced to the hospital ship in July it wasn't anything serious. I don't guess I told you all much about what I had because I didn't know myself. I had a temperature and all the symptoms of malaria but I didn't have malaria. I was feeling better two days after I reached the ship. It was pretty easy for me. In fact, I skated for a few weeks. Believe me, July sure did go by fast for me.

Our flight was canceled three times at Cam Ranh Bay. When I arrived in Da Nang I stayed there for one day. I bet you all could find it on the Vietnam map you have at home. After I got to Freedom Hill I ran into a bunch of guys from Mike Company who was going back to Ross. So instead of taking a chopper we started hitchhiking to Baldy. There were several trucks going that way so we got a ride on one. There wasn't a convoy leaving LZ Baldy that night so we stayed at the base camp all night. The next morning we took a chopper from LZ Baldy to Firebase Ross. I got back just in time to be sent to the field the next day. At least I got to sign the pay roster.

Well, when I got there I asked the mail clerk if I had any mail and he said that he had sent it all to the USS Sanctuary that morning. That was just my luck. Now it'll take about two weeks to get back to me. I should have it though when you get this letter. I got some letters this last week and Mom said something about some pictures she had sent. Well, I haven't got them yet but I'm looking forward to it. I can't wait to see all of them.

Speaking of pictures, I've got two rolls taken to send home. I may do that tomorrow. Right now our squad is on an OP (observation post). We were choppered up yesterday onto a mountain called LZ Ryder. It's just a little piece from Ross. It's a fire support base up here and we were sent up for security. They said we'd be up here for about two weeks before going back into the lowlands. To give you all an idea, we're southwest of Da Nang, about thirty miles away. In fact, all the 7th Marines are up here. By the way, did you all see in the papers about the middle of July where the 7th Marines found all that stuff in the Que Son Mountains? Well, that was us. They came out with it about a month later in the papers over here.

Have you all got the cruise book I sent? I started not to get one but I thought it might bring back memories after I get out of the Corps. That was all the 3rd Battalion, 7th Marines, while we were at Baldy. When I got back to LZ Ross, Hawkeye was leaving for R&R in Hawaii. This past week we've been pretty busy but maybe we'll have some spare time up on this mountain.

Well that about does it relating to what I've been doing. Guess we'll be up on Ryder for two weeks and then go back down to work in the valleys. I hope everyone back home are doing okay. Dad, how is the tobacco crop coming along? I imagine it's getting pretty good size by now. Guess you're already thinking about how you're going to get it in the barn. Wish I could help but you all will probably find enough help. I guess ole Jimmy Howard will have to give a hand this year being as he's got some of his own. So your sows are pigging again! Seems like no time since you wrote and told me about them the last time. Hope you have good luck with them.

Up on this hill the guys that fire the big artillery guns have a pig for a mascot. You can probably guess what its name is. You guessed it, "Arnold." It's not too big, but it's fat as a pig. Ha ha! They don't get too big over here. The only things that are big over here are the insects and rodents, that's about it.

Well Larry, glad to hear you went camping this summer. I should have sent you some C-Rations for your chow. Ha! Man Larry, you better live it up while you can. Already it's August again. I'm glad, but I bet you wish time would go by slower, as school is rapidly approaching. It sure is hot now but in September the monsoons will cool things off a little. I just heard over our squad radio that we are going to get paid today so I may just put this letter in the envelope with the check. I kept out about 96 dollars so the check will be around one hundred dollars. Mom, when you go to put the check in the bank take out what you think will cover the cost of getting the film developed. Like I say, I have a couple more to send home and that soon adds up and I don't want you all to be paying for it.

Well I'll sign off for now so until next time I'll say good-bye and hope this finds everyone doing just fine.

As always,
Fred

A chopper landed on FSB Ryder as announced over the radio and a pay roll officer got off with pay checks for those who had signed up for them. He would stay the night and then catch a chopper back the next morning. That gave me the opportunity to not only receive a pay check but to get it inside the envelope with my letter. Some Marine came around collecting the mail to go out on the morning chopper. I felt relieved that my letter would be on its way to my loved ones back home. As it became dark I went back inside the bunker to settle down and attempt to get some rest. I laid my poncho liner out on the cot and used my poncho as a pillow. I laid back and started to doze off.

A black Marine in my fireteam was laying on his cot across from me. He looked over and saw me preparing to get some shut eye. "Hey Fenwick," he said. "Why are you laying down at the position of attention? Are you going to sleep that way? Just look at you. You're so gungy, you sleep at attention." Then he got the attention of another Marine who was laying on a cot just to poke more fun at me. "Hey, look at Fenwick," he said. He's sleeping at the position of attention. His thumbs are along the trouser seams, his hands are curled into a fist, and his feet are at a forty-five degree angle. Just like in boot camp. He's a motivated Marine, ain't he?"

"Yeah," the Marine responded, "Fenwick sure is Gung Ho."

I opened my eyes and looked down the length of my body and noticed that I was in fact at a somewhat modified position of attention.

"Hell, I didn't even know I was at attention," I responded. "I'm just in a

Cruise Book photo of PFC Fenwick 1970.

relaxed state. What else can you do? You can't roll over in this damn cot, it's too narrow."

"Yeah man, we know," the black Marine replied. "You're just gungy to the max."

"Well, at least it's comfortable," I said.

The next morning when the sun came up I went to visit the two hole shitter that I had cleaned out the day before. Although the stench in the outhouses could be a little on the raunchy side, it was better than digging a hole in the dirt with my E-tool as we had to do in the bush. There was even real honest to goodness toilet paper to use instead of the small compressed packs that came in our C-Ration accessory packs. I returned to the bunker and decided to shave and chow down on some C-Rations. Since any can of shaving cream would take up too much room in my pack, I used a bar of Dial soap to create lather for my face. I had a Gillette Techmatic safety razor with a replaceable band-blade cartridge. It seemed dull on my rough chin stubble but I managed to shave with it.

After I shaved and had eaten some peanut butter and a can of ham and eggs for breakfast, Travieso came to our bunker. He told us that we were going to go out on a listening post and spend three days and nights in a bunker outside of the perimeter. He explained that our entire 3rd squad would be going out and that we would set up an observation post in the day time and a listening post at night. Basically we were to hang loose at the bunker and keep a watchful eye out for the enemy attempting to infiltrate our perimeter. We would not have to go out on patrols.

We got our gear packed up and walked together in a column down into a ravine and back up on the other side of a hill. The bunker we were to stay in was built of sandbags and the floor was not under ground, but rather flat with a contour of the ground. The sandbag roof was held up by pieces of strong plywood boards. We all moved inside the bunker and got settled into our own little plot of ground. It was crowded with the entire squad inside the bunker, but we managed to make do with what we had. We made out a watch schedule. The Marines would take turns sleeping during the day and writing letters or just playing cards. We had some spare time on our hands to carry on conversation that no one else outside our little domain would understand what we were talking about.

The next night I had the mid watch. I sat on top of the bunker peering into the darkness and watching the lights from villages flickering in the valleys below. The wind was blowing calmly and it was a comfortable warm evening. It was a tranquil time for me. Even the mosquitoes didn't seem to bother me too much. I could vaguely hear one Marine snoring inside the bunker. I stretched out on top of the sandbags and they still felt warm from the day sun. I could hear the lullaby of crickets in the grass and the grass seemed to sway back and forth to the wind like waves of an ocean. As I lay back quietly with my head resting on my helmet that I used for a pillow my eyes became very heavy.

The next thing I knew my entire body jerked and twitched as I began to fall into a deep sleep. I realized that there could be serious consequences if I allowed myself to fall asleep so I bolted up in a sitting position. I scanned the area to see if there were any suspicious sights or sounds. Satisfied that there was nothing unusual, I looked at my watch for the time. I realized that I had missed firing the M79 in which we were to fire a HE round down the hillside every fifteen minutes. I picked up the grenade launcher and fired out a round. It exploded and things got quiet again.

I could hear the Marine snoring even louder now inside the bunker. I felt that I must try my best to stay awake so some VC wouldn't be able to sneak up on the squad and slit our throats. I became more attentive and thought of Hawkeye back in Hawaii watching the girls prance down the beautiful beaches. As Marine lingo would have it, "He owes it to his body." That is, he owes it to himself to enjoy life. Enjoying life in Vietnam was something you had to do when the opportunity presented itself and just try to make the best of it.

I was relieved from watch at approximately 0400. In a few hours I heard the rest of the squad stirring about at around 0700. I remained curled up in my poncho liner still sleepy from the mid watch. One of the Marines asked if I was getting up. I rolled over onto one side and whispered, "No."

Travieso then responded that I had had mid watch and to let me sleep. Then I heard voices talking about going back into the CP to get some water and some C-Rations to last us a few more days. They formed up outside the bunker and their voices disappeared. I could still hear Travieso talking to someone and then they were in the middle of a card game of back alley.

I spoke from under my poncho liner, "Now I've seen everything. Here you all are playing cards at 0730."

Travieso looked up and said, "Hey Fenwick, want to play a game of back alley with us?"

"Naw, don't think I will. I'll just lay here until I have to get up to take a leak or something," I replied lazily.

"Don't let us disturb you," Travieso said. "You can lay there as long as you want. It's gonna be another slack day for us anyway."

It wasn't long until the group of Marines from the squad returned with some water in plastic jugs and C-Rations. Then the bunker became full of conversation. I decided that it wasn't any use to try and sleep any longer, so I got up, went outside to take a leak, and then prepared a meal outside the bunker. I had the time now to cook it up nice and slow so I could have a warm meal. I thought I would splurge a little and fix some hot cocoa from a pack I had been saving. I pulled the cigarettes out of the ace (accessory) pack and hollered into the bunker if anyone wanted them. About three Marines spoke up almost immediately, so I tossed the cigarettes in the entrance of the bunker. They started scrambling for the cigarettes.

I laughed out loud and said, "You guys are worse than the gook kids."

One of the Marines responded, "Hey Fenwick, if you don't want your cigarettes, give them to me."

I replied, "No problem, but when Hawkeye gets back, you'll have to fight with him. I keep him supplied with my cigmos."

Instead of three days out on the observation post it turned out to be six days. We enjoyed the slack time. One morning Travieso answered a radio call from the 3rd platoon radio operator back at FSB Ryder.

I heard him say, "Roger that, I'll send him right over. Then Travieso looked at me and said, "Fenwick, they want you over at the CP, Right now!"

"Who wants to see me?" I asked.

"The platoon commander wants to see you. You need to get over there ASAP!" Travieso reiterated.

"What's this all about?" I inquired. "What did I do?"

"I don't know, but you must be in big trouble," Travieso said. "The lieutenant didn't seem too happy."

"Well hell," I responded. "I can't figure out what I did wrong."

"Hope it's nothing that has happened back home," Travieso replied.

"Yeah," I agreed. "That's all I need."

I picked up my rifle and my cartridge belt and started around the outside the bunker. Inside I heard Travieso whispering to some of the Marines but I never paid any attention to him. They seemed awful jovial that I was in some kind of trouble. I didn't take the time to ask what was going on. I grabbed my rifle, helmet, and a bandoleer of ammo and headed down the trail toward FSB Ryder. I did not need any security with me since FSB Ryder was only a short distance away from the OP.

I dropped out of sight down into the ravine and up the other hillside. As I was nearing the perimeter lines I gave a yell out that I was a friendly. Permission was given to enter through the barbed wire perimeter by one of the Marines in our platoon. I looked around and saw our platoon commander standing with the company commander and a small group of Marines close by. I feared the worse. Something bad had happened back home on the farm, I just knew it. I reported to the lieutenant without haste.

I carried my M16 at sling arms with it slung over my right shoulder. Not knowing what to expect I decided to render a hand salute to the lieutenant. I stepped in front of the platoon commander and assumed the position of attention. Then I reached across with my left hand, grasped the rifle sling just above my right hand, released my right hand from the sling, and executed a hand salute. We never rendered a hand salute to officers in the bush because if the enemy were to see an officer being saluted, he would become a prime target.

"Sir, PFC Fenwick reporting as ordered," I said.

"Order Arms!" the lieutenant commanded. He did not return my salute.

I lowered my right hand smartly to my right side, re-grasped the sling at the original position with my right hand, released the sling with my left hand, and returned it smartly to the position of attention.

"Yes, Fenwick," he replied, "Got a surprise for you, you're gonna get promoted."

With a surprised inflection in my voice I responded, "Promoted?"

"Yep, we're going to make you a lance corporal," the lieutenant said while grinning.

"All right, Sir," I said, "will do."

"You come on down and join this little formation we've got going on and the company commander will come through the rank and promote each Marine," said the lieutenant.

"Aye Aye, Sir," I responded.

It was a total shock. I had all sorts of things running through my mind on my way to see the lieutenant. I had hoped that nothing bad had happened to any of my family members. But now those thoughts gave way to what I would be doing as a newly promoted lance corporal. It would be more responsibilities, that was for certain. I walked down a small embankment to take my place in a single rank of about six Marines. Before I reached the formation the company gunnery sergeant got my attention.

"Didn't anybody ever teach you not to salute officers in the field?" the gunny asked.

"Yes, Gunny," I said, "it won't happen again."

"It better not," he replied. "Now take your place in ranks.

I moved to the single file of Marines and took my place in an empty spot reserved for me. We were called to the position of attention by the gunny and the company commander came in front of the first Marine to promote him. The gunny read the warrant and the company commander congratulated the Marine on his promotion. He stepped over to the next Marine and repeated the sequence.

I happened to think that the gunny had got on my case for saluting an officer in the field and yet we were called to the position of attention to receive our promotions. I was trying to make some kind of sense to it. Then the company commander came in front of me, presented me with the promotion certificate, shook my hand, and congratulated me on my accomplishment.

"Keep up the good work Lance Corporal Fenwick. Along with this promotion there will be additional responsibilities."

"Thank you, Sir," I said modestly.

When he stepped over to the next Marine, my platoon commander came in front of me. "Congratulations," the first lieutenant said. "A job well done. I expect some good things to come from you."

"Aye Aye Sir," I replied.

They continued down to the end of the file and promoted the last Marine. Then they took their positions in front of the formation and the company commander gave a short talk about how additional responsibilities come with the rank. Then he once again congratulated us all on our promotions. The company commander and platoon commander walked away from the formation going back to their bunkers on FSB Ryder. The company gunnery sergeant came in front of me.

"Well Marine," he said, "since you need to get back to your observation post outside the perimeter, I will start with you first." Just then he turned me sideways and belted me a good punch to my right arm. Then he turned me in the opposite direction and belted me a good blow in the left arm. "It's an old Marine Corps tradition to pin the stripes on in this manner," he said. "Wear those crossed rifles with pride, lance corporal."

"Okay Gunny," I responded, "I will."

The chevrons of a private first class in the Marine Corps have only one stripe. When I was promoted to lance corporal, the chevrons had one stripe with crossed rifles beneath the stripe. It was a sign of additional authority and leadership responsibility when a PFC got promoted and wore the lance corporal chevrons. It signified that you were experienced and not a boot or "newbie" any longer. I relished the idea.

After the field promotion ceremony I began to walk back along the trail returning to my squad. I was feeling overjoyed. I tucked my promotion warrant under my flak jacket. I knew that it may wrinkle under my flak jacket but that would be better than getting it wet from the sweat on my arms. I approached the squad at the sandbagged bunker where we had set up the observation post. Travieso was standing on the outside and called for the other squad members to join him. They emerged from the bunker and stared at me in an uncomfortable manner.

"Well, did you get you're ass chewed by the lieutenant?" Travieso asked with a smile.

"No," I replied, "I got promoted."

"Yeah, we already know," stated Travieso. "Come here, Fenwick. We're gonna pin your stripes on in the traditional Marine Corps fashion."

"Wait a minute," I said, "you mean to tell me you knew all along that I was getting promoted?"

"That's right," Travieso said. "Come here and standby for a knockout."

I knew what was coming. The old Marine Corps "beat the Marine who just got promoted until he is so black and blue that he won't be able to lift his arms for days" tradition.

"Wait a minute," I said again.

"What now?" Travieso asked impatiently.

"Yeah, what now? the other Marines chimed in as they balled their fists and pounded them together.

One Marine said, "Come on Fenwick, you know what comes next. I may be gentle, but I kinda doubt it."

"Yeah, okay," I responded. "Just give me a few seconds to put my promotion warrant in my pack. I don't want it to get damaged."

Wagenbaugh who had a big grin on his face answered up, "Dah only thang dat's gonna git damaged is you, Fenny. Now git yo ass o'er here."

Travieso said, "Okay you guys, let him put his warrant away."

I knew that was my queue to get to my pack while I had the chance. I hurried inside the bunker, found my pack among all the loose gear laying about, and slipped my promotion warrant down inside. I would take the time later to put it in some plastic so the damp air and rain wouldn't get to it. I dreaded going back outside of the bunker but it was either I go out on my own or be dragged out by my fellow squad members eager to pin my stripes on. I exited the entrance, but before I could rise up completely to the standing position, I was grabbed by two Marines, one on each side of me.

The entire squad began gathering around me as I slowly backed away. It was no use. Travieso and Wagenbaugh got first "dibs." Travieso was on my right side and Wagenbaugh was on my left side. They grabbed both my arms with their left hand at my elbow and they drew back their right fists. They let me have it in the meat of the arms at the same time. The jolt jarred my entire body. The pain on the right side where Travieso had hit didn't seem as bad as the left side. I guessed that Travieso, as my squad leader, had cut me a huss while Wagenbaugh was out to prove a point. He had made sure that his knuckles had hit me at an angle which caused more pain than hitting straight on. When they were finished, they shook my hand and congratulated me on my promotion.

Then two more Marines grabbed me by the arms and commenced to wail the hell out of me. They hit my arms as hard as they could, turned me around and did it again. Eventually the whole squad got a turn. Some would

Fire Support Base Ryder. Photo taken from Mike 3 Charlie Observation Post. This is where I was promoted to Lance Corporal.

double up their fists and hit me straight on while others would ensure that their knuckles landed in the right place that caused the most pain.

After the squad had finished, my arms were so sore that I could barely move them. My bruises and soreness would last for over a week. I wished that I would never get promoted again. I knew that along with the rank came additional responsibility and I wasn't sure if I was ready for that at this juncture of my combat tour. I did believe, however, that because of my past experience in Vietnam, I could handle any leadership challenge.

I received a letter from home during mail call later that day. I also heard that Hawkeye had returned from R&R. He had been assigned as radioman for our 3rd platoon. He was back at FSB Ryder but I would have to wait until we went back into the perimeter before I could get in touch with him. We also heard that he had gone to Oregon from Hawaii which was unauthorized.

I hoped that he would not get busted if someone in the higher echelon ever found out about it.

I found time to write home again to my mother and father after the soreness in my arms subsided a bit. When I stuffed the letter in the envelope, I inserted the promotion warrant, without mention that I had been promoted. I just wanted to see if they would figure it out for themselves by reading the citation.

August 8, 1970

Hello Mom, Dad and Larry

How are things back around Springfield, Kentucky? Guess it's the same thing going on and I don't guess much has changed. I got Mom's letter today and was really happy to get it. You don't know how much I enjoy getting letters. I really like to read what's going on back there and Mom tells me about everything I wonder about. We get mail up here on this mountain about every two days and sometimes once a day.

When we go back to the lowlands around the 14th, we should get mail about every third day. Sometimes I carry letters around with me for several days at a time and read them over and over. Then when mail call comes in again, I burn the old ones. I must say I'm always looking for a letter from home. It kinda builds up my morale.

Speaking of mail, I never got the mail that I should have received while I was in the hospital. Maybe it will catch up to me in the next couple weeks. Also I haven't gotten the pictures Mom sent to me but I am looking for them. I got the two pictures you sent to me that I took at Cam Ranh Bay. It looks like they might have turned out good after all. Just keep the rest of the photos. I'll see them when I get home. You've probably got the other two rolls of film I sent in by now. I know you could crown me, but do like I say and take the money out of my checks. I've got one more roll of film to send home and that will be all for awhile. There is no place around here to get any more film. I should have several pictures by now anyway. I have to tape my old instamatic camera together, but I guess it still takes good flicks.

Well it sounds like you all have been pretty busy lately. I imagine by now all the work is caught up except for putting in the tobacco. Hope you can get it in without any trouble. I can't realize that the summer has gone by so fast. I hope the rest of my time over here goes as fast.

Larry, won't be long until you'll be going back to school. Guess you'll be in the 7th grade won't you? I'll be glad when you get in high school. Maybe by then I'll be out of this "Green Machine" they call the United States Marine Corps. Hey, take it easy on the piano! Don't beat it to death. I want to bang on it when I get home too. Ha! Maybe we can make up another tune like our hit single, "Groovy Mood."

Dad, Mom said it's pretty dry back there now. Maybe you'll get a good rain by the time you get this letter. It must be getting pretty close to the monsoons over here because every evening around five o'clock it comes up a rain cloud. It doesn't rain too much though, not yet anyway. The next day it's just as dry as if it hadn't rained at all.

By the way Mom, don't send me any more sausage in the mason jars if you haven't already. I don't think I would go for them much now. Besides I've gotten use to C-Rats and we get good chow when we go back to the rear. So just hold off on sending me any food or anything unless I ask for it. Right now I'm doing pretty good. Most of the letters I get, people ask me how I'm feeling. Well I'm a little better than my old self. That trip to Cam Ranh Bay did me good.

That blonde headed guy didn't leave the company. He just went on R&R but got back today. I haven't gotten to see him yet. He's now the platoon radioman. I may end up as squad radioman, but I hope not. There's another guy in the squad who wants that position. Hawkeye went to Hawaii on R&R but he also went on back to the States to Oregon where he lives. He wasn't supposed to do that, but what the heck, I'm glad he got a chance to go home. Don't think it cost him much either.

Well there's not much going on over where I am now. It'll get a little more exciting when we leave this mountain. Right now all we do is go on OP's (observation posts) for twenty-four hours and go on working parties in the mornings at the firebase. It's nothing hard though.

So we're just waiting now till the 14th when we go back down to the valleys. I guess I'll close for now and let you all get back to farm business. I will write later on. So until next time, bye for now, and everyone take care.

Yours most affirm,
Fred

Mike 3 Charlie was relieved from the Observation Post by another squad and we walked back into the perimeter of FSB Ryder. We made our way to the bunkers which we had previously occupied. Our squad noticed that some of the Marines from Mike Company were tearing down a few of the bunkers. The rumor was that the artillery battery was getting ready to disband from FSB Ryder in a couple of months and the grunts from Mike

Company were being utilized as working details to help tear down the bunkers. The thought process was that when the day finally came for the artillery battery to disband, there would be nothing left behind at FSB Ryder, not even one single sandbag. They were going to bombard the hill to bits once all the equipment and supplies were taken off.

It seemed premature to start tearing down the bunkers this early if they were not moving off the hill for another couple months. Something just didn't fit. Why the haste? In the back of my mind I figured that the artillery battery was leaving sooner than they wanted the grunts of Mike Company to know. We were not to question it, just go with the flow. We just carried out our orders and directions from one day to the next. We began to get very busy with the chores assigned to us.

One day Travieso came by my bunker looking for me and said, "Hey Fenwick, I need you for another working party."

"Don't tell me its burning shitters again," I replied. "Hell, I'm a lance corporal now. Don't I have any privileges?"

"Not yet," he replied. "Until you have a fireteam of your own, you will have to sweat like the rest of the peons. Besides, this is not burning shitters, this is dumping trash over the hill from the mess hall."

"All right Travieso," I conceded, "point this peon in the right direction."

Travieso laughed out loud and replied, "Just get your peon ass moving down to the mess hall, Fenwick. I'm sure one of the cooks will take charge of the slop detail.

I had heard the term "peons" used many times by Marines. It was Marine lingo which meant the ranks of lance corporal and below. The peons were the ones who did all of the menial and dirty work that those of higher rank were exempt from. It wasn't until you reached the rank of corporal that you were considered a noncommissioned officer and reaped small benefits that went along with the rank and experience in the Marine Corps.

I proceeded to the mess hall, checked in with the cook in charge of the working party, and received instructions on what needed to be done. There were already grunts from other platoons carrying out boxes of garbage and trash. I lifted what I could and followed the others to where they were throwing it over the hillside not far from the mess hall. The dump for the LZ was a real steep embankment over the side of the mountain. With one heave a box of trash would roll and tumble down the hill and finally come to rest about fifty meters from the top of the hill. Someone had stretched a rope around some trees along the side of the garbage dump. After we finished throwing all the trash over the side, we would hold on to the rope, proceed down the embankment, walk into the center of the garbage, and then set fire to it in several places. Then we would climb back up the hill while holding on to the rope and stand at the top and watch it burn. Sometimes Vietnamese kids would appear and rummage through the garbage. They would also try to put out the fires so they could get their little hands on anything that they could salvage.

The artillery battery had adopted a pig for a pet and mascot that roamed freely throughout the fire support base. He was used to all the hustle and bustle of Marines carrying out their duties and was very much at home in their midst. Whenever garbage was taken out from the mess hall the pig always got his fair share of the leftover food scraps. He was running around my legs as I was carrying trash from the mess hall to the trash pit.

I threw some food scrap down for the pig and said to one of the other Marines helping on the working party, "Old Arnold is wondering around up here on FSB Ryder like he owns the place."

"Yeah," he answered, "he got the name from the TV show Green Acres."

I responded, "Yeah, I know it well. We used to watch that show all the time when I was a kid back home. It's a suitable name for this lazy old pig."

"These Marines from the Artillery Battery are going to fatten him up and then slaughter him," the Marine said while toting a box of garbage.

"You're shitin me," I said. "Well, I hope we are here for the big pig roast."

"These old boys up here will probably scarf him up without us even knowing about it," the Marine replied.

"Yeah, too bad Arnold," I said as I reached down to pat him. "Gonna be fattened up and end up in one of the shitters we'll have to burn. If you only knew your final destination you'd get the hell off this mountain."

I rubbed the pig's back and he just stood there eating and seemed to be enjoying the attention. I punched the pig gently. He let out an oink and moved his butt sideways while still eating. He seemed to be fattening up pretty good and why not with all the scraps from the mess hall. I pondered for a moment, instead of naming the pig Arnold, they should have named him Grunt.

I started daydreaming as I continued to tote boxes of trash to dump over the hillside. Cherry Hill Farm popped into my mind. I remembered back to the times on the farm when we would kill about six hogs in the fall. I used to really enjoy the task and especially eating fresh sausage and tenderloin. My father would prepare and season the meat in various ways. He would take the hams and lay them on an old wooden table in a room we called the back room. He covered them all over with table salt making sure every bit of the ham was covered. Then he would cover the hams with a paper grocery bag, run a wire through the small bone end, and hang them on wooden rails that were mounted from two wooden beams. The hams would cure and keep for years in this manner. The longer they cured, the better tasting they were when cooked. My mother had promised me, that when I got home from Vietnam, she would fix me one of the hams that had been curing for a couple of years. I couldn't wait to taste it. I would have to wait for a few more months however, before I would get the opportunity to gorge myself with her great country home cooking.

After the working detail had finished we ate some hot chow at the mess hall. I thought it tasted real good. They had prepared mashed potatoes, green beans out of the can, and canned ham. It seemed ironic to be eating ham slices after feeding old Arnold the pig. The ham from the mess hall tasted good but I knew it could not compare with the cured hams back home. We even had some milk which was quite a treat to get milk out in the bush. I thought to myself as I ate sitting down on a rock, these Marines in the artillery battery really know how to feed themselves. They should be in the grunts so that they would have to eat C-Rations all the time.

After chow I went back to the bunker and lay down on my cot for a little while. I heard a noise under my cot. I rolled onto my right side and looked under the cot. There were two rats scurrying around that were about ten inches long. Great big varmints, I thought. They were attempting to climb up the legs of the cot. I grabbed my rifle and with the butt of the weapon tried to hit them in the head. I got one as he squealed and whirled about and to my surprise raised up on his hind legs. It seemed as though the rat was defying me in its own animalistic way. I managed to connect with the rifle butt knocking the rat to the ground. I immediately finished him off with repeated blows to the head. The other rat ran into the sandbagged walls of the bunker. I stood up and searched for it. I could hear it moving behind the sandbags but I could not get to it. I decided to give up and lay back down.

A few minutes passed and I heard a few more scurrying noises about in the bunker. The other Marines joined in trying to kill the rats and we managed to get one more. I grabbed them by the tails and carried them out of the bunker and tossed them outside of the perimeter wire. When I reentered the bunker the other Marines were devising other methods of trying to capture the rats. We laughed at the various techniques that we were brainstorming.

One Marine playfully suggested a booby trap using a can of ham and eggs with a frag grenade, sort of a do-it-yourself rat trap. We figured that we would most likely end up dead instead of the rats. Since I had done a little trapping while I was growing up on the farm, I thought that we might get one if I set a rabbit snare. I gave up on the idea, however, for not having ready access to the materials needed. We decided to ignore the creatures. I believed that the rats were increasing their movements and boldness because of all the bunkers being torn down on the hill.

That night as I lay on my cot I felt something on my boot. I raised my head from underneath my poncho liner and saw a large rat gnawing on my boot next to my toes. I kicked it with as much force as I possibly could while still laying down and it scurried off and into the sandbags. I continued to try and sleep but then one of the rats ran across my chest. I bolted to an upright position, but it was too late. The rat had disappeared into the sandbags. It seemed as though the rats were playing a game with me.

Throughout the night I could feel something nibbling on my boot but I

Sitting on top of our bunker at Fire Support Base Ryder. The rats were so bad inside the bunker that it was better to be on the outside.

was too tired to concern myself. I would twitch from time to time to scare the creatures off and I would hear them scurrying about across the dirt floor of the bunker. I decided to curl up in my poncho liner wrapping it around my body real tight so that they could not get on the inside. I feared one might gnaw on my flesh without me knowing it. These pesky rodents had to carry some sort of disease and I didn't want to get medevaced to another hospital or worse end up dying from some disease infected rat. I continued to try and scare off my intruders throughout the night which caused a very restless sleep.

The next morning I awoke to the sunlight coming through the opening of the bunker and looked at one of my boots. One of the rodents had managed to attack me in my sleep and had gnawed a hole right through the leather by my big toe. That was awful close, I thought. Guess I would have to cover up with my poncho and poncho liner in the future. I could not believe that one had nibbled its way right through the tough leather on my boot. Good thing I slept with my boots on during the night. Then when I looked at my other boot, it too had a gnawed out hole in the leather just above the heel. The other Marines began to complain that the rats were a nuisance all night long.

I went outside of the bunker and watched the sun rise. I inspected my boots again and began talking to myself and cursing the rats. I knew whenever I stepped in a puddle of water, or it rained, or I was walking across a rice paddy that my boots would quickly fill with water. I would just have to air my feet more often. Sometimes it would take weeks just to get a set of utilities or boots sent out from the rear. I opened a can of beef and rocks and fixed me some coffee. An early morning breakfast fit for a king, I thought. I sipped my coffee out of a C-Ration can. I would be glad when we got off this mountain and away from the rats. As I sat enjoying the view and eating my C-Rations I heard footsteps coming up from behind me.

"Hey Fenwick, you son of a gun," the voice said.

I recognized it immediately. I looked over my shoulder and saw Hawkeye walking toward me in his own slouched manner as if he had a heavy load on his back. I saw his blonde hair glistening in the sunlight. He reminded me of my younger brother, Larry, who also had blonde hair when he was young.

"Come on over here cotton top," I said. "Have a seat and let's shoot the breeze for awhile."

Hawkeye sat down beside me. I offered him a sip of coffee. He took the C-Ration can filled with coffee and took a sip. "Mighty fine coffee for an amateur," he said. "I can make coffee that will make the hair stand on your head."

"Gimme my coffee back," I said as I reached for the can.

"Not yet, Hawkeye replied, just one more sip. Humm, good to the last drop."

We began talking about his R&R in Hawaii and Oregon. Hawkeye said that as far as he knew the platoon commander did not know that he went back to Oregon instead staying in Hawaii like he was supposed to. He said that if the platoon commander were to find out that he probably wouldn't do anything about it anyway. He said that you don't want to come down hard on a Marine who could someday save your ass in combat. He was now the platoon radio operator which meant he would always be within eye contact of the platoon commander. That in itself was a good reason not to be hard on Hawkeye. So it looked as though Hawkeye would not get into trouble after all. I was glad because he was a good guy who never meant anyone any harm. As the platoon radio operator, Hawkeye and I would now only see one another from time to time when we were in a defensive posture and not moving. It was consoling however, to know that my best friend would be close by when I needed someone to talk to.

It wasn't long until Travieso came by and joined us.

As he approached the spot where we sat talking, Travieso said, "Hello Hawkeye, how's it hanging?"

Hawkeye looked at him and replied, "Oh, it's still hanging."

"How are you doing Fenny?" Travieso continued.

"Doing all right I guess," I replied. "Didn't sleep worth a fart last night. The rats were attacking me all night. What I wouldn't give for a decent nights sleep."

"I told you there are some big ass rats up here on this mountain," Travieso said. "These bastards are large enough to drag you off this hill."

"I know," I said. "One of them stood up on its hind legs as if to fight me last night, but I managed to kill the bastard. Look what one did to my boots?" I showed him the holes in my boots.

Travieso and Hawkeye laughed out loud.

Travieso said, "These fuckin rats are really pests. That's all right though, we'll be moving off this mountain tomorrow morning. That's what I came by to tell you."

"Where are we going this time?" I asked while contemplating the worst.

"It looks like we are going down into Sniper Valley. We will be there for about twenty-five days. Gonna chase Charlie again," Travieso said.

I was glad. Finally I would get away from all the rats. They were becoming more aggressive with each passing day. We sat around talking about the day when we might be pulled out of Vietnam. Some of the other units had already been pulled out. We reckoned that the U.S. government had finally come to their senses about this war. We doubted seriously if the South Vietnamese military would be able to defend their country without American support. We had seen the ARVN (Army of the Republic of Vietnam) in combat action before. They did not seem very well organized, trained, dependable, or disciplined. We felt that South Vietnam would surely fall to the communist if the American forces were to withdraw out of Vietnam. But for the meantime, we still had a job to do.

"Sniper Valley, huh?" I said out of the blue. I wondered how many firefights awaited Mike Company in the next few months ahead.

"Oh, by the way, Fenwick," Travieso interrupted. "I've got some word for you. You're gonna have some more responsibility now that you are a lance corporal. You are now the 2nd fireteam leader. You've got two lance corporals and one PFC. You'll have to look after them like I look after the squad."

"Congratulations," Hawkeye said. "Now you've got your own fireteam. Before you know it you will be a squad leader."

Travieso responded, "Yeah, he can take my place when I leave this God forsaken country. I'm getting awful short, you know. Hell, I'm not short, I'm next. Well Fenny, let your fireteam know who is boss and get them ready to move out tomorrow. I've got to get back and have a meeting with the platoon commander. You guys take care, I'll talk with you later."

Travieso departed from us and then Hawkeye decided he had better get back to the platoon radio. He had left another Marine in charge of the radio while he came to visit with me and to shoot the breeze.

"Take it easy Hawkeye," I said as he walked away.

"I'll take it any way I can get it," replied Hawkeye.

I went into the bunker and explained to the Marines that I was now their fireteam leader. They were merely content knowing that one of them was not assigned the additional responsibility. Things were beginning to change for me now, I could sense it. There would be more responsibility that would require extra attention to detail and leadership. I would have to make decisions that would determine the life and death of the fireteam. I hoped that I would always make the right decisions.

That afternoon I decided to write home while I had the chance. I knew we would be going into Sniper Valley and didn't know when I would be able to write again. Back into the bush, I thought. Back to the booby traps, mines, firefights, and chasing the elusive enemy. Our slack time on FSB Ryder was about over for awhile.

August 13, 1970

Hello Mom, Dad and Larry,

How does this find you all? I hope you are in good health and spirits. I have some time so thought I'd write a couple of lines. We've been pretty busy up on LZ Ryder where this fire support base is. They're moving off the mountain within the next few months and we're tearing down all the bunkers. They ain't going to leave anything up here. Guess they'll leave it like they found it, nothing on it. Except it'll be a little battered because they're going to have air strikes on it as soon as they leave.

We leave tomorrow into the lowlands again. It's called Sniper Valley. Another valley we stay in a lot is Happy Valley but there's sure nothing happy about it. We have worked in an area called Elephant Valley and we also operate in the Que Son Mountains a lot. We really cover a big area. We'll be in the bush for twenty-five days or longer. Don't guess we'll even get a rehab. I imagine we'll look pretty shabby by the time we get back to LZ Ross. We should go back to the rear around the 10th of September. I will be glad when Larry's birthday gets here in September. From then on out maybe we can slack off a little before we get ready for a stand-down.

Well guess you all have noticed that I'm a "Lance Corporal" now. I got promoted the other day but my promotion warrant is dated the 5th of August. That will mean a little more pay and some more responsibility. I was assigned as the 2nd fireteam leader about three days ago. I have three men under me that I'm responsible for. Two are lance corporals and one a PFC. Now I can give a few orders instead of always receiving them. Of course no one likes a boss who is always giving orders. I'll do my job though and maintain my cool. Really it's quite easy for people to get along with each other over here. Besides they're depending on the leaders to make the decisions to keep them going. There are some really good dudes over here. This place makes us realize and appreciate the better things in life that we were accustomed to.

Well I'm finally getting my back mail from the hospital, although I still haven't gotten the pictures Mom sent. I sure am looking forward to seeing them. Guess I'll close for now since we may have to go on a working party pretty soon. There's not much going on right now, but we should see some action in a couple of days. Being occupied all the time sure passes the time quick. So I'll say by for now, hoping everyone is doing okay. I will be thinking of you always.

Yours truly,
Fred

I prepared my fireteam that afternoon in order to be ready to move out around noon the following day. We were going to go hump down the side of the mountain from FSB Ryder to look for a cave. It was suspected that the enemy had a cave at the foot of the hills and was occupied by NVA or VC. We prepared for the company move by drawing ammunition, rations, supplies, and all the other gear we would need for combat.

Travieso came over to the bunker where my fireteam was busy preparing our packs for departure. "What are you mumbling about, Fenwick? he asked.

While still stuffing my haversack with all sorts of gear I replied, "This damn ole pack I've got won't hold crap. We have all these resupplies of 60mm mortar rounds, M60 machine gun ammo cans, frag grenades, trip flares, M16 ammo, blooper rounds, and claymore mines. On top of that I have to cram in six days of C-Rations, my utility jacket, poncho, poncho liner, skivvies, letter writing gear, and shaving kit. I just can't fit them all in here. The damn straps on the pack are too short also. I'd like to have one of those gook packs that some of the other Marines are carrying around. The Vietnamese packs with all the extra pockets are so much better than our own haversack. I don't know why the Marine Corps don't have packs like that."

"Yeah, know what you mean," Travieso responded. "You have to kill a gook and take his pack in order to get one. We don't have them in our supply, only these dinky haversacks. The damn gooks have better packs than we do. Do you want a gook pack?"

"Yeah, you damn right, I'd like one," I replied

"I'll get you a gook pack," Travieso said as he started to leave the bunker.

A fire caused by air strikes at Happy Valley in the Quang Nam Province.

"Where are you going?" I asked.

Without turning back he said, "Don't worry about it, I'll get you a gook pack."

I was beginning to get a little concerned. "Where are you getting it from? You're not gonna steal one from another Marine, are you?"

While ducking his head under the entrance of the bunker Travieso turned around and headed back toward me. He sat on the edge of my cot.

"Give me your pack!" he commanded.

"What are you going to do with it?" I asked.

Travieso replied, "All I'm going to do is trade."

"Nooo! Don't do that!" I exclaimed. "No one in their right mind will trade a gook pack for a haversack. You know that these Marines in artillery don't have any gook packs so you'll have to get it from someone in Mike Company."

"Do you want a gook pack or not?" Travieso asked in an impatient manner.

"Sure, I'd like to have one, but not that way," I replied.

"Give me your pack and I'll be back in a minute," he said as he grabbed my pack away from me and dumped the contents onto my cot.

"Damn, Travieso," I said, "you're gonna get us both in trouble."

Ignoring my last remark Travieso left the bunker with my pack in his hand. In about half an hour Travieso returned waving a large gook pack in his hand and grinning from ear to ear.

In disbelief I asked, "Where is my pack?"

"I just traded it with another Marine," Travieso replied as he threw the pack for me to catch.

"Did the Marine say it was okay to trade?" I asked.

"Yeah, of course, no problem," said Travieso. "Just go ahead and pack it up."

As I began to stuff some of my gear into the outer pockets of the pack I noticed a name written across the back in black letters. "This pack has a name on it Travieso," I commented. "Are you sure the Marine said it was okay to trade with him?"

"You worry too much," Travieso replied. "Have I ever stirred you wrong before?"

I answered, "No, but there is always a first time for everything, but if you say it is okay, then I trust you. Wow, this is all right! I will have room to spare. Damn, Travieso, this is a really good pack!"

"You owe me one, Fenwick," Travieso said while exiting the bunker.

"Okay," I said, "you got it."

The next day at around 0900 on 14 August, word was passed by the Mike Company CP to saddle up. We were to begin our descent down the sides of FSB Ryder. We now had a different platoon commander. The current company commander would not be going with us. He remained at FSB Ross preparing for his departure for duty in Okinawa. Filling in as company commander was my former platoon commander. He was now the Executive Officer for Mike Company. He was a competent infantry officer and had arrived in country about a month before I had. I liked and respected him as a combat leader.

The front column was moving at a slow pace and our platoon was directly behind the lead platoon followed by another platoon that was bringing up the rear. We would stop and then move forward in an accordion effect. It wasn't long until I reached the incline of the hill descending below the crest. It was beginning to get a little steep and the ground was rocky with small loose pebbles. I was now about one hundred meters outside of the perimeter. We stopped again and with the weight of the pack I decided to place the bayonet of my rifle in the ground and lean on it for support. It was a habit I had gotten into each time we stopped because of the heavy pack digging into my shoulder muscles.

I was daydreaming when all of a sudden there was a heavy thump to the back of my head. I tumbled about eight feet down the side of the hill scraping my elbows and shins on the rocks as I slid. When I came to a stop I managed to look up to see what had hit me. I saw this tall muscular black Marine standing up the hill towering over me. One of my canteens had come off my cartridge belt during the fall and was laying on the ground about three feet away. My feet slid on the small gravel as I started to climb back up. I picked up my canteen off the ground and managed to climb uphill to where the Marine was standing.

I was bent over slightly trying to compensate for the heavy gear on my back. Just as I was about to raise up he pushed me again with both his hands. I lost my balance and again began sliding down the incline. I landed about the same place as before. This time I was a bit more dazed than the first fall. My rifle had come loose from my grasp and my helmet had gone flying off my head. It lay face up on the side of the hill. I wondered why it hadn't continued to roll further down the hillside and into the brush below. I was also lucky that my M16 was still close by.

"Motha fucka!" the black Marine yelled. "I'm gonna kill you, you sons-a-bitch. You stole mah pack you goddamn motha fucka!"

I saw our new platoon guide, who had replaced Sergeant Eiland, approach the black Marine.

"What the hell is going on here?" he demanded from him.

The black Marine began to curse and point his finger at me. "Dis motha fucka done gone and stole mah fuckin pack, that sons-a-bitch. I'll kill dat motha fucka!" he yelled.

"What are you talking about man!" the platoon guide yelled back. "This is his pack."

I glanced at Travieso standing on top of a little knoll uphill from the black Marine. He just stood there not saying a word but had seen the entire incident.

"Travieso," I yelled out in anger, "you traded my pack with this Marine didn't you?"

"Trade mah fuckin ass," the black Marine cut me off. "You stole mah fuckin pack. I wont my goddamn pack back. Dat's my motha fuckin pack. I even have my name on the fucka."

I grabbed my rifle and helmet and started back up the hillside for the third time. When I got to where the black Marine was standing he lunged toward me and pushed me again in the chest. I was ready for him this time as I braced myself by leaning forward to resist rolling back down this steep incline. I stopped only a few feet away. I looked up and saw that the platoon sergeant had his left arm out in front of the black Marine cautioning him to "knock it off."

Now I was pissed. I laid my M16 on the ground, threw my helmet on the ground, took the pack off my shoulders, and gave it a heave. I sprang up this time in anger ready to go toe-to-toe with this Marine and kick his ass. I started back up the hill to avenge my attacker.

Before I could reach him our platoon sergeant had made his way to the commotion and was standing next to the platoon guide and the black Marine. "I want to know what the hell is going on here!" the platoon sergeant snapped. "We're here to fight the enemy, not ourselves."

"Dis mah fucka here stole my goddamn pack," the black Marine responded. "I wont my fuckin pack back. Dis white honkey ass switched his rinky-dink pack for my gook pack. His fuckin pack won't hold shit. I looked for my pack all night long and couldn't find it. Dat one he's got on has my name on it. Can't you see it?" the black Marine yelled.

The platoon sergeant looked at me and asked angrily, "Did you take this Marine's pack?"

"I thought it was traded for my pack," I replied.

"Does the pack you're carrying belong to you or not?" the platoon sergeant asked.

"I had a haversack, probably the one he has on now," I answered. "I thought he traded packs with me through another member of my squad." I looked up at Travieso standing uphill from me. Travieso simply looked away without saying a word. "Okay, I'll give him his pack back," I said not wanting to create any more havoc.

The platoon sergeant responded by saying, "We don't have time to be trading packs now. Just carry it on down the hill. The next time we stop for any period of time you two can trade packs. You two understand?"

"Mah fucka, betta gives me my pack back," the black Marine said in anger.

"You know, I'm getting pretty sick and tired of being called a mother fucker, you asshole," I quipped.

The staff sergeant was quick to intervene. "Okay that's enough! Both of you knock it off! Do you hear me?"

"Yeah I hear," replied the black Marine.

"Yes staff sergeant, I understand," I said.

"Good", the platoon sergeant answered, "now let's saddle up and move out!"

As we headed out in column the black Marine walked faster than the others trying to catch up to his squad that had not stopped moving forward. As he bounced along I couldn't help but notice my small pack on his back. He was a large and robust Marine with wide shoulders and the small pack looked odd on his back. It was also apparent that he had been clumsy in packing all the equipment and attaching it to the pack. I was used to the small haversack and would manage to tie things to the pack in a manner that looked half way decent. He had things dangling all over the place as he had been used to cramming everything into a larger and much better gook pack.

At one point I thought it humorous about how awkward he looked. Then I thought about what had happened and Travieso taking his pack and giving it to me. If the same thing had happened to me, I would be a little angry myself.

Mike Company finally stopped in a small clearing about half way down the side of FSB Ryder to take a break. I would use my break time to try and locate the black Marine with my pack. I walked forward asking Marines who were laying on the ground with their backs resting on their packs if they had seen the Marine. Each one pointed toward the front of the column. I finally spotted him sitting on the ground in a grassy area that he was using for shade. My pack lay on the ground in front of him.

As I approached him I took the gook pack from my shoulders, laid it at my feet, knelt down, and started unfastening the straps.

"Okay, I'm ready to trade packs now. I'm really sorry that this happened. It was all a mistake. I had told my buddy that I would like to have a gook pack and I assumed that he had traded packs with someone. I didn't know that he had stolen it from you. I thought that you had agreed to a trade."

With a leering look he said, "Go ahead and put all your shit in this rinky-dink pack and put my stuff back into my gook pack."

"Okay, no problem," I said.

I repacked my stuff into the haversack and his gear into his original gook pack. I apologized again but only received an evil look from him. I felt bad about what had happened and returned to join my squad looking for Travieso. I found him chowing down on a can of apricots.

"Travieso, why in the hell didn't you say you stole his pack?" I asked annoyingly.

"What in the hell am I to say?" Travieso replied. "That I stole his fuckin pack? You are the one who wanted a gook pack in the first place. I got you one didn't I? The subject is closed as far as I'm concerned."

"Thanks a lot for nothing," I answered Travieso. "Now I've got my old pack back and I've got more gear than I know what to do with. I might be shit canning some of it because I don't have the room in this dinky haversack. From now on Travieso, don't do me no more favors."

"Fine by me!" Travieso snapped.

I was not really mad at Travieso. His heart was in the right place. It just showed me what lengths he would go to in order to take care of his squad. I hoped that we could remain on good terms.

We got the word to move out so we threw our heavy packs on our backs and started forward. This time our platoon, Mike 3, took the lead. We had not moved very far through the dense foliage until a Marine observed one enemy in green utilities in a cave. Mike 3 engaged the enemy with small arms fire and killed him. Another NVA managed to escape. After we searched the area we found that the cave was a hospital with a small dispensary. There were also three packs containing assorted medical gear and documents that were found in the cave along with hot food already served on dishes. It appeared that this hide out was used as a feeding place for the enemy. The medical gear was to be evacuated to the rear for further evaluation.

We were once again given the word to saddle up and move out. My fireteam started to pass by the entrance of the cave. I took notice that there was a rusted out American made M60 machine gun. The NVA/VC had either killed some American serviceman or had obtained the machine gun though some other means. Now that it was recovered, it would most likely be classified as unserviceable, because of the heavily embedded rust.

We moved into an area about twenty-five hundred meters southeast of FSB Ryder. From this position we conducted search and clear operations in conjunction with CUPP and Popular force units for about two days. The acronym CUPP meant Combined Unit Pacification Program. It consisted of Marines and South Vietnamese soldiers working together. We had only minor contact with the enemy.

At around 1800 on 16 August we arrived at our night position and dug fighting holes, sleeping holes, and prepared fields of fire. From here Mike Company conducted several night and early morning patrols without contact. My squad was located at grid AT965335, a village Loc Trung (5) was just to our north. The elevation on this small knoll was about 90 feet above sea level so my squad simply named it Hill 90 for a lack of a better term.

The following morning on 17 August at around 1030 a CH-46 resupplying Mike Company drew small arms fire while attempting to land. Two UH-1E Gunships and two OV-10s attacked the suspected enemy position which was about 500 meters southeast of the company's position. An aerial observer reported movement in the same vicinity and a two squad patrol went to investigate. Several were seen entering a cave, however only one Vietnamese female about 25 years old was apprehended and returned to the company position.

That same day at around noon, my squad, Mike 3 Charlie, was sent out on patrol to check the area once again. We formed up in column formation on Hill 90 and proceeded down the slope to where the ground was level. This was my first patrol as a fireteam leader so I wanted to make sure I was always on the alert. We veered southeast toward the area where the resupply chopper had received sniper fire earlier that morning. As we moved slowly along some vegetation we soon came to some rice paddies and crossed over them toward the area.

Travieso had been given certain checkpoints to cover. From past experience we had learned our lesson to make sure that we in fact hit each and every checkpoint. As we moved from one checkpoint to the other we would notify the platoon radio operator of our whereabouts. We did not want a fire mission called in on a checkpoint, if we were still at that location, as it had happened under the leadership of my first squad leader. Travieso followed orders in a professional manner and his main concern was to look out for the welfare and safety of his men. He was very dedicated and responsible although he was a little rough around the edges.

We moved along in a column with about fifteen meters in between each man. We came into a clearing passing through rice paddies and into some treelines. We walked into some heavy over growth. Everyone was quiet as we moved with great caution and knowing that our point-man was on the alert looking out for mines and booby traps along the trail. Each time we stopped our tail end Charlie would face about 180 degrees and visually scan the area behind us so the enemy didn't sneak up on us. There was never a patrol that we didn't ensure we had flank and rear security.

We turned to the east and then north and started to circle back toward the hill where the company was located. As we headed back to the southwest we could get out of the rice paddy and walk along the vegetation along the sides. It wasn't long until we could see the base of the hill where Mike Company was located. There had been rumors that we were going back to FSB Ross for three days of rehabilitation. As we began to approach the hill we heard over the squad radio that we were going to hump back to FSB Ross.

After hearing this Travieso said, "Great, we're going back to the rear after all, three more days of rehab."

The squad began to rejoice about the fact that we were going back to the base camp so soon again. There would be showers, beer, and clean clothes. Travieso checked his map and told us that it looked like it was about six klicks back to the base camp.

"Hell, don't they have choppers anymore? I'm tired of humping everywhere we go," I moaned.

Just then a familiar voice came over the radio net. It was Hawkeye, our platoon radio operator. "Mike 3 Charlie, This is Mike 3, Over."

Our squad radio operator replied, "Mike 3, This is Mike 3 Charlie."

"Roger, be advised that you need to get on back to the perimeter as soon as possible. We will be moving out for the base camp in a few mikes. We have already started to pack it up. Over."

"Roger that!" our squad radio operator acknowledged.

We commenced to walk a little faster. The next transmission we heard over the radio was coming from the company commander's radio operator to the Mike Company mortar section. The company commander had given the mortar section permission to fire off any extra HE mortar rounds before returning to the base camp. They were to use this time for target practice and fire in the direction where the resupply chopper had received sniper fire.

We could not believe what we were hearing. They were actually going to fire off mortar rounds so that the mortar section and all the other Marines who helped carry the heavy rounds would not have to hump them back to the rear. That was good news for our squad to be spared of the extra burden.

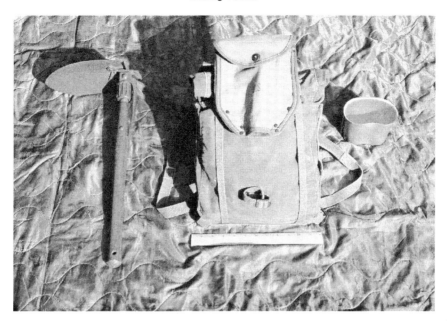

Marine Corps Haversack. The M1941 pack system could be converted into five different configurations. We used the smallest and lightest in Vietnam which consisted of only the haversack. It was called a Light Marching Pack. Photo represents a comparison of size to the E-Tool and canteen cup. The haversack was hardly adequate for the amount of ordnance, chow, and equipment we had to carry on our backs.

We would strap four or five mortar rounds to our packs in addition to the usual ordnance.

The ammo I carried consisted of mortar rounds, machine gun ammo, bandoleers of M16 ammo, about eight hand grenades, claymore mines, trip flares, and other miscellaneous ordnance. In addition, I carried the essential combat gear such as six to eight canteens full of water, poncho, poncho liner, rations, entrenching tool, and all the other essentials for survival. I also carried personal items such as a sleeping shirt, utility jacket, shaving kit, and letter writing gear. It was quite a bit of gear to carry on our backs.

Within the mortar section of the CP group there was a black Marine who was nicknamed "Thumper." He was very fast in setting up the 60-millimeter mortar tube. Upon receiving map grid coordinates of an enemy position over the radio he could set up the mortar tube, align the sights on target, and fire off the very first mortar round in a matter of seconds. He did this with the help of an assistant gunner (A-Gunner) who would hand Thumper the uncased mortar rounds. Each time a mortar round was dropped into the tube and it engaged the firing pin, the mortar rounds would fire into the air with a rapid "thump-thump" sound. Thus, the nickname emerged.

It was approximately 1420 when our squad began moving along the base of the hill. We were close enough now to hear the radio transmissions and the echoes of the Marines actually talking over the radios. From the mortar section we heard the transmission, "Outgoing!"

I heard the sounds of 60mm mortar rounds being fired right over the top of our heads. They were being fired to the east and southeast and landing in the rice paddy. I wondered why they hadn't waited until our patrol was completely out of the line of fire. As our squad headed back up the slope toward the crest of the hill I saw two mortar tubes firing off mortar rounds that were spaced about twenty-five meters apart. The mortar tube on the left seemed to be firing in a northeast direction while the mortar tube on the right seemed to be firing east and south east.

The first rounds impacted about 450 meters away from our perimeter. I noticed that the rounds began to walk in the rice paddy with the tube on the left traversing right and the tube on the right, Thumper's tube, traversing left. The left tube started firing its rounds first with the rounds impacting on target. After the left tube had fired about five rounds, the right tube commenced firing and it looked as though one round impacted near the right flank of the target with two or three others impacting to the left of the first round.

Thumper was firing off the mortar rounds very rapidly. The mortar section Marines were opening the casings of the rounds and stripping the fins of one or two increments. This determined how far the round would travel. They would then place the rounds in stacks ready for the A-Gunner to feed the rounds into the tube. Thumper had initially used the bi-pods attached to the mortar tube to stabilize it during firing. He would use the sights on the mortar tube to aim in the direction where he wanted the rounds to hit. Thumper and his A-Gunner were firing off the rounds just as fast as they could. Thumper was telling his A-Gunner to hurry up and feed the tube faster and faster.

The process of rapidly firing off the mortars was just not going as fast as Thumper desired. He placed an asbestos glove on his left hand, removed the bi-pods from the tube, and held the mortar tube with his left hand. He began to drop rounds into the tube with his right hand without the aid of the bi-pods. Thumper started grabbing the rounds and was dropping them in the tube by himself in a rapid succession. Some of the Marines in the CP group and around the perimeter saw him in action and yelled out, "Get some, Thumper! Get some!"

With the jolt derived from each round fired the tube began to cant backwards. Now he had no elevation or range adjustment on the sights which was required to send the rounds out of the CP area and onto the target area. I caught sight of my sleeping hole when a Marine near the CP yelled in a frightening manner, "Short Round! Short Round! INCOMING!"

Some of the mortar rounds had gone straight up into the air and the lack of trajectory brought them straight back down. At this time a mortar round impacted approximately one hundred meters from the mortar position in the direction of the target followed immediately by five or six rounds that impacted in the company position. There were also two rounds that impacted to the rear of the mortar position. As the first round impacted, the Marines who had been preparing to move out began diving for cover and looking for their flak jackets and helmets. Some made it to their fighting holes but others did not. One round exploded right in the center of the company CP.

Our entire squad dived down an embankment leading to the top of the hill. I slid uncontrollably down the side of the hill for about fifteen feet. My helmet had slid over my eyes and I placed my hands interlocked behind my neck hoping to keep any shrapnel from penetrating this vulnerable part of my body. Mortar rounds exploded on the hill as shrapnel flew over my head. In those seconds as the mortar rounds were exploding all around me it was the most fearful moment of my life.

I began praying the Our Father because I feared this was the end of my life. In a split second I recalled the poem I had sent home to my parents titled Letter from Vietnam and was thankful that I had written it. I was completely helpless and vulnerable to the flying shrapnel. I thought of my mother and said her name out loud, "Momma, help me!" I continued to pray as the mortar rounds impacted this knoll and the ground shook underneath me. The sounds of the explosions were deafening.

Finally the pounding of the mortar rounds were silent. We all knew that the last mortar round had fallen from the sky. I felt a stinging and burning sensation in both elbows so I removed my interlocked hands from behind my neck and took a look. Both of my elbows were oozing blood from scraping them on the loose rocks. I had dirt and debris mixed in with my blood soaked elbows. I realized at this moment that I was okay and that I was going to live. Then I heard the eerie sounds of moaning, screaming, and yelling coming from within the company's perimeter.

The entire hill was now consumed with chaos and cries for help. "CORPSMAN! CORPSMAN! CORPSMAN UP! Oh God, Help me! Someone get a corpsman! We need help over here, ASAP! Oh no, my leg, I can't feel my leg? What's happened to me? Oh God, my arm! Help me! Help me! Don't let me die!"

Now Marines began running to the aid of their buddies. The nerve-shattering sounds of moaning and screaming continued. Most of the casualties occurred within the company command group, including the company commander in the immediate vicinity of the mortar pits, when one round struck vegetation and detonated approximately four feet above the ground. A second round impacted between the mortar pits and was the second most damaging round that resulted in two KIA.

I heard my platoon sergeant arbitrarily barking orders. "Leave him alone Doc. He's dead. We need you over here. Get over here and fix this one, hurry up! Quickly! Hey you, Marine, grab your poncho and tighten it over his chest, he has a bad sucking chest wound, Move it!"

The squad leaders also joined in to assist the platoon sergeant and barking orders and directions. "Give me some Marines up here with tourniquets and battle dressings. Hurry up we need help. Corpsman! Corpsman Up! Let's go, we've got some wounded over here. Let's move people, Hurry up!"

There was mass confusion on the top of the hill. Marines were running and dodging one another while on the move. They were grabbing battle dressings, web belts, ponchos, and anything else they could get their hands on to stop the bleeding. Marines were assisting the corpsmen by tying arms and legs with tourniquets and dressings. Some arms and legs were mangled into bloody slabs of meat. The company commander had been hit, but it was not life threatening. The company gunny had also been hit. Marines were laying all over the hill in pain. Some moaning and groaning, others yelling and screaming. The corpsmen began to administer shots of morphine to ease the pain and shock and to quiet the sounds of anguish.

Our platoon corpsman and I attended to a wounded Marine with a serious leg wound. As we were bandaging him up, he said, "Don't let me die! You hear me? Don't let me die! Then he paused for a moment and gritted his teeth in pain. He looked at me and asked, "Where is my rifle? I need my rifle." I assured him that his rifle was close by his side. Marines were trained from boot camp to never let their rifle out of their sight. Their very lives would depend on the individual weapon while wearing the Marine Corps uniform. It was a Marine's life-blood. "God, help me!" he screamed.

We secured the tourniquet on the Marine's leg and the corpsman began to fill out an information tag that would accompany the wounded Marine back to the rear. The corpsman looked up and noticed that I was bleeding from both elbows.

"Are you hurt?" he yelled out over the yelling of the other Marines.

I answered him saying, "Nah, just a couple of scratches. I dove for cover from the incoming mortar rounds and slid down an embankment on my elbows. I'll be all right."

"Okay, if you say so," the corpsman replied. "Go ahead and help the others. I'll finish up on this one."

I glanced at the top of the hill and saw the confused state of urgency and panic of the Marines. I saw a group of Marines close by attending to a wounded Marine. I picked up the Marine's rifle that the corpsman and I had been treating and ran over to see if I could help. I knew that all the individual rifles and pistols would have to be sorted out later. When I got to their huddle, the Marines stood up and began to carry the wounded Marine to the top of the hill. One of our platoon squad leaders yelled for me to pick up the Marine's rifle and pack and to bring it to the top of the hill.

I did as I was instructed and picked up any fallen equipment that was accidentally dropped by the group. I passed by Hawkeye and noticed that he was okay and that he was glued to the radio handset monitoring the transmissions. He did not notice me as I passed by him with my arms loaded with weapons and equipment. I dropped the gear in a predesignated stack. The Marines of Mike Company then staged the KIA and WIA in a centralized location on top of Hill 90.

The two dead Marines were placed side by side and covered with ponchos. The wounded were positioned not far away and attended to by Marines and company corpsmen. They were categorized as emergency, priority, and routine medevacs. At about 1427 I heard the company radio operator calling the base camp for medevac choppers. It was not long until we all heard the sound of medevac choppers. Whomp, Whomp, Whomp, Whomp!

The sound of helicopters was always a welcome sound while in the bush. The Marine helicopters and their crews were appreciated by all Marines. They meant everything from transportation, resupply of water and rations, mail delivery, ammunition delivery, and most importantly, medevacs. Two CH-46 Sea Knights arrived on scene at 1442. It had only taken them approximately fifteen minutes to fly from FSB Ross. I thanked God they were on their way to get these Marines out.

The medevac choppers landed at which time twenty-one of the most serious cases were evacuated. At approximately 1455, the Commanding Officer, 3rd Battalion, 7th Marines arrived on the scene. I believe the Battalion Commander suspected friendly on friendly fire. After questioning Marines in leadership positions the Battalion Commander decided to impound the weapons and remaining ammunition and caused all items to be moved to FSB Ross where they would be under the control of an investigating officer. His Ch-46 was used to evacuate the remaining casualties. The overall evacuation was complete by around 1515.

The strong gusts of wind and flying debris peppered my face as the last chopper rose into the air. I turned my head and closed my eyes. I struggled to maintain my sense of balance as the force of the wind pressed against me. Suddenly the wind subsided and I lifted my head to watch the choppers disappear out of sight over the rice paddies and hills. Still half in a daze from all the commotion within the last hour, I headed back to my sleeping hole.

The results of this catastrophe kept racing through my mind. Mike Company had shelled itself with its own 60mm mortars. Because of this serious incident, we had 2 Marines KIA and 30 Marines WIA. Of the wounded in action, 12 were emergency medevacs, 3 were priority medevacs, and 15 were routine medevacs. In addition, the Viet Cong woman prisoner had been killed by the mortar explosions.

I found my sleeping hole and combat gear even though it was totally unrecognizable to me. My poncho liner that I had covering my sleeping hole had been blown down the hillside. It was tangled around a bush. The medevac choppers had landed near my sleeping hole and the wind gusts from the choppers had blown all my personal belongings about. I knelt down and stared at my gear. There was shrapnel scattered about. I began to pick up the big pieces and throw them away from my gear. Some of it was still warm to the touch.

My poncho was punctured with holes of different sizes and shapes. My pack had small punctures throughout. One piece of shrapnel had ripped a hole the size of a golf ball right through the top of the pack. Another piece of shrapnel had penetrated the center of the pack leaving a hole with torn and ripped material in a diameter the size of a grapefruit. I checked my six canteens. All were punctured by shrapnel except two and the water had seeped out and onto the ground. The incoming shrapnel, the water from my canteens, and the wind from the choppers, had destroyed my letter writing gear. I realized that I was a very lucky Marine to be alive. I could have stayed back and slept on my pack that day. As fate would have it, Mike 3 Charlie was sent out on patrol that afternoon. I thought that God had protected me and spared my life that day. I began to whisper some prayers; Our Father's, Hail Mary's, and Glory Be's.

I was interrupted by the voice of our platoon corpsman. He was walking around the platoon's sector and checking to see if the Marines were okay before we started our march back to the base camp. He approached me from behind.

"Fenwick, are you sure you are okay?" he asked again.

"Yeah Doc, I'm fine," I replied.

"Let me see those elbows," he commanded.

"That's okay Doc," I answered. "My elbows will be fine. Just a lot of stinging but they are sore as hell."

"Don't let me have to pull rank on you," the corpsman said smiling. "Now let me see those elbows!" I stood up and bent both arms so the Doc could see my elbows. "You've got a couple of nice little scrapes but you will live. They are a bit deep and will get infected if you don't take care of them. Those are prime spots for jungle rot."

"What do you suggest Doc? I damn sure don't want jungle rot," I said.

"Well," the corpsman responded. "First wash them with water from your canteens to get the dirt out then apply some gauze and keep them dry. When they scab over, make sure you don't pick at the scabs. That's about the best I can do."

"I've only got two canteens of water left Doc," I explained to him. "I'm afraid if I use what little water I have left to wash my wounds I may totally run out before we get back to the rear."

"Damn, Fenwick," he replied sounding a bit irritated. "Make up your mind! Get jungle rot, or die of thirst!"

"Okay Doc, I get the point," I said.

I reached for a canteen and began to clean my elbows. I felt the stinging sensation of water and dirt in my open wound but there was little I could do except take the pain. My elbows were sore and bruised. Others had been less fortunate than I.

"Hey Fenwick," the corpsman said as I attempted to clean my scraped elbows. "I can put you up for a Purple Heart. After all, you were wounded in combat."

"Yeah, right Doc," I replied sarcastically.

"I'm not kidding," he said. "The other wounded Marines will be put up for Purple Hearts. You just wait and see. You might as well be one of them."

I hesitated for a few seconds and then replied, "I thought you had to be wounded by the enemy in order to get a Purple Heart, not just be in combat. Besides, all I did was duck for cover and ended up scraping my elbows on the rocks."

"Who's to know?" the Doc asked. "As far as I'm concerned you got wounded in combat."

"I would know," I told the corpsman, "you can't be serious."

"Serious as a heart attack," the corpsman responded, "don't you want to go home with a Purple Heart?"

"Nah, that's okay Doc," I said. "There are Marines who deserve the Purple Heart because they were wounded by the enemy. It just wouldn't be right. If I'm gonna get a Purple Heart in Vietnam, it will be because I earned it."

"Suit yourself," the corpsman replied. He walked off to check on the adjacent Marines. I knew deep within that the Doc was just full of crap. You don't get purple hearts by diving for cover while being shelled by your own unit.

We gathered our belongings, placed them in our packs, and stood by to move out. I did not cover my wounds with gauze as the corpsman had suggested. I wanted to keep what bandages I had in case there were other casualties. We were ready to start our hump back to the rear but instead we just sat in place for what seemed like a long time.

I walked over to Travieso and asked, "What the hell are we waiting for? It will be dark by the time we start moving."

"Your guess is as good as mine, "Travieso answered.

"Don't they know we can trip all kinds of mines and booby traps in the dark?" I said angrily.

"Don't guess they do," replied Travieso. He seemed a bit out of it, so I walked away and left him alone with his personal thoughts. No one was acting themselves after the mortar incident.

At about 1600 we heard that another chopper was coming in to land. This time the Regimental Commander and the Commanding General of 1st Marine Division was coming to our position to determine what had happened. The Commanding General discussed the situation with the Regimental and Battalion Commander. It seemed that the majority of personnel questioned in Mike Company believed that they were subjected to an enemy mortar attack. I never got a chance to be questioned so I could not tell what I had seen with my own eyes. The fact remained that whatever Marines wanted to believe, we were mortared by our own mortar section.

Finally the CG, Regimental Commander, and Battalion Commander departed our position by helicopter. It was now close to getting dark by the time we were to start humping back to the rear. I wondered why we were walking back to FSB Ross during the hours of darkness. It made no sense to me. We could have stayed the night and then humped back the next day to avoid tripping mines or booby traps. The senior platoon commander was put in charge of the company as we started to hump back to the base camp. After this ordeal, all the Marines just wanted to get the hell off this hill.

As we moved along in column formation down the side of Hill 90 some started talking about the company party we would have when we got back to the rear. It was as though nothing had ever happened, just another day in the Nam. As I walked along in column at the base of the hill, I momentarily looked back over my left shoulder toward the west to get one last look at Hill 90 in the Que Son Valley. I realized at that moment that this incident would remain a vivid memory and lasting visions for the rest of my life.

At about 2000 we started receiving about 50 rounds of AK47 fire from about 200 meters to the northeast across a rice paddy. BBBRROOWWW... Ratatat..tat! One corpsman was wounded in the leg. The 1st platoon returned fire and broke contact. The corpsman was quickly medevaced and we then continued on our night movement. We walked for over an hour and came upon a dirt road leading back to FSB Ross. The company commander decided that we would follow the road to expedite our movement. At around 2115 I heard an explosion up ahead. WHOOMPH!"

Everyone hit the deck. The point man had somehow seen a warning sign for a booby trap and while trying to locate it, detonated the booby trap. A medevac chopper was called by one of the radiomen. Mike Company stopped and rested on the road side waiting for the medevac choppers to arrive. As the choppers approached, the pilots were shining their spotlights on the ground. What prime targets for Charlie, I thought. It was announced over the radio that there were 4 WIA.

I wondered how so many could have been wounded by a single booby trap unless the Marines were just too close together in the darkness. The word was passed that we needed to keep it spread out while on the march. It wasn't long until the 4 wounded Marines were on their way to FSB Ross for medical aid. Why was this entire thing happening? Why us? Was all of Mike Company going to be wiped out in a single day? Would we ever make it back to the base camp alive? Would I ever see another beer or hamburger again? Would I ever see my mother and father again? Questions and thoughts raced through my mind.

We were halted in place for what seemed to be an eternity but it was only about an hour. At around 2300 we heard over the radio that tanks would be coming from the base camp to escort us back safely. We were to walk in the tracks made by the tanks to avoid stepping on mines. This seemed like a logical solution at the time. As we moved out again one of the tanks hit a mine and one of its tracks had been blown off. The tank crew had been shaken up and wounded but none seriously. Finally, approximately five to six tanks arrived. They turned around facing down the road leading to the base camp. Everyone was given strict orders to walk in the imprint of the tracks on the road and not to walk to either side. We all felt that this should do it. We should make it back to the base camp safely. That was not to be however, because another tank hit a mine.

After inspecting the incident, it was determined that the mine had been hand detonated by a VC. They traced the wire to the spot where Charlie had been waiting and hiding for just the right opportunity. Now he had vanished into the night. I thought that the VC probably had crawled into a spider trap or tunnel nearby after he had detonated the mine. The acting company commander made a command decision that we would set up a perimeter in the treeline and wait for morning before attempting to move back to the base camp. Maybe this way we could see mines and booby traps as we moved slowly along. We moved off to the side of the road and the squad leaders were called up for a meeting. Our squad position for the night was designated.

We dug in and posted a fifty per cent alert through the rest of the night. The tanks departed to return to the base camp. I never knew if they made it back without further incident that night. By the time I finished my fighting hole I was extremely tired and sleepy. I luckily managed to get the first security watch in my foxhole. The rest of the fireteam would share the watch until sunrise. While standing watch I expected the unexpected. I tried my best to stay awake because I knew that Charlie was in the immediate vicinity. I struggled to keep my heavy eyelids open.

I began to contemplate the sequence of events for the day. From the time our own mortar rounds started dropping into the CP on Hill 90, to the time that the NVA/VC ambushed us, our company had dwindled from almost one hundred to about sixty men. It was a good sized platoon. I estimated that during this period of about nine hours, the Marines of Mike Company suffered the loss of 2 killed, 34 wounded, and one wounded Navy corpsman. It didn't look good either for the three Marines that were priority medevacs who were in serious condition.

Morning dawned with a cloudy overcast. It was 18 August 1970. I was just happy to still be alive. I thought of home and realized that it was already night time back home in Kentucky. I sat upright in my sleeping hole eating a small unheated can of ham and eggs with peanut butter. We heard over the radio that we were heading back to FSB Ross. We packed our gear and headed down the road toward the base camp. As we humped along the road Hawkeye somehow managed be right behind me in column formation. I glanced back at him from time to time. His pack appeared very large and heavy with the PRC-77 radio strapped to it. He had screwed a whip antenna onto his radio for transmitting at greater distances but for the hump back he had folded it into sections and had them tied in a bundle. It was very strenuous and difficult carrying our heavy equipment while humping down the dirt road. I thought we would never reach FSB Ross.

Just as we began to turn off the road approaching the base camp I turned about and took a picture of Hawkeye. He was in no mood for pictures as we had all been through a rough ordeal. We finally made it back to the base camp that morning in one piece. We were physically and mentally exhausted. We would spend three days back at FSB Ross for a period of rehabilitation. We would need every day to recuperate from our mental anguish.

Travieso told us to move into the hooch and get a good nights rest. Tomorrow we would have a formation to honor our dead. Not many of us got much sleep that night. A few Marines went to the club to drown in their sorrows. I preferred to be alone and to recollect my thoughts about the recent fatalities in Mike Company. I attempted to dispel the horrific events as merely a bad dream, but I knew deep down that the thoughts would always haunt me. I lay back on my cot with my fingers interlocked and under my head. I stared at the ceiling deep in thought. Flashbacks of the last two days went through my mind. I started to hear a Marine's transistor radio playing a slow song. I listened to the lyrics. It was "Bridge Over Troubled Water" by Simon and Garfunkel. A tear ran down the side of my face and into my left ear. I did not wipe it away. Soon I drifted off into a light sleep.

The next morning after breakfast the company fell out in formation. Two M16 rifles were stuck in the ground with their bayonets and helmets placed on top to represent the dead. A few of the less seriously wounded Marines from the day before joined us in ranks as the Battalion Chaplain read names off a piece of paper. He began his benediction and prayer by saying, "Oh God, in your divine wisdom and power, look favorably upon our fallen comrades and grant them eternal rest."

I thought I became a full-fledged man that day on Hill 90 at the age of nineteen. If nothing else, I had become a better man, a man who would learn to appreciate life and the blessings we reap each and every day we are alive. I would respect my fellow Marines both past and present and understand the ultimate sacrifices we pay to God, Corps, and Country. My life would be forever changed. I found out the hard way about "Medevac Mike." Not only had Marines been medevaced because of mines, booby traps, and enemy aggression, it was now by our own carelessness. What a price to pay for defending one's Country.

The rehab we spent in the rear at FSB Ross gave us a chance to wash our clothes, take showers, eat chow under the mess tent, get haircuts, clean our weapons, and down some warm beer. The time in the rear passed us by very quickly and before we knew it we were heading back out to the bush. It was the same ritual each time. Get up early, go to chow, draw weapons from the armory, fall in with the rest of Mike Company, get issued rounds and ordnance, get six days of rations from the squad leader, and then get inspected to make sure we had all our gear.

I hated the packing part. There was so much to carry and items had to be fastened to the pack in such a way that it was equally balanced on both sides. I proceeded to the armory to draw my rifle. On the other side of the hooches I heard the drill instructor voice of the company gunny. He was yelling at Thumper for him to get to the armory and draw his weapon in order to go back to the bush. I really didn't know what all the commotion was about.

Thumper would not accompany us on this next operation. Due to the negligence indicated in the investigation on the part of the mortar section leader and two mortar gunners, the convening authority referred their cases to an Article 32 investigation. Thumper could face a court-martial for his negligence on Hill 90. He had told the company gunnery sergeant that he was "not" going back to the bush. Not only did he know that he was pending disciplinary action, there were rumors floating around Mike Company that Thumper feared going back to the bush because some Marines might take revenge. The company gunny ordered Thumper to draw his .45 pistol from the armory and to get his gear ready. Thumper was told he had no choice in the matter.

Thumper went to the armory as ordered and checked out his pistol. He was in the line ahead of me. I was just getting ready to step up to the cage door to draw my M16 when I heard, "Pooww!" It scared the hell out of me. I almost hit the deck but caught myself. My first thought was that it was incoming from the enemy. Then I thought someone had an accidental discharge. My ears were ringing from the pistol going off so close and in confined quarters.

I looked behind me and saw Thumper holding his left hand and blood pouring from it. He had taken his .45 pistol, loaded it with ammo, placed the barrel in the palm of his left hand, and pulled the trigger. He had said that he was not going back into the bush. Now he wasn't, for sure! He was rushed to the Battalion Aid Station for medical attention. We continued to prepare for the bush as if nothing out of the ordinary had happened. I never saw Thumper again.

August 19, 1970

Hello Mom, Dad and Larry,

How is everyone back home? I hope in A-1 condition. For myself I'm doing fine. We left LZ Ryder about a week ago and have been near Sniper Valley ever since. On our way down the side of the mountain from Ryder we found a gook hospital. We got one gooner, but one got away. They had a lot of medical supplies and even some sort of a mess hall.

We'll be in the bush this time for about twenty days before we get back to the rear. At least it won't be too bad humping in the flat lands, just the heat. Now it's cooling off a little over here. It gets so it rains every evening at about five o'clock now. But I'm prepared for it. I had finally got me a rain jacket that really helps out. It sure comes in handy. I also have the pants for it but I hardly ever use it. I probably will though when the heavy monsoons hit.

Well I got Mom's package yesterday and was glad to get it. Everything went over good. I let the guys in the squad try the canned sausage paddies. My squad leader really dug into them. He said they're "Number One." Thanks for the package, I really appreciate it. I don't imagine I'll need anything else for awhile.

Well I got all my back mail yesterday and had about twenty letters. Like Mom had said, I hardly knew what each person had said. I'll probably read them all over several times.

By the way, I got the pictures you had sent. They are really good. I'm going to keep these instead of sending them back home. I think maybe I can put them together with my writing gear and some plastic cover to keep them from ruining. They really brought back memories. They kinda made me homesick for awhile. Everyone looks real good in them. I'm sending some pictures home that Janice sent me. She sent me two rolls of film which I had taken about two months ago. I'm going to send them home because she sent them all for me to keep. She kept some too though.

Well, I'll close for now. Hoping everyone is doing fine. I want to get this off on the next chopper. Will write later on. Thanks for the pictures.

Yours truly,
Fred

On 20 August Mike Company went back out to the bush. This time we had a new first lieutenant company commander. He had been the 2nd platoon commander prior to being assigned as company commander of Mike Company. We departed FSB Ross and headed out to the vicinity of Sniper Valley. On the first day out the company was conducting a daytime move when one of our squads in the 3rd platoon saw four enemy in a treeline. They commenced firing with small arms but the enemy got away. After the squad searched the area they found one wounded enemy and six enemy packs. The enemy and packs were sent back to the rear.

That afternoon Travieso gathered the squad together and told us that we would be setting up an ambush for the night. He told us to prepare our gear and that he would get with the platoon commander to find out the coordinates where we were to set in. We were to remain overnight and come back into the perimeter the next morning. We filled our canteens, made sure we had enough ammunition, cleaned our weapons, and got some chow to take with us just in case we had to stay out longer than anticipated. A machine gun team was also assigned to the squad.

As the sun set we formed up and began to move out in single file. We moved quietly and slowly since it was now beginning to get dark in order to be aware of any booby traps that might be in our path. We arrived at the position that we were to set in for the night and to set up a hasty 180 degree perimeter, a semicircle similar to a half moon. Watches were assigned for the night so that two Marines would be on watch at any given time. The rest of the squad, would just lay out on top of the ground in order to try and get some sleep, if we could. There would be no digging of fighting holes or sleeping holes. We did not want to call attention of our position to the enemy prematurely.

We must have been in this position for about two hours. I was just beginning to get into a comfortable position laying on the hard ground when I heard a spoon fly off a grenade. Then there was a loud explosion not far from me. "WHOOO... OOOOMMMM!" A grenade had detonated. I scrambled from my prone position and rolled onto my stomach clutching my rifle at the ready for contact with the enemy. My first thought was that they were right on top of us. A Marine in the squad yelled, "Gooks in the open!" The squad began firing frantically and the sounds of machine guns opened up. I saw vague figures running away from our position, obviously VC. We could not tell if we had killed or wounded any of the enemy. Travieso radioed back to the CP. He requested a call for fire and provided instructions for the 60 millimeter mortars to drop rounds to our direct front.

After a few minutes of waiting an illumination spotter round burst in mid air to determine if the mortars were on target. It appeared that the spotter round was about one hundred fifty meters off target. Travieso called back to readjust the fire. In the meantime we continued to sporadically fire our rifles, blooper, and lob out grenades. The next round from the mortars hit in the vicinity of where we thought the enemy retreated. Travieso was heard saying, "Fire for effect!"

He told us to keep close to the ground since we did not have any cover to protect us from any shrapnel. We stopped firing to take cover. Six HE rounds exploded about one hundred meters from our position. We could hear the sizzling steel whizzing through the air. I hoped that none of the mortar rounds would fall short and onto our own position. Travieso then radioed back and told them to "Check Fire!" The mortars stopped firing. The area to our front was peppered pretty well with the HE rounds, but of course, we would not be able to go out and see if we got any confirmed kills until daylight.

The excitement died down and we were told by Travieso that we would remain on one hundred per cent alert for the rest of the night. We were cautious and tried to maintain some sort of silence. When we talked to one another, we whispered in low voices. We heard some Marines open fire back at the perimeter on the other side but it subsided as quickly as it had started. Evidently some of the VC got close to the perimeter of the company CP and the Marines had opened fire. We had no idea how many VC were in the area but we did know that they were scurrying about in the darkness of the night trying to probe our positions.

We now had a black Marine in the squad from New York. He was notorious for throwing grenades at every little noise during the hours of darkness. Ever chance he got he would throw a grenade and most of the time would not yell "Outgoing" as a warning to his fellow Marines. His rationale was that he was trying to keep the enemy at bay and prevent them from sneaking up on him. He felt a protective barrier within the bursting radius of the grenades if he could toss one out from time to time. Everyone in the squad would comment that he would throw a grenade if he heard the wind blow. It was all meant in a jokingly manner. Thus, he earned the nickname, "The Mad Fragger."

As we lay still in our position, we heard an explosion that was too close for comfort. "KAA... WHOOO... PPH!"

Then we heard a Marine moan, "Goddamit." It sounded as though he was actually praying the word. "Who the hell threw that fuckin grenade," the voice asked angrily? Trying to fuckin kill me?"

It had happened that a private first class in my fireteam had crawled beyond our hasty defense and was making a noise as he moved along the ground. The Mad Fragger heard movement to his front and had lobbed a grenade almost on top of him. He had mistaken the suspicious movement as a VC. Then there were sounds of punching, fighting, moaning, and swearing as the two Marines engaged in their own type of warfare. I could vaguely see that the PFC was on top of the Mad Fragger punching him. All the while he was yelling that the Mad Fragger had tried to kill him. There had not been an awful lot of affection between the two ever since they had first met.

Travieso and another member of the squad broke up the fight. Travieso could be heard telling the Mad Fragger that he had to watch what he was doing and at least holler "Outgoing" before he lobbed a grenade so that everyone else would know what was about to happen. Luckily the Marine had not been injured. But he was very shaken up. He didn't have one scratch from the shrapnel. The grenade had landed only a few feet from him, but since he was hugging the ground, the bits of metal exploded up and away from his body. He was more deafened and frightened than anything else.

The Mad Fragger spoke up in protest. "Well the dumb son-aw-bitch had no business crawling out past our perimeter. What the sam hell were you doing out there anyway?"

The Marine replied in anger, "I was trying to move to another location when you fragged my ass!"

The whole squad could be heard snickering and laughing about how the

Marine who had almost gotten fragged had made the statement. The Mad Fragger and the Marine joined in the laughter as well. We all agreed that the Marine should not have been beyond the perimeter of our hasty defense. The fact remained however, that he was really shaken up. The squad leader designated another position for him far away from the Mad Fragger.

As soon as day broke we patrolled the area to check for any signs of confirmed kills. We could see trails of blood on the ground but obviously the wounded and killed were dragged away from the area. We reported back to the perimeter. Travieso told the platoon commander what had happened the night before and that there were no confirmed kills to speak of.

That afternoon Mike 3 Charlie went out on another patrol. We didn't mind because it meant that we would not have to go out of the perimeter that night to set up an ambush. It was much better to remain inside our company perimeter defenses, because on an ambush, it was only our squad out in the open to help ward off any would-be attackers. There were only six of us on this particular patrol.

As we crossed a rice paddy the point man alerted us and we spotted 2 VC hiding in a treeline and then saw two VC running into the bush. We killed both of them with small arms fire and captured the other two. We brought them back to the perimeter to be sent to the rear for interrogation. We also confiscated an AK47, two pistols, and a hand drawn map of Da Nang. I thought the map was interesting and tried to study it to figure out what the enemy's intent was. I did not reach a determination as we had to turn everything over to the platoon commander so the items could be analyzed by our intelligence back in the rear.

One day a resupply chopper arrived at our position and Travieso got on board to go back to the rear. His time in the Nam had come to an end. He was going home. We all had said our goodbyes and the squad members envied him as walked up the helicopter ramp with his M16 dangling by his right side and his heavy pack on his back. He would be missed. I stood at my fighting hole and watched the chopper lift into the air. Soon it was out of sight as it flew over the jungles and rice paddies heading to the rear. And just like that, Lance Corporal Travieso was out of my life.

I was now the Mike 3 Charlie Squad Leader. It dawned on me that times were changing. Corporal Ka-Bar had rotated back to the States the end of June. We had new members that had since joined the squad from the States. I knew that I would not see Corporal Ka-Bar or Travieso ever again. They would back in the real world having survived the tour in this hell hole called Vietnam. Hawkeye was still the platoon radio operator and our experienced squad leader had just left us behind. I knew that I could never be the tactical expert in the bush as Corporal Ka-Bar and Lance Corporal Travieso, but I figured my experience thus far would see me through. I now had a squad under my charge and looked forward to the challenges ahead. My squad would never be the same without the original members and without my bud-

Mike 3 Charlie checking out a village for VC. We were augmented at times by other squads and machine gunners. Little Vietnamese girl is paying us very little attention while she prepares bread.

dy, Hawkeye, by my side. I still had opportunities to talk with Hawkeye, but I now had responsibilities of my own. Mike 3 Charlie as I once knew it would be no more. I just knew that I would never forget those guys, not ever!

While we were in our defensive position, squads were sent out in different directions and ours ended up going through a nearby village. As it happened an OV-10 Bronco observation aircraft from above spotted a hooch and directed us toward it via radio contact. We found nothing suspicious but I got a kick out of watching a little Vietnamese girl laying out slices of bread on a rack. This gave us a chance to fill our canteens from a well near the hooch. While some were busy filling their canteens others were digging into stacks of rice for any hidden weapons. In the meantime, Marines were posted as look outs. Most of the papasans were VC or VC sympathizers. We hardly ever found many males around when checking the hooches. They were probably hiding underground or setting out booby traps.

We returned to the company perimeter and worked in this area sending out various patrols during the day and ambushes at night. We had a chance to relax somewhat even though we stayed busy. We even got a change of pace in our eating habits. Some long rations were sent out to us from the base camp. These long rations were dehydrated food in which water had to be added before consumption. Initially it looked as though one meal would not be enough, but after adding water, it was sufficient to fill our stomachs. One day Hawkeye and I decided to mix two meals together and cook them in his helmet. His steel pot became a cooking pot. It turned out to be a gourmet feast with the help of a little hot sauce.

The 1st squad of our platoon went out on patrol and started receiving sniper fire. They returned fire and since they could not see anything they continued with their patrol. Once again they received sniper fire. Their corpsman was hit by enemy fire. They called for an Aerial Observer and it passed several times dropping the onboard ordnance and then called for an artillery mission. The corpsman was medevaced to the rear for treatment.

On another occasion someone in the company perimeter observed a Vietnamese female studying the perimeter. A fireteam was sent to investigate her intentions. She was in her early twenties and had no ID. She was sent back to the rear so she could be interrogated. I was impressed by the fact that the Marines were so vigilant to detect her suspicious behavior that may have saved some lives in the long run.

While my squad was on a daytime patrol we took four sniper rounds from a nearby village. I directed the squad to sweep the area and we spotted a Vietnamese female about 1000 meters away carrying a rifle. We moved to that area while watching for mines and booby traps. As we swept through the area where we had seen the woman we found four women. One of them had pack strap marks on her shoulders. We called back to the platoon commander and ended up bringing them back to the perimeter. A chopper was called the women were sent back to the rear for interrogation.

While our 3rd platoon was on a security patrol one Marine hit a booby trap. It was a M26 grenade buried in the ground with a can pushed down on top of it. Three Marines were WIA and had to be medevaced out. Then as our platoon moved to a position to be a blocking force someone discovered a booby trapped M26 grenade with a trip wire tied to a branch that ran across the trail. The booby trap was wired so that a slight movement of the branch would detonate the booby trap. We blew it in place. When Mike Company began to relocate its position and while on the move someone tripped a booby trap. It was laying on the deck and was set off by a pressure firing device. The result of the detonated booby trap was one KIA and four WIA. They were all medevaced out.

Taking a break while on patrol. You had to make use of any available shade in the sweltering heat.

There were a lot of booby traps in this area and we had to constantly be on the lookout. I instructed my point man to be especially watchful for anything suspicious on and near the trails. I cautioned him not to take any chances regarding booby traps and risk his life and the lives of his fellow Marines. He assured me that he would keep his "eyeballs peeled" at all times. I wanted to do everything I possibly could to avoid any of the Marines in my squad from tripping a booby trap. I kept reminding them to be aware of their surroundings.

The next morning I was called to the CP by my platoon commander. He informed me that I was to be reassigned to the company mortar section. After the mortar incident of friendly on friendly, the mortar section was short on experienced personnel. I knew very little about the mortars, but figured I would learn. My tenure as a squad leader this time was short lived, at least for the time being. I had eagerly accepted the challenge as a squad leader but

I knew I had to be put where I was needed the most.

I began training within the mortar section and started off as an ammo bearer and then A-Gunner. The only advantage of being in the mortar section was that we traveled within the CP boundaries and did not go on patrols or ambushes. The disadvantage was humping the heavy mortar rounds, base plate, mortar tube, and tripods, in addition to our usual gear. I became quite proficient at my new assignment. In case of immediate calls for fire support we practiced setting up the mortar tube, aiming on targets, and firing off the first round, all within nine seconds.

The next day at about 0730 I heard on the radio that the 2nd squad from Mike 3 was going out on a daytime patrol. This was the 3rd platoon that I had just left in order to join the mortar section. While on patrol a Marine in Mike 3 Bravo tripped a booby trap. The booby trap was a M26 grenade with a two foot long trip wire across the trail. The end result was that a Marine was KIA and there were two Marines that were WIA. A medevac chopper was called and completed for all the Marines within a matter of minutes. We all liked and respected the Marine who was KIA. His home state was Alabama. He was easy going and had a great sense of humor. He died on 27 August 1970 while serving his country and the Marines of Mike Company in the Quang Nam Province, South Vietnam.

The same day yet another two booby trapped M26 grenades with five foot trip wires were found. One booby trap was hooked to a tree limb while the other was stretched across the trail. They were blown in place. I figured I had better write a letter home while I was still alive for this area had booby traps all over the place.

August 27, 1970

Hello Mom, Dad and Larry,

As I sit under my poncho I have put up for shade, I thought I'd drop you a few lines. It's cooling off a little since it's almost sundown. I started a letter later this afternoon but couldn't finish it because my paper was wet from sweat. It sure gets hot over here during the day. But don't guess it'll be long before we'll be wanting the sun to pop out when it starts raining. It usually rains at night over here now.

Guess everyone around home wonders why I'm not writing. Well, for one thing, I can hardly find the time and for another I'm running out of paper. I have to save it so I can write home to you guys. It's hard to get paper out here in the field and we haven't returned to the rear for awhile either. But don't send me any because by the time it gets here I will have some more. Just tell everyone I'm thinking of them.

The latest scoop I heard was that we're going to stay here in Sniper Valley for another five to six days. After that I don't know what we'll be doing but on 6 September we're supposed to go back up on LZ Ryder for a couple of weeks. I sure hope we do. They're tearing the firebase down and I imagine we'll be tearing down bunkers too. Of course you never know if what the "lifers" pass is straight scoop or not. A lot of times they say one thing and do another. But if we should go back to Ryder for a couple of weeks, even if we have to tear down bunkers, it will be better than being down here in the lowlands.

Well, I was taken out of the squad the other day and was put into the mortar team. We travel and stay with the CP (Command Post). It's a lot better and I'm kinda glad I'm not in Mike 3 Charlie any more because almost everyone is new and they don't know anything that's going on. I was trained to be a machine gunner back in the States and now I'm a mortarman. One thing about this place over here is we get a lot of experience. So far I've been a squad radio operator, carried the blooper (M79 grenade launcher), been a fireteam leader, and now I'm in mortars. I was even a squad leader, but they said they needed someone in the mortar section and the lieutenant picked me.

I've been over here for six months now. Guess you might say I'm half way. Now I can start going down hill although I never keep up with the time. I hardly know what the date is. I usually have to ask someone. I have not heard from Donald for a long time. He did not tell me about him building a base up on a mountain. I imagine he's pretty busy.

Larry's probably in school by now. Hope he ain't got no "bada-lac" for a teacher. He should have our company gunny as a school teacher. I guarantee that Larry would learn something then. He used to be a drill instructor at Parris Island. Did you all ever get the cruise book I sent in? You never said anything about it. It has pictures of the 7th Marines.

Well, Mom and Dad take it easy. Guess Dad is working in the tobacco about now. Hope you get it in the barn without any trouble. I'll let you all go for now. The artillery back at Ross is firing on a hill so believe I'll watch the show. It's getting dark anyway. So until next time I'll say so long and hope everyone is doing fine. By the way I got the pictures of you all awhile back and have them together with my letter writing gear. I look at them every time I write a letter. I must say they sure are good. I like the one of Mom and Dad in the front room. You should have taken them out in the yard though, or maybe in the tobacco or corn patch. Ha ha! Bye for now, everyone be good.

Always thinking of you,
Fred

As I got comfortable in the mortar section I always took notice of when a patrol was going out from Mike 3, my old platoon. I missed the Marines in a way and was curious as to what they were up to without me being there. The mortar section was okay for me, but I was trained as a machine gunner, and I had not been assigned to a machine gun team yet. I asked from time to time but was always told that the machine gunners had enough personnel. Since being a machine gunner was my forte, I longed to get my hands on a M60 once again. Even carrying the gun, or tripods, or spare barrel bag, or heavy cans of ammo was better in my mind than carrying the heavy base plates, mortar tubes, and heavy mortar rounds.

Our mortar section was practicing setting up the gun one day when I heard over the radio that Mike 3 Charlie was going out on patrol. I listened to the radio traffic in between gun drills. As my old squad moved along a river someone tripped a M33 booby trap but it did not detonate. It was fixed with a tripwire and set in front of a man-made cave which had been blown up. The squad blew it in place.

The next day I heard that they were going out again on patrol. This time I sat by the radio and listened to the transmissions. They found another booby trapped M26 grenade. It had the pin pulled and was hanging half way out of a colored smoke can so that moving of the can would cause the booby trap to detonate. It also was blown in place. I wondered when I would be hearing that Mike 3 Charlie had casualties from tripping a booby trap. I wished that we could get out of this place.

Sometime during the month of August a letter company in the battalion was responsible for losing a complete book of numerical shackles and one AN/PRC-25 radio. This was not good because our communications had been compromised if the enemy got their hands on them. I got to where I would sleep next to the radio that we had in mortars, just to keep an eye on it, and to hear what was going on within Mike Company. I had spent many days not knowing what was going on or where we were located. We just moved and set in position when we were directed to do so. I enjoyed being in the know for a change.

We finally got back to the rear at FSB Ross on 2 September for some much needed rehabilitation. We did the usual ritual in the rear such as taking showers, cleaning weapons, laundering, shining our boots, getting hair cuts, and attending formations. Each night we had a chance to go the enlisted club. This was our time to relax. While we were in the rear we found out that two other Marines had died from wounds received from the mortar incident on 17 August. One was a corporal and the latest casualty was a sergeant. This brought the total to 4 Marines KIA and 28 WIA. I hoped that the mortar section that I was assigned to would be more careful in the future.

We sensed something strange happening back at FSB Ross. There was a lot of talk about disbanding the 7th Marines involvement in Vietnam. Bunkers and hooches were slowly being dismantled. Trucks were seen moving

Photo taken from Fire Support Base Ryder. Bald spots on the knoll in the center of picture is Hill 90 where Mike Company shelled itself with its own mortars resulting in 4 USMC KIA, 28 USMC WIA, and one female Vietnamese detainee killed.

supplies out of the area to Da Nang. There was also talk of an upcoming operation called "Nebraska Rapids" that would go from 5-8 September. We understood that we were to sweep through villages looking for Vietnamese Communist Infrastructure (VCI) and local guerrillas. The terrain would be mostly rivers, streams, paddies and flat land. We were to conduct search and clear operations and assist an ARVN Division to open and improve Highway 535 from LZ Ross to a place called Hiep Duc.

The bad news came when our company commander told us that we would be going back to the bush to an area around Sniper Valley again. This area had been known to be crawling with NVA, VC, and guerillas. Through the hustle and bustle of preparing for our next operation I managed to write a letter home.

September 3, 1970

Dear Mom, Dad and Larry,

Well, how does this find everyone back home? Hope you are all doing fine. Now that it's September I guess everyone is slowing down a bit. But from Mom's last letter it seems that in awhile Dad will be putting the tobacco into the barn. Sure hope it turns out good and you get it in with no problem. Wish I could have seen the farm this summer. I bet everything is real pretty now. When I get home in February the snow should be around. But compared to this weather right now I wish I was covered with it. Not long from now it'll get a little cooler because of monsoon season.

We came back to the rear yesterday but are leaving tomorrow the 4th. If we get lucky we may go up on Ryder again but they say we may be going to Sniper Valley. Well, the 7th Marines are being pulled out but don't get excited, I won't be going with them. The ones who are due to rotate before November 30th are the only ones who will be going home. They're supposed to start getting things together around September 27th and leave about the 2nd week in October. I will be joining either the 5th or 1st Marines. Hope I can get into a decent company. By then I won't have many more months to do over here. I'm going down hill now. I'll tell you more about the pullout later on but right now no one knows too much.

I have to go now. If we get to go to Ryder later on maybe I can write a longer letter. Oh! By the way, don't bother sending me those sausages. I really don't need them now. I'll clean up on them when I get home.

As ever,
Fred

P.S. Here is a picture of one of my buddies and squad leader. He's not my squad leader anymore but he was for three months. Now I'm in the mortar section. The background is a typical site where there aren't many rice paddies. It was just on a little high ground where we stayed at night.

Instead of going back to the bush the next day we left on the 5 September. Reveille went very early that morning at around 0400. We were to be heli-lifted to our area of responsibility at about 0630. As Mike Company began forming up in a clearing at Firebase Ross, preparing to go to the bush once again, Hawkeye came to where I was in the mortar section. I had already packed away all my personal gear and organized the mortar rounds on my pack and had a huge canvas bag full of HE rounds, illumination, and white phosphorus which the Marines called "Willie Peter." I was looking over my gear wondering how in the world I was going to manage to carry it all.

Hawkeye yelled out to me, "Hey Fenwick! Take those heavy ass mortar rounds off your pack and give them to the other Marines in the mortar section. You are going to be the squad leader for Mike 3 Charlie when we go into Sniper Valley."

"What are you talking about Hawkeye? I asked. "I was assigned to the mortar section not long ago. What's going on?"

Hawkeye responded, "Seems the platoon commander wants you to head up the 3rd squad again. He wants someone in charge that has been in country for awhile and is a combat veteran."

"Oh great," I replied, "I wish they would make up their minds whether they want me as squad leader, mortarman, blooperman, radioman, or whatever!"

Hawkeye chuckled at my comment and said, "Yeah, you must have done a good job before as squad leader if the lieutenant wants you back again. You've been here long enough to know the ropes by now. After all, those new Marines in Mike 3 Charlie need your leadership. Your squad combat experience is not being utilized if you're stuck in the mortar section."

I started removing the mortar rounds from my pack and gave them to the other Marines in the mortar section. They were not pleased that they would have to share the extra burden. I walked away with Hawkeye and he told me that the lieutenant wanted to see me right away to give all the squad leaders a brief before we left Firebase Ross.

The 1st and 2nd squad leaders from the 3rd platoon were already huddled around the platoon commander. He told me the reason for taking me out of mortars at the last minute and then handed me a map of the area where we were going to. He then began briefing us.

"The choppers will be here to helo us out to our AOR in about an hour," the lieutenant said. "When we land get your people out fast and set up in a 360 hasty defense around the choppers. Each squad will have a machine gun team attached to you. It is imperative that you set in quickly because it could be a hot LZ. There have been reports that Charlie is all over the area. We will be looking for a NVA unit that has filtered into the area from the north. Be advised that this is a "Free Fire Zone." In other words when we get hit you direct your fire on anything that moves. There will be no friendlies in this area. Be very cautious and attentive. This may be our last major operation and I want all my Marines to come out of this thing alive. I wish you all the best of luck. Just keep talking to me either by radio or verbally as we move into this area so that I will know your whereabouts. Check your squads closely and ensure they have all the ammunition they need and are aware that we are not going on no picnic. This is serious business. Are there any questions?"

The other two squad leaders asked the lieutenant some questions about medevacs for the wounded, resupply, forward edge of the battle area, and the like. I did not have any questions for the platoon commander.

"No questions, Fenwick?" the lieutenant asked.

"No Sir," I stated, "let's do it!"

"I'm expecting great things from you Fenwick, as squad leader," the lieutenant continued. "The 3rd squad needs your expertise and leadership!"

"Roger that, I'll do my best Sir," I replied.

We broke up from the squad leader's meeting and started back to our formation in ranks. As I passed by Hawkeye manning the platoon radio he said, "Get some, Fred! I'll be talkin at you on the radio."

"Hold on to your nuts, Hawkeye," I responded, "we're getting too short to get our balls shot off."

We both laughed and I returned to the 3rd Platoon and gathered the 3rd squad together to brief them on what was to come. We readied our equipment and the company moved down to the landing zone to await the choppers.

Soon the skies were filled with choppers flying our way. They were accompanied by the usual amount of Huey Gunships and Cobras. The choppers landed and there were droves of Marines loaded down with combat gear getting aboard the choppers from the various platoons. It was now our platoon's turn to scramble aboard. I directed my squad in single file leaning our bodies against the gusts of wind from the rotors of the chopper. When we had all taken a seat I directed the squad to turn their weapons upside down so that the barrels were resting on the floor of the aircraft. I remembered this from all the other times I had boarded a chopper. This was a precaution in case a weapon was accidently discharged inside the chopper the round would not strike a vital part of the aircraft. We had already locked and loaded with full magazines. I felt in charge and felt comfortable with the responsibility.

We were off flying in formation. I managed to sneak a peak outside one of the windows. It looked like a flock of geese flying south for the winter. The skies were full of choppers. I tried to study my map and the grid coordinates where we were heading but the ride was a little bumpy. After a few minutes of flying in a straight line our chopper began to circle. I knew this was it. We would be touching down in just a few moments. I yelled to the squad over the humming of the engine and rotors to make sure they double-timed off the aircraft when it landed and to set up a hasty defense around the landing zone. We would be taking the northeast side of the boundary. I saw one of the new Marines take his selector switch off safe and had his hand on the pistol grip of the weapon. I got his attention by pointing at him from my seat and told him to place the selector switch back on safe.

I yelled out to the squad, "Don't take your weapons off safe until you clear the ramp after we land." We don't need an accidental discharge in this chopper."

A new private first class was sitting next to me. He was gripping his weapon so tight I could see that his blood veins were swelling up on the back of his hands. He appeared to be petrified and was just staring into space. I told him to just relax and that everything would be okay. Then I remembered the words that my platoon sergeant had told me the very first day I was in a firefight. I decided to mimic him to an extent.

You're scared ain't you?" I asked.

"No Sir," the PFC replied.

I repeated myself, "I said you're scared ain't cha?"

"No Sir," the PFC quipped again.

"Damit, you're scared, ain't you?"

"Yes, Sir!" he finally said.

"I'm scared too," I said calmly and with purpose. "You don't have to deny it. It's only natural. I'm scared, you're scared, and so are the other Marines out here. Every time we get into a firefight and every time a chopper touches down into unknown territory I feel like shittin my drawers. Just take it easy, it'll all be over before long."

The new Marine relaxed the grip on his pistol grip and forced a smile. It wasn't long until we were on the ground. The chopper landed on a clearing surrounded by trees. The back ramp dropped to the ground and I began barking orders.

"Okay you guys, this is it. Move out! On the double!" The Marines stood up and were right behind each other as they cleared the ramp. To my surprise they followed my previous instructions to the letter as they took a left turn away from the chopper and ran toward the treeline. "Keep it spread out!" I yelled. I began to point at the various positions that we were to assume for security. "1st fireteam, over here, 2nd fireteam, set up in this position facing outboard, 3rd fireteam take up this position covering our flanks!" I managed to get the squad set in a hasty defense and to connect with the other squads on our left and right flanks. Fortunately, the landing zone was not hot. Mike Company assembled and started moving to our objective in a column formation.

At around noon the 1st squad went out on patrol. They observed three huts with 12 Vietnamese in them. When the squad began to question them, they indicated they would like to relocate to a resettlement hamlet. There were five women, ranging in age from 15 years to about 67 years, and seven children ages three to seven years. We would find out later that the refugees were escorted to the district headquarters for questioning and determination of their status and then were allowed to leave by district personnel before they were questioned. The refugees entered Lahn Thuong and stated they wished to resettle because they had been driven from their own village. They were once more escorted to the Que Son district and turned over to the National Police.

Meanwhile a squad in the 1st platoon discovered eight natural caves on the north side of Hill 270. In one cave they discovered a pair of scissors, one ammo pouch, one pack, one illumination parachute, and one bandoleer of M16 ammunition. The gear was evacuated and the caves were not destroyed due to their size.

The next day I took the squad out on a daytime patrol at about 0900. The platoon guide wanted to come along just to see what was going on. He told me he would not interfere with my duties as a squad leader but that he would be close by if I needed him. We came upon a large rock formation on the northwest side of Hill 270. Upon further investigation it was determined to be a cave complex. I set up security around the sides of the rock formation and went to see the platoon guide.

"So what's your plan now?" the platoon guide asked me.

"Well," I said, "I'm assigning you as the squad leader for awhile."

"What do you mean?" he asked.

I replied, "I need you to fill in for me as squad leader while I go down into the caves and check them out. I'm volunteering to be a Tunnel Rat."

"Are you sure you want to do that?" the platoon guide asked.

"Yes," I said. "Everyone else in the squad has stuck their heads into caves and tunnels so I figure it is about my turn to check out the underground. After all, these entrances are large enough for a six foot grunt to crawl down into. It was hard for me to fit in any of the previous spider traps and tunnels but I can get through this one. I will be out in about thirty minutes or so.

"Roger that," he said. "I'll keep an eye on things outside. If you find anything, we'll have to get you more people down there to help out."

"Okay," I replied, "here goes nothing."

I borrowed the .45 caliber pistol that our blooperman was carrying. I checked the magazine and ensured a round was in the chamber. I would take it off safe as I entered the cave. I walked over to the entrance and began to crouch to ease myself inside the opening.

I heard the platoon guide say, "Don't take any chances down in there. We are getting too short in Nam for this kind of stuff, besides, I don't want to take your job as squad leader. I'm satisfied as the platoon guide."

"See you in about thirty mikes," I said.

I dropped down into the cave. I could see fairly well from the sunlight peeking through the big boulders. The entrance was small at first and I was moving slowly while being on the lookout for any pit vipers that the enemy may have tied to the sides. They were known to do that so the venomous snakes would bite any unsuspecting Tunnel Rats. I was also checking where I crawled to avoid any mines or booby traps. I began to think of my mother and father back home on the farm. They would have been scared to death if they knew what I was doing. I didn't know why I was doing it, only that I had a mission to accomplish.

The entrance opened up to where I could stand up. I couldn't believe my eyes. I had stumbled upon a cave that had beds and cooking pots. It could accommodate a lot of NVA/VC. I drew the pistol out in front of me expecting any minute to have to take on an enemy platoon. I just hoped that I could exit quickly enough if a firefight started in the cave. I eased forward and looked around. I scanned the area and could not find any sort of enemy presence. They were either deeper in the cave complex or had seen us coming and high tailed it into the hillsides. I figured it would be best not to play hero and to go get the rest of the squad.

I exited the cave the same way I entered and told the platoon guide what I had found. He suggested that the squad disperse and search the caves in two teams. I agreed and we set about investigating our find. The platoon guide and I stayed outside to maintain security. While the Marines were searching, the platoon guide and I began to talk about different things. I enjoyed the fact that he was a sergeant and yet was so down to earth when it came to speaking to a lance corporal. I thought, that if I ever got to be a sergeant, that I would treat Marines with dignity and respect that they truly deserve.

Mike 3 Charlie had made a good find. We had discovered 10 caves in the rocks on the north side of Hill 270. The caves were large enough to sleep a total of 100 people. A search of the area revealed six beds, four cooking pots, two M26 grenades, a canteen cover, an Army pack, two saws, four fish traps, one M16 magazine with 11 rounds, freshly cut wood and straw, and 20 pounds of rice. There was a stream in one cave. We believed the caves had been occupied as recently as two days before. All captured equipment and material was destroyed.

Later that afternoon Mike Company was moving to a night defensive position. A Marine detonated a Surprise Firing Device (SFD). Seven Marines were wounded resulting in three emergency, two priority, and two routine medevacs. The device was believed to be an eight inch artillery round rigged for pressure detonation and buried in the ground. After medevacs were completed the area was swept for other devices and set up our night defensive position.

The next day while Mike Company was on a sweep we started receiving about 50-75 rounds of enemy small arms fire. One round hit a Marine's helmet resulting in only a bloody nose. We returned fire and swept through the area finding two mortar rounds. They were destroyed in place. The Marine who had been shot in the helmet was a very lucky Marine. His helmet had saved his life.

It seemed Operation Nebraska Rapids was completed as quickly as it had begun. The operation was terminated on 8 September. Mike Company remained in the local vicinity for a few days working alongside the Vietnamese RF (Regular Forces) and PF (Popular Forces). Our company perimeter was right next to them. There had been talk that they were not very good to work with because they were undisciplined. The rumors were confirmed because at night they were seen cooking their meals over open flames and drinking and talking loudly. In general, they were having a good time among themselves.

Our company commander became angry because the Vietnamese Army would not listen to what he told them. Needless to say, during that short time we received a few mortar and rocket attacks because of their carelessness. The company commander finally told the RF and PF leaders, that if they did not put out the camp fires at night and keep down the noise, our company would move completely away from them. They did not listen and consequently we got permission to move to a different location.

Their reckless attitudes and unprofessional behavior was in reality a hazard to our very existence. It left little doubt in our minds that South Vietnam would surely fall into the hands of the North Vietnamese Army when the Americans left and the RFs and PFs had to defend themselves. We also noticed that during these few days our Kit Carson Scouts would at times dig shallow sleeping holes and at other times dig deep fighting holes. When they dug their holes deep the Marines normally did the same. Somehow the Kit Carson Scouts seemed to know when we were about to be hit by mortars and rockets.

One morning as my squad was on a patrol we spotted two NVA/VC with packs and weapons moving to our southwest. We pursued them and were taken under enemy small arms fire. We commenced firing back with all we had. After we reported the spot report back to the platoon commander an air strike was called. An Aerial Observer and fixed wing soon arrived and dropped ordnance on the target. We also called for a 106 fire mission. When it was all over we searched the area and did not find any sign of Charlie. The elusive enemy had dodged our fire power once again. They were probably deep underground waiting for their next opportunity to pop up and fire at our Marines.

That afternoon a squad from the 1st platoon found three Vietnamese youths walking in tall grass. One of the youths took off running. The squad leader called for him to stop and he did. A search of the three children resulted in finding one HE blasting cap and a three inch wire. Two of the children were approximately 10-13 years old. Mike Company detained the older youth and sent him to the battalion rear for questioning.

I awoke one morning and started eating a can of ham and eggs with crackers. I wondered what day it was in the Nam. I asked one of the squad members and he said it was 13 September. "Huh?" I whispered to myself. "Today is my younger brother's birthday." I could celebrate it before he does since the time difference between Vietnam and Kentucky was about eleven hours ahead. I figured I'd eat a couple of chocolate candy discs (the Marines called them shit disks) that came with my C-Rations to celebrate Larry's birthday. As I chowed down on the chocolate discs I hoped that all was well back on the home front.

As I sat cleaning my M16, I was summoned by the platoon commander. We were going on a platoon size patrol that would last most of the day. The Popular Forces would be going along with us. At around 0900 we found eight caves that were approximately 6'X5'X15'. We searched the area but did not find anything unusual. We continued on our patrol. About an hour and a half later we received approximately 150 rounds of semi-automatic and automatic fire from the enemy about 100 meters to our north. We returned fire with small arms and then swept the area. It amazed me that we still had not killed any enemy.

At around noon our platoon and Popular Forces were still on the search and clear operation. When we entered a village, two females in black pajamas were detained. They were about 25 to 30 years of age and did not have any identification on them. There were also five children that we safeguarded. The village was searched and we found an abundance of rice and miscellaneous documents. The PFs stated that the documents contained information revealing the names of VC in the area and other information. At this time, one enemy male was spotted carrying a rifle. The enemy fired at the PFs who returned fire with small arms. A heavy volume of fire erupted from about 200 meters to the west. Our platoon returned fire with M16s, M60 machine guns, and M79 grenade launchers.

As we were about to move forward, the explosions could be seen all around us. The enemy was firing mortars on our position but we could not see them. We could only hug the ground hoping that one of the rounds would not drop in our hip pockets. I heard our own mortars returning fire. They were putting out a large volume of fire in the direction where we suspected the enemy fire had come from. "Thump! Thump! Thump!" the mortars sounded off. It was a familiar and welcomed sound for the Marines. I mentally pictured myself scrambling about getting the rounds ready for the mortar tube, had I still been in the mortar section. Seemed they were doing quite well without me.

The enemy fire stopped momentarily. We were given the order to advance into the treelines in order to keep the enemy from getting any closer than they already were. It was good that the rice paddy was dry and free from a lot of mud. I made sure that my squad was prepared to continue the mission. I got an ammo count and casualty report from the fireteam leaders. Everyone in the squad was okay. No one was wounded and we still had plenty of ammo.

Then I thought of Hawkeye and where he might be. I got close to our squad radio operator and reached for the handset in order to try and reach him. Instead the net was blaring away with priority transmissions. I heard someone calling for an Aerial Observer and an air strike. I decided against getting on the net and wait until things quieted down a little. As I handed the radio handset back to the radio operator I heard a familiar voice on the other end.

"Mike 3 Charlie, Mike 3 Charlie, This is Mike 3, SITREP, Over," came the squeaky voice. I knew instantly that it was Hawkeye.

"Mike 3, This is Mike 3 Charlie, You common dog," I said. "We're A-okay down here. How bout you, Hawkeye."

"No problem," came Hawkeye's reply. I gave him an accurate Situation Report and as we signed off I felt relieved that Hawkeye was all right. I realized that we may have strayed from proper protocol in our radio transmissions but Hawkeye was my buddy. Besides, we had been in country now longer than most of the other Marines and we felt a little cocky.

We began to move through the rice paddy and we could see the village now about three hundred meters ahead. The platoon reorganized on line with the squads in wedge formations. As we crossed the open rice paddy we began to receive fire from the treeline on our right flank. As the squad moved forward we would duck in behind rice paddy dikes while the rounds were whizzing over our heads. RPG Grenade Launchers were being fired from the village. Our machine guns and mortars opened fire on the village.

The squad radio operator told me that an air strike was on the way. The 1st and 2nd squads were slightly ahead of us at this point and were catching all the heat of the battle. My squad was bringing up the rear but we were receiving sporadic fire from the treeline about fifty meters away. I directed my squad to concentrate fire into the treeline to pin down the enemy. It wasn't long until there was quiet within the adjacent treeline.

The platoon commander was now only a few feet from where I was. He yelled that we were to leap and bound to a position further up the rice paddy and that we would sweep through the treeline. I began barking commands to the fireteams to leap and bound from one rice paddy dike to the other as we inched our way to the treeline. "1st fireteam, prepare to move out, move out! 2nd fireteam, prepare to move out, watch your right flank, move out! 3rd fireteam, hit and roll. Let's move it!"

I followed behind the 2nd fireteam because I wanted to be there to coordinate their fire power nearest the trees where we had received the enemy fire. I bolted forward in a crouched running stance while enemy rounds were being fired in all directions. An enemy rocket hit in the middle of the rice paddy about fifty feet to my front. The ground shook from the blast as I dove behind a rice paddy dike along with the 2nd fireteam. We raised our heads above the dike and began spraying the area to our right front with M16s. We began to receive heavy fire as rounds were hitting the dike on the other side of us. All we could do at this point was to curl up behind the dike. There was a small bush on top of the dike and a round from an AK47 stripped the leaves. It was a distinct sound that I had learned to recognize. It was from an enemy's weapon who was trying to kill me or anyone else that got in his path.

Through all the excitement I had not noticed that my right leg was stretched straight out from the rear of the dike. Another round hit in the mud only six inches from my ankle. I pulled my leg up under my buttocks and cuddled in behind the dike hoping that an enemy round would not find its mark. Periodically I would rise up over the dike trying to put a volume of fire into the treeline. The heavy volume of fire from the enemy had now reduced to only sporadic fire. The lieutenant, laying several feet away from me, began to pass the word that we were to move forward for the next paddy dike. I passed the word to the rest of my squad as we stood up and commenced our forward movement. The other squads were advancing in the same direction.

As I moved forward, the lieutenant yelled, "Fenwick, your right flank. That gook is still moving and he's got a chi-com underneath him. Shoot him!"

I turned immediately to my right with my rifle at the ready and saw the NVA. He was laying on the ground a few feet from a rice paddy dike. He was wounded and was squirming about. He was dressed in blue colored uniform and it dawned on me that we were in contact with the North Vietnamese Regulars. His arms were tucked underneath his stomach and I could see that he was holding a chi-com. I clicked my M16 selector lever from semi-automatic to automatic fire. I aimed low and pulled the trigger. "BBBRROOWWW." The rounds ripped through the NVA from his waist to his head. Before I knew it my magazine was empty.

In the heat of the moment I reached for another magazine and locked and loaded. This time I put the selector lever back on semi-automatic and fired a three round burst into his head to make sure he was dead. I thought that even with him being wounded that he may be able to pull the pin on the chi-com. I stopped firing and looked at the withering body. The unsightly figure lay on the ground with the chi-com still clutched in his hands. He had been prepared to blow himself up in an attempt to take a Marine down with him.

The platoon commander yelled out, "Dammit Fenwick, how about some fire discipline? You don't have to use an entire magazine on one gook. Save your ammo because it looks like we're gonna need it."

"Roger that!" I yelled back. "Guess I got a little excited. He was too close for comfort."

"Just watch your fire discipline," the lieutenant remarked.

"Will do," I replied.

I glanced down at the dead NVA once again. The entrances of the three round bursts were small where they had entered his head but they left a big gapping hole in the back of his head. Brain matter was scattered on the rice paddy ground. I thought to myself, what a horrible death. I soon realized however that this NVA would have killed me or other Marines if given the chance.

The lieutenant hollered again, "Fenwick, forget about him, lets move on!"

"What about the chi-com underneath him, lieutenant?" I yelled out. "If we leave it here the NVA can use it some other time."

"Screw the chi-com," he said. "Let's get the hell out of here!"

We began to advance forward to another rice paddy dike and we could now see the village ahead of us. NVA were seen fleeing the village and disappearing into a treeline. Some were still trying to fire back in our direction while on the run. We continued firing in that direction. Some of them dropped to the ground while some managed to escape. It looked like they were partly subdued and were running for cover.

An Aerial Observer came on station and flew over and around the village. I could now hear F-4 Phantom jets at a distance and I knew that an air strike was imminent. We were ordered to take cover behind the rice paddy dike. One of the jets could be seen coming in over the trees. I could see the helmet outline of the Marine pilot and copilot as they dropped two 500 pound bombs in the village. WHOOOMMM! WHOOOMMM! The earth quivered and shook from the explosions. I peered over the rice paddy dike to see if anymore NVA were running out. Instead of NVA, I saw pigs, chickens, and water buffalo running out of the village. I knew that this area was a "free fire zone" meaning anything that moved was fair game. In my wildest dreams I could not have imagined what happened next.

Some unknown Marine in the platoon who was up ahead yelled out, "Shoot that fuckin water buffalo! Then another Marine shouted, "Shoot dem fuckin pigs!"

As a water buffalo ran across the rice paddy several machine gunners opened fire and killed the animal. You could hear the cheers as the water buffalo stumbled to the ground. Then a rifleman opened up on some pigs running across our fields of fire. I heard a Marine yell out "Yee Haa!" Then another could be heard bellowing, "Get Some, Get Some!" Then chickens became targets. It was a free for all, not a free fire zone. I could not believe the Marines were actually killing the animals. What if there were women and children in the village. I prayed that we would not sweep through the village. With this much disarray in the ranks it would have been a disaster. It was no telling what the Marines would have done.

A second jet came in for a low strike. Again it was tree top high. The Marines who had opened fire on the animals stopped firing to watch the bombs hit. It dropped two more 500 pound bombs into the center of the village. WHOOOMMM! WHOOOMMM! Pieces of thatched roofs and debris flew high into the air. The ground shook and rocks and dirt was falling all around us. Smoke was rising from the village. I began to think how much the grunts loved the close air support. Just then a piece of shrapnel hit in some standing water in the rice paddy only about two feet from me. It smoked and sizzled in the water and mud. In the meantime the jet circled in the air aiming for another strike.

As the bombing continued, for some unknown reason, I reached out to touch the jagged metal which was about sixteen inches long and about four inches wide. I happened to think to myself what great damage a large piece of metal like this could do to the human body. As I touched it for a split second it burned the end of my forefinger. This was the second time I had touched hot shrapnel out of curiosity and got burnt. Maybe this time I would learn my lesson.

Another air strike came in and dropped napalm on the village. This time the entire village was engulfed in flames. There was nothing but fire and flames. For the moment our firing had ceased. In all this excitement word was passed by the platoon commander for the Marines to immediately stop firing at animals. We moved forward and set up a 360 degree defensive perimeter around the burning village. I could hear all sorts of chatter on the radio. Marines were talking and the Popular Forces were talking. They were trying to get some kind of body count so I went about my business at hand with my squad. I had my squad face outboard for security.

One of our Kit Carson Scouts was a huge and robust man for a Vietnamese. He was seen questioning a woman prisoner. From what I could gather and from listening to the Marine interpreters, this woman was a nurse for this particular NVA unit. She had been shot in her right arm at the elbow. One of the corpsmen had applied a tourniquet to her upper arm a few inches above her elbow. Her forearm seemed to be dangling at the elbow with only a small portion of muscle and bone. The woman was not crying but her face was very pale barely any expression or sign of pain. I figured she was probably in a state of shock.

The South Vietnamese interrogator kept questioning her but she would not respond. As he smacked her in the face she uttered something in a low voice and he smacked her again. It was obvious that he was not getting anywhere with his interrogation. He became angered and frustrated. This time he grabbed her right forearm that was dangling down from the elbow and twisted it. She stumbled backward and flinched in pain, but still did not say a word. I thought the oversized Kit Carson Scout was going to yank her whole arm off.

The platoon commander saw what had happened and yelled at the Kit Carson Scout to get away from her. The Kit Carson Scout retaliated by talking back to the platoon commander in Vietnamese. A different Kit Carson Scout went up to the larger interrogator and tried to pull him away from the woman. Both were yelling and screaming at each other in Vietnamese.

The lieutenant stepped up to both of them and yelled, "Didi mau! Didi mau!"

Reluctantly both Kit Carson Scouts moved away still jabbering Vietnamese in very angry voices. The larger one who had been interrogating the NVA nurse was now giving the lieutenant very dirty looks for breaking up his interrogation. Some of the new Marines could not believe the brutality of the Kit Carson Scout, while others who had been in country longer, took it with a grain of salt.

The wounded NVA nurse was soon loaded aboard a chopper along with two other prisoners. I would never know if the NVA nurse would survive as she had lost a lot of blood and her face was as white as a sheet when they loaded her onto the chopper. The captured weapons and equipment were also loaded onto the choppers. What little remained in the village was completely searched and we ensured that there was not a hooch standing. What was not destroyed by the bombs was set on fire by the Popular Forces.

We spent the next day working the area around this village looking for bunkers, tunnels, and traces of the NVA. Our time was spent running ambushes, patrols, and calling in artillery and air strikes on pre-designated targets. We had very little sleep during this time. One morning we moved into another area and came upon another small village. A search was conducted immediately and everybody was rounded up into a group. Like all the other villages we had searched there were no males to be found in this one either. We made them sit on the ground.

The huge Kit Carson Scout spotted two women within the group and claimed that they were VC. After a few minutes of questioning the women, he suggested that they be taken back for further interrogation. There was a lot of yelling back and forth in Vietnamese and the usual pulling and tugging. A few Marines who knew a little of the Vietnamese language interpreted for me what was being said. The women were pleading not to be taken away from the village. They feared they would be killed by the NVA if they returned after being seen with the Americans.

In spite of their protests, the Kit Carson Scout had convinced the platoon commander that the two women were VC and they were taken back to the rear on a chopper. We then moved on further away from the village and into a clearing. The company set up a defensive position in the tall elephant grass. A few hours later a chopper was coming in to land at our position. One of the Marines popped a smoke grenade to designate the area where the pilot was to land. Not only did the chopper have resupplies, but the two Vietnamese women who had previously been taken away, returned on the same chopper.

Our Kit Carson Scout gathered around them and asked, "Ong o xa nao?" (What village are you from?) The two women pointed in the direction of their village. Then he asked, "Viet Cong con o tai day khong?" (Are the Viet Cong still here?)

The two women replied, "Da co!" (Yes). Then they got down on their knees and began tugging on the Kit Carson Scout's trousers and pleading with him not to return them to their village.

The Kit Carson Scout stepped back pushing the women away and said, "Toi se khong lam hai ong dau." (You will not be harmed) Dung len! (Stand up) Tin Vao chung toi (Trust us).

In the meantime the two women continued pleading that if they remained in the area they would surely be killed by the VC or NVA. By now the Kit Carson Scout was loosing his patience. I could tell by the inflection of his voice.

While waving his hands for them to get away, he yelled, "Didi mau! Didi mau!" The women finally got on their feet and started walking toward the bushes in the direction of their village. We were told that not much derived from the interrogation at the rear and that these women could return to their village.

Since my squad was about to leave the company perimeter on patrol, the platoon commander instructed me to ensure that these two women were safely escorted back to their village. We followed them into the elephant grass and bushes as they proceeded very slowly. Occasionally they would turn around and try to walk back in the direction we came from. We would latch on to their arms and force them to walk along with us for we were given the assignment to take them back. We finally arrived at the village and I motioned with hand and arm signals for them to remain there. Then I told the point man to continue on our patrol. As we walked out of the village the women seemed very scared to be back in their own village.

Mike 3 Charlie hit all of our checkpoints and after the last one we headed back toward the company's defensive position. I made a command decision that my squad would return by way of the village. It would be easier walking than in the tall elephant grass and rice paddies. Besides, I wanted to check on the two Vietnamese women that we had dropped off at the village. On our way back I positioned myself as the fourth Marine in our squad for command and control purposes. As we approached the village my point man proceeded around the corner of a grass hooch and came upon a small group of women and children. Some were crying and others were just staring in silence. The point man gave the signal for the squad to halt.

"You guys are not going to believe this," he said out loud for the squad to hear.

"What's the matter?" I asked him.

"You'd better come here and see for yourself," the point man replied.

I walked forward and some other Marines in the squad moved forward with me just out of curiosity. I approached the point man from behind and then stepped along his right side. We both stood there speechless for a few seconds. On the ground in front of us were the mutilated bodies of the two Vietnamese women. Their upper body had been stripped naked and the bodies were positioned on their backs. Both breasts had been cut off. Each woman had one breast positioned on their stomachs and one breast was placed over their genital areas. Their limbs and chest had wounds which looked like they were inflicted with very sharp objects. It appeared they had been stabbed to death. Their bodies were covered with blood but we recognized the faces of these women as the ones we had escorted back to the village, and ultimately to their death. Their eyes were still open as they lay there motionless. Flies began to circle and land on their bodies. We finally grasped why these two women had protested not to be taken back to their village. They had foreseen their unfortunate fate. It made my squad sick to our stomachs. I was mad as hell, but I didn't show my anger to the squad.

I figured that whoever did this would have degraded and mutilated their bodies even more if my squad had not reentered the village. The wounds were fresh and I thought that they may have heard us coming and went underground. We knew that the enemy was in the area and possibly close by. It was obvious that this brutal killing had taken place only moments earlier. I gave the order to check every hooch. I told my squad to be very careful not to trip any booby traps. Pots, pans, floor mats, and everything else was turned over during our search. One Marine found a trail leading into the dense vegetation and into a treeline but we found no tunnels or other signs in the grass huts that would lead us to the VC/NVA. They were most likely deep underground and would resurface after our patrol left.

I called back on the radio and reported the incident to the platoon commander and asked if we could head down the trail to see if we could find the murderers. I was told that there was nothing else we could do on this particular patrol and to get back to the perimeter. I felt sorry for the women and children who were squatting down next to the bodies and crying. It must have been total hell to always live in fear. As we walked back toward our company CP the visions of these two killed women kept flashing in my mind. I wished I could get my hands on the Bastards who had killed them. I wanted to go out on patrol the next day and hunt them down like the animals they were.

That afternoon Hawkeye and I were sitting around talking. Out of the blue, a transmission was heard over the radio that Mike Company would be moving back to FSB Ryder. It was sheer bliss to hear the news.

"Hot damn, we're going back to Ryder," I said to Hawkeye. "Rat infested bunkers is better than staying in this hot ass valley."

"You can say that again," Hawkeye replied. "We can see old Arnold the pig one more time. Also we can get us some hot grub from the mess hall and sit around shootin the breeze."

"How bout burning shitters," I said laughing. "What do you think about that, Hawkeye?"

"About time we got a little break," Hawkeye replied with a grin on his face.

The next day we were choppered up to FSB Ryder and relieved Lima Company of the responsibility for the defense of FSB Ryder. The same chores were attended to such as going out on the observation post, listening posts, and work details. By coincidence I found myself in the same bunker where I had been before. Only this time it was not made of sandbags, but rather ammunition boxes. All the sandbagged bunkers had been torn down and replaced by wooden crates. The rat community seemed to have grown

Lance Corporal Fenwick in Sniper Valley with an air strike in the background. It was so hot it melted my camera film. A barely visible squad is crossing the open area to check for the enemy.

while we were humping in the valleys. You could see rat dumplings scattered all around the bunkers. We joked about keeping a big stick close by at night in order to do hand to hand combat with the rats.

I asked one of the artillery Marines if he had seen Arnold. I wanted to see if it had grown any.

"Oh yeah, Arnold," the Marine replied. With a sneer on his face he added, "We ate him about a month ago. Now that was some mighty fine eatin. Dem boys at the mess hall did a real good job of cookin him."

"Damn," I said. "You scoundrels! I was hoping to see him one more time before the Marines ate him. I didn't even get a bite." I wasn't sure if I was disappointed by not being a part of the pig roast or if I just missed the animal.

"Someday we might get ourselves another pig," the Marine said.

"You'll never have another Arnold," I replied. "He reminded me of some of the old pigs we have back on the farm in Kentucky."

The next few days became lackadaisical for Mike Company. The day to day duties were somewhat less intense and we had some spare time to sleep, eat, and write letters. One of the Marines from the artillery battery had a guitar and Hawkeye and I would sit around him in a little group every chance we got. We would sing songs of the times.

One of my favorites was the "House of the Rising Sun." One could hear our voices in unison singing along as the Marine strummed the guitar. We would chuckle at the lyrics and the differences of pitch from us singing along. Hawkeye couldn't carry a very good note. I would tease him by saying, "Hawkeye, what did you do with that money your mother gave you for singing lessons?" At this point in our tour, we didn't care if we could carry a tune. We were just happy to have the chance to be together, have some fun, and sing to the strumming of the guitar. If for no other reason, we were singing to escape from the reality of war, even if it was for a few precious moments.

September 15, 1970

Hello Dad,

How is everything with you? Hope you are in good health and spirits. I got your letter yesterday and was glad to get it. Mail is one thing that every guy over here looks forward to, especially if it's from someone in the family. You said that you were having trouble with your back in the letter. Well, I hope it's not too bad. I don't imagine cutting tobacco helps it any either.

Guess by the time you get this letter your tobacco will be in the barn or just about anyway. I bet help is awful scarce this year especially since the summer months are over with. Most guys that could help are either in school or working at public jobs, but the way you and Mom talked, seems like most of your normal help is working somewhere else. Oh! well, you'll get it in.

That corn blight must be pretty bad. Probably the same thing will happen next year but I sure hope not. I was just wondering if you are really going to sell your sows. It would be bad if you had to, but I guess if corn is so high, then it's not much you can do about it. The old farm would seem empty without a few pigs running around and rooting up the place.

How is the farm life nowadays? Guess it's about the same thing, can't make money for spending it. I wonder how Jimmy Howard likes farming. Guess he helped you out quite a bit this summer, didn't he? Wish I could have helped you this year but you know how it is. I've got plenty to do over here. I wonder if what we are doing will ever amount to anything.

Well Dad, we were choppered up on LZ Ryder. We were in a pretty bad spot so I'm glad we got out of there. We had been there about twenty days. If you ever hear of Sniper Valley, we were working around that area. So now we're up here on a mountain that has a fire support base on it. How long we'll be here I don't know, but I suppose till stand-down which is about the 27th of this month. Stand-down is when the company starts getting ready to pull out. I may leave sooner than that though since I'm being transferred to another unit.

I'm hoping I can go to the 1st Marines which work in the area around Da Nang. With my luck though, I'll probably go to the 5th Marines and be in the same area I am now. I think Mom misunderstood me when I said that around September the 13th I'll be out of the bush. What I really meant is that we might have gone to the rear, which is LZ Ross. If we did it would only be for about two days to get cleaned up and back out again. Instead of going back to the rear we were choppered up here on LZ Ryder. But at least it's sure better than being in the bush. I guess I'll be in the bush as long as I stay over here unless I get lucky when I get transferred. It is awfully doubtful though. "Grunts," like me, usually stay in the bush for eleven and a half months. In other words, the ground stompers.

As you know I'm a squad leader now so I won't be doing much up on this mountain. Mostly all we do is go on working parties that range from cleaning up trash to cleaning out shitters. Yes we even have the outdoor type toilets up here. Usually in the bush, well all the time in the bush, we dig a hole. Guess you might say it's a "cat hole" and just big enough for the person who digs it. We never dig a big hole for the entire company because we move so often. Every two days I go on an OP (observation post) for two days at a time. It's not bad. In fact, I kinda like it. All we do out there is lay around all day, but at night we set up watches so we can keep an eye out for Charlie. It's about the distance from the house back home to the old tenant house. We have hooches made out of ammo boxes. Right now I'm sitting on a box writing this letter.

I guess maybe I can catch up on my writing while I'm up here. The big guns go off pretty often so if you see an ink mark all the way across the paper, it's because one of the guns went off. Ha! They fire about twenty rounds each fire mission. Well like I said I don't know how long I'll be up here but I guess for at least a week. I'll let you all know where I go when I get transferred.

Well Dad, guess I've about run out of things to tell you so I'll close for now and let you get back to the farm chores. Take it easy and don't work too hard. I'll be thinking of you all real often.

As ever,
Fred

"Hey Fenwick," the familiar voice of Hawkeye could be heard. "Let's go up to where the big guns are and watch the artillery battery do a fire mission. They are going to fire a few rounds out into Sniper Valley."

"Why, is there enemy activity out there?" I asked.

"I imagine so or they wouldn't waste the rounds," Hawkeye replied. "They're getting ready to fire now. Come on, let's go."

I stuffed the letter to my father in an envelope, licked it, and sealed it. I would have it ready to go out with the next chopper. Hawkeye and I walked up the hill crest to where the Marines manning the 105mm howitzers were getting ready. One Marine began shouting commands. "STANDBY... READY... FIRE!"

KABOOM! The first big gun went off, followed by a second, as it rippled down the line of howitzers. Four of the big guns were putting lead on target. The ground beneath us trembled and shook from each blast. We could hear the whistling of the rounds as they streaked through the air and then landed on target. WHOOOSSS! WHOOOMMM!

We were joined by other members of the squad as we sat on the ground to witness the spectacle. Hawkeye and I watched with great enthusiasm. It was something to do to break up the monotony.

After about five minutes of firing, one of the Marines yelled, "Kiss... my... ass! You all done killed an elephant?"

Turning to Hawkeye I asked, "Did you hear that? He said they killed an elephant. I haven't seen no elephants here in Vietnam, have you?"

"I ain't seen any, but they have them here," he replied. Hawkeye got up on his feet and said, "Let's go take a look."

I got up and followed him walking toward the Marines who were doing the firing. One of the arty Marines was standing back at a safe distance from the howitzers and looking down range through a pair of binoculars.

Hawkeye asked, "Hey Marine, did they really kill an elephant out there in Sniper Valley?"

"Shit yeah," the Marine replied. "Look through these and see for yourself." He handed the binoculars to Hawkeye.

In the meantime, the Marines around us were cheering and clapping their hands. Hawkeye and I took turns looking through the binoculars. As far as we could see into the valley with the aid of the binoculars, we saw that there was in fact, a dead elephant. One of the rounds had actually killed it.

Handing the binoculars back to the Marine I asked jokingly, "Why kill an elephant instead of killing the NVA?"

"Fire a few of those rounds into Antenna Valley," Hawkeye suggested. "That's where Charlie is." Hawkeye looked at me and asked, "Fenwick, you know where our next AOR is going to be?"

Shaking my head in disbelief I replied, "Don't tell me, Antenna Valley, right?"

"You guessed it," Hawkeye said while nodding his head and smiling sheepishly. "We're moving out day after tomorrow."

"Hot damn," I replied. "Here we go again. That place is crawling with NVA and VC."

We walked back to our hooch at a slower pace than going up to see the howitzers fire. We were dreading going back down into Antenna Valley. I had been in Vietnam now for about seven months. Even though there was talk of pulling the Marines out I knew that I was destined to stay in the bush looking for the enemy. I didn't have a good feeling about this one. I had just written a letter to my father and I was beginning to think of the farm and how I would love to be back there even if we did have backbreaking work. At least there I could drive the farm tractor which I had loved to do. We spent the rest of the day talking about Antenna Valley. Late in the afternoon we sat around and played cards as the sun went down. It was getting dark so we decided to quit our game. I set the watches for the remainder of the night.

We spent the next day preparing for our move to Antenna Valley. We all felt that this would be our last time on FSB Ryder. Hawkeye and I were sitting around talking while I put some items in my pack. The platoon commander approached me. It was odd because he was carrying a PRC-77 radio with him. You just didn't see a platoon commander lug around a radio. He placed the radio on the ground in front of me that was attached to a pack frame.

"Lance Corporal Fenwick, you will be carrying this radio tomorrow. You will be our platoon radio operator, and you Hawkeye, will be the company radio operator. The company radio operator is sick and he will be evacuated out of here today.

"What about my squad?" I asked the lieutenant.

"The 1st fireteam leader will be the squad leader," he replied.

"Roger that," I said. "This may be my last time as squad leader since Mike Company is getting ready to stand down and get out of Nam."

"That may be true," the lieutenant agreed. He then turned around and proceeded back to his bunker. I reached for the radio to inspect it and to perform an operation check.

"Hear that?" I asked Hawkeye. "Being assigned a platoon radio operator really came at an opportune time, just when we are going back down into Antenna Valley. It didn't get that name for nothing. The enemy goes for the radio operator first and the platoon commander second. I hear that there has been a sharp rise in casualties of radiomen in the bush from hostile fire during this month. Oh well, guess time will tell if our luck holds out. When I was undergoing machine gun training, we were told by our instructor that a machine gunner's life expectancy once a machine gunner opened fire, is 6 seconds. What is the life expectancy of a radio operator?"

Hawkeye patted me on the shoulder and said, "Just keep a low profile Fred, you'll be okay."

I replied, "How can I keep a low profile when I'm six foot tall and the whip antenna is about eight feet above my head."

"Let me show you how it's done," Hawkeye replied. "Take the antenna, break it down into sections, leave the base in the air, and strap the rest on your pack." He then knelt down on his knees demonstrating what he was talking about.

Then he looked at me and saw that I was a little concerned. "Don't worry," he said. "I'll be in the rear if you need me."

"Thanks for your confidence," I replied.

"Do you still remember all of the phonetic alphabet?" Hawkeye asked.

"Yeah," I responded.

"Let's go over them now just to make sure," he suggested.

We both sat on the ground side by side with our legs crossed. Hawkeye began to quiz me. "A is what?" he asked.

"Alpha," I replied. "This is too easy. I think I know them all already so just stop me if I get one wrong."

Hawkeye said, "Okay then, go as far as you can and I'll help you if you need it.

"Okay," I replied, "here we go, Alpha, Bravo, Charlie, Delta, Echo, Foxtrot, Golf, Hotel"… I continued down the letters but got hung up on X.

"I can't remember the letter X for some reason," I said.

"Common, think Fenwick," he said. "What do you get if you go to the hospital with a broken bone?"

"Oohhh, okay," I said. "X-ray! The last two are Yankee and Zulu.

"Very good Fred, you're a natural," Hawkeye replied.

We went over various other radio procedures and protocol until he was sure that I knew how to call in a medevac. That afternoon after chow, I had some spare time so I wrote another letter home while we were still at FSB Ryder. Since my last letter was addressed only to my father, this time I would write a personal letter to my mother.

September 16, 1970

Hello Mom,

Well how does this find you doing these days? Hope you're doing just fine. I got your letter the same time I received Dad and Larry's. Was sure glad to hear from you all. I really enjoy getting a letter from you. As I think about it, somehow I don't believe you all are getting all my mail. You mentioned that you have not received the Cruise Book which I sent about a month and a half ago. Also I sent Larry some little beads that go around your neck and he did not mention it in his letter. They were just small ones so they should have made it without any trouble. He also did not mention the article I sent about "The Grunt." Oh well, they were not that important, but I was just wondering why some of my mail hasn't reached home. It must be a problem that occurs over here.

Like I told Dad in the letter, I'm up on LZ Ryder again. This is the same mountain I was on once before. We were supposed to be here for a week but we're getting ready to move off Ryder tomorrow. Shortly after that I'll be getting ready to be transferred to another unit. The company is supposed to leave around the second week in October but will start getting ready about the 27th of this month. I may leave the company before then since I'm going to another unit. While I'm getting transferred I don't guess I'll get any mail until I get to where I'm supposed to go. I'll write and tell you my new address when I get there. Guess I'm kinda getting ahead of myself, but the 27th isn't that far away.

I've been over here for about 7 months now. Time seems to be going pretty fast for me. Before you know it, I'll be heading home. February seems to be pretty far off but the way these last 7 months have gone by it won't be long to go. I just hope I can get in a decent company when I leave this one. I'll probably still be in the bush. Mike Company is just not the same anymore. At first it was all right, but now we've got a lot of boots just from the States, plus some boot lieutenants. They just don't seem to know what's going on. They think they're back in the States.

I heard from Donald the other day. He seemed to be doing fine. He mentioned some hills which he was on while he was here. He said that they were not too far from Da Nang. Our paths must have crossed on Hills 848 and 290. Also our paths must have crossed in the area about thirty miles southwest of Da Nang and about the same distance west of Chu Lai. At least I think its Chu Lai. I can see the lights at night from up here. We had a full moon last night and it sure was pretty.

Yes Mom, I liked the toothpaste you sent. In fact, I still have some. I saved a little for the time on Ryder. Sometimes, but not very often, they bring up some SP's (special packs) that contain toothpaste, cigarettes, candy, shaving gear, and other items during our resupply. Usually the toothpaste we get out here is Colgate. In the bush I usually use salt out of the C-Ration accessory packs, but its not too often I get to brush my teeth. Most of the time, we are short on water. I carry six canteens now, but I still try to save all I can, because we never know if a chopper will resupply us. Sure wish I could have a drink out of the old well at home. I guess I'll have to wait for awhile. Believe me, that is the best tasting water anywhere. I also liked your pickles. They were really good.

Well Mom, guess I'd better go now. I'll write to you all later.

I'm trying to catch up on my writing while I've got the chance. In another week, don't guess I'll have the time to write for awhile. Someone said that we might find out today if the ones not going back to the States will leave, but I doubt if we do. So I'll let you go for now, I hope everyone is doing fine.

As ever,
Fred

I was awakened the next morning by a CH-53 setting down on FSB Ryder. I sat up and rolled my poncho liner off of me. I had not slept in one of the bunkers made of ammo boxes but rather was content to sleep in the open under the stars. My back and shoulders ached slightly from the hard ground. My poncho liner was wet with the morning dew. I began brushing my teeth and then stood up to see what the chopper was doing coming in this early in the morning. It was around 0600.

I could see Marines running about around the chopper and fastening ropes and nets to the under carriage. The chopper lifted slowly into the air hovering in one spot for a few seconds. Then the ropes tightened and it lifted into the air carrying with it one of the big guns. Before long another CH-53 flew in and had dropped off a small bull dozer. Almost immediately the Marine driving the dozer started around the top of the hill leveling off the ground. More choppers began to come in, each with a different load or taking something out.

Mike Company was now carrying empty ammo crates to a spot on the hill and stacking them up in a huge pile. They began to burn the pile of boxes and flames and smoke bellowed from the stack. We were tearing down the improvised bunkers. What we could not manage to tear away from the bunkers in the ground, the dozer would level the spot. The top of FSB Ryder looked like a plowed field by the time noon arrived.

We received the word that Mike Company was now ready to get off the mountain. Hawkeye came over to where I was and told me to change the radio battery and handed me three new batteries.

He started back to the CP and said, "Hey Fred, I'll give you a radio check when I get back to my radio."

"Roger, Dodger," I replied.

I replaced the battery and packed away the extra ones in my pack. I also secured the radio to the pack frame and ensured the whip antenna was in place. I got a hissing sound on the radio when I turned it on. Then I adjusted the volume. I could see Hawkeye up on the hillside and gave him the thumbs up that I was ready.

I heard Hawkeye's voice over the net. "Mike 3, Mike 3, This is Mike, Romeo Charlie, Over,"

I replied, "Roger Mike, I hear you Lima Charlie, Hotel Mike, Over."

Hawkeye transmitted, "Roger Mike 3, I have you the same, Mike, Out."

Romeo Charlie was Marine lingo which meant "Radio Check." Lima Charlie meant "Loud and Clear" and Hotel Mike meant "How Me." It wasn't exactly correct radio procedures but the radio operators had come up with the lingo long before my arrival in Vietnam.

We were now ready to go back to Antenna Valley. We were choppered into the valley and we began to hump. It was interesting being the radio operator because I could always be apprised of all situations just by listening to the transmissions on the radio between the company commander and platoon commanders. The only bad part was the extra weight of the radio and the batteries along with all the other gear that I had to carry.

Over all we spent about another week in Antenna Valley. The company would set up sensors at night up in the hills on trails. That way we would be able to detect any foot movement from the enemy. On a few occasions the CP heard enemy movement and artillery was called to bombard the area. I believed that this tactic aided us in keeping a safe distance from the NVA and thus only encountered minor sniper and mortar fire from the enemy.

One day as we were walking along a crest overlooking the valley we heard the sound of an enemy sniper rifle. Crrraaaccckkkk! The bullet whizzed about ten feet directly above my head. I flinched while still in the upright position. A couple of seconds later another enemy round hit the dirt a few feet away from me followed by the muffled sound of the enemy weapon in the distance. I immediately dropped to the ground. Then I heard the platoon sergeant yell, "Keep your heads down, there's a sniper down in the treeline!"

I hollered out to anyone who might care to hear what I had to say. "Well, no shit! The fucker is aiming for me. I've got to get rid of this damn PRC-77 radio!"

The platoon sergeant yelled out, "Ah, don't worry bout it, Kentucky, he can't hit nothin."

"Easy for you to say," I retorted. "You're not carrying this big ass radio with this big ass whip antenna."

The staff sergeant just looked at me and laughed out loud. "You shor do have a Kentucky accent," he commented. He always seemed to be cool and calm even in the heat of battle.

"Yeah, staff sergeant," I responded, "and you gotta Samoan accent." We laughed as if nothing out of the ordinary was happening.

As we crouched down for cover we heard that the Marine snipers attached to Mike Company were going to engage the enemy with one of our own sniper rifles. Soon there were two Marine snipers waking through the column of Marines until they reached my location.

"Which direction did the sniper fire come from?" one of the Marine snipers asked me.

"To my right flank," I responded. "He's probably about three hundred meters out."

The Marine sniper with the M40 Sniper Rifle lay down on top of a large rock. It was a good position to rest his weapon. The other Marine sniper tried to locate the enemy with a strong pair of binoculars. Suddenly another round zoomed past our heads. The Marine with the binoculars yelled out that he had seen where the enemy fire had come from. The Marine sniper on the rock started to aim through the scope affixed to his rifle. I could see that he was taking his time moving the barrel back and forth in order to pinpoint the enemy sniper. Then another enemy shot rang out that echoed through the valley.

The Marine sniper said in an unconcerned tone of voice, "I've got him located. He's in a fuckin tree. Don't worry about it. I'll get that mothafucker."

In the meantime the company had halted because of the sniper fire. Hawkeye came up to me from nowhere and was inquiring what was going on. I gave him the details and we both sat down and peered into the direction that the Marine sniper was aiming. We waited for the Marine to fire. We waited and we waited. It seemed like a long time.

"Hey Hawkeye," I asked, "What's taking so damn long?"

He replied, "Well appears that he is trying to get a real good shot the first time, so he don't skedaddle on us."

"Yeah," I replied, "but by the time he aims in and pulls the trigger the gooner will be long gone."

"Only thing we can do now is just wait and see," Hawkeye continued.

Almost as suddenly as Hawkeye had finished speaking, the Marine sniper fired his weapon. I could see that the rifle kicked back into his shoulder with a mighty jolt. Poooowwww! The sound of the sniper rile rang out and the round was on its way. We waited for the 7.62x51mm NATO Full Metal Jacket to find its mark. The Marine sniper settled his weapon back down on the target while looking through the scope with one eye.

He said in a slow sarcastic voice, "I got that gooner mothafucker. We don't have to worry about his shit no more."

There were sighs of relief among the Marines who had witnessed the Marine sniper at work. About five Marines had gathered around to observe the "one shot, one kill." We all stood up to look out in the direction where he had fired. We took turns looking through the binoculars. When it came my turn, I peered through the binoculars and scanned the area. Then at a distance I saw a withering body dangling from a tree limb about twenty feet off the ground. As I tried to zoom in with the binoculars the body fell to the ground and landed near the tree trunk. It reminded me of hunting squirrels back on the farm.

I spoke up while still peering through the binoculars, "He fell out of the tree and hit the ground. There's no movement." Everyone around me began cheering.

"Nice job," a Marine was heard saying, "we won't be bothered by that fuckin gook no more."

The Marine sniper took his right forefinger, wet it with his saliva, and stroked the front sight of his weapon. "Another notch for my stock," he replied boastingly.

Before we started to move again I took one more section off my whip antenna and fastened it to my pack. I had raised the height of the antenna while on the move because I was having problems hearing the radio transmissions. Since Charlie had taken a few pot shots at me I decided that I should not make myself a prime target for the enemy snipers. We ended up next to a river. We set up the usual security defenses. One day I was sitting under my poncho liner and heard a radio transmission from the base camp. Some choppers would be arriving the next day to take us back to the rear. Excitedly I ran over to Hawkeye who was laying next to this radio.

"Hey Hawkeye," I said. "Did you hear that over the radio? We're going back to the rear again."

"I heard it," Hawkeye replied, "Maybe they're pulling us out of here for good."

"I sure hope so," I responded. "Maybe we can get the hell out of this valley. You can hardly breathe here. It's so miserably hot and humid." I sat down across from Hawkeye who did not move from his position.

"Yeah, maybe we can go back and get a warm soda," Hawkeye said. "A cold shower would be nice too."

"Don't even mention it," I commanded. "My mouth is watering just thinking about a soda and I am beginning to really need a shower."

"Know whatcha mean," Hawkeye replied. "When we get back to the world, it will take months to get this dirt and grime off our bodies. I dream of just sitting in a tub of warm water for hours on end."

"I will never take things for granted anymore," I said. "People in the world don't know how good they have it."

"Yeah, you got that right," Hawkeye said pondering.

Hawkeye and I could sense a whole new attitude within the company. We realized that it would not be long before we would be pulled out of Vietnam. Mike Company, as we knew it, would be no more. Even our spot reports seemed to take on an almost comical and lackadaisical demeanor. One report in particular stated that while Mike 3 was set in a defensive perimeter that several noises were heard. After a 60mm mortar mission we swept the area but ended up with negative results. It was believed that an elephant had made the noises.

One night as Hawkeye and I were sitting around next to our improvised bush hooch talking, we saw some flares in the sky from a hillside in the distance. There were green tracers, red tracers, yellow flares, and white illumination lighting up the sky. The whole hillside opened up at the same time. The fireworks in the sky looked like a 4th of July celebration. We sat back and watched the spectacle.

I looked over at Hawkeye and said, "I wonder what the hell is going on up there. They must really be in a hot firefight."

Hawkeye replied without even turning his head, "No, I don't think so. I think that unit over there has just found out that they are going to be pulled out of Vietnam. You know lately they have been pulling units out left and right."

Watching the sky I replied, "It sounds good, and it looks pretty good, but I'll believe it when I see it."

For at least an hour we sat watching the fireworks. Rumors circulated throughout the rest of the evening that we were in fact pulling out of Vietnam. There were all sorts of discussions among the Marines about what we would do when we got back to the States. The scuttlebutt (rumor) was that units were being withdrawn slowly out of Vietnam on a rotation basis and that arrangements were being made. In the meantime, they would turn control over to the South Vietnamese Army. The plan was that by 1974 every American unit would be withdrawn from the blood soaked soil of Vietnam.

The next morning we boarded choppers heading back to the rear at FSB Ross. We settled into our hooches and I asked Hawkeye if he wanted to go to the armory with me to check out my SKS. He accepted my invitation and walked with me to the armory. I was excited about checking out my SKS that I had turned over to the company first sergeant while I was in the bush and our base camp had been LZ Baldy. It was to be a prized souvenir to take home which would enhance the stories I could tell the rest of my life. It would be "lasting visions" of a war in which we won the battles, but lost the war.

I was hoping to clean the weapon while I had some spare time. Hawkeye was going to help me clean it. We walked up to the Marine behind the armory counter and I proudly announced, "I am here to claim my SKS."

"Do you have a SKS stored here?" the Marine armorer asked.

I responded, "Yeah, I tagged it with my name and unit while I was I was in the bush and the Mike Company First Sergeant brought it back for me. Now I'm here to claim it, well actually, I just want to check it out and clean it for the time being. I'll take it back home with me when I get ready to rotate."

I gave him my name and unit and he walked away to look for the weapon. Very shortly he returned and said, "Spell your name for me, will you?"

While spelling my last name carefully and slowly I replied, "F.E.N.W.I.C.K."

The Marine leaned over the counter and said, "Well, Fenwick, I hate to tell you this, but you don't have a SKS here. The first sergeant rotated back to the States about a month ago.

"You gotta be shitin me!" I exclaimed. My heart sank. "You mean to tell me that the first sergeant took my SKS, the one I got off a gook I killed out in the bush? That son-of-a-bitch! Can you look again for me?"

"The SKS is not here," the armorer replied. "Wish I could help you out, but like I said, the SKS is not here and the first sergeant is long gone."

"Just take one more look," I pleaded.

The armorer turned around, walked around the rifle racks, and stood in front of an empty rack. He pointed at the rack and said, "All our gook weapons would be stored here in this rack. As you can see there is no SKS. Sorry man."

I turned and looked at Hawkeye. "Ain't this a bitch," I said with anger. I felt so cheated and depressed that another Marine would do this to me and a senior Marine at that. "So much for my souvenir," I said with complete disgust.

Hawkeye in an attempt to console me said, "Well, maybe you may get lucky enough to get another one."

As I walked toward the armory door to go back to our hooch I commented to Hawkeye, "To tell you the truth, I hope I will never have that opportunity again."

Hawkeye followed behind me and said, "Yeah! I know what you mean. It's a damn shame!"

"I ain't believing this shit," I said as if talking to myself. What's say we go to the E-Club and have a Black Label Beer?" I suggested to Hawkeye.

"Sounds good to me," Hawkeye replied.

We sat and talked in the club for awhile. I had a few choice names for the transferred first sergeant over a few beers. I just could not believe that the Mike Company First Sergeant, who was a senior enlisted Marine with a pay grade of E-8, would do such a thing. He was supposed to set the example for all junior enlisted Marines. Hawkeye offered to me that maybe one of the Marines working in the company armory or even another Marine may have rotated and took my SKS. He also hinted that it may have gotten lost when the company armory moved from LZ Baldy to FSB Ross during the first week of July.

I was not in a position to speculate. All I knew was that I blamed the first sergeant. After all, he was the one that I handed my SKS over to while I was in the bush. The fact remained that I would never get my hands on it ever again. I had devilish thoughts for the one who illegally took it from me. I thought to myself that whoever stole my SKS would one day have it mounted on a wall in their home. I could imagine all the lies that could be told about the war trophy and how it was obtained. I could not imagine how anyone could live a life of lies. I was really upset that another Marine had stolen my SKS.

We spent the next few days doing our usual routine in the rear. We took long showers, got clean clothes, and even managed to get haircuts. We were beginning to look like shaggy dogs since we had been in the bush for so long. The higher echelon came down with a quota stating that the Marines who wished to remain behind in Vietnam could stay. They would be assigned to a CAP (Combined Action Platoon) unit. Their job was to stay in a specified village and act as security. They would also provide medical attention to the local villagers who needed it. The other remaining Marines would be transferred to Okinawa.

I talked with Hawkeye and I asked if he was going to Okinawa with me.

"Well, I don't know, I kinda like it here. I don't mind volunteering for one of these CAP units," Hawkeye said.

"You are crazy as hell!" I exclaimed. "We've got a chance to get out of here, and you want to go to a CAP unit?"

"I don't know, I may change my mind later," Hawkeye replied while smiling. "At least I'd like to give it a try. I'm not ready to leave Nam yet."

"Suit yourself, but I was hoping we could have some good times in Kin Ville, Okinawa. You know the place, the little town just outside the main gate at Camp Hansen."

"Yeah, I know," Hawkeye replied, "been there, done that."

"Then you owe it to your body to have a good time, right?" I asked.

"Yeah, "I owe it to my body," Hawkeye said. I laughed at his unconcerned expression.

A couple of days later the signs of us withdrawing out of the area became more and more evident. Everyone was ordered to go to supply and claim our seabags. They had been stored in supply since we arrived at Mike Company. Our bags were filled with handfuls of moth balls. I felt that my uniforms might be ruined because of the hot and humid weather. I feared that they would be covered with mold and mildew. Surprisingly, however, when I emptied them out of the seabag, I noticed that my clothes were in mint condition, except for the smell of moth balls.

I returned to my hooch and saw Hawkeye rummaging through his seabag. As I dropped mine on my cot I said to Hawkeye, "Looks like we are heading out to Okinawa in the next few days."

Hawkeye looked at me with a strange face and said, "Well, I've already talked to the company commander. I'm going to be assigned to one of the CAP units."

"You didn't," I said in disbelief.

"Yeah, I want to stay here for a little while longer," Hawkeye replied.

"Well hell, are you sure you're doing the right thing?" I asked. "I hate to leave you over here in Nam, Hawkeye. I wouldn't mind staying with you but its time for me to move on. I've got a cousin in Okinawa. We joined the Marine Corps together and I would like to see him again. Also my brother Donald is there."

"By all means, don't follow me. We've been following each other long enough," Hawkeye replied while still digging in his seabag. For myself, I don't have much to go home to right now. I'm just going to play it by ear. I think a CAP unit would be good."

"You know that they get hit by the NVA and VC on occasions, don't you?" I asked.

"Yeah, I know," Hawkeye replied. "It's just the chance I'll have to take. I don't mind it here. It would be a change from the grunts humping everywhere. I will just be in a village and probably won't have to move all the time. I might even set up permanent residence here."

We both laughed. Then there was a moment of silence between the two of us. We suddenly realized that it was the end of the line for us to be fighting side by side in Vietnam. We were not talking in our usual jovial manner. It was almost like we could not find the right words to say to each other. We had formed a close friendship. We had shared our thoughts, our fighting holes, our letters from home, and even the food we received through the mail. Something in the back of my mind told me that I would not see Hawkeye again after Vietnam since he lived in Salem, Oregon and I was from Springfield, Kentucky.

During the last few days, Hawkeye and I reminisced about the times we spent together. We had our last few laughs as we talked about our uncertain future ahead of us and the reality of the war we had experienced. There were times where we barely had much to say to one another. Our minds were preoccupied in deep thoughts. I think we managed to say all we needed to say before we would go our separate ways.

I had learned a lot from this Marine I called Hawkeye. I admired him for his bravery and unselfish willingness to help others. He had been cool and calm in handling all critical situations. Even in the heat of battle, Hawkeye displayed professionalism, maturity, and sound judgment. He was an inspiration for me and I considered him as brother and the best friend I would ever have. We had suffered together and had laughed together. We had been a team and formed an unending bond. We had shared the same combat experiences and feared for our lives together in operations such as "Pickens Forest" and "Nebraska Rapids." We had been together during the various campaigns that our unit had participated; Vietnam Winter-Spring 1970 01Nov69-30Apr70, Sanctuary Counter-offensive 01May70-30Jun70, Vietnam Counter-offensive VII 01Jul70-30Jun71. I knew that he would always be in my thoughts. I felt deeply saddened and heart broken that I was leaving my "foxhole buddy" behind in Vietnam.

The Reality of War

THE following tribute to the infantry "Grunt" was written in 1970 by an unknown author and appeared in the *Stars and Stripes* newspaper in Vietnam. The original version related to the Army grunt. I copied it down on a sheet of paper and inserted a few of my own words in order for it to relate specifically to the Marine Corps Infantryman. I sent it home for safe keeping on 13 August 1970 in a letter to my brother, Larry. I doff my cap to the original author.

THE GRUNT

Con Thien, Vietnam – "This may be your finest hour, for you are about to meet a GRUNT.

Doff your cap, if you will; wave a flag; choke back a sob in your throat; wipe away a tear from your eye, for this is the man who is fighting your war.

He is the Marine up front, the one who is sticking his nose in the mud each day, everyday.

He is the one who sees the enemy at twenty-five yards. He is the one who knows what it feels like to be shot at close range by small arms.

He is the one who dies a thousand times when the night is dark and the moon is gone. And he is the one who dies once and forever when an enemy rifle belches flame.

If you have ever slogged through a sticky rice paddy or waded a stream carrying sixty rounds of ammunition, six canteens, a rifle and a pack with enough field rations and spare clothing to last a week, you know why they call him a "Grunt!" It's fairly obvious.

But look at him well and know him, for he is really something. He wears, in dirty dignity, a helmet, flak jacket and a faded uniform. His hands are ripped and torn from contact with barbed wire and elephant grass. His wrists are swollen from mosquito bites.

His pockets are full and his boots are mud-caked and his eyes never stand still; they move and squint and twitch. He is nervous, aware of enemy sound. For he operates in a never-never world where the difference between death and one more tomorrow often depends upon what he sees or does not see, what he hears or does not hear.

The "Grunt" is the man who lives as close to war as it is possible to get. His rank varies, mostly he is a Private First Class, Lance Corporal, Corporal, or a Sergeant.

He likes air support because planes give him a measure of protection. He likes the artillery outfits because they can knock the bejabbers out of an enemy platoon. He cares about supply outfits only to the extent that they can provide him with something to eat and more ammunition to shoot.

He lives first for the day when his tour will be up and he can get out of this country. He lives next for an opportunity to take an in country R&R. He'd like to get his hands on a can of cold beer because it would drive the heat from his throat and ease the corroding pain in his gut. He'd like to feel the softness of a woman.

But he is a "Grunt" and if he can live through today, then there will be tomorrow. And if he can live through enough tomorrow's there will be the R&R, the cold beer, the feel of a woman, and end of his tour.

The "Grunt" as he stands in dirty, muddy majesty, is as fine a fighting man as the United States has ever produced. He is young, tough, intelligent, and he knows how to kill.

But he is a lot more than that. There is something of the builder in these young men. They speak, sometimes of what must be done to South Vietnam to make it right and workable. They speak, sometimes, of government and how it must work. And, if you are lucky, you may get a "Grunt" to speak his mind about the war.

He may tell you many things in language largely unprintable, but it may or may not be surprising to learn that, for the most part, he believes in the purposes that put him here. And that is something, because if you take the "Grunt" out of his muddy, water filled fighting holes, remove his helmet, his flak jacket, his field uniform, take away his rifle, clean him up and dress him a sports shirt, slacks and loafers, you've got the kid who was playing on last year's High School basketball team.

HE'S A NATIONAL ASSET TO BE CHERISHED."

As a Marine Corps Infantry grunt in Vietnam this writing had a special meaning for me. When I read it in the Stars and Stripes newspaper, I could really relate to it. All the Marines who had a MOS (Military Occupational Specialty) of Infantry were considered to be grunts. I was only 19 years old when I stepped off the plane at Da Nang on 6 March 1970. I had graduated from high school in 1969, and after helping my father on the farm through the summer months, I joined the Marine Corps on 23 September of that year.

Vietnam was a life changing experience for me. I believed in what I was doing and I thought that it was the right thing to do. While assigned to Mike Company, 3rd Battalion, 7th Marines, this infantry battalion trudged through the rice paddies, jungles, and mountains of Vietnam looking for the elusive enemy. The grunt was someone who saw the enemy up close. He was the one who was on the front lines. He saw first hand the killing and maiming of human life. I had two kinds of anxiety when I was in Vietnam. One was a feeling of not knowing what was going to happen next and the other of thinking that the next enemy round might have my name on it.

The natural environment and weather conditions presented a challenge to overcome. The weather most of the time was hot, dry, and humid. On other occasions it would be wet and cold, especially during the monsoons. The monsoons made life miserable for the Marines because they had to sleep in the mud. I was wet most of the time. We were either wet from the heat and humidity or from the overnight dew. When the monsoon season began we were either wet from the rain or from our own body perspiration. These were the main reasons why many Marines had trench foot and jungle rot. It was very hard to keep your body dry.

Setting in fighting holes at night was a struggle, not only because we were expecting the enemy to overrun our position, but we also had to endure the annoying menace of insects that lurked in the darkness. During the day the flying insects did not bother us as much. My worst despised insect was the mosquito. These pestering dive bombers would fly into your ears, eyes, land on your arms and hands, and pierce right through the material of our jungle utilities. I managed to get a small mosquito net that was designed to fit only over a person's head. I used it on occasion when I was sleeping but somehow the mosquitoes would always manage to find their way inside the netting for a feast. They were the most detested insects to the infantry grunt. For the time I was in Vietnam, there were approximately 188 cases of malaria within 3rd Battalion, 7th Marines.

I soaked my arms and the nape of my neck and face with insect repellent. This would deter them for only a short period of time. Due to continuous perspiration the repellent would become virtually non-effective. There were times when it would not have been prudent to swat at the mosquitoes. Any commotion or slight movement could be detected by Charlie. This was especially true at night when sitting in an ambush, listening post, or security around the perimeter. We sometimes had no choice but to allow the annoying pests to feed on our blood at will.

Our intense concentration on any movement and the fact that we were so tired all the time would make the endurance of the mosquitoes easier to cope with. We got to the point where we would just ignore them since it was utterly hopeless to keep the thousands of the mosquitoes at bay. After a long night of being pierced by these blood sucking insects I would have many large whelps on my arms and legs the following morning. Sometimes we wouldn't even realize they had bitten us so much during the night. Fortunately, we were provided malaria pills that were distributed by the Navy corpsmen on a regular basis. It was left up to the individual to take those very large pills but I took mine as often as we received them.

I used to watch the mosquitoes land on my arms, far too many to count. They resembled a swarm of bees. I would just watch them bite and draw my blood and then watch my blood soaked sweat trickle down the sides of my arm. I just could not win the battle. To get my revenge, I would at times wait for hundreds of them to settle on my arms and then in a continuous sweeping motion rub the palm of my hands over my forearms. The persistent ones would be mashed while others buzzed slightly off my arms only to light again. My arms would be an ugly red from mashing the mosquitoes.

Red ants were also everywhere. Seems that every time I dug a fighting hole or sleeping hole there would be red ants running around. I would lay on my poncho in my sleeping hole and feel them biting me all over while I tried to sleep. You somehow trained yourself to block out the pain of the stings. At times we would have fun with the ants. As we would watch an army of red ants scurrying about on the ground in a long line, we would spray them with insect repellent. It was flammable so we would light the repellent with a match and set them on fire. We would watch the line of ants burn in the short lived flames. What was left of the colony simply altered their route.

The disadvantage to this method of engagement was that Marines would find themselves getting too carried away and as a result would squirt all of their valuable insect repellent on the ground. This proved to be unwise since a Marine would find himself short of insect repellent when he needed it the most. Like the mosquitoes, their bites would leave welts on our skin. The itch was almost unbearable and scratching did not help. Many times infection would be the result as Marines scratched the spot excessively.

Snakes were other reptiles that we had to watch out for especially the poisonous ones. Vietnam had a variety of snakes but the poisonous ones were the spitting cobra, bamboo pit viper, and the Malayan pit viper. The smaller snakes could bite without a person realizing it. The bamboo vipers could be found almost everywhere.

One morning I was laying on my poncho half asleep. I felt something moving on my chest. As I slowly opened my eyes, I saw a snake curled up on my chest with its beady eyes staring at my face with its forked tongue flicking in and out. I instinctively sat up while at the same time flinging the snake off of me with both hands. I sprang to my feet and went about ten feet in about a split second. I looked to see if the snake was still by my gear. I saw him crawling off quickly into the bushes. He was about two inches in diameter and estimated to be about three feet long. Its color was green with shades of brown and black. I didn't know what kind of snake it was and I didn't care. I was just grateful it hadn't bitten me in the face. While we stayed in this defensive posture I did not get much sleep for thinking of the snake. I didn't know if it was poisonous or not.

Another encounter with a snake was when I took off my boots to powder my feet. I decided to lay back on my pack to get a little rest and ended up dozing off for a few minutes. When I awoke I started to put my socks and boots back on. A small snake was in one of my boots. I held up my boot by the sole and flung the intruder into the bushes. I thought that was a close call but I realized that I had best check the insides of my boots before slipping into them. Although snakes were abundant in Vietnam, we rarely had a casualty from actual snake bites while in the bush.

The ones who had to be extra careful of poisonous snakes were our "Tunnel Rats." The VC and NVA had tunnels dug all over South Vietnam. They would live in these tunnels and hide from us. They would store their rations, munitions, and weapons in these underground complexes. When we discovered an entrance to a tunnel we would designate a Tunnel Rat to go into the hole to find Charlie. Poisonous snakes were sometimes tied and placed at the entrance of these holes. The first Marine down into the tunnel had a chance of getting bitten by a poisonous snake. We would always toss in two or three hand grenades into these holes before attempting to crawl into the tunnel. I knew of only two incidences whereby Marines were bitten by snakes upon entering a tunnel. That is not to say however, that other units did not experience snake bites while checking out the VC tunnels.

Although we were cautioned to stay away from the Vietnamese civilians when they were selling sodas by the roadsides or near villages, some of the Marines were so hot and thirsty from the heat, that they could not resist the temptation. Marines occasionally would purchase sodas with MPC (Military Payment Check), which was legal Vietnamese tender. A soda would at best be partially chilled but most of the time they were just warm. The taste of the sodas however, was much better than warm water treated with iodine tablets that we carried in our canteens.

I saw Marines gulp down an entire bottle of soda very quickly without any pause or hesitation. The Vietnamese were not to be trusted because you never knew who were VC sympathizers. I had heard of incidents where the hard core sympathizers would mix crushed glass in the sodas. This was deadly because if a Marine drank crushed glass in a soda it would result in internal bleeding. That was basically the goal. If a Marine had to be medevaced and was put out of commission there would be one less warrior on the battlefield to contend with.

The Navy corpsmen assigned to the infantry line companies were as brave as they come. They did an outstanding job of looking after the Marines and tending to the sick, lame, and wounded. They were respected by all the Marines of Mike Company, for they knew that the corpsmen would risk their very own lives, for the life of another Marine. They were truly "brothers-in-arms." There was at times a shortage of Navy corpsmen in the field with us. The lack of replacements made it impossible to rotate them out of the field. We normally had anywhere from six to seven corpsmen attached to

Mike Company which kept them very busy.

The perseverance of self protection on a daily basis was also a reality of war. We always had to be on the lookout and on guard to detect mines, booby traps, pungi pits, and trip wires. We were also conscious of wearing helmets, flak jackets, and digging suitable fighting holes. Whenever we moved from one position to another we would normally travel about six klicks or 6000 meters. In layman's terms this was 3.72 miles. This may not seem like a lot of ground to cover in one day, but when your pack, equipment, weapons, and ordnance ranged from 80-100 pounds, it would definitely take its toll. This was especially true when it was so unbearably hot and humid.

The entire company would move to a different location about every three days. As soon as we reached our new position, "pos" as we called it, we would start to dig fighting holes and sleeping holes. The ground at times was rock hard. My E-Tool had a wooden handle. One side was a shovel and the other side a pick. The pick came in handy especially in the lowlands and mountains. We would always dig a fighting hole and a sleeping hole. This was our only protection from the incoming enemy rockets and mortar fire while we were in the bush and away from the base camps.

I had large blisters on my fingers and palms from digging in the hard ground. My squad leader saw them one day and ordered me a pair of gloves from our battalion supply. The light-weight green and gray gloves had perforations throughout the leather fabric for ventilation and a wrist strap to adjust the fit. They were a real blessing and I used them extensively while digging fighting holes and sleeping holes. They really helped save my hands from so many blisters. As with any soft material however, they eventually wore out.

My hands had been used to a lot of digging and hard work on the farm, but digging in the rock hard soil with a small wooden handle E-tool, was more than enough to cause blisters. Sweaty hands caused the open blisters to sting and burn. When we moved to another location we would also have to fill in the holes that we dug so that the VC would not be as tempted to place mines and booby traps in and around them. I saw Marines wounded and killed from booby traps placed inside old fighting holes.

When we dug fighting holes we would also clear fields of fire. This was done in order to clear out bushes and shrubbery for a clear line of sight on avenues of approach. These imaginary avenues were the most likely routes that the enemy might take in order to invade our defensive perimeter. We would also dig a large hole within the company perimeter in order to bury the used C-Ration cans and cardboard boxes so the Vietnamese could not use them. Large pits were also dug out in the dirt for emplacing our heavy guns such as machine guns and mortars. Consequently, the Marines in Mike Company spent a lot of time digging with their entrenching tools.

Ask any Marine grunt and he will tell you what the lingo "humping" means. When a Marine strapped on his heavy haversack pack that was loaded down with combat gear and equipment, and then hiked to another location, the slang word for it was humping. It was the primary means of getting from one place to the other on foot. To a grunt walking was a way of life. As long as you held the MOS of "03 Infantry" you would always hump. We stopped periodically while on the move for short breaks. I normally kept my bayonet affixed to the end of the rifle. During breaks I would stick the bayonet into the ground and lean on the rifle pistol grip while standing. The Marines did this to ease some of the heavy weight and pressure from the thin pack straps digging into our shoulders.

One day I was moving along in column and came to within the company command post. Our forward movement paused and as usual I stuck my bayonet into the ground to lean on my weapon. I looked up and saw the company commander and the company gunnery sergeant sitting on the ground watching us move slowly past. The company gunny took the opportunity to scold me for doing that. He warned me that the bayonet on my rifle was not meant to be stuck in the ground in that fashion and that I might break the pistol grip of the M16 by leaning on it. I resented his remarks but gripped my rifle by the carrying handle and moved on. Although some Marines had slings on their weapons we did not use them much. While in the bush it would sometimes be impractical to carry a rifle at sling arms. We mostly carried our M16s by the carrying handle, at port arms, or at the ready position.

The straps from the heavy pack would dig into my shoulder muscles causing soreness and stiffness. The amount of time for the breaks while on the march varied with the mission. Breaks for rest and recovery time could be between ten minutes to half an hour. Even during the longer breaks we would usually keep our packs on our shoulders. The Marines would sit on the ground while leaning back on the pack for support. This helped elevate some of the pressure on our shoulders and back. When we did get the word to move out, the command was, "Saddle Up!" The weight on the backs of the Marines was simply too great to stand straight up. Some rolled over on their knees and muscled their way to stand erect while others asked for help by grabbing a Marine's outstretched hands to help pull him up. Many miles of our journeys were covered on foot.

While in our defensive positions it was imperative that we took the time for personal field sanitation and hygiene. This included powdering our feet, drying our socks, shaving, brushing our teeth, cleaning and lubricating our weapons, and tending to insect bites and jungle rot. An iodine solution came as a component of the first aid kit. It was useful in the treatment of jungle rot. The corpsmen used a special cream to aid in the healing process but it was difficult to keep the skin dry and clean so the ointments could be effective. This was hard because of the constant perspiration, rain, and mucky environment.

While one Marine disassembled his weapon for cleaning, another would remain on watch. Each pair of Marines would take turns to clean their weapons. This was done to ensure that there were always rifles fully assembled to return fire on the enemy if necessary. It was very important to keep our weapons, magazines, and ammunition clean. It proved to be valuable because if we engaged with the enemy the chances of our weapons malfunctioning would be minimal. Rifle bore cleaner and a compound called LSA (lubricating oil, small arms), was used for this purpose.

Sometimes we would get lucky and Mike Company would set up a defensive posture next to a river. We would take turns, usually by squads, going into the water to bathe and wash the grime off our bodies. We would always post a Marine on the river bank as security to watch out for Charlie. It was never a problem in getting a Marine to be posted as security because we would always get a volunteer. For the Marine on security it was a little quiet time for himself although he was constantly scanning the immediate area for any suspicious movement. He could also enjoy watching the spectacle of his fellow Marines frolicking in the river. He in turn would get a chance to bathe as soon as the first Marine came out of the river.

Swimming in a river was a rare opportunity for the Marines to thoroughly enjoy themselves. It had its drawbacks but the good out weighed the bad. If a Marine wondered too close to a log or tree roots near the river bank, he would emerge from the river with huge leeches attached to his body. We also had to be on the lookout for snakes and other critters that made the river their home. Some Marines, when seeing they had a leach on them, would try to remove the blood sucking vermin by just pulling them off. This was not always a good idea. The head of the leach could be left embedded in the skin and cause an infection. Some Marines used a sharp pocket knife to poke at the critter in order for it to let go. Others used a straight pin or needle that they had in their sewing kit. Still others just rubbed them with sand or dirt, anything to get them off.

When we were in the rear for rehabilitation we could take outdoor showers. At LZ Baldy there was a small shower made of plywood. It was about a four foot square enclosure. A small tank inside the shower was approximately eight feet off the ground. In order to take a shower a bucket of water had to be fetched from a "water buffalo," also called a water bull. This was a 400-gallon potable water tank that could be trailer-mounted and towed behind a M35A2 2-1/2 ton cargo truck. Once the bucket was filled with water it was poured into the small tank inside the shower.

A dangling rope attached to the tank regulated the flow of water. As the water drained from the bottom of the tank, a Marine could pull and release the rope, in order to soap up and use the water sparingly. It was a little tedious to let a little water cover your body, cut off the flow, soap down, and then repeat the process. An over anxious Marine would find himself covered with soap and the tank out of water. Then he had two choices, refill the tank with a bucket of water, or dry off while the soap was still clinging to his body. Most elected to just dry off and not put up with the hassle of fetching another bucket of water.

At LZ Baldy there was normally a line at the showers especially when the entire company had just returned from the field. You would have to fill a bucket of water and then wait for the ones taking showers to finish. Instead of waiting so long, my squad made it a point to just go down to a flowing rice paddy to take a bath. The water was clear running over the dike and had formed a fairly large pot hole. The water was about chest high and about half the squad could bathe in it at one time. We would also wash our clothes in it which was something we could not do back at the showers.

At Firebase Ross they had a shower unit set up that was run by a generator. A large rubber tank of about a thousand gallons was pre-staged and the water was pumped into the shower outlets. There were about twelve sockets where the water was dispensed and the Marines could stand on wooden pallets while there was a continuous jet stream of spray. We could normally get a half decent shower that way, however the generator would be turned off if every shower head was not being utilized. Therefore, all twelve shower heads would have to have someone under it before the Marine running the generator would allow the water to be pumped. I witnessed a few of the Marine generator operators get royally chewed out by the grunts when the water was turned off in the middle of a shower. After all, the grunts had been in the bush for sometimes thirty or more days and rated to have at least one good shower while back in the rear.

Also in the rear we would visit the camp barber for haircuts and we would even shine our boots. We would have personnel inspections, weapons inspections, and in general prepare three days for our return to the bush. During the time we were in the rear; we could socialize at the Enlisted Club. We had at least one company "beer bust" in which we would barbeque and have beer on ice, sodas, steaks, hot dogs, and hamburgers.

If we were lucky enough to be in the rear when they had a USO show it would be the main attraction. It was nice to break up the every day monotony and escape from reality from time to time. One time a USO show came to LZ Baldy when Mike Company was in the rear. Whenever a band was scheduled it was normally a Filipino band. The bands traveled from the Philippines to play at various American base camps throughout Vietnam. This particular band was on a small stage that had been prepared by the rear echelon personnel. The Marines in attendance sat on wooden benches that faced the stage.

While the band was playing their first musical set we received incoming mortar rounds from the hills in the distance. The rounds began to land inside the compound. Everyone dove for a trench that had been dug around the stage. There were some bunkers and fighting holes scattered throughout the area in which the Marines took cover. Taken by sudden surprise and fear, the Filipino band left their instruments on stage, and dived for the trench as well.

The bombardment subsided after a few minutes and the Marines began to crawl out of the fighting holes, trenches, and bunkers. They took their same seats on the benches facing the stage. Most appeared as if nothing had happened. They elected to ignore Charlie's continual harassment. The band reluctantly returned to the stage after some Marine motivational persuasion. The band started to play once again to the cheers and cat calls from the Marines. The band had brought along two good looking Filipina go-go girls to keep them excited.

During this one USO performance we received incoming three different times. On the third time some shrapnel flew through the air all around us while we hugged the ground in the defensive positions. When the barrage had ended we returned again as usual to watch the show. The band noticed that one of the drums had been pierced by some shrapnel along with the base guitar. They immediately packed their equipment and proceeded to depart the area as quickly as possible. All the while the Marines were laughing and booing their cowardly behavior. I suppose it had become second nature for us. We had to have a little incoming to spruce up our lives.

One of the bad things about going back to the rear was that some of the Marines were able to get their hands on marijuana. The Vietnamese locals would appear at the perimeter fence and proposition some of the Marines to buy their "grass." There were always that ten per cent of Marines that tended to go astray and get into trouble. Most knew the consequences but didn't really care. Some Marines who bought the marijuana got caught while others did not. Those who got caught were punished under the UCMJ (Uniform Code of Military Justice).

At times they would smoke the pot while on hole watch back in the rear. There would most likely be some stoned Marines somewhere around the perimeter at any given night. It usually would be some of the rear echelon personnel that would entice some of the Marines in our company to try it. Although it wasn't a big problem within Mike Company it did exist to a degree. The good thing was that they could not get their hands on it while we were actually in the bush for twenty or thirty days at a time.

A story circulated throughout the enlisted ranks, of a Marine who made it a habit to get enough marijuana while at LZ Baldy, to last a few days in the bush. One morning when one of his buddies checked on him in his foxhole, he found the dead Marine. Sometime during the night a VC had slipped up on his position and managed to slit his throat while he slept. He had been noticed the night before smoking a joint while on security watch. You could never let your guard down, especially at night. Alertness was the key to survival during the night. Marijuana had no place in a foxhole, perimeter watch, or anywhere else in Vietnam. There were a few unfortunate men who lost their lives because of their defiant attitude of not conforming to military rules and regulations that governed the military service regarding drug use.

When a Marine found himself a little spare time he had to use it wisely. Some took the time to relax and write letters to their loved ones. Others liked to listen to music on their transistor radios. There were always weapons cleaning going on. Time off to do as one wished was hard to come by. We spent a lot of time out on patrols, ambushes, or moving as a company or platoon to other defensive positions. Marines would try to sleep in the day time but at night there was always a minimum of a fifty per cent watch. This meant that out of every two men, one would have to be awake, and on alert.

The Marines could manage to find time for some much needed sleep during the day but it was never a sound sleep. One would undoubtedly be interrupted in some form or fashion. It could be that you were called on to go on a work detail or choppers could be flying in and out of the perimeter. It could be that jets were flying overhead bombarding an area around us or an artillery battery shelling likely enemy locations. It could be that a squad out on patrol ran into enemy contact and you could hear the firefight at a distance. It could be that we were fighting off insects, rodents, ants, snakes, and the like. It could be the rain hitting your poncho or that you had chills because you were soaking wet. It could be that is was just too hot and humid to sleep. It was always something.

Every grunt I saw seemed to be drained of energy. Some were irritable, appeared very tired, and had black rings under their eyes from the lack of sleep and rest. Their facial skin seemed to be sunken in and sunburned from the hot tropical sun. Many had lost so much weight that their trousers were too big for them around the waist. They had a certain stare that when you talked to them they would look right through you. It was known as the grunt stare, the stare of a very tired combat veteran.

Constant radio communications were essential. Without communications there would not have been air strikes, artillery, no resupply choppers for chow and water, no ammunition, and no letters from home. There would not have been medevac choppers to take out the sick, wounded, and killed Marines. There would not have been the R&R out of country or the rehabilitation back in the rear. A Marine's mere existence depended on voice communications. A squad could possibly be totally annihilated without a good radio and no one would have known what had happened until it was too late. The adjacent friendly units had to be contacted so that we did not fire our weapons on them by mistake or they fire on us. The SITREP (Situation Reports) during the night let everyone in the company know that all was secure at our position or that there was enemy movement.

The enemy was also very good at scrambling the transmissions and interpreting what was said. Consequently, each Marine had to be careful what he said over the radio net, especially when engaging with the NVA. I saw a Marine in Antenna Valley that got shot right through the radio on his back. The communist aimed at the radio operators in order to knock out communications and cause confusion within the unit. If we were lucky we would get another radio to replace the one destroyed. The unfortunate thing was that there was a dead Marine that had been lost to sniper fire because he was carrying a PRC-77 squad radio. We would get another Marine from within our ranks to take his place regardless of his training or Military Occupational Specialty.

If a Marine had ripped and torn utility trousers or T-shirts, while in the bush, a replacement issue would have to be ordered through the supply system. This was done by utilizing the chain of command. It was the same procedure for any kind of military gear. The individual Marine informed his fireteam leader what he needed, the fireteam leader informed his squad leader, and the squad leader informed the platoon guide. The platoon guide consolidated the gear requests for the entire platoon and then sent them through the proper channels until they ended up at battalion supply back at the base camp.

To save time sometimes the squad leader just asked everyone what they needed and reported that to the platoon guide. Sometimes it would take weeks for a replacement item to arrive in the bush. When you finally got your order delivered by chopper, you could just about bet that it would be the wrong size. Regardless, we had to take what we got. I saw Marines wearing utility trousers that had both knees completely out, no material in the seat of the trousers, or trouser legs just dangling around the legs from being torn and ripped. It reminded me of a bunch of hobo's without a home.

We would set up hooches in the bush or at least that's what we called them. They were our own personal free style living quarters. Mainly it consisted of a poncho laid out on the ground and the poncho liner tied to some bushes, trees, sticks or anything else available to get it about two or three feet above the ground. This shelter would help serve to keep the intense heat off during the day. It could be arranged to suit each individual's life style.

Some were sloppy housekeepers with gear adrift and some would be a little neater. The pack or the utility shirt was normally used to serve as a pillow. I used to fold up my utility jacket on the pack for a pillow during the day but found it necessary to wear it at night. This was because even in the "Nam" it got a little chilly when the sun went down. The long sleeves on the utility jacket also helped to keep some of the crawling bugs and flying mosquitoes from making mince meat out of my bare arms.

I arranged my gear in my hooch so that if I had to jump into my fighting hole, I would have my weapon, magazines, or any other ordnance at my finger tips. I would sleep with my rifle under my arm or under my legs. I ensured that I never walked away anywhere without taking my M16. These hooches were self-made and they served the purpose. Of course, when we were in the bunkers in the rear or on fire support bases, we would have to contend with the rats. Although there were cots to sleep on at the fire support bases there was always something that did not make life as pleasant as one hoped.

We never dug company or platoon straddle trenches to relieve ourselves in the bush, instead, we dug individual catholes. The dimensions of a cathole by the book is probably around one foot long, one foot wide, and 6-12 inches deep. Most of the catholes that Marines dug would average about six inches deep and 4 inches wide, just enough to cover the stool. This was due to either laziness or the ground was too hard. So if you were not careful you could step right in the middle of someone's crap. A cathole should be at least 100 yards away from the unit. In Vietnam, there was no way a Marine was going to wonder off 100 yards outside the perimeter by himself.

We would have to save toilet paper from our C-Ration accessory packs to accumulate enough for one use. Sometimes one might need two or three individual packs of toilet paper to do the dirty deed. One little packet, as small as it was, would not be enough. When we went outside of friendly lines, we would have to make sure that even if security was posted, a rifle or pistol would be taken with us. This was an avoidance countermeasure not to be totally surprised by the enemy with your pants down. Charlie was not patient enough nor was he courteous enough to allow a Marine time to relieve himself before he tried to kill you. He didn't care if you were taking a crap or not.

One June day as I sat under my poncho liner hooch I could smell a lingering foul odor. It got stronger when the wind shifted in my direction. I could not figure out where it was coming from. It was not long until I noticed my platoon sergeant heading my way with his E-tool in hand. He was a staff sergeant and a Samoan Marine. He was a short, stocky, and very robust. He came to within about five feet from my poncho liner that I had tied to some bushes over my head. He dug a cathole quickly, dropped his trousers, and squatted down to take a crap. I peered at him through the bushes from under my poncho liner. I realized that was where the foul order had been coming from.

"Hey, staff sergeant," I said. "You're not going to take a shit right there are you?"

"Yeah, I'm gonna take a shit," he replied.

"Hell, that's what I've smelled all this time. Have you been covering your holes?" I asked.

"Yeah, I've been covering them. Don't worry about it," he replied. Directly there was a sigh of relief coming from the staff sergeant.

"Holy Cow," I said in protest. "It smells like shit over here where I have my hooch."

Standing up and pulling up his trousers he said in response, "Dat's cause it is shit, goddamit! Whut do ya expect it ta smell like, roses?"

"Why don't you go outside the lines like everybody else," I asked in anger.

"Don't tell me where to take a shit, there, PFC. I'll take a shit wherever I please," he replied.

"Okay," I retorted. "Go right ahead, but how would you like it if I took a shit right next to your sleeping hole?"

He covered his cathole and then walked away slowly swinging his E-tool in his right hand and stuffing the extra toilet paper in his cargo pocket.

"A little whiff-o-shit won't harm you Marine," he said as he walked away.

"If all the Marines around the perimeter took a dump in the CP, everyone would be sleeping in it," I said loudly.

The platoon sergeant mumbled something under his breath about not being able to take a decent crap in the bush without getting chastised by some smart ass private first class. On his next outing with E-tool in hand, I did notice that this time he went outside the perimeter to relieve himself. Maybe I had gotten my point across that I was angry at the fact that he had relieved himself so close to my hooch. I glanced around my surroundings to see if there was a better location to make my bush hooch. On second thought, I figured that I was just too comfortable in my little domain to be bothered by the smell of a pile of crap. I would definitely make it a point not to settle in at our next position anywhere near the staff sergeant.

I used to run out of writing paper while I was in the bush. There were a couple of times when I would write to my sister, Janice, and use C-Ration toilet paper to write on. Actually, it worked better than expected. The toilet paper from the accessory packs was course enough to write on legibly. It was about a four inch by four inch square and I did not have any problem writing on it with my pen. Even though the paper was of very poor quality for doing the job it was intended for it had rendered another service for me.

Water was another vital means of our survival. If you could do without anything else in Vietnam, you had to have safe drinking water in order to survive. There were various ways of obtaining water. We could fill up plastic water jugs from a river or stream, treat it with iodine tablets for purification, let it stand for at least thirty minutes, and then fill our canteens for drinking. If we were just passing through a river, stream, or flowing rice paddy, the Marines wading in the water would remove their helmets, scoop up a helmet full of water, and pour it over their sweaty heads, faces, and backs. By the time a Marine reached the other side, he had managed to fill one or two of his canteens, while still on the move.

Water was precious since we never knew when we might have another chance to fill our canteens. Occasionally, depending on our location, we would get some pre-filled water jugs from the rear that was sent out on the resupply choppers. This method of resupply was very limited and did not happen very often. We were mostly on our own to find other sources of water when the water jugs became empty. Patrols were usually organized to scout the area for more water.

On one occasion I was down to my last canteen of water when Hawkeye and I was standing security for the Combat Engineers next to a pagoda. We were sitting under a small grass hooch that had no sides, just a grass roof supported by four small poles. It began to rain and the water began dripping

CH-53 Sea Stallion landed in a rice paddy to transport Mike Company back to the rear for three days of rehab. Some Marines are carrying plastic water jugs.

off the grass roof and onto the ground. I managed to fill two canteens with the rain water dripping from the grass roof. I tasted a canteen of water and it tasted like straw. The rain became heavier so I poured out the two canteens that I had filled. I placed all six of my canteens under the dripping water. Hawkeye thought it was a good idea and did the same on the opposite side of the hooch. I filled each canteen to the top. After the water was treated with iodine tablets I tasted it once again. It still tasted like straw even after the roof had been washed off by the rain. I drank the water anyway regardless of what it tasted like. I had to make do with what resources were available at the time.

Some of the best tasting water available was from the wells in the villages. An empty C-ration fruit can, tied to a long rip cord, could be lowered deep into the well to fetch the water. Whenever our squad passed through a village we would always fill our canteens from the village wells and drink from a fruit can. Some of the Marines did not put halogen tablets into their canteens. They figured that if the local villagers could drink the well water without any treatment, it should be safe to drink. I made it a habit to purify my drinking water no matter where it came from. I had been medevaced to the Cam Ranh Bay Army Hospital after drinking impure water from a stream and had learned my lesson. It had been a bad experience for me. I had always tried to keep all my canteens full to the very top when possible and treat the water with the iodine tablets. Besides fearing the unknown, the second worst fear was being without water.

While in the bush, if we were to stay in one specific area for several days, the C-rations might be supplemented with SP's (Special Packs). These cellophane packs came in cardboard boxes which were about a three foot square and contained all sorts of goodies. There was letter writing gear, candy, cigarettes, razors, pens, and other assorted health and comfort items. When these boxes were flown in by chopper, the items were evenly distributed throughout the squads and platoons. By the time everybody got their fair share of the supplies, one Marine might end up with two packs of cigarettes, two or three candy bars, and perhaps a writing tablet. Sometimes along with the SP's we would receive large cans of apple juice, grape juice, or orange juice. A single Marine would manage to get a half canteen cup of juice. I did not smoke so I always gave my cigarettes to Hawkeye.

The Meal, Combat, Individual (MCI) was the official name of the combat rations issued from 1958-1980. The Marines simply called them C-Rations. There were different types of C-Ration meals. Twelve small boxes containing the meals came in a cardboard box about two feet long and one foot wide. The cases were wrapped with two strands of bailing wire. Marines used the open end of their rifle flash suppressor (located on the end of the barrel), their E-tools, bayonets, and Ka-bars, to break the wires. Besides the twelve meals in the box there would be about six P-38 can openers, known to the Marines as a "John Wayne."

There were three different units; B-1, B-2, and B-3.

The B-1 unit consisted of: Meat Choices (in small cans), Beef Steak, Ham and Eggs (Chopped), Ham Slices, and Turkey Loaf. The fruit choices were Applesauce, Fruit Cocktail, Peaches, or Pears. It also had Crackers (7), Peanut Butter, Candy Disc (Chocolate, Solid Chocolate, Cream, or Coconut, and an accessory pack.

B-2 Units consisted of: Meat Choices (in larger cans), Beans and Wieners, Spaghetti and Meatballs, Beefsteak (with Potatoes and Gravy), Ham and Lima Beans, Meatballs and Beans. It also had Crackers (4), Cheese Spread (Processed, Caraway, and Pimento), Fruit Cake, Pecan Roll, Pound Cake, and an accessory pack.

B-3 Units consisted of: Meat Choices (in small cans), Boned Chicken, Chicken and Noodles, Meat Loaf, Spiced Beef. It also contained Bread (White), Cookies (4), Cocoa Beverage Powder, and Jam.

All units contained an accessory pack that included; Plastic Spoon, Salt, Pepper, Instant Coffee, Sugar, Non-dairy Creamer, 2 Chicklets Gum, Pack of 4 cigarettes (either Winston, Marlboro, Salem, Pall Mall, Camel, Chesterfield, Kent, Lucky Strike, or Kool), Moisture Resistant Matches, and one Toilet Paper.

We would mix the meals to suit our tastes. It was dining cuisine at its finest. Being seasoned Marine grunts, we knew how to spruce up a common meal. When we found the time we preferred to spice up our C-Rations which helped relieve the monotony of having the same taste day in and day out. Sometimes four or five of us would get together and prepare a variety of meats and cook them in a steel helmet over an open flame. Tabasco sauce or "hot sauce" was our favorite means of seasoning and was regularly used by the Marines when available. Just about every Marine had his own bottle of hot sauce in his pack. When our gourmet meal was finally heated we would fill our canteen cups for our share of the feast. It was well worth the effort to take the time and prepare a meal this way. We could never prepare a meal in this manner over an open flame at night because we would surely draw enemy fire.

We called one concoction of a drink, "mocoa." This was instant coffee and cocoa powder mixed together. It made for a pretty good cup of Joe. Coffee could be heated in one of our empty fruit cans. Some Marines even improvised a wire handle for their so-called coffee mug and carried it around with them in their pack. It prevented them having to make a new cup every time they wanted a cup of coffee. The Marines had the standard issue heavy gauge stainless steel canteen cups, but a drink mix would take less time if heated in a tin can.

I also used to take my powdered cream and mix it in peaches, fruit cocktail, pears, or applesauce to give it added flavor. We would heat our chow with trioxin heat tablets which was issued separately from the C-Ration cases. These heat tabs were officially called "fuel, compressed, trioxide, ration, heating, chemical." The heat tab was placed in a do-it-your-self cooking stove made out of C-ration cans, ignited, and the can of food to be cooked placed on the stove. The heat tab was about an inch and a half from the bottom of the can to be heated. It was important that this heating chemical be used with adequate ventilation because the fumes would irritate your eyes and make breathing difficult. I saw many Marines run from out under their hooch after inhaling the toxic fumes. These heat tabs would burn approximately three minutes which was just enough time to heat a canteen cup of coffee or a can of chow.

To make a cooking stove we took the smaller cans which contained items such as pound cake or crackers, removed the contents, and made a cooking stove out of them. We would use a John Wayne can opener to make several holes around the top and bottom rim sides of the can. Then at the bottom rim of the can we would cut about an inch and a half line on two sides of the can and push the sides in. This allowed ventilation to get to the trioxin heat tab. Some Marines carried a church key and used the can opener end to puncture holes around both the top and bottom rims. This actually worked better than using the John Wayne, but not all Marines could get their hands on a church key. Once a stove was made it was normally carried in the pack so it could be used over and over again without making a new one every time you wanted to heat a meal.

If Marines could get their hands on C-4 (plastic explosives, carried in one pound bars), they would use it instead of heat tabs. Although C-4 was handy in blowing up mines and booby traps it could also be used for cooking. A small piece cut from the putty textured explosive would burn very hot and very fast. In a matter of seconds a Marine would have a large can of meat bubbling over at the top of the can. I have seen Marines drop their meals in the dirt because they were holding on to the bare end of the peeled back lid and it got too hot to hold. Most used a cut piece of cardboard off the C-ration cartons to protect their fingers when grasping the lid of the can being heated. Although it was hard to come by, some fortunate Marines who did manage to obtain C-4, had no problem in heating a meal.

Another field ration that was not as readily available in the bush was called "long rations." At least, that is what the Marines called it. The contents came in a robust tin foil wrapper that resembled a very small sandbag. The bag was so strong that you almost had to use a Ka-bar knife or bayonet to cut open the package. The food was dehydrated so all we had to do was to add water, stir, and eat. It was a lot faster to fix a meal but the drawback was that it required a lot of precious water from our canteens. The accessory pack included with the long ration meal contained candy bars. Other than the candy bars the choices of food was about the same as the C-ration meals.

One very hot day we were in the bush in a defensive perimeter. A CH-46 helicopter was en route to drop off resupplies. I was assigned to the ten man working detail to help off load the supplies. As the chopper approached one of the senior Marines in the work detail tossed out a yellow smoke grenade. This was to mark the position where we wanted the chopper to drop the supplies. There was a large cargo net swaying beneath the chopper's belly and the pilot hovered into position. After the cargo net was dropped to the ground the chopper ascended high into the air and turned 180 degrees to head back to the base camp.

The working detail scrambled to unfasten and pull back the cargo net. We began to separate the rations, water, and ammunition. As we sorted the supplies we noticed some strange boxes. There were several five gallon cardboard containers that we didn't know if they were food or accessory packs. A closer inspection determined that they contained "ice cream." We

CH-46 Sea Knight helicopter landing with resupplies. These choppers were the life blood for the Marines.

opened a box because it was sagging in the middle and the melted ice cream had begun to run down the sides of the box. The ice cream had almost completely melted. There was only one thing to do, we summoned the Marines to bring their canteen cups to get some of the melted ice cream. I never saw Marines move so fast scrambling to find their canteen cups.

One by one they appeared from all sides of the perimeter and dipped their canteen cups into the now liquid ice cream. It was like dipping a glass into a punch bowl. Some Marines were too impatient to find their canteen cups and just cupped their hands into the ice cream to get a slurp. We opened all the ice cream boxes and it was a spectacle to see all the Marines dipping their canteen cups into the sweet liquid. All the boxes were vanilla flavor. The company gunnery sergeant within the vicinity of the CP yelled out, "One frag grenade will kill you all! Spread out and get back to your fighting positions!"

After seeing our attempts to save the precious dessert was futile, the working detail dumped the remaining contents on the ground and stacked the boxes for disposal. We never knew if the permanent personnel back at the base camp mess hall sent the ice cream out to us in an attempt to lookout for our welfare or if it was just a practical joke. That was the last time I saw ice cream delivered to the bush. I had heard that the company commander radioed back to the rear and told them not to send anymore ice cream to the field. If nothing else, it gave us something to talk about.

One time our defensive position was located closer to Da Nang. We were positioned on top of a knoll overlooking an Army camp. They considered themselves as being in the bush. We set up very quickly and when I looked down toward the Army camp I could not believe my eyes. The camp was set up with field tents that had cots inside to sleep on. When the Army infantry came back from patrols they slept off the ground. There was also a mess tent with hot chow. I located Hawkeye and told him that this must be the "Life of Riley" and that we had joined the wrong branch of service.

"Yeah, they have the good life," Hawkeye said. "Maybe we can sneak a little chow from the mess tent. I'll bet if we got to know some of them on a friendly basis we could trade things, tit for tat."

"Sounds good to me," I responded, "but I doubt if they will trade anything for C-Rations."

The platoon commander very quickly passed the word that we were not allowed in or around the tents of the Army camp. This did not stop some of the Marines who managed to sneak down the hill for a hot meal. The soldiers really didn't have a problem with the Marines coming into their camp. Even though the Army was so close that you could smell the aroma of cooked food coming from the mess tent, I was content to eat my own C-Rations. For I didn't want to get in trouble after the Army camp was put off limits for us.

All the letters that I received from home while in Vietnam were torn up and burned. I did this because I did not want to get captured knowing that some communist VC or NVA might have gotten their hands on any of my personal letters. I felt it was privy information and for my eyes only. I therefore avoided having them fall into any enemy hands and allowing them to spread propaganda to my family members. The last thing I needed was for the enemy to obtain my home address and write letters to my parents.

I had heard stories that as a prisoner of war they would write to your mother and father and tell them that you were captured and that you were being tortured. I just could not allow this to happen and cause undue torment for my parents. I figured that if I ever did get captured, at least I wouldn't have my home address on me. I made it a point to destroy every letter that I received from home because I thought it best under the circumstances. There was nothing I hated more, than to watch the letters that I had received from my loved ones, go up in smoke.

When I did receive letters from home it took several days and some-times weeks to reach me. By the time I finally got to read the letter it was old news. At times I would be reading mail that was two to three weeks old. I had wished often that I could contact my parents by phone but I never had that opportunity. When I mailed a letter from Vietnam I merely wrote "free" in the top right hand corner of the envelope. Uncle Sam was good about that. As long as you were in a combat zone all the personal letters could be sent free of charge. We never needed stamps.

When the resupply choppers flew into our company area we would get excited knowing that we would be getting the ordnance and ammunition required to keep Charlie at bay. We would at times get water in plastic jugs to quench our thirsts. Also we would get food to fill our bellies and mail to boost our morale. Of all the things we received during resupply, the letters from home were the most welcome.

Reading about what my mother, father, and younger brother were doing back in Kentucky on Cherry Hill Farm was a total delight. My mother never let me down. She wrote to me very often and her words of love, encourage-ment, concern, wisdom, and advice kept me inspired and motivated to make it out of Vietnam in one piece. As I read each of her letters to me I could almost hear her saying the words. She was a remarkable woman and I loved her with all my heart. She was always on my mind.

Half way through my tour we got a brand new second lieutenant as our platoon commander. He was fresh from The Basic School at Quantico, Vir-ginia. He decided that he would lead a platoon size patrol and set up an am-bush very early in the morning. He wanted to be in place waiting for the en-emy no later than 0400. He briefed all the squad leaders the night before and told them to meet with him again at 0330 the morning of the ambush. He gave them a Five Paragraph Order. The squad leaders said it was strictly by the book. The combat briefing was best remembered by the acronym "SMEAC." It stood for Situation, Mission, Execution, Administration and Logistics, and Command and Signal. Under each element certain details were covered about the mission at hand. Although there were different types of combat orders the breakdown of the Five Paragraph Order went like this.

1. SITUATION. The situation paragraph contained information on the overall status and disposition of both friendly and enemy forces. It contained three subparagraphs:
   a. Enemy Forces. This subparagraph contained essential infor-mation concerning the enemy's composition, disposition, location, capabilities, limitations, and recent activities of the enemy. The acronym SALUTE was used.
      1) Size – enemy squad, platoon, etc.
      2) Activity - enemy digging in, bivouacking, etc.

3) Location - six digit grid
4) Unit – VC, NVA, etc.
5) Time – when the enemy was last observed
6) Equipment – AK47s, RPGs, Mortars, etc.

b. Friendly Forces. This subparagraph contained essential information concerning the mission of the next higher unit, location and mission of adjacent units, and mission of non-organic supporting units. Information in this subparagraph can be remembered with the acronym HAS.

1) Higher
2) Adjacent
3) Supporting

c. Attachments and Detachments. Non-organic units attached (+) and/or organic units detached (-) from the unit.

2. MISSION. This paragraph provided a clear and concise statement of what the unit was to accomplish. The mission statement was the heart of the order and should answer the following five questions (the five W's): Who, What, When, Where, and Why.

3. EXECUTION. The execution paragraph contained the information needed to conduct the operation. The paragraph was divided into three paragraphs:

a. Concept of Operations. This was a general explanation of the tactical plan. It included a brief scheme of maneuver from start to conclusion, type of attack, and fire support plan.

b. Tasks. The specific missions that were to be accomplished by each subordinate element of the unit. It was the subordinate's unit mission statements.

c. Coordinating Instructions. The specific instructions and tasks that were applied to two or more units. Information given included order of movement, planned combat formations, tactical and fire control measures (i.e., phase lines, check-points), and any other tasks that pertained to the mission.

4. ADMINISTRATION AND LOGISTICS. This paragraph contained information or instructions pertaining to rations and ammunition; location of the distribution point, corpsman, and aid station; handling of prisoners of war; and other administrative and supply matters.

5. COMMAND AND SIGNAL. This paragraph contained instructions and information relating to command and communications (control) functions. It contained two subparagraphs:

a. Signal. Gave signal instructions for the operation such as frequencies, call signs, pyrotechnics, challenge and password, and brevity codes.

b. Command. Identified the chain of command and their location (including the corpsman) before, during, and after the operation.

Very early the following morning I could hear my squad leader, Travieso, arguing with the second lieutenant that we could not set an ambush in the area he had designated on the map. He told the lieutenant that it was smack dap in the middle of a rice paddy. He also suggested that we set the ambush closer to the village that was about a klick away.

"No!" exclaimed the lieutenant as he pointed his pin light on the map. "We must set in as I have indicated on the map." The squad leader continued to argue saying that we could not set up in an open rice paddy. "Listen, lance corporal," the lieutenant replied. "I'm giving the orders around here and this is where we are going to set in. Is that understood?"

"Sir, Yes Sir," the squad leader responded. "Sir, What ever you say, Sir."

The squads were then assembled and we started to move out in the dark. On our way to the location we passed by a Vietnamese man and women sleeping on the ground just off the trail. We could see by the moonlit sky that they had made their sleeping mat out of C-Ration cardboard. They were snuggled up against one another dressed in what looked like black pajamas. A couple of Marines purposely went off the trail and harassed them by kicking them and waking them up from their slumber. It was not uncommon to see Vietnamese sleeping in the open in this manner.

We finally arrived at the spot on the map where the platoon commander wanted to set up the ambush. The squad leaders began to set up each squad in their designated sectors and fields of fire. We soon discovered that we were in fact waist deep in water on the edge of a rice paddy. When I got to the position where I was to remain for the ambush the water line was right up to my cartridge belt. The cattails and reeds shot up from the top of the water about a foot over my head even while I was standing. I couldn't believe we were going to wait out an ambush until dawn in this muck.

I asked Travieso if I could move back further to set up where the water was not as deep. He told me that wouldn't work because everyone had to be on line to avoid shooting our own people in a firefight. I had to tie in with two other Marines on my left and right. I could not stand for hours like that so I squatted down onto the water. The bent over reeds and cattails helped to keep me somewhat afloat without too much effort. My canteens were only partially full with water so the air pockets inside helped to make my cartridge belt act like a semi-floatation device. I had to make an extra effort to keep my rifle up high enough to keep it from submerging under the water.

It was quite miserable setting up an ambush at the edge of a rice paddy. Once in awhile I would have to reposition myself because I was sinking into the mud. I'd shift left or right in order to pick another spot and sit down again onto the reeds. Each time I moved bubbles would come up from the mud and the smell was almost unbearable. It was like standing in a sewer. I noticed that my bandoleer of M16 magazines fully loaded had slipped down into the water. That was the last thing I needed was for my ammunition to malfunction because it was wet. I repositioned the bandoleer high up on my shoulder so the water could run out of the magazines.

The moonlit landscape provided a beautiful light bouncing off the water. In the light there were vast swarms of mosquitoes and gnats flying around. The mosquitoes were relentless and unbearable. They were in my eyes, ears, hair and biting me all over my upper body. I turned the collar of my utility jacket up to cover part of my neck and rolled the sleeves down but it was no use. There was nothing I could do except take the bites and stings. Only the lower part of my body that was submerged in the murky water was free from the relentless torment.

There was no telling what was lurking around my feet and legs. I just knew I would be covered with leeches and I expected that a snake might invade my territory. I was so mad I didn't even know who the Marines were to my left and right. I began to silently curse the second lieutenant. How could he be so stupid as to set up an ambush in waist deep rice paddy water? As time passed slowly by I heard myself verbally cursing the lieutenant out loud. The Marines around me were not happy campers either. I think I heard every profanity word that was ever created and some that had not yet been created.

We sat in this position until day light which was about two hours. There would be no enemy contact on this ambush, not in waist deep water and muck. One of the squad leaders who was loud enough for everyone around him to hear said, "This is bullshit, lets get the fuck out of this rice paddy. We're right in the open and water is up to our chests." This sparked several other protests from the Marines because we were sitting and standing in the mud and water. Finally, the lieutenant gave the order to move back to the CP.

We started to hump back to the perimeter in single file. All the Marines were soaked up to their waist line and nasty smelly mud clung to their boots. We were now on dry land for a change. The Marines started pulling up their trousers legs looking for leaches. You could hear them cursing as they pulled them off. We started following a trail that was going up a small hill. The ground had small loose rocks to walk on and there were bushes on both sides of the trail. Marines could still be heard complaining even though we were heading back to the CP.

The 1st squad was in the front of the column and they decided to stop on the trail and take a rest. The lieutenant was just behind them and had taken a seat on the ground just a few feet off the trail. As the Marines from the other two squads walked past the lieutenant to take the lead, some started telling the lieutenant that he was a stupid boot officer with no common sense. They said that he could not read a map and didn't know how to set up a proper ambush. The lieutenant ignored their comments and was frantically looking over his map with a compass in hand trying to figure out where we were. A couple of daring Marines cursed at him as they walked passed and spat on his boots.

To my surprise, the lieutenant did nothing. He just inclined backward with his back resting on a large rock. He was still pretending to look over his map for it was obvious he did not know what he was doing. He stuffed his map in his trouser cargo pocket and sat with his head down. He looked at the saliva on the tips of his boots. He looked up and made eye contact with me just as I started to pass him. It was if he was expecting me to spit on him as well. I did not. I figured the lieutenant had learned a lesson, the hard way. He must have realized that he had made a mistake and now was losing control and discipline over his men. He most likely wished that he had listened to the more experienced squad leader when he briefed them earlier that morning.

When we got back inside the perimeter with the rest of the company the second lieutenant called for Travieso to give him some pointers about map reading. Travieso was selected instead one of the other squad leaders because he was more experienced and had a reputation of knowing his stuff in the bush. Our new platoon commander wanted a refresher course in land navigation and how the bush Marines set up proper ambushes. Some of our squad members heard this and you could hear a few sneers and laughs. At first Travieso was somewhat reluctant, but then as he and the lieutenant sat on the ground, Travieso started plotting grids with the compass and asking the lieutenant questions. It was what Travieso did best, shared all his experience with other Marines in need. He was a great Marine combat veteran and squad leader. By the time Travieso was done with the platoon commander, he was confident that the lieutenant could read a map, set up ambushes, call in close air support, and request medevac and resupply choppers.

The next time Mike Company was on the move, our squad noticed that the lieutenant had affixed rank insignia to the front of his helmet. It was a gold bar which indicated second lieutenant.

A few of the Marines had some comments to make. "You can tell he's a boot lieutenant," a Marine said. "You just don't wear "butter bars" or any other rank insignia on the front of your helmet. That's a bullseye as far as Charlie is concerned.

Travieso approached him and said, "You've gotta take that bar off your helmet, lieutenant."

"Why?" the lieutenant asked. "That's where I've been instructed to wear it."

Travieso replied, "You can wear it on your helmet if you want to, but I'm gonna tell you like it is, Sir. A sniper's bullet will have your name on it. There are a few choice targets that Charlie prefers as prime targets. Just to name a few; radio operators, machine gunners, point-man, tail end Charlie, and most of all second lieutenants wearing a shiny gold bar on their helmets that glitter in the sunlight. So you can wear it if you want, lieutenant. Just stay far enough away from me so that I don't catch a stray sniper round."

Feeling a bit bitter over the boldness of Lance Corporal Travieso's remarks, the lieutenant swore under his breath. He removed his helmet, took off the insignia, and put it in his pocket. While walking away Travieso grinned at the lieutenant. "Stick close to me, lieutenant, and you may learn a few things here in the Nam." The squad thought it was nice of Lance Corporal Travieso to "square away" the platoon commander once again. As time progressed the lieutenant began to pick up a few valuable tricks of the trade. After he realized that there was more to being a leader than just barking orders, he began to learn from the squad leaders and became quite effective. He eventually smoothed out the rough edges like anyone else who had just arrived in country.

One day while on a patrol my squad saw six VC with AK47 rifles running across a rice paddy. We were out of range with our M16s and wanted to get closer before they disappeared into the treeline. They were about eight hundred meters away. The squad leader was the first one I had when I first arrived in Mike Company. He gave us the command to double time across the rice patty so we could catch up with the enemy. We took off running after them as fast as we could. Our helmets were bobbing up and down to where we could barely see where we were going. We soon began to tire and became short of breath because of the heat and humidity. We started firing as we ran forward. The VC kept running since we could not take good aim while running. A few of the Marines dropped back in total exhaustion. Our pursuit after the enemy stopped abruptly because we now had two Marines who were suffering from heat exhaustion and one from head stroke. A medevac chopper had to be called in to medevac the Marine out who was suffering from heat stroke.

The VC had escaped into the treeline. We didn't get one kill. The squad leader was later reprimanded by the company gunnery sergeant for ordering the squad to double-time in the intense heat. We learned our lesson the hard way, that in temperature in excess of over one hundred degrees, we could not run with full combat gear and still be effective. It made me think of all the forced marches that we went on while in boot camp and infantry training. Those 15-20 mile hikes were designed for speed, however, speed was never a factor in moving from one place to another in Vietnam when you were on foot. There were just too many mines and booby traps.

On another occasion, as the company was moving together on our way to another position, we entered a small wooded area overlooking some rice paddy fields. Suddenly we saw five VC running with weapons on the opposite side of the dikes and quite a distance away. The command was given to open fire on our right flank in the direction of the enemy. My squad opened up with semi-automatic and automatic fire. They were trying to put lead on target and were not taking well aimed shots. A few Marines were firing sporadically from the hip (John Wayne style) and others with the butt of the rifles under their armpits instead of into their shoulders. We watched as the VC entered a treeline unharmed. We had missed our target of opportunity.

The company gunny came back from the front of the column to where all the firing had taken place. He asked if we got any gooks. One Marine said that they all got away.

He began to rant and rave at us. "How were you firing those weapons, on automatic, Right?"

One Marine told him that we had done just that. He began to cuss and raise all hell with us. It was followed by a lecture from the former drill instructor.

"Whenever you fire at the enemy at a distance use sight alignment, sight picture, and trigger control. Just like you were taught in boot camp. You can't hit shit with your weapons on automatic at long distances. Do you people think you're John Wayne or something? Now you men settle down and start aiming in properly on your targets. I can't believe you all let every one of those gooners get away without hitting one."

He grabbed a M16 from one of the squad members and demonstrated what he meant by sight alignment, sight picture, and trigger control. He shoved the M16 back at the Marine and walked back to the front of the column. As he walked away I noticed the sawed off shotgun that the gunny carried with him in the bush in addition to his .45 pistol. He never carried a M16 rifle. He claimed that the Marines of Mike Company were there to protect his ass from Charlie. He had various rounds such as slugs, buck-shot, and bee hive. When we used to get into a firefight we would occasionally hear the Gunny fire the shot gun which had a distinctive sound. It gave us more motivation and spirit to continue through the battle knowing that the Gunny was fighting along with us. He was as tough as nails but respected by all of Mike Company. I would never forget him.

Here a lesson was learned once again. We would have to aim in at the enemy in order to make direct hits. Without any killed or wounded VC and NVA, we were expending ammo for nothing. The squad leader would always try to emphasize fire discipline which meant that we were to conserve our ammunition. We never knew when we might need it most.

One of the things that intrigued me was when air support was called in during contact with the enemy and the jets dropped napalm on the target. It could be that it was dropped on enemy troops in the open, in treelines, or on entire villages. Napalm was nothing more than a polystyrene, benzene, and gasoline mixture that produced flames and fire which engulfed all life where it exploded. An enemy hit with napalm would either be burned alive or die from suffocation. The ground would shake and all that could be seen would be fire and smoke. It was a welcome smell for the grunts, for they knew that Charlie could not possibly survive when engaged in a direct hit. At times we could see smoldering and burning bodies that the napalm had hit. The combination of burning flesh and hair, however, gave off a very unpleasant order up close. The smell of napalm to all the Marines established our presence as being superior to the VC and NVA. It was truly the smell of victory.

When we received enemy fire from a village we would immediately return fire. Sometimes we would call for additional fire support in the form of fixed wing, helicopter, or artillery. After the firing ceased we would proceed into the village and search everything in sight. We would throw grenades into bunkers and tunnels. We would look for mines and booby traps. We would look for pungi pits and other devices used to inflict casualties on the Americans. A designated Tunnel Rat within the unit would proceed into the tunnels looking for the elusive enemy. All the huts were checked. Things were turned upside down looking for weapons and ammunition. Containers of rice were searched by using the bayonet attached to the rifles and swirling it around to determine if anything was hidden underneath. If the containers were too deep they were simply dumped on the ground to check the very bottom of the container. This did not make the mamasans very happy. Some would get down right hostile.

If there was an overabundance of rice, for the size of the village, it was determined that the NVA and VC were using the village to hide out. Stock piled rice was burned. If a village was a real hot spot with obvious signs of heavy enemy presence the order was given to burn the grass huts to the ground. Before we did this, we made sure that the women and children were out of harms way. It was terrible to watch the faces of the women and children as their homes went up in flames. We could only offer that we were doing it for their own good so that Charlie would move on and leave them alone.

We would question the villagers and attempt to gain more information about the enemy. We were interested in the size of the enemy forces, activities that were taking place around the village, their location, whether they were NVA or VC, the time they were last observed, and the equipment they were armed with. Most of the time, the villagers would not talk. They were holding back information because they were either NVA sympathizers or VC themselves. Some feared that if they talked they would be tortured and killed. They also kept quiet because we were simply invading their homes. Whatever the reason, there was not much information that could be gathered through the cooperation of the villagers. The Kit Carson Scouts would manage to get a little more information than the Marines since they were Vietnamese themselves and spoke the native tongue.

The villagers feared for their lives on a daily basis. They never knew what the next day might bring. The VC or NVA could show up and make life a living hell for them or the Marines would show up and destroy their village. When we entered a village, the villagers could have been cooking food, drawing water from one of the wells, eating, sleeping, or kids running around. No matter what they were doing at the time, the Marines disrupted their daily activities to gain full control. The mamasans would sometimes try to ignore us, so that we might leave quickly, but we took our time to check everything suspicious.

We would enter their hooches, check their shelves, look under mats, and scatter cooking utensils about. We would check all baskets for ordnance and explosives. Most of the time, we did not see any men except for the old papasans. Everyone was a suspect. The North Vietnamese would intimate and threaten the locals, especially the men. They terrorized the villagers in order for them to join in the fight to support communism. If they refused, their families could be tortured and killed right in front of their eyes.

There was always that sense of awareness and being on the alert for dangerous situations such as mines, booby traps, pungi pits, spider traps, snipers, dud rounds, and the like. A cautious behavior was a must at all times. The Marines themselves were at times our own worst enemy. Some would knowingly discard gear which they felt was too heavy to carry. This might include such items as claymore mines, grenades, and mortar rounds. If this type of ordnance was discovered by the enemy they could make good use of it against us.

There was a land mine called a "Bouncing Betty." It was buried underground and when stepped on it became armed. When pressure was released for about 3 seconds it launched the canister upward. This antipersonnel mine had two charges. The first propelled the explosive charge upward about 4 feet above the ground and the second detonated the device. The bouncing betty would maim as well as kill. It was meant to cause maximum shrapnel wounds to the chest and head and was very demoralizing to troops. We had to constantly be on the lookout for such devices.

There was an expression that the Marines could always be heard saying. It was, "Pay Back Is A Medevac." If we killed any VC or NVA we felt it was justified since they were maiming and killing fellow Marines. We were there to do a job. The only way to accomplish that mission was to follow a stanza found on the enlisted Marine promotion warrant. "I will follow such orders and directions as may be given from time to time by superiors acting accordingly to the rules and articles that govern the discipline of the Armed Forces of the United States of America." Killing the enemy was a job that had to be done. After all, we were defending our country and the spread of communism.

Our last mission in the Que Son Mountains was to locate the caves that had been gassed in the preceding months and to make sure that they had not been reoccupied by the enemy. Word had spread throughout the chain of command, that the gas used earlier in the caves, was supposed to last for many years. "Not a living creature will be able to survive in the gassed caves for eight years," they had said. To our surprise, we found five VC living in the caves even after the caves had been gassed. I managed to get a closer look at the caves on this last mission. My squad retracted the VC from the caves, destroyed the rice, confiscated two M60 machine guns, and gathered up a few grenades. The rice was destroyed by burning and the enemy was sent back to the rear for interrogation.

The cave occupants had taken large bamboo poles, split them in half, and attached joining poles that ran from a stream down past the caves. This was their means of obtaining water by crude man-made water gutters. Obvious rocks had been placed in small circles on the ground where they had been cooking food. There were empty salmon cans thrown all around the caves. It looked as though they were well organized and somewhat comfortable in their surroundings. The Nuclear, Biological, and Chemical Warfare personnel were called upon once again to re-gas the caves. They boasted this time that this particular gas would last for twelve years. I wondered however, how soon the NVA and VC would be right back in the caves after the gassing, making them their homes and hideout.

While I was out in the bush we got some Stars and Stripes newspapers with a resupply chopper. They were passed out and I got my own copy since some in the squad were not too interested. I glanced through the paper and started reading an article written about Corporal Martin and his dog Rebel. We must have had a combat journalist along with us on this operation up in the Que Son Mountains because a picture was taken as well. I cut out the article for safe keeping. The picture that appeared in the newspaper showed Corporal Martin with his bush hat on his head and holding on to the wounded dog. The caption under the picture read: "Cpl Israel Martin comforted his scout dog, Rebel, when the dog was hit by a sniper in Vietnam. The valiant dog later succumbed to his wounds, but he had saved the lives of a Marine patrol."

The newspaper article told the story of how Rebel got killed. It was written as follows.

REBEL
Da Nang—Rebel is dead. His tour in Vietnam came to an abrupt end shortly after he was hit by enemy sniper fire. He sacrificed his life to save his fellow Marines.

Rebel, one of many scout dogs serving with Marine units in the field, was doing his job—finding Charlie. On his last operation, Rebel and his handler, Cpl Israel Martin, were attached to "M" Co., 3/7, operating in the Que Son Mountains.

Rebel's last day started as he led a routine patrol with Martin. After traveling through dense jungle foliage into a small clearing, he stopped to sniff the air. He alerted Martin just as the enemy sniper opened up.

The dog faltered only slightly, though gravely wounded. On command of his handler, he attacked the hidden enemy soldier.

Quickly following the short, scream-punctuated battle that followed, Martin rushed to the side of his K-9 friend.

Beside Rebel, Martin found the sniper's death dealing weapon, slashed by Rebel's teeth.

Following immediate first aid, administered by a corpsman with the patrol, Martin and Rebel were medevaced to the rear. There Rebel died of the wounds he had received while protecting the lives of his Marine buddies.

Although Rebel is dead, his memory lives on with the men of "Mike" Company who accompanied him on his last patrol."

Chapter 10

The Other Side of the Orient

THE day came when I left behind LZ Baldy, Firebase Ross, Medevac Mike, and my foxhole buddy. I felt proud of the fact that I had served my country in the Vietnam War in Mike Company, 3rd Battalion, 7th Marines, 1st Marine Division. Now it was time to set another course. Just as I was getting used to being in one unit it was time to transfer to another. I had no idea what my next duty assignment on Okinawa might be like.

Mike Company had been heli-lifted on 26 September 1970 from FSB Ross to the 9th Engineer Cantonment in Da Nang to conduct stand down activities. The Marines being transferred to Okinawa spent the next two days in Da Nang in order to process for our departure from Vietnam. There were sixty-five other Marines along with me that were leaving Vietnam for good. On the second day we were taken to the Da Nang Air Terminal. This was the same airport that I had flown into when I first arrived in Vietnam months before.

Inside the terminal we were corralled into a large holding area. The Marines were spread out and lined up in rows with their seabags at their feet. We were told by the Marine Customs Agents to dump our seabags for a customs inspection. I had a few grotesque pictures of dead VC that I had taken while I was in the bush and had hidden them in the very bottom of my shaving kit. The shaving kit was placed at the bottom of my seabag to avoid confiscation at customs. I had been told by other Marines, that if you didn't want the airport customs to confiscate pictures of this nature and of other items of contraband, the bottom of the seabag was the best place to pack them. I honestly did not think that the Customs Agents would unzip and look in my shaving kit. After emptying the contents the Customs authorities began to search through everyone's belongings.

A corporal approached me wearing a Customs badge on his uniform. He began digging through my uniform articles and throwing them about in a haphazard manner. As he rummaged through my gear I noticed that one of the Customs Officials had confiscated some sea shells from a civilian that was receiving the same inspection as the Marines. He began to beg the Customs Official to let him keep the sea shells. He was refused and the shells were thrown into a large box. Needless to say the civilian was furious, but there was nothing he could do about it.

Meanwhile, the corporal made his way through every stitch of clothing that I had laid out on the floor. I had only emptied half of my seabag in an attempt to avoid him getting his hands on my pictures. He got irritated and told me to dump the remaining articles on the floor. This I did with reluctance. He came upon my shaving kit and picked it up. He unzipped it and removed my razor and soap case. He peered further into my shaving kit and then looked me in the eye.

"Well, what do we have here?" he asked with a sneer. He pulled the pictures out and began flipping through them rapidly. "These are contraband," he said. "I'm gonna have to confiscate these Marine. Looks like you have taken some nice pictures of dead gooks."

"Can't I keep them?" I asked. "It cost me money to buy the film and get them developed."

"No," he rejected my request, "I can't do that." He then tossed the pictures behind him and into a box that contained other items he had taken from other Marines.

"Hey, corporal," I said. "I'm going home now back to the world and those pictures were my lasting memories of Vietnam. Not all of them are of dead gooks. I have some squad photos in the stack as well. Please let me take them with me."

"Nope, I told you I can't do that," he replied. "It's against regulations."

Out of desperation I asked, "How much will you take? I'll pay you something if you will just let me keep them."

The corporal quickly looked me in the eye and said, "Do you want me to lock you up for bribery?"

I quickly answered, "No, corporal, I don't want no trouble. I just want to keep my squad pictures."

"I don't care what you want, lance corporal," he interjected. "If you try to bribe me again I'll put you in hand cuffs. Now put your stuff back into your seabag."

I packed my things back into my seabag. I could just barely fasten the strap at the top of the seabag as I had packed it very tight for the trip to Okinawa. I was sweating now from the heat and humidity inside the terminal after struggling to repack my seabag. After all the Marines had been inspected and packed up we began to stack our seabags for loading and wait for the airplane to arrive. After I had placed my seabag on the stack I looked and saw the corporal and other Customs Inspectors rummaging through the confiscated articles. I moved closer to the counter where they were gathered and could hear their conversation.

"Well what did you confiscate?" one asked of another.

"Look at this!" one of them declared. "I got some pop up flares, some AK47 rounds, and a trip flare. Can you believe this shit?"

"Yeah," the corporal replied. "I got me some great photos of some dead gooks, just look at these."

They began scanning through my photos. Almost all of them were black and white. Each of the customs Marines were sorting through the stack of photos and claiming some for themselves.

"Those dirty bastards," I said out loud. "They are picking through my pictures and are going to keep them for themselves."

One of the Marines standing next to me said, "Yeah, I see what you mean. These assholes confiscate all our stuff and keep it for themselves."

The longer I stood and watched them picking through my pictures the angrier I got. I approached the counter that they were standing behind while rummaging through the confiscated items.

"What the hell is going on?" I demanded. "I thought those pictures were contraband and that they were to be discarded. Now I see that you all are helping yourselves to my pictures for your own personal use. I want those pictures back! They are mine!"

"You are out of line lance corporal," the corporal retorted. "These photos are contraband." Then he told the other Marine Customs Agents that I had tried to bribe him.

A sergeant looked at me and said, "You had best move along Marine or else you will be in a lot of trouble."

Being persistent I replied, "Well at least let me have the pictures that I took of my squad. Not all of them are of dead gooks."

"No way," the corporal replied as he and the others turned away from me and started walking toward a back room. They were laughing and carrying on as they entered the room. In that large area they had many shelves full of confiscated items. I overheard one of them say that he had been looking all over for sea shells like the ones he had confiscated from the civilian and that now he would not have to look any longer.

I was extremely bitter, but at the time, I did not know of anything else to do. I sauntered back to the waiting area feeling totally disgusted and mad at myself for not mailing the photos to my sister, Janice. She would have kept them for me. I knew that the Marines conducting the customs inspection would go through every bit of confiscated materials and pick out what they wanted for themselves. I thought to myself that they would most likely get back to the States and have all sorts of war stories to tell their children and grandchildren. They would have to be the ones to live with their lies. I could understand customs confiscating the various types of ordnance at the airport but it seemed to be taking things to the extreme by taking individual photos. These Marine customs officials had never been in the bush or experienced combat, but yet they could play hard nose with the Marines when they departed Vietnam. It made me sick to my stomach and disgusted with the whole customs process.

By now I was getting used to being messed over by those senior to me. My souvenirs had been taken away from me while I was aboard on the USS Sanctuary, I had been cheated out of my SKS rifle when it was stolen from me, and now my most treasured pictures of my squad had been confiscated right in front of my eyes. Luckily, I had sent other pictures home through the mail, but none of them were of the true faces of death. One particular picture that was confiscated had been taken with Hawkeye, Corporal Ka-Bar, Travieso and me, sitting next to four dead VC that we had just killed. We were taking a break and eating some C-Rations. The photo that we all posed for depicted the true reality of war.

We finally boarded a commercial plane bound for Kadena Air Force Base on Okinawa. The engines roared a different sound than what I was used to. It was a lot different than the propellers of helicopters and fixed wing bombers. The plane taxied down the runway and on 28 September 1970 my "Freedom Bird" lifted off the Da Nang Airport runway and away from the Vietnam coastline.

As soon as the plane lifted off the runway I thought of Hawkeye. He had volunteered to stay behind in Vietnam and provide his services in a CAP unit. The Marine Corps concept was to combine a squad of Marines with local Popular Forces and assign them a village to protect. It basically denied the enemy a sanctuary in the local villages. Hawkeye would be virtually living among the local villagers. He was still in a very dangerous environment. I feared for his safety, but applauded his bravery. He would be missed.

My thoughts returned to the aircraft cabin. I kept staring at the American women stewardesses on the plane, as the Marines would jokingly say, "Round Eyes." It had been months since I had seen an American woman. Three stewardesses made up the crew that served the aircraft. All the Marines on board were beckoning for special attention. There was teasing throughout the journey to Okinawa. Basically we were a happy bunch. The women appeared to enjoy the attention or perhaps they were used to Marines like us leaving Vietnam. We all enjoyed the flight.

After a two and a half hour flight we landed on the runway at Kadena. All the Marines cheered as the wheels of the airplane touched down on the runway. We made our way inside the terminal to await our seabags to be off loaded. After we received our seabags we had to go through another customs inspection. Once again all the contents of our seabags were emptied and inspected. This time an Air Force Customs Official did not even look in my shaving kit. Just my luck, I thought. It was a hassle to try and stuff all my gear back inside my seabag for the second time. I wondered how many more inspections we might have to go through.

We walked outside to board buses that were waiting for us. It was very hot and humid on Okinawa. We loaded our seabags and boarded the military buses. We rolled down all the windows. The drivers headed out of the terminal and onto the highway. We passed through some small towns. I was tired but couldn't keep from looking out the windows at the Okinawans going about their daily chores. The local people seemed very busy rushing from one place to another. They took little note of the passing buses with all the American Marines aboard. We were still in our jungle utilities.

I looked out a window to see the position of the sun just to reaffirm that we were heading north. After about an hour we stopped at Camp Hague. This was the same base that my cousin and I had said our good-byes when I left for Vietnam. We spent the rest of the day being processed and receiving orders. Some of the Marines would be going to Camp Hansen and others to Camp Schwab, a base on the northern most part of Okinawa. When I received my orders they were stamped Camp Schwab. I would be going to 3rd Battalion, 9th Marines.

It wasn't until around 2100 that the Marines going to Camp Schwab finally boarded a bus. I thought they had forgotten about us. We passed by Camp Hansen and I peered out the windows at the town of Kin Ville. I had once bar hopped in Kin Ville with my brother, Donald, just prior to heading for Vietnam. I could see the neon lights glistening in the darkness and the flashing signs of Bars, Bars! Girls, Girls!

The buses continued on and we arrived at the main gate at Camp Schwab. I figured it must have been at least about twenty-six miles from the Kadena Air Force Terminal to Camp Schwab. I had finally made it to my destination. As we went through the front gate a Marine lance corporal on sentry duty knew that we were from Vietnam for we were still wore our jungle utilities. He was wearing the traditional green sateen utilities and his uniform was very neatly pressed and starched. He saluted us as we passed the sentry booth and held his salute until the end of the bus had passed. He was extending a greeting of respect for the combat veterans returning from Vietnam. I appreciated the fact that an enlisted Marine was saluting other enlisted.

When the bus came to a stop we got out and assembled in formation. Even while standing on the dimly lit asphalt we stood out from the rest of the Marines in our jungle utilities. Some Marines were scurrying about to escort us to our assigned units. They were wearing starched sateen utilities, starched covers (headgear), and spit-shined boots. I remembered the time when I was up on FSB Ryder and the rats had eaten holes in the toes of my jungle boots. Fortunately, I had received a new pair while in the bush that had been sent out on a resupply run from FSB Ross. Now my second pair of jungle boots was worn as much as the first pair. I looked down at my jungle boots as a comparison to the spit-shined boots. The toes and heels of my jungle boots were brown and scuffed right down into the leather. When they were first issued they were black with green canvas on the sides. The canvas material was brown also from the sun, mud, and general wear and tear of being in the bush. We were scruffy looking compared to the Camp Schwab permanent personnel. As we stood in formation waiting for one of the Marines to take us to our units, I made the statement, "So this is the real Marine Corps!" A Marine in ranks responded, "Yep, spit-shined boots and all."

A staff sergeant, who was the Officer of the Day, took roll and made us aware of which units individual Marines would be going to. The sixty-five

Marines that had made the journey with me from Vietnam to Okinawa was now about to be broken up and assigned to different units at Camp Schwab. The next thing I knew a group of about twelve Marines were being lead away with seabags in hand to join their unit. I wondered if I should have been in the group. I didn't know exactly what was going on.

Then a lance corporal came over to where I was and said that he would be escorting me and two other Marines to the Lima Company barracks. The other two Marines gathered around and we lifted our seabags to our shoulders and started to walk behind him. He offered to carry my seabag, but I figured that I had come this far without help, so I might as well carry it myself. We walked along a sidewalk that passed along a bluff and from the moonlit night I could see that we were right on the beach. I could hear the waves splashing down below. It was a pretty sight but by now my mind was on something else. I couldn't wait to drop my seabag and climb into a nice soft bed. I really needed the sleep before reveille the next morning.

We entered the barracks and walked down the center of the squad bay. Wall lockers were positioned along both sides and I could tell that the Marines occupying the barracks had their racks in behind the wall lockers forming four man cubicles. The lance corporal pointed to two empty racks and told the other two Marines that had accompanied me from Vietnam that they were to sleep there for the night. He gestured for me to follow him outside the barracks and into another barracks running parallel to the one we had just left. We entered in the center, turned left, and passed by the shower stalls and head. I peered in as I walked by. Honest to goodness urinals and commodes, I thought. No more digging cat holes for awhile.

We continued on and passed two cubicles on the left and right. At the third cubicle on the right the lance corporal moved a small black curtain to the side and disappeared on the other side. He stuck his head back out and gave a motion for me to enter.

"Come on in," he said, "here is your rack."

I ducked under the curtain and dropped my seabag on the concrete floor. I noticed it was shinning from a wax that had been highly buffed. He put his hand on the top rack and told me this was to be my home for as long as I was in Lima Company. He then showed me an empty wall locker that I could use to hang my uniforms. He started to undress as I turned the combination on my lock in order to open my seabag. I could barely make out the combination numbers on my lock because he had not turned on the squad bay lights. All the Marines were in their bunks sound asleep. I managed to get my seabag unlocked by the moon light coming through the windows.

"I take it you stay here also," I whispered.

"Yeah," he replied. "I'm right across from you on this top rack."

He placed his foot on the rack below and heaved up and into the top bunk. He reached for the sheets and covered himself up to his waistline. There were two fans blowing in the cubicle. It was hot even at night time.

"By the way," he said, "my name is Callahan, what's yours?"

"Fenwick," I responded.

"Glad to meet you Fenwick," Callahan continued.

"Likewise," I said. We both shook hands.

"We should be in the same squad," he said. "You are a 0331, ain't you?"

"Yeah," I replied. "I was trained as a machine gunner, but I haven't been in a machine gun team since I left infantry training. I used the gun on several occasions in Vietnam, but I was never assigned to a machine gun team. They made me a rifleman instead. Now I can get back to my MOS. I love firing the M60."

"Yeah, me too," Callahan responded. "Trouble is that here we train a lot, clean the gun even if it's not dirty, go on forced marches, and have all kinds of inspections. You will definitely get your fill of the M60. Well, I will see you in the morning. We had better get some shut eye. Reveille goes at 0530 in the morning."

I looked at my watch. It was just past midnight. I locked my seabag in the wall locker, got undressed, hung my camouflage utilities over the end of the rack, and crawled into the top rack. The squeaking of the rack springs caused the Marines in the bottom two racks to stir and moan. In only a few seconds they were sawing logs again. I didn't have any sheets, a pillow, or a blanket. I would have to go to supply the next day to sign for them. I folded up my utility jacket to act as a pillow and lay back on the bare mattress. It wasn't long until I fell asleep.

The next thing I knew the squad leaders were going from cube to cube waking up the Marines in the squad bay. I could hear the sound of flip-flops moving slowly towards the head and then the sound of flushing water, commodes, and sinks. It was a strange but pleasant sound. I rolled over to one side facing the partition in the cubicle. Now I have my own little apartment, I pondered, but with three other roommates.

I managed to peer out from under my heavy eyelids and glanced at my watch. It was 0535, reveille. I had wished that I could remain in the rack all day but I knew that was not to be. I was still very tired from the travelling the day before. A lance corporal appeared in the cubicle coaxing the other Marines to get out of the rack. With sleepy eyes and still yawning Callahan told him that I had just arrived at midnight. I rolled over to see who he was talking to.

"Hi," he said to me, "I'm Foster, your team leader."

"Fenwick," I replied.

He reached out and we shook hands. "Welcome to Okinawa," he said. "Callahan will get you all checked in today and then I will tell you what goes on around here and what training we have coming up. We're supposed to go on a float aboard ship around November, but right now not too many people know what's going on. We should hit some pretty good liberty ports. You're just coming back from Vietnam, huh?"

"Yeah," I responded, "got here late last night."

"Well listen, Fenwick, if you want to stay in the rack until our formation at 0700 you can, but our chow formation goes this morning at 0600."

"Thanks anyway, I responded, but I'm starved. I think I will go to chow with you guys this morning."

"Very well then, but you only have about twenty minutes to shit, shave, and shower."

"No problem," I said.

When I crawled out of the rack there was barely enough room to move around without bumping into one another. The cube was only about eight feet wide and ten feet long. In addition to that the two double bunks occupied most of the space.

"Tight quarters here, huh?" I gestured.

"Yeah," Callahan said, "we just have to improvise and make do with what we have."

The other Marines in the cubicle started introducing themselves. Hill was from Ohio, Trump was from New Jersey, and Callahan was from Oregon. Although Trump had a rack in our cubicle, he was in a different gun team than ours, but he was still in our squad. After the introductions I dashed into the head and began to shave and clean up. Some of the other Marines looked at me curiously since I was a new face in the crowd. After shaving, I went back to the cubicle and put on my jungle utilities. The word was given to fall out in formation for chow.

Callahan showed me where our machine gun team was to fall in formation within the platoon. He told me that I would be in the 3rd machine gun team, 3rd squad. I happened to realize that Lima Company was the 3rd infantry company within the 3rd battalion. I remembered that while in Vietnam I was in the 3rd squad, 3rd platoon, and 3rd infantry company within the 3rd battalion. In boot camp I was in the 3rd recruit training battalion. I figured that the number 3 might have a play in my destiny and either a lucky or unlucky number, as fate would have it.

The platoon guide marched us to chow in platoon formation. The morning air felt good to the skin but I knew we were in for a hot and humid day. It seemed strange to march as a unit on the hard surface road. There was no dust or mud as it had been at the base camps back in Vietnam. We rounded a corner and veered to the left. The formation was stopped just outside the mess hall double doors. We filed off in single file. I got to a small metal table where a Marine private first class was sitting in a metal chair. He was checking everyone's meal cards. In order to eat in the mess halls, all the Marines had to have a meal card issued by the respective company office.

"I just arrived here last night. I haven't been issued a meal card yet," I explained.

"You can't eat in the mess hall without a meal card," he responded.

"Like I said, I haven't had a chance to check in to the company yet. I am going to do that today," I said.

"Sorry," he said in a girlish manner. "No meal card, no eat."

I was not in the mood for no foolishness this morning. "I ought to pull you across this desk and pound the crap outta you, you little jackass!" I yelled. "I told you I have not checked in to the company yet. I don't need no bullshit from a knucklehead PFC, you hear me you little bastard!" I reached across the desk with my right hand and grabbed the PFC by his shirt collar. I twisted his utility jacket up into a knot. His eyes opened wide and his mouth fell open with surprise. Just then, Foster grabbed my arm.

"Don't worry about it Fenwick," he said. "You wait here and I will talk to the Mess Chief."

I still had the PFC in my grasp. Foster told me to let go of the PFC and I did so reluctantly. Foster then walked down to the serving line and began speaking to a corporal that was dressed in mess whites. All the while I was standing in front of the table staring the PFC in the eye. I was mumbling that I would whip the tar out of this slimy little private first class. The Marines behind me in the chow line backed away for they just knew I was going to beat the hell out of this Marine. Foster returned quickly and informed me that the Mess Chief said it was okay to eat without a meal card. I walked past the PFC looking him dead in the eye. If looks could have killed, he would have been dead. I heard Callahan tell Hill and Trump that I was one Marine not be messed with.

"Yeah, he's a Vietnam Vet," Hill said. "He's liable to kill you."

I went through the serving line and filled my tray. The food looked very appetizing. I had creamed beef on toast, scrambled eggs, pancakes, hash brown potatoes, and a serving of oatmeal. I also picked up a banana and apple from the fruit bar. Then I filled one glass with milk and the other with orange juice. What a feast, I thought. I might even be able to gain some weight before I go home. I did not want my mother to see me looking like I did because I looked like a walking skeleton. After a few minutes of eating, I realized that I would not be able to finish even half of the chow that I had put on my tray. My stomach must have gotten smaller and my eyes were too big for my stomach. I left the mess hall stuffed.

We straggled back to the barracks. Straggled was a term the Marines used that meant that we did not have to be marched in formation. After cleanup of the barracks we fell out in company formation. I looked down the line of platoons and saw the other two Marines dressed in the same camouflage utilities as me. We stood out among the rest of the company whose attire was sateen utilities, starched covers, and spit-shined boots. After the company commander received the report from the first sergeant, the formation was turned over to the company gunny. He rattled on for about fifteen minutes telling the entire company the plan of the day. In the next few days we would go to the gas chamber. I thought about gassing the caves in the Que Son Mountains. Now it would be my turn to get gassed.

We went back into the barracks and the Marines began to get ready for the chores of the day. Callahan was to take me around to the company office and get me properly checked in. The Marines in my cubicle were laughing about the look on the PFC's face at the mess hall when I grabbed him by the collar.

"That guy was scared shitless of you Fenwick, were you going to choke him?" Hill asked.

"Damn right," I said with a smile. "I put up with enough bullshit just coming back here from Vietnam and I was still tired from the trip. I'll be damned if I let some whimp of a PFC give me a ration of crap."

"Yeah," said Trump. "He sure was a whimp, did you guys see the look on his face when Fenwick grabbed him. I thought he was going to crap all over himself."

Some of the other Marines in the squad began coming by the cubicle introducing themselves to me. I was glad that they were taking such an interest. I noticed that they were all admiring my jungle utilities. At first they drove me crazy with all their questions about Vietnam. I was the only one in the platoon who had been in combat.

"How many VC did you kill?"

"Is it as bad as they say it is down south?"

"How was it like over there?"

"How many Marines did you see come back in body bags?"

"You ever get a body count?"

"How many confirmed kills did you get?"

This went on and on. I thought that in Okinawa that I could put some of the memories to rest. The continual bombardment of questions got to me at one point so I decided to step outside the barracks that overlooked the crashing waves of the ocean. I guess I was trying to find some peace and quiet. I sat down on the bluff and looked out over the sandy beach. I was thinking to myself that it sure was not like this with my squad in Vietnam. These boots did not know the first thing about combat. The "real action," they called it. Callahan and Trump found where I was sitting on the bluff and joined me.

"If you don't want to talk about Nam, that's okay with us," Callahan said. "It must have been hell seeing your buddies blown up and sent back in body bags.

"Yeah," Trump added. "We understand, we won't pester you anymore."

I lowered my head looking down at the ground under my feet. "You're right," I responded. "I really don't want to talk about it now, maybe some other time."

"Well, I'd better get you checked in to the company office," Callahan replied. "You want to get paid this payday, don't you?"

"Hell yes," I said. "There's a cold beer at the E-Club with my name on it."

"Now you're tawkin," Callahan said.

After the first day the platoon finally stopped asking questions about Vietnam. It was business as usual. I understood their interest but I wanted to put it all behind me now. We had a black staff sergeant who was our platoon sergeant for Weapons Platoon. On the second day he came to the barracks and entered the squad bay. He was checking all the cubicles and making comments about us living like pigs and for us to get things squared away. He raised the curtain we had at the entrance of our cubicle and stepped inside. Callahan was sitting on a bottom rack and I was standing next to my open wall locker. By now I was wearing my sateen utilities that had been stored in my seabag at LZ Baldy while I was in the bush. I had still been unable to pick up all my other dress uniforms that had been stored at Camp Hansen months before. The platoon sergeant pulled the door back so he could inspect.

"How long you been here, lance corporal?" he asked.

"This is my second day," I responded.

"Your second day and you still don't have your seabag unpacked. What are you waiting for?" he asked.

"I couldn't find enough clothes hangers," I replied.

"Well, I see that you found enough to hang up those jungle utilities," the platoon sergeant quipped. "Those utilities are not authorized here on Okinawa. You have to turn them into supply, ASAP!"

"Can't I keep them, staff sergeant?" I asked politely. "I wore these in Vietnam and would like to hang on to them."

The platoon sergeant stated, "No, you can't keep them. You have to turn them in. Are you deaf? I don't want to repeat myself again. Do you hear?"

"I will not wear them," I replied in a more unpleasant tone. "I have worn them for several months in Vietnam and I only want to keep them for sentimental reasons. All the supply personnel are going to do is throw them in the trash."

"I'll be back this afternoon and those fuckin jungle utilities had best be gone," he quipped.

He threw back the curtain and stormed out of the squad bay. I reached inside my wall locker and took my utility jacket off the metal close hanger. Angrily, I placed it on my top rack with the buttons facing down. I folded both sides in toward the center, extended the arms down, and folded it in half. Then I reached for my utility trousers and folded them as well. I grabbed my sateen utility cover and put it on my head.

"Going down to supply now?" Callahan asked.

"Nope," I responded, "the Post Office."

"The Post Office?" Callahan asked with a surprised look on his face.

I replied, "Yep, the platoon sergeant wants these jungle utilities gone, and that's exactly what I'm going to do. In a few days they will be at Route #2, Springfield, Kentucky."

"Sending them home, huh?" Callahan asked. "I don't blame you. The platoon sergeant will never know anyway. I'll never tell."

"Thanks Callahan," I said, "I'll be back after I find a box and mail my utilities home."

On my way to the base Post Office I began to think about what had just occurred. The more I thought about it the more irritated I got. I could not believe that I was not allowed to keep the jungle utilities that I had been wearing in Vietnam. Even though they were now not going to be a part of my required military issue, I simply could not fathom why I was not allowed to keep them. Was it because of some stupid regulation or was the staff sergeant just trying to screw with me. While contemplating my predicament, I happened to think that I should have mailed my pictures home that had been confiscated at the Da Nang airport. If I had, I would still have them. I figured that I would just mail my utilities home as I was sick and tired of Marines in a position of authority taking things from me. I looked down at the jungle boots I was wearing as I walked. I wore my jungle boots in Vietnam, so why not turn them in to supply also? It just didn't make sense.

I managed to get an empty cardboard box from the Post Exchange. It was just about the right size. I packed my jungle utilities in the box and headed for the Post Office. I had to ask a few Marines on the way to point me in the right direction. I arrived at the military Post Office and asked one of the Marines if they had any tape to seal up the box and a pen to write the address with. To my surprise the postal Marine was very helpful. I taped the box shut without even putting in a note to my parents and wrote my return address and home address on the front. I was in a real hurry so I could get back to the squad bay without anyone knowing. I had enough cash on me to pay for the shipment. The postal Marine behind the counter stamped it and told me it would probably take about six to seven days to reach Kentucky. I told him that was quite all right.

On my way back to the barracks I wondered if I would get into trouble for not carrying out the staff sergeant's directions. He had said that he wanted them gone, and as far as I was concerned, they were gone. I felt that the Marine Corps at least owed me a pair of jungle utilities, a pair that I had already been issued. I had been cheated out of my SKS rifle, Vietnam souvenirs, and personal pictures. I was not about to let them cheat me out of my jungle utilities. I had finally salvaged a part of my sentiments. I received no repercussion from the platoon sergeant since he never knew that I had mailed them home.

October 1, 1970

Hello Mom, Dad and all,

Well! You'll never guess where I'm at. I was pulled out of Nam on the 28th of September along with sixty-five other guys and sent to Okinawa. I never knew a thing about it until they called our names out. It was sure a surprise. Some stayed and were going to the 1st Marines and a few went back to the States. I wanted to stay in Nam, believe it or not, because the 1st Marines would have been a lot better. Well anyway, I had to pack up all my stuff and come with them. We flew over on an American Airlines plane, so it only took two and one half-hours. After being processed we got to the unit at around 11:00 p.m. There are only a couple of guys that are still with me from Nam.

I'm at Camp Schwab and I guess it is about a twenty minute drive from where Donald lives. He said that he lived only a few miles out of Kin Village and we passed by there on our way to Camp Schwab. I called the place where Donald works today but he had already gone home. The Marine I was talking to said he'd tell Donald I called the first thing in morning, so I imagine I'll get to see him before long.

They told us we are going on a cruise in November. That will really pass the time quickly and by the time we get back, I'll be ready to come home. In a way I don't like this place. We're back to the silly games we had in ITR. The platoon went to the gas chamber today but I didn't have to go because I was checking in. I have to go to about fifteen places just to tell them I'm here. I still haven't done it yet. Maybe we can finish up tomorrow.

We're having a big inspection this Monday and I still haven't gotten my clothes I had stored at Camp Hansen. Well I'm not worrying about them because the less I have, the less I have to lay out for inspection. Some of the things I don't like are the formations, shined boots and brass, plus having starched utilities. They said we can wear trousers not starched, but we've got to have them starched for inspections.

I know I'm not going to like it here, for awhile at least, until I get all my gear squared away. But I'll make the best of it. Guess in the long run its better than being shot at. I'm in a Weapons Platoon and I am in a machine gun squad. I got back to my old MOS. I've almost forgotten some of the things about the machine gun. Guess I'll pick them back up as I go along.

As far as liberty goes, that means time off, we won't have any for a few weeks. They just had to have these darn inspections when I got here. They sound liberty at about seven o'clock at night, but it's only around on base. Right now we don't get much of that but they did manage to get liberty tonight. I stayed behind to shine my dress shoes. You should have seen them when I took them out of my seabag. They even had mold on them. I'm hoping I can send the plaque home which I got when I left Nam. It's pretty nice. I also have the Cruise Book of the 3rd Battalion, 7th Marines that I was talking about. The farts in the mailroom back at LZ Ross never did mail it.

Guess I've earned about five ribbons now. Most of the guys here have only two so I'm three ahead of them. Next week I'm supposed to qualify again with the rifle only this time with the M16 instead of the M14. I hope I can do good.

Well, guess I'll close for now. Just wanted you to know I have a change of address now. So bye for now, write when you can, I'll do the same.

As ever,
Fred

I finally got in touch with Donald at the unit where he worked. We made plans to go fishing the following Monday. I was granted special liberty for that day in order to meet with a family member. He was to pick me up at my barracks on Monday morning and then drive to a fishing pier south from the Camp Schwab main gate. I remained on base and anxiously waited for the first time that I could get off the military installation for a little "libbo." That was Marine lingo for off base liberty. I also was very excited about seeing my brother again.

At the time my brother, Donald, was a Marine staff sergeant and had served two complete tours in Vietnam as a combat engineer. His first combat tour of duty in Vietnam began in September 1965 at the onset of the war and continued through 1967. He had served with Alpha Company, 3rd Engineer Battalion, 3rd Marine Division. He saw combat in such operations as Hastings, Prairie I, Prairie II, Texas, and Virginia. Donald had spent a lot of time on the Rockpile which was a rock outcropping near the demilitarized zone of South Vietnam.

That Monday morning I was up at the crack of dawn to get dressed and ready to go. I could have gone to the mess hall with the platoon, but in anticipation of the day ahead, I had already dressed in civilian attire. The Marines were in utilities as it was just another work day for them. Civilian attire was only authorized in the mess hall on weekends so I did not take the time to get in the proper uniform for chow. I was just too pumped up anyway to eat chow. I hadn't picked up a fishing rod since I had left home and joined the Marine Corps. I wondered what kind of a fisherman I would be. I felt for sure I would be a little rusty. Donald had told me on the phone that he had plenty of rods and bait.

The platoon was out of the barracks. Only the squad bay duty noncommissioned officer and I remained on deck. As I sat on my footlocker, waiting for my brother to arrive, I finally heard the back door of the barracks open and then close. I figured it must be him since all was quiet in the squad bay. I looked at my watch. It was about 0830. I stood up and peered around the curtain that hung at the entrance to my cubicle. I saw my older brother walking down the squad bay toward me and slowly turning his head from one side to another searching for my cubicle. I noticed the deep dark tan that Donald had on his face and arms. He undoubtedly had been spending a lot of time outdoors. Our eyes finally met and we both smiled at each other. We approached each other in the center of the squad bay and vigorously shook hands. We were both excited to see one another after those long uncertain months while I was in Vietnam.

After a few moments of casual conversation I told Donald that I had to check out with the Duty NCO. He walked with me and watched me sign out of the log book. I placed my liberty card and special liberty chit in my wallet and we proceeded out one of the side doors. We walked along the sidewalk leading from the barracks down to the asphalt roadway. I made sure I walked on the left side of my brother to show respect. I had learned that while in boot camp.

The stairway was about forty feet down an embankment. I could see his car parked across the road. It was the usual Japanese made car, old but reliable. Donald got in the driver's seat while I walked around to the passenger side. I had to wait until he could reach across the seat and open the passenger door from the inside. He said the door knob didn't work. I sat down and began to curiously look around the interior to see what instruments were included in this Japanese made car. I smelled the aroma of stale ale in the air. On the floor board in the back seat there were empty beer bottles and cans.

"Smells liked a brewery in here," I said.

"Yeah," Donald replied with a grin. "I've already christened her." We both laughed. "Wait till you hear the engine purrrrr," he said as he turned on the ignition. The car started and he let it idled and then revved the engine several times. "Sounds like a kitten purring," he said. "Ain't that nice?"

"I hope those chip monks under the hood get us to where we're supposed to go," I replied.

"This old gal won't let us down, she's my sweetheart," he said as he patted the dash board with one hand.

We drove along the road passing the barracks and buildings on Camp Schwab and approached the main gate. The Marine sentry on duty waved us through the gate with sharp snappy movements. Donald waved at him as we passed by. We came to a stop not too far from the sentry booth. Donald checked left and right for any oncoming traffic and then turned left. We headed south along a winding road toward Kin Ville which was about ten miles away. We were busy talking back and forth which made the car ride seem very short. It wasn't long until we arrived at Kin Ville.

Donald took a left turn and proceeded down a street toward a fishing pier that was on Red Beach. He drove his car as close as he could to the pier and parked. We grabbed his fishing rods, reels, and a cooler and headed to the end of the pier. We found a good spot to fish and sat the cooler down on the pier. Then we started to assemble his rods and reels and baited the hooks.

We cast our lines into the water. The ocean water was crystal clear and was dark blue. By now the rays of the morning sun bounced off the water. It was finally my time to relax and enjoy life for a change.

"How about a nice cool beer?" Donald asked.

I replied, "This time of the morning?"

"Why not?" he said.

I conceded and decided I might as well have a beer with my older brother. After all, we were going to celebrate my return from Vietnam. "All right then, Donald. That sounds good to me. It's been quite awhile since I had a nice cold beer, especially before noon."

He chuckled and then handed me a larger than normal beer bottle. It was a quart size. I held it with two hands while he popped the top with a church key. I could have used one of those in Vietnam. On one end of the church key was a bottle opener and on the other end a can opener. He then opened one for himself. I took a good mouthful of the brew. It had a strange bitter taste, but was satisfying nonetheless.

"How do you like it?" Donald asked while wiping his lips.

"Little bitter," I said holding the bottle up to inspect the writing on the label. Guess I'm just used to the Black Label Beer we had in Vietnam. It does taste pretty good though. Different, huh?"

"Yep," he replied while taking another gulp, "this is good old Okinawan beer."

I held the bottle up closer to my eyes and read the label. "Orion!" I exclaimed.

"Good old Orion beer," Donald said, "it'll tickle your fancy."

I knew this was going to be quite an interesting day. I was not used to drinking beer in the middle of the morning. I had a few more sips. The more I sipped, the better it tasted. It wasn't long until we saw the ends of our rods bobbing up and down. We just knew it would be the catch of the day. We both reeled in our lines and saw that we had caught two small pin fish approximately three inches long.

"Gonna be one of those days," Donald said as he unhooked his fish and threw it back into the water.

"I sure would like to tangle with old grand daddy fish," I said while also tossing my catch back into the water. "It's been a long time since I had a large fish on my hook."

"We'll just have to wait and see," he said. "Sometimes if you're lucky enough you can hit a school of fish and catch some pretty good size ones."

"What kind of fish are in these waters?" I asked. I reared back with the rod and threw the bait out as far as possible. Donald cast his line as well.

Donald started naming some of the fish in the ocean. "Oh, let's see, there are groupers, blues, flounders, blow fish, sting rays, sharks, and uhh, hell, all kinds of fish. You never know what you have on your line until you reel it in." He reached for his beer bottle and gulped down another mouthful of Orion beer. "We may not catch enough fish to make a meal, but we've got enough Orion to last all day," Donald said.

We both raised our beer bottles toasting one another and began to laugh. We sat down on the concrete pier letting our legs dangle off the sides and patiently waited for our bait to be taken. We talked about Vietnam, Okinawa, our Fenwick family, Cherry Hill Farm, and exchanged some of our personal experiences during our tours overseas. My stories about combat in Vietnam could not compare to the gut-wrenching details of Donald's encounters. He had been exposed to extreme hardships and was blessed to have survived two back to back tours in Vietnam.

At around 1400 we realized that we had caught what we thought was a mess of fish, in other words, one meal to feed at least two people. The sun was now beating down and the sea breeze began to increase. We had stripped off our T-shirts earlier to get a tan, but now it was beginning to feel a little chilly so we put our shirts back on. I noticed that my shoulders and stomach were somewhat red from the sun. Here it was in the month of October and we had gotten slightly sunburned. I thought to myself that this time of the year back in Kentucky was the fall of the year and that it would be quite chilly by now. On Okinawa I was fishing off the pier and getting sunburned.

We gathered our belongings and fishing gear and put them in the car. Donald drove away from the pier calling it a day for our little fishing spree. He zigzagged through the streets of Kin Ville.

"Where are we going now, Donald?" I asked.

"I'm going to show you my house in Kin Ville," he replied.

I responded saying, "Good, I've always wanted to see where you live. It's a Japanese style house ain't it?"

While not taking his eyes off the road Donald replied, "Yep, sure is. I got all the conveniences of home. Even got my own outdoor benjo ditch."

"You mean you don't have running water or a commode?" I asked jokingly.

"Hell no," he laughed. "When in Okinawa, do as the Okinawans do." He pulled off the side of the road and came to a stop. It appeared to be a very small country store away from the neon lights of Kin Ville. "Got to get some more Orion to stock up on," Donald said as he got out of the car.

I followed him into the store and asked, "You mean to tell me they actually sell beer in a store like this"?

"Yeah," he said, "they have just about anything you need."

While in the store I offered to pay for the Orion beer, but he insisted that it was his treat. We both got back into the car with several large quarts of beer. Donald took a bottle and handed me one as we continued our journey to his abode.

"The beer is a lot cheaper in these little country stores than they are in town," he said. "Hell, sometimes in the bars you have to pay about two dollars just for one beer. The Okinawans are really cleaning up from the American GI's. If it wasn't for people like me who drink their beer they would dry up and blow away."

"Guess you keep them in business," I snickered.

Donald smiled and said, "Yeah, I've invested my money in the Okinawan economy. Hell, I should run for Mayor."

We both laughed at the idea of Donald being Mayor of the town of Kin Ville. He ended up driving down a narrow alley which was the center of Kin Ville. As we drove along slowly, I glanced at the signs and neon lights through the windows and windshield of the car. I was fascinated at the neon signs even though they were not turned on in the middle of the afternoon. I knew that when darkness fell on this little town of Kin Ville, that the lights would be flickering and flashing enticing Marines to enter the establishments and spend all their money. I read out loud some of the signs as we passed by. "Girls, Girls, Girls! Floor Show, Live Entertainment! Ladies of the Night! Bath and Massage! Club Lucky! Club China Night! Seven Club!" Donald and I laughed as I read some of the signs out loud.

"How much for short time?" I asked inquisitively.

"Only ten dolla," Donald replied smiling. "We'll come back to town after I show you my house and we get something to eat."

By now I was feeling pretty good from drinking the Orion beer on an empty stomach. We joked and laughed as we continued on our way. It was good to hang out with my older brother. He could be so funny at times and was always cracking jokes. He turned into another narrow alley and we began passing Japanese style houses. He came to a stop, turned off the ignition, and got out of his door. I estimated that Donald lived about a mile and a half from the front gate of Camp Hanson.

Donald said, "Well, Freddy, this is it. Home sweet home."

He gathered up the beer in his arms to take inside. I got out of the car and curiously looked around noticing that all the houses were very closely packed together with hardly much space in between. They all looked very similar in design.

"Which one of these houses is yours?" I asked.

"Right through that iron gate," Donald responded as he pointed a finger.

I looked in the direction he was pointing and noticed that there was a walkway leading through a black gate and up to a sliding glass door to his house. A banana tree was growing just on the other side of the fence. It had very small green bananas hanging in clumps throughout the tree.

"I see you have your own home grown bananas Donald," I said.

"Wait till you see my palm tree growing in the back yard," he replied while grinning.

I opened the gate following Donald's instructions and we walked up the walkway and onto the porch. Fumbling with the beer bottles he managed to slide the door open. He proceeded in first and gave a motion for me to come inside.

"Come on in Freddy," he said, "make yourself at home." He sat the beer bottles on the floor and removed his shoes and placed them meticulously on a mat near the door. I had a few beer bottles of my own so I did likewise by setting them on the floor and taking off my shoes.

"Old Okinawan custom," Donald said.

We then picked up the beer bottles and went into the small kitchen to place them in the refrigerator. He reached inside and pulled out two cold beers and handed me one. I looked inside the refrigerator and noticed that he had some snack food but it was mostly stocked with Orion beer and a couple of whisky bottles.

"Well, looks like you have plenty of beer on hand," I said with a smile.

Donald agreed, "Yeah, I have to keep a good supply on hand in case we get hit by a typhoon. Sometimes those things last for days."

He began telling me about the last typhoon that almost blew his roof off and how the thin walls of his house were swaying to the gusts of wind. We managed to make our way into the living room and sat down at a small coffee table in the center of the room. He sat on one side and I sat on the other facing each other. He folded his legs and placed his feet under his buttocks.

"This is the way the Okinawans sit," he said with a snicker.

I pulled my feet up under my legs. "Must get uncomfortable after awhile," I said.

"Not really," he responded, "you get used to it."

We continued to drink our Orion and he began showing me some pictures that he had taken on the island. I fumbled through them slowly trying to pick out every detail. Then he showed me his stereo, a very unique piece of gear he had explained. It had the capability of picking up overseas stations. I was amazed at the various countries that he was receiving while turning the dial. After we played with the stereo for awhile we fixed a bite to eat. I was very hungry at this point but I tried not to show it by eating slowly.

As Donald finished the last swallow of his beer, he said, "How about a shot of ole Jim Beam?"

Thinking it might be a bad idea to mix beer and whisky I responded, "I don't know, this beer is doing a number on me as it is. I don't know about drinking whisky along with it."

"Hell, Freddy, relax!" Donald exclaimed. "Stay here tonight and I will take you back to Camp Schwab tomorrow."

"Oh, I don't know," I replied, tomorrow is a work day and I don't want to put you out and be an inconvenience for you."

"Are you shittin me," he said. "If you don't stay I'll just sit here and stare at the four walls. With that he got up, went into the kitchen, and returned with two glasses and a bottle of whisky. He poured me a drink and then one for himself. He held up his glass in a toast.

"Kanpai," he said as he clanged his glass against mine.

"What is the meaning of Kanpai?" I inquired. "I've done forgot."

"That's Okinawain language for toast," he replied.

"Guess you have learned quite a bit of the language, huh Donald?" I asked.

"Oh, some," he replied. Then he began speaking the language in a musical sort of manner. "Moshi moshi, that means Hello. Konbon wa, that means Good Evening. He continued on. Konnichi wa, means Good Day. Ohayo (gozaima su) means Good Morning. Sayonara means Goodbye." I couldn't believe that this ole country boy from Kentucky was speaking the Japanese words fluently.

I became a little light headed and began to slur my speech. Donald laughed at my comical state. The beer and whisky was taking me away from all the cares of the world. It was just me and Donald talking about old times and enjoying the time and family conversations together.

"Hey, Donald, I gotta take a piss," I said. "Where is the head?"

"Just outside that side door," he replied. "Just piss right into the benjo ditch."

I got to my feet. I stumbled momentarily. One of my legs had fallen asleep while sitting with my legs crossed like an Okinawan. I could feel the tingling sensation and it was hard to walk a straight line.

"Freddy, you're drunk as a skunk," Donald said laughing.

"No I'm not," I replied. I Then I began to fake my drunken state by weaving from side to side.

"Hell fire, Freddy, we still have to paint the town tonight. Maybe you ought to slow down some," Donald said.

"Hell no, I'm okay, I'm fine, never felt better, in my entire whole life," I replied. I began to sing one of our favorite songs, "Pistol Packin Momma." Our mother could play that tune on the piano with such an upbeat that everyone listening would be patting their feet on the floor. As I approached the side door I repeated a stanza of the song while slurring the lyrics.

I proceeded through the side door and stepped out into the open air. A warm and humid breeze was blowing. It felt good to step out into the fresh air. I saw the benjo ditch that was running along the length of his property. It was covered by concrete slabs that were about a two foot square and sectioned off. An open gutter type carving had been formed in the concrete and was about five feet long and terminating into a six inch diameter hole.

When I returned, I asked Donald, "How do you take a crap out there in the benjo ditch. Do you have to try and aim for the hole?"

Donald responded, "Of course, if you miss the hole, you can always flush it down with a bucket of water. Don't worry Freddy, after all this Orion beer and whisky, you'll be able to crap through a key hole at thirty paces."

Out of curiosity I began to slowly scan the interior of this small little Japanese house. Nice little place, I thought. The living room was only about

well liked within the platoon. The Marines considered him to be unfair, obnoxious, and boisterous. He would rant and rave over matters of no importance. They felt that he used his rank to intimidate the platoon. He would continuously bark orders and degraded those that he reprimanded.

Our gear was staged with Marine security from each platoon while the company went to chow. We called them gear guards or chow guards. After chow we put on our equipment and started off on a twenty-two mile hike. Since I was the gunner of the 3rd gun team, I was responsible for carrying the M60 machine gun. Other members of the gun team carried the spare barrel bag and tripod.

We passed through the main gate and headed south along the same hard surface road which Donald and I had driven when we went fishing. The company was divided into two columns with one on each side of the road. The company commander, a first lieutenant, seemed to be walking as fast as he could. It was hard to try and keep the rigorous pace and to maintain close interval between each Marine. I looked around at the Marines in my platoon. They were carrying heavy mortar tubes, base plates, M60 machine guns, spare barrel bags, tripods, and 3.5 rocket launchers. This was all in addition to our packs and rifles.

After about the tenth mile the machine gun on my shoulder seemed to weigh a ton. The weight of the M60 was 23.15 pounds, but when I carried it with full combat gear, it seemed much heavier. I held one bi-pod leg of the barrel with my right hand and rested the balance of the weapon on my right shoulder. At times I would alternate hands and shoulders. At one point I balanced the machine gun at the top of my pack which allowed me to have both hands free. I could then pull the front straps of my pack up and out in order to relieve some of the pressure on my shoulders. All of a sudden I heard this screaming voice coming from behind.

"What the hell are you doing? Hold that weapon right, you'll drop the damn thing and break it if you don't hold on to it." I looked behind me and saw Sergeant Buttplate.

"The gun will be all right on my pack," I replied to Sergeant Buttplate. "I have it balanced evenly so it won't fall off."

"I said carry that fuckin gun right, Marine!" He sped up his pace in order to catch up to me.

"I have been carrying the gun right for the last ten miles, but now it's heavy. I need some relief on my shoulders," I said.

"The only relief you'll get is my boot up your ass if you don't do as I say. Now carry that fuckin gun in a proper manner and that's an order!" Sergeant Buttplate yelled.

"Shit fire," I declared as I repositioned the machine gun on my shoulder. "Can't even carry my M60 machine gun on a hump without being yelled at."

"Anymore crap out of you Marine and I will write you up on charges; disrespect, disobedience of a lawful order, and failure to follow instructions from a noncommissioned officer, do you understand me?" He continued to yell pointing his index finger at me.

"Yes, I understand, Sar... geant," I replied sarcastically. I could sense the anger in my tone of voice.

"You had best say that with respect!" he yelled.

I did not respond. What an asshole he was, I thought to myself. Just then another Marine caught his attention on the opposite side of the road. The Marine was slowing down his pace leaving a small gap in the column. Sergeant Buttplate immediately crossed the road and began yelling while waving his hands about.

"Close it up! Close it up! What's the matter Marine, your pussy hurts? Huh? I want this column ass-hole-to-belly-button. Then he yelled out, "Now tighten it up!"

Callahan was directly behind me in the column. He had witnessed the exchange of words between Sergeant Buttplate and me.

"Hey, Fenwick," Callahan said. "Don't worry about him. He's a real horse's ass. He does this kind of stuff all the time. He thinks he's God's gift to creation."

"He acts like he's got a corncob up his ass," I replied. "I'd like to smack him across his face with this machine gun, but I know that he would love to see me court-martialed."

"The best thing to do is just ignore his dumb ass," Callahan continued.

"Yeah," I responded, "but I sure would like to catch him in a dark alley. I'd fix his wagon for sure."

Sergeant Buttplate was still scurrying up and down the column chewing out Marines and treating them like they were in boot camp. The company commander was still walking rapidly and never once looked back.

"I don't know if I will take too much of this kind of crap," I told Callahan. "This guy has never been in combat and he acts like a blooming idiot in handling his men."

"He's about a shithead all right," Callahan agreed.

We reached the eleven mile mark and sat down on the side of the road to take a break. A heavy set staff sergeant was our company gunny. I heard the sound of the company jeep and some hollering going on. I looked up and saw the staff sergeant riding on the passenger side of the jeep and barking orders for the straggling Marines to close it up and keep it tight.

"So this is garrison life in the Marine Corps," I said to Callahan and the others. "The company commander thinks he's a fuckin deer, the platoon sergeant has his head up his ass, and the company gunny is riding in a jeep while we are humping our asses off. So this is leadership by example. That company gunny needs to get his fat ass out of the jeep and hump just like the rest of us."

The Marines agreed with me. After powdering my feet and changing socks, we saddled up again and started back to Camp Schwab.

"Let me carry that gun for awhile," Callahan suggested.

"Not on your life," I replied. "I'm the gunner, so I'll carry it all the way, even if it kills me."

"You don't have to," he said, "we can all take turns."

"Never mind," I said. "Ain't no biggy. I'd end up carrying the spare barrel or tripod anyway. Besides, I'd rather carry the gun."

"Okay, Callahan said, "but if you get tired just let me know."

We humped the rest of the way back without another break. I could not believe that we had to be pushed so hard. We were supposed to take a ten minute break after every hour of hiking, but policy could be deviated from, I reckoned. When we reached the barracks we had to clean the weapons before we turned them back into the armory. Inside the cubicle I took my boots off. I had large blisters on both feet. I used a needle from my sewing kit and punctured the blisters and squeezed the fluid out of them. What a way to make a living, I thought.

We spent the rest of the week cleaning weapons. We would bring the M60 and M16s into our barracks cubicle and clean them there. We pulled out our olive drab footlockers from underneath the bottom racks and spread out all our weapons cleaning gear so the entire gun team could have access to it. We used all kinds of cleaning solvents and lubricants which worked good for lubrication but did not clean the carbon enough to pass inspection. We found out that if you wanted to pass inspection with the M60 you had to use regular gasoline. It would definitely take off the caked on carbon. While cleaning weapons for hours on end we enjoyed listening to the radio. A popular song at the time was "All Right Now" by an English rock band called Free. We would be cleaning the weapons while listening to the song and then break for chow. When we returned to the barracks from eating chow, the song would be playing once again on the radios. I did a lot of weapons cleaning listening to that song.

We also conducted close order drill, personnel inspections, and gun drills with the M60 machine gun. The purpose of the gun drills was to give team members complete confidence in our ability to put the machine gun into action with precision and speed. We rotated duties and billets during our training to ensure every member of the gun team became proficient with all the other positions. In this way, any Marine could fill in for another at any given time. Precision and speed were our primary goals, but we never sacrificed precision for speed.

Within our team we trained with the squad leader, team leader, myself as the gunner, and one ammunition bearer. The squad leader's equipment consisted of binoculars and a compass. The team leader had the tripod and one bandoleer of ammunition. As the gunner, I carried the machine gun with gun platform and the attached pintle, one bandoleer of ammunition, and a combination wrench. The wrench was used to tighten the gas cylinder on the barrel of the gun when it became loose from continuous firing. The ammunition bearer carried the spare barrel case, traversing and elevating mechanism, and one metal ammo can of pre-linked 7.62 mm NATO cartridges.

For our drills the gun team would form on line with approximately five paces between members. The squad leader would give all the commands while the team leader repeated them to his team. We would go through a series of motions and inspection of our equipment and then on the command "Action," we would start the procedure of setting up the gun as rapidly as possible.

As the gunner, I would reach and grab the M60 by the carrying handle with my right hand and a bandoleer of 100 pre-linked ammunition with my left hand. Then we would all double time forward to a predesignated position where the gun was to be mounted. I would run directly behind the team leader who was running with the tripod. The team leader then held the tripod up over his head and pulled outward to spread the legs. He would then mount the tripod on the ground at the designated spot. When I arrived at his location I would get down in the prone position, place my bandoleer of rounds to the left of the tripod, lock the pintle into the well of the tripod, raise the rear sight of the gun, and then assume the prone position once again. The team leader would then receive the traversing and elevating mechanism from the ammunition bearer and hand it off to me. After receiving the T&E from the team leader, I would fasten it onto the gun and lock it to the tripod. Then I would open the cover, insert the linked ammunition into the feedway, close and latch the cover, and pull the bolt to the rear until it locked in the open position. Once I had completed these actions I would signal to the team that I was ready to commence firing by yelling out, "UP!"

The sequence was then followed by changing the barrel while the team leader assisted. The team leader had a duel role of assistant gunner commonly referred to as the A-gunner. Each team member had his own inspection and movements in order to properly set the gun up for firing. We practiced the entire sequence until we got to within ten to twelve seconds. The whole idea was to set up the machine gun as quickly as possible and to work as a team.

The following Sunday I caught a bus down to Camp Hansen to locate Donald in the barracks. He was supposed to have duty that weekend but I could not seem to locate him. I walked outside the main gate into Kin Ville to see if he was at his house. He was not home either. After walking the streets for awhile, I decided to see if I could find my cousin. From the letters I had received from him while I was in Vietnam, I knew that he was with the military police, and that his unit was at Camp Hansen also.

After asking several Marines who were wandering about on the base, I finally found the barracks where he stayed. The Duty NCO told me that he was on duty at Hanoko, a little town just outside the main gate at Camp Schwab. So without further adieu, I got on another bus heading back to Camp Schwab. I asked the driver to let me off at the entrance to Hanoko. It was only walking distance to the main gate and I knew that I would be able to walk the rest of the way back to my barracks if I could not find him.

I walked down each narrow street trying to locate him. It was a very small town and I covered some of the streets twice. I felt that I was searching in vain so I went inside a small bar. As I sat down on a bar stool I placed my Kodak Instamatic 124 camera on the bar in front of me. I looked down at the small scratched up camera that I had taped together. I thought to myself that it had been a good investment for only five dollars while I was in Vietnam.

I asked the mamasan tending bar to give me a beer. She reached inside a cooler and pulled out an Orion. I sipped the brew, quenching my thirst. I paid her and then looked around at the decorated interior. I could see oriental ornaments throughout and various posters hanging on the walls. There was a group of six Marines drinking in a corner and four girls sitting with them. They seemed to be having the time of their life.

"Buy me one drinki," I heard one of the girls say to a Marine. I watched as he pulled out his wallet and gave her a ten dollar bill. She walked up to the bar next to me and ordered a rum and coke. As the bartender fixed her drink they laughed and talked in their native tongue. The girl turned to face me and winked one eye. I smiled and then looked away not wanting to cause a confrontation with the other Marines. While the two women were conversing, I managed to get a few sneak peeks at the girl standing next to me.

She had long straight black hair, brown eyes, and wore a silky red dress exposing her cleavage. I noticed her high cheek bones and flat nose. Her arms were tanned and her hands appeared to look unusually rough. I figured that this was probably from working in the fields during the day. She returned to the table with her drink and gestured to the Marine that she would keep the change. I figured it was at least eight dollars. After a bit of teasing, the Marine let her keep the change. A very high priced tip, I thought.

I finished my beer and was ready to call it a day. We were supposed to have a hike the next day so I didn't want to stay out too late. When I walked outside the bar I noticed that the sun was beginning to go down. The streets were now full of drunken Marines stumbling from one bar to the next. They were somewhat rowdy but no one seemed to pay much attention to them. I saw a few Marines on duty as Shore Patrol to try and keep the Marines out of trouble. I noticed a couple of MP's walk around a corner down a street so I decided to ask them if they knew my cousin. I walked rapidly and caught up with them. I gave a corporal my cousin's name and explained what he looked like. He told me that he knew him and that he was walking the beat with another MP in Hanoko."

"Do you know where he might be now?" I asked.

"Wait just a minute and I'll contact him on the radio," the corporal replied. He reached and pulled out a walkie-talkie from the side of his black MP belt. I listened as he spoke over the radio.

"Echo Three Foxtrot, this is Echo Four Mobile," he said. I could hear a transmission over the radio.

"Roger," he replied. "What is your location? I have someone here who wants to see you. It's your cousin."

He talked back and forth a little more and then told me to walk down a street to my left and that I would run into him.

"Thanks a lot," I told the corporal, "I really appreciate it."

"Don't mention it," the corporal responded.

I started to walk down the street and saw two MP's rounding the corner about fifty feet away. I recognized my cousin right away.

"Hey, you son-of-a-gun!" I yelled. "Long time, no see!"

My cousin stared at me from the distance and said, "Hello, Freddy, how the hell are you?"

We began to walk a little faster toward each other and ended up in the middle of the street shaking hands.

"Damn it's good to see you again Freddy," my cousin said.

"Likewise," I said. "How ya been anyway? I went to your barracks and they told me that you were on duty in Hanoko, so I decided to try and look you up."

With a big grin on his face he said, "It's good to have you back. Did you see much action in Vietnam?"

"Oh, just a little here and there," I responded, not wanting to boast or brag.

"I've been wanting to go over there but now I hear that they are pulling out most of the units. Is that true Freddy?" he asked.

"Yes," I said. "That's why I'm here now, 3rd Battalion, 7th Marines were pulled out."

"What are my chances of going over to Vietnam now?"

"Not good," I answered. "I think you've missed out on your opportunity to see combat action in Vietnam."

"Oh well," he replied, "maybe I'll get to be in the next war."

"Yeah, maybe," I said. "We'll probably both be in the next war, but for right now, I've seen enough."

We walked along while talking about our parents and home back in Kentucky. Suddenly there was a sound of a loud explosion somewhere down one of the streets. My first instinct was to drop immediately to the ground. I didn't quite hit the pavement, but I was close to it. While still in a stooped position I yelled out, "What the hell was that?"

My cousin was a little stunned at my reaction. "Take it easy Freddy," he said. "You're not in Vietnam. That's just some clowns with cherry bombs. They like to terrorize the Ville. Most of them are Vietnam Vets strutting their stuff."

WHOOOM! There was another explosion.

"Gotta go Freddy," he said as he turned about and started to run down the street with his partner.

"Wait just a minute!" I yelled.

He stopped and turned around. I raised my camera and took a quick snap shot of him. "Okay," I laughed. "Go gettum."

He swirled around and started to race down the street. He held the baton dangling from his holster on his left side with his left hand to keep it from interfering with his running. He placed his right hand over the pistol holster on the right side of his belt to keep his revolver from falling out. I followed behind them walking at a fast pace just to see what was going on. I was curious what he and the other MP was going to do with a bunch of rowdy Marines.

When I arrived at the scene my cousin and the other MP's had joined forces and were rounding up about ten Marines in the crowd. They were walking them toward the MP Sub-Station and had confiscated the remaining cherry bombs from the would-be hoodlums. The cherry bombs would not cause much damage, however they definitely made some loud noises.

As my cousin and the group passed by me I hollered, "I'm gonna go now. I see you have work to do."

"Okay Freddy," he replied, "come visit me at the barracks next weekend and I'll take you to BC Street."

"What's at BC Street?" I asked as I still followed along with them.

"Have you heard of "Suck-a-Hotchi Alley," commonly known as Whisper Alley?" he replied.

"Oh, yeah," I said laughing. "Now I remember. Sucki-Fucky, Five Dolla?"

"You got it," he replied, "I'll show you a good time."

"Okay, see you later," I said.

We waved goodbye to each other. I returned to my barracks and prepared my gear for the hike which was scheduled for the following morning and hit the rack. The next day we humped for only two miles but at a very rapid pace. My feet were still burning from the twenty-two mile hike the week prior. I looked forward to getting on ship so we wouldn't have to hump as much. That night I felt the need to write home.

October 15, 1970

Hello Mom, Dad and Larry,

How is everyone around home getting along? I hope just fine. Guess it's getting cool back there now, but over here it gets to about 85 degrees during the day. When I get home it'll probably be pretty cold, but I won't mind. The quicker I get out of this place the better I'll like it. To tell you the truth, I'd rather be in Nam.

Here at Camp Schwab things are about like ITR. Well, anywhere you go here it's the same way. Maybe when we get on the float in late November things will slacken off a little. People have told me how nice Okinawa is. Well, so far, they can have the whole damn island. I know they don't do the things that the grunts do. We're always training.

We get up at 5:30 a.m. and fall out for PT, that is, physical training. We do about fifteen minutes of exercises, then we fall back in the barracks and clean up. Then chow goes and I make every chow formation. Ha ha! Wish I had a good home cooked meal of Mom's, but that will have to wait for awhile. We usually have a few classes during the day. If it's not one thing it's another; like a hike, cleaning our weapons, or drilling. We went on a short hike today, just two miles out and two back, but the lieutenant leading the formation almost ran the distance instead of walking. Of course, he doesn't have the stuff we have to carry.

I'm the machine gunner of the team so I carry the M60 machine gun everywhere we go. The other day we went on a twenty-two mile hike, but I survived. Also we run about three miles every other day and we had a PFT (Physical Fitness Test). Almost like boot camp in many ways. It doesn't bother me though because I just play along with them. We've been going to the field for a few days at a time to play war games. Trouble is, what we do here, I wouldn't dare do in Vietnam.

Well, guess I've said enough about this island for awhile. Guess I'll just do what I can for another four months. One good thing about being here is that we get liberty almost every night, but I've been pretty busy these first few weeks. I'm aiming to see Donald this weekend if I can. Mom, you were asking how Donald looked. Well he hasn't changed a bit. He's still the same old Donald I've always known.

No Mom! I won't have to go back to Nam. I couldn't go even if I tried because they're pulling Marines out of Nam. Mom, you also wanted to know about my ribbons. Well come to find out I only have 4. Another one is supposed to come through, but whether it ever will I don't know. One is the National Defense Service Medal which is red and yellow with red, white, and blue stripes. One is the Vietnam Service Medal which is green and yellow with three red stripes. I have the Republic of Vietnam Campaign Medal for being in Nam over 6 months. It's green and white with the number 61 on it to represent when the Marines first landed in Nam. The most senior one is the Combat Action Ribbon for being in direct combat with the enemy. It is blue, yellow, and red with small red, white, and blue stripes in the center.

Well I guess I'll close for now. Don't guess you all think I like it here. All I can say is that I'll do my best since there's no other choice. They say the cruise is really nice so I'm looking forward to that. So until I get a chance to write again, I'll say good-bye and hope this finds everyone doing fine.

As ever,
Fred

Lima Company spent the next few weeks in the field practicing and re-hearsing company tactics. When we moved from one position to another we dug fighting holes and set up defensive positions. The other platoons went out on simulated ambushes and patrols. Within the Weapons Platoon, the machine gun squads, mortar section, and 3.5 rocket launcher section, took turns being attached out to the various squads within the company. This way we could alternate training with the rifle platoons and also provide general support for the company in the defensive positions. My squad's first assign-ment was to set in with machine gun interlocking fires within the perimeter. Range cards were prepared by the team leaders and inspected by the squad leaders and platoon commander. Foster became the squad leader and I moved up from the gunner to team leader.

We moved to a new location one day and began to dig fighting holes that were inspected by the platoon commander. He wanted to make sure that the holes were in strict accordance with the "Manual," that is, so deep, so wide, with a concealed parapet around the front of the holes. As I dug my hole I thought about all the hasty fighting holes that I had dug in the soil in Vietnam. No one measured the holes there. Somehow we had sensed how deep to dig our holes depending if Charlie was in the vicinity. I dug my hole faster and faster and then without realizing what I was doing, I dug out a sleeping hole as well.

Foster approached me and asked, "What the hell are you digging that for, Fenwick?"

I stopped abruptly, scratched my head in disbelief, then threw my E-tool on the ground.

"Damned if I know," I said, "I must have gotten carried away."

"What exactly is it?" he asked.

"Oh, it's a sleeping hole," I replied. "We used to dig these in Vietnam to keep the incoming shrapnel from penetrating our bodies while we slept or rested.

"Well, Foster said," There ain't any VC or NVA here. We won't be get-ting any enemy incoming so you are just wasting your time."

"Yes, I agree with you," I said, "can't kill anyone using blanks for bul-lets anyway."

We both laughed at the idea that we were parading around in the field playing war games. On occasions when the Marines ran out of blank rounds during our exercises, they would verbally holler out, "Bang Bang, or Buda Buda Buda." It seemed so corny and asinine to me at the time.

While I sat back in my fighting hole eating some C-Rations, down in the bushes I began to hear some rustling. Then I heard the voice of a woman. Suddenly an old Okinawan woman emerged carrying a large basket on her back. She approached me and awkwardly removed the basket from her shoulders and sat on the ground in front of me. She then opened the top and I could see that she had lined it with plastic and ice and was selling sodas. I looked into the basket and could see the coca-cola bottles laying in the half melted ice.

She offered me one and I gladly accepted. Wouldn't have to worry about chipped glass in these sodas, I reckoned. She opened the top for me with a bottle opener and then held out her hand for some money. I didn't have any Japanese yen on me so I gave her an American dollar bill. She was more than happy to receive payment which was most likely three times what she was asking for. I drank the cold soda while I continued to eat my C-Rations. It was a good combination, one that I had not been used to. I had always settled for water while eating C-Rations.

The woman tried to talk to me in her native tongue but I could not understand very much. All I knew was that she was a very nice old woman. She finally picked up her basket of goodies and went from Marine to Marine selling sodas. The platoon commander found out that she was in the area and told the section leaders to run her off and to not allow us to drink the sodas. In his opinion, we were on military maneuvers and needed to keep our attention focused on any enemy activity. Enemy activity, I thought. What enemy activity? At any rate the Marines continued to purchase sodas from the woman and she eventually had to leave because she had been run off by those in the position of authority. She waved to us as she passed by us heading back into the dense brush.

On our last day of the field exercise, the company commander had this bright idea that we would take a hill by double-timing up to the foot of the hill while wearing gas masks, and then continue our assault to the top. At our rallying point we began to run with full combat gear. When we got to the bottom of the hill everyone was tired and began to fall out. The Marines started taking off the smothering gas masks. He ranted and raved with the platoon commanders for the Marines to don their masks. We started off again, this time to the top of the hill. The Marines could barely breathe with the gas masks strapped to their faces. My chest burned for lack of oxygen as I tried to suck in fresh air. After we reached the top of the hill, word was finally passed that we could remove our gas masks. All the Marines were totally exhausted and sweating profusely. I wondered what foolishness the company commander would try on our next phony assault. Running to an objective was unheard of in Vietnam.

That next Saturday back at Camp Schwab, my gun team decided to take a sponsored tour of the southern part of Okinawa. We caught a bus down to Camp Hansen and then boarded a tour bus. We did not know exactly where the tour bus stopped, but we proceeded to the "Cave of Virgins." It was somewhere near the capital city of Naha. As we all took pictures from the entrance of the cave, I noticed the writings on a sign that was posted for tourists.

The story told to us at the time, was that during World War II, American soldiers had seen some girls fleeing into the cave and ignored the soldier's commands to stop. When the Americans reached the cave there were loud noises coming from within. The soldiers figured that the enemy soldiers were held up inside the cave, so they demolished it with the use of flame throwers. When the war ended, it became known that inside the cave there were about seventy young girls. All were teenagers and most had been nurses. Their remains were still undisturbed at the bottom of the cave.

We moved on to "Suicide Cliff" and walked through the underground annexes and bunkers that the Japanese had built to defend the island. Radios, maps, chairs, and quarters still remained undisturbed. They were roped off so the tourists could not tamper with the remains of that long fought war. This was also the spot where two Japanese Generals committed suicide so that they would not be captured and lose face. Also the women threw their babies off the cliff and onto the reefs and water below, and ultimately leaping themselves off the sides to their deaths. As I stood on the cliff of history past, I looked across the water to the east and had a vision that my home was somewhere many miles away off in the distance. I longed to get back there.

Our next stop was in the city of Naha. I felt like a fish out of water when I got off the bus and looked around at the tall buildings and the hustle and bustle of city life. We formed together and proceeded down an alley into a meat market. They were selling chickens and pigs right on the streets. The venders wanted us to come into their clothing stores, but we were more fascinated with the sights and were not that interested in shopping.

After a few hours we decided to go into a movie theater and watch a movie that we had seen advertised on a bill board outside. Once the movie started, we realized that we had made a mistake, for the entire movie was in the Japanese language. After only a few short minutes we decided to continue on sight seeing throughout the city. We stopped at a restaurant and ate some chicken fried rice. Callahan smothered his rice with catsup. The waitress thought he was a mad man for treating rice in this manner. We all laughed as we joined in and squirted catsup all over the rice. Actually it tasted real good.

On the next day I went back to see Donald for a short while and then stopped off at Camp Hansen to see my cousin. When I walked in on him he was buffing a waxed floor in the recreation room around a pool table.

"Well," I announced, "I'm here to take you up on that offer to go to BC Street down in Koza." Koza was about twelve miles south of Camp Hanson.

While still buffing the floor he replied, "I was beginning to wonder if you were going to show up. Where have you been?"

"Out in the field playing war games," I responded.

"Didn't you get enough of that in Nam?" he asked.

I said, "Oh yeah, but you know how it is. In the grunts the training just never stops. We do the same old stuff over and over."

"You should do like I did," he exclaimed. "Hell I got tired of that stuff so I changed my MOS to the Military Police field."

"What's the matter," I laughed, "can't hack the grunts?"

"It's not that," he said, "I just want to do something in the Marine Corps that I can benefit from when I get out."

"Yeah, know what you mean," I said. "What the hell am I training for in the grunts? Don't know of anyone who hires assassins or mercenaries, do you?"

"Not off hand," he laughed with a chuckle. "Freddy, give me a few more minutes on this floor and I'll get ready to paint the town with you."

I replied, "Okay, but hurry up. I can hear BC Street a-callin-us."

I sat down on a sofa and watched TV while he was finishing up on the floor. I became quite interested in watching a Sumo Wrestling Match. The traditional stomping and parading around seemed to be a bit similar to American professional wrestling, with one exception, the Japanese were dead serious about what they were doing. The commentator had said that they eat several times a day and make it a point to drink as much beer as possible in order to have a big belly to bump each other with. I wondered how the wrestlers could even move about in the ring while weighing almost three hundred pounds each. Their costumes seemed to be as much a part of the bout as their ability.

"Hey, I know what I can do when I get out of the Corps," I said. "I can drink beer and eat all day like the Sumo Wrestlers and show these Japanese how to really wrestle."

"I can see it now," my cousin replied. "A three hundred pound trained drunken killer in the attack."

I laughed out loud at the idea. He gestured for me to come with him to his room while he dressed to go out on liberty. He had a two man cubicle like mine at Camp Schwab, but it seemed a bit cozier.

"Looks like you have really decorated your room," I said.

"Yeah," he shrugged. "Home away from home, but for not much longer. Do you realize Freddy that we have been overseas for almost a year now? We are really getting short over here."

"Oh yeah," I replied. "I can't wait to see Cherry Hill Farm again. I'd also like to taste some of that good old Kentucky Sterling Beer and Oertels'92 beer."

"You've got that right," he said. "One of those favorite Kentucky beers would really go good right about now."

"They sure would, but guess we will have to settle for this Okinawan Orion beer for tonight. Hurry up, I commanded, time's a-wastin."

He finished getting dressed and we walked out to the main gate to catch a taxi to Koza. We talked of old times we had spent together on our way to BC Street and he attempted to inform me of what to expect once we got there. We arrived at Koza and started down a narrow street. My cousin was giving the cab driver directions. As we took a left turn he told the driver to stop the cab while speaking in the local language. As we reached for our wallets in order to pay the "Honcho" driver for his services, he said, "This is it, the world renowned Whisper Alley."

"Seems to me you've been here before," I laughed.

"Oh, only a few times with some buddies, just out of curiosity," he replied smiling.

We split the cost of the taxi fare and the driver drove away. We began walking down the somewhat deserted alley still mumbling away. As we talked, I noticed the buildings on both sides of the pavement. They looked like they had not seen paint for years. The exterior framework was a rusty brown and made of course wooden planks. I could see that some of the rooms were very dimly lit. The small square windows had iron rods running down the center and behind the bars were metal sheets. It looked as though we were walking through a jail house. The stench of the benjo ditches that ran along the sides of the pavement on both sides lingered in the still night air.

"I thought you told me that there are all kinds of ladies of the night down here on BC Street," I said. "Hell, I haven't seen one woman since we got out of the cab. Besides a few stray Marines walking down this alley, it appears to be a ghost town."

"Hold your horses," my cousin replied. "We haven't got to the heart of the action yet."

About that time one of the metal sheets could be heard being slid to one side. I turned my head toward the right side of the street where I had heard the sound. We both stopped and looked in through the bars and could see a tiny room dimly lit on the other side. There was one Okinawan girl staring at us from behind the bars. I could see that in the room behind her that there were other girls sitting around in chairs, some in shorts, others in bathing suits, and still others in sexy night gowns.

"Psssst! Psssst!" came a whispering sound from the girl at the window.

"Hey Marine, you want short time? I give you good time. I sucky-fucky, five dolla."

"Did you hear that?" I asked. "This girl wants to drop our pants for only five dollars."

"Oh yeah," my cousin replied, "That's about the going price for Puntang. That's what the Marines call "Rice Pudding." We both laughed.

"Well, Freddy, are you gonna take her up on her offer? Only five dolla," he said laughing.

"No, not me," I replied. "I might catch the black syphilis and my pecker fall off. I've been through enough already. I don't want that to happen."

Two other Marines had now approached us and began peering into the window at the girls. "Hey, you guys gonna go inside and get laid?" one of them asked.

"Ain't no way," I replied, "they look a little ugly to me."

"Hell, the uglier they are, the less chances of catching the clap," one of the Marines responded. "The good looking ones are the ones that get the clap because they go through an entire battalion in one night."

"You might have a point," I agreed.

"Well, I don't know about you guys, but we came here to get laid and that's what we are going to do," he continued.

The two Marines went to the door and two of the girls let them inside. Without closing the door, a girl began talking to the Marine possibly discussing the price. I could see that no action would take place without the money up front. He handed her a few dollars and to our surprise, the girl pulled down his trousers and began to get to work right then and there. The other Marine was led out of sight back into the room. Other girls were now at the door coaxing us to come inside.

"Well, what do you say Freddy?" my cousin asked.

"I say we get the hell out of here," I replied.

We continued down the street and now girls were popping their heads out of the windows on both sides of the street asking us to come inside. We gazed at the girls as we passed by.

"Pssssst, psssst, sucky-fucky," some girls could be heard saying. My cousin stopped and held out his right arm to stop my forward movement.

"Well, what do you think about these ladies?" he asked.

I looked at the elderly women that were whispering behind the barred windows. They had to be at least sixty years of age. Their faces were rough and wrinkled. I saw a few of the women smiling at us and licking their tongues around the outside of their lips.

"I give you good sucky," one of them said.

In disbelief I said, "You've gotta be shittin me. All these women don't have any teeth."

"All the better for a delightful sucky," my cousin laughed. "At least they can't bite your root off."

"That's not what I'm afraid of," I responded, "let's get the hell out of here!"

I had to grab my cousin by his right arm and pull him down the street he was laughing so hard. He had always been a sort of a prankster.

"Now I know why they call it Whisper Alley and Suck-A-Hotchy Alley," I said.

My cousin did not answer. He was too busy laughing. We ended up checking out the local bars. As we passed one club, a male Okinawan was standing outside the doors yelling, "Floor show, floor show! Come inside! See topless and bottomless girls on stage! Floor show, floor show!"

We went inside, sat down, and ordered two Orion Beers. There was an oriental dancer on stage without a top prancing around. We tried to talk to each other over the loud jukebox music. It became a yelling match. As we sipped on our beers the dancer took off her panties and started rolling slowly across the stage on the floor.

"Hot dam," I said. "This is the Life."

"Relax, Freddy," he said. "You've been tromping around in the jungles of Vietnam too long. It's time for you to enjoy yourself. Welcome to BC Street, an Okinawan paradise."

Soon a different girl took the stage. I sat curiously as she strutted around the small stage wearing a flimsy see through gown. One could tell that she did not have any underwear beneath that gown. There was not much left for your imagination. She swayed to the rhythm of the music moving closer to the edge of the stage. Moving up to one of the Marines in the front row, she took off his glasses and while dancing, rubbed them all over her private parts. The crowd roared with laughter.

She returned the glasses to the Marine, wiped them slightly with her gown, and placed them back on his ears and nose. She then bent forward and kissed him on the forehead. The Marine slumped back in his chair pretending that he was in a daze. She then asked a Marine for a dollar bill. She rolled it up tightly and then squatted down over it and picked it up. The audience clapped and cheered. What a way to make a living, I thought to myself.

I could no longer stand the very loud music so I gave a motion for us to leave. My cousin took me to a Japanese style restaurant where they cooked the food right in front of us. That was the best part of the night. My cousin had to prove to me that he could use the chop sticks as well. After dinner we decided to head back to the barracks. I had enjoyed the night out on the town but figured I would stay away from BC Street in the future. It was just not my cup of tea. When we got to Camp Hansen, we said our good-byes. Then he got out of the cab and started walking through the main gate.

"See you after my cruise," I called out to my cousin.

"Yeah, Freddy," you take care of yourself. "I'll see you when you get back."

I found time during the next few days to write home. I was now getting ready to deploy on a cruise to Singapore, Philippines, and back to the coast of Vietnam. I wondered if we might land on the shores of Vietnam. God forbid, I thought.

November 17, 1970
9:00 p.m.

Hi Mom, Dad and Larry,

How is everyone getting along now that the tobacco is in the barn? I imagine you all are pretty glad it's stripped off the stalk.

Hope it sells real good at the market.

For myself, I'm doing fine but have been awful busy this last week. We're having all kinds of inspections before we go on ship. We had a big one today and got inspected by the colonel and he seemed like he was pretty well satisfied. We were the first company in the battalion to pass his inspection, so I guess we did pretty good.

Well, I moved up to a team leader now instead of being a gunner. I just have two men under me now, but things may change around now that we're going on a ship. Usually there are four guys in a gun team. I'm kinda glad to get back to carrying a rifle instead of always carrying the heavy machine gun.

I looked at the calendar today and counted one hundred three days left overseas. By the time you get this letter I'll be a two digit midget, in other words, getting pretty short in time left overseas. When I get back from the cruise I'll have thirteen days left, so it won't be long until I get on that silver bird back to the States.

I got some pictures back the other day which I took around the barracks. I'll send them home when I get the time. I had bought a cheap little album from a mamasan in town. She wanted three dollars for it, but she finally sold it to me for a dollar and a half. You can usually talk these people down on their prices if you try hard enough.

By the way, I saw Donald last Sunday. I went to his house and two Marines were renting it out. They told me to see a mamasan that worked in a bar at Kin Ville. I went to talk to her and she knew where Donald had moved to. She was pretty nice. She took me to where he was in a taxi cab and I paid the fare which was about fifty cents and the driver went on back. After awhile Donald and I took her back to the bar.

Donald lives in a Japanese style house about a mile out of Kin Ville. It has about three rooms. He has a small TV and just about everything that goes in a living room back home. He has mats on the floor instead of a rug. The front doors slide open and closed, and as you look in, there is a table that he eats on. It is about as big as the coffee table Mom has in the front room. It's not like the houses in the States of course, but it's nice and comfortable. Shoes come off before entering too. Ha!

We had fried chicken, rice, fried potatoes, and believe it or not pop corn and beer for supper. He had tried to contact me one other Sunday, but my liberty card had been pulled, because I had messed up on an inspection. That Sunday I could not get off Base. The reason they pulled my liberty card was because I had marked my name in my underwear in the wrong place. This place is really that way. That's why I'll be glad to get out of here.

Well, I have to go now so everyone take care and be good. Bye for now and I'll see everyone in about three months or so.

Yours truly,
Fred

On Sunday 22 November 1970 we began to move our belongings out to an open field in preparation for loading aboard the ship. We could see the ship anchored off shore. We were to have a clothing and equipment inspection prior to movement to the ship. The entire battalion was instructed to form up as companies and to open ranks in order to dump our seabags for inspection. This we did and waited for the battalion commander to walk through the ranks.

It just so happened that the battalion commander had previously passed the word that "under no circumstances" would any Marine be allowed to bring civilian attire aboard the ship. When he spotted several Marines within the battalion that had brought along civilian clothing anyway, he became extremely angry and chewed out all the company commanders. They were ordered to tell all the Marines who brought civilian clothes in their seabags to take them back to the barracks. He also stated that if he caught any Marine with civilian attire aboard the ship that he would personally throw them overboard. Luckily, I had followed orders and did not have to return to the barracks. When the Marines returned to the formation, they were again chewed out by the battalion commander for not following orders.

We were finally choppered by CH-46s aboard the USS Iwo Jima LPH-2. The LPH stood for Landing Platform for Helicopters. That afternoon we settled into our compartments. It was cramped and stuffy down in the belly of the ship. The racks were very close together and were stacked four racks high. When a Marine lay down in his rack he only had about six inches of room in between him and the rack above. Someone had said that if the Marine on the top rack became seasick, the vomit would spill over onto the racks below. I was to find out that this would become a true statement.

The following day we set sail for Subic Bay, Republic of the Philippines. We ran into some rough seas while traveling from Okinawa to the Philippines. After a few days the ship pulled into the Subic Bay harbor and docked. At night the horizon was lit from the city lights of Olongapo City. We knew there would be no liberty for us this first night in port, but we hoped that the battalion commander would let us all go out on the town the following day.

The next morning passed quickly since we were cleaning weapons and our compartments. We also had classes given by the corpsman on venereal diseases. This Sailor had been to Subic Bay once before and knew of the various diseases that could be contacted. Evening rolled around and there was no word of liberty for our battalion. The Sailors aboard the ship had left earlier that morning in civilian attire and very few had returned when it started to turn dusk.

Then we heard on the intercom that liberty had been sounded for the Marine Air Wing unit that had embarked on the ship with us. The Marines within 3rd Battalion, 9th Marines, began to grow restless and eager to walk down the gang plank. Some of the troops began asking questions about liberty call for the BLT (Battalion Landing Team). The platoon commanders were summoned to a meeting with the company commander. The battalion commander had passed the word that there would be no liberty for the Marines of the BLT for the next few days.

The Marines complained about the decision but we were to follow his orders. Finally after seeing that the complaining was getting us nowhere we decided to settle down and play cards and watch TV that we had in the berthing areas. Time was spent writing letters and in general carrying on with outlandish conversations.

The following morning at around 1000 liberty was sounded for the Sailors. Then at around 1500 liberty was once again sounded for the Marine Air Wing. We would watch them, dressed in civilian clothes, walk down the gang plank and disappear out of sight on their way to Olongapo. While my platoon was cleaning weapons on the hanger deck, we heard what sounded like a riot on the other side of the ship. There were several Marines who had gathered around in a huddle near the gang plank and were ranting and raving in a boisterous manner. Some of us rushed over to see what all the commotion was about. When we got to where the crowd had gathered they told us that the battalion commander had been seen dressed in civilian attire and going off the ship.

"I can't believe this shit," a Marine said. "We got our asses chewed out for trying to bring civilian clothes on ship while all the time the battalion commander had civvies in his luggage. What a crock!"

Someone else joined in, "Yeah, this is unsat. We couldn't bring civilian clothes, but its okay for the lifers. Piss poor leadership example," he continued.

Now a corporal joined in the protest, "These lifers can go out on liberty but the peon enlisted is stuck back here on ship. We should walk down the gang plank in utilities and say to hell with these lifer sons-a-bitches."

Just then some of the Staff Noncommissioned Officers arrived and began to disperse the crowd of Marines. They were barking orders for the men to return to their platoon areas.

One of the gunny's made a statement, "We all know that it is bullshit, but I won't have a mutiny on our hands. The Staff NCO's will have a talk with the Officers and find out what the hell is going on."

Everyone returned to their areas and we could see that the Staff NCO's had joined together and were walking away together to talk with the respective company commanders. That evening when the battalion commander returned to the ship there were a few Marines who awaited him at the top of the gang plank. They began to jeer him as he stepped foot aboard the ship. Without saying a word the battalion commander hurriedly proceeded to his quarters and called for a meeting with the company commanders.

After about two hours the company commanders returned. Our company commander of Lima Company informed us that we would be allowed to go on liberty the following morning with a few stipulations. First of all, everyone must have civilian clothes which meant that we would have to rush to the PX at Subic Bay Naval Base and buy clothes. Second, liberty call would commence at 1000. Thirdly, liberty was to be secured at 1800 because the next day we were to disembark from the ship and be transported to our billeting area. We all returned to our racks still somewhat bitter about not being allowed to bring civilian attire aboard the ship in the first place.

The next morning there was a mad dash to the Duty NCO to have the individual liberty cards signed out. We all had them all checked out before the time liberty was to commence. The entire battalion was gathered around the gang plank when the clock stuck 1000. Marines were all crowded around one another pushing for the exit. It took several minutes for Callahan, Trump, Hill, Foster, and I to get to the gang plank. We rushed to the PX and started trying on civilian clothes. We bought the first pair of trousers, shirt, and shoes that would fit half way decent. Then we returned to the ship to change clothes and to secure our sateen utility uniforms. It was not long until we were headed toward the Main Gate that was manned by the Marines stationed at Marine Barracks, Subic Bay. They checked our military ID cards and liberty cards and then we walked hurriedly down the sidewalk. After only a few feet we came upon the bridge that separated the Main Gate from Olongapo City.

When we neared the center of the bridge we heard voices coming from over the side of the railing. We stopped and looked down at the dirty river below. It had a very unpleasant odor. We could see numerous small boats floating in the river a few feet from the bridge. The boats were approximately ten feet long and each was anchored by the use of ropes in the front and back. Inside the boats were three or four small Filipino boys dressed only in trunks or shorts. A pretty teenage Filipina girl also stood in the middle of the boats. The girls were dressed in lavish white dresses.

"Hey Marine, throw me one peso," a boy nearest to us yelled out.

"Throw one coin into river and I dive for it, then I give to the pretty lady. Okay?"

We laughed and joked about what the young boy was willing to do for a little pocket change. I was intrigued knowing that even more adventures awaited me on the other side of the Orient. This was an Orient at peace. A Marine a few feet away from us flipped a coin out from the bridge and into the water. Three young boys dived into the water from different boats. After about thirty seconds, one of them emerged with the coin, swam to his boat, and tossed it into a tin can. We could not believe that the boy had actually found the coin in the dirty and murky river. He had held his breath for what seemed like a very long time.

"Thank you Marine, thank you," he said as he wiped the dirty water away from his eyes with both hands. "Souvenir me one more peso."

"Let me try one," Foster said. He took out a coin and flipped it into the water. Immediately about four boys and now one small girl dived into the water. The boy, who had initially got our attention, emerged with the treasure. He held up his hand to prove that he had retrieved the coin, thanked us, and then swam to his boat and crawled in. He tossed the coin into a tin can as well.

"Ain't that something," Callahan said, "I can't imagine them being able to find anything in that nasty water."

Foster replied, "Hell, that's only one of the ways they try to make a living for themselves. It don't matter if its pesos, or nearly worthless centavos, they have to make a living somehow. The nice looking girls in the boats probably sell their bodies at night, as prostitutes. Anyway, you guys know what they call this river here in Olongapo? None other than, Shit River. That's cause raw sewage is dumped into this channel."

Hill spoke up, "Yeah, that's the nickname the Americans gave it, but what do the Filipino's call the river, anybody know?"

Callahan replied, "Who cares? I'm okay with the name. Now let's get on with it. I want to check out some good looking Filipina honey-co's today."

"There you go Callahan," Foster said, "You're letting your hard dick override your brain housing group."

As usual Trump had to top it off with his favorite quotation, "Yeah, Callahan, you'll get over like the dog."

We laughed and continued across the bridge. As we reached the other side of the bridge Foster stopped and turned around forcing all of us to come to an abrupt halt. We listened to what he had to say.

"Well this is Magsaysay Drive. You guys better take your wallets and put them in your socks. There are pickpockets all over this city. They will rob you blind and you won't even know it."

We all agreed with him. Without haste and almost simultaneously we removed our wallets from our trousers pockets, placed them in our socks, and then pulled our trouser legs back down.

"Sounds like you have been in Olongapo before," I said to Foster.

"Yeah," he said, "This is my second cruise to the Philippines. You guys stick next to me and I will keep you out of trouble."

"Listen to him," Hill interrupted, "he's the old salt of the Orient."

We walked on the right side of the street. As we walked along I took notice of some of the bar and club names. There were names such as New Mexico Club, California Club, Grand Ole Opry Club, and Old Grand Dad Club. As we proceeded on into the city I noticed the heavy traffic of motorcycles and jeepneys. The jeepneys were the most popular means of public transportation in the Philippines that were originally made from U.S. military jeeps left over from World War II. They were known for their rich and colorful decorations and crowded passenger seating. They became a symbol of Philippine culture.

To me the jeepneys were comical looking. The front resembled an ordinary jeep and the rear was assembled in such a manner to accommodate eight or more people. There was a roof covering the bed while the sides were open. The vehicle was colorfully painted on the sides with a touch of individualism. Each vehicle had a design of its own. I saw no dividing lines on the streets and witnessed the jeepneys swaying in and out of the traffic sometimes coming all the way across the road from the opposite side. The traffic moved slowly under the heat of the sun, bumper to bumper.

Foster who was feeling in charge at this moment said, "These people drive like maniacs over here. What ever you do, stay off the streets."

There were neon signs and the billboards hanging above our heads along the streets. Being as it was in the middle of the day there were no flashing lights but we could read the names of the various bars. As we walked along the sidewalk I began to lag behind the rest due to my curiosity. Two young girls, around the age of six years old, came up to me and walked with me. A girl was on each side of me and they held my hands as we walked. Although I thought they were so cute and sweet, I gestured for them to move away, but they persisted. I told them to "Didi Mau", which was Vietnamese and not the Philippine Tagalog language.

"Where are you going Marine? I will take you there," one of them said.

"No, that's okay," I replied, "I will go with my friends."

They continued to pull on my hands as if guiding me to my destination. Again one of them asked, "Where are you going?"

I yelled to Foster who was several paces ahead of me. "Hey, Foster, where are we going? These two little girls are driving me crazy."

Foster kept walking but turned his head back over his shoulder and said, "We're going to the Oriental Club."

He then noticed me walking with the two little girls, and said "Hey Fenwick, better get rid of the two girls. They looked like trouble to me."

"Ohhh, come on Foster," I answered. "They look like they are about six years old. What trouble can they cause?"

Foster replied, "You can't trust any of these people over here."

Immediately it dawned on me that these very same words of advice had been frequently addressed to the Marines in Vietnam. I became disappointed with myself for letting my guard down and being so complacent.

"Get away from me and leave me alone," I said with anger in my voice. I pulled both hands away from their grasp. The young girl holding my right hand let go but the one on the left persisted to hang on to my hand. Almost immediately I felt my watch sliding off my wrist. Before I could react, the two girls were running away from me amid the crowd of people. The girl holding my left hand had stripped my watch right off my wrist.

I turned around and yelled in anger, "Come back here with my watch, you little bitch!"

They continued running through the crowd and was soon out of sight. Foster and the others were now entering the Oriental Club.

I yelled to Foster waving my hand. "Hey Foster, wait a minute! Those little girls stole my watch. Let's see if we can catch them."

Foster paused at the door and said, "Forget it, Fenwick. Your watch is history. We could search for months and still not find those two girls. After all, they all look the same to me."

"Well hell," I said while walking toward Foster. "I ain't believing this shit."

"You should have listened to me," Foster said shaking his head. He put his arm around my neck and said, "Ooohh well, just forget it. Come on in the Oriental Club and I'll buy you a beer."

I was surprised to see that the bars were open for business in the middle of the day. It was dark inside as we stepped out of the sun light. There were no dancing girls at this time of the day so we each drank a lukewarm San Miguel beer. We left after that and continued walking along the sidewalk. We came upon a small fenced in area. There was a small boy trying to sell us some ducklings. We all stopped and hovered around him. The boy placed a small duckling into Foster's palm. We began to pass it among ourselves to have a feel of the soft silky coat of feathers.

By the time Hill got to hold the duckling he cried out, "Damned duck shit in my hands." He almost dropped the bird transferring it from one hand to another. We all laughed at his comical expression and at the same time felt lucky it did not happen to us. Callahan took the duckling away from Hill and handed it back to the boy.

Trump asked, "Why in hell are they selling ducks on the streets for?"

"Give the boy enough pesos to buy it and I'll show you," Foster said.

Out of curiosity, Trump reached into his wallet and pulled out two pesos. He handed the money to the boy.

Foster said to Trump, "Now that you have bought the duck, you can do the honors."

"What do you mean?" asked Trump.

"Its time for you to feed the alligator," Foster laughed.

Trump had not been able to see the four foot alligator laying in a pool of water. "Holy crap!" Trump exclaimed in disbelief. "I can't feed this duck to no alligator. It's inhumane."

"Then let me do it," Foster replied.

Without hesitation he snatched the duck from Trump's hands and threw it into the pool of water. The duckling began swimming frantically in circles. The alligator moved swiftly towards the duck and gulped down the little bird in one swallow.

With a pitiful and disgusted look on Trump's face he said, "There just ain't no justice." We snickered at his remarks and continued to head toward the next bar. Time passed quickly.

Finally Foster said, "It's 1700, time for us to head back to the ship. We don't want to miss movement and end up in the brig feeding on bread and water."

With that we walked hastily out of the bar, down the sidewalks, across the bridge, through the main gate, up the gang plank, and onto the ship. For the next few hours we talked about what we might do the next time we pulled liberty in Olongapo City.

The next day we off-loaded the ship and took buses to the Upper SLF (Special Landing Force) Camp which was only about a half hour drive. It was perched high upon a hill which seemed like a mountain for us. We settled into our barracks which were the old Quonset hut style. We secured our weapons and prepared our gear to go to the field. Our battalion was scheduled to conduct field training and maneuvers for the next five days.

I stepped outside of my Quonset hut and sat down on a set of wooden steps. I had a new deck of cards that I was shuffling in order to practice the art. I was never much of a card player, but I was intrigued at how some of the Marines could shuffle the cards when playing. As I shuffled the cards, I would occasionally glance around at my surroundings. I noticed a sidewalk that came half way down the hillside and then all of a sudden stopped without connecting any other sidewalks or barracks. I thought it odd that the builders did not finish the job.

Out of curiosity, I put my cards aside and walked around to where the sidewalk started at the top of the hill. As I walked down the sidewalk I thought that it was very nicely done with the exception of not being completed. I came to the very end and noticed that the final square of concrete had been carefully squared on the corners and along the sides. Being a bit puzzled, I momentarily stood at the end of the sidewalk and looked back behind me. I still couldn't figure it out why the construction had suddenly stopped in the middle of the hill.

I stepped off the edge and onto the grass. As I watched where I was stepping, I noticed that some inscription was carved at the very end. I turned around and moved some of the high grass aside with one foot to see if I could see what it said. In total surprise, I saw that part of the inscription read, "Don Fenwick." I knew instantly that it was Donald, my brother back on Okinawa. He obviously had been involved with laying this sidewalk at the Upper SLF Camp. I had to run back to the barracks to tell my buddies. Callahan and Hill walked with me to the end of the sidewalk. They were amazed at seeing my brother's name carved in the concrete.

"Small Marine Corps," Callahan said.

"Yeah," I responded. "It sure is. My brother has left his mark in the

Philippines."

I went back to the barracks and sat down to write Donald a letter and tell him what I had stumbled upon. I was so excited that I went back out to the end of the sidewalk and trimmed the grass from around the last concrete slab, as if to claim the territory for the family. I would write to my parents also to inform them of my discovery in the Philippines.

November 29, 1970

Dear Mom, Dad, and Larry,

Well how's everyone doing now-a-days? Guess the cold weather makes it kinda rough but that's the way it goes. It's hot over here. I'd say it gets up to around 85 degrees during the day. Looks like I'll miss most of the winter back home but I'll probably feel some too since March isn't exactly summer.

By the way, I'm off Okinawa now and on the cruise. As a matter of fact I'm sitting at an SLF Camp in the Philippines right now. There are huts here we stay in. We're going to be in the Philippines for about 5 days and then board ship to start sailing around again. We'll be in the bush all five days but I really don't care since it's so warm. Listen, if you all don't hear from me for a couple weeks at a time, don't think nothing of it. Most of the time I stay pretty busy and can't find time to write, but I'll write whenever I get the chance.

Mom, I got your letter today and was glad to get it. We hadn't had any mail since we got on ship, but we should get it pretty regular now. You said you hope I don't get seasick. Well, to tell you the truth I was seasick for about a day while we were on our way here. That ship is always rocking back and forth. Besides we ran into some 18 foot waves. It was about like riding a rollercoaster. The ship we're on is the USS Iwo Jima. It's a pretty big ship. It has a big flight deck on top for helicopters. The only sea life I saw on the way here was a few flying fish.

Our quarters on ship are real tight. We have about 149 people in a compartment about the size of the kitchen, living room, hall, and dining room back home. The racks are 4 high so it's pretty crowded.

Donald didn't see me off because I got on a chopper and flew out to the ship. I saw him the Sunday before that though. I will probably get to see him again while I'm at Okinawa for the 12 days I'll be there after the cruise. Guess what? I have 90 days left. Not that I'm counting the days but just thought I'd tell you all how short I'm getting. Ha ha!

There's a sidewalk here by the barracks that has Donald's name on it. I know he must have poured the cement for it. It's got, S/Sgt Don Fenwick Alpha Co, on it. There is something else, but I can't think of it right now. So Donald and I will have seen about the same places over here. You know what they say, "History repeats itself."

Well won't be long until the tobacco will be sold. Hope that Dad gets a good price for it. Listen Mom, I know its getting close to Christmas now, but I'm going to ask you not to send me anything. I can't send you all anything, so I don't want you to send me something. Besides, I haven't got any room for anything and we keep moving from one place to another. I'd feel better if you didn't send me anything at all. Okay? I'll be thinking of everyone around that time so you all take care until then. Hope you all had a Happy Thanksgiving.

In a way I'm glad I don't get too much mail because I can hardly find time to answer the letters. Don't get me wrong though, I always enjoy hearing from someone, especially from home. Well I'll close for now. We have to get up pretty early tomorrow. So until I board ship again, which will be about 5 days, I'll say bye for now and hope this finds everyone doing fine.

As always,
Fred

On Monday the battalion was choppered out to the field for training exercises. Weapons Platoon was attached out to the various platoons within the company but our squad managed to stay together within the same platoon. The chopper I was on landed on a knoll. The Marines quickly exited the aircraft, joined forces with other Marines on the ground, and set up a 360 hasty defense around the LZ. For me, it was old hat. I had grown accustomed to riding in the back of a CH-46, touching down on a LZ, running off the ramp with full combat gear, and then setting up a defensive perimeter. Fortunately, this LZ would not be hot. We were only on a training operation. I wondered how this company might react if they got out of the choppers and received enemy fire as I had in Vietnam. Most of the men in the company had never seen any type of combat.

The battalion CP set up for command and control. We started out as a company separate from the rest of the battalion, but we knew they were close by. Radio contact was made with the battalion CP as our company walked off the knoll and down into a valley. It reminded me of the jungles of Vietnam. The scenery was about the same. Unconsciously I started to look for mines and booby traps but it dawned on me that there were no enemy troops about. I was amazed that I still had the thoughts of combat lingering in my mind even though I had been out of Vietnam for a couple of months. I supposed that it might take me quite awhile to forget about the past.

We ended up passing through a mountain village. A few of the children came out of their grass huts to get a better look at us. They seemed timid and shy. Maybe they had never been American troops coming through this area before. We crossed a cultivated plot of land next to one of the huts. All of a sudden an old man came running out ranting and raving in his native tongue. We could not understand what he was saying but we all knew that he did not want us trespassing through his fields. Whatever he had planted, we were intruding. He began waving his hands at us in order to ward us off. Some of the Marines continued to walk through the field while others veered off and into the grassy area. The old man seemed somewhat contented that he had at least conveyed his message of disapproval to the Marines.

As I passed by the grass huts I noticed a petite teenage girl. She had long shiny black hair, big brown eyes, and her skin was dark from the tropical sun. There were a few other smaller boys and girls standing around her. She was speaking to the children as if in the position of authority and holding the others back from getting too close to us. I reached in my cargo pocket of my trousers and threw a can of crackers in their direction. They scrambled for it and immediately started inspecting the can. Then they came closer and begged for more. I realized that I shouldn't have given them any chow. If I wasn't careful I would have a whole swarm of kids around me which wouldn't settle too well with my superiors. I shouted to them "Didi Mau," but realized that I was speaking Vietnamese and not Tagalog. Fortunately, we continued to move away from the village and I lost sight of the children.

We ended up on top of a hill and began to dig fighting positions. We prepared fields of fire and range cards for the gun teams. It was very hot and humid and I felt my T-shirt wet from sweat. After our preparation was completed, we settled back to eat some C-Rations. One infantry squad went out on a simulated patrol and was to make contact with the company commander periodically. After about an hour the radio operator radioed back and informed the rest of us that they had found a huge waterfall with a hole of water that was perfect for swimming. They asked for permission to take a break and go for a swim. To our surprise, the company commander granted the request.

The Marines within our perimeter began to ask their superiors if they could also go for a swim also. Eventually the company commander granted permission. We were to proceed to the waterfall one squad at a time. It seemed like a long time before my squad got its turn to go for a swim. We headed out in patrol formation and went straight for the waterfall. We had received the map coordinates provided to us by the squad who had initially found it. When we arrived at the waterfall we estimated it was about fifty feet high. Crystal clear water cascaded into a large pool at the base of the falls. The pool looked as though it was about twenty feet in circumference. Foster had to be the first one in. He dived into the water from a huge rock.

When he surfaced he said, "Damn! This water is cold, but it sure feels good. Come on in you guys."

Callahan was next to dive into the water.

"How deep is the water?" Chief asked Foster, who was now doing the back stroke.

"There ain't no bottom to this pool of water," Foster answered. "I couldn't even begin to touch bottom."

"Great!" Chief yelled. Chief climbed up an embankment and came to stand on a big rock at about middle ways up the falls. He came to the very end of the rock and put his arms up and out to his sides. "Here goes a swan dive!" Chief yelled out to everyone.

"You had best be careful," Trump hollered. "You might hit your head on a rock and kill your fool self!"

"Not to worry!" Chief yelled back. "I can clear these rocks and Foster already said that there was no bottom to be found in the pool!"

"Let's make sure," Foster said. "Let's all swim around here for a bit and see if we can touch bottom anywhere here in the pool."

We all jumped into the pool. The water practically took my breath away because it was so cold. About six of us swam around and dived down in the water trying to touch the bottom. Except for the sides of the pool, there was no bottom to be found.

"Okay!" yelled Foster to Chief. "You're all clear. Let's see your swan dive!"

Chief dove in the most beautiful swan dive and plunged into the water. After a few seconds he emerged and yelled out, "That was great! I'm gonna do that again. Come on you guys. You don't know what you're missin."

Three more Marines climbed out of the pool and scurried up the embankment. They took turns diving into the water with their own personal techniques of diving. We were having one heck of a time until the Marine monitoring the radio told us that we were instructed to come back to the CP. It was another squad's turn to cool off. We hated to leave but knew that another squad was waiting. We returned to the CP and began to set up our shelter halves for the night. We were now sweating from the humidity. We wanted to go back to the waterfalls but that would have to be another day.

We set up the watches as darkness fell upon us. At around 2100 we heard screaming from the other side of the perimeter. Everyone was stirred by the commotion. Word was passed that some Filipinos were running through the perimeter trying to steal our M60 machine guns, M16 rifles, or anything else they could lay their hands on.

Foster arrived at my machine gun team to check on us. "The fuckin Hucks are coming through the perimeter!" he yelled out in the darkness of night. "Take the slings off your weapons and wrap them around your legs or arms. Break out your E-tools. They are trying to steal our weapons. If any of them commie bastards come close to you, knock the crap out of them with your E-tools. Whatever you do, don't let them get your weapons."

I could sense the anxious Marines as their excitement grew more intense. Everyone armed themselves with their E-tools and waited to ambush the intruders. We were merely on a training exercise and only had blank ammunition to fire. Even if we did have live ammo we couldn't have used it on the so-called Filipino Hucks. It was an international incident just waiting to happen. We did get approval, however, to ward them off with our E-tools. Seemed a little odd to me that combat trained Marines had to resort to entrenching tools to protect themselves. It was quite a contrast from being in an actual combat zone as compared to a training exercise in garrison.

Although it was dark, the moon provided enough light to make out the silhouettes of Marines standing around the perimeter. All of a sudden one Filipino came dashing through the perimeter right in front of us. He tried to grab the M16 service rifle that Hill had wrapped around his arm by the sling. Hill fought him off in a split second and the Filipino ran to Callahan trying to take his weapon. Callahan swung at him with his E-tool, but missed.

"Somebody get that motha fucker!" Callahan yelled.

The Filipino then started running in my direction. Trump swung at him and missed also. By now the intruder was getting a little frantic. He approached me while looking in the opposite direction. I swung the broad side of my E-tool and caught the Filipino up side the head. He staggered backward but somehow managed to gain his senses. He started to run out of the perimeter. I threw my E-tool and hit him in the small of the back. He screamed with pain but continued to run into the darkness.

"OOH-RAH!" the squad yelled out in unison.

"Look at old Fenny," Foster said. "He is hell with that E-tool. He scared the hell out of that Huck, that's for sure."

Callahan agreed, "Yeah, you ever play baseball, Fenwick? Seems like you are good at pitching and hitting."

I couldn't resist telling Callahan a little story. "As a matter of fact, I used to play hard ball in the seventh and eighth grades. I was our pitcher and could throw a mean fast ball. The fast ball was the only pitch I had mastered but I was accurate and used to burn up the catcher's mitt. One time I threw a no-hitter while we were playing a rival school. We beat those guys thirty-two to nothing. I loved seeing the puff of smoke fly out of the catcher's mitt followed by the swing of the batter. I was just too damn fast for them. I never threw no E-tools, this is my first try at that."

"Well, you haven't lost your touch," Callahan replied.

We were told that the Hucks were considered to be a communist group that hid out in the mountains and at times terrorized the small villages with their antics. Now that we were in their area of control I supposed that they would at least try to steal our weapons. Senior ranking Marines had told us that the Hucks would not cause us any harm and that they only wanted our weapons. I was not taking any chances. I unfastened the sling at the butt end of my M16, loosened the sling, wrapped it around my right leg, and then refastened it to my rifle. I would sleep that way. If a Huck was going to grab my weapon and run off, he would have to drag me along with it. As things quieted down we all decided to settle down for some sleep while keeping a fifty per cent watch through the night. All through the night and into the early hours of the morning, the Hucks attempted several times to run through our lines and steal a weapon.

The following morning the platoon commanders checked to see that every Marine had his own weapon. The Hucks had failed, at least for the night. We began to stir and prepare a meal of C-Rations for breakfast. For the rest of the day we would send out patrols. We all hoped that we would be able to go swimming at the waterfall once again. A little later in the morning a group of women and teenage girls approached the perimeter from all sides. They were trying to sell sodas and some fish and rice to us. Hill managed to trade a can of fruit cocktail for some rice and a soda. The word was passed not to buy anything from them, but Hill had already eaten the rice.

"Ask them for some balut," Foster said to Hill.

"Hill replied, "No thanks, I'm not eating an unhatched chicken. I've heard about those things. But to tell you the truth, this rice ain't too bad."

"You had better watch that stuff," I told Hill. "You might get sick from eating that junk. No tellin what they have in it."

"Yeah," added Foster, "you know that they use human feces to fertilize the rice fields, don't you?"

"I think I might be sick," Hill said in disgust. We were amused and laughed at him.

Patrols were sent out through the course of the day. Much to our dissatisfaction, we did not get to go for a swim in the beautiful waterfall during the day. That night we were all ordered to pick up every weapon, carry them to the CP, and bury them. A working party of Marines dug a huge 360 degree hole and the company weapons were all stacked in the center. Several ponchos were put together to cover them up and then dirt was thrown around the outer edges. There would be six Marines posted throughout the night to guard the weapons.

This was the first time I had ever seen a Marine unit actually collect weapons and bury them in order to keep someone from steeling them. But I had to keep reminding myself that I was in garrison and not in actual combat. I wondered how a unit that conducted training exercises in this manner was ever going to be effective in combat. In my mind, the leadership was setting the Marines up for failure.

As darkness fell again that night, the Hucks once again ran through the perimeter searching for weapons to steal. It was if they knew that we would not harm them. The Marines were having a ball trying to hit them with their E-tools. Finally the Hucks figured out that all the weapons were placed in one stack and covered up. About four of them ran all at once and tried scrambling for the weapons. The Marines on guard managed to fight them off. Then the guard was doubled. Callahan and I stood watch with other Marines between 2300 and 2400 but it was quiet during that time.

The next morning the company commander decided we had better move to another location to avoid weapons being stolen by these pesky Filipinos.

Before we relocated to another position, we were given permission to go to the waterfall for one last swim. It was great. It was the most beautiful spot I had ever seen. My entire machine gun section really enjoyed the peace and tranquility of this waterfall somewhere in the jungles of the Philippines. We stayed in the field for a few more days conducting battalion size operations. The Hucks did not attempt to steal our weapons again.

Back at the SLF Camp we packed our gear and returned to the ship. We departed port on 5 December at approximately 1800. As we cruised through the harbor, we could see the night lights of the city of Olongapo. The lights glittered like a gem stone in the dark. We wondered when we might pull liberty again in this tropical paradise. We thought we were heading straight for Vietnam, but instead, we sailed around the Philippine Islands for a few days.

We occupied our time by running PT (physical training), cleaning weapons, classes, fishing off the fan tail, and providing working parties for various duties. During PT we ran around the flight deck for three miles. Six times around the flight deck was equivalent to one mile; consequently we would run eighteen times around the deck. At times it was difficult to balance ourselves due to the movements of the vessel caused by the waves.

The BLT managed to pull off a couple of beach landings while we were still off the coast of the Philippines. In between all the training, on and off the ship, I managed to find time to write a letter home.

Dec. 8, 1970

Hello Mom, Dad, and all,

I got Mom's letter today and was glad to get it. I guess everyone thinks I've forgotten about them but really I haven't had much of a chance to write. Sorry I haven't written sooner but that's the way things go. Like I said before, if you don't hear from me for awhile at a time don't worry, because I'll be doing fine. Just busy that's all.

Well guess you got my other letter by now. I mailed it about a week later. We spent 5 days in the bush and then came in and got on ship the next day. Right now we're sailing around the Philippines. We'll be here until the 13th then head south. We may stay off the coast of Nam for a couple of days and then on to Singapore. We're supposed to be there Christmas.

Today we got on choppers and made a beach landing here at the Philippine Islands. We're going to do the same thing tomorrow, so we'll get up pretty early. We got up at 3:30 this morning. It's nothing hard about making a landing, but it's silly in a way. We do the same things over and over again.

The ship life is okay, but kinda crowded. They always have us doing something. Like doing what we did today out in the bush, cleaning up the place, inspections, and a lot of other bullshit. I'll be glad when I get out of this company.

I've had fun so far on the cruise though and it's some really interesting sights. I went into town with some other guys and had a pretty good time. Remind me to tell you all about Olongapo when I get back. That sure is a wild town. Don't worry, I go along with several buddies whenever I go into town. Mostly, I stayed on base at the ship yard.

Well I guess I'd better go for now. If anyone asks about me just tell them I'm doing just fine and that I don't have much time to write. We can talk when I get home. By the way, I got 82 days left. Ha ha!

Mom, don't send me anything for Christmas. We haven't got any room on ship for nothing. We can't even eat chow in our quarters, so you see, they're pretty strict.

Since I can't send you all anything, I'm going to put 40 dollars in this letter, so you all can divide it up and get what ever you want. Do me a favor and spend it, okay? Let ole Larry have a share too. Like I say, the three of you can divide it up.

So I'll let you go now, I'll be thinking of everyone real often.

As ever,
Fred

Even after our beach landings we remained off the coast of the Philippines. I had no idea where we were. Our daily routine consisted of an early reveille, cleanup of our berthing area, chow, classes, cleaning weapons, and physical training. If we had any downtime the Marines played card games and wrote letters home.

During this time I received a letter from Okinawa. It was from my brother, Donald. It was in reply to my letter informing him about the sidewalk at the Upper SLF Camp with his name on it. He knew exactly what sidewalk I was referring to. He wrote in his letter to me that at the time he was off ship with the Combat Engineers. They had started working on the sidewalk to connect the barracks and in the middle of the project they were called back to the ship. He had poured the concrete for it one morning and prior to heading back to the ship he had etched his name in the wet cement. His ship then pulled out of port that afternoon. He said he never saw it after the forms were taken off and wanted to know how it looked. Consequently, he had never made it back to the Philippines to finish the job.

One day our ship received food supplies from two other ships that had sailed from Subic Bay. We got a kick out of watching the Sailors transfer the cargo from one ship to the other. They did this by using ropes and pulleys. After all our new supplies were brought onboard the supply ships steamed back toward the direction of Subic Bay. I had been instructed to provide a working detail from my team to carry frozen foodstuffs down into the huge refers (refrigerators) in the belly of the ship. After a few minutes I decided to check on my Marines. They were sweating from packing boxes back and forth and stacking them neatly in the refers. I joined in to assist them with the task. It was hard work, but when we had finished, the Sailors rewarded us with some strawberry ice cream.

December 13, 1970

Hello Mom, Dad, and Larry,

Today is Sunday and we're not doing much so thought I'd send a few Christmas cards while I have the chance. After the 14th we'll have to wait until we get to Singapore before we get mail or they pick ours up. We should get to Singapore around the 23rd and stay for Christmas. Right now we're sailing around off the coast of the Philippines. We'll leave here the 14th, go off the coast of Nam for about a week, and then on to Singapore. I'm really looking forward to seeing Vietnam again. Ha! I'll be glad to get to Singapore and get some liberty there.

We keep pretty busy on ship but the time passes pretty fast. We have an inspection tomorrow by the lieutenant colonel of the battalion. I don't sweat the "ole man" though, because he puts his trousers on just like everybody else. The "lifters" don't bother us much on ship. I guess it's because over half the company is getting short and just don't care about anything. Most of the guys go home in January or February, so I guess the company will be pretty small by the time we get back to Okinawa.

Well, guess I'll close for now. There's not much going on around here. So until next time I'll say so long and hope this finds you all doing just fine. May you have a Happy Christmas.

As ever,
Fred

After a few days at sea, the Captain of the Ship finally told us that we were in the Gulf of Tonkin, off the coast of North Vietnam. We were to remain in the middle of the Gulf and be prepared to go ashore if ordered by higher command. We floated around in circles. Each time we wandered out to the flight deck we tried to see land but there was no land in sight. By now there were approximately six other ships that accompanied the USS Iwo Jima. All the ships in the Task Force were referred to as the 6th Fleet.

One morning at around 0900 I went up to the flight deck alone. I wanted to stand out on the catwalk and look out across the deep blue waves of the ocean. The waves in a rhythmical motion crashed into the sides of the ship with enough force to shake the vessel. I began to peer down into the depths as far as the naked eye could see. Several large eels, about six feet long and approximately four inches in diameter, were spotted swimming beneath the white caps of the waves. When they almost reached the top of the water they would slither back down and out of sight. I was amazed at the spectacle. This was no place to go for a swim, I thought to myself.

Further across the rolling waves a school of dolphins were playfully swimming in the distance. Then some flying fish broke the surface of the water. They glided in mid air for what seemed to be at least five seconds then plunged back into the water with movements ever so graceful. Another school of porpoise joined in very close to the fish. I wondered what other aquatic life might lie in the depths beneath the ship.

Prior to departing the catwalk, I reached into my utility pocket and pulled out a quarter. I looked at the date of the coin. It was 1969, the year I had entered the Marine Corps. I made a wish, and without looking back, I tossed the coin over my right shoulder and over the side of the ship. I knew that the twenty-five cent coin that I had fondled, would lay at rest on the bottom of the Tonkin Gulf, for all eternity.

As I entered my quarters, I heard blaring from the loud speaker.

"General Quarters...General Quarters...All Hands Man Your Battle Stations!" For the Marines, General Quarters meant that everyone would stay in the berthing area, close the hatches, and standby in case we had to go ashore. For the Sailors, it meant that they would actually man the battle stations throughout the ship. I used to watch them practice. The Navy personnel would run about frantically and designated personnel would take up their positions next to the three inch guns. Other Sailors manned their positions on the flight deck.

"Wonder what the hell is going on?" Callahan asked.

"Must be just another drill," Foster answered.

Hill added, "Yeah, they do this crap all the time. What we need is a real war!"

We all gathered around a group of tables in the center of the compartment. Some Marines were watching the black and white TV while about six Marines played a card game of back alley. After a few minutes, the platoon commander entered the compartment and walked over to where we were gathered. He motioned for all of us to listen up.

The platoon commander said, "All right Marines, this is the real thing. We may be loaded aboard the choppers on the flight deck in the next couple of hours heading for the shores of North Vietnam."

"North Vietnam?" one of the Marines stated out loud. "What the hell are we going to do against the entire North Vietnamese Army. Hell, there ain't no friendlies for hundreds of miles."

"That's right," said the lieutenant. "We might have to hit the beach, but at least we will have Naval Gunfire to cover our six. I have to go back for a staff meeting. I want all of you to draw weapons and ammunition and standby to move out. No one is to wonder around the ship without my permission. Do you all understand?"

We all shook our heads in the affirmative. He then began explaining to the section leaders what he wanted done. Sergeant Buttplate immediately began barking orders while the lieutenant was still talking.

"All right, you knuckleheads," Sergeant Buttplate began. "Listen up! You will all go with your section leaders. The section leaders will take you to the armory to draw weapons and then to the supply point to draw ammo. After you draw your ammo I want you to beat feet back to the compartment and I want the team leaders to report to me with an ammo count and accountability of all your people. I don't want anyone lollygagging around. Now, let's get it done. Mortars will go first, followed by the machine gun section, and then the assault section. Let's move it!"

It was understood that the section leaders were supposed to be in charge of their sections, but Sergeant Buttplate began randomly barking orders for the entire platoon. Mortars went to the armory first and after about five minutes our section leader escorted the machine gun section to the armory. Then we went to the supply point and were issued M60 and M16 ammo. The section leader told me to take my gun team back to the compartment and said that he would join us in a few minutes. When we returned to our compartment the Marines in my gun team began to question me about what to do or expect in case we hit the beach in full combat gear.

Hill asked, "Hey Fenwick, what are we going to do if we hit the beach? I've never been in combat. What type of a position should we set up on the beach?"

"I know one thing," Callahan joined in, "I am going to stick right on your ass, Fenwick. You've been in Vietnam and you know your stuff. If I have to fight, I want to do it next to a combat vet."

Coming up from behind me, Foster put his right arm around my shoulder and said, "I may be squad leader, but when we hit the beach, you tell me what to do Fenny. I can take orders with the best of them. I know you have seen combat and we want to stick close to you. What do you say?"

"Take it easy guys," I said to them calmly and boldly and with a bit of pride. First of all let's see how much ammo we have between us and perform an inspection check on our weapons. We need to ensure that our weapons are ready to rock and roll when we hit the beach."

"Listen to old Fenny," Foster interrupted. "He is just as calm as anything. Hell, I'd follow you right into an enemy machine gun nest."

Our conversation was then interrupted by the commanding voice of Sergeant Buttplate. He yelled out, "Who the fuck is the 3rd machine gun team leader?" I looked and saw that Sergeant Buttplate was standing with a group of NCO's, obviously boasting what he would do once we hit the beach.

"I am the 3rd team leader," I responded.

"Well, Crazy," he responded, "didn't I tell you to report back to me after you received your ammo for an ammo count and accountability of your people?"

"Yes," I answered, "I was just getting ready to get a count on the ammo and perform a weapons inspection."

"Well, take your sweet ass time," he scolded. "We ain't got all fuckin day. Hurry it up!"

Callahan and Hill looked at each other and rolled their eyes. We started to count the cans of machine gun ammo and M16 rounds.

"That son-of-a-bitch," Foster said under his breath. "We ought to stuff a hand grenade up his dumb ass when we hit the beach."

For about two hours we waited for further instructions. Finally the platoon commander returned to the compartment and instructed us to start forming up on the flight deck ladderwell in single file. Once we were in position on the ladderwell, our machine gun section leader squeezed his way through the maze of Marines, and then broke us down into helo sticks. There were about twenty Marines assigned to each wave.

One of the Marines in the platoon could be heard saying, "This is bullshit. This is only a drill. Hell, the engines on the choppers are not even turning."

"I think you are right," another Marine responded, "this is just another way the Squids play games with the Marines."

Just then the rotors on six helicopters started turning. It became difficult to carry on a conversation over the loud sounds of the CH-46 choppers.

"Looks like we're going in for real, Fenwick!" yelled Foster over the roar of the engines.

Trump was sitting next to me on the ladderwell. He reached and tapped me on the shoulder and said, "Looks like we're gonna hit the beach. I'm sticking close to you, Fenwick. That way, I'll be over like the dog." I just smiled.

After about twenty minutes of churning the sounds of the engines died down to an idle and then turned off. Word was passed from one Marine to another that we were to turn in our ammunition and weapons and return to our living quarters. This particular mission was not to be. The higher echelon obviously had planned another scheme of maneuver or it was merely a drill after all. Most of the Marines believed that they made it look like it was for real so we would take it more seriously. We continued to float around in circles drilling several times a day. We talked about what we would do, if in fact, we did hit the beach in North Vietnam.

One day we heard the ship's announcement that we were steaming to Singapore and that liberty would be sounded upon arrival. We were scheduled to arrive at Singapore during the Christmas period. Everyone was excited about the idea of spending Christmas in a foreign port. We could not wait to step foot on dry land once again. The thought of going on liberty in Singapore was a real morale booster for our Weapons Platoon. I was anxious to explore another city in the Orient.

On our way to Singapore the machine gun section was cleaning weapons on the hanger deck. Our section leader came by and asked for volunteers to go on Brig Guard Duty. Trump and I thought it might be a skate job so we enthusiastically volunteered for the opportunity. I did not think the section leader would pick me for I was a team leader. To my total surprise, he selected Trump and I for the job. We were elated.

We were to report to the Navy Turn-Key at the ship's brig for further instructions. He was the enlisted Sailor in charge of the brig. The Turn-Key told Trump and I that we would be working four hours during the mornings, four hours at night, with the following two days off. After a few days as brig guard, Trump and I grew accustomed to our new duties. On our days off, Sergeant Buttplate made sure that we worked within our own platoon, instead of being off from duty as the Turn-Key had instructed. Sergeant Buttplate did allow us the afternoon off just prior to assuming the brig guard duties. This gave us a chance to "square away" our uniforms prior to being posted at the brig.

Initially there were three Marines confined in the ship's brig. Two of them were restricted to meals which consisted of only bread and water. The confined Marines tried to coax us into sneaking chow from the mess hall. Trump and I declined because we enjoyed this type of duty away from our platoon. We agreed not to risk it by taking any chances with the prisoners.

We were to arrive at Singapore around 22 December and liberty was scheduled for the few days we were to be in port. The ship anchored in the harbor and it seemed as though it was about a mile and a half from the shore. The Captain of the Ship warned us that an American ship had not been allowed a port call in Singapore for the past two years. He briefly explained over the intercom system that the last American ship that docked at Singapore stirred up a lot of problems between the local government and American government. Apparently, the American servicemen had caused frequent fights in the city and were considered a "nuisance" by the locals. He said that the Singapore government was giving us another chance and that we must be on our best behavior.

Before liberty was given to our platoon, we were to have a weapons inspection conducted by Sergeant Buttplate. The day we anchored off shore we spent the entire day cleaning the M60 machine guns, individual M16s, spare barrels for the guns, and all the gun accessories. That afternoon Sergeant Buttplate was to inspect the machine gun section. He forewarned us that if any Marine failed his weapons inspection their liberty would be secured for the entire time we were at Singapore.

During his inspection, Sergeant Buttplate was being over scrupulous in finding carbon on the weapons and it was obvious that he was excessively concerned with minute details. I questioned his motive. Was he doing this for his own vindictiveness or was he merely doing his job as a platoon sergeant. He had inspected the 1st and 2nd gun teams and already had secured four Marines liberty. When he got to our gun he could find no discrepancies. He thoroughly checked the spare barrel, traversing and elevating mechanism, and tripod. He was trying very hard to find inspection discrepancies. He looked disappointed as if expecting to secure our liberty like he had the others.

At this point he reorganized his thoughts. It was so obvious that he had come up with one of his bright ideas as if a light bulb had been turned on. He grabbed a combination wrench and unscrewed the gas cylinder nut and removed the gas cylinder extension. He then slid the gas piston out of the gas cylinder. In addition, he removed the safety wire and gas port plug and inserted his little finger into the gas port plug. This additional procedure was to be done only by authorized ordnance personnel. We could not believe our eyes at his actions. He raised his curled hand in the air and pointed with the tip of his little finger. We could see a trace of carbon on the tip of his finger.

With a smirk look on his face he said, "Well, well, well! Look at what I have found. A dirty machine gun! I bet you didn't expect me to look into the port plug, right? Who is the team leader here?" As if he didn't already know.

"I am," I answered, while realizing what was coming next.

He stood up and said, "Well, Fenwick, looks like this dirty weapon has just cost you your liberty in Singapore. You are responsible for this dirty weapon because you are the team leader."

I felt a strong feeling of anger and a hot flush to my face but I tried to maintain my composure. I told Sergeant Buttplate, "It will only take me a few minutes to clean it. I'll do it myself. Just don't secure my liberty."

Sergeant Buttplate replied in a sarcastic manner. "Okay Fenwick, not a problem. I will let you clean it by yourself. You can clean it today, tomorrow, and every day thereafter until we leave Singapore. Besides, you won't have anything else to do because you are restricted to the ship and your liberty has been secured."

I was so mad and frustrated that I could not see straight and could not find the words to verbally retaliate. My first instinct was to punch him right in the mouth for he had a smirk on his face that he was enjoying watching my reaction. Then I thought to myself that I wouldn't give him the satisfaction. He would have loved to have put me up on assault charges and visit me in the ship's brig. He was just a conniving sergeant who had to show the Marines around him just what a bad ass he could be. For some reason he did not see eye to eye with me from the very first day we met. I think he resented the fact that I was a lance corporal and a Vietnam Vet and he was a sergeant and had never seen combat. Whatever the reason, he had to prove that he was superior in rank and position.

The next day I joined several other Marines at the top of the ship's gangplank. Their liberty had also been secured by Sergeant Buttplate. We watched the Marines and Sailors leave the ship. There was a lot of enthusiasm and laughter as they walked down the gangplank to head into Singapore on liberty. Some of members of the platoon gave remarks of compassion and sentiment to those of us left behind. At the bottom of the gangplank they boarded small boats operated by the local people for transportation to the dock. Foster, Callahan, Hill, and Trump waved to me from the boat as it slowly moved away from the ship heading toward the dock.

I spent the rest of the day cleaning and polishing the M60 machine gun that had cost me my liberty. The other Marines left behind were from the machine gun section as well. I kept very much to myself that afternoon and wondered what my buddies might be up to as they pulled liberty in Singapore.

That evening at around midnight I was awakened from my slumber when my buddies returned from liberty. They straggled in the berthing area still talking about what they had seen in town and where they would go the following day. Foster and Callahan leaned over my rack and told me about their excitement while Trump and Hill crawled into their racks.

"Why don't you sneak out with us tomorrow?" Foster suggested.

"Yeah," Callahan added, "we might be able to pick up your liberty card from the Duty NCO and Sergeant Buttplate won't know anything about it."

In my sleepy stupor I murmured, "Nah, you know I'm restricted to the ship for the time we are in Singapore. If I get caught out in town, I might not see land again for the entire float. It might be our return to Okinawa before I'm authorized to get off this ship."

"You only live once," Foster replied. "You have got to get off the USS Iwo Jima and see Singapore, you just have to. You may never have the chance ever again, not in this lifetime."

I responded by saying, "Foster, I appreciate your intentions, but I don't want to be secured to this rocking ship when we get back to the Philippines. Better to be safe, than sorry."

"Yeah, guess you're right, Fenwick," Foster replied. "That damned Sergeant Buttplate. We saw him in town, drunk on his ass. He has no self decency. I was hoping he would get locked up by the local police."

"Not a chance," Callahan said, "looks like we're stuck with him until we rotate back to the States."

"That's it!" Foster exclaimed excitedly.

"What do you mean?" Callahan asked.

Foster replied in confidence, "The best time for you to sneak off the ship is when Sergeant Buttplate is out in town on liberty."

"Are you kidding me?" I asked. "It would be my luck to see him walking down the sidewalk. Then I would be in a world of shit."

Foster suddenly lost his enthusiasm. "Yeah, Fenwick, you're right. Bad idea, I guess."

"Don't concern yourself with me," I replied, "I'll be okay."

With that Foster and Callahan crawled into their racks and soon fell asleep. I watched with envy as they crawled out of their racks the next morning and dressed for their liberty. The liberty uniform was khaki trousers, khaki short sleeve shirt with ribbons and badges, khaki garrison cover, and to top it off, black combat boots. I was beginning to feel depressed as I witnessed my buddies iron their uniforms and spit-shine their boots. My khaki uniform was at the bottom of my seabag and stuffed into one of the very small compartment wall lockers. I felt that I would never have the chance to wear them, at least not in Singapore.

Now with only two days left before the ship would sail out of the Singapore harbor, all I had seen up until this point was the bay from the flight deck and the small cramped compartment in the berthing area. Callahan, Foster, and Trump, became persistent that I should go ashore with them. I was skeptical about their idea but yet tempted to go along with their lame brained idea. I could imagine myself in town with the gang.

"Come on Fenwick," Foster said. "Get your khakis out of your seabag and iron them. You are going into town with us whether you want to or not."

Reluctantly I answered Foster, "No thanks, I had better remain aboard the ship. I don't want to get into more trouble than I already am."

"Listen, Fenwick, I am your squad leader. You get those khakis out and iron them right now," Foster commanded with a serious look on his face. "You don't want to be run up in front of the old man for failing to obey an order from your superior, do you?"

"You bullshit too much, you know that Foster," I said with a smile.

"I am dead serious," he continued. "I am leaving for a few minutes and when I return you had best have that uniform squared away."

"Better listen to your squad leader," Callahan added. "Come on, I'll help you."

Half heartily I unlocked my wall locker and pulled my seabag from it. I dug my hand into it and pulled out what I was looking for. Callahan pressed out my shirt and trousers while I started to shine my boots. All the while I protested slightly saying that I could get into all sorts of trouble. Foster returned with a smile from cheek to cheek. He handed me my liberty card.

"How did you manage to get this?" I asked dropping what I was doing.

"Piece of cake." Foster responded. "It pays to know the Duty NCO and he has also already agreed not to log you out on liberty or back in off liberty. That way, if Sergeant Buttplate checks the log book, your name won't be in it."

Foster smiled and gave a slight wink to Callahan. He was very pleased with himself on his accomplishment as if patting himself on the back. They began to talk about what they would be doing in town. As the conversation progressed my excitement grew and I began to move along faster getting into my uniform.

"Are you ready, Fenny?" Foster asked me. "Don't worry, Sergeant Buttplate is already in town. He's probably drunk on his ass by now. Hell, if he does see you, he probably won't even recognize you. Besides, Singapore is a big city. We will get lost in the crowd."

I finished getting into my khaki uniform and was ready to go. I looked at Foster and asked, "Hey Foster, what in the hell are we waiting for? Ooh-rah! Let's get going!"

"Ooh-rah!" my buddies responded in unison.

When we reached the Officer of the Day at the top of the gangplank, we saluted, and requested permission to go ashore.

"Lance Corporal Fenwick requests permission to go ashore," I sounded off feeling very confident.

"Permission Granted," the Officer of the Day replied as he returned a hand salute.

He was a Navy Chief dressed in the Navy's khaki uniform of the day. The other Marines walked about half way down the gangplank, faced aft, and saluted the national ensign that was flying in the breeze. I hesitated momentarily concentrating on the small local boats that awaited us at the bottom of the gangplank.

"Come on Fenwick," Foster said. "How about facing aft and saluting old glory. You act like this is your first time off the ship."

"It seems like it," I responded as I rendered the proper salute and continued down the gangplank.

We boarded a boat and were soon underway to the shore. The sky above us was overcast and the temperature was warm and humid with a slight breeze. When we arrived at the dock we got off the boat and started walking down the boardwalk. There were several vendors trying to sell us just about everything imaginable. A man about middle aged approached us with about twenty wrist watches around each forearm.

"I hab goode watches for you," he said. "These are verrie goode watches. You buy, huh?"

"How much?" I asked.

"This one only thirty dolla American, this one only twenty-five dolla American," he continued as he selected through the watches on his forearms.

"Do you have any for ten dollars American?" I asked. I was attempting to use the custom of bargaining for a reduced price. To my surprise he immediately pulled off a nice looking watch and put it up to my ear.

"Dis a verrie nice watch for only ten dolla American," he said.

I examined the watch carefully and held it up close to my ear listening to the ticking sound.

"Five American dollars," I said, pushing my luck a little further.

"No, no, too cheap," the man retorted shaking his head. "Ten dolla and you have dis bootiful watch."

"No thank you," I said grinning, "I have a watch back at the ship. I don't need two watches."

"Okay, okay, eight dolla American," the man persisted.

"Humm, I don't know," I said in a low tone of voice. "Not bad for a watch that ticks. I'll take it!"

"Thank you," he said as he took the money from me. While I walked away he continued to pester other Marines and Sailors coming ashore from the ship.

"That watch will not last you two weeks," Foster proclaimed. "I'll bet it falls apart on your wrist, you'll see.

"I don't know," I replied feeling good about my purchase. "It looks like a pretty good watch to me, a ticking jewel of the Orient." I snickered as I put the watch in my right front trousers pocket instead of on my wrist. I had learned my lesson in Olongapo. Mentally I dared someone to try and pick-pocket my watch in my front pocket.

We continued walking and soon came upon an open market. We decided to stroll along and get a good look at the shops. Vendor stalls lined both sides of the street. There were live chickens and ducks in small compact cages. Pigs were kept in vine weaved cages. Some peddlers were busy slaughtering chickens. They would then drop the fowl into large pots of hot scalding water. After a few minutes they would remove them and swiftly pluck the feathers.

There was a Singaporean man with a huge potbelly standing behind a wooden block that was about waist high. Several local women were standing around him while he was busy with his meat cleaver. He swung the cutting edge of the knife with his right hand in an almost rhythmic manner. He chopped up various cuts of meat, quickly wrapped them, and handed them to his customers. Then he collected payment for his services and rendered the appropriate monetary change back to the women. I could not help but smell the familiar and distinctive odors that I had grown accustomed to back on the farm. My mother had prepared a Sunday chicken dinner in about the same manner. From the cutting off of the chicken's heads, placing them into boiling water, to the plucking of the feathers; the sights, sounds, and smells came back to me.

We spent about an hour in the market alone. Hill had a good camera and was taking lots of photographs of anything that tickled his fancy. We finally ended up in a poor side of the city. The people were very curious since they had not seen American servicemen on their streets for over two years. They seemed to be admiring our uniforms. I was the only one wearing the most ribbons in our little group and some of the locals got even closer to me in order to peer at them.

Foster began pointing at my ribbons as we walked along saying, "This is a war hero. He fought in Vietnam killing those commie gooks."

"Knock it off," I told Foster. "These people might resent you using the word gook."

"Hell," he continued, "ain't they all gooks over here in the Far East?"

"Not even," I replied while feeling a bit disdainful about his remark. "Most of the people over here are just like us. They are hard working and trying to make a living to survive from one day to the next."

Callahan agreed with me, "Yeah, not everyone is communist. Besides, they will treat you right if you treat them with a little respect and decency."

"Okay, okay, I get your point," Foster answered, "now spare me from all the preaching, will you?"

We looked down the street and saw two Marines heading in our direction. They were members of our squad. One went by the name of Pinoy. He was a Filipino by nationality who had joined the Marine Corps while still in his homeland. The other Marine we simply called Chief as he was a Navajo American Indian and the 1st gun team leader.

"Hey Pinoy!" yelled Foster. "What are you guys up to?"

Pinoy replied, "We're just out looking at the maganda (Tagalog for beautiful) women. I never saw as many different nationalities."

"You got that right," agreed Chief. "This city has Chinese, Filipinos, Malays, Taiwanese, Far East Indians, and who knows what other races. This is a single Marine's paradise."

"What do you all say we go get a piece-a-ass?" Pinoy asked.

"Aaahh, so you want, sucky-fucky, huh GI?" asked Foster. "You horny little bastard."

"That's right," replied Pinoy, "I want to gilling-gilling a maganda woman."

"So where do you intend on going?" Callahan asked.

"I thought we might get in a taxi and tell the cab driver to take us to a Skivvy House," Pinoy replied without hesitation.

"Listen to him," Foster interjected. "He don't want to waste no time in a bar. He just wants to get on with it."

"Well, what are we waiting for?" Chief asked. "I'll flag down a cab for us."

"We all can't fit in one taxi," I responded. "We'll have to get two cabs. There are seven of us."

"No we won't," Foster said. "I've done it before. As long as you have the money to pay for it, these cabbies will take you there."

While we waited for a taxi to pass by a small boy approached us and showed us pictures of three girls that looked to be in their early twenties.

"Do you want to fuck my sistas," the boy asked us in unbroken English.

"Look at this," Trump said while holding all three pictures in his hands. "These girls don't look too bad but I seriously doubt that they are all his sisters."

"No, I don't think so either," Callahan said, "maybe we should take the little guy up on it, though."

"How much?" Hill asked inquisitively.

"Only thirty dolla," the boy replied.

"Thirty dollars?" Chief shouted out. "Hell, ain't no pussy worth that."

"Okay," the boy replied, "twenty-five dolla."

"The price of meat is too high," Foster told the boy. "Better tell your sistas to look somewhere else."

"Maybe you like to see donkey fuck, live on stage," added the boy.

"Donkey fuck, did you all here that?" Hill asked.

Pretending to be ignorant, Trump asked, "What's a donkey fuck?"

"Ooohhh, don't be silly," Foster replied. "Just add one and one together and you get two. It's a woman on stage making love to a donkey."

"How in the hell can any woman make love to a donkey?" Trump asked.

"Easy," Chief answered, "the woman has to have a big pussy."

We all giggled and laughed. It was the way Chief had said it. Just then Chief managed to flag down a taxi. We all crammed ourselves into the cab. I noticed the shocked expression on the cab drivers face as all seven of us piled into his little taxi, but he was content to take us where we wanted to go.

"Where do you want me to take you?" the driver asked.

Pinoy replied, "Take us to a skivvy house where there are nice women that want to screw our brains out."

"You want nice girls?" the driver asked.

"Hell yeah, we want nice girls," Chief answered. "We don't want to screw no donkeys."

We chuckled at Chief's sense of humor. He was turning into a regular comedian.

The cab driver said, "Okay, I know veddy good place. Lots of nice girls there. All are veddy pretty."

"How do you know, Honcho?" I asked. "You been there before?"

Nodding his head with a big grin, the driver said, "Ooohhh, yes, many time before."

"Sounds like the place we want to go," said Callahan.

The driver zigzagged through the traffic for what seemed like a half hour.

"Hell fire," I finally said now growing uncomfortable with the long drive. "We may never find our way back to the ship. This guy might take us into the boonies and get us rolled."

"Relax, Fenwick," Foster said, "ain't nobody gonna roll seven bad ass Marines."

"Famous last words," I replied.

The taxi finally came to a stop. We peered out of the windows and saw some steps leading up to a house on some wooden poles.

"This is it," the driver said. "Dese girls show you good time. Enjoy your stay."

"Don't worry about that," Pinoy said, "that's what we plan to do."

We paid the cab driver and started up the steps. At the top of the steps two girls who had seen us get out of the taxi were standing between the railings and raising their skirts high up above their knees. They made sure we got a peek of their panties.

"Hot dam, looky here," said Hill. "These babes are hot to trot and are not too bad looking either."

"This be the place," Pinoy said with a big grin on his face.

As we entered a room filled with chairs and couches, the hostess approached, invited us to sit down, and asked if we wanted anything to drink. She told us that the first drink was complimentary with no charge. Everyone ordered a beer except Pinoy.

"Why don't you get a beer?" Chief asked Pinoy.

"Not now," Pinoy said, "I don't want to be drunk when I dive into some pussy."

"This guy cracks me up," Foster said. "Go ahead and order a beer anyway. Hell, I'll drink it for you. After all, it's free."

Pinoy ordered the beer and the woman returned with two girls helping her carry the round of cheer.

"Oh boy!" exclaimed Foster. "Good ole Tiger Beer."

I looked at the label. I was about to sample still another type of brew of the Orient. The label had a picture of a tiger that seemed to leap out at you.

"This is a fancy label," I said, "I wouldn't mind keeping the bottle as a souvenir."

"Listen to Fenny," Foster said. "Next thing you know he will want to take one of these oriental beauties back to the States with him."

"Don't worry about that," I replied. "I'm going back to the States the same way I came over, just me and my seabag."

"And a case of the clap," Trump added.

We all laughed. Just then Pinoy asked, "Where are all the women? All I see is just these two. I don't want sloppy seconds. Hell, there are seven of us."

Instantly the hostess clapped her hands loudly several times and into the room walked about twelve girls. Some were dressed in short dresses while others wore bathing suits.

"Gentlemen," she said, "take your pick from these lovely ladies of pleasure."

"Ooohh, Noooo, Look at these beauties," Hill said. "I think I have died and gone to heaven."

"What are we waiting for?" Pinoy asked. He got to his feet and walked up to the girls. He walked slowly up and down the line of girls trying to make his decision.

"Well, what's taking so long?" I asked.

"Hell, these girls are so pretty, I don't know which one to choose," Pinoy responded.

"Let me show you how it's done," said Chief as he walked directly to the center of the girls and covered his eyes with his hands. He then paced up and down, uncovered his eyes, and took an unsuspecting girl by the hand.

He winked at us as he led her off into another room.

"Wait a minute," Pinoy said abruptly, "If I'm not careful you guys will take all the good looking ones."

"Better make your mind up," Foster said laughing.

One of the girls standing just in front of Pinoy leaned forward and whispered something in his ear. Almost instantly Pinoy was following her into another room. He was looking back over his shoulder and smiling at us as she led him away.

"Well Fenny, how about you?" Foster asked. "Gonna wet your whistle or not?"

"Don't think so," I replied. "When Trump said that I might go back to the States with a case of the clap, it kinda made me wonder. I don't need no VD now. I'm getting too short for that."

"That's the way," Trump said. "Avoid the temptations of the flesh. You'll thank me later."

"Yep, think you're right. I think I will sit right here and drink my Tiger Beer," I said.

"Me too," stated Foster. "I've got a girl back in Pennsylvania. Don't want to spoil a good thing."

Realizing that the rest of us were not interested, the hostess clapped her hands once again and the girls disappeared out of sight. We ordered another beer and surprisingly enough the woman would not accept payment. After about twenty minutes Chief returned and sat down with the rest of us. Pinoy returned shortly after and took a seat on the couch next to me.

I looked at Pinoy and laughed out loud.

"Tell me something, Pinoy," I said. "What did that girl whisper to you that made you pick her over the others?"

Pinoy replied, "She told me she has a tiger in her pussy."

"What, a tiger?" I asked.

Pinoy answered me saying, "Yeah, she told me she had a real live tiger in her tank. Can you believe that?"

"Well, did she?" I asked smiling.

"She sure did," Pinoy said laughing.

"How do you know, did it attack you?" I asked while edging him on.

Pinoy held up his fingers and showed me how the muscles had contracted back and forth while they were behind closed doors. "That's what she meant by a tiger. It grabbed me and wouldn't let go."

The other Marines sitting around burst into laughter. We teased Pinoy about his confrontation with a tiger and he seemed to enjoy the attention. After about another five minutes we decided that we should go to one bar before calling it a night. Foster asked the hostess if she could call a taxi for us and she cheerfully obliged. She was such a graceful hostess even though she was running a brothel. While some of us stood at the bottom of the steps to await the taxi, Hill, Chief, and Pinoy stayed at the top with their arms around two of the girls. After about fifteen minutes the taxi arrived and we all squeezed in again. We waved to the girls as we rode away.

"Take us to a nice bar," Foster told the driver.

"Yeah," added Callahan. "Let's go party."

Acknowledging with a nod the cab driver zigzagged down streets making turns along the way. We ended up on the main street where we had first entered the city.

"Hey, this is all right," I said to the others. "At least now I can find my way back to the ship."

"You sound like you want to go back now, do you?" Foster asked.

"I think Fenwick is afraid that Sergeant Buttplate might see him out here and get into trouble," Trump interjected.

I responded by saying, "All I know is that I will be in heap of trouble if I get caught out in town. This is too close to the ship for comfort."

"Don't worry about it," Foster said. "I will take the blame. After all, it was me who got your liberty card."

"Well, hell, let's go," I said. "I owe it to myself to see Singapore."

"That's the spirit," Chief said. "Don't worry about it, we'll cover for you, but you ain't gonna see much of Singapore bouncing from one bar to the next."

Answering Chief I replied, "I've seen enough of the scenic sights during the day. I might as well enjoy the night at some Slop Chute with my liberty buddies."

"Roger that, Callahan said, "let's check out this last place and then head back to the ship."

We entered the bar and saw several oriental girls. Some were in a little group sitting in one corner. We gathered around a table and pulled up two more tables and extra chairs in order to connect them into one long table. We sat down and ordered a round of Tiger Beer. As we sat looking around at the girls and listening to the music from a jukebox, one Marine from our squad entered through the doors. We waved to him and he came over to the table.

"What brings you here?" Foster asked. Foster knew that the Marine had been seeing one of the girls on a regular basis.

"Oh, I thought I would just drop in and see what is going on," the Marine responded.

Foster replied, "Yeah, right, we know that you have been popping that pretty girl over in the corner. Tell her to come over here and join us."

"Don't think so," the Marine said, "you guys will be drooling all over her."

"Listen to him," Chief said. "He thinks we want his girl. We already got a piece-o-ass. We just want to eye-ball her. Ain't no harm in that, is there?"

"No, I don't guess," the Marine answered.

He waved his hands for her to come to the table and to sit next to him. The Marine had taken an empty seat on my right hand side. As she approached the table, I politely scooted over to sit in the chair to my left in order to free up a chair for her.

"Look at ole Fenny," Foster said, "what a gentleman."

"He's no gentleman," Callahan responded, "he just wants to sniff her perfume and gaze at her cleavage."

"Since when can you read my mind," I said to Callahan.

The girl sat down and asked if we wanted the other girls to sit with us around the table.

"Not really," Foster said, "you're the prettiest girl in here."

She acknowledge the compliment with a coyly grin and then rested her head on the Marine's shoulder.

"Ahhhhh, ain't that sweet," Trump said, "these two are in love."

"Looks like wedding bells to me," I added.

The Marine held her right hand in his left and started stroking the top of her hand with his right.

Foster asked, "Did you ever see such love birds?"

The Marine leaned over the table and whispered to Foster in a low voice, "Foster, this ain't no ordinary girl, she is something special."

We could tell that Foster was getting impatient with the Marine for being such a pansy and this girl having him wrapped around her little finger. "I bet you not only lay her, but eat her snatch as well," Foster said loudly. "Where is your decency?"

We laughed. The Marine stood up, grabbed his girl by her hand, and led her away from the table. They started out the door.

"Have a good time," Foster shouted. "Better hope you don't catch the clap."

Feeling a bit sorry for the Marine, Hill spoke directly to him, "See you back on the ship."

Foster polished off his beer in a few gulps and placed the empty beer can hard on the table. We finished our beer as well and I suggested that we head back to ship.

"I want to get in my rack before Sergeant Buttplate realizes that I am missing," I said.

"Take it easy," Foster answered. "How can you enjoy yourself thinking about that asshole?"

"It's not that," I said, "I just think I've had enough for one day."

"Is everyone ready to split?" Foster asked.

"Yeah," Chief answered, "Let's make tracks."

We got to the docks and boarded the small boats that took us back to the ship. I could see the night lights of the city as we made our way across the bay. When we got to the top of the gangplank, we saluted the Officer of the Day.

"Request permission to come aboard," we all said in unison.

"Permission Granted," the Officer of the Day replied as he returned our salutes.

We proceeded to the Duty NCO to turn in our liberty cards. Foster reminded him not to log me in off liberty since I had not signed out in the first place. We returned to our compartment, talked about our day for a few moments, and then we were in our racks sound asleep. The next morning was Christmas Day. We ate breakfast in the mess hall and when we returned to our compartment everyone was getting ready to hit the town again.

"I think I will stay back today," I said. "I guess I've seen enough of Singapore."

"Hell, we've just begun," Foster said. "We still have lots to see."

"I know," I responded, "but I don't want to push my luck any further."

"That does it," Foster said angrily. "I'm going to go and see the section leader and ask his permission for you to go on liberty. This bullshit has gone on long enough."

"Don't concern yourself about it, Foster," I said. "We've only got one more day in port."

"All the more reason to hit the town for one last time," he told me.

Without saying another word, Foster left the compartment. He returned about twenty minutes later and told me to get into my liberty uniform and that our section leader had granted me liberty.

"Did you remind him that Sergeant Buttplate has secured my liberty?" I asked.

"Of course, he knows that," Foster said. "If you don't believe me go ask him yourself."

"That's okay," I responded, "I believe you."

"Then what are we waiting for?" Callahan asked.

"Where is Trump?" I asked while looking around.

"You should know," Foster said. "Today he has to go back on Brig Guard duty."

"Oh, that's right," I said, "I almost forgot that I have brig duty again starting tomorrow."

This time there would be only four of us on liberty, Callahan, Foster, Hill, and me. As we neared the gangplank Foster noticed that the section leader was coming up the steps from the mess hall.

"Tell Fenwick that you have approved his liberty for today," Foster said to him.

"Yeah, that's right," our machine gun section leader said to me. "You've been restricted to the ship long enough. Besides, today is Christmas. Go and enjoy yourself. I will clear it with Sergeant Buttplate. You guys have a good time."

"Thanks a lot," I said.

When we arrived at the dock the same vendors approached us again trying to sell their goods. I saw the guy who had sold me the watch the day before.

I looked at him and pointed to my newly acquired watch and said, "It's still ticking."

"Aahhh," the man said smiling, "Goode watch, huh? You buy another for your girlfriend?"

"No thanks," I said. "I don't need another watch. Besides I don't have a girlfriend."

We walked past the vendors ignoring their pestering to buy something. We walked into town stopping once in awhile at some bars for a quick drink and a snack. We continued to see as much of the city as possible before it got dark.

At around 2000 we decided to see what the Singapore Hilton Hotel looked like inside. We went through the doors and got on the elevator. It must have been at least twenty floors to the roof top balcony. When we reached the top floor the elevator door opened. We strutted out full of excitement to be on the roof top. Suddenly we noticed that everyone was dressed in formal attire and most of the men wore coats and ties. We stopped in our tracks looking around and felt out of place since we were wearing our khaki uniforms and boots. Even Foster, the rambunctious one, made the comment that we had better leave.

Just then a very tall and nice looking oriental girl wearing a long formal dress approached us. She asked if we wanted a drink or a seat.

"No thanks," Foster replied. "Don't look like we are dressed for the occasion. We'll be leaving now."

"Don't leave," the girl said as if pleading for us to stay. "You dressed okay. No matter. All are welcome to stay."

"That's awful nice of you," Callahan said.

"Yeah," added Hill, "we might just take you up on it."

"Look, they even have a live band up here," I said. "Let's go sit down and listen to the music."

"Good luck trying to find a seat," Foster said, "Looks like they are all taken."

"I will find table for you," the girl told us.

We all looked at one another and shrugged our shoulders. She led us to a table in one corner next to the railing which ran along the perimeter of the roof top. We momentarily gazed out over the city and down the wall of this huge hotel. We saw people walking on the streets down below in the street lights and seemed to resemble ants from a distance. We were awed at the view of the city lights.

The oriental girl brought us a round of Tiger Beer. She accepted payment and we told her to keep some of the change. Then she said to us, "If anything you need, call me. I come right over. Hab good time. Enjoy! Then she turned and walked away.

"Wow," Callahan said, "they sure grow them pretty here in Singapore."

"I'm with you on that, Callahan," I responded. "She is beautiful."

We sat and talked while listening to the band. There were several people dancing on the dance floor. Hill decided that he wanted to dance. He went from one table to the next asking women to dance with him. Finally, after about the fifth try he lead a nice looking girl onto the dance floor.

"Look at ole Hill," Callahan said. "he's a real ladies man."

"Yeah," Foster answered. "I think I will try that too. Hell, I haven't danced to a live band in a long time."

He was immediately up on his feet and was soon on the dance floor having the time of his life. Callahan and I were contented to just sit back and watch. We enjoyed looking out over the city as we leaned back against the balcony railing. It was a beautiful place to be, I thought. After about two hours we all decided to go to the Nelson Bar that we had been to the night before. It was the same bar that the Marine from the squad was seeing one of the girls. We walked in like we owned the place, sat down at the bar, and ordered a round. After a few minutes we decided to sit at one of the tables.

Just then Callahan said, "Oh no, we have company. Look who is sitting in the corner with those girls."

We all looked in the direction that Callahan was staring and saw that Sergeant Buttplate was there laughing and carrying on with the ladies. He was too busy to notice us.

"Let's split this place," Hill said. "Next thing you know he will be over here trying to bum drinks from us."

Foster answered, "What are we going to do, just stand up and walk out? He is surely to see us."

"What the hell," I said, "Let's stay right here and drink our beer. It's a free country ain't it?"

Callahan replied, "Fenwick's right, let's just ignore him."

It wasn't long until Sergeant Buttplate noticed us but we began to talk a little louder ignoring his presence.

"Hey you guys!" he yelled from across the room. "How bout buyin your old sarge a drink. I'll have a Tiger Beer over here."

Foster yelled back that he should buy his troops a round of cheer since he made more money than we did. To our surprise Sergeant Buttplate stood up and shouted at the bartender. "Give me a round of cheer for my troops," he said. "I will drink these Devil Dogs under the table." He moved to the bar and paid for the beer. With two beers in each hand he moseyed over to our table. He sat the drinks down and passed them around. Then without saying a word he walked around the table and approached me from behind. "What in the same hell are you doing out in town on liberty, Fenwick?" he whispered in a low voice.

Before I could answer, Foster spoke up. "The machine gun section leader granted Fenwick liberty on our last day in port. He said he would clear it with you."

"Clear it with me?" he asked angrily. "I'm the one who makes the deci-

sions in my platoon. I restricted Fenwick to the ship and now he has disobeyed my order. I'm gonna write your ass up. Instead of skating as a brig
guard you will be on bread and water," Sergeant Buttplate said to me. He
gave me a mean stare and put his face closer to mine.

"Why don't you leave him alone?" Callahan said in a low tone of voice.
"Just because you found carbon on the team's gun you have to make an example of him. Anybody could find carbon in the gas port cylinder, besides,
we are not even supposed to remove it, only qualified armory personnel.

Sergeant Buttplate leaned on the table and pointed his finger at Callahan. "Who do you think you are trying to bullshit, Callahan?" Sergeant
Buttplate asked. We all know that we take those apart to keep the weapon
from malfunctioning, so don't give me that shit about qualified personnel."

"You should have restricted the entire gun team and not just Fenwick,"
Hill interrupted.

"Shut up, Hill." Sergeant Buttplate said. "If I want any shit out of you I
will unscrew your head and dip it out with a gourd."

Foster tried to take charge of the situation. "Look, Sergeant Buttplate,
"The fact remains that the section leader gave Fenwick liberty and we have
all had a little too much to drink. Why don't we just drop it? We can discuss
this tomorrow with our section leader."

"You're not in command here, Foster," Sergeant Buttplate said as he
took a drink from the beer he had sat on the table in front of me. "I give the
orders around here and right now I am ordering Fenwick back to the ship
and his ass will burn come tomorrow." Sergeant Buttplate looked at me and
said, "Now Shithead, back to the ship, on the double."

All the while the talking was going on around me I had elected to keep
quiet and stare ahead in anger. Now I could feel my temper beginning to
flare and I knew I wouldn't be able to control it. I stood up, faced Sergeant
Buttplate, and put my face close to his.

"Let me get a couple of things straight, Buttplate," I said angrily. I
stared into his eyes and had intentionally not called him sergeant. "First of
all, I don't cotton to an Indian Giver who buys me a beer and then drinks it
himself. Second, my name is Fenwick, Lance Corporal Fenwick to you, and
I am not Shithead. Third, I am not intimidated by your measly threats of disciplinary action especially since I have authority to be out on liberty. And
lastly, if you don't back off right now, I will beat your ass right here in front
of God and everybody. Now if you feel froggy, leap you son-of-a-bitch!"
There was a moment of silence. My buddies could not believe what I had
just said. "Well, what do you say Sergeant Buttplate? You want a size eleven
boot up your ass sideways? I've about had all I'm going to take from you for
one night."

"Calm down, Fenwick," Sergeant Buttplate said in a low tone of voice. I
was only joking."

"The joke is over," I said, "and I just told you I am lance corporal to you and I mean it!"

"Okay, okay, lance corporal," he replied. "Let me buy you another beer."

"Keep your money," I replied, "now just leave us alone."

Sergeant Buttplate returned to his table and soon left from the bar. Out of anger he pounded his fist on the door on his way out. The other Marines could not believe that I had talked to him in the manner that I had.

"I'll bet he don't mess with you anymore," Foster said to me. "Did you see the look on his face when you said you would kick his ass? It was great."

"We've got ourselves a real mean team leader," Callahan said. "Remind me not to piss you off, Lance Corporal Fenwick."

"I think I'm in a world of shit," I said.

They laughed as we continued talking about the encounter. After another drink we headed back to the ship. I realized that I had been out of line with Sergeant Buttplate, but sometimes a person had to make a stand. The next morning the routine went on as usual. I saw Sergeant Buttplate just prior to me assuming brig guard duty but there was no mention of any retaliation. In fact, he seemed quite friendly. I thought that maybe he was just suffering from a hangover and didn't want to deal with me. I figured it was a matter of time before I went up for non-judicial punishment.

That same day the ship pulled anchor and we were steaming for the Philippines once again. The waves worsened the further we sailed out to sea. I felt a little woozy down in the belly of the ship next to the brig but managed to keep from throwing up. I could feel the pounding of the waves against the hull of the ship. Trump relieved me at around midnight and I was glad to hit the rack and get some shut eye.

About the second day at sea I felt my body being rolled around in my bunk. I felt like I wanted to throw up and jumped from my rack and ran into the head. I hugged the commode for a few minutes. The coolness of the bowl felt good to my hands. I decided that I needed to get to the hanger bay for some fresh air. When I got to the open hanger I looked out across the rolling ocean. The waves seemed as though they might wash across the hanger deck in any second. I leaned forward and joined a few other Marines that were throwing up over the roped off railing. I tried to get to the front of the line so that the wind would not blow vomit in my face from other Marines.

I heard one of the Marines say that the eighteen foot waves were really getting to him. An old crusty looking Navy Chief and a few other Sailors were laughing at the Marines heaving away. They seemed to be immune to the rocking of the ship or they had just simply gotten used to it. As I passed one of the Sailors heading back to my compartment, I noticed that one was a Navy corpsman.

"Doc," I said, "ain't there anything that will keep you from getting seasick?"

"As a matter of fact there is," the corpsman replied. "If you go to sick bay someone will give you some seasick pills that will calm your stomach."

"Outstanding," I said to the Doc, "thanks for the advice."

Then the Navy Chief spoke up. "Son, this seasick business is all in your head. If you were an old salt like me, it wouldn't bother you."

"Chief," I said, "if this is all in my head, I wonder why my stomach keeps me running for the side of the ship."

Just then the pain and dizziness hit me again and I ran back to the side of the ship to throw up. I could hear laughter in the background and the Sailors talking about my dilemma. I managed to get to sick bay and took two of the so-called seasick pills. They did not seem to do any good. Must all be in my mind, I thought. I returned to my bunk. I dreaded the time when Trump would come to get me so I could take over the watch at the brig.

That night I carried a tin can down to the brig with me just in case I had to throw up during the night. I had the dry heaves all through the night. The next day I was off duty for a couple of days. I was assigned Duty NCO for the company. I figured that if I had to be at my post during the night, that I might as well try to write a letter home. As I wrote the letter, I had my tin can within reach, just in case.

December 30, 1970

Hello Mom, Dad and all,

Well I have duty tonight so thought I'd drop you a few lines while I'm not doing much. Its kinda quiet around here now since everyone is in the racks. It's about two o'clock in the morning now. All I have to do is to ensure the guys on restriction signs in. They're held in the company area for some reason or other. They just can't leave the area or go anywhere without someone knowing it.

I have been a brig guard now for about a week. It may last through the cruise. It isn't too bad. I work four hours in the mornings and four at night, but get off two days. During that time I go through the same routine as the platoon does, except I don't have any details or watches to do. We're supposed to go to the bush for five days when we hit the Philippines again. I hope I have guard so I don't have to go. If I do go, then we'll have to take all our gear with us back to the same camp we were before. It sure is a hassle unloading this ship, but you know how the Marine Corps is.

Well we were in Singapore last week and to tell the truth, it wasn't what I expected it to be. It was a pretty city but not much to do. I had a good time though and saw some pretty sights. I have a picture in this letter that was taken on Christmas day. It's in a bar in Singapore. Don't get the impression that I spent all my time in bars cause I didn't. Mostly we walked the streets but occasionally dropped in to have a snort. Ha ha! When this picture was taken we were heading back to the ship. Small boats took us from the ship to the pier because we couldn't get that close to port.

We left there on the 26th and should be back in the Philippines tomorrow. We had eighteen feet waves all the way from Singapore and there were plenty of sick guys. I was one of them! I got some seasick pills from the Doc and I feel better now. This darn ship is always rocking back and forth. If you're not careful your chow tray at the mess hall will slide right off onto the floor. It has calmed down a lot now. I guess we must be near the coast.

We'll spend about a week here, about five days being in the bush, and then head out for Hong Kong. I'm really looking forward to going there. I've heard a lot about it. Guess we'll get a couple nights of liberty while we're here. Everyone looks forward to that.

Well guess that's about all I have for now. So I'll let you all go until the next time. Hope everyone had a nice Christmas and a prosperous New Year to come.

As ever,
Fred

Once again the USS Iwo Jima pulled into port at the U. S. Naval Base Subic Bay, Philippines. It was New Years Eve. That afternoon liberty was sounded for the entire battalion. It was about 1800 before we managed to get organized and get out on liberty. Our little band-of-brothers went ashore and walked down to the Sampaguita Enlisted Men's Club that was near the main gate of Subic Bay. It was a short walk from the club and into Olongapo. During happy hour at the club the beer was ten cents a can. We could save our hard earned money by first patronizing the naval base club prior to heading out into the city.

After stacking a pyramid of beer cans on the table we decided that the great city of Olongapo was calling us. We made our way through Marine Security at the main gate and crossed over the bridge into town. We were now traipsing down Magsaysay Drive for the second time. Our designated liberty uniform was khaki shirt with ribbons, khaki trousers, and black spit shinned dress shoes.

As we walked along in the crowd passing all the clubs and bars, a male Filipino in his middle thirties, yelled at me from the steps of a bar.

"Hey, you, Marine, look what I have," the Filipino said. He held up a Combat Action Ribbon. "I took it off your uniform," he laughed as he held the ribbon above his head and waved it from side to side.

I looked down at my ribbons that I had mounted and placed exactly one eighth of an inch and centered above my left breast pocket. All my ribbons were still in tact. I looked back at the man and he began to laugh along with

Fenwick pictured on the left while on liberty in Singapore. Christmas Day 1970.

a few of his buddies.

"I will get your ribbon!" he yelled again as we continued to walk past him.

"You'll play hell getting my ribbon," I said boldly.

The other Marines walking with me thought it was funny. The Filipino had played a joke on me. As we moved along slowly I began to dislike the fact that the Filipinos couldn't seem to walk a straight line without bumping into us. I began to feel that they might dirty my uniform, a uniform that I took pride in wearing. It wasn't long until I saw the same man standing on the steps of another bar. As we approached, he held up a Combat Action Ribbon for the second time.

"Look Marine," he said, "see what I have?"

"You can't get me to fall for that trick again," I replied.

"Go ahead, Marine," he said laughing. "Look at your ribbons. I have it, don't you see?"

"Suck balut eggs!" I replied boastfully. I had learned quickly that balut eggs were fertilized duck or chicken eggs with a nearly-developed embryo inside and eaten in the shell by the Filipino people.

Just then Callahan turned around and said, "Hey Fenwick, that bastard does have your ribbon. Yours is missing."

"Not you too," I said to Callahan.

"He's right," Hill said as he joined in. "He has stolen your ribbon right off your ribbon bar!"

I glanced down at my ribbon bar. Sure enough my Combat Action Ribbon was missing. "That son-of-a-bitch!" I yelled out. "That fucker did take my ribbon. Give it back, you dumb asshole." I started through the crowd to get to the man but he quickly ran and disappeared down a back alley while his buddies were all laughing. One held up a different ribbon and told me to look and see if I was missing it. I looked down but that ribbon was still on the ribbon bar.

"I'm gonna kill these little commie bastards!" I yelled out as I started to pursue at them. They all dispersed quickly and disappeared into the crowd.

Foster grabbed my arm. "Wait a minute, Fenwick," he said. "You don't want to go off half cocked chasing these idiots around. That's all they want you to do, follow them into a back alley, and then they will roll you and take your money."

"They will die trying," I said angrily.

"Come on, Fenwick," Callahan interrupted. "This is no time to play hero. We would rather have a live hero than a dead one in our gun team."

"He's right," insisted Hill, "just forget about it."

"Oh well, guess you guys are right," I agreed. "But now I have to walk around town all night missing one ribbon. I'm out of uniform."

"We won't tell," Foster answered. "Hell, let's get a cold San Miguel beer."

We walked into the nearest bar and sat down. Several girls approached us trying to sit with us and asked that we buy them drinks. We refused having just gone through the experience outside with the prankster Filipino men. We just wanted to watch some boobs and ass bounce around on stage and perhaps listen to some music. There were sounds of firecrackers being set off outside.

"Get ready," Foster said, as he leaned over the table. "They're getting ready to celebrate the New Year. I heard from a Sailor that they really get into the spirit with the firecrackers on the streets."

Just then some teenage Filipino boy tossed a cherry bomb into the bar. BOOM! The cherry bomb exploded as I was sipping on my bottle of beer and caught me totally off guard. Instantly, I dove for cover knocking over the bottle of beer and spilling it all over the table. For a split second I thought I was back in Vietnam. My ears were ringing from the loud noise made by the cherry bomb.

"Holy shit!" Foster yelled, not flinching a muscle. "Take it easy Fenwick, it's only a cherry bomb. It went off under that empty table. A cherry bomb won't hurt you. It just makes a lot of noise."

Still out of my chair I looked at my Marine buddies who had not moved from their seats at the table. "Damned thing sounded like a booby trap to me," I said.

Most of the girls were now laughing that I had been scared by the cherry bomb. "Shut the hell up, you slimy little sluts," I yelled out as I regained my composure and sat back down. I felt confused and embarrassed. The girls were still laughing and making fun of me in their native language, Tagalog. For an instance they all seemed to take on the appearance of Vietnamese women. Their loud cackling and high pitched laughter made me angry. I thought to myself, who do these bar hookers think they are to laugh at me? They had no damn right as far as I was concerned. I could sense that everyone in the bar was staring at me and I felt uncomfortable with my surroundings. Even a couple of Sailors sitting over in a corner were eyeballing me. "Let's get the hell out of here," I demanded loudly.

"Okay," Foster and Callahan said in unison.

"What about our beers?" Hill asked.

"Give them to the whores," I replied angrily, "I'm outta here."

As we walked out of the door, Callahan touched me on the shoulder as if to console me but I abruptly jerked away. He immediately withdrew his hand.

"Try to relax, Fenwick," he said. "These cherry bombs and firecrackers will most likely go on all night."

"I know," I responded, "but I'll be a nervous wreck by the time I get back to the ship."

"Just remember you are not in Vietnam," Foster added. "There are no mines, booby traps, or the enemy trying to kill you. We are your buddies and we will take care of you. You know, Semper Fi, Gung Ho, and all that gungy stuff."

"I can't help but be a little jumpy," I replied, "but I do appreciate the camaraderie."

I was still a little dazed and nervous. I felt my hands trembling from the excitement so I stuck them in my trousers pockets for a brief period. Then I realized that Marines were not allowed to walk around with hands in their pockets so I removed them. As we walked along through the dimly lit streets the firecrackers and cherry bombs could be seen and heard throughout the city of Olongapo. Kids were running around lighting firecrackers and throwing them at the feet of passing pedestrians.

I told my Marine buddies, "Those little commie bastards better keep away from me. I'll smack the hell right out of 'em."

"Come on, Fenwick," Foster replied. "You can walk in the middle of us. That way we can keep you out of trouble."

Just then a cherry bomb exploded right behind us. It caught me by surprise once again. It was very loud. Again I ducked violently. I knew that it was a cherry bomb but I just could not control my instincts. "Hot damn!" I yelled out. "I don't know how much of this crap I can take. I may have to go back to the ship and see Olongapo some other time."

"No, no, you'll be okay," Foster said trying to assure me that everything was all right. "Let's go into this Club and we can stay off the streets for awhile." Everyone agreed.

The neon sign above the entrance read East Inn Club. The first floor appeared to be a hardware store but there was a long flight of stairs leading up to the second floor. As we began walking up the steps there were three Filipina girls standing at the top raising the hemline of their dresses. We proceeded past them and found a table in one corner of the bar. We ordered drinks and began talking about New Years back home. Some of the girls began pestering us but we left them alone for they were as ugly as sin. We saw Chief, Patuba, Swanie, and Kartum, and other members of the squad enter the bar. They had seen us walking into the Club and had decided to join us. They gathered around our table and ordered their drinks.

As we laughed and talked, Patuba said, "Let's try one of the balut eggs."

"Not me," said Swanie, "I tried one of them the last time we were in port and it made me sick as a dog."

"Me neither," added Kartum, "I ain't gonna eat one of those things."

Foster said, "Come on you guys, it's only a little unhatched chicken still in the egg. They are delicious!"

"Oh yeah," I said with sarcasm. "That's all I need right now is to eat an unhatched chicken while drinking San Miguel Beer. I think I'll pass."

"No balls eh?" asked Patuba. "Let me show you how it's done."

He yelled at the bartender to bring him some balut. It wasn't long until a girl brought the eggs over on a platter.

"Um um good," Patuba announced. "Just what the doctor ordered."

"If you eat those things, you might need a doctor," I replied.

Everyone started to laugh. Without any hesitation, Patuba cracked a hole at one end of an egg and sucked the unhatched chicken from within into his mouth. With a motion of trying desperately to swallow the morsel he managed to get it down. He immediately took a huge swallow of beer. Rubbing his mouth with one hand and his stomach with the other he said, "You guys should try one, they ain't too bad."

"That's sick," Kartum said, "ain't no way I'm gonna eat an unborn chicken with the feathers still on it."

"Let me show you how," Foster interrupted. He repeated the procedure and after a struggle managed to swallow the chicken.

"Oh, what the hell," Hill joined in. "Give me one of those things."

Hill cracked the egg, swallowed the morsel, and then took a long drink from his beer bottle. "Man, this is awful," Hill finally said. "Why did you all let me do that?"

We erupted in laughter. Hill began to feel sick and his face turned a ghost white. "Gotta go to the head," Hill screamed as he held both hands over his mouth. He could not find the door to the bathroom right away so he began to run about frantically. All the rest of us were rolling in our chairs laughing at him. Foster pointed him in the direction of the head and we could hear Hill throwing up inside.

"Okay, Fenwick, your turn," Foster said.

"Yeah, go for it," Patuba added.

"Not me," I said, "seems a waste of good beer."

"Come on, Fenwick, have some balls," Patuba insisted.

The other Marines around the table joined in trying to coax me into trying to eat one of the balut. I took one of the eggs off of the platter and peeled back a hole at one end. I could see the feathers of the unhatched chicken and the beak of the bird. It was surrounded by bloody tissue.

"Not on your life," I said, "ain't no way."

"Go ahead," Foster coached me on. "If you swallow it, I will buy you beers the rest of the night."

"Ain't no free beers worth eating this," I replied.

The other Marines began to taunt me. They all started chanting, "Machine Guns! Machine Guns! Blood and Guts! Semper Fi! Do or Die!"

I took the egg and sucked the contents into my mouth and held it there for a moment. I knew that my facial expression was one of total disgust. The Marines laughed so hard they cried. Finally I swallowed the morsel. It seemed to get lodged about midway down my throat. I tried to drink beer to finish its journey into my stomach. I felt the morsel reach my stomach. Then all of a sudden it started back up again. I dashed to the head holding the vomit with both hands. I could hear laughter from the table of Marines. I hugged the commode. This delicacy was now where it was supposed to be, down the toilet. I returned and took a drink of San Miguel beer and swished it around in my mouth like mouthwash.

"I will never listen to you guys ever again," I said.

They laughed uncontrollably for what seemed like a very long time. Finally we left the East Inn Club and began walking along the streets while passing one bar after another. The Filipinos were now continuously throwing firecrackers as we walked along. They were getting on my nerves but there was little I could do about it. We wandered around aimlessly and someone noticed that we were on Rizal Avenue. At some point we agreed to begin making our way back toward the Main Gate at Subic Bay. We came upon a club called the Acapulco Nite Club Delgado. The Marines in our group wanted to go inside for one last drink before heading back to the base.

We got seated around some tables that we had pushed together. The bar girls began sitting in our laps even though some of us were resisting. They seemed to be a nuisance to me. All I wanted to do was to sit and talk, but now each Marine began talking to the girl that was either sitting in his lap or next to him. By now our little party of "liberty hounds" consisted of about eight Marines.

The girl that was sitting in Callahan's lap began to rub him on his private parts. He leaned over to me and whispered in my ear. "I'm gonna have to go and ball this girl. She's making me too hot," he said.

"Better not," I replied, "what if you catch venereal disease?"

"Yeah, guess your right," he said, "but I just might have to take the chance if she don't leave me alone."

I laughed and Callahan sat back still chatting with her. I noticed that she was now blowing in his ears. It wasn't long until Callahan leaned back over to me and said, "I'm going. I'm gonna take this girl home and bang her like she has never been banged before."

"You're not getting a cherry girl you know," I said to Callahan. "She has been around the block a few times. Every Battalion Landing Team that comes into port she gets laid, not to mention all the horny Squids from all the ships that hit port."

"Oh well," Callahan said, "guess I will just be another statistic." He stood up and started to walk away with the girl.

"I will see you back on ship," I told him.

"No, don't leave me," he replied. "This won't take long. I'll be back in a few minutes."

"I'll give you thirty minutes and then I'm heading back to the ship, I replied.

"Okay," Callahan agreed, "thirty minutes."

After about forty-five minutes of waiting I became uncomfortable knowing that my buddy Callahan had disappeared into the night by himself. I could have kicked myself for letting him wonder off on his own. I got up from the table and told the other Marines that I was going back to the ship and hit the rack. They tried to get me to stay a little longer and I started to, until a firecracker went off in one corner of the bar. That was all it took for me to decide to leave. As I started to walk away from the table, Callahan returned.

"Okay, Fenwick, I'm ready," he said.

"Thought you might take all night," I replied.

"I didn't do anything," Callahan said. "She took me to her room and she had a baby in there. I just couldn't do it in front of the kid so we just sat and talked. Let's get on back to the ship."

"You are one helluva guy," I told Callahan.

We both walked together down the streets, across the bridge, through the main gate, and walked up the gang plank of the ship. We went straight to our berthing area and crawled into our racks. The next day was New Years Day. The battalion commander declared it a holiday routine for all hands. Consequently we did not do any training. Instead, the Marines just hung around the compartment waiting for off base liberty to be sounded later on in the afternoon. Callahan and I decided to stay on ship in order to prepare our gear for the field.

The BLT moved to the SLF Camp the next day and we set up once again the Quonset Huts. Once we had secured all our gear, liberty was sounded at around 2100. There was a delay because the company commander ensured that we had cleaned our barracks and weapons before he would sound liberty call. When liberty was finally sounded there was a mad dash to catch taxies to the bottom of the hill and to the Subic Bay Main Gate. Callahan and I got tired of waiting for a taxi amidst all the other swarms of Marines from the battalion, so we decided to remain at the SLF Club which was just a short walk from the Quonset Huts.

We spent the night drinking San Miguel Beer and listening to a live band. There were several Filipina girls that worked in the Club as entertainers, in other words, girls that would sit with you, talk with you, and dance the night away. They were not allowed to leave with any of the servicemen, unless of course, one happened to have a silver tongue. Callahan and I were content to just relax and drink a few beers before turning in for the night. I thought it better than running around on the streets of Olongapo.

We spent three days somewhere in the hills of the Philippines conducting training exercises. The terrain was very similar to that of Vietnam. The time passed quickly and before we knew it we were back aboard ship. We settled back into our usual compartments of the ship, same racks, and same small wall lockers. The ship set sail and almost all of the battalion of Marines stood on the hanger deck to watch Olongapo disappear out of sight. There were a few Sailors that stared at the coast also while remembering the good times they had in port.

We found out that the battalion left port with two AWOL (Away Without Leave) Marines. They were probably shacked up with some oriental beauties. We would most likely pick them up when we returned to Subic Bay. By then they both would have run out of money. The ladies of Olongapo would say, "No Money, No Honey!" There would be two more in the ship's brig that Trump and I would have to guard. Better them than me on bread and water, I thought. I reckoned that as the ship sailed from the Subic Bay harbor that the two AWOL Marines could care less if they "missed movement."

While we were out at sea, the Marine that had gone with the pretty girl in Singapore, came down with the clap. He assured us that he did not touch a woman in Olongapo. He told us that he was faithful to his bar girlfriend back in Singapore and that they had been writing letters back and forth. We got a kick out of teasing him about his dilemma. "See what happens when you muff dive on a bar girl," Foster said to him. "You get VD of the mouth." It just so happened that the Marine also had a big fever blister on his lip which made the taunts even worse.

We got word that we would be heading to Malaya and that we would be out to sea for approximately thirty to forty days before hitting port. The word was passed that there were flood victims near Port Swettenham and that our choppers were to fly in supplies. Port Swettenham would later be named Port Kelang Malaysia. It is the leading port of Malaysia on the Strait of Malacca, midway between the major ports of Pinang and Singapore. It is the port of Kuala Lumpur, the capital if Malaysia, which is twenty-three miles east-northeast from the port.

My birthday, 8 January, passed unnoticed. I was now twenty years old. I had seen a lot in the past year or so. I figured that I had become a man in more ways than one. Not only was I seasick on my birthday from the eighteen foot waves, but we all had to get inoculations on that day. That made me even sicker. What a way to spend a birthday, I thought.

January 9, 1971

Dear Mom, Dad and Larry,

How has everyone been getting along lately? I hope you're in good health and spirits. For myself, I'm doing just fine except I'm getting sort of tired of this ship rocking back and forth. A lot of guys get sick including me at times, but I've pretty well got used to it now. I got some seasick pills from the Doc and when I feel a little dizzy I take one. They help out some. The only time I get a little sick is when we run into eighteen foot waves.

Well I guess everyone back home thinks I've forgotten about them, but I haven't. I just don't have much of a chance to write. Usually we can't write anyway because the ship rocks so much. We can be eating chow and the trays will slide right off on the floor if you're not careful. It's funny at times when everybody's chairs start sliding into one corner.

Well, the last letter I wrote I said we were supposed to spend about five days in the bush in the Philippines. We got there on a Thursday and didn't go to the field until Monday, so we had some days of good liberty there. The name of the town is Olongapo. I've had some good times there but one has to be pretty careful. We were in the field three days but then one morning they told us to pack up and that we were getting back on the ship. We finally loaded aboard at about six o'clock that night and then we left port.

So right now we're on our way to Malaysia. They've had some bad floods there and we're going to help the people out a little. Of course we won't leave the ship I don't guess, but the choppers we have on board will fly supplies and food to them. I think we're heading pretty close to Singapore again. Right now we're going around the tip of South Vietnam, so that's why this letter is free. I bet you all thought I was back in Nam! We should get to where we're going either tomorrow or the next day. After this mission is all over I suppose we'll head for Hong Kong. At least I hope so.

Well Mom, I got your package on January 1st. I really enjoyed it. Thanks a lot for everything. Don't guess I'll have to buy any more writing gear now until after I get home. Yesterday was my birthday but I didn't do much. The ship was rocking so much they called off the training schedule for the day. So I lay in the rack most of the afternoon. Of course I got a birthday present. Everyone had to get two inoculations. Ha!

Well, I'll close for now. I'll be home in another forty-nine days and we can talk then. So I'll say bye for now, hope everyone is doing fine.

As ever,
Short Timer Fred

We finally got close enough to Malaysia that the helicopters could fly supplies in for the flood victims. The ship never did pull into port for some unknown reason. At times we could see land, but we would drift back out to sea and go around in circles. We were accompanied by about six other ships. The Marines made use of the downtime by playing basketball on the flight deck, conducting physical training, playing cards, and fishing off the fan tail.

At one point we got so bored that we threw boxes off the fan tail and then fired at them with the machine guns mounted on tripods. That turned out to be an exciting day. All the Sailors wanted to fire the machine guns but we told them it was part of our training. We offered to let them fire the machine guns if they would let us fire their anti-missile guns. Of course, that was a deal that could not be made. On about the fourth day at sea, a ship arrived from Subic Bay to join us. There were about eight new Marines that were to be assigned to our battalion.

One morning at around 0900 we got word that the new Marines were coming from the other ship to join our battalion. They were to be flown on a CH-46 Sea Knight helicopter. Some of the Marines in our berthing compartment decided to go up to the flight deck and watch the chopper fly in. They wanted to get some fresh air and greet the Marines as they off loaded the chopper. Callahan and I went along with them to break the monotony.

We stood on the catwalk awaiting the chopper to arrive. It wasn't long until we could see the chopper lift off of the other ship. The chopper was in the air and began its path to our ship. Everything seemed to be going as planned, just another routine mission. Then as the chopper approached the flight deck of the USS Iwo Jima it started to descend in altitude. The CH-46 flew lower and lower toward the waves of the ocean. It became apparent to us that the pilot was having trouble with the aircraft and that it would not reach the flight deck.

"Oh, noooo!" a Marine yelled out. "It's gonna crash!"

The other Marines and I watched helplessly as the aircraft fell into the ocean with the propellers still turning at high speed. The body of the chopper began to sink into the water. We could see that the passengers were escaping from both sides of the aircraft.

"God forbid!" I yelled. "Those Marines are gonna get sliced to pieces by the propellers!"

"For Christ Sakes," Callahan added, "what can we do to help them?"

"There's not a thing we can do for them," I responded, "except pray."

We watched grimacing as the Marines were trying to swim out of the propellers path. Somehow the pilot had managed to cut the engine just prior to hitting the water and the propellers stopped as they bounced off the water in a convulsion like manner. Now the aircraft was beginning to sink and we could see that a couple of the Marines were being pulled down with the suction. We felt so helpless.

We looked and saw that a CH-46 aboard our ship was revving its engine and getting ready for a desperate attempt to pick up survivors. By now the chopper that had crashed in the water had disappeared out of sight. Callahan and I started counting the Marines floating and swimming in the water. We counted over and over again. We could count twelve of them. We assumed that eight of them were the new joins, two were the crew chiefs, one was the pilot, and one was the co-pilot.

"I think that's all of them," I said excitedly.

"Yeah," responded Callahan, "looks like they might make it if the rescue chopper gets to them in time."

We watched our chopper lift off the flight deck. It flew out and around in a circle. Then it hovered only about twenty-five feet above the swimming Marines. A rope ladder was tossed over one side and then another rope on the other. The Marines in the water helped the ones that were struggling the most onto the ladders. They began to slowly climb up the ropes and the crew chiefs pulled them into the hovering chopper. Then very slowly the others began to climb up the ropes. When the last one clung on to the ladder, the chopper lifted up slightly and moved toward the flight deck of our ship.

Callahan and I ran over to be of assistance. The Marines that were clinging onto the ropes climbed down into the arms of waiting Sailors and Marines. When they had cleared the chopper it veered over to a different location on the flight deck and landed. The other drenched Marines came walking slowly out of the rear of the chopper. The propellers came to a stop. Everyone on the flight deck cheered loudly as the Marines and helicopter crew came off the aircraft. They had made it. No one was seriously hurt. It was a successful rescue attempt.

Callahan and I tried to console two of the newly joined Marines. They nervously complained that all their uniforms and gear was lost with the chopper when it sank. Everything they owned was stuffed into seabags.

"Don't worry about that," I told them, "you are all lucky to be alive."

"Thank God for that," Callahan said. "Come on and go with us. We'll help you around the ship and try to find out what company you are supposed to go to."

As it turned out, Lima Company ended up with the two Marines that we had talked to. Some of the other Marines in the platoon that were about their size gave them some utilities, skivvies, socks, and boots. The section leader put in an order to get them new uniforms but it would take weeks for them to arrive. The request for uniforms would have to go through the Subic Bay supply channels and we currently going around in circles somewhere off the coast of Malaysia. The two Marines thanked Callahan and me for our hospitality.

"Not a problem," Callahan said, "we take care of our own."

"He's right about that," I added, "if you need anything, don't hesitate to call on us."

It wasn't long until the ship started to steam for Hong Kong. Our mission was completed in Malaysia. After a days journey all the ships turned around and headed back in the opposite direction. The Captain of the Ship made a surprise announcement.

"All hands on deck...All hands on deck...Our port call in Hong Kong has been canceled... There has been a change of orders...You will be briefed as soon as more details are received from higher command."

"I wonder what is going on now," Foster said to Callahan.

"Don't know," replied Callahan, "looks like we are going back to Malaysia."

"Either that or we are going back off the coast of Vietnam," I added.

"Why do you always look on the glum side?" asked Foster. "It's almost as though you want to go back to Nam,"

"No, not me," I replied. "I just want to face reality. After all, the USS Iwo Jima is still part of the Task Force for the Vietnam Counteroffensive Phase VII."

Foster looked at me and said in reply, "Wow, I'm impressed. You are really on top of things."

The Captain of the Ship made an announcement over the intercom. He stated that we were heading for the coast of Cambodia on some special operation. He also informed the ship's personnel that he was not at liberty to divulge any further information.

"Here we go again," Foster groaned.

"Yeah," I said. "Old Charlie must be acting up again."

"Maybe we will go in this time," Hill said nervously.

"Whatever our future holds, we might as well relax for awhile," I said. "It will probably take us a couple of days to reach Cambodia."

"Yeah, you're right," added Foster, "let's play a game of back alley."

The next day I had to go on brig duty again. I escorted one of the prisoners to the mess hall to eat the noon meal. His bread and water rationing had ended. We went through the line and got our chow. I followed him to the table where we were to eat. I sat down and watched the prisoner go get his milk and return.

"I'm going to go get some juice to drink," I said to the prisoner, "don't go anywhere."

"Hey Man," the prisoner responded, "where do you think I can go on this ship? Can't dive overboard and swim to port. Hell, we're miles from shore."

"Yeah I know," I answered, "I just don't want you wandering around without me being with you."

"I'll be right here when you get back," the prisoner said while forcing down his chow rapidly.

I walked over to the milk machine and found the juice. I poured me two glasses and as I started to walk away, Trump spoke to me from behind.

"How's it going, Fenwick?" he asked.

"Oh, all right, I suppose," I replied. "When do you come back on brig duty?"

"Tomorrow," he said. "I'll be relieving you first thing in the morning."

"Sounds good to me," I said.

"Mind if I join you at your table for chow?" Trump asked.

"You know you're always welcome at my table Trump," I responded. "Only thing is we will have to keep company with one of the prisoners that I escorted up from the brig. He's off bread and water now."

"What prisoner?" Trump asked.

"The one sitting over at the table in the corner," I replied.

"I don't see no prisoner," Trump whispered.

"The one right over."... I stopped speaking abruptly. I looked and saw that the prisoner was not at the table and that his tray had been taken away.

"Holy crap," I said in a low voice. "That damned asshole has disappeared on me. Hell, I never will find him. My ass is grass if anybody finds out that I let a prisoner escape."

"Calm down, Fenwick," murmured Trump. "He couldn't have gotten too far. He has to be somewhere on this ship."

"Don't say a word to anyone Trump," I ordered, "I'll find him if I have to search this entire ship from top to bottom."

"Let's eat chow and then look for him," Trump suggested.

"Are you crazy?" I snapped. "Here I have a prisoner roaming around loose on the ship and you want to think about eating. You go ahead and eat but I am going to find this knucklehead."

"Okay, okay," Trump responded, "let's get on with it."

I emptied my tray of food in a frenzy and poured out my drinks into the garbage can. Trump was stuffing his face with food as he dumped his tray also. I started out of the mess hall. What if one of the superiors saw the prisoner running around loose, I would really be in trouble, I thought.

"Wait for me!" Trump called out.

We started searching together. We walked rapidly through the hanger deck and then up to the flight deck. We checked the catwalks, no sign of him anywhere. We then went down into the compartments. We decided that we must split up in order to cover more territory. I went immediately to the boiler room. After searching in this very hot place I thought that the guy would have to be an idiot to hide down here. I was now wet from sweat. I searched down in the passageways, checked the heads, and went down to the ship's store. Still the prisoner was not to be found. I went through some of the other company compartments. Some of the Marines asked what I was doing in their area but I did not divulge the real reason. After about an hour of searching I went back to the hanger deck. I saw Trump walking towards me.

"I've searched all over," Trump said. "I even went back down to the brig but he did not show up. He is hiding from us somewhere."

"Now I've done it," I said seriously, as I sat down next to one of the fork lifts that was chained down on the hanger deck. Trump squatted down next to me and then leaned back against the wheel.

"Let's think this thing over," he said, "if you were a prisoner, where would you hide aboard ship?"

We began to contemplate.

"I know," I said excitedly.

"Where?" asked Trump.

"Just think about it," I continued. "Where do we go where it is nice and quiet, no one bothers us, where we have platoon classes from time to time, and you can sleep all day without anyone knowing your whereabouts?"

"Is this a riddle or what?" asked Trump. "I give up, where?"

"The Crows Nest at the fore of the ship," I exclaimed.

"Now why didn't we think of that earlier?" Trump asked.

"Because we were to busy trying to save my ass," I said, making Trump smile.

We bolted up and walked briskly up the ladderwells and went through the metal door that led to the Crows Nest. Once inside we both saw the prisoner laying asleep on the coils of the large rope that was affixed to the ships anchor.

"Now we have him." I exclaimed.

"Let's beat his ass," Trump said in anger.

"I'll handle this," I said.

I walked up to the sleeping prisoner. "Reveille...Reveille...Reveille... Shit-for-brains!" I shouted.

The prisoner jumped up from his sleeping position. "What's going on man?" the prisoner asked still in a sleepy daze.

"Listen Numbnuts," I continued. "Why did you leave the mess hall without me? Do you want me to kick your ass all over this ship?"

"Wait a minute," he replied. "I didn't mean nothin by it. I just wanted to play a little game with you."

"Well, the game is over now," I scolded. "You're going back to the brig right this minute. If you say just one more word, I'm gonna put your ass on bread and water."

"Please, not that," the prisoner replied. "I'm really sorry. I didn't mean to put you to any trouble."

"It's too late, you already have," I replied angrily. "I told you not another word and now you have disobeyed my order by running your sewer mouth. It's going to be bread and water for you. Now get your ass in gear and walk in front of me back to the brig. One little false move and I will kick your ass!"

"All right, all right," the prisoner replied.

As we walked down the ladderwells Trump followed behind me. "Let's beat his ass anyway, Fenwick, just for GP (General Purposes)."

"No, that's okay," I said. "He will get tired of bread and water."

"Can you legally do that?" Trump whispered in my ear.

I replied, "No, but this guy will learn not to mess with Lance Corporal Fenwick. I dare him to say one word about this little incident to anyone."

We escorted the prisoner back to the brig and I opened the door with the turn-key. Then I gave him a slight shove on the shoulder to help him along getting back inside his jail cell. Then I slammed the door shut and locked it with the key. "Remember that sound," I told the prisoner, "because you will not hear it open for you again to go to the mess hall when I am on brig duty."

"Same goes for me," Trump added.

I was very hungry by the time the evening meal was served. I had totally missed the noon meal while searching for the prisoner. I went to the mess hall on my own and left the prisoner in his cell to have bread and water. I was still angry about the little practical joke he had played on me. I had just hoped that he would not say anything to any superiors because he was now supposed to be off bread and water and allowed to eat meals in the mess hall. When this happened they were about ready to be released from the ship's brig and sent back to their respective companies.

The following morning Trump arrived at the designated time to relieve me of watch. He had already gotten paid and told me they wanted me to report for pay call. I went to the berthing area and received my pay. I decided to write a letter home and send my mother my paycheck. It was quite noisy down in the compartment with the Marines carrying out their normal duties of sweeping and swabbing the floors and emptying the trash. I decided to go back to the brig to write my letter as it was nice and peaceful there. No one ever checked on us at the ship's brig except for a few Sailors from time to time.

I entered the brig door and Trump was too busy making a log book entry to say anything. I sat down on an old dirty mattress that was placed on the brig floor. I opened up my plastic pouch that contained my letter writing gear and prepared to write a letter.

"Is our little buddy behaving himself?" I asked Trump.

"Oh yes," Trump said, "he won't give you any more trouble."

"Have you given him breakfast yet?" I asked smiling.

"Yeah," said Trump. "He's good to go until the next meal. The loaf of bread is over here next to me. You'll have to get him some water."

"Not a problem," I replied, "but you still have to feed him the noon meal. I don't relieve you until this afternoon, remember?"

I started writing the letter. Trump was trying to carry on a conversation as I wrote. I talked with him briefly and then said, "How do you think I can concentrate on writing home with you talking all the time?"

"Okay, okay," Trump replied, "I won't say another word."

After I wrote another line he began talking again. "I can see right now that this is going to be a short letter," I said. "By the time I write one page it will be time for me to relieve you from watch."

"Makes the time go by faster for me," Trump replied laughing.

January 15, 1971
0900

Dear Mom, Dad and all,

I'm sitting at the brig now but I don't go on duty till 3:00 p.m. I just thought I'd come down here where it's quiet and get away from the company awhile. On duty days we don't have to do anything that the rest of the company does. All three of us brig guards are down here now.

We got paid this morning so I thought I'd send a little money home. We are still in combat waters and that's why the mail is still free. I don't know how long we'll be off the coast, but for several more days I suppose. Not to scare you or anything but we're off the coast of Cambodia. The choppers are flying some kind of missions back and forth but they won't tell us what they're doing. We should be back to the Philippines around the 27th of this month. Now I don't know if we'll get to Hong Kong or not.

Well, I have to close for now. I want to get this money order in the mail. Tell me if it gets to you. We haven't got any mail for two weeks but should get some soon.

Bye for now,
Fred

We spent the rest of the week just floating around in the ocean. We could tell that the ships were at times just steaming around in circles. No one knew of the mission that the fleet of ships was trying to accomplish off the coast of Cambodia. The fleet commander ensured that all hands were virtually left in the dark. Boredom became a dominant factor. The morale of the men began to decrease. All we could see was ocean as far as the eye could see. We tried to make the best of the situation by playing card games, conducting platoon and company training, and anything else to keep us occupied. It seemed that the majority of the time was spent in the chow lines or taking cat naps during this time of uncertainty.

Trump and I would go up on the bow of the ship and sunbathe. He would bring along his trumpet and play a few tunes for me as the ship rocked back and forth. His favorite song was "Leaving on a Jet Plane." He would also blow his instrument at reveille each morning to motivate the Marines. At times a few Marines would tell him to knock off the noise but it was understood that they were only joking. Most liked the sound of the trumpet, especially at night when he sounded Taps at 2200. When he played Taps no matter what the Marines were doing in our compartment they all became quiet in order to listen to the solemn sound of the trumpet. It was a certain feeling of reverence among the young Marines who had a love for their country and respect for our fallen comrades in a time of war.

One day it was learned that we were floating in the Gulf of Siam which was later named the Gulf of Thailand. Time dragged by and we looked forward to the day that we would be able to step foot on land once again. We would not make it to Hong Kong on this cruise. That had been our plans, but whatever was going on in Cambodia, it would take precedence over liberty in Hong Kong.

Because of the boredom most of the Marines wrote several letters home. We enjoyed it when a Marine in the squad received a package from home. Everyone shared like we were brothers. We became very close and learned about individual experiences prior to coming into the Marine Corps and what their future might hold. I was counting down the days for I knew that it wouldn't be too long before the cruise would end and I would be on my way home.

January 21, 1971
0800

Dear Mom and Dad,

We got mail the other day so I got the letter that Mom wrote me. I thought at first you had written a book. Sure did enjoy reading it. How is everyone doing around home? Hope you all are doing okay. Guess the winter is getting a little boring but really it won't be long until spring. Hope it's not too cold when I'm home in March. I'm used to warm and humid weather now.

We're still sitting off the coast of Cambodia but should head back for the Philippines around the end of this month. We're in a gulf called the Gulf of Siam. I don't mind just floating around out here but its beginning to get tiresome. Now I'll be glad when we get back to the Philippines. If I'm lucky I'll be going back to Okinawa after we hit port. My name is on a list to go back after we hit port but you can never tell. They may just keep me until the float is over. Any way you look at it though, I'm getting short. Don't guess I'll see Hong Kong but I don't really mind. I'm kinda getting tired of this darn ship although we haven't seen really rough waters since we got here.

Mom, I was just thinking about my driver license. If you haven't already sent it to me, then just keep it until I get home. If I do go to Oki from this cruise, then I probably won't get any more mail out here on ship. I'll let you all know if I go to Oki or not. I'd like to go back to Oki a little early anyway to get my gear squared away and run around a bit.

That's a bummer about me returning home in March and Donald coming home in April. Oh well! Guess that's how the ball bounces. I don't know where I'll be stationed as of yet, but I don't even think about it right now.

Dad, I was sorry to hear that the hams and bacon spoiled in the old back room. Sounds like you weren't alone. At least you managed to keep some of it. Ever once in awhile I think of that two year old cured ham hanging up in the back room. Ha!

Right now I'm at the brig again and we have three prisoners. Two are on bread and water. I like brig guard because it gives me a chance to get away from the company. I'll be glad when I check out of the company to go back to Oki. I've never seen such a messed up company.

Well, guess I've said about all I know to say right now. As usual, there's not much going on. So I'll sign off now and write later on.

Yours most affirm,
Fred

On or about 26 January the ship started back on its way back to the Philippines. All the other ships accompanied us. We were going back for resupplies and a few days of liberty. We were to be in port for approximately ten days.

When we arrived at Subic Bay, the battalion off-loaded and went up to the SLF Camp once again. Because we had one prisoner aboard ship, all the brig guards were told to stay back on the ship. This suited Trump and I just fine. We could be away from the company for awhile and not have to do the training out in the bush. I began to expect word that I would be going back to Okinawa, but the word never came.

On our off days, Trump and I went to the Sampaguita Club on base at the naval base in Subic Bay. We found out that we could have just as good a time in the enlisted club than out in town where we would spend all our money. For one U.S. dollar, we could get pretty well lit. Sometimes the beer was only ten cents during happy hour. We liked sipping on cocktails such as the Mai Tai and Singapore Sling. Decent girls from Olongapo came into the club at night as entertainers. They were not allowed to leave the club with anyone and we were told they had to undergo a screening process to have access to the naval base. We enjoyed talking with the girls and finding out about their background and their way of life. There was a live band nightly and we always managed to dance the night away. Some of the Filipino bands were very good imitators. They played country, rock, and pop music.

On other occasions we would frequent the base snack bar for a greasy hamburger and French fries. It was a welcome change from the mess hall food aboard ship. The base at Subic had more recreational facilities than we had previously realized. There was horse back riding, swimming pools, softball fields, go-cart rides, gyms where the Marines and Sailors played basketball and weight lifted, and a variety of other indoor and outdoor recreations. We thought that it would be paradise if we could ever be stationed at Subic Bay like the Marines permanently assigned to the Marine Barracks.

After only five days in port, the order came that the ship would be pulling out again, this time off the coast of Vietnam again. Our venture away from the company was short lived. When everyone got back to the ship, Trump and I found out that we would have a total of eight prisoners to watch while we were out to sea.

Two of them were the Marines that went AWOL when we had left the port the previous time. They had returned because they had run out of money, and when you run out of money in Olongapo, "No Money, No Honey!" The others had gotten into trouble by not being back to the base on time when liberty secured for the battalion or they stayed the entire time out in town.

The ship began to pull out of port. I stood and watched as one stray Marine ashore came running up frantically to catch the ship. It was too late. We were too far out for the Captain of the Ship to go back and he probably wouldn't have anyway. We were all sure that he had to put up with this routine each and every time the ship pulled into a foreign port. Besides, what is one Marine non-rate to him. If it had been one of the Navy Officers, he would have still left him standing on the dock. That was the way it had to be.

To everyone's surprise, another Marine from a different line company dived overboard and swam to the dock. When he got to the dock he turned around, waved to us, and yelled that he would see us when we came back into port. Then I saw a Filipino girl grab him by the arm and led him off. What an idiot, I thought. He would get into all sorts of trouble for just one Filipina girl.

I turned away as the shore was now getting further away. I looked and saw a long line down the hanger deck. From seeing this every time we pulled out of the Subic Bay port, I knew that it wasn't the chow line. All the Marines and Sailors were lined up to visit sick bay for venereal disease. Seemed they never would learn their lesson and stay away from the bar hookers.

After a few days we were floating off the coast of Vietnam in the Gulf of Tonkin. I remembered the time I had tossed a quarter over my shoulder and into the blue sea below. It is still down there, I thought. I reached into my pocket and tossed another quarter into the murky depths. Some wishing well this has turned out to be, I pondered, while looking out over the horizon.

I inquired as to when I might be going back to Okinawa. My platoon sergeant told me that I had a good chance of going back when we pulled back into port at Subic Bay. I could only hope that I would be on that Freedom Bird back to the States before long.

February 4, 1971
1200 noon

Dear Mom, Dad and Larry,

What's happening around home these days? Guess everyone is getting tired of winter but can't say that I blame you. It's been raining all day here and pretty cool for a change. By the way, we're back out at sea again. You can probably guess where we're at since the mail is free again.

I think in the last letter I told you all that we were heading back to the Philippines and were going to be there until the 10th. Well, we only stayed about five days and everyone had to get back on ship and take off again. This ship gets around the fastest I think I've ever seen. Anyway we're off the coast of Vietnam again, but we haven't been able to see land. They never tell us what's going on. I think they are trying to keep us in suspense.

While we were back in the Philippines, I stayed on ship while the others off-loaded and went to the SLF Camp. The reason I stayed back was because we had a guy in the brig so all the brig guards had to stay back. It was a pretty good deal, but I think the guys that went to the SLF Camp got more liberty than we did. We had one day off and one day on so that wasn't too bad. I had a pretty good time when I did go out on liberty. When we left PI this time we had eight prisoners in the brig. Now we have five that are in from fifteen to thirty days. Right now I'm at the brig and things are pretty quiet. Everyone is crashed, asleep, in other words.

There's not much going on right now that is too exciting and guess I'll let you go for now. We can talk when I get home. They don't tell us what's going on but it really doesn't matter to me because the days just keep on going. I'll be so glad when I get out of this company, "Leaping Lima," we call it. Well, bye for now, I'll write later on. Everyone be good and take care.

As ever,
Fred

A couple of weeks passed and I was told by my section leader that I needed to check out of the company and to pack my seabag. He told me that the next time we hit port in the Philippines that I would be flying back to Okinawa and get ready to depart for the States. I was elated.

I checked out of the company and turned in my rifle and all of my 782 gear which was referred to as "War Fighting Equipment." I was glad to know that I may not have to use it again in combat. The section leader also told me that I was taken off brig duty and that I would just hang around doing virtually nothing until we docked. I felt that I was now going to be free from all the training and clean up details that the company performed on a daily basis.

I watched one day as the resupply ships came along side of our ship. I wondered why we were getting resupplied in the middle of the ocean if we were heading back to Subic Bay in a few days. I figured that the ship must be getting very low in food and supplies. It was the first time that I wasn't assigned in some way to help with the resupply. I felt very short on my tour and a bit salty. Since I was not involved in off-loading the resupply ships I decided to go down into the compartment and watch a little TV. It gave me a chance to write another letter home.

As I was writing my letter, Sergeant Buttplate came down into the compartment.

"What the hell are you doing down here, Fenwick?" he asked.

"I'm all checked out of the company so I thought I would relax and write a letter home," I answered."

"So you're all checked out, eeh," he replied with sarcasm. "From what I just overheard the lieutenant talking about, it looks like you may get extended awhile longer."

"You're pulling my leg, Sergeant Buttplate," I said, not looking up from my paper.

"You had best check with the lieutenant," Sergeant Buttplate added. "You may not be leaving as soon as you think."

As I continued to write my letter my concentration was broken. I could not help from thinking about what Sergeant Buttplate had said about me being extended. I put my pen down and went to find the platoon commander. He was still standing on the hanger deck with my section leader. The rest of the machine gun section was sitting on the hanger deck cleaning their weapons just in front of them.

"Hey guys, here comes short-timer Fenwick," Hill exclaimed. "How are you doing, short-timer?"

"I could be better," I replied, not looking at him.

I then heard Foster tell Hill to shut up. It appeared that the rest of the platoon had overheard the conversation between the section leader and the platoon commander about me being extended on the cruise.

"Tell me something," I said to the lieutenant. "Am I leaving when we get back to port or not? Sergeant Buttplate said that I may be extended. Is that right?"

"As it looks right now, yes," he replied. "We haven't gotten definite word but it looks like all the Marines that are supposed to rotate back to the States may be extended until the cruise is over."

"What a crock-a-crap," I blurted out. "I can't believe this. Here I am all packed up and checked out of the company and now I'm told I may be extended."

Listen Lance Corporal Fenwick," the lieutenant said. "It seems that if the ones that are due to rotate back to the States leave early, the battalion will be under strength for the remainder of the cruise and the battalion commander does not want that. Also they think there is a transportation problem of getting you guys back to Okinawa from the Philippines."

"I understand about a possible transportation problem, but because only a few Marines will be rotating back, I can't see that just a few will be missed," I responded.

"Well, the battalion commander does not see it that way," the lieutenant replied. "He probably has received his orders from higher authority."

"Well, hell," I said angrily. "What do I do now that I am checked out of the company?"

"Just hang loose," the lieutenant replied. "We will let you know if you get extended as soon as we find out."

"Well, I might as well help you guys clean the guns," I said while I squatted down beside Callahan.

"Oh, no you don't," said Callahan. "We've got it. You can go back to screwing off. We don't need you anyway. Besides I'm bucking for team leader in your place," he said smiling. The other Marines would not let me touch the gun to help clean it so I went back down into the compartment. I felt a bit disgusted so I put my letter writing gear away. I would try and write later.

The next day was supposed to be the day that I was to leave but I knew that would never happen. I performed the duties along with the rest of the platoon. A few of my buddies tried to boost my morale but I told them that I was okay. After all, I had seen disappointments before. I managed to get a little free time during the day so I decided to finish my letter home that I had started the day before.

February 20, 1971

Dear Mom, Dad and Larry,

How has everything been going for you? I hope pretty well. I got Mom's letter yesterday that was dated the 1st of February and it was good to hear from home. It was the first mail we got since around the 2nd of this month. Guess everyone thinks I've forgotten them, but really I never feel much like writing. Seems like I'm busy all the time, but that's what makes time go by fast.

I'm doing just fine only I sure would like to see land again. We've been out at sea for about twenty days now. Still off the coast of Nam but there's not much going on. They never tell us anything around here. I imagine you all know more about what we're doing here than I do. I don't care though because time is passing pretty fast.

Well folks, I was supposed to have left for Okinawa yesterday but didn't get to. I had my seabag packed and ready to go and had already checked out of the company. They said if the ones that rotate leave now they will have less than a battalion is supposed to have. Also I think transportation is a problem. So now they're talking about extending us until after the float is over. It was supposed to end the 15th but this Vietnam deal came up. I can't see that we're doing much good out here in the water, but of course, I'm only a "peon." The big wheels run the show!

So don't look for me around the end of this month. It may be April before I get home now or it may be sooner. Right now no one knows whether we'll be extended or not, but it's a good chance we will. One thing about it though, whenever we do hit land again, I'll be on my way. In a way, I sort of hope I do get extended for about a month so Donald and I will be home together.

Since I'm checked out of the company I don't do much now. I turned in my rifle and all my fighting gear. I just hope I don't have to check back into the company. I'm even off brig duty now. I'll miss bullying the prisoners around. Ha!

Well, I'll close for now and let you know more when I find out. So everyone be good and take care. I'll see everyone before long, either one way or the other.

As ever,
Fred

P.S. Mom, if any mail comes to the house for me, just save it for me until I get home. I have some friends that got my home address and are going to write to me. Also, if the driver license comes in, save that also. Thanks a lot.

The next day the machine gun section leader came to see me in the berthing compartment.

"Well, Fenwick, I hate to be the one to tell you this, but you need to check back into the company. All of the guys that are due to rotate have been "involuntarily extended" until the cruise is over. Sorry about that," he added.

"Ah, that's okay," I said glumly. "I didn't want to leave this floating prison anyway. Besides, maybe I can help out the gun team so that they can continue to march when I'm gone."

"That's a real fine attitude," the section leader added. "I wish I had more

Marines like you in the machine gun section. I'm gonna miss you when you're gone."

"Thanks," I said. "Now, what is the plan of attack for today? It's time to get back to the routine of things around here again."

After I got over the initial shock of not being able to rotate back to Okinawa after my hopes had been built up, I settled back into the same daily routine. I tried not to think about it in order to pass the time more quickly. I got to where I would PT on the flight deck alone and at times play a game of basketball with my buddies. We even managed to check out some rod and reels and fish off the fan tail. I never caught anything but it was just another way to pass the time. I started working on a suntan up on the flight deck every chance I got. I wanted to impress my folks back home in Kentucky when I showed up on their door step during March with a tan. By that time the cruise would be over.

February 24, 1971

Dear Mom, Dad and Larry,

Hope this finds everyone doing just fine and taking it easy. Guess it's still pretty cold back there now. The way Mom talked in her last letter I don't think I could stand it that cold. I've been used to the warm climate for over a year now. Hope you all didn't have much trouble this winter. I imagine the water pipes froze once in awhile but that's to be expected.

We're still off the coast of Vietnam but are not doing anything. No one knows when we'll leave from here but I don't imagine it'll be too much longer. We've already been here for about twenty-three days this last time. We should head for Okinawa after this.

I'm sending some money home. I was saving some for when I started back to the States but I don't guess I'll need it for awhile. I may be home earlier than April but right now it looks like it'll be around then. One thing for sure is I won't leave from over here when I'm supposed to. My rotation date is this Sunday. "It won't be long until I'll be starting on my second tour." Ha! You know, this is the first I've seen anyone extended past their rotation date. But you know how my luck runs, "Always getting the "Green Weeney." In case you don't know what I mean by that, ask Jimmy Howard. He probably knows. Tell everyone I'm sorry for not writing but I'll be home before long anyway.

Well there is not much going on to tell about, so I'll close for now. So everyone be good and take care. I'll be thinking of you.

As always,
Fred

Three days later we received our pay checks. I figured I had better send some money home before I ended up blowing it all in port. There was nothing to spend it on anyway while floating around in the South Pacific seas. I was trying to save as much as I could for when I went home on annual leave. I imagined that I would get at least thirty days leave when I went home.

February 27, 1971

Hello everyone,

    Hope this finds you all doing fine and in good health. I'm sending home some more money. We got paid today again and I really don't need so much money out at sea. I don't know if I'll be here for another pay day or not but I really don't care. I didn't want to go home until April anyway. We get paid at the first of the month and at the end of the month. I got a little more than usual this time since we're getting combat pay. Whatever comes back from the income tax just keep it for your own use. I got Mom's letter yesterday and she said it was thirteen dollars and something.

    Well, I have to close for now. I'll write a longer letter later on. Maybe tomorrow, since it's Sunday.

Yours most affirm,
Fred

After another week of just bouncing around in the ocean I got really bored. The higher command would not tell us anything and we spent a lot of time conducting field days of our living areas and common areas. I got so sick of watching the Marines play card games. Trump and I managed to escape to the flight deck when flight operations were not going on to relax, talk, and work on our tans. We enjoyed looking out over the open seas. Once in awhile we would see dolphins, flying fish, sea snakes, and the like swimming in the ocean. It was good just to have some piece and quiet. Sometimes we would do physical training on the flight deck or play basketball. Since six laps around the flight deck were equal to one mile, I would count out eighteen laps around the USS Iwo Jima for my three mile runs.

    I figured my time was getting really short overseas. It would not be long before the cruise would end and I would see my family once again. I longed for that day, although I would miss leaving my Marine buddies behind. I decided to write one last letter home in hopes of getting back home before I needed to write another one. After all, we would soon be heading back to Okinawa before too much longer. If I wrote a letter home within three weeks of departing, I probably would never get the reply from home. I might be gone before it reached me.

March 6, 1971

Dear Mom, Dad and Larry,

    Well here it is the 6th already and everything is going good over here. The time is really passing fast and the faster its goes the better. I'm doing just fine. I hope the same is true for everyone back home.

I got off the ship yesterday for the first time in over a month. We all loaded up on choppers and flew around for about an hour. I took my camera up with me to take some flicks, but we were in a big CH-53 chopper and I couldn't see much. We did it yesterday and today too. The reason we did it today was to show off in front of some Admirals that came aboard.

Today we cleaned weapons and are getting ready for the colonel's inspection on Monday. I'm ready for it. I haven't done too much to impress the "old man" but I don't really care. You should see some of these nuts just from the States. They're shining their boots and brass, ironing their trousers and shirts, and just anything to impress him. I don't need to impress him myself because you don't get a darn thing out of it. Besides I'm too "salty!" Ha! He's a pretty good guy though. We even see each other in church. Yes, believe it or not I go to church. It's just a small Chapel on ship, but we usually have mass in the library. It holds about twenty people, but it's usually room for everyone. Guess I'll go tomorrow.

If this letter sounds a little mixed up, it's because it's about eight different tape recorders going around me and each one playing a different song. I never need a radio or tape player because there is always plenty of music coming from the other Marines in the compartment. It's still as crowded as ever been but I've gotten use to it. I won't know how to act when I get to where I can turn around without bumping into someone.

Well, I have to go now. Our platoon has duty tomorrow so I'd better get some sleep. I'm sorta tired since I played basketball today and did PT on the flight deck. So I'll close now and hope this finds everyone okay. I'll see you all before long.

As ever,
Fred

Enclosed within this letter was a memo that one of the clerks who worked in the company office taped on my wall locker. He knew that I had been due to rotate back to the States on 28 February and posted it as a practical joke since I had been "involuntarily extended." The text of the memo was indicative of the times.

S H O R T?
Leaving the Marine Corps Soon?
... a few things you should know.

The GI Bill Gives You:
  (1) If you're single, $175.00 per month for up to thirty-six months to go to college, business school, technical school, or grad school. More money if you have dependents.
  (2) If you're single, $108.00 per month for the first six months apprenticeship or OJT. $81.00 per month for the next six months. More money if you have dependents.
  (3) Financial assistance to get a high school diploma without charge against your basic entitlement. You'd still have the thirty-six months of payments for college.
  (4) Payment for any educational, vocational, or trade schooling so long as it is VA approved.
  (5) HOME LOANS, in order to purchase, make repairs, or re-finance. The VA will back you for as much as sixty per cent of the loan you need. This applies to farms as well.
  (6) HOSPITAL CARE, even if your condition did NOT develop while you were in the Corps, the VA will cover your hospitalization if you swear under oath that you cannot pay for it.
  (7) JOB COUNSELLING. Need work? Your local VA will help you find a job, place you in training programs, administer employment tests.

EARLY OUT PROGRAMS
You can get an early release if you have a non-critical MOS (Grunts are non-critical) and fall into one of these categories:
  (1) Arrive back in the world with one hundred twenty days left on active duty.
  (2) Accepted into a state's police academy (up to ninety day cut).
  (3) School cut: if you have been accepted at college, vocational or technical school, you can get as much as a three month cut. But the earliest you can leave the service is thirty days before the start of classes. You must be attending full time, not summer school. This does apply if you're overseas.

PROJECT TRANSITION
If you are in CONUS with four to six months left on your enlistment, get into Project Transition. You are put into a training program run by civilians to qualify you for a job on the outside. Training programs are in such things as mechanics, repairs, sales, etc. If you successfully complete the training, the company offers you a job. (You get into the program only if your CO says the unit can accomplish its mission without you.)

FEDERAL SKYMARSHAL

The US Government is hiring veterans to be plainclothed guards aboard commercial airliners to prevent hijacking. You need to:
(1) Be at least twenty-one.
(2) Have no serious police record.
(3) Have at least two years of college or similar post-high school training.
(4) Have no physical defects.

What do you get? Starting salary between $5853. and $8098. Civil Service benefits. Friendly stewardesses for company.

HIGH SCHOOL DIPLOMA may be gotten while you're in the service by means of the GED test. However, you can also take the GED as a civilian by making arrangements through you State's Education Department, you still wind up with a high school diploma.

After I had placed my letter in the outgoing mailbox I decided to rest for a bit in my rack. That afternoon a huge and violent storm hit the fleet of ships. I wondered up to the flight deck to see what the weather looked like. The ship was rocking back and forth and from side to side. It was hard to stand up. The wind was blowing fiercely and the torrents of rain felt like hail. The clouds were the blackest I had ever seen. I figured the berthing compartment would be the safest place to ride out the storm and returned to my quarters.

We were right in the middle of a typhoon for about three days. The ship was rocking back and forth so much that just about everyone on board was seasick, including the Navy "Old Salts." The rocking ship had no mercy on anyone. Marines began to vomit while laying in their racks. Some were on the top racks and the vomit came down onto the racks below. The floor was covered with vomit, but the Marines that were not feeling too sick tried to keep the compartments clean. Some of the Marines went to the mess hall and got some large empty coffee cans so they could throw up in the cans. This way they could heave into the cans instead of drowning their fellow Marines in the racks below them. It was a real mess!

At around 0530 on the second morning of the storm I was trying to sleep in my rack. It was 8 March 1971. I had been tough to sleep the night before. I could feel the steady rocking of the ship. It was tossing my body back and forth. I tried to get out of bed, but I felt dizzy and started to throw up. I laid back down hoping that the feeling would soon subside. I figured that I had another half hour before reveille would sound. The Duty NCO would wake us up in the compartment each morning at 0600, so I knew someone would be around in a few minutes.

I began to hear moans and groans of waking Marines throughout our berthing area. Then some Marine said, "You are on report!"

I tried to rise up from my rack to see what was going on but the sickness hit me again. I lay back down and swallowed my own vomit that was trying to escape. It tasted terrible. Just then I felt a Marine shaking my shoulder.

"Wake up Marine," the voice commanded. "What is your name?"

I looked and saw that it was a tall lean Marine wearing a green duty belt with a Marine Corps brass waistplate. He was a corporal and was assigned as Duty Noncommissioned Officer for Lima Company. We were always told that the Duty NCO was the direct representative of the commanding officer when in a duty status.

"I'm getting up," I wearily commented. "I'm feeling really seasick. Are you holding reveille?"

"I asked, what is your name?" the Duty Noncommissioned Officer repeated.

"Fenwick," I replied. "Why?"

"What is your rank?"

"Lance Corporal," I responded.

"What is your service number?"

"What do you mean what is my service number? What is this anyway," I asked?

"You are on report for sleeping past reveille. Now what is your service number?"

"What do you mean I'm on report for sleeping past reveille?" I asked. "What time is it anyway?"

"0630," the corporal snapped.

"Damn," I said, "didn't you wake anybody up at 0600?"

"I'll ask the questions. Now what is your service number, Marine?" the Duty NCO demanded.

"Look," I now said enraged with anger, "if you want my service number, you can go check my Service Record Book, because I'm not giving it to you."

"Have it your way," the corporal said, "but you are still on report."

"Kiss my ass!" I exclaimed.

The Duty NCO then went from rack to rack taking down names. Someone asked Sergeant Buttplate if the Duty NCO came through at 0600 to wake up anyone.

"No," he said, "but that does not relieve you of the responsibility to get out of the rack on time."

"I ain't believing this shit," I murmured to myself. "What the sam hell is going on in this screwed up infantry company? They don't call it "Leaping Lima" for nothing."

The Duty NCO had failed to wake us up when he was supposed to at 0600, and now he was putting everyone on report, that was still in the rack at 0630. I managed to crawl out of my rack and went to the head. Even before I could relieve myself I had to throw up in one of the commodes. On report for sleeping after 0600, I thought to myself. Thirty damned minutes! The leadership in Lima Company must be nuts! I figured that the Duty NCO had been given his orders from the first lieutenant, our company commander. No other Marine would have pulled off such a ludicrous caper like that on their own volition.

After morning chow, Sergeant Buttplate came into the compartment and called off a list of names that had to go and see the company commander. There were about nine of us who were to face Nonjudicial Punishment, commonly known as Captain's Mast or Office Hours. We all went to the deck where the company office was located. We stood in a group until the company first sergeant came out of his office and ordered us to stand in single file up next to the bulkhead. One by one he called us in and read us our rights. Then he told us to standby and wait to see the company commander.

About five Marines went in before me. It took about five minutes for each one before they came out shaking their heads in disbelief. We tried to find out what kind of punishment the company commander had given them but the first sergeant rushed them out. Then it was finally my turn.

"Report to the company commander for Captain's Mast," the first sergeant commanded.

I walked into the lieutenant's office and stood three paces from his desk at the position of attention.

"Sir, Lance Corporal Fenwick reporting to the company commander as ordered," I said.

"Lance Corporal Fenwick," the lieutenant said. "You are suspected of being in violation of Article 92 of the Uniform Code of Military Justice in that Lance Corporal Fenwick, having knowledge of a lawful order issued by the Commanding Officer, Company L, Battalion Landing Team, 3rd Battalion, 9th Marines, 3rd Marine Division, to get up at 0600 reveille, an order which was his duty to obey, did, on board the USS Iwo Jima, on or about 0630 710308, fail to obey the same, by wrongfully sleeping past 0600. How do you plead, Lance Corporal Fenwick, Guilty or Not Guilty?"

"Sir," I responded, "I would like to explain the circumstances surrounding this accusation."

"I didn't ask you for an explanation, Lance Corporal Fenwick," the lieutenant interrupted. "I asked how do you plead? Guilty or Not Guilty."

"If it was failure to wake up at 0600, I plead guilty," I replied. "If it was disobedience of a written order to get out of the rack at 0600, I plead not guilty since the Duty NCO never did wake anyone up in the berthing compartment until 0630."

"I hear a plea of Guilty, so I find you Guilty," the lieutenant interjected.

"Wait a minute, Sir," I said. "How can the men be expected to get up at exactly 0600 each morning if the Duty NCO does not make an attempt to wake anyone up at that exact time. We rely on him because none of us have alarm clocks aboard ship. Besides, almost all the Marines were sick as dogs this morning. They had been vomiting all night long,"

"I have rendered my decision," the lieutenant snapped. "And now I will award the following punishment. You are to be restricted to the company area, messing facilities, place of worship and sick bay for a period of 14 days without suspension of normal duties. The restriction to the company area is suspended for 3 months, at which time, unless the suspension is sooner vacated, the punishment will be remitted without further action. This will be a permanent entry in your Service Record Book. Do you have any questions, Lance Corporal Fenwick?"

"Yes Sir," I said with distinct anger in my voice. "What exactly do you mean by suspended for three months?"

The lieutenant looked at the first sergeant in a manner that indicated that I should already know what that meant. With a smirk on the lieutenant's face he replied, "That means you will not have to be restricted to the ship for a period of three months, unless you fuck up again. In that event, the suspension will be vacated and you will have to carry out the restriction. Also you have the right to appeal my decision. That is, if you feel that the punishment awarded was unjust or disproportionate to the offense committed, you have five days to submit an appeal in writing. Do you understand?" the lieutenant asked.

"Not really, Sir," I said. "But it really doesn't matter. As soon as we get back to Okinawa I will get out of this screwed up company."

"That's all, Lance Corporal Fenwick, you are dismissed!" shouted the lieutenant.

I gave the first lieutenant an evil eye and walked out of his office. I did not do any fancy about face that I had been taught in boot camp to show respect for authority. As I left his office, I heard the lieutenant tell the first sergeant, "Every Vietnam Vet thinks he is too good to be awarded nonjudicial punishment." I was very angry at this point and turned around to confront the lieutenant.

The first sergeant blocked me from reentering the lieutenant's office. "Better let it go," the first sergeant told me. "Best thing for you to do is to get back to your berthing area."

I realized that if I did something to the company commander out of rage, that Trump would be guarding me in the ship's brig. So I swallowed my pride and let it go. I returned to my rack and lay down. I stared at the mattress above me only inches from my face. I vowed that if I ever got out of this screwed up Lima Company, 3/9, that I would never be back. After I told my Marine buddies what had happened they became bitter as well.

The day came when the USS Iwo Jima returned back to Okinawa after about four months at sea. Finally the cruise was over and we moved into the same set of barracks at Camp Schwab. The following week seemed to drag by. I checked out of the company and awaited my port call, in other words my plane ticket back to the States. I grabbed every opportunity I could to lay outside of the barracks and get a tan. I had realized that it was March and that it would be cold back home. I wanted to surprise everyone when I arrived home slightly brown from the sun in the Orient. The sun was just hot enough for a nice even tan. The Marines in the platoon went about their business and did not bother me because they knew I would be leaving soon. I did manage to see my cousin and Donald one more time before I left the Island and told them that I would see them back in the real world.

Chapter 11

Coming Home

THE day arrived for me to depart Camp Schwab for the airport at Kadena Air Force Base. I said goodbye to all my Marine buddies in the machine gun section and wished that I could see them again in the States. I knew deep down that I would never see these guys again. They were scattered out across America in states such as Ohio, Pennsylvania, New Jersey, and Oregon. It was sad for me to leave them behind but I was anxious and overjoyed to be going home to my loved ones.

As my bus passed by Camp Hansen, Kin Ville, and Camp Hague, I reflected back to the first week in March 1970 when I had first arrived on Okinawa. I had seen things that most people could only imagine, been to places that most people could only dream of, and had done more things than some people would do their entire lifetime. I had been through a lot but I had gained the experience necessary to serve me well in the Marine Corps.

Getting through customs at the Kadena Air Terminal was a blur for me as I had other things on my mind. I finally got on board the plane and found my seat by a window. I could feel my heart beating fast in anticipation. The plane lifted off the runway and it wasn't long until it became a smooth glide over the rich blue waters below. I looked out the window as the plane soared higher into the clouds and soon the small Okinawain Islands below were out of sight. I remembered my brother, Donald, who was still on Okinawa. I wished that one day my family could all get together and have a family reunion. I thought about each family member and realized how much I loved each and every one of them. I snapped out of my daydreaming and a sigh of relief came over me. I was finally going home. The date was 19 March 1971.

The plane flew from Kadena to Hawaii and then on to Norton Air Force Base which was located about three miles from San Bernardino, California. From here my tickets had me going to Saint Louis, Chicago, and then Louisville, Kentucky. I had a night layover at Norton so I decided to get in touch with my sister, Janice, who still lived in San Clemente, California. She was all excited and said that she and her husband, Steve, was going to drive up to Norton and pick me up. I thought it was a bit out of my way but my sister insisted. She explained that Norton Air Force was only about sixty miles from where she lived and that they could be there in a couple of hours.

I decided to visit with them as I did not know when I would be back through California again. My sister Janice had met Steve while I was ending up my tour in Vietnam. Steve had enlisted in the Marine Corps and was honorably discharged as a sergeant. He had served a tour in Vietnam with 2nd Battalion, 9th Marines during 1968. Steve had also been an infantry grunt. He had been through some very tough and traumatic times in Vietnam.

I waited for Steve and Janice to drive all the way from San Clemente to Norton Air Force Base. When they arrived Janice was so excited. I could hardly get a word in edge wise. She would laugh and then she would cry. She seemed so happy that I was safe and sound. I met Steve for the first time. He was a handsome sort of guy. He was tall, thin, with black hair, and a dark complexion. He was Samoan and I could detect his native accent when he spoke. He seemed like a very nice guy but I did not quite know how to act around him because he had gotten out of the Marine Corps as a sergeant and I was still a lance corporal. The ride back to their little apartment was nice. It gave us a chance to catch up on things and to get acquainted.

Janice fixed us lunch and we sat and talked through the afternoon. At around 6:00 p.m. Steve told my sister it was time for a "Boy's Night Out." She agreed as Steve and I got dressed to go and paint the town. He knew of a bar in downtown San Clemente where we could hang out, have a few beers, shoot some pool, and put quarters in the jukebox. We arrived at the bar and Steve paid for the beers. He would not hear of me paying for a beer myself. He wanted to welcome me back home.

We started playing pool, but I told him I was not very good at it. Steve began to teach me the fundamentals of the game.

"Looks like you have been around the pool table a few times," I said to Steve.

"Yeah, I hold my own I guess," he replied.

I started to ask him about meeting my sister. He had nothing but good things to say about her. Then I became curious about his native country of Samoa. He started explaining about the customs, food, and entertainment of the country. He said he really missed Samoa and would like to go back and visit one day. He didn't think he would ever go there and live but he did have family there. Then the subject of Vietnam came up. He asked about my experiences in Vietnam as he shared some of his experiences. The more I talked with Steve the more I grew fond of him. I knew that my sister Janice had made a good choice with Steve. They should do well together, I thought.

Steve put a quarter in the juke box and selected a song.

"You like Conway Twitty?" Steve asked.

"Yeah, I guess," I replied.

"This is the new song by Conway Twitty," he said. "It's called Hello Darlin'. I could listen to it all night long."

The song began to play and we listened to the first few verses without saying too much. With authority Steve hit the last remaining eight ball with the queue ball. The eight ball went straight for the corner pocket and sank out of sight. He walked around the pool table to where I was standing. I was nonchalantly holding the pool stick in a vertical position with the base of the pool stick resting on the floor.

"Nice shot," I said to Steve.

Steve placed his left hand on my right shoulder and said, "Freddy, I'm glad you made it back from Vietnam okay."

I felt tightness in my throat but managed to control my emotions.

"I'm glad you made it back okay too Steve," I replied.

We had a few more beers and decided to head home for the night. Janice was sound asleep when we arrived at around midnight. Steve headed off to bed and I made myself at home on the living room couch. It wasn't long until I was asleep but I would turn ever so often to adjust my position during the morning hours. Janice woke up early the next morning and went straight to the kitchen. It wasn't long until I smelled fresh made coffee. She came and sat on the floor beside me. When she saw that I wasn't really asleep she asked if we had a good time at the bar. I told her it gave me the chance to really get to know Steve better. She said that she knew it would, that's why she went along with it. But she still felt a bit cheated not to have spent that precious time with me.

"Come on in to the kitchen Freddy," she said. "I'm gonna fix you some toast, bacon, and eggs. They are not as good as Momma makes, but they are okay." How do you want your eggs?"

"Scrambled would be fine Janice," I replied.

As we sat eating breakfast and talking, Steve got up to join us. I began to make plans for catching my next plane connection to head home. We agreed on a time that we should leave the apartment and after breakfast I made sure all my belongings were packed sufficiently in my seabag. The ride to the airport was sad for me because I didn't know how long it would be before I ever got to see Steve and Janice again. They lived so far away from Kentucky. The time flew by. The next thing I knew, we are saying our goodbyes and I was back on a plane heading for Kentucky. When I got off the plane in Louisville, my brothers Jimmy Howard and Larry were at the airport waiting for me. I had a big lump in my throat when I saw them. Jimmy Howard told me that when he first saw me get off the plane in Louisville, that he thought I looked like a walking skeleton. That was because I had lost so much weight. I told him that I had tried to fatten myself up while I was in Okinawa to regain the weight I had lost in Vietnam. Evidently, I still had a long way to go.

It was a thrilling ride for me, from the airport, to the "old home place." I was filled with excitement and anticipation of seeing my parents for the first time in over a year. We made small talk about the weather, spring time, hunting, fishing, and the like. Our trip of fifty-eight miles from the airport to home took us about an hour. As we turned off the main road of US Highway 150 and into the driveway, I saw the huge white house with the green tin roof glowing in its majesty. I was anxious to see everyone again as I let out a sigh of relief. I was back home at last on "Cherry Hill Farm."

When the car got to the top of the hill, I looked out the windows trying to see the barns, garage, cellar top, and fields. I was amazed at how good it really looked even though it was early spring. I started to scan the back porch for my Mom and Dad. Jimmy Howard's car came to a stop. We got out of the vehicle and just then my mother and father stepped out onto the back porch. I felt the throbbing in my heart as I tried to hold back the tears.

"Freddy, Freddy," my mother said with quivering lips. "Welcome home! You're a sight for sore eyes!"

I walked up the steps of the porch and we embraced. I was afraid that it was just a dream, but now safe in my mother's arms, I was convinced that this day was for real.

"My, my, Freddy", my mother said as she leaned back to look at me. "It's good to have you home. I've spent many nights praying for you. Me and Daddy thank God that you're home safe and sound."

I saw the tears swelling up in my mother's eyes but I was trying to be brave. "It's good to be home Momma," I replied. That was about all I could get out in one breath without my voice cracking. "Momma, you really look good," I uttered. I felt a little awkward as I didn't know exactly what to say after being away from home for so long.

"You look pretty good yourself," she said, while still not taking her eyes off me.

My father was standing close by. He reached out to shake my hand. That was his style. No mushy stuff for my father.

"Welcome home, Freddy," he said.

"Thanks Daddy," I replied, "it's good to be home."

My father said jokingly, "I hope you will be here long enough to help me weed the tobacco beds. I know how you enjoy that job," he said while grinning.

"Well, sharpen a pocketknife for me, Daddy. I'm ready to go to work," I replied.

We all laughed. It was a moment I had long awaited for. To be with my family once again was truly a dream come true. This was a moment that I had always pictured in my mind during the lonely times in Vietnam and Okinawa when I missed them so much. There was a brief moment of silence as we stood on the back porch and then my mother broke the silence as she placed her hand on my arm.

"Come on inside, Freddy, and get something to eat," she suggested.

I followed her through the back porch door and through a small hallway that led into the kitchen. My father walked just behind me. I was in a state of bliss, a feeling which I had not felt for a long time. Going to boot camp after high school was my first time away from home. This moment of reunion with my mother, father, and younger brother was so real and genuine. My parents were so sincere and elated that I was home. I would always cherish their love for me. No matter where the Marine Corps would take me, I knew that they would be there to always welcome me home.

I entered the kitchen and it was like a ray of light had just hit me in the face. The old farm kitchen was just like it was when I had left to go to boot camp. The memories started coming back. I glanced around the kitchen at the four walls and took note of the items on display. I noticed the old bread box that we had in the family for so long, the farmer's almanac calendar hanging on the wall, the vanity mirror we had screwed into the wall, and the pictures on the wall. My father used to use the vanity mirror to shave with a straight razor, shaving cup, and old fashioned brush. I looked at my favorite spot where I used to sit and eat at the table. The three old wooden chairs along the outside of the table and the two on each end looked very homey and comfortable. On the opposite side of the table next to the wall was a wooden bench that could accommodate about four adults, more if it was filled with children.

The display of food dishes and bowls on the old wooden table caught my eye. I quickly scanned over the dishes, Mom's country home cooking at its best. There was cornbread, biscuits, gravy, pinto beans, corn, mashed potatoes, hominy, lima beans, beets, country ham slices, sausage, tenderloin, and fruit salad. On the kitchen counter my mother had prepared iced tea, coffee, and a jam cake. The food was fit for a king.

As usual, my father started the meal with a prayer of grace. "Bless Us Oh Lord, And These Thy Gifts, Which We Are About To Receive, From Thy Bounty, Through Christ Our Lord, Amen."

We all made the Sign of the Cross and then dug in. It was customary at the table to grab a plate in front of you, get what you wanted, and then pass it to your left. I had done it so many times before but this time was different. I smelled the aroma of each plate as it came in front of me and I passed it to my left. My plate ended up being so full that I couldn't fit anything else on it even before all the plates and bowls made their way toward me. As we ate, I raved about the taste of Mom's home cooking and compared it to all the C-Ration meals I had consumed. I named a few of the choice C-Ration meals and said that they couldn't hold a candle to Mom's home cooking. My mother, being a very modest person, insisted that it was just another meal and nothing fancy.

After dinner my father gave a motion for the men of the house to go into the living room so we could talk. We all stood up from the table and we followed him into the living room. He took a seat at his favorite recliner chair. Jimmy Howard sat in a straight back chair and Larry and I sat on the couch. This was the same room where my mother and father slept so there was also a large bed, two dressers, and a TV in the room. The wood stove was still up and sat in the middle of the floor. My father said he would be taking down the old stove since it was beginning to warm up for spring.

My father began the conversation by asking questions about my trip over from Okinawa. He wanted to know what airports I stopped off at on my way home and how long it took me to fly home. He seemed very interested as I explained my journey from Okinawa. I told him that I estimated the actual flying time in the air was about twenty four hours. If I counted the time when I first got on the bus at Camp Schwab, Okinawa until I stepped foot on the back porch, it would be around two solid days of travel time.

"My gosh, Freddy," he said. "That is an awful long way. I don't know how you did it. When I was a courtin' your mother in a horse and buggy, it took me the biggest part of the day to travel to and from our house on Tick Creek Pike to Harrodsburg, Kentucky. By the time I got to Harrodsburg to see her, it was time to come back home. I can't imagine how long it took you to fly over from Okinawa."

He started to ask a few questions about Vietnam. "I guess it was pretty rough over there in Vietnam wasn't it Freddy?" he asked.

"Yeah, at times it could be rough," I responded. "But overall I had some pretty good Marine buddies to look after me. I had a close buddy I called Hawkeye from Salem, Oregon. He really helped me out and he was my best friend. We were together through thick and thin. He really kept my mind off the war and we did a lot of things together. We would read each others letters from home and share the care packages that we received. We also shared the same fighting hole. I called him my "foxhole buddy.""

"Where is he now?" my father asked.

"The last time I saw him he had orders to a Combined Action Platoon," I replied. He had a choice of leaving Vietnam and going to Okinawa with me or staying in Vietnam. He decided he wasn't quite ready to go home yet so he chose to stay in Vietnam for a few more months.

"I wonder why he did that," my father said.

"I'm not real sure," I responded. "I think deep down Hawkeye wanted a little more time away from the hectic pace of an infantry unit and re-gather his composure and sanity before he came back home. He arrived in Vietnam a few months before I did and I think he just needed time to unwind. By now, he should have left Vietnam for good."

"Do you think you will ever see him again?" my father asked?

I answered, "Well, it's a small Marine Corps, but I doubt if I will ever see him again. He doesn't have too much longer left in the Marine Corps on his enlistment and he was talking about settling down in Salem, Oregon. I doubt if I will ever get to Oregon."

My father commented, "Well, I sure hope so. That would be a real shame if you never saw him again. Where did you say he went to in Vietnam after you left?"

"Oh, sorry," I replied. "He went to a CAP Unit. They call it a Combined Action Platoon. It basically consists of a Marine rifle squad and a Navy corpsman combined with a Vietnamese Popular Force platoon. Their job is to provide local security for the villages that they are assigned to. The Marines live in the villages and train with the local militia. They go out on patrols and ambushes just like they would if they were in an infantry outfit. Most of the Marines assigned to these CAP units volunteer for the duty and Hawkeye volunteered for it. I told him he was crazy for doing it."

"He's got a lot of guts," Jimmy Howard said.

"Yep, a lot of guts," I answered. "There is none braver than my old foxhole buddy."

Jimmy Howard mentioned some of the buddies that he had when he was in the Marine Corps. He had been stationed at Camp Lejeune in North Carolina and Hawaii. He went to boot camp at Parris Island, South Carolina just like our older brother Bobby and I had done. Donald was given a choice of Parris Island or San Diego, so he chose San Diego. The Marines used to jokingly refer to San Diego boot camp Marines as, "Hollywood Marines," but no one in the family would ever call Donald that. He was a far cry from being soft. He was an old salt and tough as nails. Bobby had been on ship most of his enlistment. He could tell some stories as well about his old buddies.

I glanced over at Larry who was sitting on the couch next to me. "Larry," I said, "I guess you are next to join the Marine Corps and uphold the family tradition." At the time Larry was thirteen years old.

"I don't know," Larry responded, "we'll have to see."

I heard my mother's voice in the kitchen. "No, I don't think Larry will join the Marines. Four sons in the Marines are enough."

Then I realized my mother had been in the kitchen the whole time cleaning up the mess, putting away the leftovers, and washing and drying the dishes. She had done that three times a day for as long as I could remember. I felt so guilty that the men were sitting back on our haunches and talking while she was slaving away in the kitchen. It had been an old fashioned routine for the farmers. The attitude was that the men worked all day in the fields and that the wives were to have dinner on the table and take care of the kids. I felt sorry for my mother and wanted to get up and help but I didn't want to walk away from my father either. I thought that if I ever got married that I would at least help my wife around the house because I had seen what my mother had to go through her entire life.

My mother finally came into the living room after the chores were done. Larry and I scooted over on the couch to make room for her. She sat down beside me on my right side. I could tell that she was exhausted from all the cooking and cleaning up. I told her it was probably time for her to go to bed and get some rest. I suggested that I should turn in myself because it had been such a long journey from Okinawa. She told me that if I wanted to go to bed to go ahead but that she was going to stay up for a bit longer. I figured I might as well sit and talk for a spell although I was extremely tired.

She asked how my visit was with Janice and Steve. I told her that they picked me up at the airport and that I spent the night with them. I told her they were doing just fine and that I was glad I took the time to see them. My mother said she wished that they were not so far away and living in California. I made the comment that Janice would probably end up staying out there for good.

My mother said over and over how glad she was that I was back home. She told me she had prayed day and night for my safe return and now her prayers had been answered. She wanted me to assure her that I would never go back to Vietnam again.

"Freddy, you won't have to go back to Vietnam again, will you?" she asked.

"No, I shouldn't have to go back," I responded. "I have orders to Camp Lejeune. Besides, they are beginning to pull the troops out of Vietnam."

"Yes, I saw that on the TV," she replied. "I wonder how long it will take them to pull all the servicemen out of there."

"Well, I'm not sure," I responded, "but I would imagine a few years."

"A few years?" she said in disbelief. "Goodness Gracious!"

"Yeah, I know," I replied, "it won't happen over night."

"Well, my mother said, "I just can't wait to hear that all our boys are out of that damned place."

My mother never swore so when she said the word damned, I knew she was fed up and angry about the Vietnam War. She had been through some very trying and stressful years. Not only did she have to manage and hold her family together on the home front, she feared for the very lives of two of her Marine sons. She had already prayed with reverence for my brother, Donald, who had served two complete tours in Vietnam. Then when I went to Vietnam it was almost too much. She was a mother in grief, praying for her sons to return safely home, from the agony of war.

With a cracking and shaky voice my mother said to me, "Freddy, I just don't think I will be able to make it if you or Donald goes back to Vietnam. It will just be too much for me to take."

I looked over at my father sitting in his recliner. He slowly wiped away a tear. My mother wiped away a tear as well. I could feel the wetness of my eyes and tried to hold it back.

"Don't worry Momma," I said with a quivering voice. "I will not go back to Vietnam."

Jimmy Howard sensed the time was right for him to get back home. He got up and said he had better get going so I could get some sleep. I stood up and walked behind him as he passed through the kitchen on his way out the back door. I thanked him for picking me up at the airport. He told me he was glad to do it and that he was glad that I had made it back from Vietnam and Okinawa. It made me feel good inside and very proud to be a part of this Fenwick family. I had always loved my brothers and sisters, but since my return from overseas, I was beginning to appreciate them even more.

I decided to hit the rack and went upstairs to my designated room. Larry had taken my old room downstairs when I shoved off to go to boot camp. I knew he always had an eye on that small little room to claim as his own when I left. It was cold upstairs because there was no heat. Only the kitchen and living room downstairs were heated in the winter time. They were heated by burning wood or coal in the old black stoves.

My mother had placed about five blankets on my bed just in case I got cold. I stripped down to my skivvies and climbed under the blankets. It was cold at first but soon I was nice and toasty. I smelled the fresh aroma of the blankets and sheets. My mother would hang all the clothes out on the clothes line to dry, even in the winter. It made them smell so good. It was quite a different aroma than what I had been used to with the military green wool blankets, mattress covers (Marines called them fart sacks) and white sheets. I took a deep breath and let it out.

Before I fell asleep I wanted to thank God that I had finally made it home safe and sound. I had been through recruit training at Parris Island, infantry training at Camp Geiger, jungle training at Camp Pendleton, combat in Vietnam, a cruise from Okinawa, and I didn't have a scratch. No purple heart, no posthumous award, and still had all my limbs. I was very lucky and fortunate. Other Marines had not been so lucky. I thanked God that I was alive and with my loved ones. I said several "Our Father's, Hail Mary's, and Glory Be's, before I drifted off to sleep.

I awoke violently around midnight. Perspiration was dripping down my neck and my entire chest and back was sweating. I had sprung up in the sitting position. My wet T-shirt was soaking wet and the cold air sent chills through my body. I took my shirt off and wiped my neck, chest, and what I could reach of my back. Then I laid back down recalling why I woke up this way in the first place.

I had been dreaming about Vietnam. It was at night and pitch black. I couldn't see anything. I was hugging the ground in my sleeping hole with my helmet over my head and my flak jacket very tight around my chest. We were being mortared by the VC and they were throwing chi-coms at our positions. A mortar round exploded right next to my head and the shrapnel ricocheted off my helmet. Then a chi-com grenade landed inside my sleeping hole and rolled underneath me. I was jumping out of the sleeping hole when I woke up.

I wondered why I was having nightmares in the safety of my parent's home. They had seemed to subside somewhat and become less frequent while I was on Okinawa and aboard ship. There were times however, that I must have awakened the entire squad bay and berthing compartment when I would yell out in my sleep. I figured that for this night it must have been the conversations that I had previously with the family that sparked the nightmares. I fell back to sleep.

At around 2:30 in the morning I again jerked out from under the covers. This time I let out in a loud voice, "Goddamit!" Again I had been dreaming that I was back in Vietnam. This time the dream placed me in a mountain stream. I was filling my canteens from the flowing water and taking big gulps of water. I kept feeling clumps of something in the water as I drank it. As I rounded a big boulder I saw four dead VC laying in the water with the water running through their mouth and out their asses. I had been drinking a mixture of body parts. I had screamed out loud in my sleep.

I hoped that I had not awakened my mother and father downstairs. I listened carefully and heard my father stir around in bed for a bit. Then I heard their voices but I could not make out what they were saying. They were mumbling something to each other at 2:30 a.m. I must have disrupted their sleep when I yelled out.

Out of the blue I began to think about my squad, Mike 3 Charlie, in Vietnam. I remembered surprising the four NVA while they slept and killing them on the spot. I recalled capturing my very own SKS semi-automatic carbine and then some Marine stealing it from me. I remembered my squad sitting next to the NVA we had just killed and eating C-Rations. We even took pictures as if nothing had ever happened, some of which were confiscated at the Da Nang Air Terminal. Then I realized that I must put the thoughts of Vietnam behind me. I was home now. I must try to forget about the past. I wished that daylight would soon come.

I heard my mother banging away in the kitchen at about 6:00 a.m. I decided to get up and go downstairs. I got dressed and headed down the long winding stair steps, down the hallway, and turned left toward Larry's room. The downstairs bathroom, the only one in the house, was adjacent to his room. My mother had the space heater turned on. It felt nice and warm. After I had gone to the bathroom I proceeded through the dining room and entered the kitchen door. As soon as I opened the door the aroma of fresh baked biscuits and fried sausage filled the air. I took a deep breath. I wished someone would invent an air freshener that smelled like this. My mother was already preparing breakfast at the crack of dawn. She was standing over the old gas stove frying up some fresh sausage paddies.

"Good morning Momma," I said.

"Good morning Freddy," she replied as she turned back to look at me. "Did you sleep good last night?"

I responded by saying, "I slept great Momma."

"Are you sure?" she asked. "Did you have enough of blankets last night?"

"Yes," I said. "I probably had too many blankets cause I woke up sweating last night."

"Well, take some of them off," my mother suggested. "I just figured you would get cold since you have been used to warm climates overseas."

"I will," I replied, "don't worry, I'll be fine."

"Now sit down there at the table Freddy and eat some breakfast. Would you like coffee this morning or juice. I just finished making the coffee in the percolator. This old percolator makes the best tasting coffee."

"Yes," I said. "I will have some coffee."

She poured me a cup of coffee. It sure did smell good.

"Now there's cream and sugar on the table Freddy, just help yourself."

After I had added cream and sugar to the cup of coffee I sipped it slowly. Very tasty, I thought. Too bad we couldn't get this kind of coffee in our C-Ration accessory packs. It wasn't long until she placed the biscuits, sausage, jam, and butter on the table.

"I'm gonna fry you up some eggs, Freddy," she said. "How do you like them?"

"I'll take my usual," I replied. "Hard!"

In a few minutes she handed me three hard fried eggs and asked if I wanted anything else for breakfast. I told her that what she had fixed was more than enough. I heard my father stirring in the next room and getting out of bed. After he finished dressing in his work clothes he entered the kitchen and immediately headed for the door leading to the bathroom.

"Good morning Freddy," he mumbled as he passed by the table.

"Good morning Daddy," I replied.

Before he opened the door to the Dining Room he asked, "Did you sleep okay last night?"

"Yeah, I slept okay," I said. "It sure was good to sleep in a comfortable bed for a change."

While he was going to the bathroom my mother sat down at the table next to me sipping on her coffee. "Freddy," she said, "Sunday, Larry and I are going to Saint Rose Church for the 9 o'clock Mass. Do you want to go? You don't have to if you don't want."

"Sure, I'll go to church with you," I said. "I have been going quite regularly anyway while I was on ship."

"Don't guess you ever got the chance to go to Mass while you were in Vietnam, did you?" she asked.

"Actually I did," I replied. The Navy Chaplains would say Mass on Sundays when we were in the rear at the base camps and they would also visit us out in the bush from time to time."

"Oh, that was nice of them, wasn't it?" she asked.

I replied by saying, "Yeah, one time I went to Mass, had communion, and then found out after the Mass that it was a Protestant Service instead of Catholic. I don't guess the priests at Saint Rose will hold that against me."

"You know, Freddy, I don't think it really matters one way or the other," my mother replied. "As long as you pray and believe in the Lord I don't think it matters what religion you are."

"Yeah, me neither," I said. "Well, Momma, what do you think I should wear to church on Sunday?"

"Oh, you can wear just about anything," she answered. "What about your uniform. You would look real nice in your Marine uniform. Is it too much trouble to fix?"

"Not at all," I responded. "In fact, it would be an honor and privilege to wear my uniform. I will dig it out of my seabag and work on it today and get it ironed out for Sunday. Right now it is in the middle of my seabag."

"I will iron it for you," she said. "I want to see what it looks like. Oh Freddy," she said with a sigh, "I am so proud of you."

"I'm proud of you too Momma," I replied.

My father had poached eggs, a bowl of oatmeal, and toast for breakfast. After we ate I put on my combat boots, blue jeans, and a grey sweat shirt with the letters "USMC" on the front. I would accompany my father to the barn in order to feed the cows. I borrowed a coat from my father. It fit just perfect so I figured we were about the same size. We proceeded through the back yard and opened the small gate leading to the barn lot. My father started calling the cows.

"Whook Sook Sook Sook! Whook Sook Sook!"

The Black Angus cows were down near the tobacco barn about five hundred yards away. They all looked up and began mooing loudly. One of the cows started walking up the rock road leading up to the stock barn. She was followed by another cow then another until the whole herd was moving in our direction. The young white-faced calves kicked and frolicked alongside their mothers. As they started through the barnyard gate my father started counting each of the cows and then the calves. When I was growing up on the farm I had seen him count the cows over and over to make sure nothing had happened to any of them.

Following behind the herd of Black Angus cows was a large red and white Herford Bull. He moped along in no particular hurry. The Herford had a slight shine to its red hide and had two large horns. They were known to be very docile animals unless another bull happened to get into the herd. The bull's head was huge and his forehead had curly white hair. He was a sight to behold.

"So, Daddy," I asked, "You traded in your Holstein milk cows for Black Angus, huh?"

"Yep," he answered. "With you gone, it was only me and Larry milking the thirty cows night and day. We just couldn't do it anymore. I decided to just raise the Black Angus and sell the calves in the fall of the year. The only problem is now I get a paycheck in the fall of the year and not every two weeks like it was when I was selling milk. It all seems to work out in the long run."

"Why didn't you get a Black Angus bull to breed the cows?" I asked.

"Because a Black Angus bull is meaner than a Herford Bull," he replied. "All they want to do is fight. They will tear down your fences just to get to your neighbors cows. Besides, the Black Angus calves are smaller in size if bred with a Black Angus Bull. If you breed the cows with a Herford, the calves are larger. That means they weigh more at the market, and the more they weigh, the more money you get from them."

"Sounds like you got it all figured out," I said.

"Whook Sook Sook Sook!" he hollered out without answering.

They were still feeding silage out of the silo during this time of the year although it was almost depleted. We went inside the barn and climbed over into the feed way that lead to the base of the silo room.

"Well, Freddy," my father said. "You can have your old job back. Climb up in the silo and throw me out some silage. I will feed the cows."

"Oh boy," I replied. "My old job back. Does it pay anymore than it used to? I used to do it for free."

My father just laughed. I entered the silo room and headed up the chute. After about the fourth door I climbed into the silo. There was a pitchfork already stuck in the silage. I looked up at the top tin roof of the silo. It had been filled all the way to the top in the fall and they had fed it all winter long to the cows. The silage and hay was enough for the cows to survive on during the long cold winter months.

I remembered back to all the years that I had emptied all the silage out of the silo all by myself. I used to throw it down the chute at the evening milking and leave enough stacked up for the morning feed. I looked down at my spit-shined combat boots. I should have worn an old pair of shoes that my father had in the back room. I hated to mess up my spit-shine, but now it was too late. I could work on them before I left to go to Camp Lejeune.

"What-er-ya-waitin-fer," my father shouted up the chute from down below. "Let's get this silage fed. We're burning daylight!"

I thought to myself, Yep, best not burn any daylight. Every precious moment was valuable on the farm to get all the chores done, and it wasn't even summer yet. I jabbed the pitchfork into the silage, bent over to lift the heavy stuff, and slung it down the chute. After a few minutes of throwing out the silage I got so hot I had to come out of my coat. Then it wasn't long until I shed my sweat shirt as well. I didn't know which was worse, digging foxholes or throwing out silage. I reckoned I'd settle for throwing out silage for the moment. I was now back in my element. I was enjoying just being on the old farm again.

I heard two scoops down at the base of the chute. I knew that Larry had made it down to the barn to help out with the chores. It must have been rough for him as a little kid to help my father keep the farm going when I left for boot camp. He had worked very hard balancing school work and the farm chores. Before we always had at least two or more siblings helping out on the farm, but when I left, Larry was all by himself. He must have felt very lonely during those times. I knew, however, that one day he would grow up and choose a life of his own. I also knew that there might be a lot of mental pressure on him to join the Marine Corps as well since all four of his older brothers had been Marines.

After feeding the cows we went back to the house. I asked Larry if he would join me to look around the farm again. He agreed to take me on a grand tour of the farm so I went and got my camera so I could take some pictures. We walked down the rock driveway and turned right and entered the old garage/tool shop. My parents parked their car in the garage and my father also had a lot of tools inside. I looked around at all his tools. He had some antique ones such as a cross cut saw, the old tomahawks and spears used for cutting tobacco, an old time hand operated tobacco setter, and a hand drill bit kit that had been handed down by his father. There were also two old ice boxes that had been used many years before to keep meat from spoiling. When he built the garage he had to cut down a large locust tree. He had left the stump which was about three feet high and about three feet in diameter. He had anchored his antique anvil on the stump. We all thought that was pretty ingenious.

Larry and I left the garage and went to unlock the large gate leading to the barn lot. It was wide enough to drive a car or tractor and wagon through. I noticed a stenciled sign they had nailed to the fence post. It was about a 2X3 foot sign. The inscription read: "No Fishing, No Hunting, No Exceptions, Don't Ask." My father had gotten a little fed up with people coming around and wanting to fish in the three lakes we had on the farm. They would leave fish hooks and fishing line on the banks of the lakes, drive through the fields when the ground was muddy, and climb and mash down the fences on the property. He decided to put up the sign when the cows would come to the barn with fish hooks dangling off their legs.

We made our way to the tobacco barn. We opened up the small door and entered. There were four other large sliding doors that were large enough to drive tractors and wagons through loaded with tobacco. My father also had a lot of tractor equipment in the barn. There were items such as plows, cultivator, corn planter, an old elevator used to transport bails of hay up to the loft of the stock barn, and the infamous tobacco setter. The barn rails were empty for the tobacco crop had sold on the market in the fall.

We left and walked over the hill and down to the newest lake that had been dug. It was a beautiful sight, just like I remembered it. Walnut trees grew on a hillside above and below the lake. Water was flowing gently down the spillway and into a small branch leading down to another lake. We walked up the hill, climbed a fence, and came to a grassy knoll overlooking the back fields and the two lakes. I sat down to look out at the beauty of the farm. I asked Larry to take a picture of me sitting in the grass overlooking the farm. As he got into position with the camera, I started having flashbacks and visions of Vietnam. I stared out over the rolling fields of grass the farm. I remembered all hard work I had put in to the farm work. I recalled the elephant grass, the rice paddies, the mountains, the villages, and the rice paddies of Vietnam. I was glad to be home, so glad to be home.

"Are you ready?" Larry asked.

"Huh?" I replied still daydreaming.

"Are you ready for me to take the picture?" Larry asked again.

"Yeah, sure," I responded.

Larry took the picture and I got on my feet. I could have stayed on top of this knoll all day. We proceeded down the hill to the lake we called the back lake. I had caught a lot of bass, blue gill, and croppy in this old lake. I remembered back to the days when I was a kid. We had caught a nine pound catfish in a river while noodling. Since we didn't want to be bothered cleaning the old catfish, my father decided that we should let him go in the back lake. We had placed the fish in a tub of water for transport to the back lake in order to release it. We placed the tub in a small trailer hitched to the tractor and off we went.

When we arrived at the lake I grabbed the catfish with my right hand by the mouth and placed my left hand under its belly. I waded out into the water under my father's watchful eye until the water was about knee high. I glided the catfish back and forth under the water to revive it. I finally let it go and the large catfish swam slowly into the deep water. "Goodbye little catfish," I had said, "we will never see you again." As the years passed no one ever saw the catfish again. There were hard core fishermen who claimed that one day they would catch the old "grand daddy fish" that I had once let loose in the lake.

Larry and I walked up the hollow back toward the house that had a branch running its length. Somehow even in the driest of times the branch would have water in it. It was a favorite place for the old cows to cool off with the water and the shade of the trees. There were walnut trees, hickory trees, buckeye trees, sycamore trees and the like down through the hollow. I used to go squirrel hunting with my father's single shot 22. caliber rifle when I was younger. I remembered once when I shot at a squirrel and two fell out of the tree. I had told my father I killed two squirrels with one shot. His comment was that the squirrels were up in the tree "friggin." That's the only way I could have killed two with one shot.

We came up the hollow and walked up the dam of the oldest lake that was closest to the house. This was the lake where we got our bath water from and the lake where I had almost drowned as a kid. Sometimes it was nasty with algae and the cows would go into the lake to drink. While they were there they had to relieve themselves as well. Also when I was growing up the hogs would go into the lake to wallow. It was a mess, but we swam in it, fished in it, and took baths in it. I knew why my father had not put up a fence around the lake to keep the farm animals out. It was because the only running branch on the farm just didn't have enough water to support the livestock.

Our tour of the farm was about finished. We proceeded to the house and just opposite a small pond near the tobacco barn was the old red bull laying on the ground. I told Larry I wanted a picture of me standing near the old bull. He took a picture and then said that the old bull was so gentle that he would allow me to sit on him for a picture. I sat on the bull and he started to get up. I immediately jumped off and Larry snapped another picture. "Guess he don't cotton much to strangers," Larry said laughing.

I had enjoyed the tour of the farm. It brought back many precious memories. I missed the farm life. The work was hard but I had gotten used to it over the years. It was a way of life. It was the backbone of my very existence. I could always fall back on my experiences of hard work, discipline, motivation, morality, patriotism, and brotherhood to help me along the path that destiny had in store for me. But now there would be no more farm work, just a commitment to God, Corps, and Country.

That afternoon I started to work on my uniform for the Sunday church service. I pulled my wool blouse out of the seabag, unfolded it, and laid it on the bed. My ribbons on the blouse were still in tact and had not been damaged by my seabag being thrown around at airports. I took out my trousers, shoes, and each article and accessory I would need to get in the proper uniform. As always, there would be a lot of pride for me to once again wear the "Marine Green Uniform."

My Winter Service Alpha uniform was made of wool serge green fabric that was 100 per cent cotton. My wool green coat, commonly referred to as "blouse," consisted of a wool green belt with brass buckle, a pair of black branch of service insignia with eagle, globe, and anchor for the collars, red and gold lance corporal rank insignia on the sleeves, Marksmanship Shooting Badge 1/8th inch above the left breast pocket, and my ribbons 1/8th inch above my shooting badge. The wool green garrison cap had a black screw-post service insignia with eagle, globe, and anchor. The wool green trousers were worn with a khaki web belt with brass buckle and tip. I had a long-sleeve khaki wool shirt that was worn with a khaki necktie and Marine Corps brass necktie clasp with emblem. I had a pair of black leather dress shoes that was worn with black dress socks. I wore white boxer skivvy shorts and a white crew neck T-shirt.

I had devised a system in getting my uniform ready for wear. First I would check the entire uniform and cut off any loose threads, commonly referred to as "Irish Pennants" by the Marines. Then I would check each and every garment starting with the garrison cover, also known as "Piss Cutter." I would check for cleanliness and proper alignment of the service insignia. I would move on to the coat and check for proper spacing with a ruler. Then I would check the trousers, shirt, tie, and socks. Once I was sure everything was perfect, I would press the uniform to make sure it had crisp creases. Then I would break out a can of Brasso and a rag and shine all the brass accessories. I would save the leather dress shoes for last. Then I would break out a small can of Kiwi boot polish and a rag and commence to "spit-shine" my shoes. My goal was to get the shoes so shiny I could see to comb what little hair I had on my head. There were even times when I cut Irish Pennants off of my dress shoes.

Sunday rolled around and I got up in time to get dressed for church. I had told my mother that I would skip breakfast and have a bite to eat when we returned home after mass. In the kitchen I used the sink and vanity mirror to shave. My mother was running around trying to get ready herself. I asked if Larry was up and she said that she had to go and wake him. While I shaved she woke up Larry and it wasn't long until Larry was also scurrying about trying to get ready.

I went back upstairs to get into my uniform. When I had finished dressing I looked at myself in the dresser mirror. I turned sideways and then turned around to look back and check my uniform from behind. The uniform looked and felt good. I checked my trousers length to make sure that the back of the trousers leg was resting on the junction formed by the heel and sole of the shoe. Then I checked the alignment of my wool green brass belt buckle. We referred to it as the "M-Buckle." I checked and adjusted my ribbons. Although I knew they were measured perfect, I had to check them just for GP, "General Purposes." I stepped back so I could see my entire figure in the mirror. I was sharp. I was squared away. I was proud. But most of all, I was a Marine. I did a left and right face on the carpet just to hear my heels pop. Then I executed an about face, took my garrison cap off my head, and proceeded down the steps to impress my mother.

I opened the door to the kitchen. My mother was dressed and was standing at the table checking her purse to make sure she had everything. She looked up and saw me in my uniform. She stopped digging in her purse and just stood there staring. Then she placed her right hand over her heart and stepped back a step as in being in total shock.

"Freddy, Freddy," she said. "You sure do look nice. That uniform is beautiful. I know beautiful is not the right word to use but it is the prettiest sight I have ever seen. You look so good in it."

"Thanks Momma," I replied, "You look pretty sharp yourself."

"Naw," she said, "it's just something I dug out of the closet."

I took a good look at her. She wore a navy blue dress that had white ruffles on the end of the sleeves and around the neck. It looked very nice on her. She also wore black shoes with stockings. Over her left breast she had pinned on a white and red corsage. She had her red hat laying on the table next to her purse.

"Let me see you with your red hat on Momma," I said.

"Oh, Freddy," you just want to make fun of me, don't you?" she asked.

"Not at all," I commented. "I just want to see how good it looks on you with your navy blue dress."

"Oh, all right," she conceded. She put the red hat on. It was really red. "Well, how does it look?" she asked.

"Beautiful," I replied, "just beautiful."

"Oh, Freddy, you are just making that up, ain't you?" she asked.

"Nope, it looks real good on you," I responded. "We will definitely be turning some heads when we walk into church this morning."

"That's what I'm afraid of," she replied. Then after a pause she said again, "Freddy, I just can't get over how good you look in that Marine uniform. I am so proud of you. I am proud of all my sons and daughters."

"Thank you Momma," I said.

I was very proud of my Marine Corps uniform and my mother was very proud of my accomplishments. I offered to drive to church so we loaded up in the old Chevrolet and headed out. On the way to Saint Rose Catholic Church, my mother told me about a family of Springfield, Kentucky who had lost a son in Vietnam. He was a soldier and had been killed in February 1970 at the age of twenty. I told my mother that I had arrived in Vietnam during March 1970. It was a shame that his life had to come to such a tragic end. Even though a year had passed since his death, the memory of that fateful day was still vivid in the minds of the Saint Rose Parishioners.

We soon arrived at the parking lot on the church compound. I felt very proud knowing that I would be seen in church with my mother and younger brother. As we walked toward the church my mother slipped her right arm under my left arm. I held my forearm up as if escorting her to the door. It was a little awkward for me because I was not used to such soft hearted gestures. Then I felt as if I was going to bust. I didn't want to walk into church with tears flowing down my cheeks. Somehow I managed to control my emotions once again. There was no better place to be than having my arm wrapped around my mother's arm. I felt I had sampled a little piece of heaven.

As we entered the church we proceeded to the holy water and blessed ourselves. I could sense that we were being watched and I looked out over the congregation. Slowly people started turning their heads and staring at us. We walked down the right side of the aisle, genuflected, made the sign of the cross, and took our usual seats about the fourth pew from the back of the church. It was a small pew next to a large pillar. We had sat there so many times before that they should have reserved it for the Floy Fenwick family.

We knelt down and began saying some prayers. I stared straight ahead, but my peripheral vision told me that a lot of eyes were upon us. I could imagine what was going through their minds, a son who has fought in Vietnam has made it home alive to his mother. Then again they could have been checking out my uniform or how pretty my mother was in her navy blue dress, red hat, and corsage. Whatever the reason, soon they returned to their praying and waited for the Priest to come out and say Mass.

It dawned on me how many times my mother had been on her knees in this church praying the rosary for Donald and me to come home safe and alive. I gathered my thoughts together and began to thank the Lord for this day. I thanked Him for leading me home and for finally giving my parents a peace of mind.

I felt a little uneasy throughout the entire mass as people around still made an effort to look back and stare. We went to communion and as I walked up the side of the pews to return to my seat I could see that both sides of the church were looking my way. I saw quite a few folks that I had known when I was growing up and attending St. Rose Church regularly. I had seven years of school at the St. Rose Elementary School and some of my acquaintances were still around. Some I realized would never leave Springfield, Kentucky.

When the mass had ended we walked out of the church and back toward the car. Several people came up to us, said hello to my mother, and shook my hand to welcome me home. One of them was my uncle on my father's side of the family. I had gone to boot camp and infantry training with his son. He would also be coming home from Okinawa before long.

"Well, Well, Floy," you sure do look nice today," he said. "You are all dressed up."

"Oh I just grabbed the first thing I saw in the closet," my mother responded modestly.

"Well, you sure do look awful pretty," he said.

My mother answered my uncle saying, "Oh, thank you, but I'm not the one dressed up. Look at Freddy. Doesn't he look nice in his Marine uniform?"

"He sure does," my uncle remarked. "He looks like a general or something." He shook my hand. "Welcome back, Freddy, it's good to have you home.

"Thanks," I replied, "it's good to be back."

"I bet it's rough over there," he said.

"Yeah, it can get a little rough at times," I replied.

My uncle then told us that he was glad that his Marine son did not go to Vietnam and that the family couldn't wait to see him again. He bid us farewell and then another man approached me who I did not recognize.

"It's a crying shame that our boys have to go over yonder and fight in that foreign land," he commented. "I don't see why they don't put an end to all this bloodshed and bring our boys home."

I was in no mood to debate about the Vietnam War so I agreed with him and said I had to be getting home. We got to the car and I was relieved that church was over. When we arrived home my mother, father, and I posed for a few pictures by the steps of the front porch and then standing in front of one of the red chimneys. We didn't know if any family members would show up to visit on this being my first Sunday back from overseas, but I knew they would come. Once the family found out I was back we would have a houseful of relatives. I dreaded all the questions that would be asked of me regarding the Vietnam War. I just wanted to put it all behind me and enjoy my thirty days leave at home. I went upstairs and changed back into my casual civilian attire.

When I came back downstairs my mother had changed clothes also. She

Father, Mother, and Lance Corporal Fenwick upon his return from Vietnam and Okinawa, March 1971.

had put on a pretty yellow dress. She asked me to go with her to the front room where the piano was. We walked into the room and she reached up on the wall and took down a small frame. In it was the poem titled "Letter from Vietnam" that I had written to my parents on 1 April 1970 while serving my country in the Quang Nam Province, South Vietnam. It was a clipping out of the local newspaper, the Springfield Sun.

As I glanced over the stanzas I remembered back in time to the very day that I had written the poem. It was still very vivid in my mind. I had felt the need that particular day to show my parents how much I really loved them because I had doubts if I would make it out of Vietnam alive. She had saved all of the letters that I had written while in Vietnam and had them bundled together with a rubber band. In the stack of letters was the "original" hand written poem that I had written. I stood there in the front room, with my mother by my side, as I had visions of my tour with the Marines of "Medevac Mike" and "Mike 3 Charlie."

I wondered about Hawkeye who was assigned to a CAP Unit when I had departed Vietnam. I had always hoped and prayed to God that he would return home safely. After a few days at home I received a letter from him. He wrote a short letter stating that he was back in Oregon and planned to settle down there. I wrote him back and wished him all the best. I was so happy that Hawkeye had made it out of Vietnam alive. I knew that I would never forget him.

Before the little hand on the clock struck eleven that morning, my brothers and sisters and all of their children started arriving. They all had large families. It wasn't long until the house was full of relatives. Fortunately it was a nice spring day and warm outside so the kids could venture out in the front and back yard to play. The men sat around and talked while my mother and my sisters helped out in the kitchen. At least my mother had some good help. All of my sisters were hard workers and they knew how to cook. They had learned from the best. I heard my mother make the comment that everyone was there except Janice out in California and Donald who was still in Okinawa.

For this special occasion my mother kept her promise to me. She had prepared a two year old ham that had been hanging in the back room. The longer it cured the better tasting it got. We sat down to a meal that was out of this world. There was country ham, fried chicken, mashed potatoes, gravy, green beans, pinto beans, deviled eggs, cornbread, biscuits, coleslaw, and other trimmings. For dessert there was coconut pie, jam cake, fruit cocktail, and blackberry cobbler. The blackberry cobbler was my favorite. My mother really knew how to make it the old fashioned way.

After the big meal all the ladies chipped in to clean up the dishes. The men went out to the front porch and sat around and talked. That's when the questions about Vietnam began to come up in conversation. I would try to make my answer short and to the point without carrying on too much. I didn't want to boast or brag like I had heard other Vietnam Vets. I found out that those Vietnam Vets who liked to show off and brag about their combat tour really didn't do much while in country. In other words, they probably never knew what being in the bush meant since they spent all their time back in the rear.

My brothers and father would listen intently when I explained about the customs of the Vietnamese, the Okinawians, and the Filipinos. They also enjoyed hearing about the rice paddies, the mountains, the beautiful valleys, the majestic sunsets and sunrises, and the beautiful tropical beaches. Once in awhile as we were talking about the weather, farming, being overseas and the like, the subject of Vietnam would pop up. I understood however, that my relatives were merely curious and had my best interest at heart. I just hoped the conversations would not spark more nightmares.

The women finally finished up in the kitchen. They joined us on the front porch. I was still entertaining questions about some of my experiences overseas. Up to this point it was all about me. My mother and sisters listened in but they also had a knack for changing the subject. We all talked and laughed for quite awhile. I began to catch up on some of the happenings around home. I loved hearing my mother talk. She had that special country twang of an accent and she could come up with the greatest one liner expressions. Some of her most often used personal expressions of excitement were "Well, I Swanie To You! Goodness Gracious! Well, Did You Ever? Lord Have Mercy!"

Finally one of my sisters, Nancy, asked my mother to play the piano. She did not want to do it at first but she was encouraged by my other sisters Joann and Carolyn. My mother gave in and all the women got up and went into the front room. The men remained behind still rambling away in conversation. Then we heard my mother playing the piano through the front room window. It sounded so nice and comforting. We couldn't help but stop talking and take notice. After a few minutes my father suggested that we all go in to hear her play a "piece" or two. We went inside and found a seat to sit back and listen to her piano playing. My mother had learned to play by ear when she was a child. She had never had a piano lesson, but she really had a special talent and knack for making the old piano sound great.

She played songs such as "Precious Memories, The Old Rugged Cross, Amazing Grace, Rock of Ages, Little Brown Church in the Wildwood, Over There, God Bless America, Lonesome Me, You Are My Sunshine, Red River Valley, Mockingbird Hill, She'll Be Coming Around The Mountain, Little Brown Jug, and Pistol Packin' Momma. When my mother began to play Pistol Packin' Momma, which was my favorite, I stood up and walked over to the piano and stood beside her to watch her play. I watched as her short stubby fingers went up and down the keyboard with style and grace. It was so motivating for me. When she had finished, she looked up at me and said," Now here's a little something especially for Freddy." She began playing The Marine's Hymn. She played it so beautifully and with so much pride and joy. Tears came to my eyes as she continued playing through the verses. It was very touching and sobering.

We had thoroughly enjoyed my mother playing the piano. After she finished my relatives decided that they had best be getting home. They started to gather their children and one by one they all drove out of the driveway. My mother, father, Larry, and I remained. Now I would have some piece and quiet for awhile. I would have a chance to really have some quality time with my mother and father over the next few weeks.

The next day I challenged Larry to a game of basketball up in the hay loft of the stock barn. We used to play up there all the time especially in the winter time. Sometimes we would have to restack some of the bails of hay in order to clear a space to shoot at the basket. The barn loft floor was hardwood which made it perfect for bouncing a basketball. We got to the barn loft and Larry dribbled the ball toward the basket and sank a layup.

"Gimme dat ball," I said with authority. Larry laughed and threw me the basketball. I dribbled it back about 25 feet from the basket, squared up, and fired up my first shot. I missed the entire rim. I used to shoot set shots from that distance and split the net quite often. "One more time," I said to Larry. He threw the ball back to me and I fired it toward the basket again. This time it bounced off the front of the rim. "Okay, Larry." I exclaimed. "I've got the range and elevation locked on. This is it. Let me see the ball one more time." I fired it up this time making sure I followed through with the shot. The basketball traveled at a high arch and split the net. That was an awesome sound for me. It brought back memories when I played as a freshman and a starting guard on the Fredericktown High School basketball team. We were called the "Fredericktown Bluejays." Larry and I played a game of basketball. It was just like the good old days. I was home and I was having fun. No worries and no cares.

Over the next few days I decided that I was a grown man and that I should be doing grown up things. I asked to borrow my father's car to go to a nearby town called Lebanon and visit "The Golden Horseshoe." It was a bar and dance lounge about nine miles away that all the high school kids used to hang out on Friday and Saturday nights. At around six o'clock that evening I walked into the bar area and noticed only a handful of people at the bar. It was too early in the evening for the band to perform. I walked up to the bar and sat down.

The bartender walked up to me and asked, "Can I help you?"

"I'd like a rum and coke please," I replied.

He looked at me and said, "Let me see some ID."

I reached into my pocket, pulled out my wallet, and handed him my military ID card. He flipped it over and read the date of birth on my card.

He handed it back to me and said, "You're not old enough. You're only twenty. I can't serve you no mixed drink, you're under age, son."

"What do you mean I'm under age?" I asked in disbelief. I grabbed my ID card back from him.

"You've gotta be twenty-one to get a mixed drink. You're only twenty," the bartender replied.

At that moment I felt a flush of warmth go over my cheeks. It had never really dawned on me that I would receive such a response in a bar. I was so accustomed to getting service at any bar while being overseas and getting either mixed drinks or beer.

"Why?" I asked. "Do you have to be twenty-one to be a man or to fight for our country?"

"Yeah, in this club you do," the bartender responded.

"Look," I said, "I've just got back from overseas and all I want is one mixed drink and I'll be on my way."

"I can serve you a beer partner, but you're not getting no mixed drink," the bartender replied casually.

I started to rationalize with the bartender. "The way I look at it, if I can go to combat and fight for my country and for people like you, I should be able to get a mixed drink. I've travelled all over the Far East and I have never been denied a mixed drink in any bar."

"I don't care where you've been," the bartender snapped. "You ain't getting no mixed drink here. You wanna beer or not?"

By this time a few patrons began staring in our direction. One of the patrons in the far corner of the bar shouted out, "What the hell, give the boy a mixed drink. He's earned it. I'll bet you've been to Vietnam haven't you son?" he asked.

"Yes, I have," I replied without looking back at him.

"I've heard it's really rough oer' dar fightin dem commie gooks. Ain't that right?" he questioned. I did not respond. "Bartender," the patron shouted, "Give dat boy a mixed drink and put it on my tab."

The bartender then began serving another customer ignoring his remark. I got up from the stool and shoved my ID card back into my wallet.

I spoke directly to the bartender, "You can take your beer and shove it up your ass."

The bartender did not reply. I turned and walked out of the Golden Horseshoe. I got into the car and drove home very slowly. All the way home I was furious. What a place to come home to, I thought. So this is the real world. This is the world that I wanted desperately to come home to. I kept thinking about the lackadaisical attitude of the bartender. It made me angry that I couldn't get a shot of spirits after putting my life on the line for my country. I finally calmed down and reckoned that laws were established for a purpose and that I needed to adhere to the regulations. After all, I was a Marine and a United States citizen to boot. I was proud to be an American.

On the drive home I felt so alone. I started to miss my Marine liberty buddies. I thought about them all, those I knew in Vietnam, and those I knew in Okinawa. I would miss them. I did not realize that I had arrived home until I drove off the main road and swerved into the driveway. I parked the car in the garage and walked to the house and went upstairs to my room. I got undressed and lay on my bed. My first night out on the town turned out to be depressing. Before long I drifted off into a light sleep.

As time passed I began to realize that I was back to reality where I had first started. People around went about their daily routine and there were times when I felt lost among them like I was a stranger in the crowd. I was no longer under any pressure, in fact, I was too free. The close camaraderie which I had attained while overseas seemed to disappear. My only fall back was my family and fond memories.

There were still many questions posed to me about my experiences in

Mother and Lance Corporal Fenwick shortly after returning from overseas. Mother prayed night and day that my brother and I would return home safe from Vietnam. Her prayers were answered.

Vietnam. When neighboring folks and relatives dropped by the house my father was ever so proud to announce that I had just returned from Vietnam. I never did say too much or take part in much discussion. As time passed members of my family soon realized that it was probably best not to bring up the subject. I kept busy attempting to refamiliarize myself with Cherry Hill Farm. It seemed so long ago since I had left home. I walked around the house reminiscing about the good old days. Through the barns I wandered thinking back and remembering the hard work of milking cows and taking care of the tobacco crops. I found myself in the middle of the tobacco patch where my destiny to go to Vietnam had first begun.

There was a farm sale out on Russell Lane off the East Texas Road that my father wanted to go to. They were selling the farm and all the equipment.

My father, Larry, and I went to the sale and were looking through the equipment that was to sell at auction. My father seemed to know just about everyone at the sale. He had been to many farm sales in the past. Even if he didn't buy anything it gave him a chance to meet other farmers and talk about the weather, crops, and farming in general.

Out of the crowd came a first cousin of my father. He was known for always being a jokester and a prankster. He was full of life and full of fun. He walked strait up to me and with a serious look on his face he shook my hand. "Freddy, I'm sure proud to see you home son." It gave me a nice warm feeling to be appreciated. It was the way that he had said it that meant so much to me. Larry told me that he would always remember his gesture because at that time a lot of people around the country didn't give Vietnam Vets the respect that they deserved. It made us both very proud.

As the weather warmed up even more, Larry and two of his nephews, my brother Bobby's two oldest sons, decided to go camping on the farm back near the old hollow. There was a huge acorn tree up on the hill close to the branch that ran the length of the hollow. They would be able to frolic in the water and play amidst the towering trees.

They loaded up the small trailer that was hooked to the Massy Ferguson 150 tractor and drove to the back of the farm to set up their tent. They were capable of taking care of everything on their own so I left them alone to have fun. I had played with them when I was a kid, but now since I had left home, I figured I would break away from playing with the kids. Night fell and my mother worried if they would be okay camping out. I assured her that they would be fine and that they were old enough to take care of themselves. Larry was a teenager now and had lived on Cherry Hill Farm his whole life. He knew all the ends and outs. He had become very independent.

The next day rolled around and I helped my father feed the cows. When we returned to the house we sat down on the back porch. He had an old wooden bench that he sat on. He took out some Red Man Chewing tobacco and put a big wad in his mouth.

"Freddy, do you want a chew?" he asked.

"Yeah, Daddy, I'll have a chew," I replied.

I took a pinch out of the pouch and put it in my mouth. I gave the pouch back to my father. He sat on the corner of the bench where he could spit off the edge of the porch. As we talked I had to keep getting up off the bench and walk to the edge of the porch to spit my tobacco juice. I decided that it would be best if I sat on the porch steps where I could talk with my father and spit at the same time. I enjoyed hearing his stories about farming. He could come up with some good ones. Some I had heard over and over but it was a pleasure to hear him talk. He had a lot of memories about work on the farm and making ends meet to barely make a living.

"What are you going to do when your time is up in the service?" he asked.

"I don't really know," I replied. "I can get out around September 1972. I wouldn't mind having a farm. Not a big one, just one about thirty acres or so. I would like to be able to work a public job and raise a few crops and maybe have a few cows."

My father pulled out his pocket knife and started sharpening it on the leather of one of his shoes. Then he spit some tobacco juice off the side of the porch. "Well, you are more than welcome to stay right here if you want," my father exclaimed. "We have those three rooms upstairs where you could stay. You could help me out on the farm and take a share of the profits. It wouldn't be much but at least you would have a roof over your head and free room and board."

"Sounds good," I said. "But eventually I would have to get out from under Momma's skirt tails, so to speak, and get out on my own. I still have some time to do in the Marine Corps so I won't worry about it for now."

"Think about it," my father replied. "You will always have a home to come to as long as I am alive and still kicking."

"Thanks, Daddy," I said, "I really appreciate that."

We continued talking about farming until my father mentioned that we should probably check on Larry and his nephews while they were on their camping trip. I told him that he didn't have to walk to the back of the farm. Instead, I would get the .22 rifle and look for some squirrels down the hollow. I would check on them as I passed by to see if everything was okay. He told me that the best way to go was behind the old lake. He had seen a bunch of squirrels running across the tree limbs down that way.

I went to the dining room to where the gun cabinet was hanging on the wall. I pulled the .22 rifle off the rack and opened the pull down door to get a box of .22 long rifle shot cartridges. When I walked out on the back porch I pulled back the lever of the rifle and loaded one round in the chamber.

"Don't let that single-shot .22 get away from you, Freddy," my father cautioned.

"Don't worry," I responded. After having fired the M14 rifle, M16 rifle, M79 Grenade Launcher, .45 caliber pistol, 60 millimeter mortar, and M60 machine gun, I think I can handle this .22 rifle."

My father laughed. "That's a lot of guns!" he exclaimed.

I began walking down the back yard on my way to the barn lot where I would cross to go in behind the old lake.

"Be careful back there, Freddy!" my father yelled out.

"Okay Daddy," I said, "I will."

I came to the hollow and started walking along the upper bank looking up in the large trees for some squirrels. I thought to myself that if I were to kill any squirrels that I would end up having to clean them which could be a chore in itself. I had done it many times before when I was growing up on the farm. When we dressed out the squirrels my mother would fry them up just like fried chicken. I decided that I would just enjoy the peace and quiet and this nice spring day outdoors. If I saw any squirrels I would either by-pass them or shoot next to them just to scare them a bit. I began to have all sorts of thoughts and memories of being on the farm. My thoughts were far removed from the Marine Corps and war. It was so calm and serene to just walk alone down this beautiful hollow that I had spent so much time in be-fore.

I soon caught sight of the camping tent the boys were staying in. I could hear talking and laughter as I neared the tent.

"Hey you guys," I said. "I see you all survived the night in the jungle. How did it go?"

They all started telling me about how much fun they were having camp-ing out and that they must do it again. They were going to stay another night before they packed it in. They were not going to starve to death, that was for sure. They had brought along a cooler with sodas, water, hot dogs, potato chips, sandwiches, candy bars, and the like. I told them I just wanted to check on them to make sure they were okay and that I was going to continue down the hollow squirrel hunting. They bid me farewell as I continued walk-ing in the warm sunlight.

I got about two hundred feet from their tent when I heard a loud explo-sion. "POOW!" I immediately dropped to the ground. I lost my grip on the .22 rifle and it lay in the dirt right next to me. It took me by complete sur-prise. I didn't know what it was. At first I thought it was a booby trap. Then the thought of a sniper crossed my mind. I heard the boys back at the tent just laughing and laughing. They thought it was so funny that they had scared me and I had dropped to the ground in such a manner.

I grabbed the rifle and headed back toward the tent. When I got there they were still laughing.

"What in the hell was that?" I asked angrily.

"It was just a firecracker," Larry said. "We brought some with us to let off. I guess we scared you pretty bad didn't we?" All three of them were still laughing at the way I hit the ground.

"Well, it's not funny," I snapped. "The next time you want to fire off a firecracker, you had better let me know first, you hear?"

"Okay," Larry replied, "we didn't mean to scare you."

"You didn't scare me," I replied, "just let me know when you are going to light one of those damn things."

I turned around and continued to walk down the hollow. I could still hear snickering as they could not control their laughter. I did not hear them set off another firecracker as I neared the back lake and decided to give up on squirrel hunting. I went straight back to the house. Larry told me later that he had realized the real reason I had hit the ground upon hearing the firecracker. He said he was sorry. I told my little brother that it was okay.

One day a man that my father knew came to the farm. My brother Bob-by and his sons, my father, Larry, and I were down at the tobacco barn. We were talking about one thing and then the other. My father told the man that I had just got back from Vietnam.

"Did you kill any of those gooks over there?" he asked.

Normally I was always responsive, polite, and respectful to my elders. But the way that this guy had said it rubbed me the wrong way. I did not answer him and turned away. My father was a bit shocked and surprised by my reaction and quickly changed the subject. I told Larry later, "I could have killed that stupid son-of-a-bitch." I guess the reason it made me mad was the fact that this guy had never been in the service and had never been in Vietnam. In my mind, if you hadn't been fighting in Vietnam, you had no right to call them gooks."

My leave at home was rapidly coming to an end. I decided to go back to the spot up on the knoll overlooking the two back lakes for the last time. I walked through the fields and came to the very spot where Larry had taken a picture of me. This time there was no camera, just me in the flesh to reminisce about the past and think about the future. It was now April and the grass had turned green after the long winter months.

Under a mild sun I watched the Black Angus cows grazing in the pasture by the lake. I sat down on the ground in a crossed ankle position. The ground was slightly wet from the overnight moisture where I sat but it did not bother me. There was a slight chilly breeze in the air and the cold air momentarily sent chills up my spine as I was only wearing a sweat shirt and jeans. I had my jungle boots on which reminded me of the times I had walked through the rice paddies, mountains, and jungles of Vietnam. Life seemed so tranquil on the farm.

As I sat deep in thought, I realized that my strife and anxiety regarding the Vietnam War was all behind me now. My next assignment was the 2nd Marine Division at Camp Lejeune, North Carolina. It crossed my mind with uncertainty that I might end up in combat again during my enlistment in the Marine Corps. I daydreamed that one day I would like to travel back to the Orient. It was so beautiful over there.

My experiences in Vietnam had made me see things in a different perspective. The life which I was so accustomed to on the farm was taken away from me when I joined the Marine Corps. Now that I was home I could not seem to fit into the cycle of life as I thought I would. If I were getting out of the Marine Corps it may have been different, but I had a few more years to go on my enlistment. My attitudes and priorities could change by then.

I realized that I had grown up in my own way, a way in which my parents would not have planned. I had willfully chosen my own destiny. As I sat on this grassy knoll, I did not mind. Now I could say that I had done my patriotic duty. I thanked the Lord for having such a loving and caring mother. She had been my inspiration and my hope as she had prayed with utmost reverence for my safe return. Her letters and care packages had kept me motivated. She would always have a special place in my heart.

I had no conscience of the passing time as I sat and pondered in peaceful serenity. My mind began to wonder and flashback to the days of Vietnam. I missed my "foxhole buddy." The time that I had spent Vietnam with my infantry squad was an experience I wished to cherish for the rest of my life. I did not know why I was withdrawn from talking about it. I supposed that it could have been that I felt others might not understand. It could have been that the memories were just too personal to part with. The sight of maimed and dead Marines, and the dead bodies of the enemy, was more than enough to haunt me for the rest of my life.

My ears seemed to pick up the slightest sounds around me and the louder noises like the sounds of firecrackers, shot gun blasts, and even the backfire of vehicles could send me diving for cover. The slightest noise during my sleep would arouse me to a scream. I had often wondered if the enemy had any feelings, but just like us, they had to fight to survive. If I should come face to face with the enemy, it would be a situation of one of us surviving, and choosing life over death.

My tour in Vietnam was over, but the memories would always remain. As much as I had looked forward to coming home, I missed the closeness of Mike 3 Charlie. I did not know what lay ahead of me on my next assignment. What would 2nd Marine Division be like? What would be the next conflict and where? Would we march off to another war?

I did not question if our presence in Vietnam was right or wrong. We were stopping the spread of Communism, doing our duty for the love of Corps and Country. I had hoped that all the pain and suffering was not in vain and that I would profit from my experiences if ever faced with a similar situation.

One thing was for certain. No matter what I would do, no matter where I would go, no matter how old I would get, I would always have memories of my personal experiences in Vietnam. Those Lasting Visions, they will never subside.